DIGITAL PSAT/NMSQT® PREP 2024

468 - 471

Editor-in-Chief
Heather Waite

Contributing Editors
J. Scott Mullison, Ethan Weber, and Melissa McLaughlin

Special thanks to our faculty authors and reviewers
Michael Collins, Bonnie Wang, Jo L'Abbate, Aisa Diaz, Mark Feery, Boris Dvorkin, Michelle Hunt, Steve Cisar, Gordon Spector, and David Staples

Additional special thanks to
Nancy Greenspan; Isaac Botier; Laurel Hanson; Brian Carlidge; Jessica Gleicher; Amy Zarkos; Alexandra Strelka, MA; Heather Wilcox; Megan Buckman; and the countless others who made this project possible

© 2023 by Kaplan North America, LLC

Published by Kaplan North America, LLC dba Kaplan Publishing
1515 West Cypress Creek Road
Fort Lauderdale, FL 33309

10 9 8 7 6 5 4 3 2 1

ISBN: 978-1-5062-8732-4

Kaplan North America, LLC print books are available at special quantity discounts to use for sales promotions, employee premiums, or educational purposes. For more information or to purchase books, please call the Simon & Schuster Special Sales department at 866-506-1949.

TABLE OF CONTENTS

GO ONLINE
www.kaptest.com
/moreonline

How to Use This Book

In January of 2022, the College Board announced a major revision to its PSAT test. Instead of the traditional pen-and-paper test, this new test was announced to be both completely digital and adaptive by section. This book is designed to help you achieve your highest score on this new digital PSAT in the fall of 2023 and beyond.

We, at Kaplan, understand that your time is limited and that this book is hefty, but nobody expects you to read every word. Nor do we expect you to go in order. If you need more work on the Reading and Writing section than on Math, for example, then feel free to skip over the math chapters. The most efficient way to use this book is to spend the most time on those areas that give you trouble, starting with those that are tested most often. If you're not sure, use the "How Much Do You Know?" pretests we provide in each chapter to figure out how much time to spend on that material.

Chapter Organization

Most chapters start with the previously mentioned "How Much Do You Know?" section that helps you get a sense of how comfortable you already are with the material in the chapter. Answers and explanations follow immediately in the "Check Your Work" section. Each lesson in a chapter starts with a question typical of the way that the PSAT tests a given topic and ends with a set of practice questions called "Try on Your Own." There is yet another practice set at the end of each chapter called "How Much Have You Learned?" to reinforce the concepts explained in the chapter. Answers and Explanations for the "Try on Your Own" and "How Much Have You Learned?" sections are found at the end of each chapter for easy reference.

Practice Test

While the new PSAT is digital, we are including a paper test at the end of this book to help you learn about the test and be able to practice even when you are not online. The Practice Test has full answers and explanations and demonstrates the adaptive structure of the digital test.

You're Already on Your Way

You already have many of the skills you'll need to excel on the PSAT, but you'll need to adapt those skills to the structure of the exam. This book will teach you to adapt your math, reading, and writing skills to solve questions more efficiently and to confidently tackle even the toughest PSAT questions.

Extra Practice

This book will help you answer the most common questions on test day, but there is even more practice for you online. We highly recommend that you make use of both your book and digital resources.

Digital Resources

To access the online resources that accompany this book, follow the steps below:

1. Go to **www.kaptest.com/moreonline**.

2. Have this book available as you complete the on-screen instructions.

3. Once you have registered your book, sign into your online resources at **www.kaptest.com**.

GO ONLINE

www.kaptest.com
/moreonline

Are you registered for the PSAT?

Kaplan cannot register you for the official PSAT. If you have not already registered for the upcoming PSAT, talk to your high school guidance counselor or visit the College Board's website at **www.collegeboard.org** to register online and for information on registration deadlines, test sites, accommodations for students with disabilities, and fees.

The PSAT/NMSQT is generally administered on only two days in mid-October. Be sure to register well in advance of your test date. Your high school guidance counselor may also have more information about registering for the PSAT. Homeschooled students can contact the guidance office of a local high school to make arrangements to take the exam at that school.

Don't Forget Your Strengths

As your test date approaches, shift your practice to your strengths. Let's say you're good at geometry. You might not need the instructional text covering geometry in this book, but in the final week before your test date, you should still do a few geometry practice questions. Think about it: your strengths are your most reliable source of points on test day. Build that confidence in the final stretch. And just as if the PSAT were an athletic event, get plenty of sleep in the days leading up to it.

Let's Get Started

Want to get a feel for the PSAT before you start studying? Take the Practice Test at the back of this book. Otherwise, start by identifying the sections of the test you think will give you the most trouble. On test day, you'll be glad you did!

PART 1

THE PSAT AND YOU

CHAPTER 1

INSIDE THE PSAT

The Digital PSAT

In January 2022, the College Board ™ announced that the PSAT would be changing. Beginning in the **fall of 2023**, the PSAT will no longer be a pencil-and-paper exam. With the exception of certain student accommodations, all students will take the digital PSAT on a computer. (The SAT will be offered digitally beginning in the spring of 2024.)

The changes to the PSAT are more substantial than a simple change from bubbling in answers on a paper answer sheet to clicking your answer choices on a computer screen. Perhaps most significantly, the test makers have **shortened the PSAT by about 45 minutes**. This is good news for test takers like you! You'll still receive a score out of 1520 that can help you qualify for scholarships and assess your readiness for the SAT, and not only will you have a shorter total exam time, but you will also have fewer questions to answer—and more time to spend per question.

The digital PSAT format has other helpful new **features**—such as a built-in graphing calculator, text annotation tools, a timer, a zooming tool, and the ability to "cross out" answer choices you want to eliminate—that will make it easy for you to navigate the test and manage the questions.

Finally, the PSAT is not just becoming shorter and digital; the **questions** themselves have undergone changes as well. These changes are geared toward making the test more accessible. The Reading and Writing passages and the Math questions are generally becoming shorter in length, making it easier for you to focus in on what the questions themselves are asking. This book will explain every PSAT question type in detail and teach you simple methods and strategies to help you tackle every question efficiently. Whether you've taken the "old" PSAT or this is your first time taking a standardized admissions test, this book will help give you the confidence you need for PSAT success.

Where and When to Take the PSAT

The PSAT is offered every year in mid-October. It is administered at your high school, not at a testing center. Homeschooled students can sign up at the nearest local high school. Most high schools administer the exam on a Wednesday; some offer it on a Saturday. Some high schools recommend that their sophomores take the test for additional practice, but sophomores who take the PSAT are not eligible to qualify for the National Merit Scholarship unless they are in an accelerated program and are preparing to graduate the following year. However, some schools will administer the test to their students only once (at the beginning of junior year). If this is the case, sophomores wanting to take the PSAT need to get permission from their guidance counselors.

Why Take the PSAT?

The PSAT/NMSQT stands for the Preliminary SAT/National Merit Scholarship Qualifying Test. It has three main functions:

1. The PSAT is excellent practice for the SAT. The PSAT contains slightly easier Reading and Writing passages and tests fewer advanced math concepts, but it contains the same types of questions. The PSAT also measures your score against those of your classmates and peers across the country, just as the SAT does.

2. Taking the PSAT also gives you a chance to qualify for several scholarship programs, most notably the National Merit Scholarship Program. Aside from the possibility of receiving tuition for college, the National Merit Scholarship program gives you recognition that is an impressive addition to your college applications.

3. The PSAT can help you stand out to colleges. Many schools purchase lists of high-scoring students and encourage these students to apply. A great score on the PSAT could get you noticed by colleges and earn you small perks like meals during visits and waived application fees.

More than two-thirds of the top 50,000 scorers on the PSAT are recognized by the National Merit program and sent letters of commendation. Only juniors who take the PSAT are eligible for National Merit Scholarships. The top 16,000 scorers become semifinalists, and approximately 15,000 semifinalists become finalists. Finally, about 7,600 National Merit finalists receive National Merit Scholarships, with each award being up to $2,500 a year toward a college education. Many high scorers who don't receive National Merit Scholarships are awarded merit scholarships from the schools to which they apply based on their high scores. Whether you qualify as a Commended Student, a Semifinalist, a Finalist, or a full-fledged National Merit Scholar, it's definitely worth noting this achievement on your college applications.

For more information on the National Merit Scholarships and Special Scholarships, visit **www.nationalmerit.org**.

PSAT Structure

The PSAT, like any standardized test, is **predictable**. The more comfortable you are with the test structure, the more confidently you will approach each question type, thus maximizing your score.

The digital PSAT is **2 hours and 14 minutes** long. The PSAT is made up of mostly multiple-choice questions in two main sections: the Math section and the Reading and Writing section. Each section is divided into **two modules**.

SECTION	MODULE	ALLOTTED TIME (MINUTES)	TOTAL TIME (MINUTES)	QUESTION COUNT	TOTAL QUESTION COUNT
Reading and Writing	Module 1	32	64	27	54
	Module 2	32		27	
Math	Module 1	35	70	22	44
	Module 2	35		22	
Total			134		98

The two-module format divides each section into two parts, each timed separately (see table above). Once you submit your answers for the first module of either the Reading and Writing or the Math section, you won't be able to return to that module. This is because the digital PSAT is an **adaptive test**. In other words, your performance on the first module of each section will determine the difficulty level of the second module you'll take.

PSAT Scoring

As you just learned, the PSAT is adaptive. How well you do on your first module determines the questions you see in the second. This is often called a multi-staged test. Doing well on the first module, also known as the routing module, will send you to a higher difficulty second module. This will give you a chance to earn the very top scores for a section (either Reading and Writing or Math). Bear in mind that even if you are routed to an easier second module, you can still earn a competitive score on the PSAT. Don't spend time trying to figure out which difficulty level you were routed to; this will only waste your brainpower and time. Your focus should be to do your best on every question, regardless of which module it is in. While their exact formula is proprietary, your total score is based on how you do on both modules of Reading and Writing and both modules of Math. There is very likely an overlapping range of scores possible for students routed to the easier or harder second module.

You will receive one score ranging from 160–760 for Reading and Writing and another for Math. Your overall PSAT score will range from 320–1520 and is calculated by adding these two scores together.

The PSAT also gives you a percentile ranking, which allows you to compare your scores with those of other test takers. For example, a student who scored in the 63rd percentile did better than 63 percent of all others who took that test.

How to Maximize Your Score

You'll find advice on test-taking strategies below and in the section management chapters at the end of the Math and the Reading and Writing sections of this book. In addition, make sure to read the instructional text in the lessons throughout this book for those topics you feel less confident about, and then work your way through the lesson's practice questions. There are hundreds of practice questions in this book, and they are very similar to those that you will see on test day. Practice will not only improve your skills, but it will also raise your confidence, and that's very important for test day success. Remember, you can use this book in any order you like, and you don't need to use all of it. Prioritize additional review on those topics from which you'd benefit the most.

The PSAT Math Test

The PSAT Math section consists of two modules of 22 questions each. Of these 22 questions, there will be 2 pretest questions that the College Board will use for research purposes while the other 20 will count toward your score. These pretest questions are not marked in any way that is visible to you, so it is in your best interest to try your best on every question you see. You may use the provided built-in graphing calculator or your own approved calculator on every question. Questions across the section consist of both **multiple-choice** and some **student-produced responses**, on which you will type in your answer. About 25%, or 11 of the questions, will be student-produced responses, and the rest will be 4-option multiple-choice questions. With 44 questions to answer in 70 minutes, this gives you about a **minute and a half per question**.

	ALLOTTED TIME (MINUTES)	QUESTION COUNT
Module 1	35	22
Module 2	35	22
Total	70	44

QUESTION TYPE	QUESTION COUNT
Multiple-Choice Questions	~33
Student-Produced Responses	~11
Total	44

About a third of the questions in the PSAT Math section will be **word problems** that are situated in a real-world context; the rest will be straightforward math questions. The PSAT Math section includes questions in **four major content areas**: Algebra, Advanced Math, Problem-Solving and Data Analysis, and Geometry and Trigonometry.

PSAT MATH SECTION CONTENT AREA DISTRIBUTION	

Algebra
(13–15 questions)
	• Solving, creating, and using:
	  • Linear equations
	  • Linear functions
	  • Linear inequalities
	  • Systems of linear equations
	• Making connections between different representations of linear relationships

Advanced Math
(12–14 questions)
	• Interpreting, solving, creating, and using:
	  • Equations with absolute value
	  • Equations with radicals
	  • Quadratic equations
	  • Exponential equations
	  • Polynomial equations
	  • Rational equations
	  • Other nonlinear equations
	• Making connections between different representations of nonlinear relationships between two variables

PSAT MATH SECTION CONTENT AREA DISTRIBUTION	

Problem Solving and Data Analysis
 	
(7-9 questions)
	• Solving questions involving:
	  • Ratios
	  • Rates
	  • Proportions
	  • Units
	  • Percentages
	• Analyzing and interpreting data, including distributions and scatterplots
	• Calculating and interpreting:
	  • Probability and conditional probability
	  • Mean, median, and range
	• Comparing distributions' standard deviations

Geometry and Trigonometry
 	
(4-6 questions)
	• Solving questions involving:
	  • Area and volume
	  • Lines, angles, and triangles
	  • Right triangles and trigonometry

The PSAT Reading and Writing Section

The PSAT Reading and Writing section will focus on your comprehension, reasoning, and editing skills with questions based on short academic passages taken from a variety of content areas.

The PSAT Reading and Writing section consists of two modules of 27 questions each. Of these 27 questions, there will be 2 pretest questions that the College Board will use for research purposes, while the other 25 will count toward your score. These pretest questions are not marked in any way that is visible to you, so it is in your best interest to try your best on every question you see. All the questions in this section are 4-option multiple-choice questions. With 54 questions to answer in 64 minutes, this gives you about a **minute and 10 seconds per question**.

	ALLOTTED TIME (MINUTES)	QUESTION COUNT
Module 1	32	27
Module 2	32	27
Total	64	54

Each question on the PSAT Reading and Writing section is accompanied by a **short passage**, usually a paragraph in length. Some questions may have two short passages about the same topic, and a few questions will have a bullet point list of notes about a topic. Passages will draw from literature, history/social studies, the humanities (topics such as the arts), and science. Some questions will also be accompanied by a graphical representation of data, such as a graph or table.

The PSAT Reading and Writing section includes questions in **four major content areas**: Information and Ideas, Craft and Structure, Expression of Ideas, and Standard English Conventions.

PSAT READING AND WRITING SECTION CONTENT AREA DISTRIBUTION	

Information and Ideas
 	
(12–14 questions)
	• Using reading comprehension, analysis, and reasoning skills to answer questions about:
	  • Main ideas
	  • Details
	  • Command of Evidence (text and graphs/tables)
	  • Inferences
	• Interpreting, evaluating, and integrating ideas

Craft and Structure
 	
(13–15 questions)
	• Using reading comprehension, analysis, and reading skills to answer questions about:
	  • The meaning of words in context
	  • The purpose of texts
	  • Connections between related texts

Expression of Ideas
 	
(8–12 questions)
	• Using revision skills to answer questions about:
	  • Synthesizing ideas to achieve rhetorical goals
	  • Making effective transitions

Standard English Conventions
 	
(11–15 questions)
	• Using editing skills to follow Standard English conventions, including:
	  • Sentence structure
	  • Punctuation
	  • Verb agreement
	  • Pronoun agreement
	  • Modifier agreement

Test-Taking Strategies

The PSAT is different from the tests you are used to taking in school. The good news is that you can use the PSAT's particular structure to your advantage.

For example, on a test given in school, you probably go through the questions in order. You spend more time on the harder questions than on the easier ones because harder questions are usually worth significantly more points. You also probably show your work because your teacher tells you that how you approach a question is as important as getting the correct answer.

This approach is not optimal for the PSAT. On the PSAT, you benefit from moving around within a section. If you come across tough questions, it's most efficient to save those until the end. This allows you to answer the easiest questions for *you* before attempting *your* most challenging ones. Similarly, showing your work on the PSAT is unimportant. It doesn't matter how you arrive at the correct answer—only that you select the correct answer choice.

The strategies discussed below can be used in both the Reading and Writing section and the Math section of the digital PSAT.

Strategy #1: Triaging the Test

You do not need to complete questions on the PSAT in order. Every student has different strengths and should attack the test with those strengths in mind. Your main objective on the PSAT should be to score as many points as you can. While approaching questions out of order may seem counterintuitive, it is a surefire way to achieve your best score.

Just remember, you can skip around within each module, but you cannot return to work on a module once you've submitted your answers for that module.

To triage a section effectively, do the following:

- First, work through all the easy questions that you can do quickly. Skip questions that are hard or time-consuming. Use the digital test's tool to **flag** any questions you are initially skipping. Before you leave the question, you might want to mark a guess, just in case you don't have time to return to it.
- Second, use the **module review screen** to return to any questions you skipped. Work through the questions that are doable but time-consuming.
- Third, work through the hard questions.

Strategy #2: Elimination

If you can determine that one or more answer choices are definitely incorrect, you can increase your chances of getting the correct answer by paring the selection down.

To eliminate answer choices, do the following:

- Read each answer choice.
- Use the digital test's **elimination tool** to cross out any answer choices that you determine are incorrect.
- If only one answer choice is left, select it and move on.
- If more than one answer choice remains, remember that there is no wrong-answer penalty, so take your best guess.

The specific lessons in this book will teach you about the different incorrect answer types that commonly appear on the PSAT. When you see one of these incorrect answer types, you can quickly eliminate it.

Strategy #3: Strategic Guessing

Each multiple-choice question on the PSAT has four answer choices and no wrong-answer penalty. That means if you have no idea how to approach a question, you have a 25 percent chance of randomly choosing the correct answer. Even though there's a 75 percent chance of selecting the incorrect answer, you won't lose any points for doing so. And often, you'll be able to eliminate one or more choices as incorrect (see Strategy #2 above), improving your chances of getting the correct answer even more. The worst that can happen on the PSAT is that you'll earn zero points on a question, which means you should *always* **at least take a guess**, even when you have no idea what to do.

When guessing on a question, do the following:

- Try to strategically eliminate answer choices before guessing.
- If you are almost out of time or have no idea what a question is asking, pick a **Letter of the Day**. A Letter of the Day is an answer choice letter (A, B, C, or D) that you choose before test day to select for questions you guess on.

- If a question is taking too long, skip it and guess. Spend your time on those questions that you know how to do; don't allow yourself to get bogged down in fighting it out with a question that is too time-consuming.
- Leave yourself a few minutes before you run out of time on each module to check the **module review screen**. Make sure you have an answer selected for every question.

Strategy #4: Living in the Question

As discussed above, the digital PSAT is an adaptive test. This means that your performance on the first module of the Math section or the Reading and Writing section will determine the difficulty of the second module you see in that section. On any adaptive test, it can be tempting to try to guess how you performed on the first module based on the questions you are seeing on the second module. However, it is important to **keep all your focus on answering the current question**.

People are typically not great at assessing their own test performance in the moment. We tend to focus on the questions that we found difficult rather than on the questions we answered easily. Thinking too much about your overall performance during the test will draw your attention away from where it needs to be: **answering as many questions correctly as you can** *on your current module*. Don't attempt to make guesses about how you're doing during the exam. Don't attempt to try to identify which questions are operational questions that count and which are the two-per-module pretest questions that are used for research. Don't attempt to determine whether the test has adapted to harder difficulty questions or think about what that means for your overall score during the test. Instead, take action that will help you continue to improve your score: focus on the question you're on. Take confidence in your preparation and in the Methods and strategies you'll learn throughout this book, and apply your skills to each individual question as you encounter it.

Practicing for the PSAT

Every time you complete a set of questions, apply the strategies from this chapter: flag questions you find too time-consuming and return to them if you have time while keeping an eye on the clock. Eliminate incorrect answer choices, strategically guess if you need to, and keep your focus on the current question. Make sure you answer every question.

PART 2

PSAT MATH

CHAPTER 2

PREREQUISITE SKILLS AND CALCULATOR USE

LEARNING OBJECTIVES

After completing this chapter, you will be able to:

- Identify skills necessary to obtain the full benefits of the Math sections of this book
- Use efficiency tips to boost your test day speed
- Distinguish between questions that need a calculator and questions in which manual calculations are more efficient

Math Fundamentals

Test Prerequisites

This book focuses on the skills that are tested on the PSAT. It assumes a working knowledge of arithmetic, algebra, and geometry. Before you dive into the subsequent chapters where you'll try testlike questions, there are a number of concepts—ranging from basic arithmetic to geometry—that you should master. The following sections contain a brief review of these concepts.

Algebra and Arithmetic

- **Order of operations** is one of the most fundamental of all arithmetic rules. A well-known mnemonic device for remembering this order is PEMDAS: Please Excuse My Dear Aunt Sally. This translates to Parentheses, Exponents, Multiplication/Division, Addition/Subtraction. Perform multiplication and division from left to right (even if it means division before multiplication) and treat addition and subtraction the same way, as shown here:

$$(14 - 4 \div 2)^2 - 3 + (2 - 1)$$
$$= (14 - 2)^2 - 3 + (1)$$
$$= 12^2 - 3 + 1$$
$$= 144 - 3 + 1$$
$$= 141 + 1$$
$$= 142$$

- Three basic properties of number (and variable) manipulation—commutative, associative, and distributive—will assist you with algebra on test day:

1. **Commutative:** Numbers can swap places and still provide the same mathematical result. This is valid only for addition and multiplication. For example:

$$a + b = b + a \rightarrow 3 + 4 = 4 + 3$$
$$a \times b = b \times a \rightarrow 3 \times 4 = 4 \times 3$$

BUT: $3 - 4 \neq 4 - 3$ and $3 \div 4 \neq 4 \div 3$

2. **Associative:** Different number groupings will provide the same mathematical result. This is valid only for addition and multiplication. For example:

$$(a + b) + c = a + (b + c) \rightarrow (4 + 5) + 6 = 4 + (5 + 6)$$
$$(a \times b) \times c = a \times (b \times c) \rightarrow (4 \times 5) \times 6 = 4 \times (5 \times 6)$$

BUT: $(4 - 5) - 6 \neq 4 - (5 - 6)$ and $(4 \div 5) \div 6 \neq 4 \div (5 \div 6)$

3. **Distributive:** A number that is multiplied by the sum or difference of two other numbers can be rewritten as the first number multiplied by the two others individually. This does *not* work with division. For example:

$$a(b+c) = ab + ac \rightarrow 6(x+3) = 6x + 6(3)$$
$$a(b-c) = ab - ac \rightarrow 3(y-2) = 3y + 3(-2)$$

$$\text{BUT: } 12 \div (6+2) \neq 12 \div 6 + 12 \div 2$$

Note: When subtracting an expression in parentheses, such as in $4 - (x+3)$, distribute the negative sign outside the parentheses first: $4 + (-x - 3) \rightarrow 1 - x$.

- Subtracting a positive number is the same as adding its negative. Likewise, subtracting a negative number is the same as adding its positive:

$$r - s = r + (-s) \rightarrow 22 - 15 = 7 \text{ and } 22 + (-15) = 7$$
$$r - (-s) = r + s \rightarrow 22 - (-15) = 37 \text{ and } 22 + 15 = 37$$

- You should be comfortable manipulating both proper and improper fractions.

  - To add and subtract fractions, first find a common denominator, then add the numerators together:

$$\frac{2}{3} + \frac{5}{4} \rightarrow \left(\frac{2}{3} \times \frac{4}{4}\right) + \left(\frac{5}{4} \times \frac{3}{3}\right) = \frac{8}{12} + \frac{15}{12} = \frac{23}{12}$$

  - Multiplying fractions is straightforward: multiply the numerators together, then repeat for the denominators. Cancel when possible to simplify the answer:

$$\frac{5}{8} \times \frac{8}{3} = \frac{5}{\overset{}{\underset{1}{\cancel{8}}}} \times \frac{\overset{1}{\cancel{8}}}{3} = \frac{5 \times 1}{1 \times 3} = \frac{5}{3}$$

  - Dividing by a fraction is the same as multiplying by its reciprocal. Once you've rewritten a division problem as multiplication, follow the rules for fraction multiplication to simplify:

$$\frac{3}{4} \div \frac{3}{2} = \frac{\overset{1}{\cancel{3}}}{\underset{2}{\cancel{4}}} \times \frac{\overset{1}{\cancel{2}}}{\underset{1}{\cancel{3}}} = \frac{1 \times 1}{2 \times 1} = \frac{1}{2}$$

- Whatever you do to one side of an equation, you must do to the other. For instance, if you multiply one side by 3, you must multiply the other side by 3 as well.

- The ability to solve straightforward, one-variable equations is critical on the PSAT. For example:

$$\frac{4x}{5} - 2 = 10$$
$$\frac{4x}{5} = 12$$
$$\frac{5}{4} \times \frac{4x}{5} = 12 \times \frac{5}{4}$$
$$x = 15$$

Note: $\frac{4x}{5}$ is the same as $\frac{4}{5}x$. You could see either form on the PSAT.

You will encounter **irrational numbers**, such as common radicals, on test day. These are numbers that cannot be expressed as the ratio of two integers (i.e., they have no equivalent fraction). You can carry an irrational number through your calculations as you would a variable (e.g., $4 \times \sqrt{2} = 4\sqrt{2}$). Only convert to a decimal when you have finished any intermediate steps.

Mental Math

Even if you're a math whiz, you need to adjust your thought process in terms of the PSAT to give yourself the biggest advantage you can. Knowing a few extra things, such as the below, will boost your speed on test day:

- Don't overutilize your calculator by using it to determine something as simple as $15 \div 3$ (we've seen it many times). Save time on test day by reviewing multiplication tables. At a bare minimum, work up through the 10s. If you know them through 12 or 15, that's even better!

- You can save a few seconds of number crunching by memorizing **perfect squares**. Knowing perfect squares of the numbers through 10 is a good start; go for 15 or even 20 if you can.

- **Percent** means "out of a hundred." For example, $27\% = \frac{27}{100}$. You can write percents as decimals (e.g., $27\% = 0.27$).

- The ability to recognize a few simple fractions masquerading in decimal or percent form will save you time on test day because you won't have to turn to your calculator to convert them. Memorize the content of the following table.

FRACTION	DECIMAL	PERCENT
$\frac{1}{10}$	0.1	10%
$\frac{1}{5}$	0.2	20%
$\frac{1}{4}$	0.25	25%
$\frac{1}{3}$	$0.333\overline{3}$	$33.3\overline{3}\%$
$\frac{1}{2}$	0.5	50%
$\frac{3}{4}$	0.75	75%

- Tip: If you don't have the decimal (or percent) form of a multiple of one of the fractions shown in the table memorized, such as $\frac{2}{5}$, just take the fraction with the corresponding denominator ($\frac{1}{5}$ in this case), convert to a decimal (0.2), and multiply by the numerator of the desired fraction to get its decimal equivalent:

$$\frac{2}{5} = \frac{1}{5} \times 2 = 0.2 \times 2 = 0.4 = 40\%$$

Graphing

- Basic two-dimensional graphing is performed on a **coordinate plane**. There are two **axes**, *x* and *y*, that meet at a central point called the **origin**. Each axis has both positive and negative values that extend outward from the origin at evenly spaced intervals. The axes divide the space into four sections called **quadrants**, which are labeled I, II, III, and IV. Quadrant I is always the upper-right section, and the rest follow counterclockwise:

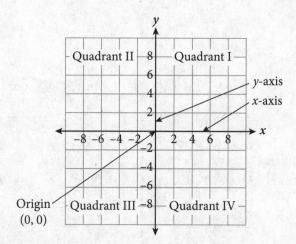

- To plot points on the coordinate plane, you need their coordinates. The **x-coordinate** is where the point falls along the *x*-axis, and the **y-coordinate** is where the point falls along the *y*-axis. The two coordinates together make an **ordered pair** written as (x, y). When writing ordered pairs, the *x*-coordinate is always listed first (think alphabetical order). Four points are plotted in the following figure as examples:

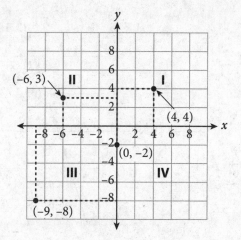

- When two points are vertically or horizontally aligned, calculating the distance between them is easy. For a horizontal distance, only the *x*-value changes; for a vertical distance, only the *y*-value changes. Take the positive difference of the *x*-coordinates (or *y*-coordinates) to determine the distance—that is, subtract the smaller number from the larger number so that the difference is positive. Two examples are presented here:

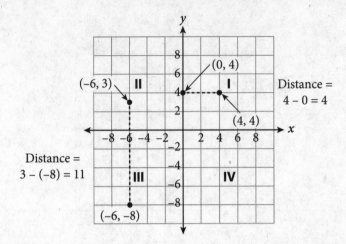

- Two-variable equations have an **independent variable** (input) and a **dependent variable** (output). The dependent variable (often y), depends on the independent variable (often x). For example, in the equation $y = 3x + 4$, x is the independent variable; any y-value depends on what you plug in for x. You can construct a table of values for the equation, or you can graph the equation on your calculator. For example:

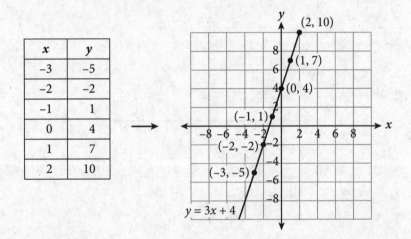

- You may be asked to infer relationships from graphs. In the first of the following graphs, the two variables are year and population. Clearly, the year does not depend on how many people live in the town; rather, the population increases over time and thus depends on the year. In the second graph, you can infer that plant height depends on the amount of rain; thus, rainfall is the independent variable. Note that the independent variable for the second graph is the vertical axis; this can happen with certain nonstandard graphs. On the standard coordinate plane, however, the independent variable is always plotted on the horizontal axis.

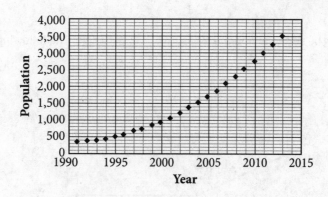

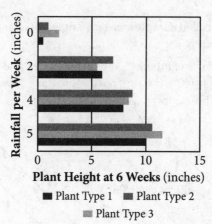

- When two straight lines are graphed simultaneously, one of three possible scenarios will occur:

  1. The lines will not intersect at all (no solution).

  2. The lines will intersect at one point (one solution).

  3. The lines will lie on top of each other (infinitely many solutions).

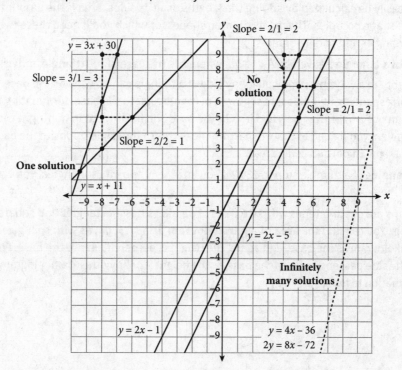

Geometry

- **Adjacent angles** can be added to find the measure of a larger angle. The following diagram demonstrates this:

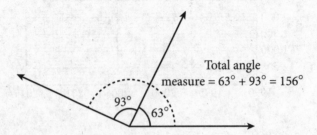

- Two angles that sum to 90° are called **complementary angles**. Two angles that sum to 180° are called **supplementary angles**.

- Two distinct lines in a plane will either intersect at one point or extend indefinitely without intersecting. If two lines intersect at a right angle (90°), they are **perpendicular** and are denoted with ⊥. If the lines never intersect, they are **parallel** and are denoted with ‖. For example:

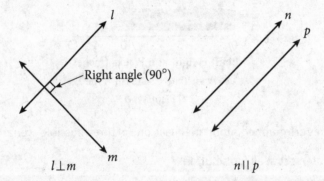

- **Perimeter** and **area** are basic properties that all two-dimensional shapes have. The perimeter of a polygon can easily be calculated by adding the lengths of all its sides. Area is the amount of two-dimensional space a shape occupies. The most common shapes for which you'll need these two properties on test day are triangles and parallelograms.

- The **area (A) of a triangle** is given by $A = \frac{1}{2}bh$, where b is the base of the triangle and h is its height. The base and height are always perpendicular. Any side of a triangle can be used as the base; just make sure you use its corresponding height (a line segment perpendicular to the base, terminating in the opposite vertex). You can use a right triangle's two legs as the base and height, but in non-right triangles, if the height is not given, you'll need to draw it in (from the vertex of the angle opposite the base down to the base itself at a right angle) and compute it.

- The **interior angles** of a triangle sum to 180°. If you know any two interior angles, you can calculate the third.

- **Parallelograms** are quadrilaterals with two pairs of parallel sides. Rectangles and squares are subsets of parallelograms. You can find the **area of a parallelogram** using $A = bh$. As with triangles, you can use any side of a parallelogram as the base, and again, the height is perpendicular to the base. For a rectangle or square, use the side perpendicular to the base as the height. For any other parallelogram, the height (or enough information to find it) will be given.

- A **tangent line** touches a circle at exactly one point and is perpendicular to a circle's radius at the point of contact, as shown here:

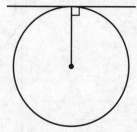

The presence of a right angle opens up the opportunity to draw otherwise hidden shapes, so pay special attention to tangents when they're mentioned.

- A shape is said to have **symmetry** when it can be split by a line (called an **axis of symmetry**) into two identical parts. Consider folding a shape along a line: if all sides and vertices align once the shape is folded in half, the shape is symmetrical about that line. Some shapes have no axis of symmetry, some have one, some have multiple axes, and still others can have infinite axes of symmetry (e.g., a circle):

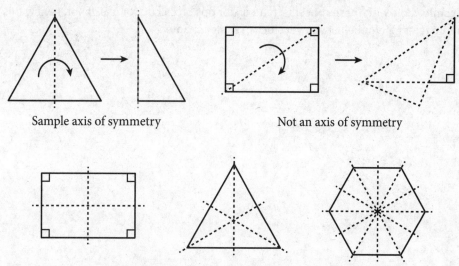

Sample axis of symmetry   Not an axis of symmetry

Sample shapes with corresponding axes of symmetry

- **Congruence** is simply a geometry term that means identical. Angles, lines, and shapes can be congruent. Congruence is indicated by using hash marks. Everything with the same number of hash marks is congruent:

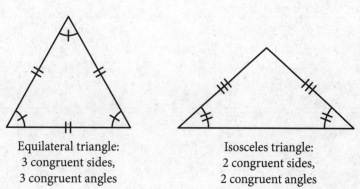

Equilateral triangle:
3 congruent sides,
3 congruent angles

Isosceles triangle:
2 congruent sides,
2 congruent angles

- **Similarity** between shapes indicates that they have identical angles and proportional sides. Think of taking a shape and stretching or shrinking each side by the same ratio. The resulting shape will have the same angles as the original. While the sides will not be identical, they will be proportional. For example:

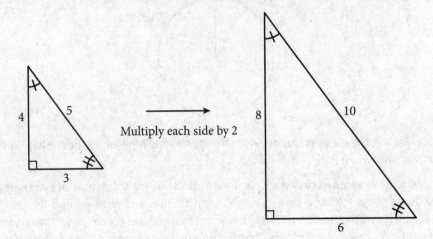

Multiply each side by 2

- If you're comfortable with these concepts, read on for tips on calculator use. If not, review this lesson and remember to refer to it for help if you get stuck in a later chapter.

Calculator Use

Calculators and the PSAT

Many students never stop to ask whether using a calculator is the most efficient way to solve a problem. This chapter will show you how the strongest test takers use their calculators strategically; that is, they carefully evaluate when to use the calculator and when to skip it in favor of a more streamlined approach. As you will see, even though you can use a calculator, sometimes it's more beneficial to save your energy by approaching a question more strategically. Work smarter, not harder.

Which Calculator Should You Use?

The PSAT allows four-function, scientific, and graphing calculators; additionally, it features a built-in graphing calculator. No matter which calculator you choose, start practicing with it now. You don't want to waste valuable time on test day looking for the exponent button or figuring out how to correctly graph equations. Due to the wide range of math topics you'll encounter on test day, **we recommend using a graphing calculator**.

A graphing calculator's capabilities extend well beyond what you'll need for the test, so don't worry about memorizing every function. The next section will cover which calculator functions you'll want to know how to use for the PSAT. If you'd prefer to use your own graphing calculator, you'll want to get the user manual; you can find this on the Internet by searching for your calculator's model number. Identify the calculator functions necessary to answer various PSAT Math questions, then write down the directions for each to make a handy study sheet.

When Should You Use a Calculator?

Some PSAT question types are designed based on the idea that students will do some or all of the work using a calculator. As a master test taker, you want to know what to look for so you can identify when calculator use is advantageous. Questions involving statistics, determining roots of complicated quadratic equations, and other topics are generally designed with calculator use in mind.

Other questions aren't intentionally designed to involve calculator use. Solving some with a calculator can save you time and energy, but you'll waste both if you go for the calculator on others. You will have to decide which method is best when you encounter the following topics:

• Long division and other extensive calculations
• Graphing quadratics
• Simplifying radicals and calculating roots
• Plane and coordinate geometry

Practicing **long computations** by hand and with the calculator will not only boost your focus and mental math prowess but will also help you determine whether it's faster to do the work for a given question by hand or reach for the calculator on test day.

Graphing quadratic equations is a big reason why many students get a fancy calculator in the first place; it makes answering these questions a snap! This is definitely an area where you need to have an in-depth knowledge of the functions of the calculator you'll be using on test day. The key to making these questions easy with the calculator is being meticulous when entering the equation.

Another stressful area for many students is **radicals**, especially when the answer choices are written as decimals. Those two elements are big red flags that trigger a reach for the calculator. Beware: not all graphing calculators have a built-in radical simplification function, so consider familiarizing yourself with this process.

Geometry can be a gray area for students when it comes to calculator use. Consider working by hand when dealing with angles and lines, specifically when filling in information on complementary, supplementary, and congruent angles. You should be able to work fluidly through most of those questions without using your calculator.

If you choose to use **trigonometric functions** to get to the answer on triangle questions, make sure you have your calculator set to degrees or radians as required by the question.

In short, be sure to understand how the calculator that you will be using on test day works, whether that's your own approved for use on the test or the one included with the College Board's testing application. You can get more practice with the College Board's included calculator by taking a Practice Test on College Board's website.

To Use or Not to Use?

A calculator is a double-edged sword on the PSAT: using one can be an asset for verifying work if you struggle when doing math by hand, but turning to it for the simplest computations will cost you time that you could devote to more complex questions. Practice solving questions with and without a calculator to get a sense of your personal style as well as your strengths and weaknesses. Think critically about when a calculator saves you time and when mental math is faster. Use the exercises in this book to practice your calculations so that by the time test day arrives, you'll be in the habit of using your calculator as effectively as possible.

CHAPTER 3

THE METHOD FOR PSAT MATH QUESTIONS

LEARNING OBJECTIVES

After completing this chapter, you will be able to:

- Efficiently apply the Math Method to PSAT Math questions
- Apply the Backsolving strategy
- Apply the Picking Numbers strategy

How to Do PSAT Math

PSAT Math questions can seem more difficult than they actually are, especially when you're working under time pressure. The method we're about to describe will help you answer PSAT questions, whether you're comfortable with the math content or not. This method is designed to give you the confidence you need to get the correct answers on the PSAT by helping you think through each question logically, one piece at a time.

Take a look at this question and think about how you would attack it if you saw it on test day:

> The Collins Library is one of four public libraries in Madison County. Of the 15,000 books in Collins Library, 58% are fiction. If the other three libraries are similar to Collins, then how many nonfiction books are held by public libraries in Madison County?
>
> (A) 6,300
>
> (B) 25,200
>
> (C) 35,600
>
> (D) 60,400

Many test takers will see a question like this and panic. Others will waste a great deal of time reading and rereading without a clear goal. You want to avoid both of those outcomes.

First, ask yourself, **"What is the question asking?"** In other words, what do the answer choices represent? In this question, they represent *the number of nonfiction books in all the public libraries in Madison County.*

Second, ask yourself, **"What does the question tell me?"** In other words, what information did the test makers give you? Here, you know that 58% of the 15,000 books in Collins Library are fiction, that Collins is one of 4 libraries in Madison County, and that all 4 libraries are similar.

Third, ask yourself, **"What strategy is best for me?"** The answer to this question is personal. What works best for you might not work best for other test takers, and vice versa. The answer choices to this question are far apart, so you might consider rounding 58% to $\frac{6}{10}$ and estimating. Alternatively, you could use your calculator to make precise calculations easily. If you decide to use your calculator, start by finding the percentage of nonfiction books: $100\% - 58\% = 42\%$. Next, calculate the number of nonfiction books in Collins:

$$\text{Nonfiction total in Collins Library: } 0.42 \times 15,000 = 6,300$$

Finally, ask yourself, **"Am I done?"** This step is an important step. Does your answer make sense? Did you answer what the question asked? Panicked students who skip this step might see choice (A) and incorrectly select it.

You're not done yet! You calculated the number of nonfiction books in *Collins*, but the question asks for the number of nonfiction books *in Madison County*. There are 4 libraries in Madison County—Collins and 3 others that are similar—so you need to multiply your answer by 4:

$$6,300 \times 4 = 25,200$$

Again, ask yourself, **"Am I done?"** This time, you are! You want the number of nonfiction books in all public libraries in Madison County, and that's what you calculated. The correct answer is **(B)**.

Here are the steps of the method we just used:

THE METHOD FOR PSAT MATH QUESTIONS

STEP 1 What is the question asking?

STEP 2 What does the question tell me?

STEP 3 What strategy is best for me?

STEP 4 Am I done?

The amount of time you spend on each step may vary from question to question. The question above, because it is an in-context word problem, required a fair amount of analysis in steps 1 and 2, but choosing an approach (step 3) was straightforward; the calculations were quick to do on a calculator, so most students find no need to estimate. Other questions will require less thought in steps 1 and 2, but will benefit from a careful strategy decision in step 3. Step 4 is always quick, but you should always do it: just stop for a moment to make sure you answered the question that was actually asked and that the answer makes sense to you before selecting or entering your response. Doing so will save you from mistakes on questions that you know how to do and should be getting credit for.

There are several approaches you can choose from in step 3: doing the traditional math, as we did in the question above; Picking Numbers; Backsolving; estimating; or taking a strategic guess. In the next two examples, you'll see Picking Numbers and Backsolving in action.

Here's another example. This one is not an in-context word problem, so steps 1 and 2 require less mental energy, but pay attention when you get to step 3:

Which of the following expressions is equivalent to $\dfrac{6x + 8}{x - 1}$?

Ⓐ $6 - \dfrac{14}{x - 1}$

Ⓑ $6 + \dfrac{8}{x - 1}$

Ⓒ $6 + \dfrac{14}{x - 1}$

Ⓓ $\dfrac{6 + 8}{-1}$

Step 1: What is the question asking?

An expression equivalent to $\dfrac{6x + 8}{x - 1}$.

Step 2: What does the question tell me?

Only the expression $\dfrac{6x + 8}{x - 1}$.

Step 3: What strategy is best for me?

Here's where it gets interesting. The creator of this question may be expecting you to use polynomial long division to solve. But if you don't know how to do polynomial long division (or find it very time-consuming), there's no need to panic. You could use an alternate approach called **Picking Numbers** that will work just as well: choose a number to substitute for x in the question, then substitute the same number in for x in the choices and see which one matches. Like this:

Pick a small number for x, say 2. When $x = 2$, the original expression becomes the following:

$$\frac{6x + 8}{x - 1} = \frac{6(2) + 8}{2 - 1} = \frac{20}{1} = 20$$

Now, plug $x = 2$ into the choices:

A) $6 - \dfrac{14}{x - 1} = 6 - \dfrac{14}{2 - 1} = 6 - 14 = -8$

Not 20, so eliminate (A).

B) $6 + \dfrac{8}{x - 1} = 6 + \dfrac{8}{2 - 1} = 14$

Eliminate (B).

C) $6 + \dfrac{14}{x - 1} = 6 + 14 = 20$

This is a match. When using Picking Numbers, it is possible that another answer choice can produce the same result, so check (D) to be sure there isn't another match when $x = 2$. (If there is, go back and pick another number to distinguish between the choices that match.)

D) $\dfrac{6 + 8}{-1} = -14$

Eliminate (D).

Step 4: Am I done?

You found the equivalent expression, so yes. Only **(C)** is a match, and therefore it is correct.

When picking numbers, use numbers that are **permissible** and **manageable**. That is, use numbers that are allowed by the stipulations of the question and that are easy to work with. In this question, you could have picked any real number because x was not defined as positive, negative, odd, even, a fraction, etc. A small positive integer is usually the best choice in this situation. In other questions, other kinds of numbers may be more manageable. For example, in percents questions, 100 is typically a good number to pick.

Try one more:

A child is arranging plates of apples to serve at a party. If the child places 6 apples on each plate, there will be 5 apples left over. In order to place 7 apples on each plate, with no apples left over, 5 more apples are needed. How many apples does the child have to arrange?

(A) 32

(B) 41

(C) 56

(D) 65

K

Step 1: What is the question asking?

The number of apples the child has.

Step 2: What does the question tell me?

Two unknowns (the number of plates and the number of apples) and sufficient information to set up a system of equations.

Step 3: What strategy is best for me?

You could set up the system of equations, but it might be faster to use a technique called **Backsolving**: plug the answer choices in for the unknown and see which one works. Here, you need an answer choice that will leave a remainder of 5 when divided by 6. Choices (A) and (C) don't meet this condition, so the answer must be (B) or (D). (The highest multiple of 6 that's less than 32 is 30, and the highest multiple of 6 that's less than 56 is 54, both of which leave a remainder of 2, not 5.)

Check (B). If there are 41 apples, and they are distributed 6 to a plate, there will indeed be 5 apples left over since $41 \div 6 = 6 \, R5$. Now, what happens in the other situation? With an extra 5 apples, there should be enough to distribute 7 to a plate with none left over. But $41 + 5 = 46$, which is not evenly divisible by 7. There would be 4 apples left over. Eliminate (B).

Step 4: Am I done?

You've now eliminated every choice but **(D)**, so it must be correct—you don't even need to test it! For the record:

If there are 65 apples and they are distributed 6 to a plate, there would indeed be 5 left over since $65 \div 6 = 10 \, R5$. With an extra 5 apples, it should be possible to distribute them evenly to 7 plates, and this is in fact what happens: $65 + 5 = 70$, which is evenly divisible by 7.

Although it wasn't the case in this question, when backsolving, it often makes sense to start with (B) or (C) in case you can tell from the context whether you'll need a larger or smaller answer choice if the one you're testing fails. For example, if you test (B) and it's too big, then the answer must be (A).

Now, it's your turn. Be deliberate with these questions. If there is analysis to do up front, do it. If there is more than one way to do a question, consider carefully before choosing your approach. And be sure to check whether you answered the right question. Forming good habits now, in slow and careful practice, will build your confidence for test day.

Try on Your Own

Directions

Take as much time as you need on these questions. Work carefully and methodically. There will be opportunities for timed practice later in the book.

1

$$4 + \sqrt{y + 2} = 7$$

What is the value of y?

(A) 3

(B) 7

(C) 9

(D) 11

2

A truck can carry 8,000 pounds. The equipment needed to load and unload the truck must travel with it and weighs 1,500 pounds. The trailer will be loaded with x containers, each of which weighs 300 pounds. How big can x be without exceeding the truck's capacity?

(A) 5

(B) 15

(C) 21

(D) 26

3

An appliance store sells a certain vacuum cleaner for \$450. The vacuum cleaner sells online for $\frac{7}{10}$ of the price. A department store sells the vacuum cleaner for $\frac{6}{5}$ of the price. How many dollars more is the price at the department store than at the online retailer?

(A) 135

(B) 180

(C) 225

(D) 315

4

A stack of 50 kitchen serving trays forms a column that is approximately $7\frac{1}{4}$ inches tall. What is closest to the number of kitchen trays that would be needed to form a column that is 14 inches tall?

(A) 70

(B) 83

(C) 100

(D) 113

5

Last month, Keith ran 18 more miles than Mick ran. If they ran a total of 76 miles, how many miles did Keith run?

(A) 29

(B) 38

(C) 42

(D) 47

6

If $\dfrac{3x}{2y} = 6$, what is the value of $\dfrac{y}{2x}$?

(A) $\dfrac{1}{8}$

(B) $\dfrac{1}{2}$

(C) $\dfrac{2}{3}$

(D) 1

7

x	y
1	$\dfrac{5}{3}$
3	3
5	$\dfrac{13}{3}$
7	$\dfrac{17}{3}$

Which of the following equations relates y to x according to the values in the table?

(A) $y = \dfrac{2}{3}x + 1$

(B) $y = x + \dfrac{2}{3}$

(C) $y = \left(\dfrac{2}{3}x\right)^2 + 1$

(D) $y = \left(\dfrac{2}{5}\right)^x - \dfrac{3}{5}$

8

In a restaurant's kitchen, c cakes are made by adding s cups of sugar to a mix of eggs and butter. If $s = 3c + 5$, how many more cups of sugar are needed to make one additional cake?

(A) 0

(B) $\dfrac{1}{3}$

(C) 1

(D) 3

9

A bowling league charges a one-time membership fee of \$25, plus x dollars each month. If a bowler has paid \$53 for the first 4 months, including the membership fee, what is the value of x?

(A) 4

(B) 7

(C) 10

(D) 13

10

If $x > 0$, which of the following is equivalent to $\dfrac{3}{\dfrac{1}{x+5} + \dfrac{1}{x+3}}$?

(A) $(x+5)^2$

(B) $\dfrac{3(x+5)(x+3)}{2(x+4)}$

(C) $3(x+4)$

(D) $\dfrac{(x+4)}{(x+5)^2}$

A Note about Student-Produced Responses

You will see questions without answer choices throughout the Math chapters of this book, starting in the next chapter, and on the PSAT itself. Instead of selecting an answer choice, you'll enter your responses to these questions into a box that looks like this:

It is possible that such a question may have more than one possible answer, such as the two roots of a quadratic equation. In that case, only enter one of the answers; either one will receive credit. For a positive answer, you can enter up to 5 characters; for a negative answer, you can enter 6 characters (which includes the negative sign). Do not enter symbols like dollar signs, percent signs, or commas. You can enter answers as either a fraction or a decimal (with or without the leading zero); the decimal point will count against the 5 or 6-character limit. If the answer is $\frac{1}{2}$, you can enter 1/2, 0.5, or .5.

Some types of answers require a bit more care. If your answer is a decimal longer than the allotted space, you can either round it or truncate it at the 4th digit. A mixed number must be entered as either an improper fraction or a decimal; anything to the left of the fraction bar will be read as the numerator of a fraction. The table below shows some examples of acceptable and unacceptable answers.

ANSWER	ACCEPTABLE	UNACCEPTABLE
$\frac{5}{9}$	5/9 0.555 0.556 .5555 .5556	0.55 0.56 .555 .556
$-4\frac{1}{4}$	$-17/4$ -4.25 -4.250	$-4\ 1/4$ $-41/4$

If you arrive at a fraction for an answer that will not fit into the space provided in the student-produced response box, such as the seven characters needed for $\frac{901}{990}$, enter the decimal equivalent of the fraction into the box using the rules above.

Reflect

Directions: Take a few minutes to recall what you've learned and what you've been practicing in this chapter. Consider the following questions, jot down your best answer for each one, and then compare your reflections to the expert responses that follow. Use your level of confidence to determine what to do next.

Think about your current habits when attacking PSAT questions. Are you a strategic test taker? Do you take the time to think through what would be the fastest way to the answer?

_____

_____

_____

Do word problems give you trouble?

_____

_____

_____

What are the steps of the Method for PSAT Math and why is each step important?

_____

_____

_____

Expert Responses

Think about your current habits when attacking PSAT questions. Are you a strategic test taker? Do you take the time to think through what would be the fastest way to the answer?

If yes, good for you! If not, we recommend doing questions more than one way whenever possible as part of your PSAT prep. If you can discover now, while you're still practicing, that Picking Numbers is faster for you on certain types of questions but not on others, you'll be that much more efficient on test day.

Do word problems give you trouble?

If word problems give you trouble and are an area of opportunity for you, get into the habit of taking an inventory, before you do any math, of what the question is asking for and what information you have.

What are the steps of the Method for PSAT Math and why is each step important?

Here are the steps:

Step 1. *What is the question asking?*

(Understanding what you are asked is key to being able to answer it correctly.)

Step 2. *What does the question tell me?*

(Taking an inventory is especially important in word problems.)

Step 3. *What strategy is best for me?*

(Taking a moment to decide which approach will be the fastest way for you to get to the answer will ultimately save you time.)

Step 4. *Am I done?*

(Making sure that you solved for the right thing will save you from missing out on points on questions that you know how to do and should be getting credit for.)

Next Steps

If your approach to most questions in the "Try On Your Own" section generally resembled that of the experts using Kaplan methods and strategies, and if your responses to the Reflect questions were similar to those of the PSAT expert, then consider the Method for PSAT Math an area of strength and move on to the next chapter. Do keep using the method as you work on the questions in future chapters.

If you don't yet feel confident, review those parts of this chapter that you have not yet mastered and try the questions you missed again. As always, be sure to review the explanations closely.

Answers and Explanations

Try on Your Own

1. B

Difficulty: Medium

Category: Advanced Math

Getting to the Answer: The question asks for the value of y given an equation in terms of y. You could try backsolving, but it would be helpful to first simplify the equation by subtracting 4 from both sides to get $\sqrt{y+2} = 3$. Now, check the answer choices, starting with (B) or (C). If the answer you choose is too large or too small, you'll know which direction to go when testing the next choice.

(B): $\sqrt{7+2} = \sqrt{9} = 3$. This is the correct answer.

If you prefer the algebraic approach, here it is:

$$\sqrt{y+2} = 3$$
$$y + 2 = 3^2$$
$$y + 2 = 9$$
$$y = 7$$

Again, **(B)** is the correct answer.

2. C

Difficulty: Medium

Category: Algebra

Getting to the Answer: The correct answer will be the biggest possible value of x, or the number of containers a truck can carry without exceeding its cargo capacity. To answer this question, organize the information you know. The capacity of the trailer is 8,000 pounds. However, equipment that is already on the trailer weighs 1,500 pounds, so there is only $8,000 - 1,500 = 6,500$ pounds of remaining capacity. Each container weighs 300 pounds, so divide 6,500 by 300 to determine the maximum number of containers that can be packed: $\frac{6,500}{300} = 21\frac{200}{300} = 21\frac{2}{3}$. Partial containers may not be packed, so round down to 21, which is **(C)**.

3. C

Difficulty: Medium

Category: Algebra

Getting to the Answer: The question asks for the difference between the prices of a vacuum cleaner at a department store and at an online retailer. You know the price of the vacuum at an appliance store, that it costs $\frac{7}{10}$ of the price at an online retailer and $\frac{6}{5}$ of the price at a department store. Determine the two unknown prices: $\frac{7}{10}(450) = 315$ and $\frac{6}{5}(450) = 540$. You're not done yet; the question asks for the difference between the prices, not either individual price, so subtract them: $540 - 315 = 225$, which is **(C)**.

4. C

Difficulty: Easy

Category: Problem-Solving and Data Analysis

Getting to the Answer: You need to determine how many trays would be in a stack 14 inches tall, given that 50 plates make a stack $7\frac{1}{4}$ tall. You could use the given information to determine the height of each tray, and then divide 14 by that height to see how many plates are needed. However, this is a good opportunity for estimating. Notice the relationship between the stack of $7\frac{1}{4}$ inches and the height of the stack asked about: 14 is very close to twice $7\frac{1}{4}$, so you will need nearly twice the 50 trays given in the question. Thus, 100 is the correct answer, which is **(C)**.

5.   D

Difficulty: Medium

Category: Algebra

Getting to the Answer: You're asked for the number of miles that Keith ran; you're told the total number of miles run by Keith and Mick and that Keith ran 18 more miles than Mick. There are two unknowns (the miles each person ran) and enough information so that a system of equations could be formed. So, traditional algebra could be used to solve this system of equations.

However, there is a more efficient way to answer the question: examine the answer choices to see which answers make sense for Keith's distance. The question states that Keith ran 18 more miles than Mick; thus, Keith must have run more than half of the 76 miles that the two of them ran. Since one-half of 76 is 38, you can eliminate (A) and (B) immediately.

Now you just have to check either (C) or (D). For (C), if Keith ran 42 miles, then Mick ran $42 - 18 = 24$ miles, and $42 + 24 = 66$ miles, which isn't correct. Thus, **(D)** is the correct answer. For the record, if Keith ran 47 miles, then Mick ran $47 - 18 = 29$ miles, and $47 + 29 = 76$, which is correct.

If you are curious about the algebraic approach, let k represent the number of miles Keith ran and m represent the number of miles Mick ran. Since Keith ran 18 miles more than Mick, Mick ran 18 miles fewer, or $m = k - 18$ miles. They ran a combined 76 miles, $k + m = 76$. Substitute the value for m from the first equation into the second and solve:

$$k + (k - 18) = 76$$
$$2k - 18 = 76$$
$$2k = 94$$
$$k = 47$$

Again, this matches **(D)**.

6.   A

Difficulty: Medium

Category: Algebra

Getting to the Answer: You're asked for the value of an expression involving x and y, and you're given an equation in terms of x and y. You could manipulate the given equation with algebraic operations until it looks like the expression, but instead, try picking numbers. Pick a simple number for y and solve for x. Hopefully, x will also be easy to work with so you can plug them into the expression you are trying to find. Say $y = 1$; this gives $\frac{3x}{2(1)} = 6$, or $3x = 12$. Dividing both sides by 3 gives $x = 4$. Both numbers are very manageable, so plug them into the expression $\frac{y}{2x}$. This yields $\frac{1}{2(4)} = \frac{1}{8}$, which is **(A)**.

7.   A

Difficulty: Medium

Category: Algebra

Getting to the Answer: The correct answer will be an equation describing the relationship between x and y, several values of which are given in a table. Notice that for every increase of 2 in x, y increases by $\frac{4}{3}$. Thus, the relationship is linear, meaning you can eliminate (C) and (D). To determine whether (A) or (B) is correct, substitution could be used. However, note that if y increases by $\frac{4}{3}$ for every 2 unit increase in x, then dividing both values by 2 shows that y increases by $\frac{2}{3}$ for every 1 unit increase in x. This is the definition of slope, and the only equation that is a line with a slope of $\frac{2}{3}$ is **(A)**.

8.   D

Difficulty: Medium

Category: Algebra

Getting to the Answer: You need to determine how many extra cups of sugar would be needed to make one more cake. You're given a linear equation in terms of s and c. Pick a number for c; say $c = 2$. This means that $3(2) + 5 = 11$ cups of sugar are needed for two cakes. Now, try $c = 3$: $3(3) + 5 = 14$ cups of sugar needed for 3 cakes. To go from 2 cakes to 3 cakes, 3 additional cups of sugar were needed, which is **(D)**. You can try $c = 4$ to confirm: $3(4) + 5 = 17$, which is another 3 cups of sugar.

9. B

Difficulty: Medium

Category: Algebra

Getting to the Answer: The question asks for the value of x, which is the monthly fee for a bowling league; you're given the cost of a four-month membership, which includes a one-time membership fee. Try back-solving, starting with (B) or (C). If the answer you choose is too large or too small, you will know which direction to go. Multiply the answer choice by 4 and add the $25 membership fee.

(B): $\$7 \times \$4 = \$28 \rightarrow \$28 + \$25 = \$53$. This is a match, so **(B)** is the correct answer.

Algebra could also be used here:

$$\$25 + 4x = \$53$$
$$4x = \$28$$
$$x = \$7$$

Algebra again leads to $7, which is **(B)**.

10. B

Difficulty: Medium

Category: Advanced Math

Getting to the Answer: The correct answer will be an expression equal to the one given in the question, which also specifies that x must be positive. Try using the picking numbers strategy. Pick something easy, like $x = 1$: $\dfrac{3}{\dfrac{1}{1+5} + \dfrac{1}{1+3}}$.

This simplifies to $\dfrac{3}{\dfrac{1}{6} + \dfrac{1}{4}} = \dfrac{3}{\dfrac{2}{12} + \dfrac{3}{12}} = \dfrac{3}{\dfrac{5}{12}}$.

This can be rewritten as $3 \times \dfrac{12}{5} = \dfrac{36}{5}$.

Now, plug 1 in for x in each of the answer choices to see which one gives you the same value:

(A): $(1+5)^2 = 36$. Eliminate.

(B): $\dfrac{3(1+5)(1+3)}{2(1+4)} = \dfrac{3(6)(4)}{2(5)} = \dfrac{72}{10} = \dfrac{36}{5}$. Correct! Just to be sure, check the other two answers.

(C): $3(1+4) = 3(5) = 15$. Eliminate.

(D): $\dfrac{(1+4)}{(1+5)^2} = \dfrac{5}{6^2} = \dfrac{5}{36}$. Eliminate.

Since **(B)** is the only answer that matched the calculated value, it must be the correct answer.

ALGEBRA

LINEAR EQUATIONS AND GRAPHS

LEARNING OBJECTIVES

After completing this chapter, you will be able to:

- Isolate a variable
- Translate word problems into equations
- Match an expression or equation to a real-life context, table, or graph
- Calculate the slope of a line given two points
- Write the equation of a line in slope-intercept form
- Discern whether the slope of a line is positive, negative, zero, or undefined based on its graph
- Describe the slopes of parallel and perpendicular lines

Math

How Much Do You Know?

Directions

Try the questions that follow. Show your work so that you can compare your solutions to the ones found in the "Check Your Work" section immediately after this question set. If you answered the question(s) on a specific topic correctly, and if your scratchwork looks like ours, you may be able to move quickly through the lesson covering that topic. If you answered incorrectly or used a different approach, you may want to take your time on that lesson.

1

$$\frac{1}{2}(3x + 17) = \frac{1}{6}(8x - 10)$$

Which value of x satisfies the equation?

(A) -61

(B) -55

(C) -41

(D) -35

2

A rental car costs $54.95 per day, taxed at a rate of 6 percent, with an additional one-time, untaxed environmental impact fee of $10. Which of the following equations represents the total cost, in dollars, c, for renting the car for d days?

(A) $c = (54.95 + 0.06d) + 10$

(B) $c = 1.06(54.95d) + 10$

(C) $c = 1.06(54.95d + 10)$

(D) $c = 1.06(54.95 + 10)d$

3

What was the initial amount of water in a barrel, in liters, if x liters remain after y liters were spilled and 6 liters were added?

(A) $x - y + 6$

(B) $y - x + 6$

(C) $x + y + 6$

(D) $y + x - 6$

4

Price of One Can	Projected Number of Cans Sold
$0.75	10,000
$0.80	9,000
$0.85	8,000
$0.90	7,000
$0.95	6,000
$1.00	5,000

Which of the following equations best describes the relationship shown in the table, where *n* indicates the number of cans sold and *p* represents the price, in dollars, of one can?

Ⓐ $n = -20{,}000p + 25{,}000$

Ⓑ $n = -200p + 250$

Ⓒ $n = 200p + 250$

Ⓓ $n = 20{,}000p + 25{,}000$

5

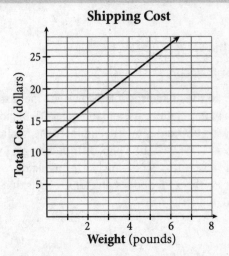

Shipping Cost

A freight company charges a flat rate to deliver a package, plus an additional charge for each pound the package weighs. The graph shows the relationship between the weight of the package and the total cost to ship it. Based on the graph, how much would it cost to ship a 25-pound box?

Ⓐ $37.00

Ⓑ $48.00

Ⓒ $62.50

Ⓓ $74.50

Check Your Work

1. A

Difficulty: Easy

Category: Algebra

Getting to the Answer: Look for a way to make the algebra manipulations easier (and quicker). Begin by multiplying both sides by 6 to eliminate the fractions. So, $3(3x + 17) = 8x - 10$. Then, distribute to get $9x + 51 = 8x - 10$. Combining like terms yields $9x - 8x = -10 - 51$, and solving for x reveals that $x = -61$, which is **(A)**.

2. B

Difficulty: Medium

Category: Algebra

Getting to the Answer: Use the information in the question to write your own equation, then look for the answer choice that matches. Simplify your equation only if you don't find a match. Start with the cost, not including tax or the environmental impact fee. If a car is rented for d days at a daily rate of $54.95, the untaxed total is $54.95d$. There is a 6% tax added to this amount, so multiply by 1.06 to get $1.06(54.95d)$. The $10.00 environmental impact fee is not taxed, so simply add 10 to the expression. The total cost is $c = 1.06(54.95d) + 10$, which matches **(B)**, so you do not need to simplify.

3. D

Difficulty: Medium

Category: Algebra

Getting to the Answer: Write an equation in words first, then translate from English to math. Finally, rearrange your equation to find what you're interested in, which is the initial amount. Call the initial amount A. After you've written your equation, solve for A.

Amount now (x) = initial amount (A) minus y plus 6:

$$x = A - y + 6$$
$$x + y - 6 = A$$

This is the same as $y + x - 6$, so **(D)** is correct.

You could also pick numbers to answer this question.

4. A

Difficulty: Medium

Category: Algebra

Getting to the Answer: The answer choices are given in slope-intercept form, so start by finding the slope. To do this, substitute two pairs of values from the table into the slope formula, $m = \frac{y_2 - y_1}{x_2 - x_1}$. Keep in mind that the projected number of cans sold *depends* on the price, so the price is the independent variable (p) and the projected number is the dependent variable (n). Using the points (0.75, 10,000) and (1.0, 5,000), the slope is:

$$m = \frac{5,000 - 10,000}{1.00 - 0.75}$$
$$= \frac{-5,000}{0.25}$$
$$= -20,000$$

This means that **(A)** must be correct because it is the only one that has a slope of $-20,000$. Don't let (D) fool you—the projected number of cans sold goes *down* as the price goes *up*, so there is an inverse relationship, and the slope must be negative.

5. D

Difficulty: Hard

Category: Algebra

Getting to the Answer: In a real-world scenario, the y-intercept of a graph usually represents a flat fee or an initial value. The slope of the line represents a unit rate, such as the cost per pound. The y-intercept of the graph is 12, so the flat fee is $12. To find the cost per pound (the unit rate), substitute two points from the graph into the slope formula. Using the points (0, 12) and (2, 17), the unit rate is $\frac{17 - 12}{2 - 0} = \frac{5}{2} = 2.5$, which means $2.50 per pound will be added to the cost. The total cost to ship a 25-pound box is $12 + 2.50(25) = 12 + 62.50 = 74.50$, which is **(D)**.

Math

Solving Equations

LEARNING OBJECTIVE

After this lesson, you will be able to:

• Isolate a variable

To answer a question like this:

$$\frac{1}{3}(3x + 12) = \frac{1}{6}(5x - 12)$$

Which of the following values is equal to x?

(A) −36

(B) 4

(C) 12

(D) 20

[handwritten: $2(3x +12) = 5x+2$]
[handwritten: $6x+24 = 5x -12$]
[handwritten: $x = -36$]

You need to know this:

Isolating a variable means getting that variable by itself on one side of the equation. To do this, use inverse operations to manipulate the equation, remembering that whatever you do to one side of the equation, you must do to *both* sides.

You need to do this:

It usually makes sense to proceed in this order:

1. Eliminate any fractions.

2. Collect and combine like terms.

3. Divide to leave the desired variable by itself.

Explanation:

Eliminate the fractions by multiplying both sides of the equation by 6:

$$\left(\frac{6}{1}\right)\frac{1}{3}(3x + 12) = \left(\frac{6}{1}\right)\frac{1}{6}(5x - 12)$$

$$2(3x + 12) = (5x - 12)$$

In order to collect all the *x* terms on one side, you'll first need to distribute the 2 on the left side of the equation:

$$6x + 24 = 5x - 12$$

Next, subtract 5x from both sides:

$$x + 24 = -12$$

Finally, subtract 24 from both sides:

$$x = -36$$

Therefore, **(A)** is correct.

$\frac{8}{7}x - .324 + 7.55 = 38$

$\frac{8}{7}x = 30.7684\cdots$

$x \approx 8.9$

$12x + 9 = -6x - 3 + 25$

Try on Your Own

Directions

Take as much time as you need on these questions. Work carefully and methodically. There will be an opportunity for timed practice later in the book.

1

HINT: Since the answer choices in Q1 involve decimals, convert the fractions to decimals.

$$\frac{8}{7}\left(x - \frac{101}{220}\right) + 4\left(x + \frac{8}{9}\right) = 38$$

Which approximate value of x satisfies the equation shown?

- (A) 4.3
- (B) 4.6
- (C) 6.6
- (D) 6.8

2

If $3(n - 2) = 6$, then what does $\frac{n-2}{n+2}$ equal?

$3n - 6 = 6$
$n = 4$

1/3

3

$$\frac{7(n - 3) + 11}{6} = \frac{18 - (6 + 2n)}{8}$$

In the equation shown, what is the value of n?

- (A) $\frac{38}{17}$
- (B) $\frac{38}{11}$
- (C) $\frac{56}{11}$
- (D) $\frac{94}{17}$

4

If $36 + 3(4x - 9) = c(2x + 1) + 25$ has no solution and c is a constant, what is the value of c?

- (A) -3
- (B) 3
- (C) 6
- (D) 12

5

HINT: Is there a way to make the fraction easier to work with for Q5?

If $x = \dfrac{a + \frac{1}{2}b}{a + b}$, which of the following expresses b in terms of a and x?

- (A) $b = \dfrac{2a(1 - x)}{2x - 1}$
- (B) $b = \dfrac{2a(1 - 2x)}{4x - 1}$
- (C) $b = 2a(1 - x)$
- (D) $b = 2a(1 - 2x)$

$\frac{7n - 10}{6} = \frac{18 - (6 + 2n)}{8}$

Word Problems

LEARNING OBJECTIVES

After this lesson, you will be able to:

- Translate word problems into expressions and equations
- Match an expression or equation to a real-life context, table, or graph

To answer a question like this:

A gym sells two types of one-year memberships. Package A costs $325 and includes an unlimited number of visits. Package B has a $185 enrollment fee, includes five free visits, and costs an additional $4 per visit after the first five. How many visits would a person need to use for Package B to cost the same amount as Package A?

Ⓐ 30

Ⓑ 35

Ⓒ 40

Ⓓ 45

You need to know this:

PSAT word problems test your understanding of how to describe real-world situations using math equations. For some questions, it will be up to you to extract and solve an equation; for others, you'll have to interpret an equation in a real-world context. The following table shows some of the most common phrases and mathematical equivalents you're likely to see on the PSAT.

WORD PROBLEMS TRANSLATION TABLE	
ENGLISH	**MATH**
equals, is, equivalent to, was, will be, has, costs, adds up to, the same as, as much as	$=$
times, of, multiplied by, product of, twice, double	$\times$
divided by, out of, ratio	$\div$
plus, added to, sum, combined, increased by	$+$
minus, subtracted from, smaller than, less than, fewer, decreased by, difference between	$-$
a number, how much, how many, what	x, n, etc.

You need to do this:

When translating from English to math, *start by defining the variables*, choosing letters that make sense. Then, *break the question down into small pieces*, writing down the translation for one phrase at a time.

Explanation:

The phrase "how many visits" indicates an unknown, so you need a variable. Use an intuitive letter to represent the number of visits; call it v. The question asks when the two memberships will cost the "same amount," so write an equation that sets the total membership costs equal to each other.

Package A costs \$325 for unlimited visits, so write 325 on one side of the equal sign. Package B costs \$4 per visit (not including, or *except for*, the first 5 visits), or $4(v-5)$, plus a flat \$185 enrollment fee, so write $4(v-5) + 185$ on the other side of the equal sign. That's it! Now, solve for v:

$$325 = 4(v-5) + 185$$
$$140 = 4v - 20$$
$$160 = 4v$$
$$40 = v$$

The answer is **(C)**.

250   130

CHAPTER 4
LINEAR EQUATIONS AND GRAPHS

Math

Try on Your Own

Directions

Take as much time as you need on these questions. Work carefully and methodically. There will be an opportunity for timed practice later in the book.

6

The price for an insurance policy includes a fixed administrative fee and a <u>percentage</u> of the value of the car, v. If the price is given by the function $T = 0.02v + 25$, then the value 0.02 best represents which of the following?

(A) The fee for the administrative expenses

(B) The value of the car

(C) The total price of the policy

(D) The percentage of the value of the car

7

A cell phone plan has a service cost of $50 per month. Additionally, while the first 2 gigabytes of data are free, each subsequent gigabyte costs $8. Each text message sent also costs $0.10. Which of the following represents the monthly cost in dollars, c, if g represents the gigabytes of data used (where $g \geq 2$), and t is the number of text messages sent?

(A) $c = 50 + 8g + 0.1t$

(B) $c = 50 + (8g - 2) + 0.1t$

(C) $c = 50 + 8(g - 2) + 0.1t$

(D) $c = 5{,}000 + 800g + 10t$

8

HINT: For Q8, determine the expression for the standard plan before attempting to build the entire equation.

An unlimited video game rental package costs $250 for 3 months and allows customers to rent as many games as they want. The standard rental package has a flat fee of $130 and costs $4 per rental in the 3-month period. How many rentals on the standard package would it take for both packages to equal the same price over 3 months?

(A) 2

(B) 30

(C) 96

(D) 120

9

On Mondays, a produce stand sells watermelons at a 20% discount from the normal price of $0.60 per pound. Which of the following represents the total cost, c, if a customer buys four sweet potatoes at $0.79 each and a watermelon weighing p pounds on a Monday?

(A) $c = 0.2p + 0.79$

(B) $c = 0.48p + 3.16$

(C) $c = 0.6p + 0.79$

(D) $c = 0.6p + 3.16$

.2

K   47

10

HINT: For Q10, if *a* arrows hit the inner circle, how many hit the outer circle in terms of *a*?

In an archery match, an archer gets 8 points if the arrow hits the inner circle of the target and 4 points if it hits the outer circle. Which of the following equations represents the total score, *p*, if, out of 12 arrows, *a* arrows hit the inner circle and the rest hit the outer circle?

Ⓐ $p = 8a$

Ⓑ $p = 8a + 4$

Ⓒ $p = 48 + 4a$

● $p = 96 - 4a$

12

a

$P = 8a +$

Linear Graphs

LEARNING OBJECTIVES

After this lesson, you will be able to:

- Calculate the slope of a line given two points
- Write the equation of a line in slope-intercept form
- Discern whether the slope of a line is positive, negative, zero, or undefined based on its graph
- Describe the slopes of parallel and perpendicular lines

To answer a question like this:

What is the equation of the line that passes through the points $(2, -4)$ and $(-2, 2)$?

A) $y = \frac{3}{2}x + 1$

B) $y = \frac{3}{2}x - 1$

C) $y = -\frac{3}{2}x + 1$

D) $y = -\frac{3}{2}x - 1$

You need to know this:

The answer choices in this question are written in slope-intercept form: $y = mx + b$. In this form of a linear equation, m represents the **slope** of the line and b represents the **y-intercept**. You can think of the slope of a line as how steep it is. The y-intercept is the y-coordinate of the point where the line crosses the y-axis. If the point where the line crosses the y-axis is $(0, b)$, the y-intercept is b.

You can calculate the slope of a line if you know any two points on the line. The formula is $m = \frac{y_2 - y_1}{x_2 - x_1}$, where (x_1, y_1) and (x_2, y_2) are the coordinates of any two points on the line.

A line that moves from the bottom left to the top right has a positive slope. A line that moves from the top left to the bottom right has a negative slope. A horizontal line has a slope of zero, and a vertical line has an undefined slope.

Some PSAT questions ask about parallel or perpendicular lines. Parallel lines have the same slope, while perpendicular lines that are not parallel to the axes have slopes that are negative reciprocals.

You need to do this:

- Find the slope of the line.
- Write the equation in slope-intercept form, substituting the value of the slope you found and one of the known points for x and y.
- Solve for the y-intercept.

Explanation:

In the question, $m = \dfrac{-4 - 2}{2 - (-2)} = \dfrac{-6}{4} = -\dfrac{3}{2}$. Of the answer choices, only (C) and (D) have negative slopes, so rule out (A) and (B).

To find the y-intercept of the line, write the equation for the line in slope-intercept form and plug in one of the known points for x and y:

$$y = -\frac{3}{2}x + b$$

$$2 = -\frac{3}{2}(-2) + b$$

$$2 = 3 + b$$

$$-1 = b$$

Therefore, **(D)** is correct.

Another way to solve this question would be to plot the two points, graph the line, check where it crosses the y-axis to find the y-intercept, and count how many spaces the line moves down for each space it moves to the right to find the slope.

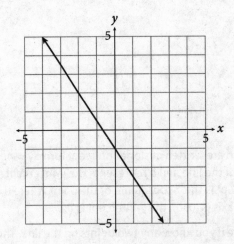

Try on Your Own

Directions

Take as much time as you need on these questions. Work carefully and methodically. There will be an opportunity for timed practice later in the book.

11

HINT: For Q11, remember that parallel lines have the same slope and perpendicular lines have opposite sign reciprocal slopes.

A line *t* is perpendicular to $y = -\frac{3}{4}x + 5$ and passes through the point (3, 5). What is the equation of line *t*?

$\frac{4}{3} + 5$

(A) $y = \frac{4}{3}x + 1$

(B) $y = -\frac{4}{3}x + 1$

(C) $y = \frac{4}{3}x + 5$

(D) $y = -\frac{3}{4}x + 1$

12

HINT: Convert the word problem in Q12 to an equation in slope-intercept form, $y = mx + b$.

Months after June	4	8	10
Price of Gas	2	3.33	4

In June, the price of gas starts increasing. The table shows the approximate price of gas 4, 8, and 10 months after June. If *y* is the price of gas, in dollars per gallon, and *x* is the number of months after June, which linear equation represents the correct relationship between *y* and *x*?

slope

(A) $y = 0.33x + 0.67$

(B) $y = 0.67x + 1.33$

(C) $y = 1.33x + 2$

(D) $y = 2.67x + 5.67$

13

HINT: For Q13, focus on where the answer choices differ in their equations: the y-intercept.

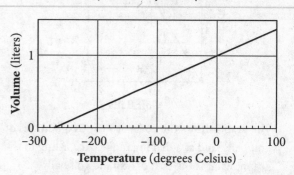

The graph shows the volume of a sample of gas as it is cooled. If *T* is the temperature of the gas in degrees Celsius and *V* is the volume in liters, which of the following equations, when plotted, could produce the graph shown?

(A) $V = 0.004T + 100$

(B) $V = 0.004T$

(C) $V = 0.004T + 1$

(D) $V = 0.004T - 0.25$

$\frac{y_2 - y_1}{x_2 - x_2}$ $\frac{10 - 2}{5}$ $\frac{4-2}{10-4}$ $\frac{2}{6} = \frac{1}{3}$

0.33

$y = mx + b$

14

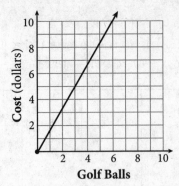

Golf Balls

The graph shows the costs of various quantities of golf balls sold at a driving range. According to the graph, what is the cost of a single golf ball?

- (A) $0.60
- (●) $1.67
- (C) $3.00
- (D) $5.00

15

For what value of y does the graph of $4x - \frac{1}{2}y = -12$ cross the y-axis?

$$\underline{24}$$

$$4x - \frac{1}{2}y = -12$$

$$4x + 12 = \frac{1}{2}y$$

$$2(4x + 12)$$

$$8x + 24 = y$$

On Test Day

Remember that the PSAT doesn't ask you to show your work. If you find the algebra in a question challenging, there is often another way to get to the answer.

Try this question first using algebra and then using the Picking Numbers strategy you learned in chapter 3. Time yourself. Which approach do you find easier? Which one was faster? Did you get the correct answer both times? Remember your preferred approach and try it first if you see a question like this on test day.

16. If $\dfrac{2(a-4)}{b} = \dfrac{4}{5}$, which of the following statements is true?

(A) $\dfrac{2a}{b} = -\dfrac{12}{5}$

(B) $\dfrac{b}{a-4} = \dfrac{5}{2}$

(C) $10a - 5b = 40$

(D) $\dfrac{a-4}{2b} = \dfrac{2}{5}$

The answer and explanation can be found at the end of this chapter.

handwritten top left: perp= -recip
parallel: recip

handwritten top right:
$45 + 27z - (9 - 18z) = -9z - 12$
$57 + 27z - 9 \cancel{} = -9z$
$48 + 27z = 9z$
$48 = -18z$ · -2.666

How Much Have You Learned?

Directions

For test-like practice, give yourself 15 minutes to complete this question set. Be sure to study the explanations, even for questions you answered correctly. They can be found at the end of this chapter.

1

Line m is parallel to line k and passes through (5, 5). The slope of line k is $-\frac{2}{5}$ and line k passes through the origin. Which of the following is the equation for line m?

(A) $y = -\frac{2}{5}x$

(B) $y = \frac{5}{2}x + 7$

● $y = \frac{5}{2}x$

(D) $y = -\frac{2}{5}x + 7$

2

Which value of x makes the equation $\frac{2}{3}(x - 1) = 12$ true?

(A) 7

(B) 9

(C) 17

● 19

3

$$\frac{5 + 3z - (1 + 2z)}{3} = \frac{-3z - 2(5 - 3)}{9}$$

What is the value of z in the given equation?

● $-\frac{8}{3}$

(B) $-\frac{61}{27}$

(C) $\frac{61}{27}$

(D) $\frac{8}{3}$

4

Sandy works at a tire store. She gets paid $70 for a day's work, plus a commission of $14 for each tire she sells. Which of the following equations represents the relationship between one day of Sandy's pay, y, and the number of tires she sells, x?

(A) $x = 14y + 70$

(B) $x = 70y + 14$

● $y = 14x + 70$

(D) $y = 70x + 14$

handwritten bottom:
$\frac{2}{3}(x-1) = 12$
$2x - 2 = 36$
$2x = 38$
$x =$

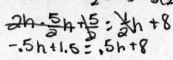

$\frac{2}{3}(3h) - \frac{5}{2}(h \cdot 1) = \frac{1}{3}(\frac{3}{2}h) + 8$ $\rightarrow h = -6.5$

$\cancel{2h} \cdot \frac{5}{2}h + \frac{5}{2} = \frac{y}{2}h + 8$

$-.5h + 1.5 = .5h + 8$

5

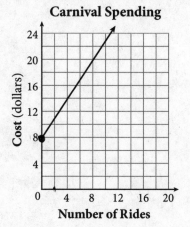

Carnival Spending

The graph shows the cost of going to a certain carnival. What does the y-intercept most likely represent?

●   A flat entrance fee

Ⓑ   The cost of riding 8 rides

Ⓒ   The cost of attending the carnival 8 times

Ⓓ   The total cost of attending the carnival and riding 1 ride

6

Depreciation, the reduction in a car's value due to use or age, begins as soon as the car is purchased and driven for the first time. If the equation $y = -0.15x + 27{,}000$ represents the estimated effect of depreciation on the value of a certain car, what does 27,000 most likely represent?

Ⓐ   The depreciation rate

Ⓑ   The current value of the car

⬤   The original purchase price of the car

Ⓓ   The value of the car after 0.15 years of ownership

7

$$\frac{2}{3}(3h) - \frac{5}{2}(h - 1) = -\frac{1}{3}\left(\frac{3}{2}h\right) + 8$$

What is the value of h in the given equation?

Ⓐ -5.5

Ⓑ 5.5

Ⓒ   There is no value of h for which the equation is true.

Ⓓ   There are infinitely many values of h for which the equation is true.

8

$\frac{9}{4}(y - 8) = \frac{27}{2}$ 

What value of y satisfies the equation? $\frac{9}{4}y = 31.5$

   $\underline{\quad 7 \quad}$ $y = 7$

9

A cybercafe charges a base rate of $25 for a year's membership, an additional $0.30 per visit for the first 50 visits, and $0.10 for every visit after that. If a customer who made more than 50 visits is charged $42.20 for a year, how many visits did the customer make?

Ⓐ   14

Ⓑ   22

⬤   72

Ⓓ   172

$42.20 - 25 = 17.2$ 50

2.2 $\frac{22}{72}$

10

A mobile phone provider charges k dollars for the first gigabyte of data used in a month and m dollars for every additional gigabyte used that month. If Jared paid $65.50 for his data use in one month, which of the following expressions represents the number of gigabytes he used that month?

Ⓐ $\dfrac{65.50}{k + m}$

● $\dfrac{65.50 - k}{m}$

Ⓒ $\dfrac{65.50 - k - m}{m}$

Ⓓ $\dfrac{65.50 - k + m}{m}$

Reflect

Directions: Take a few minutes to recall what you've learned and what you've been practicing in this chapter. Consider the following questions, jot down your best answer for each one, and then compare your reflections to the expert responses that follow. Use your level of confidence to determine what to do next.

What should you do to isolate a particular variable in an equation?

_____

_____

_____

What types of keywords should you look for when translating English into math?

_____

_____

_____

What is the most useful equation for a line in the coordinate plane? Why?

_____

_____

_____

When the PSAT gives you two points on a line, what can you figure out?

_____

_____

_____

How are parallel and perpendicular lines related to each other?

_____

_____

_____

Expert Responses

What should you do to isolate a particular variable in an equation?

Perform inverse operations until the variable is by itself on one side of the equal sign. If the equation has fractions, make them disappear by multiplying both sides of the equation by the denominator(s). If like terms appear on different sides of the equation, collect them on the same side so that you can combine them.

What types of keywords should you look for when translating English into math?

Look for keywords that signal equality ("is," "has," "was"), variable names ("Marina's age," "the cost of one bathtub"), or one of the four arithmetic operations (addition, subtraction, multiplication, and division).

What is the most useful equation for a line in the coordinate plane? Why?

The best equation is slope-intercept form, $y = mx + b$, *because it tells you the slope* (m) *and the* y-intercept (b). *Conversely, if you need to derive an equation yourself, you can plug the slope and y-intercept into slope-intercept form and you're done.*

When the PSAT gives you two points on a line, what can you figure out?

If you know two points, you can figure out the slope of the line with the equation $m = \dfrac{y_2 - y_1}{x_2 - x_1}$. *From there, you can plug one of the points and the slope into slope-intercept form and find the y-intercept.*

How are parallel and perpendicular lines related to each other?

Parallel lines never intersect and they have equal slopes. Perpendicular lines intersect at a 90° angle and they have negative reciprocal slopes.

Next Steps

If you answered most questions correctly in the "How Much Have You Learned?" section, and if your responses to the Reflect questions were similar to those of the PSAT expert, then consider Linear Equations and Graphs an area of strength and move on to the next chapter. Come back to this topic periodically to prevent yourself from getting rusty.

If you don't yet feel confident, review those parts of this chapter that you have not yet mastered. In particular, review the variable isolation example in the Solving Equations lesson and the definition of slope-intercept form in the Linear Graphs lesson. Then, try the questions you missed again. As always, be sure to review the explanations closely.

Answers and Explanations

Try on Your Own

1.   D

Difficulty: Medium

Category: Algebra

Getting to the Answer: Multiply both sides by 7 to eliminate the fraction outside the parentheses. Then, because the choices are decimals, convert all fractions to decimal form: $8(x - 0.46) + 28(x + 0.89) = 266$. Distribute to get $8x - 3.68 + 28x + 24.92 = 266$, then combine like terms to yield $36x = 266 + 3.68 - 24.92$, or $36x = 244.76$. Divide both sides by 36 to find that x is approximately 6.8, which is **(D)**.

2.   1/3, .3333, or 0.333

Difficulty: Medium

Category: Algebra

Getting to the Answer: We have the equation $3(n - 2) = 6$. Dividing both sides by 3, we have $n - 2 = 2$. Adding 2 to both sides, $n = 4$. Now substitute 4 for n in the expression $(n - 2)/(n + 2)$. Then $(4 - 2)/(4 + 2) = 2/6 = 1/3$. Enter **1/3, .3333,** or **0.333**

3.   A

Difficulty: Medium

Category: Algebra

Getting to the Answer: Start by simplifying the numerators. Don't forget to distribute the negative to both terms inside the parentheses on the right side of the equation:

$$\frac{7(n - 3) + 11}{6} = \frac{18 - (6 + 2n)}{8}$$

$$\frac{7n - 21 + 11}{6} = \frac{18 - 6 - 2n}{8}$$

$$\frac{7n - 10}{6} = \frac{12 - 2n}{8}$$

$$\frac{7n - 10}{6} = \frac{6 - n}{4}$$

Next, cross-multiply and solve for n using inverse operations:

$$4(7n - 10) = 6(6 - n)$$

$$28n - 40 = 36 - 6n$$

$$34n = 76$$

$$n = \frac{76}{34} = \frac{38}{17}$$

This matches **(A)**.

4.   C

Difficulty: Medium

Category: Algebra

Getting to the Answer: If a linear equation has no solution, the variables cancel out, leaving two numbers that are not equal to each other. Start by simplifying the left side of the equation:

$$36 + 3(4x - 9) = c(2x + 1) + 25$$

$$36 + 12x - 27 = 2cx + c + 25$$

The variable term on the left is $12x$. Because the variable terms must cancel, the right side of the equation must also have a $12x$, so it must be that $c = 6$, which is **(C)**.

5.   A

Difficulty: Medium

Category: Algebra

Getting to the Answer: Clear the equation of the fraction in the numerator by multiplying both sides by 2 to yield:

$$2x = \frac{2a + b}{a + b}$$

Now, multiply both sides by the denominator $a + b$ to clear the equation of fractions:

$$2x(a + b) = 2a + b$$

Distribute the 2x:

$$2ax + 2bx = 2a + b$$

Collect all the terms that include b on one side of the equation:

$$2bx - b = 2a - 2ax$$

Factor out b from the left side and 2a from the right side:

$$b(2x - 1) = 2a(1 - x)$$

Divide both sides by $(2x - 1)$ to isolate b:

$$b = \frac{2a(1 - x)}{2x - 1}$$

(**A**) is correct.

6. D

Difficulty: Easy

Category: Algebra

Getting to the Answer: The total insurance bill consists of a flat fee and a percentage of the value of the car. The administrative fee does not depend on the value of the car and therefore should not be multiplied by v. This means that 25 is the administrative fee. The other expression in the equation, 0.02v, represents the percentage of the value of the car times the car's value (which the question tells you is v). Therefore, 0.02 must represent the percentage, which is (**D**).

7. C

Difficulty: Medium

Category: Algebra

Getting to the Answer: You know there will be a flat fee of $50, and for text messages you'll be looking for 0.1t. This eliminates (D). If you're stuck on the data plan cost, plug in some numbers. For $g = 2$, you wouldn't expect there to be an additional fee for data usage. For $g = 3$, you'd expect to see an $8 charge, and for $g = 4$, you'd expect to see a $16 charge. The only choice that reflects this is (**C**).

8. B

Difficulty: Medium

Category: Algebra

Getting to the Answer: Set up an expression representing the cost of the standard plan. If r is the number of rentals, then the cost of the standard plan for 3 months would be $130 + 4r$. Set that expression equal to the cost of the unlimited plan for 3 months and solve for r:

$$130 + 4r = 250$$
$$4r = 120$$
$$r = 30$$

Choice (**B**) is correct.

9. B

Difficulty: Medium

Category: Algebra

Getting to the Answer: Translate from English to math. The cost of the watermelon is its weight in pounds, p, multiplied by the sale price. Since the purchase is made on Monday, the sale price per pound is: $0.60 \times 80\% = 0.6 \times 0.8 = 0.48$. This gives the cost of the watermelon: 0.48p. Now, to get the total cost, c, add the cost of four sweet potatoes, $0.79 \times 4 = 3.16$, to get the equation $c = 0.48p + 3.16$, which matches (**B**).

You could also use the Picking Numbers strategy: pick a number for the weight of the watermelon and calculate how much it would cost (on sale). Next, add the cost of four sweet potatoes. Finally, find the equation that gives the same amount.

10. C

Difficulty: Hard

Category: Algebra

Getting to the Answer: The key to answering this question is to determine how many arrows hit each circle. If there are 12 arrows total and a hit the inner circle, the rest, or $12 - a$, must hit the outer circle. Each arrow in the inner circle scores 8 points and each arrow in the outer circle scores 4 points, so the total score, p, is $p = 8a + 4(12 - a)$. This is not one of the answer choices, so simplify the expression by distributing the 4 and then combining like terms: $8a + 4(12 - a) = 8a + 48 - 4a = 4a + 48$, so the equation is $p = 4a + 48$. Rearrange the order of the terms on the right side to arrive at (**C**).

$\frac{3}{4}$ $-\frac{4}{3}$

CHAPTER 4
LINEAR EQUATIONS AND GRAPHS

Math

11. A

Difficulty: Medium

Category: Algebra

Getting to the Answer: The first useful piece of information is that the slope of the line perpendicular to line t is $-\frac{3}{4}$. Perpendicular lines have negative reciprocal slopes, so the slope of line t is $\frac{4}{3}$. Eliminate (B) and (D) because they have incorrect slopes.

Plug the values for the slope and the coordinates of the point (3, 5) into the slope-intercept equation to solve for b:

$$5 = \frac{4}{3}(3) + b$$
$$5 = 4 + b$$
$$5 - 4 = b$$
$$b = 1$$

Eliminate (C) because it does not have the correct y-intercept. Choice **(A)** is correct.

12. A

Difficulty: Medium

Category: Algebra

Getting to the Answer: The question tells you that the relationship is linear, so start by finding the slope, m, using any two pairs of values from the table and the slope formula. Next, substitute the slope and any pair of values from the table, such as (4, 2) and (10, 4), into the equation $y = mx + b$ and solve for b. Finally, use the values of m and b to write the function:

$$m = \frac{y_2 - y_1}{x_2 - x_1} = \frac{4 - 2}{10 - 4} = \frac{2}{6} = \frac{1}{3}$$

You can stop right there! Only (A) has a slope of 0.33, so it must be the correct answer. For the record:

$$2 = \frac{1}{3}(4) + b$$
$$2 = \frac{4}{3} + b$$
$$\frac{2}{3} = b$$

$$\frac{Y_2 - Y_1}{X_2 - X_1}$$

13. C

Difficulty: Medium

Category: Algebra

Getting to the Answer: Temperature, T, is the independent variable on the x-axis, and volume, V, is the dependent variable on the y-axis. Therefore, the form of the equation you're looking for is $V = mT + b$. Because each answer choice has a different y-intercept, finding b is enough to get the correct answer; there is no need to determine the slope. Although the graph is not centered around the origin, you can still find the y-intercept. In this case, it's 1. This eliminates every answer choice except **(C)**, which is correct.

14. B

Difficulty: Medium

Category: Algebra

Getting to the Answer: The x-axis represents the number of golf balls, so find 1 on the x-axis and trace up to where it meets the graph of the line. The y-value is somewhere between $1 and $2, so the only possible correct answer is $1.67, which is **(B)**.

You could also find the unit rate by calculating the slope of the line using two of the points shown on the graph. The graph rises 5 units and runs 3 units from one point to the next, so the slope is $\frac{5}{3}$, or 1.67.

15. 24

Difficulty: Medium

Category: Algebra

Getting to the Answer: The place where the line crosses the y-axis is the y-intercept, or b when the equation is written in slope-intercept form ($y = mx + b$), so rewrite the equation in this form:

$$4x - \frac{1}{2}y = -12$$
$$-\frac{1}{2}y = -4x - 12$$
$$-2\left(-\frac{1}{2}y = -2(-4x - 12)\right)$$
$$y = 8x + 24$$

The y-intercept is **24**.

Because the y-intercept of a graph is always of the form (0, y), you could also substitute 0 for x in the original equation and solve for y.

On Test Day

16. B

Difficulty: Hard

Category: Algebra

Getting to the Answer: To find the answer using Picking Numbers, take advantage of the fact that the equation is a proportion (that is, two fractions equal to each other). If $b = 5$ and $2(a - 4) = 4$, then both fractions will be the same and the numbers you've picked will be valid. Solve for a: $2(a - 4) = 4$, so $a = 6$. Now, plug $b = 5$ and $a = 6$ into the choices, looking for the one that is true:

(A) $\frac{2a}{b} = \frac{2(6)}{5} = \frac{12}{5} \neq -\frac{12}{5}$. Eliminate.

(B) $\frac{b}{a-4} = \frac{5}{6-4} = \frac{5}{2}$. This is correct, but with picking numbers, you'll want to check all of the answer choices. If you get more than one answer choice where the numbers you picked worked, try the answer choice that you didn't eliminate with new permissible numbers and repeat the process.

(C) $10a - 5b = 10(6) - 5(5) = 60 - 25 = 35$. This does not equal 40, so it can be eliminated.

(D) $\frac{a-4}{2b} = \frac{6-4}{2(5)} = \frac{2}{10}$. This does not equal $\frac{2}{5}$, so it can also be eliminated.

Since **(B)** is the only choice that worked, it is correct.

To solve this question using algebra, first cross-multiply and simplify the original equation:

$$\frac{2(a-4)}{b} = \frac{4}{5}$$
$$10(a-4) = 4b$$
$$5(a-4) = 2b$$
$$5a - 20 = 2b$$
$$5a - 2b = 20$$

Then, repeat this process for each answer choice, looking for the one that yields the same equation:

(A) $\frac{2a}{b} = -\frac{12}{5}$, $10a = -12b$, $5a = -6b$, $5a + 6b = 0$. Eliminate.

(B) $\frac{b}{a-4} = \frac{5}{2}$, $2b = 5a - 20$, $20 = 5a - 2b$. This matches and is correct.

There can only be one correct answer, so choose **(B)** and move on. For the record:

(C) $10a - 5b = 40$, $5a - \frac{5}{2}b = 20$. Eliminate.

(D) $\frac{a-4}{2b} = \frac{2}{5}$, $5a - 20 = 4b$, $5a - 4b = 20$. Eliminate.

How Much Have You Learned?

1. D

Difficulty: Medium

Category: Algebra

Getting to the Answer: This question provides an equation for a line parallel to line m and a coordinate of the point on line m, (5, 5). The slope of the parallel line, which is $-\frac{2}{5}$, is the same as the slope of line m. Eliminate (B) and (C) because they have the incorrect slope.

Plug the values for the slope and the coordinate of the point (5, 5) into the slope-intercept equation to solve for b:

$$5 = -\frac{2}{5}(5) + b$$
$$5 = -2 + b$$
$$5 + 2 = b$$
$$b = 7$$

Eliminate (A) because it does not have the correct y-intercept. Only **(D)** is left and is correct. To confirm, plug the values for the slope and the y-intercept into the slope-intercept equation to get $y = -\frac{2}{5}x + 7$.

2. D

Difficulty: Easy

Category: Algebra

Getting to the Answer: Distributing the $\frac{2}{3}$ will result in messy calculations, so clear the fraction instead. Multiply both sides of the equation by the reciprocal of $\frac{2}{3}$, which is $\frac{3}{2}$, and isolate x:

$$\frac{3}{2} \cdot \frac{2}{3}(x - 1) = 12 \cdot \frac{3}{2}$$
$$x - 1 = 18$$
$$x = 19$$

Choice **(D)** is correct.

Alternatively, you could backsolve. Say you started with (B). The left side of the equation would become

$\frac{2}{3}(9-1) = \frac{2}{3}(8) = \frac{16}{3}$, which is smaller than 12, so you would move to (C) next. Plugging in 17 gives $\frac{2}{3}(17-1) = \frac{2}{3}(16) = \frac{32}{3}$. This is still smaller than 12 since $12(3) = 36$, so the correct answer again must be **(D)**.

3. A

Difficulty: Medium

Category: Algebra

Getting to the Answer: Simplify the numerators as much as possible, then isolate the variable. Begin by combining like terms on both sides of the equation. Once complete, cross-multiply and solve for z:

$$\frac{5 + 3z - (1 + 2z)}{3} = \frac{-3z - 2(5-3)}{9}$$
$$\frac{4+z}{3} = \frac{-3z-4}{9}$$
$$9(4+z) = 3(-3z-4)$$
$$36 + 9z = -9z - 12$$
$$18z = -48$$
$$z = -\frac{8}{3}$$

Choice **(A)** is correct.

4. C

Difficulty: Easy

Category: Algebra

Getting to the Answer: When writing a linear equation, a flat rate is a constant while a unit rate is always multiplied by the independent variable. For one day of work, Sandy is paid $70, which is a flat rate and should be the constant in the equation. You can identify the unit rate by looking for words like *per* or *for each*. The clue "for each" tells you to multiply $14 by the number of tires she sells, so the equation is *pay* = 14 × *number of tires* + 70, or $y = 14x + 70$. This matches **(C)**.

5. A

Difficulty: Easy

Category: Algebra

Getting to the Answer: Read the axis labels carefully. The y-intercept is the point at which $x = 0$, which means the number of rides is 0. The y-intercept is (0, 8). This means the cost is $8 before riding any rides, and therefore 8 most likely represents a flat entrance fee, **(A)**.

6. C

Difficulty: Easy

Category: Algebra

Getting to the Answer: Because the car's value is always declining from the time it is purchased, its greatest value is its purchase price when new. The car's price at any time can be represented as the purchase price minus some value that depends on the car's age. In the given formula, $0.15x$ is subtracted from 27,000, suggesting that $0.15x$ represents the decline in value over time and 27,000 represents the car's original purchase price, choice **(C)**.

7. C

Difficulty: Medium

Category: Algebra

Getting to the Answer: Look for a way to make the math easier, such as clearing the fractions first. To do this, multiply both sides of the equation by 6, then solve for h using inverse operations:

$$6\left[\frac{2}{3}(3h)\right] - 6\left[\frac{5}{2}(h-1)\right] = 6\left[-\frac{1}{3}\left(\frac{3}{2}h\right)\right] + 6\,(8)$$
$$4(3h) - 15(h-1) = -2\left(\frac{3}{2}h\right) + 48$$
$$12h - 15h + 15 = -3h + 48$$
$$-3h + 15 = -3h + 48$$
$$15 \neq 48$$

Because the variable terms in the equation cancel out, and 15 does not equal 48, the equation has no solution. In other words, there is no value of h that satisfies the equation, so **(C)** is correct.

8. 14

Difficulty: Easy

Category: Algebra

Getting to the Answer: Eliminate the fractions to simplify the math. Multiply both sides of the equation by 4, then solve for y using inverse operations:

$$4\left[\frac{9}{4}(y-8)\right] = 4\left(\frac{27}{2}\right)$$
$$9(y-8) = 54$$
$$9y - 72 = 54$$
$$9y = 126$$
$$y = 14$$

Enter **14** in the box.

9. C

Difficulty: Medium

Category: Algebra

Getting to the Answer: Use the information in the question to set up an equation for the yearly cost. There's a $25 flat fee, a $0.30 charge for each of the first 50 visits, and an additional $0.10 cost for each of the visits over 50. So if c is the total cost and v is the number of visits, then:

$$c = 25 + 0.3(50) + 0.1(v - 50)$$
$$= 25 + 15 + 0.1v - 5$$
$$= 35 + 0.1v$$

You know the total cost for the year, $42.20, so plug that into the equation and solve for v:

$$42.20 = 35 + 0.1v$$
$$7.20 = 0.1v$$
$$72 = v$$

(C) is correct.

10. D

Difficulty: Hard

Category: Algebra

Getting to the Answer: Let g be the number of gigabytes Jared used during the month. The first gigabyte costs k dollars and the remaining gigabytes $(g - 1)$ are charged at the rate of m dollars per gigabyte. Therefore, the total charge for a month is $k + (g - 1)m$. Set this equal to the amount Jared paid and solve for g. Note that you're not going to get a numeric answer because the question doesn't give you the actual rates:

$$k + (g - 1)m = 65.50$$
$$k + gm - m = 65.50$$
$$mg = 65.50 + m - k$$
$$g = \frac{65.50 + m - k}{m}$$

This expression matches **(D)**. Note that you could also use Picking Numbers to answer this question.

$$k + (g - 1)m$$

SYSTEMS OF LINEAR EQUATIONS

Math

Math

LEARNING OBJECTIVES

After completing this chapter, you will be able to:

- Solve systems of linear equations by substitution
- Solve systems of linear equations by combination
- Determine the number of possible solutions for a system of linear equations, if any

How Much Do You Know?

Directions

Try the questions that follow. Show your work so that you can compare your solutions to the ones found in the "Check Your Work" section immediately after this question set. If you answered the question(s) on a specific topic correctly, and if your scratchwork looks like ours, you may be able to move quickly through the lesson covering that topic. If you answered incorrectly or used a different approach, you may want to take your time on that lesson.

1

$$-6x + 3y = 27$$
$$x + y = 0$$

What is the value of x for the given equations above?

(A) −3

(B) 0

(C) 3

(D) 5

2

An LED television costs $25 less than twice the cost of wireless speakers. If the television and speakers together cost $500, how much more does the television cost than the speakers?

(A) $150

(B) $175

(C) $200

(D) $225

3

At a snack stand, hot dogs cost $3.50 and hamburgers cost $5.00. If the snack stand sold 27 snacks for a total of $118.50, how many hot dogs and how many hamburgers were sold?

(A) 16 hot dogs; 11 hamburgers

(B) 16 hot dogs; 16 hamburgers

(C) 11 hot dogs; 14 hamburgers

(D) 11 hot dogs; 16 hamburgers

4

A certain student cell phone plan charges $0.10 per text and $0.15 per picture, with no additional monthly fee. If a student sends a total of 75 texts and pictures in one month and is billed $8.90 for that month, how many more texts did he send than pictures?

(A) 19

(B) 28

(C) 36

(D) 47

5

$$\frac{1}{8}q + \frac{1}{5}s = 40$$

$$zq + 8s = 1,600$$

In the system of linear equations shown, z represents a constant. If the system of equations has infinitely many solutions, what is the value of z?

Ⓐ $\frac{1}{8}$

Ⓑ 5

Ⓒ 8

Ⓓ 40

Check Your Work

1.   A

Difficulty: Easy

Category: Algebra

Getting to the Answer: Solve the second equation for y in terms of x (which yields $y = -x$), then substitute into the first equation and solve:

$$-6x - 3x = 27$$
$$-9x = 27$$
$$x = -3$$

Choice **(A)** is correct.

2.   A

Difficulty: Medium

Category: Algebra

Getting to the Answer: Translate English into math to write a system of equations with s as the cost of the speakers in dollars and t as the cost of the television in dollars. A television costs $25 less than twice the cost of the speakers, or $t = 2s - 25$. Together, the speakers and the television cost $500, so $s + t = 500$.

The system of equations is:

$$t = 2s - 25$$
$$s + t = 500$$

The top equation is already solved for t, so substitute $2s - 25$ into the second equation for t:

$$s + 2s - 25 = 500$$
$$3s - 25 = 500$$
$$3s = 525$$
$$s = 175$$

The speakers cost $175, so the television costs $2(175) - 25 = 350 - 25 = \$325$. This means the television costs $\$325 - \$175 = \$150$ more than the speakers, which is **(A)**.

3.   D

Difficulty: Medium

Category: Algebra

Getting to the Answer: Begin by translating English into math. Define the variables logically: d for hot dogs, b for hamburgers. You're given the cost of each, as well as the

number of snacks sold and the total revenue generated. Next, write the system of equations that represents the information given:

$$d + b = 27$$
$$3.5d + 5b = 118.5$$

Multiplying the top equation by -5 allows you to solve for d using combination:

$$-5d - 5b = -135$$
$$+3.5d + 5b = 118.5$$
$$-1.5d + 0b = -16.5$$

Dividing both sides by -1.5 gives $d = 11$, which eliminates (A) and (B). Plugging 11 in for d in the first equation in the system gives you $11 + b = 27$. Subtract 11 from both sides to find that $b = 16$. **(D)** is correct.

4.   A

Difficulty: Medium

Category: Algebra

Getting to the Answer: Translate English into math to make sense of the situation. First, define your variables: t for texts and p for pictures are good choices. You know that this student sent a total of 75 texts and pictures. You're also told each text costs $0.10 and each picture is $0.15, and that the bill is $8.90. You'll have two equations: one relating the numbers of texts and pictures and a second relating the costs associated with each:

$$t + p = 75$$
$$0.1t + 0.15p = 8.9$$

Multiplying the second equation by 10 allows you to solve for p using combination:

$$t + p = 75$$
$$-(t + 1.5p = 89)$$

Subtract the second equation from the first to find that $-0.5p = -14$ and $p = 28$. But you're not done yet; you're asked for the difference between the text and picture count. Substitute 28 for p in the first equation and then solve for t to get $t = 47$. Subtracting 28 from 47 yields 19, which is **(A)**.

5.   B

Difficulty: Medium

Category: Algebra

Getting to the Answer: A system of equations that has infinitely many solutions results when you can algebraically manipulate one equation to arrive at the other. Examining the right sides of the equations, you see that $40 \times 40 = 1{,}600$; therefore, multiplying the first equation by 40 will give 1,600 on the right: $5q + 8s = 1{,}600$. The first equation is now identical to the second equation, meaning z must be 5, which is **(B)**.

Substitution

LEARNING OBJECTIVE

After this lesson, you will be able to:

- Solve systems of linear equations by substitution

To answer a question like this:

What is the value of y if $5x + 3y = 20$ and $x + y = 20$?

Ⓐ -40

Ⓑ -20

Ⓒ 20

Ⓓ 40

You need to know this:

A **system** of two linear equations simply refers to the equations of two lines. "Solving" a system of two linear equations usually means finding the point where the two lines intersect. (However, see the lesson titled "Number of Possible Solutions" later in this chapter for exceptions.)

There are multiple ways to solve a system of linear equations. For some PSAT questions, substitution is fastest; for others, combination is fastest. There is also the possibility of using the test's built-in graphing calculator, although this can sometimes be more time consuming. Combination is covered in the next lesson.

You need to do this:

To solve a system of two linear equations by substitution, do the following:

- Isolate a variable (ideally, one whose coefficient is 1) in one of the equations.
- Substitute the result into the other equation.

Explanation:

Isolate x in the second equation, then substitute the result into the first equation:

$$x = 20 - y$$
$$5(20 - y) + 3y = 20$$
$$100 - 5y + 3y = 20$$
$$-2y = -80$$
$$y = 40$$

Thus, **(D)** is correct. If you needed to know the value of x as well, you could now substitute 40 for y into either equation to find that $x = -20$.

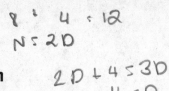

$8 \cdot 4 = 12$

$N = 2D$

$2D + 4 = 3D$

$4 = D$

Try on Your Own

Directions

Solve these questions using substitution. Take as much time as you need on these questions. Work carefully and methodically. There will be an opportunity for timed practice later in the book.

$N = 2D$

$N = 3D$

1

Clarice had twice as many nickels as dimes. When she adds 4 more nickels, she has three times as many nickels as dimes. What was Clarice's total number of coins before she added the additional nickels?

- (A) 4
- (B) 8
- ● 12
- (D) 16

2

HINT: Ask yourself: Which variable in Q2 is the easier one to isolate?

What is the value of b that satisfies $5c + 5b = 20$ and $5b - c = 4$?

CHAPTER 5
SYSTEMS OF LINEAR EQUATIONS

Math

3

$$5x - 4y = 10 + y$$
$$x - 3y = 4$$

What is the value of $x - y$ from the solution of the given system of equations?

- (A) -5
- (B) 0
- (C) 2
- (D) 5

4

HINT: Since the correct answer to Q4 requires you to know the value for r, solve for s in terms of r and substitute.

If $3r + 2s = 24$ and $r + s = 12$, what is the value of $r + 6$?

- (A) 0
- (B) 4
- (C) 6
- (D) 12

5

At a certain restaurant, there are 25 tables and each table has either 2 or 4 chairs. If a total of 86 chairs accompany the 25 tables, how many tables have exactly 4 chairs?

- (A) 7
- (B) 12
- (C) 15
- (D) 18

K 71

Combination

LEARNING OBJECTIVE

After this lesson, you will be able to:

* Solve systems of linear equations by combination

To answer a question like this:

$$6x - 5y = 21$$
$$3x + 3y = -6$$

If the lines represented by the equations shown intersect at the point (x, y), then what is the value of y?

- Ⓐ -3
- Ⓑ -2
- Ⓒ 2
- Ⓓ 3

You need to know this:

Combining two equations means adding or subtracting them. Most often the goal is to eliminate one of the variables, hence this is also known as elimination, but this technique can also be used to solve for a combination of variables (e.g., $5m + 7n$).

You need to do this:

To solve a system of two linear equations by combination, do the following:

* Make sure that the coefficients for one variable have the same absolute value. (If they don't, multiply one equation by an appropriate constant. Sometimes, you'll want to multiply both equations by constants.)
* Either add or subtract the equations to eliminate one variable.
* Solve for the remaining variable, then substitute its value into either equation to solve for the variable you eliminated in the preceding step.

Explanation:

Both variables have different coefficients in the two equations, but you can convert the $3x$ in the second equation to $6x$ by multiplying the entire second equation by 2:

$$2(3x + 3y = -6)$$
$$6x + 6y = -12$$

Now that the coefficients for one variable are the same, subtract the second equation from the first to eliminate the x variable. (Note that if the x-coefficients were 6 and -6, you would add the equations instead of subtracting.)

$$6x - 5y = 21$$
$$\underline{-(6x + 6y = -12)}$$
$$0x - 11y = 33$$

Solve this equation for y:

$$-11y = 33$$
$$y = -3$$

(A) is the correct answer. If the question asked for x as well, you would now substitute -3 for y in either of the original equations and solve for x. (For the record, $x = 1$.)

Try on Your Own

Directions

Solve these questions using combination. Take as much time as you need on these questions. Work carefully and methodically. There will be an opportunity for timed practice later in the book.

6

$$2x - 4y = 14$$
$$5x + 4y = 21$$

What is the y-coordinate of the solution to the system of equations shown?

(A) -1

(B) 0

(C) $\dfrac{7}{3}$

(D) 5

7

HINT: There's no need to solve for b and c separately in Q7.

If $-8c - 3b = 11$ and $6b + 6c = 4$, what is the value of $3b - 2c$?

(A) -27

(B) -3

(C) 8

(D) 15

8

If $6a + 6b = 30$ and $3a + 2b = 14$, then what are the values of a and b?

(A) $a = 2; b = 2$

(B) $a = 4; b = 1$

(C) $a = 1; b = 4$

(D) $a = 2; b = 3$

9

Given $2x + 5y = 49$ and $5x + 3y = 94$, what is the product of x and y?

$$\boxed{\underline{\qquad\qquad}}$$

10

Sixty people attended a concert. Children's tickets sold for \$8 each and adult tickets sold for \$12 each. If \$624 was collected in ticket money, how many more adults than children attended the concert?

(A) 0

(B) 12

(C) 24

(D) 60

Number of Possible Solutions

To answer a question like this:

$$10x - 4y = 8$$
$$8y = kx - 30$$

In the system of linear equations shown, k represents a constant. What is the value of $3k$ if the system of linear equations has no solution?

Ⓐ 20

Ⓑ 30

Ⓒ 60

Ⓓ 80

You need to know this:

The solution to a system of linear equations consists of the values of the variables that make both equations true.

A system of linear equations may have one solution, infinitely many solutions, or no solution.

If a system of equations represents two lines that intersect, then the system will have exactly **one solution** (in which the x- and y-values correspond to the point of intersection).

If a system of equations has **infinitely many solutions**, the two equations actually represent the same line. For example, $2x + y = 15$ and $4x + 2y = 30$ represent the same line. If you divide the second equation by 2, you arrive at the first equation. Every point along this line is a solution.

If a system of equations has **no solution**, as in the question above, the lines are parallel: there is no point of intersection.

One Solution

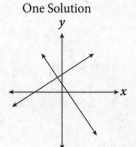

Infinitely Many Solutions

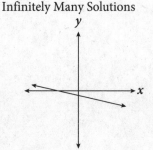

No Solution

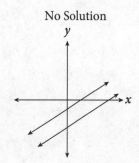

You need to do this:

- If the question states that the system has one solution and provides the point of intersection, substitute the values at that point of intersection for x and y in the equations.

- If the question states that the system has infinitely many solutions, make the x-coefficients equal to each other, the y-coefficients equal to each other, and the y-intercepts (or constant terms, if the equations are in $ax + by + c$ form) equal to each other. This will result in two equations that represent the same line.

- If the question states that the system has no solution, manipulate the equations to make the x-coefficients equal to each other and the y-coefficients equal to each other, but be sure that the y-intercepts (or constant terms) are different. This will result in two equations with the same slope but different y-intercepts, or, in other words, parallel lines.

Explanation:

Start by recognizing that for two lines to be parallel, both the x-coefficients must be equal and the y-coefficients must be equal. Manipulate the second equation so that it is in the same format as the first one:

$$kx - 8y = 30$$

The y-coefficient in the first equation, $10x - 4y = 8$, is 4. Divide the second equation by 2 in order to make the y-coefficients in both equations equal:

$$\frac{k}{2}x - 4y = 15$$

Now, set the x-coefficient equal to that in the first equation:

$$\frac{k}{2} = 10$$
$$k = 20$$

Note that the question asks for the value of $3k$, so the correct answer is **(C)**, 60.

Try on Your Own

Directions

Take as much time as you need on these questions. Work carefully and methodically. There will be an opportunity for timed practice later in the book.

11

HINT: How can the x- and y-values you are given as the solution to the system in Q11 help you find h and k?

$$hx - 5y = -15$$
$$kx + 2y = -20$$

What is the value of $\frac{k}{h}$ if the (x, y) solution of the given system of equations is $(-5, 2)$?

Ⓐ $\frac{1}{3}$

Ⓑ 2

Ⓒ $\frac{24}{5}$

Ⓓ 6

12

HINT: For Q12, if a system of equations has infinitely many solutions, what do you know about the two equations?

$$9x + 4y = 24$$
$$qx - \frac{y}{3} = -2$$

If q is a constant and the given system of equations has infinitely many solutions, what is the value of q?

Ⓐ -9

Ⓑ $-\frac{3}{4}$

Ⓒ $\frac{2}{3}$

Ⓓ 9

13

HINT: For Q13, what does it mean, graphically, when a system has no solution?

$$8x + 4y = 17$$
$$\frac{1}{5}x + zy = \frac{1}{2}$$

In the system of linear equations shown, z is a constant. If the **system** has no solution, what is the value of z?

Ⓐ $\frac{1}{10}$

Ⓑ $\frac{1}{4}$

Ⓒ 8

Ⓓ 10

14

$$3x - 4y = 10$$
$$6x + wy = 16$$

For which of the following values of w will the given system of equations have no solution?

Ⓐ -8

Ⓑ -4

Ⓒ 4

Ⓓ 8

15

$$\frac{1}{2}x - \frac{2}{3}y = c$$

$$6x - 8y = -1$$

If the given system of linear equations has infinitely many solutions, and c is a constant, what is the value of c?

Ⓐ $-\frac{1}{2}$

Ⓑ $-\frac{1}{12}$

Ⓒ 2

Ⓓ 12

On Test Day

Many PSAT Math questions can be solved in more than one way. A little efficiency goes a long way in helping you get through the Math sections on time, so it's useful to try solving problems more than one way to learn which way is fastest.

Try this question using two approaches: substitution and combination. Time yourself on each attempt. Which approach allowed you to get to the answer faster?

16. What is the value of x if $25x - 7y = 28$ and $10x + 7y + 18 = 60$?

    Ⓐ $-\dfrac{14}{15}$

    Ⓑ $\dfrac{1}{2}$

    Ⓒ 2

    Ⓓ $3\dfrac{1}{7}$

The answer and both ways of solving can be found at the end of this chapter.

How Much Have You Learned?

Directions

For test-like practice, give yourself 15 minutes to complete this question set. Be sure to study the explanations, even for questions you answered correctly. They can be found at the end of this chapter.

(handwritten: 4 8)

1

What is the value of $y - x$, if $6x - 4y = 8$ and $5y - 7x = 12$?

(handwritten: $24 - 32 = -8$)

Ⓐ −8

Ⓑ 4

Ⓒ 12

● 20

2

A bed costs $40 less than three times the cost of a couch. If the bed and couch together cost $700, how much more does the bed cost than the couch?

Ⓐ $185

Ⓑ $225

● $330

Ⓓ $515

(handwritten:
bed =
b = 3c − 40   515
c = 185
b + c = 700

100

4c − 40 = 700
4c = 740)

(handwritten top of page: $y - x = 20$ $-32 + k$ $k = 9y + 4x$)

(handwritten: $16k = -32$ $x = -2$)

3

(handwritten: $-32 = 9y + 4x$ $k = \frac{9}{16}y + \frac{1}{4}x$)

If k is a constant and the given system of linear equations has infinitely many solutions, what is the value of k?

Ⓐ −8

Ⓑ −4

● −2

Ⓓ −1

4

(handwritten: $13 = 9 + 6bx + 36x$ $-22 = 6bx + 36x$)

(handwritten: $-13 = 7y + 36x$ $9 + 6bx = 7y$)

(handwritten: $-13 - 36x = 9 + 6bx$)

What is the value of b if b is a constant and the above system of equations has no solution?

Ⓐ 6

Ⓑ 1

Ⓒ −1

Ⓓ −6

5

If $\frac{1}{8}x + 4y = \frac{11}{2}$ and $-4y - x = 12$, what is $\frac{1}{4}$ of y?

6

At a local airport, landing fees are $281 for commercial flights and $31 for private planes. One day, 312 planes landed at the airport and $48,172 in landing fees was collected. Solving which of the following systems of equations yields the number of commercial flights, c, and the number of private planes, p, that landed at the airport that day?

(A) $\begin{cases} c + p = 48{,}172 \\ 281c + 31p = 312 \end{cases}$

(B) $\begin{cases} c + p = 312 \\ 31c + 281p = 48{,}172 \end{cases}$

(C) $\begin{cases} c + p = 312 \\ 281c + 31p = 48{,}172 \end{cases}$

(D) $\begin{cases} c + p = 48{,}172 \\ 31c + 281p = 312 \end{cases}$

7

At a certain coffee store, a small bag of beans costs $2.50 and a large bag of beans costs $15. If the store sold 27 small and large bags of beans and had $155 in revenue in one week, how many small bags and large bags of beans were sold?

(A) 20 small bags, 7 large bags

(B) 7 small bags, 20 large bags

(C) 8 small bags, 19 large bags

(D) 20 small bags, 9 large bags

8

$$2x + 3y = 8 - y$$

$$x - 6y = 10$$

If (x, y) is a solution to the system of equations shown, then what is the value of $x - y$?

(A) $-\dfrac{3}{4}$

(B) $\dfrac{19}{4}$

(C) $\dfrac{11}{2}$

(D) $\dfrac{25}{4}$

9

For a wedding, a catering company charges $12.75 for each chicken dish and $9.50 for each vegetarian dish. If 62 chicken and vegetarian meals were served at the wedding and the catering bill was $725.25, which of the following systems of equations represents the number of people who ordered chicken, c, and the number of people who ordered vegetarian, v?

(A) $\begin{cases} c + v = 725.25 \\ 12.75c + 9.5v = 62 \end{cases}$

(B) $\begin{cases} c + v = 62 \\ 12.75c + 9.5v = \dfrac{725.25}{2} \end{cases}$

(C) $\begin{cases} c + v = 62 \\ 12.75c + 9.5v = 725.25 \end{cases}$

(D) $\begin{cases} c + v = 62 \\ 12.75c + 9.5v = 725.25 \times 2 \end{cases}$

10

Two turkey burgers and a bottle of water cost
$3.25. If three turkey burgers and a bottle of water
cost $4.50, what is the cost of two bottles of water?

(A) $0.75

(B) $1.25

(C) $1.50

(D) $3.00

Reflect

Directions: Take a few minutes to recall what you've learned and what you've been practicing in this chapter. Consider the following questions, jot down your best answer for each one, and then compare your reflections to the expert responses that follow. Use your level of confidence to determine what to do next.

When is substitution a good choice for solving a system of equations?

_____

_____

_____

When is combination a good choice for solving a system of equations?

_____

_____

_____

What does it mean if a system of linear equations has no solution? Infinitely many solutions?

_____

_____

_____

_____

Expert Responses

When is substitution a good choice for solving a system of equations?

Substitution works best when at least one of the variables has a coefficient of 1, making the variable easy to isolate. This system, for example, is well suited for substitution:

$$a + 3b = 5$$
$$4a - 6b = 21$$

That's because in the first equation, you can easily isolate the a as a = 5 − 3b and plug that in for a in the other equation. By contrast, substitution would not be a great choice for solving this system:

$$2a + 3b = 5$$
$$4a - 6b = 21$$

If you used substitution now, you'd have to work with fractions, which is messy.

When is combination a good choice for solving a system of equations?

Combination is always a good choice. It is at its most difficult in systems such as this one:

$$2a + 3b = 5$$
$$3a + 5b = 7$$

Neither a-coefficient is a multiple of the other, and neither b-coefficient is a multiple of the other, so to solve this system with combination you'll likely want to multiply both equations by a constant (e.g., multiply the first equation by 3 and the second equation by 2 to create a 6a term in both equations). But substitution wouldn't be stellar in this situation, either.

Note that combination may be particularly effective when the PSAT asks for a variable expression. For example, if a question based on the previous system of equations asked for the value of 5a + 8b, then you could find the answer instantly by adding the equations together.

What does it mean if a system of linear equations has no solution? Infinitely many solutions?

A system of equations with no solution represents two parallel lines, which never cross. The coefficient of a variable in one equation will match the coefficient of the same variable in the other equation, but the constants will be different. For example, this system has no solution:

$$2x + 3y = 4$$
$$2x + 3y = 5$$

Subtracting one equation from the other yields the equation $0 = -1$, which makes no sense.

If a system of equations has infinitely many solutions, then the two equations represent the same line. For example, this system has infinitely many solutions:

$$2x + 3y = 4$$
$$4x + 6y = 8$$

Dividing the second equation by 2 yields $2x + 3y = 4$, so while the two equations look different, they are actually the same.

Next Steps

If you answered most questions correctly in the "How Much Have You Learned?" section, and if your responses to the Reflect questions were similar to those of the PSAT expert, then consider Systems of Linear Equations an area of strength and move on to the next chapter. Come back to this topic periodically to prevent yourself from getting rusty.

If you don't yet feel confident, review those parts of this chapter that you have not yet mastered. In particular, review the mechanics for solving a system of equations by substitution and by combination. Then, try the questions you missed again. As always, be sure to review the explanations closely.

Answers and Explanations

Try on Your Own

1. C

Difficulty: Easy

Category: Algebra

Getting to the Answer: Translate the words in the question into equations. Let n be the original number of nickels and d be the number of dimes. That there were "twice as many nickels as dimes" means that $n = 2d$. When 4 nickels are added, the number of nickels is 3 times the number of dimes. Thus, $n + 4 = 3d$. Substitute $2d$ for n in the second equation: $2d + 4 = 3d$. Subtract $2d$ from each side to get $4 = d$. The question asks for the original number of coins. The original number of nickels is $n = 2d = 8$ and the total number of coins is $4 + 8 = 12$, which is **(C)**.

2. 4/3 or 1.333

Difficulty: Medium

Category: Algebra

Getting to the Answer: Since you're solving for b and can easily isolate c in the second equation, use substitution rather than combination. Substitute $c = 5b - 4$ into the first equation and solve:

$$5(5b - 4) + 5b = 20$$
$$5b - 4 + b = 4$$
$$6b = 8$$
$$3b = 4$$
$$b = \frac{4}{3}$$

Enter **4/3** or **1.333** and move on.

3. C

Difficulty: Medium

Category: Algebra

Getting to the Answer: Because x has a coefficient of 1 in the second equation, solve the system using substitution. Before you select your answer, make sure you found the right quantity (the difference between x and y).

First, solve the second equation for x and substitute:

$$x - 3y = 4 \rightarrow x = 4 + 3y$$
$$5(4 + 3y) - 4y = 10 + y$$
$$20 + 15y - 4y = 10 + y$$
$$20 + 11y = 10 + y$$
$$10y = -10$$
$$y = -1$$

Next, substitute this value back into $x = 4 + 3y$ and simplify:

$$x = 4 + 3(-1)$$
$$x = 4 - 3$$
$$x = 1$$

Finally, evaluate $x - y$ to find the difference:

$$1 - (-1) = 2$$

Hence, **(C)** is correct. While substitution is a valid way to solve this because the second equation readily gives you x in terms of y, you could have just restated the first equation as $5x - 5y = 10$ and, therefore, $x - y = 2$.

4. C

Difficulty: Medium

Category: Algebra

Getting to the Answer: Since the question asks for $r + 6$, substitute by solving for s using the second equation, $r + s = 12$, so $s = 12 - r$. Substitute $12 - r$ into the first equation for s to get $3r + 2(12 - r) = 24$. Distribute the 2 to get $3r + 24 - 2r = 24$. Next, combine like terms: $3r - 2r = 24 - 24$, which yields $r = 0$. Remember that the question asks for $r + 6$, not r by itself!

Choice **(C)** is correct.

5.   D

Difficulty: Hard

Category: Algebra

Getting to the Answer: Create a system of two linear equations where t represents tables with 2 chairs and f represents tables with 4 chairs. The first equation should represent the total number of *tables*, each with 2 or 4 chairs, or $t + f = 25$. The second equation should represent the total number of *chairs*. Because t represents tables with 2 chairs and f represents tables with 4 chairs, the second equation should be $2t + 4f = 86$. Now, solve the system using substitution. Solve the first equation for t in terms of f so that when you substitute the result into the second equation, you can solve directly for f:

$$t + f = 25 \rightarrow t = 25 - f$$
$$2(25 - f) + 4f = 86$$
$$50 - 2f + 4f = 86$$
$$2f = 36$$
$$f = 18$$

There are 18 tables with 4 chairs each, **(D)**. This is all the question asks for, so you don't need to find the value of t.

6.   A

Difficulty: Easy

Category: Algebra

Getting to the Answer: Quickly compare the two equations. The system is already set up perfectly to solve using combination, so add the two equations to cancel $-4y$ and $4y$. Then, solve the resulting equation for x. Remember, the question asks for the y-coordinate of the solution, so you will need to substitute x back into one of the original equations and solve for y:

$2x - 4y = 14$	$2(5) - 4y = 14$
$+(5x + 4y = 21)$	$10 - 4y = 14$
$7x = 35$	$-4y = 4$
$x = 5$	$y = -1$

Thus, **(A)** is correct.

7.   D

Difficulty: Easy

Category: Algebra

Getting to the Answer: If you're not asked to find the value of an individual variable, the question may lend itself to combination. This question asks for $3b - 2c$, so don't waste your time finding the variables individually if you can avoid it. After rearranging the equations so that variables and constants are aligned, you can add the equations together:

$$6b + 6c = 4$$
$$+(-3b - 8c = 11)$$
$$\overline{3b - 2c = 15}$$

This matches **(D)**.

8.   B

Difficulty: Easy

Category: Algebra

Getting to the Answer: Looking at the coefficients of the two equations, you'll notice that multiplying the second equation by 2 will allow you to eliminate the a terms:

$$6a + 6b = 30$$
$$-(6a + 4b = 28)$$
$$\overline{0a + 2b = 2}$$
$$b = 1$$

Solving the resulting equation gives $b = 1$. Choice **(B)** is the only choice that contains this value for b, so it must be correct.

9.   51

Difficulty: Medium

Category: Algebra

Getting to the Answer: Rather than multiplying just one equation by a factor, you'll want to multiply both by a factor to use combination. Suppose you want to eliminate x. The coefficients of the x terms are 2 and 5, so you need to multiply the equations by numbers that will give you -10 and 10 as your new x term coefficients. To do this, multiply the first equation by -5 and the second equation by 2:

$$-5(2x + 5y = 49)$$
$$2(5x + 3y = 94)$$

Add the resulting equations:

$$\begin{aligned}\cancel{-10x} - 25y &= -245\\+(\cancel{10x} + 6y &= 188)\\\hline 0x - 19y &= -57\end{aligned}$$

Solving for y gives you 3. Next, plug 3 back in for y in either equation and solve for x, which equals 17. Multiplying x and y together yields 51. Enter **51**.

10. B

Difficulty: Medium

Category: Algebra

Getting to the Answer: Translate English into math to extract what you need. First, define the variables using letters that make sense. Use c for children and a for adults. Now, break the word problem into shorter phrases: children's tickets sold for $8 each; adult tickets sold for $12 each; 60 people attended the concert; $624 was collected in ticket money. Translating each phrase into a math expression will produce the components needed:

Children's tickets (c) cost $8 each → $8c$

Adult tickets (a) cost $12 each → $12a$

60 people attended the concert → $c + a = 60$

$624 was collected in ticket money → Total $ = 624

Now, put the expressions together in a system:

$$\begin{aligned}c + a &= 60\\8c + 12a &= 624\end{aligned}$$

This equation can be solved easily by either substitution or combination. To solve for the variables using combination, multiply the first equation by 8 and subtract it from the second equation:

$$\begin{aligned}8c + 12a &= 624\\-(8c + 8a &= 480)\\\hline 0c + 4a &= 144\\a &= 36\end{aligned}$$

Plug this value into $c + a = 60$ to find that $c = 24$. Remember, the question asks for the difference between the number of adults and the number of children, so the correct answer is $36 - 24 = 12$, which corresponds to **(B)**.

11. C

Difficulty: Medium

Category: Algebra

Getting to the Answer: You are told that the solution to the system is $x = -5$ and $y = 2$. Substitute these values into both equations to find h and k:

$$\begin{aligned}hx - 5y &= -15\\h(-5) - 5(2) &= -15\\-5h - 10 &= -15\\-5h &= -5\\h &= 1\end{aligned}$$

$$\begin{aligned}kx + 2y &= -20\\k(-5) + 2(2) &= -20\\-5k + 4 &= -20\\-5k &= -24\\k &= \frac{24}{5}\end{aligned}$$

So, $\frac{k}{h} = \frac{\frac{24}{5}}{1}$, making **(C)** correct.

12. B

Difficulty: Hard

Category: Algebra

Getting to the Answer: A system of equations that has infinitely many solutions describes a single line. Therefore, manipulation of one equation will yield the other. Look at the constant terms: to turn the 24 into -2, divide the first equation by -12:

$$\frac{(9x + 4y = 24)}{-12} \rightarrow -\frac{9}{12}x - \frac{4}{12}y = -2$$

$$\rightarrow -\frac{3}{4}x - \frac{1}{3}y = -2$$

The y term and the constant in the first equation now match those in the second. All that's left is to set the coefficients of x equal to each other: $q = -\frac{3}{4}$. Choice **(B)** is correct.

Note that you could also write each equation in slope-intercept form and set the slopes equal to each other to solve for q.

13. A

Difficulty: Hard

Category: Algebra

Getting to the Answer: A system of linear equations that has no solution should describe two parallel lines. This means the coefficients of the variables should be the same (so the slopes of the lines are the same). Only the constant should be different (so the y-intercepts are not the same). The easiest way to make the coefficients the same is to manipulate the second equation. Multiplying the second equation by 40 would make the coefficients of x the same in both equations: $8x + 40zy = 20$. Now, equate the coefficients of y to get $4 = 40z$. Solve for z to reveal that $z = \frac{1}{10}$, which is **(A)**. Alternatively, you could write each equation in slope-intercept form and set the slopes equal to each other to solve for z.

14. A

Difficulty: Hard

Category: Algebra

Getting to the Answer: One way to answer the question is to think about the graphs of the equations. Graphically, a system of linear equations that has no solution indicates two parallel lines or, in other words, two lines that have the same slope. Write each of the equations in slope-intercept form, $y = mx + b$, and set their slopes, m, equal to each other to solve for w.

First equation:

$$3x - 4y = 10$$
$$-4y = -3x + 10$$
$$y = \frac{3}{4}x - \frac{5}{2}$$

Second equation:

$$6x + wy = 16$$
$$wy = -6x + 16$$
$$y = -\frac{6}{w}x + \frac{16}{w}$$

Set the slopes equal:

$$\frac{3}{4} = -\frac{6}{w}$$
$$3w = -24$$
$$w = -8$$

This matches **(A)**. Alternatively, you could manipulate the first equation to make the x-coefficients the same and then equate the coefficients of y to solve for w.

15. B

Difficulty: Hard

Category: Algebra

Getting to the Answer: A system of linear equations has infinitely many solutions if both lines in the system have the same slope and the same y-intercept (in other words, they are the same line). Write each of the equations in slope-intercept form, $y = mx + b$. Their slopes should be the same. To find c, set the y-intercepts, b, equal to each other and solve. Before rewriting the equations, multiply the first equation by 6 to make it easier to manipulate.

First equation:

$$6\left(\frac{1}{2}x - \frac{2}{3}y\right) = 6(c)$$
$$3x - 4y = 6c$$
$$-4y = -3x + 6c$$
$$y = \frac{3}{4}x - \frac{3}{2}c$$

Second equation:

$$6x - 8y = -1$$
$$-8y = -6x - 1$$
$$y = \frac{3}{4}x + \frac{1}{8}$$

Set the y-intercepts equal:

$$-\frac{3}{2}c = \frac{1}{8}$$
$$-24c = 2$$
$$c = -\frac{1}{12}$$

Hence, **(B)** is correct.

On Test Day

16. C

Difficulty: Medium

Category: Algebra

Strategic Advice: The numbers here are fairly large, so substitution is not likely to be convenient. Moreover, the y-coefficients have the same absolute value, so combination will likely be the faster way to solve.

Getting to the Answer: Start by writing the second equation in the same form as the first, then use combination to solve for x:

$$\begin{array}{r} 25x - 7y = 28 \\ +(10x + 7y = 42) \\ \hline 35x = 70 \\ x = 2 \end{array}$$

Thus, **(C)** is correct.

If you feel more comfortable using substitution, you can maximize efficiency by solving one equation for $7y$ and substituting that value into the other equation:

$$10x + 7y = 42 \rightarrow 7y = 42 - 10x$$
$$25x - (42 - 10x) = 28$$
$$35x - 42 = 28$$
$$35x = 70$$
$$x = 2$$

Note that the arithmetic is fundamentally the same, but the setup using combination is quicker and visually easier to follow.

How Much Have You Learned?

1. D

Difficulty: Medium

Category: Algebra

Strategic Advice: When a question asks for a sum or difference of variables, consider solving by combination.

Getting to the Answer: Rearrange the equations to be in the same form, with the y terms before the x terms, and then add:

$$\begin{array}{r} -4y + 6x = 8 \\ +(5y - 7x = 12) \\ \hline y - x = 20 \end{array}$$

The correct answer is **(D)**.

2. C

Difficulty: Medium

Category: Algebra

Getting to the Answer: Write a system of equations where c is the cost of the couch in dollars and b is the cost of the bed in dollars. A bed costs $40 less than three times the cost of the couch, or $b = 3c - 40$. Together, a bed and a couch cost $700, so $b + c = 700$.

The system of equations is:

$$b = 3c - 40$$
$$b + c = 700$$

The top equation is already solved for b, so substitute $3c - 40$ into the bottom equation for b and solve for c:

$$3c - 40 + c = 700$$
$$4c - 40 = 700$$
$$4c = 740$$
$$c = 185$$

Remember to check if you solved for the right thing! The couch costs $185, so the bed costs $3(\$185) - \$40 = \$555 - \$40 = \$515$. This means the bed costs $\$515 - \$185 = \$330$ more than the couch. Therefore, **(C)** is correct.

3. C

Difficulty: Hard

Category: Algebra

Getting to the Answer: The system has infinitely many solutions, so both equations must describe the same line. Notice that if you multiply the x- and y-coefficients in the second equation by 16, you arrive at the x- and y-coefficients in the first equation. The constant k times 16 must then equal the constant in the first equation, or -32:

$$16k = -32$$
$$k = -2$$

Therefore, **(C)** is correct.

4. D

Difficulty: Medium

Category: Algebra

Getting to the Answer: Rearrange the equations and write them on top of each other so that the x and y terms line up:

$$-36x - 7y = 13$$
$$6bx - 7y = -9$$

In a system of equations that has no solution, the x-coefficients must equal each other and the y-coefficients must equal each other, but the constant on the right needs to be different. Thus, for the x-coefficients, $-36 = 6b$ and $b = -6$. Choice **(D)** is correct.

5. 1/2, 0.5, or **.5**

Difficulty: Medium

Category: Algebra

Getting to the Answer: Start by clearing the fractions from the first equation (by multiplying by 8) to make the numbers easier to work with. Then, use combination to solve for y:

$$\begin{aligned} x + 32y &= 44 \\ +(-x - 4y &= 12) \\ \hline 28y &= 56 \\ y &= 2 \end{aligned}$$

Take one-fourth of 2 to get $\frac{1}{2}$; then enter **1/2**, **0.5**, or **.5**.

6. C

Difficulty: Medium

Category: Algebra

Getting to the Answer: Because the variables are defined in the question stem and because the answer choices contain the variables, the only thing left for you to do is to figure out how they relate to one another. There will be two equations: one involving the total number of aircraft that landed and one involving the total amount of landing fees collected. Add together both types of aircraft to get the total number of aircraft that landed: $c + p = 312$. Think carefully about which type of plane should be associated with which fee to get the latter. Commercial airliners are much more expensive; hence, your second equation should be $281c + 31p = 47,848$. Only **(C)** contains both of those equations.

7. A

Difficulty: Medium

Category: Algebra

Getting to the Answer: Choose intuitive letters for the variables: s for the small bags, L for the large bags. You're given the cost of each, as well as the number of each sold and the total revenue generated. Next, write the system of equations that represents the information given:

$$s + L = 27$$
$$2.5s + 15L = 155$$

Multiplying the top equation by -15 allows you to solve for s using combination:

$$\begin{aligned} -15s - 15L &= -405 \\ +(2.5s + 15L &= 155) \\ \hline -12.5s &= -250 \\ s &= 20 \end{aligned}$$

Solving for s gives 20, which eliminates (B) and (C). Plugging this value back into the first equation allows you to find L, which is 7. Choice **(A)** is correct.

8. D

Difficulty: Medium

Category: Algebra

Getting to the Answer: Because x has a coefficient of 1 in the second equation, solve the system using substitution. First, solve the second equation for x to get $x = 6y + 10$. Then, substitute the resulting expression for x into the first equation and solve for y:

$$\begin{aligned} 2(6y + 10) + 3y &= 8 - y \\ 12y + 20 + 3y &= 8 - y \\ 15y + 20 &= 8 - y \\ 16y &= -12 \\ y &= -\frac{3}{4} \end{aligned}$$

Next, substitute this value back into $x = 6y + 10$ and simplify:

$$\begin{aligned} x &= 6\left(-\frac{3}{4}\right) + 10 \\ &= -\frac{9}{2} + \frac{20}{2} \\ &= \frac{11}{2} \end{aligned}$$

Finally, evaluate $x - y$ to find that **(D)** is correct:

$$\frac{11}{2} - \left(-\frac{3}{4}\right) = \frac{22}{4} + \frac{3}{4} = \frac{25}{4}$$

CHAPTER 5
SYSTEMS OF LINEAR EQUATIONS

Math

9. C

Difficulty: Easy

Category: Algebra

Getting to the Answer: Translate English into math. One equation should represent the total *number* of meals ordered, while the other equation should represent the *cost* of the meals.

The number of people who ordered chicken plus the number who ordered vegetarian equals the total number of meals, 62, so one equation is $c + v = 62$. This means you can eliminate (A). Now, write the cost equation: the cost per chicken dish, \$12.75, times the number of chicken dishes, c, plus the cost per vegetarian dish, \$9.50, times number of vegetarian dishes, v, equals the total bill, \$725.25. The cost equation should be $12.75c + 9.5v = 725.25$. Together, these two equations form the system in **(C)**.

10. C

Difficulty: Medium

Category: Algebra

Getting to the Answer: Translate English into math to write a system of equations with t being the cost of a turkey burger, in dollars, and w equaling the cost of a bottle of water, in dollars. The first statement is translated as $2t + w = \$3.25$ and the second as $3t + w = \$4.50$. Now, set up a system:

$$2t + w = 3.25$$
$$3t + w = 4.50$$

You could solve the system using substitution, but combination is quicker in this question because subtracting the first equation from the second eliminates w and you can solve for t:

$$\begin{array}{r} 3t + w = 4.50 \\ -(2t + w = 3.25) \\ \hline t = 1.25 \end{array}$$

Substitute this value for t in the first equation and solve for w:

$$2(1.25) + w = 3.25$$
$$2.5 + w = 3.25$$
$$w = 0.75$$

Two bottles of water would cost $2 \times \$0.75 = \$1.50$, which is **(C)**.

[CHAPTER 6]

LINEAR FUNCTIONS

LEARNING OBJECTIVES

After completing this chapter, you will be able to:

- Apply function notation
- Define the domain and range of a linear function
- Evaluate the output of a linear function for a given input
- Interpret the graph of a linear function
- Write a linear function to describe a rule or data set

How Much Do You Know?

Directions

Try the questions that follow. Show your work so that you can compare your solutions to the ones found in the "Check Your Work" section immediately after this question set. If you answered the question(s) on a specific topic correctly, and if your scratchwork looks like ours, you may be able to move quickly through the lesson covering that topic. If you answered incorrectly or used a different approach, you may want to take your time on that lesson.

1

Given that $f(x) = 2x + 1$ and $g(x) = \dfrac{x + 2}{3}$, what is the product of $f(-5)$ and $g(-5)$?

Ⓐ -9

Ⓑ -1

Ⓒ 1

Ⓓ 9

2

x	$f(x)$
-2	8
-1	6
0	4
1	2

x	$g(x)$
-1	-4
1	0
2	2
4	6

For the two functions $f(x)$ and $g(x)$ given in the tables, what is the value of $f(g(1))$?

Ⓐ 0

Ⓑ 2

Ⓒ 4

Ⓓ 6

3

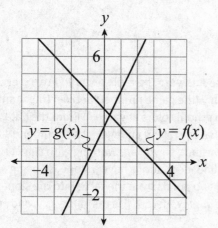

The graphs of linear functions f and g are shown. What is the value of a such that $f(a) + g(a) = 6$?

_____

4

Game	Number of Students
1	5
2	10
3	15
4	20
5	25

West Valley High School is encouraging students to wear school colors when they attend home football games. If j represents the game number and $f(j)$ represents the number of students in school colors at game j, which of the following functions best describes the information in the table?

Ⓐ $f(j) = \dfrac{j}{5}$

Ⓑ $f(j) = \dfrac{j}{5} + 5$

Ⓒ $f(j) = 5j$

Ⓓ $f(j) = 5j + 5$

5

The growth of a microbial population over time can be modeled by a linear function of the amount of time elapsed in hours. When $t = 21$ hours, the population is 8 colonies, and when $t = 35$ hours, the population is 10 colonies. Which of the following best describes $f(t)$?

Ⓐ $f(t) = \frac{1}{3}t + 1$

Ⓑ $f(t) = \frac{1}{5}t + 3$

Ⓒ $f(t) = \frac{1}{7}t + 5$

Ⓓ $f(t) = 7(t - 5)$

Check Your Work

1.   D

Difficulty: Easy

Category: Algebra

Getting to the Answer: Read carefully to see what the question is asking. You need to find the product of the results when you evaluate each function at $x = -5$. You could multiply the two functions together and then evaluate the result, but it's quicker to evaluate each function separately and then multiply:

$$f(-5) = 2(-5) + 1 = -10 + 1 = -9$$

$$g(-5) = \frac{-5+2}{3} = \frac{-3}{3} = -1$$

Now multiply to get $(-9)(-1) = 9$, which is **(D)**.

2.   C

Difficulty: Medium

Category: Algebra

Getting to the Answer: This is a composition of functions, so start with the innermost set of parentheses, which is $g(1)$. According to the $g(x)$ table, when $x = 1$, $g(x) = 0$. Then, $x = 0$ becomes the input for f. Now find $f(0)$. The $f(x)$ table shows that this is equal to 4, which is **(C)**.

3.   1

Difficulty: Hard

Category: Algebra

Getting to the Answer: At first glance, this question may seem overwhelming. However, only a limited number of possible x-values are displayed in the graph. Start with the easier values and proceed gradually to the harder ones.

First, look at $x = 0$. The notation $f(0)$ means "the y-value when $x = 0$." According to the graph, this is 3. Using similar logic, $g(0) = 2$. Since $2 + 3 = 5$, this is not correct.

Next, try $x = 1$. The graph shows that $f(1) = 2$ and $g(1) = 4$. Since $2 + 4 = 6$, this is the x-value that you are looking for. The number **1** is correct.

4.   C

Difficulty: Easy

Category: Algebra

Getting to the Answer: The table gives you two pieces of information: j (the game number) and $f(j)$ (the number of students in school colors at game j). From the data, you can see that the rate of change in the number of students is constant, so you are working with a linear equation. All linear equations have a slope, so begin there. Plug in two points from the table into the slope formula and simplify. Here, $f(j)$ is the same as y, and j is the same as x.

$$\frac{y_2 - y_1}{x_2 - x_1} = \frac{10 - 5}{2 - 1}$$

$$= \frac{5}{1}$$

$$= 5$$

Eliminate (A) and (B). Now consider the y-intercept. The y-intercept is the y-value when $x = 0$. Since the slope is not 0 (in other words, the y-values are not constant for all x-values) and the table tells you that $y = 5$ when $x = 1$, the y-intercept cannot be 5. Therefore, **(C)** is correct.

You could also plug in a point from the table to find the y-intercept. Using $(1, 5)$ results in the easiest calculations.

$$y = mx + b$$

$$y = 5x + b$$

$$5 = 5(1) + b$$

$$5 = 5 + b$$

$$0 = b$$

Again, you are led to **(C)**.

5.   C

Difficulty: Medium

Category: Algebra

Getting to the Answer: Because the slopes of all the answer choices are different, you can use the slope formula to determine which choice is correct. The number of colonies *depends* on the time elapsed, so start by writing the information given as ordered pairs in the form (time, number of colonies). Using the ordered pairs (21, 8) and (35, 10), the slope is $m = \frac{y_2 - y_1}{x_2 - x_1} = \frac{10 - 8}{35 - 21} = \frac{2}{14} = \frac{1}{7}$. The only choice with this slope is **(C)**.

On test day, you would stop here. It is not necessary to find the *y*-intercept. But for the record, the *y*-intercept can be found by plugging one of the points above into the slope-intercept equation and solving for *b*. The point (21, 8) is used below.

$$y = \frac{1}{7}x + b$$
$$8 = \frac{1}{7}(21) + b$$
$$8 = 3 + b$$
$$5 = b$$

Again, choice **(C)** is correct.

Function Notation

To answer a question like this:

$h(x) = 5x + 5$

The function $h(x)$ is defined above. Out of the statements below, which must be true about $h(x)$?

(A) $h(2) = 30$

(B) $h(8) = 45$

(C) The domain of $h(x)$ consists only of integers

(D) $h(x)$ may only be positive

You need to know this:

A **function** is a rule that generates one unique output for a given input. In function notation, the x-value is the input and the y-value, designated by $f(x)$, is the output. (Note that other letters besides x and f may be used.)

A linear function is a function that describes a line; as such, it is generally expressed in slope-intercept form with $f(x)$ being equivalent to y:

$$f(x) = mx + b$$

In questions that describe real-life situations, the y-intercept will often be the starting point for the function. You can think of it as $f(0)$, or the value of the function where $x = 0$.

The set of all possible x-values is called the **domain** of the function, while the set of all possible y-values is called the **range**. For most linear functions, the range and domain consists of all real numbers, since lines are infinitely long. However, a constant function, such as $f(x) = 4$, produces a horizontal line, since every x-value produces the same y-value, and thus has a range consisting of just that one number.

You need to do this:

- To find $f(x)$ for some value of x, substitute the concrete value in for the variable and do the arithmetic.
- For questions that ask about a function of a function, such as $g(f(x))$, start on the inside and work your way out.

Explanation:

Check each statement. For the first statement, plug in 2 for x:

$$5(2) + 5 = 10 + 5 = 15$$

This does not equal 30. Eliminate choice (A).

Check choice (B), plug in 8 for x:

$$5(8) + 5 = 40 + 5 = 45$$

That is correct. Select Choice **(B)**. On test day, you would move on, but for the record:

Choice (C) is incorrect. Since it is a linear function, any possible x-values, not just integers, will correspond with a point on the line. Choice (D) is also incorrect. You could either graph this equation on a calculator or pick an x-value to try, say $x = -10$, which leads to $h(-10) = 5(-10)+5 = -45$, to see that negative outputs are possible with this function.

Try on Your Own

Directions

Take as much time as you need on these questions. Work carefully and methodically. There will be an opportunity for timed practice later in the book.

1

HINT: For Q1, remember that $f(x)$ is equivalent to y.

If $f(x) = 2$, then what is the range of $f(x)$?

Ⓐ   No real numbers.

Ⓑ   0

Ⓒ   2

Ⓓ   All real numbers.

2

HINT: For Q2, remember that when dealing with nested functions, you should work from the inside out.

If $f(x) = -x + 5$ and $g(x) = 6x$, what is $g(f(3))$?

3

HINT: Begin Q3 by solving for $h(5)$ and $h(2)$: plug in 5 for x, then plug in 2 for x.

If $h(x) = 3x - 1$, what is the value of $h(5) - h(2)$?

Ⓐ   3

Ⓑ   8

Ⓒ   9

Ⓓ   14

4

x	$g(x)$
−4	0
−3	2
−2	4
−1	6
0	8
1	10

x	$h(x)$
−2	−4
−1	2
0	0
1	−2
2	−4

Several values for the functions $g(x)$ and $h(x)$ are shown in the tables. What is the value of $g(h(-2))$?

Ⓐ   −2

Ⓑ   0

Ⓒ   4

Ⓓ   10

5

If $f(x) = -4x + 1$, what is $f(2x + 1)$?

Ⓐ $-8x - 3$

Ⓑ $-8x + 1$

Ⓒ $-8x + 2$

Ⓓ $8x - 3$

Graphs of Linear Functions

LEARNING OBJECTIVE

After this lesson, you will be able to:

- Interpret the graph of a linear function

To answer a question like this:

x	h(x)
−2	−5
−1	−4
0	−3
1	−2
2	−1

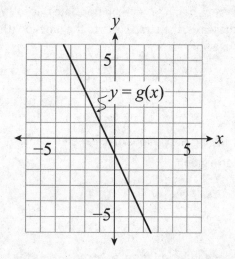

The graph shows $g(x) = mx + b$, where m and b are constants. Values for the function h are shown in the table. What is the value of $h(m)$?

(A) −5

(B) −4

(C) −2

(D) −1

You need to know this:

Interpreting graphs of linear functions uses the same skills as interpreting graphs of linear equations. For example:

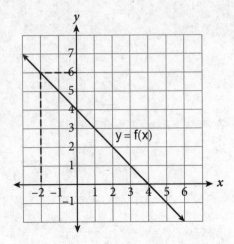

Say the graph above represents the function $f(x)$, and you're asked to find the value of x for which $f(x) = 6$. Because $f(x)$ represents the output value, or range, you can translate this to, "When does the y-value equal 6?" To answer the question, find 6 on the y-axis, then trace over to the function (the line). Read the corresponding x-value: it's -2, so when $f(x) = 6$, x must be -2.

You need to do this:

- Use the skills you learned for dealing with graphs of linear equations.
- Treat $f(x)$ as the y-coordinate on a graph.

Explanation:

The linear function $g(x)$ is given in slope-intercept form, so m represents the function's slope. You can determine the slope by visually inspecting the graph: for every unit the line moves to the right, it also goes down two, so $m = -2$. You could also plug two points from the graph of $g(x)$, such as $(-1, 1)$ and $(0, -1)$, into the slope formula: $m = \dfrac{y_2 - y_1}{x_2 - x_1} = \dfrac{-1 - 1}{0 - (-1)} = \dfrac{-2}{1} = -2$. Next, use the table to find $h(-2)$, which is the y-value of function h when $x = -2$. According to the table, when $x = -2$, $h(x) = -5$. **(A)** is correct.

Try on Your Own

Directions

Take as much time as you need on these questions. Work carefully and methodically. There will be an opportunity for timed practice later in the book.

6

HINT: For Q6, first determine $f(3)$.

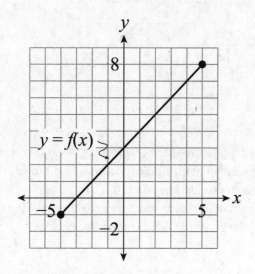

The graph of the function f is shown in the xy-plane. The equation for the function g (not shown) is $g(x) = f(x) - 6$. What is the value of $g(3)$?

Ⓐ -3

Ⓑ -2

Ⓒ 0

Ⓓ 4

7

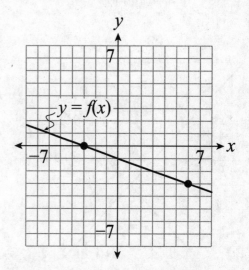

The graph of the linear function f is shown in the figure. Which of the following is the equation for f?

Ⓐ $f(x) = -3x - 1$

Ⓑ $f(x) = -x - 3$

Ⓒ $f(x) = -\frac{1}{3}x - 1$

Ⓓ $f(x) = -3x - 3$

8

HINT: For Q8, locate the *x*-value that gives the same *y*-value in each function.

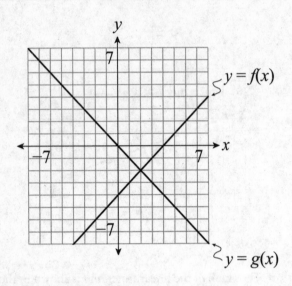

The graphs of the linear functions *f* and *g* are shown. What is the value of *a* such that $f(a) = g(a)$?

- Ⓐ -4
- Ⓑ -2
- Ⓒ 0
- Ⓓ 2

9

HINT: Begin Q9 by finding the slope of the graph of *f*.

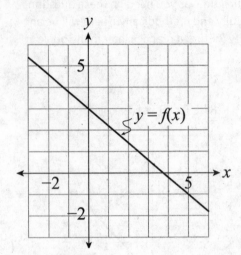

The figure shows the graph of the linear function *f*. The graph of the linear function *g* (not shown) passes through the point (0, 1). If the slope of the graph of the linear function *g* is 5 times the slope of the graph of *f*, what is the value of *g*(5)?

- Ⓐ -25
- Ⓑ -19
- Ⓒ -1
- Ⓓ 1

10

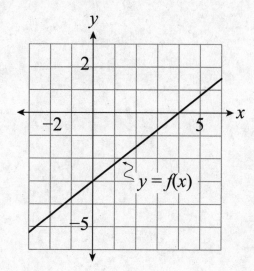

The figure shows the graph of the linear function f.
What is the value of $f(0)$?

Describing Real-Life Situations with Linear Functions

LEARNING OBJECTIVE

After this lesson, you will be able to:

- Write a linear function to describe a rule or data set

To answer a question like this:

TYPE OF MEAT	POUNDS OF MEAT PER PACKAGE	PROFIT PER POUND, IN DOLLARS
Sausage	42	1.10
Ground Beef	30	0.38
Salami	36	0.74
Bacon	32	0.50
Ham	40	0.98
Chicken	34	0.62

The number of pounds per package and the profit per pound for the different types of meat sold by a meat distributor is shown in the table. The relationship between the number of pounds per package (n) and the profit, in dollars, that the company makes per pound (p) can be represented by which of the following linear functions?

(A) $p(n) = 0.09n - 0.41$

(B) $p(n) = 0.08n - 0.82$

(C) $p(n) = 0.07n - 1.11$

(D) $p(n) = 0.06n - 1.42$

You need to know this:

Modeling real-life situations using functions is the same as modeling them using equations; the only difference is the function notation and the rule that each input has only one output.

For example, suppose a homeowner wants to determine the cost of installing a certain amount of carpet in her living room. Say that the carpet costs $0.86 per square foot, the installer charges a $29 installation fee, and sales tax on the total cost is 7%. Using your algebra and function knowledge, you can describe this situation in which the cost, c, is a function of square footage, f. The equation would be $c = 1.07(0.86f + 29)$. In function notation, this becomes $c(f) = 1.07(0.86f + 29)$, where $c(f)$ is shorthand for "cost as a function of square footage." The following table summarizes what each piece of the function represents in the scenario.

ENGLISH	Overall cost	Square footage	Material cost	Installation fee	Sales tax
MATH	c	f	$0.86f$	29	1.07

You need to do this:

In word problems involving function notation, translate the math equations exactly as you learned in the Word Problems lesson in the Linear Equations and Graphs chapter, but substitute $f(x)$ for y.

Explanation:

Note that the question asks for the relationship between the number pounds of meat per package, n, and the profit per pound, p, and that the answer choices all start with $p(n)$. Given the context, this must mean, "profit as a function of the number of pounds of meat." All the choices express a linear relationship, so you can't rule out any of them on that basis.

There are several approaches you could take to find the correct answer. One would be to recognize that all the choices are in the form $p(n) = mn + b$ (a variation of the slope-intercept form $y = mx + b$) and that you can set up a system of linear equations using the data from any two rows, such as "sausage" ($p(n) = 1.10$ and $n = 42$) and "bacon" ($p(n) = 0.50$ and $n = 32$), to solve for m and b. That approach would look like this:

$$
\begin{aligned}
1.10 &= 42m + b \\
-(0.50 &= 32m + b) \\
\hline
0.60 &= 10m \\
0.06 &= m
\end{aligned}
$$

$$
\begin{aligned}
0.50 &= 0.06(32) + b \\
0.50 &= 1.92 + b \\
b &= -1.42
\end{aligned}
$$

If $m = 0.06$ and $b = -1.42$, the correct function is $p(n) = 0.06n - 1.42$, so **(D)** is correct.

Another approach would be to use two of the pairs of data points from the table to calculate a slope; for example, using the "sausage" and "bacon" rows would yield $\dfrac{1.10 - 0.5}{42 - 32} = \dfrac{0.60}{10} = 0.06$. Because only one answer has a slope of 0.06, you can pick **(D)**.

One last approach: you could pick numbers from the table. Plug any one of the rows of data from the table, such as "bacon," into all four answer choices to check which equation will produce a profit of $0.50 per pound given 32 pounds per package:

(A): $0.09(32) - 0.41 = 2.47 \neq 0.50$, eliminate.

(B): $0.08(32) - 0.82 = 1.74 \neq 0.50$, eliminate.

(C): $0.07(32) - 1.11 = 1.13 \neq 0.50$, eliminate.

(D): $0.06(32) - 1.42 = 0.50$

Choice **(D)** is confirmed as the only one that works. It is correct.

Try on Your Own

Directions

Take as much time as you need on these questions. Work carefully and methodically. There will be an opportunity for timed practice later in the book.

11

HINT: Are there any answer choices in Q11 that you can immediately eliminate?

A biologist studying the birth rate of a certain fish uses the function $b(n)$ to analyze the fish's effect on other parts of the ecosystem, where n is the number of eggs laid by the fish over a given period of time. Which of the following lists could represent the domain for the biologist's function?

Ⓐ $\{\ldots -1{,}500, -1{,}000, -500, 0, 500, 1{,}000, 1{,}500\ldots\}$

Ⓑ $\{-1{,}500, -1{,}000, -500, 0, 500, 1{,}000, 1{,}500\}$

Ⓒ $\{0, 0.25, 0.5, 0.75, 1, 1.25, 1.5\ldots\}$

Ⓓ $\{0, 500, 1{,}000, 1{,}500, 2{,}000\ldots\}$

12

A book publisher pays writers a base fee of $2,500 for each book that it publishes, plus 5 cents per word. If one of its writers earned $8,000 from her book last year, how many words, w, did she write for the publisher?

Ⓐ 11,000

Ⓑ 110,000

Ⓒ 155,000

Ⓓ 250,000

13

HINT: How does knowing the starting height of the solution help you construct the function in Q13?

If the height of the liquid in the jar was 5 inches (in) before any pennies were added and 8.5 inches after 50 pennies were added, which of the following linear functions represents the relationship between the number of pennies, p, and the height in inches, $h(p)$, of the liquid in the jar?

Ⓐ $h(p) = 0.07p + 5$

Ⓑ $h(p) = 0.07p + 8.5$

Ⓒ $h(p) = 0.14p + 5$

Ⓓ $h(p) = 0.14p + 8.5$

14

HINT: Begin Q14 by calculating the parts per million at both 10 and 20 hours.

$c(t) = 21t + 2$

Doctors use the function shown to calculate the concentration, in parts per million, of a certain drug in a patient's bloodstream after t hours. How many more parts per million of the drug are in the bloodstream after 20 hours than after 10 hours?

15

Basic classroom supplies cost a teacher $500, and she spends an additional $25 per child in her class. The school reimburses her $5 for every student. Which function best describes the amount, in dollars, that the teacher spends per school year on supplies, given that s represents the number of students in the class?

Ⓐ $f(s) = 500 + 20s$

Ⓑ $f(s) = 495 + 25s$

Ⓒ $f(s) = 500 + 30s$

Ⓓ $f(s) = 505 + 25s$

On Test Day

The PSAT likes to test the modeling of real-life situations. Get comfortable with function notation in these questions. Remember that you can write the equation of a line as $y = mx + b$ or as $f(x) = mx + b$, where m is the slope and b is the y-intercept. Recall, the slope indicates the rate of change. Often, in questions asking about real-life situations, the x variable indicates time. In that case, the y-intercept (that is, the value of the function at $x = 0$, or $f(0)$) indicates the starting point.

16. A company plans to eliminate 10.8 metric tons of greenhouse gas emissions by the end of 15 years. If the company eliminates greenhouse gas emissions at a constant rate, which of the following linear functions f models the amount of remaining greenhouse gas emissions (in metric tons) t years into the program?

    Ⓐ $f(t) = -\dfrac{108}{75}t + 10.8$

    Ⓑ $f(t) = -\dfrac{54}{75}t + 10.8$

    Ⓒ $f(t) = \dfrac{54}{75}t + 10.8$

    Ⓓ $f(t) = \dfrac{108}{75}t + 10.8$

The answer and explanation can be found at the end of this chapter.

How Much Have You Learned?

Directions

For test-like practice, give yourself 16 minutes to complete this question set. Be sure to study the explanations, even for questions you got right. They can be found at the end of this chapter.

1

A function is defined by the equation $f(x) = \frac{2}{5}x - 7$. For what value of x does $f(x) = 5$?

Ⓐ -5

Ⓑ 2

Ⓒ 9

Ⓓ 30

2

If $f(x) = -x + 5$ and $g(x) = 2x - 1$, what is $2f(x) - g(x)$?

Ⓐ $-5x + 7$

Ⓑ $-4x + 9$

Ⓒ $-4x + 11$

Ⓓ $x + 4$

3

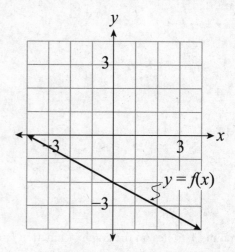

The graph of the function $f(x)$ is shown. What is the domain of the function?

Ⓐ $y \geq -4$

Ⓑ   All real numbers

Ⓒ $y > -2$

Ⓓ   The domain is undefined.

4

Jayesh requires 2,048 calories to maintain his weight when he doesn't exercise. On a certain day, he burns 231 calories for every hour he plays basketball. If the number of calories Jayesh needs to maintain his weight on this day can be modeled by the function $f(x) = ax + b$, where x is the number of hours that he plays basketball, what is the value of a?

5

Two functions are defined as follows: $f(x) = \frac{x}{4}$ and $g(x) = 2x - 1$. What is the value of $g(f(x))$ when $x = 2$?

Ⓐ 0

Ⓑ $\frac{1}{2}$

Ⓒ $\frac{3}{4}$

Ⓓ 2

6

The point $(3, 6)$ lies on the graph of function f in the xy-plane. If $f(x) = -2x + k$, then what is the value of k?

7

In a forest, the average height of the trees was 3.6 feet when they were planted. They have grown an average of 2.4 feet per year since then. A scientist uses the function $g(y) = h + 2.4y$, where h is the height (in feet) of the trees five years after they were planted and y is the number of years after the fifth year, to determine the expected further growth of these trees from the sixth year onward. Which of the following would be included in the range of the scientist's results?

Ⓐ 6

Ⓑ 10.8

Ⓒ 15.4

Ⓓ 18

8

If $f(x) = \frac{2x + 6}{4}$ and $g(x) = 2x - 1$, what is $f(g(x))$?

Ⓐ $x + 1$

Ⓑ $2x + 2$

Ⓒ $4x + 1$

Ⓓ $4x + 4$

9

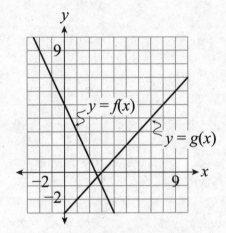

The functions $f(x)$ and $g(x)$ are graphed in the xy-plane. What is the value of $f(-2) - g(2)$?

Ⓐ -10

Ⓑ -1

Ⓒ 9

Ⓓ 10

10

To install fencing, a builder charges $15 per foot for the first 100 feet plus an additional $12 per foot thereafter. If c represents the total cost of a fence installation, in dollars, and x represents the length of the fence in feet, then which of the following functions best describes the cost of a fence that is more than 100 feet long?

Ⓐ $c(x) = 1{,}500 - 12(100 - x)$

Ⓑ $c(x) = 1{,}500 + 12(x - 100)$

Ⓒ $c(x) = 12(100 - x) - 1{,}500$

Ⓓ $c(x) = 12(x - 100) - 1{,}500$

11

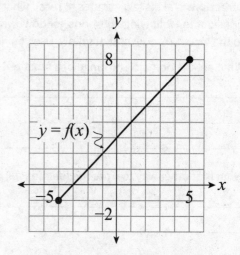

The complete graph of the function $f(x)$ in the xy-plane is shown. What is the domain of $f(x)$?

Ⓐ All real numbers greater than -4

Ⓑ All real numbers between and including -1 and 5

Ⓒ All real numbers between and including -4 and 5

Ⓓ All real numbers

Reflect

Directions: Take a few minutes to recall what you've learned and what you've been practicing in this chapter. Consider the following questions, jot down your best answer for each one, and then compare your reflections to the expert responses that follow. Use your level of confidence to determine what to do next.

What are the domain and range of a function?

_____
_____
_____

What is another way to write the function $f(x) = x + 4$?

_____
_____
_____

In the same function, what does x represent? What does $f(x)$ represent?

_____
_____
_____

What will the function look like when graphed?

_____
_____
_____

In a function whose x-value represents time, what does the y-intercept represent?

_____
_____
_____

Expert Responses

What are the domain and range of a function?

The domain of a function indicates the possible x-values and the range of a function indicates the possible y-values. In a linear function, the domain is all real numbers, and, for non-horizontal lines, the range is all real numbers.

What is another way to write the function $f(x) = x + 4$?

When you graph the function on the xy-coordinate plane, you can replace f(x) with y. This function is equivalent to y = x + 4.

In the same function, what does x represent? What does $f(x)$ represent?

In this function, x is the input and f(x) is the output.

What will the function look like when graphed?

The slope of the line is 1 and its y-intercept is 4, so it will move from the lower left to the upper right and cross the y-axis at y = 4.

In a function whose *x*-value represents time, what does the *y*-intercept represent?

The y-intercept represents the initial quantity when t = 0. Say a function represents the progress of a machine manufacturing widgets at a rate of 6 widgets per hour. The machine adds the widgets it makes to a growing pile that consisted of 12 widgets when the machine started working. If this function were graphed as a function of time, the y-intercept would be 12—the pile of 12 widgets that were there when the machine started its task.

Next Steps

If you answered most questions correctly in the "How Much Have You Learned?" section, and if your responses to the Reflect questions were similar to those of the PSAT expert, then consider Linear Functions an area of strength and move on to the next chapter. Come back to this topic periodically to prevent yourself from getting rusty.

If you don't yet feel confident, review those parts of this chapter that you have not yet mastered. Then, try the questions you missed again. As always, be sure to review the explanations closely. Finally, **go online** (**www.kaptest.com/moreonline**) for additional practice.

Answers and Explanations

Try on Your Own

1. C

Difficulty: Easy

Category: Algebra

Getting to the Answer: Recall that the function's range means all of its possible y-values. Here, the function has just one y-value, 2, so its range is 2. Choice **(C)** is correct.

2. 12

Difficulty: Easy

Category: Algebra

Getting to the Answer: Make sure you compute the functions in this composition in the correct order. Start with the innermost set of parentheses. Plug $x = 3$ into the f function and simplify.

$$f(3) = -3 + 5$$
$$= 2$$

Now, take this result and plug it into the g function.

$$g(2) = 6(2)$$
$$= 12$$

Enter **12**.

3. C

Difficulty: Easy

Category: Algebra

Getting to the Answer: First, substitute 5 into the function.

$$h(5) = 3(5) - 1 = 15 - 1 = 14$$

Next, plug in 2.

$$h(2) = 3(2) - 1 = 6 - 1 = 5$$

Finally, take the difference to obtain $14 - 5 = 9$. Choice **(C)** is correct. Caution! This is not the same as computing $5 - 2$ and then substituting 3 into the function.

4. B

Difficulty: Medium

Category: Algebra

Strategic Advice: The notation $g(h(x))$ can be read "g of h of x." It means that when x is substituted into $h(x)$, the output becomes the input for $g(x)$.

Getting to the Answer: Start with the innermost function. Use the $h(x)$ table to find $h(-2)$. When $x = -2$, the output of $h(x)$ is -4. Use -4 as the input for $g(x)$. When $x = -4$, the output of $g(x)$ is 0. Choice **(B)** is correct.

5. A

Difficulty: Hard

Category: Algebra

Getting to the Answer: This question may seem strange at first, but it employs the exact same logic that you use when evaluating something like $f(2)$. Just replace all xs in the function with the new expression in parentheses and simplify.

$$f(2x + 1) = -4(2x + 1) + 1$$
$$= -8x - 4 + 1$$
$$= -8x - 3$$

Choice **(A)** is correct.

6. B

Difficulty: Medium

Category: Algebra

Getting to the Answer: Since $g(x) = f(x) - 6$, when $x = 3$, $g(3) = f(3) - 6$. Begin by using the graph of f to find $f(3)$. At $x = 3$, $f(x) = 4$. Then substitute 4 for $f(3)$ into $g(3) = f(3) - 6$ to solve for $g(3)$. This gives $g(3) = 4 - 6 = -2$. **(B)** is correct.

7. C

Difficulty: Easy

Category: Algebra

Getting to the Answer: Use the graph to determine the equation of function f in slope-intercept form, $y = mx + b$. The function passes through the points $(-3, 0)$ and $(6, -3)$, so the slope is $\frac{y_2 - y_1}{x_2 - x_1} = \frac{-3 - 0}{6 - (-3)} = \frac{-3}{9} = -\frac{1}{3}$. Since only (C) has a slope of $-\frac{1}{3}$, **(C)** is correct. The y-intercept, the place where the function crosses the y-axis, is -1.

Alternatively, you could plug the points on the line into each of the choices to determine which equation is correct. First, plug in $(-3, 0)$.

A) $0 \neq -3(-3) - 1$. Eliminate.

B) $0 = -(-3) - 3$. Keep.

C) $0 = -\frac{1}{3}(-3) - 1$. Keep.

D) $0 \neq -3(-3) - 3$. Eliminate.

Now plug in $(6, -3)$ into the remaining choices.

B) $-3 \neq -(6) - 3$. Eliminate.

C) $-3 = -\frac{1}{3}(6) - 1$. Keep.

(C) is correct.

8. D

Difficulty: Medium

Category: Algebra

Getting to the Answer: The value of a is the x-value that gives the same y-value in each function; that is, the point at which the functions f and g intersect. According to the graph, the functions intersect at $(2, -2)$, so the value of a for which $f(a) = g(a)$ is 2. Choice **(D)** is correct.

9. B

Difficulty: Hard

Category: Algebra

Getting to the Answer: First, determine the slope of linear function f from the graph. Function f passes through the points $(0, 3)$ and $(5, -1)$. Thus, the slope of the graph of f is $\frac{y_2 - y_1}{x_2 - x_1} = \frac{-1 - 3}{5 - 0} = \frac{-4}{5} = -\frac{4}{5}$. The slope of the graph of g is 5 times the slope of f, so it is $5\left(-\frac{4}{5}\right) = -4$. Now use the slope-intercept equation,

$y = mx + b$, to determine b, the y-intercept of the graph of g. Plugging in $(0, 1)$ for (x, y) and -4 for m gives $1 = -4(0) + b$, and $b = 1$. The equation for function g is $g(x) = -4x + 1$. Thus, $g(5) = -4(5) + 1 = -19$. **(B)** is correct.

10. −3

Difficulty: Easy

Category: Algebra

Getting to the Answer: The value of $f(0)$ is the y-value of the function f when $x = 0$. The graph of the function f shows that when $x = 0$, $y = -3$. Thus, $f(0) = -3$. Enter **−3**.

11. D

Difficulty: Easy

Category: Algebra

Getting to the Answer: The domain of a function represents the possible input values. In this function, the input values are represented by n, which is the number of eggs laid by the fish over a given period of time. Because there cannot be a negative number of eggs or a fraction of an egg, the list in **(D)** is the only one that could represent the function's domain.

12. B

Difficulty: Easy

Category: Algebra

Getting to the Answer: First, figure out the function that will show you how much the magazine publisher pays its writers. The writers earn $2,500 plus $0.05 per word. So the function for earnings, E, is: $E(w) = \$2,500 + \$0.05(w)$.

Plug in what you know and solve for what you don't. The writer made $8,000 for writing one book, so $8,000 = \$2,500 + \$0.05(w)$. Now solve for w.

$$\$8,000 = \$2,500 + \$0.05(w)$$
$$\$5,500 = \$0.05(w)$$
$$110,000 = w$$

So to earn $8,000, the writer wrote 110,000 words for the publishing company. This matches **(B)**.

13. A

Difficulty: Medium

Category: Algebra

Strategic Advice: The question tells you that the function is linear, which means that you need to know the slope (rate of change in the height of the liquid) and the y-intercept (height of the liquid when there are 0 pennies) to pick the correct function.

Getting to the Answer: You already know the height of the liquid when there are 0 pennies—it's 5 inches. This means you can eliminate (B) and (D). To determine the rate of change in the height of the liquid, write what you know as ordered pairs, and then use the slope formula:

At 0 pennies, the height is 5 inches → (0, 5).
At 50 pennies, the height is 8.5 inches → (50, 8.5).

The rate of change in the height of the liquid is $\frac{8.5 - 5}{50 - 0} = \frac{3.5}{50} = 0.07$. This means that the correct function is $h(p) = 0.07p + 5$, which is **(A)**.

14. 210

Difficulty: Easy

Category: Algebra

Getting to the Answer: Evaluate the function at $t = 20$ and at $t = 10$, and then subtract the results.

$$c(20) = 21(20) + 2$$
$$= 420 + 2$$
$$= 422$$
$$c(10) = 21(10) + 2$$
$$= 210 + 2$$
$$= 212$$

The question asks how many more parts per million are in a patient's bloodstream after 20 hours than after 10 hours, so subtract $422 - 212 = 210$. The answer is **210**.

Another approach is to subtract the differences in time to obtain $20 - 10 = 10$ and multiply this number by the rate of change (21) to obtain $21(10) = 210$. This works because 21 represents the rate of increase per hour, and the question asks for the increase over these 10 hours. Either option results in **210**.

15. A

Difficulty: Medium

Category: Algebra

Getting to the Answer: The teacher spends $500 plus $25 per child, or $500 + 25s$. But she is reimbursed $5 for every student in the class, so subtract $5s$ to obtain $500 + 25s - 5s = 500 + 20s$. The correct function is $f(s) = 500 + 20s$, which matches **(A)**.

On Test Day

16. B

Difficulty: Medium

Category: Algebra

Strategic Advice: When modeling a real-life situation with a linear function, the starting point in the description is the y-intercept of the equation and the rate of change is the slope. Eliminate choices as you go; you may find that you are able to answer the question after only one or two steps. Never do more math than necessary to answer the question.

Getting to the Answer: In this question, the company is reducing the amount of greenhouse gas emissions, so the slope must be negative. Eliminate (C) and (D) because their positive slopes indicate an *increasing* function.

The starting point, or y-intercept, is the amount of greenhouse gas emissions the company plans to eliminate, or 10.8 million pounds. Unfortunately, this value is the same in (A) and (B), so you'll need to determine the slope: the amount of greenhouse gas emissions eliminated per year. Since the company wants to eliminate 10.8 metric tons of greenhouse gas emissions in 15 years, the amount of greenhouse gas emissions eliminated per year is 10.8 divided by 15.

You might expect to see a slope of $-\frac{10.8}{15}$ in the answer choices, but since decimals and fractions are generally not mixed in PSAT answer choices, the same slope will appear in a different form. You can note that the value of $-\frac{10.8}{15}$ is between 0 and -1. Of the remaining answer choices, only choice **(B)** is in that range. You can also confirm $-\frac{10.8}{15} = -\frac{54}{75}$ by using your calculator to convert the fractions to decimals: $-\frac{10.8}{15} = -0.72$ and $-\frac{54}{75} = -0.72$.

Alternatively, since the amount of greenhouse gas emissions at the end of 15 years is 0, that is, $f(15) = 0$, you could plug $(15, 0)$ into (A) and (B) to determine which equation is correct.

(A): $f(15) = -\frac{108}{75}(15) + 10.8 \neq 0$, eliminate.

Thus, **(B)** is correct.

How Much Have You Learned?

1.   D

Difficulty: Medium

Category: Algebra

Getting to the Answer: The question says that the value of $f(x) = 5$ and asks for the value of x that produces this result. This means that you are solving for x, not substituting for x. Set the function equal to 5 and solve:

$$5 = \frac{2}{5}x - 7$$
$$12 = \frac{2}{5}x$$
$$60 = 2x$$
$$30 = x$$

Thus, **(D)** is correct.

2.   C

Difficulty: Hard

Category: Algebra

Getting to the Answer: Take things one step at a time. First, determine $2f(x)$.

$$2f(x) = 2(-x + 5)$$
$$= -2x + 10$$

Now subtract $g(x)$. Be sure to distribute the negative sign to each term.

$$-2x + 10 - g(x)$$
$$-2x + 10 - (2x - 1)$$
$$-2x + 10 - 2x + 1$$
$$-4x + 11$$

Choice **(C)** is correct.

3.   B

Difficulty: Easy

Category: Algebra

Getting to the Answer: The domain of a function is all possible x-values. Here, the arrows indicate that the graph continues infinitely in both directions, so every x-value is possible. The domain of the function is all real numbers. Choice **(B)** is correct.

4.   231

Difficulty: Medium

Category: Algebra

Getting to the Answer: Linear functions have two components: slope and y-intercept. The y-intercept represents the starting amount, and the slope describes the rate of change. You are being asked for the value of a. In the equation $f(x) = ax + b$, a represents the slope. Since Jayesh's calorie needs vary depending on how many hours he plays basketball, **231** is the correct answer.

5.   A

Difficulty: Easy

Category: Algebra

Getting to the Answer: Work through nested functions from the inside out. You are asked for $g(f(x))$, so start with $f(x)$. Plug $x = 2$ into the f function and simplify.

$$f(2) = \frac{2}{4}$$
$$= \frac{1}{2}$$

Now plug this value into the outer function, g.

$$g\left(\frac{1}{2}\right) = 2\left(\frac{1}{2}\right) - 1$$
$$= 1 - 1$$
$$= 0$$

This matches **(A)**.

Note that if you had worked your nested functions in the wrong order—as you would if you'd been asked for $f(g(x))$—your final result would have been $\frac{3}{4}$, which matches (C).

6.   12

Difficulty: Easy

Category: Algebra

Getting to the Answer: Remember that $f(x)$ means y. Substitute 3 for x and 6 for $f(x)$ to find k:

$$6 = -2(3) + k$$
$$6 = -6 + k$$
$$12 = k$$

The answer is **12**.

7.   D

Difficulty: Hard

Category: Algebra

Getting to the Answer: The range of the function describes all of the possible $g(y)$ values. The question asks you to determine which number can be part of the range.

First, calculate how tall the trees are when the scientist begins to use the function. Since the trees were 3.6 feet when they were first planted and grew at a rate of 2.4 feet for 5 years, $h = 3.6 + 2.4(5) = 15.6$ feet. Having solved for h, rewrite the function as $g(y) = 15.6 + 2.4y$. Since y is greater than or equal to 0, the range will be any value greater than or equal to 15.6. Only **(D)** is larger than 15.6, so it is correct.

8.   A

Difficulty: Hard

Category: Algebra

Getting to the Answer: To find $f(g(x))$, plug $g(x)$ into the f function.

$$f(g(x)) = \frac{2g(x) + 6}{4}$$
$$= \frac{2(2x - 1) + 6}{4}$$
$$= \frac{4x - 2 + 6}{4}$$
$$= \frac{4x + 4}{4}$$
$$= \frac{4(x + 1)}{4}$$
$$= x + 1$$

Thus, **(A)** is correct.

9.   D

Difficulty: Medium

Category: Algebra

Getting to the Answer: The expression $f(-2)$ means "the y-value when $x = -2$." According to the graph, $f(-2)$ has a value of 9, while $g(2)$ has a value of -1. Therefore, $f(-2) - g(2) = 9 - (-1) = 9 + 1 = 10$. This matches **(D)**.

10. B

Difficulty: Medium

Category: Algebra

Getting to the Answer: The cost for the first 100 feet will be $15(100) = \$1,500$. This number will be added to the cost for the remainder of the fence. Eliminate (C) and (D), which subtract the 1,500 instead of adding it.

Now, consider what happens after the first 100 feet. The remaining length of fencing is the total length, x, minus the first 100 feet, or $x - 100$. Multiply by 12 to find the cost for this section of the fence: $12(x - 100)$. The complete function, then, is $c(x) = 1,500 + 12(x - 100)$. This matches **(B)**.

11. C

Difficulty: Medium

Category: Algebra

Getting to the Answer: The domain is all the x-values that will yield a value for $f(x)$. From left to right, notice that the graph goes from -4 to 5 and includes the endpoints. Thus, **(C)** is correct.

PROBLEM-SOLVING AND DATA ANALYSIS

[CHAPTER 7]

RATES, RATIOS, PROPORTIONS, PERCENTS, AND UNITS

LEARNING OBJECTIVES

After completing this chapter, you will be able to:

- Given any two values in a three-part rate equation, solve for the third
- Set up and solve a proportion for a missing value
- Use ratios to perform unit conversions
- Calculate percents
- Calculate percent change

How Much Do You Know?

Directions

Try the questions that follow. Show your work so that you can compare your solutions to the ones found in the "Check Your Work" section immediately after this question set. If you answered the question(s) on a specific topic correctly, and if your scratchwork looks like ours, you may be able to move quickly through the lesson covering that topic. If you answered incorrectly or used a different approach, you may want to take your time on that lesson.

1

A silo currently contains 1,000 bushels of grain. If a silo blower continues to fill the silo at a rate of 850 bushels per half-hour, how many bushels of grain will be in the silo after 2 hours?

(A) 2,700

(B) 3,400

(C) 4,400

(D) 5,400

2

Seven out of every 250 students who take Exam A are expected to score at least 90 percent. If 12,000 students take Exam A, how many would be expected to score at least 90 percent?

(A) 176

(B) 224

(C) 300

(D) 336

$$\frac{7}{250}^{x}$$

3

A homeowner needs 81 square feet of grass for his lawn, but the vendor sells grass by the square yard. How many square yards of grass should the home-owner purchase? (1 yard = 3 feet)

(A) 9

(B) 27

(C) 243

(D) 729

4

An oil company decreases the ethanol content of its gasoline from 15 percent to 6 percent by volume to lower the cost. If a car with a 14-gallon tank is filled with the 15 percent blend and a second car with a 10-gallon tank is filled with the 6 percent blend, how many times more ethanol is in the first car than in the second car?

(A) 1.5

(B) 2.5

(C) 3.5

(D) 4.0

14g → 15% → 14 × .15 = 2.1

10g → 6% → 10 × .06 = 2.1

$\frac{2.1}{.6}$ $\frac{2.1}{.6}$ 3.5

5

After the first week of production, Kelania decreased the number of pounds of flour she ordered for her bakery by 25 percent. The following week, she increased the number by 10 percent. What is the net percent decrease in the number of pounds of flour Kelania ordered from the start of the first week to the end of the second week?

(A) 15%

(B) 17.5%

(C) 25%

(D) 35%

6

The cost of tuition at a four-year college in 1995 was approximately $15,800. In 2020, the cost of tuition at the same college was approximately $30,100. If tuition experiences the same total percent increase over the next 25 years, approximately how much will tuition at the four-year college cost?

(A) $44,400

(B) $45,800

(C) $57,300

(D) $66,200

Handwritten work:

1 week → −25%
2 week → +10%

$$\frac{14,300}{25}$$

47.5 %

1.47.5

1995 - 2020

15,800 - 30,100
14 300

44,400

$$\frac{14,800}{30,100} \quad .475$$

47.5 ≈ 50%

30,100 × 2 = 60,200

Less then 50%

57,300

Check Your Work

1. C

Difficulty: Medium

Category: Problem-Solving and Data Analysis

Getting to the Answer: The question asks for the number of bushels of grain after the silo blower runs for 2 hours. Note that the silo initially contains 1,000 bushels. Since the rate of the silo blower is given as 850 bushels per half-hour, first convert the rate to per hour: $\frac{850 \text{ bu.}}{0.5 \text{ hr}} = \frac{1{,}700 \text{ bu.}}{1 \text{ hr}}$. Then, multiply the rate by 2 hours, the number of hours the silo blower ran, to get the number of bushels that were blown into the silo after 2 hours: $\frac{1{,}700 \text{ bu.}}{1 \text{ hr}} \times 2 \text{ hr} = 3{,}400 \text{ bu.}$ Now add this to the initial number of bushels in the silo to get the total number of bushels of grain in the silo after 2 hours: 1,000 bu. + 3,400 bu. = 4,400 bu. **(C)** is correct.

2. D

Difficulty: Easy

Category: Problem-Solving and Data Analysis

Getting to the Answer: Assign a variable, say n, to the number of students expected to score at least 90 percent when 12,000 students take Exam A. Then, set up a proportion and solve for n:

$$\frac{7}{250} = \frac{n}{12{,}000}$$

$$250n = (7)(12{,}000)$$

$$250n = 84{,}000$$

$$n = 336$$

The correct answer is **(D)**.

3. A

Difficulty: Easy

Category: Problem-Solving and Data Analysis

Getting to the Answer: Map out your route from starting units to ending units. Be mindful of the fact that the question deals with units of area (square units), so you need to multiply by the conversion factor twice. The starting quantity is in square feet, and the desired quantity is in square yards. The only conversion factor you need is 3 ft = 1 yd. Setting up your route to square yards, you get:

$$\frac{81 \text{ ft}^2}{1} \times \frac{1 \text{ yd}}{3 \text{ ft}} \times \frac{1 \text{ yd}}{3 \text{ ft}} = \frac{81}{9} \text{ yd}^2 = 9 \text{ yd}^2$$

This matches **(A)**.

4. C

Difficulty: Medium

Category: Problem-Solving and Data Analysis

Getting to the Answer: Starting with the 14-gallon tank, determine the gallons of ethanol by multiplying the percent ethanol by the number of gallons in the tank: $15\% \times 14 = ? \rightarrow 0.15 \times 14 = 2.1$ gallons of ethanol. Repeat for the smaller tank: $6\% \times 10 = ? \rightarrow 0.06 \times 10 = 0.6$ gallons of ethanol. The question asks how many times more ethanol is in the larger tank, so divide the quantities to get $\frac{2.1}{0.6} = 3.5$. This matches **(C)**.

5.　B

Difficulty: Medium

Category: Problem-Solving and Data Analysis

Getting to the Answer: Remember to avoid merely combining the percentages together. Find each change individually. You're not given a definite number of pounds of flour in the question, so assume Kelania starts with 100. To save a step with each change, calculate the total amount instead of the weekly increase or decrease. The first change is -25%; so the number of pounds of flour ordered the next week is $75\% \times 100 = 0.75 \times 100 = 75$. The second change is $+10\%$, which corresponds to $110\% \times 75 = 1.1 \times 75 = 82.5$ pounds. The percent change is $\frac{82.5 - 100}{100} = \frac{-17.5}{100} \times 100\% = -17.5\%$, which corresponds to a 17.5% decrease.

(B) is correct.

6.　C

Difficulty: Medium

Category: Problem-Solving and Data Analysis

Getting to the Answer: Find the percent increase using the formula: percent change $= \frac{\text{actual change}}{\text{original value}} \times 100\%$. Then, apply the same percent increase to the amount for 2020. The amount of increase is $30{,}100 - 15{,}800 = 14{,}300$, so the percent increase is $\frac{14{,}300}{15{,}800} \times 100\% \approx 0.905 \times 100\% = 90.5\%$ over 25 years. If the total percent increase over the next 25 years is the same, the cost of tuition will be $30{,}100 \times 1.905 = 57{,}340.50$, or about $57{,}300$, which is **(C)**.

Alternatively, if you noticed that $30{,}100 is almost double $15{,}800, then the cost of tuition in 25 years will be almost double $30{,}100, which matches **(C)**.

Rates

To answer a question like this:

Devi's bathtub, which holds 36 gallons of water when full, takes 4 minutes to empty when the plug is pulled. Ridley's bathtub, which holds 60 gallons of water when full, takes 3 minutes to empty when the plug is pulled. What is the positive difference, in gallons per minute, between the rates at which Devi and Ridley's bathtubs empty?

Ⓐ 3

Ⓑ 9

Ⓒ 11

Ⓓ 20

You need to know this:

A **rate** is an expression of the amount of something done per unit of time. Speed, for example, represents how far something travels in a particular amount of time. The general three-part rate formula is

Rate $= \dfrac{\textbf{amount}}{\textbf{time}}$, although you may see this in a number of different ways. With a little math, the equation becomes **Amount** $=$ **rate** $\times$ **time**, or you might find it helpful to use **Distance** $=$ **rate** $\times$ **time** or even **Work** $=$ **rate** $\times$ **time**. We'll use several ways in this chapter. For instance, say a cyclist rides 30 miles in 2 hours. To determine her speed (rate), plug in 30 miles for the amount and 2 hours for the time to get

Speed $= \dfrac{30 \text{ miles}}{2 \text{ hours}} = 15$ miles per hour. Since a rate also represents the work done in one unit of time, its reciprocal represents the amount of time taken to do one unit of work. The bike being ridden at 15 miles per hour takes $\dfrac{1}{15}$ of an hour to go one mile.

Like other three-part formulas, you may need to rearrange the rate formula to solve for the other two parts: **Amount** $=$ **rate** $\times$ **time** and **Time** $= \dfrac{\textbf{amount}}{\textbf{rate}}$.

Sometimes, you'll be given the rates of two separate workers attempting to complete a task, and you'll need to combine their rates to figure out how long they'd take to complete the task together. Suppose that it takes Dorian 3 hours to paint a room and Clarice 2 hours to paint a room of the same size. So, Dorian's rate is $\dfrac{1 \text{ room}}{3 \text{ hours}} = \dfrac{1}{3}$ room per hour and Clarice's is $\dfrac{1 \text{ room}}{2 \text{ hours}} = \dfrac{1}{2}$ room per hour. If they work together, their combined rate of progress is the sum of their individual rates: $\dfrac{1}{3} + \dfrac{1}{2} = \dfrac{2}{6} + \dfrac{3}{6} = \dfrac{5}{6}$ room per hour. You could then take the reciprocal to find that it would take them $\dfrac{6}{5}$ of an hour to paint one room.

There is also a simplified formula for two workers. If a and b represent the time each worker takes to complete the task and T is their combined time, then $T = \dfrac{ab}{a+b}$.

You need to do this:

- Determine which two parts of the rate formula are given and use them to solve for the third.
- If there are multiple workers collaborating on a task, use their individual rates to determine their combined rate.

Explanation:

First, find the rates at which each individual bathtub drains using the rate formula, $\textbf{Rate} = \dfrac{\textbf{amount}}{\textbf{time}}$. For Devi's bathtub, the amount is 36 gallons and the time is 4 minutes, so $\text{Rate} = \dfrac{36 \text{ gallons}}{4 \text{ minutes}} = 9$ gallons per minute.

For Ridley's bathtub, the amount is 60 gallons and the time is 3 minutes, so $\text{Rate} = \dfrac{60 \text{ gallons}}{3 \text{ minutes}} = 20$ gallons per minute. Remember, though, that the question asks for the positive difference between these rates, not either of the rates themselves. Since $20 - 9 = 11$, **(C)** is correct.

Math

Try on Your Own

Directions

Take as much time as you need on these questions. Work carefully and methodically. There will be an opportunity for timed practice later in the book.

1

The Concorde jet had a cruising speed of 1,341 miles per hour. At this speed, approximately how many hours would it take the jet to travel from New York to Paris, a distance of approximately 3,628 miles?

(A) 1

(B) 3

(C) 4

(D) 5

2

At 3:00 p.m., a climber of Mt. Kilimanjaro was at an elevation of 2,200 meters. By 7:00 p.m., she had reached an elevation of 3,000 meters. What was the climber's average rate of ascent between 3:00 p.m. and 7:00 p.m., in meters per hour?

(A) 200

(B) 400

(C) 600

(D) 800

3

HINT: For Q3, consider what happens to the distance between the two balls with each second that goes by.

Two balls roll toward each other on a flat surface. One ball rolls at a speed of 4 feet per second, and the other rolls at a speed of 6 feet per second. If the balls collide after 5 seconds, how many feet apart were they initially?

(A) 2

(B) 10

(C) 25

(D) 50

4

A container crane can unload 200 containers from a ship in one hour. Assuming a crane can operate around the clock, how many cranes would need to operate simultaneously to unload 10,000 containers in one day?

(A) 2

(B) 3

(C) 4

(D) 5

5

HINT: For Q5, combine the two rates before using the rate equation.

A water pipe can fill a swimming pool in 8 hours. A drain pipe can fully empty the same pool in 10 hours. If both pipes are open, how many hours will it take for the pool to fill completely?

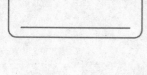

Math

Ratios and Proportions

LEARNING OBJECTIVE

After this lesson, you will be able to:

- Set up and solve a proportion for a missing value

To answer a question like this:

The projected length and width of a property to be built are 1,245 feet and 415 feet, respectively. The contractor wishes to build an exact replica scale model of the property that is 5 feet long. Approximately how many feet wide will the scale model's width be?

You need to know this:

A **ratio** is a comparison of one quantity to another. When writing ratios, you can compare one part of a group to another part of that group or you can compare a part of the group to the whole group. Suppose you have a bowl of apples and oranges: you can write ratios that compare apples to oranges (part to part), apples to total fruit (part to whole), and oranges to total fruit (part to whole).

Keep in mind that ratios convey *relative* amounts, not necessarily actual amounts, and that they are typically expressed in lowest terms. For example, if there are 10 apples and 6 oranges in a bowl, the ratio of apples to oranges would likely be expressed as $\frac{5}{3}$ on the PSAT rather than as $\frac{10}{6}$. However, if you know the ratio of apples to oranges and either the actual number of apples or the total number of pieces of fruit, you can find the actual number of oranges by setting up a proportion (see below).

Note that the PSAT may occasionally use the word "proportion" to mean "ratio."

A **proportion** is simply two ratios set equal to each other, for example, $\frac{a}{b} = \frac{c}{d}$. Proportions are an efficient way to solve certain problems, but you must exercise caution when setting them up. Noting the units of each piece of the proportion will help you put each piece of the proportion in the right place.

Sometimes, the PSAT may ask you to determine whether certain proportions are equivalent—check this by cross-multiplying. You'll get results that are much easier to compare.

$$\text{If } \frac{a}{b} = \frac{c}{d}, \text{ then: } ad = bc, \frac{a}{c} = \frac{b}{d}, \frac{d}{b} = \frac{c}{a}, \frac{b}{a} = \frac{d}{c}, \text{ BUT } \frac{a}{d} \neq \frac{c}{b}$$

Each derived ratio shown above except the last one is simply a manipulation of the first, so all except the last are correct. You can verify this via cross-multiplication ($ad = bc$ in each case except the last).

Alternatively, you can pick equivalent fractions $\frac{2}{3}$ and $\frac{6}{9}$ ($a = 2, b = 3, c = 6, d = 9$). Cross-multiplication gives $2 \times 9 = 3 \times 6$, which is a true statement. Dividing 2 and 3 by 6 and 9 gives $\frac{2}{6} = \frac{3}{9}$, which is also true, and so on. However, attempting to equate $\frac{2}{9}$ and $\frac{3}{6}$ will not work.

If you know any three numerical values in a proportion, you can solve for the fourth. For example, say a fruit stand sells 3 peaches for every 5 apricots and you are supposed to calculate the number of peaches sold on a day when 20 apricots were sold. You would use the given information to set up a proportion and solve for the unknown:

$$\frac{3}{5} = \frac{p}{20}$$

You can now solve for the number of peaches sold, p, by cross-multiplying:

$$60 = 5p$$
$$p = 12$$

Alternatively, you could use the common multiplier to solve for p: the numerator and denominator in the original ratio must be multiplied by the same value to arrive at their respective terms in the new ratio. To get from 5 to 20 in the denominator, you multiply by 4, so you also have to multiply the 3 in the numerator by 4 to arrive at the actual number of peaches sold: $4(3) = 12$.

You need to do this:

Set up a proportion and solve for the unknown, either by cross-multiplying or by using the common multiplier.

Explanation:

The ratio of the length of the real property to that of the scale model is $\frac{1,245 \text{ feet}}{5 \text{ feet}}$. You know the actual width (415 feet), so set up a proportion and solve for the scale model's width:

$$\frac{1,245 \text{ feet}}{5 \text{ feet}} = \frac{415 \text{ feet}}{x \text{ feet}}$$
$$1,245x = 2,075$$
$$x = 1.66\overline{6} \text{ feet}$$

Since the answer is a repeating decimal, you can enter it by either truncating or rounding it at the 4th digit. So, enter either **1.666** or **1.667**.

Try on Your Own

Directions

Take as much time as you need on these questions. Work carefully and methodically. There will be an opportunity for timed practice later in the book.

6

> HINT: When setting up the proportion in Q6, if the number of defective snow blowers appears in the numerator on the left, the number of defective snow blowers must also appear in the numerator on the right.

For every 4,000 snowblowers produced by a snowblower factory, exactly 8 are defective. If this remains unchanged, how many snowblowers were produced during a period in which exactly 18 snowblowers were defective?

Ⓐ 6,000

Ⓑ 9,000

Ⓒ 12,000

Ⓓ 18,000

7

In a 75-foot-long escalator, the difference in height between the two floors being connected was originally supposed to be 40 feet, but due to a calculation error, this height must be reduced by 25 percent. The angle between the escalator and the floor must not change. What is the difference in length, in feet, between the original escalator measurement and its corrected value?

Ⓐ 18.75

Ⓑ 25

Ⓒ 56.25

Ⓓ 100

8

The number of cars that can safely pass through a stoplight is directly proportional to the length of time that the light stays green. If 9 cars can safely pass through a light that stays green for 36 seconds, how many cars can safely pass through a light that stays green for 24 seconds?

Ⓐ 4

Ⓑ 6

Ⓒ 7

Ⓓ 8

9

If the total weight of 31 identical medieval coins is approximately 16 ounces, which of the following is closest to the weight, in ounces, of 97 of these coins?

(A) 5

(B) 19

(C) 50

(D) 188

10

HINT: For Q10, assign a variable as the common multiplier in the proportion of the pyramid's length : width : height, then express the volume in terms of that common multiplier.

The Great Pyramid of Giza has a square base with a side length of 750 feet and a height of 500 feet. If a student builds a scale replica using 162 cubic inches of modeling clay, what will be the height of her model pyramid, in inches? The volume of a pyramid is $V = \frac{1}{3}lwh$.

_____

Unit Conversion

LEARNING OBJECTIVE

After this lesson, you will be able to:

* Use ratios to perform unit conversions

To answer a question like this:

City A and city B are 2,000 miles apart, while city C is twice as far from city A as city A is from city B. What is the approximate distance, in inches, between city A and city C? (1 mile = 5,280 feet and 1 foot = 12 inches)

Ⓐ 4.3 million

Ⓑ 52 million

Ⓒ 127 million

Ⓓ 253 million

You need to know this:

You can use ratios to perform unit conversions. This is especially useful when there are multiple conversions or when the units are unfamiliar.

For example, though these units of measurement are no longer commonly used, there are 8 furlongs in a mile and 3 miles in a league. Say you're asked to convert 4 leagues to furlongs. A convenient way to do this is to set up the conversion ratios so that equivalent units cancel:

$$4 \text{ leagues} \times \frac{3 \text{ miles}}{1 \text{ league}} \times \frac{8 \text{ furlongs}}{1 \text{ mile}} = 4 \times 3 \times 8 = 96 \text{ furlongs}$$

Notice that all the units cancel out except the furlongs, which is the one you want.

You need to do this:

Set up a series of ratios to make equivalent units cancel. (Keep track of the units by writing them down next to the numbers in the ratios.) You should be left with the units you're converting into.

Explanation:

City C is twice as far from city A as city A is from city B, so city C is 2(2,000) = 4,000 miles away from city A. Set up a series of ratios to convert to inches (in):

$$4,000 \text{ mi} \times \frac{5,280 \text{ ft}}{1 \text{ mi}} \times \frac{12 \text{ in}}{1 \text{ ft}} = 4,000 \times 5,280 \times 12 \text{ in}$$
$$= 253,440,000 \text{ in} = 253.44 \text{ million inches}$$

Therefore, **(D)** is correct.

Try on Your Own

Directions

Take as much time as you need on these questions. Work carefully and methodically. There will be an opportunity for timed practice later in the book.

11

Jack travels 180 miles while his car uses gasoline at a rate of 40 miles per gallon. He then travels another 105 miles while his car uses gasoline at a rate of 35 miles per gallon. How many gallons of gasoline did his car consume?

Ⓐ 1.5

Ⓑ 3.0

Ⓒ 4.5

Ⓓ 7.5

12

HINT: Begin the conversion in Q12 by starting with the number that is not a rate.

Juan's air mattress deflates at a constant rate of 100 milliliters per minute. If the air mattress contains 300 liters of air, how long will it take, in hours, for the air mattress to completely deflate? (1,000 milliliter = 1 liter)

13

A sled slides down a snowy hill at a constant speed of 3 miles per hour. How fast is that in feet per second? (1 mile = 5,280 feet)

14

HINT: Be careful to use the correct units in Q14! What units are used in the question and what units appear in the answer choices?

Jorge reads at a rate of 5 words per second. If the pages of Jorge's textbook contain an average of 500 words per page, how long will it take him to read 45 pages?

Ⓐ 50 minutes

Ⓑ 1 hour, 15 minutes

Ⓒ 1 hour, 25 minutes

Ⓓ 1 hour, 40 minutes

15

Each MRI scan given at a hospital produces about 3.6 gigabits of data. The hospital computers spend 8 hours each night uploading the MRI scans to a remote server at a rate of 2 megabits per second. What is the maximum number of MRI scans that the hospital can upload each night? (1 gigabit = 1,024 megabits)

Ⓐ 15

Ⓑ 16

Ⓒ 56

Ⓓ 202

Percents

Math

> **LEARNING OBJECTIVE**
>
> After this lesson, you will be able to:
>
> - Calculate percents

To answer a question like this:

Teachers surveyed 512 students at South Side High School and of those, 12.5 percent favor math class. At the North Side High School, 24.8 percent of 625 students favor math class. What is the approximate percentage of all the students surveyed that favor math class?

Ⓐ 15.4%

Ⓑ 19.3%

Ⓒ 25.4%

Ⓓ 31.9%

You need to know this:

Percent means "per one hundred." Thus, 25% means 25 out of every hundred. For instance, 25% of 500 students can be found by setting up a proportion: $\frac{25}{100} = \frac{x}{500}$, where x represents 25% of 500 students and equals 125.

To calculate percent, you can use this basic equation:

$$\text{Percent} = \frac{\text{part}}{\text{whole}} \times 100\%$$

In the example, the whole is 500 students and the part is 125 students. Plugging the values into the equation gives $\frac{125}{500} \times 100\% = 25\%$.

Alternatively, use this statement: _____ percent of _____ is _____. Translating from English into math, you get _____% × _____ = _____. For example, "25 percent of 500 is 125" translated is "25% × 500 = 125."

In some calculations, you may find it convenient to express percentages as decimals: 25% as a decimal is 25 divided by 100 or 0.25. Thus, 25% × 500 can be written as 0.25 × 500.

You need to do this:

- Translate from English into math.
- Plug in the values for any two parts of the formula and solve for the third.

Explanation:

First, find the number of students at each school who favor math class. Start with South Side High School: 12.5% of 512 is $0.125 \times 512 = 64$. Move on to North Side High School: $0.248 \times 625 = 155$. Next, find the total number of students who were surveyed at both schools, which was $512 + 625 = 1,137$, and the total number who favor math class, $64 + 155 = 219$. Finally, find the percent of students who favor math class by using the formula:

$$\text{percent} = \frac{219}{1,137} \times 100\%$$
$$\approx 0.1926 \times 100\%$$
$$\approx 19.3\%$$

Of all the students surveyed, about 19.3% favor math class, making **(B)** the correct answer.

Try on Your Own

Directions

Take as much time as you need on these questions. Work carefully and methodically. There will be an opportunity for timed practice later in the book.

16

A company sells dolls for $20 each. It decides to offer a discount of 20 percent to see how many new customers it can attract. How much will each doll sell for at the discounted price?

- Ⓐ $12
- Ⓑ $14
- Ⓒ $16
- Ⓓ $18

17

HINT: For Q17, begin by figuring out what percent of the budget actually goes to lunch.

A high school's Environment Club allocates 40 percent of its budget for a guest speaker, 25 percent for educational materials, 20 percent to rent a hotel conference room, and the remainder for lunch. If the club plans to spend $225 for lunch, how much does it plan to spend on the guest speaker?

- Ⓐ $375
- Ⓑ $450
- Ⓒ $525
- Ⓓ $600

18

A bag of marbles contains 60 marbles that are either red, blue, or yellow. If there are 12 blue marbles, what percent of the bag is red and yellow marbles?

- Ⓐ 20%
- Ⓑ 48%
- Ⓒ 80%
- Ⓓ 88%

19

HINT: For Q19, use the percent formula. Which is the part and which is the whole?

The price for a haircut at a salon is $40. If Aiswarya tipped $p\%$ and paid the salon owner $50, what is the value of p?

- Ⓐ 0.25
- Ⓑ 1.25
- Ⓒ 25
- Ⓓ 80

20

On a 50-question exam, a correct answer is worth two points, and the penalty for an incorrect answer is a half-point deduction. If Maxim scored 70 points, what percent of the questions did he answer correctly?

- Ⓐ 24%
- Ⓑ 38%
- Ⓒ 62%
- Ⓓ 76%

Percent Change

To answer a question like this:

In the afternoon, Lisle increases her lemonade production by 25 percent. Then, in the evening she decreases it by 10 percent. What is the net percent increase in Lisle's lemonade production from the afternoon to the evening?

You need to know this:

You can determine the **percent change** in a given situation by applying this formula:

$$\text{Percent increase or decrease} = \frac{\text{amount of increase or decrease}}{\text{original amount}} \times 100\%$$

Sometimes, more than one change will occur. Be careful here, as it can be tempting to take a "shortcut" by just combining percent changes together (which will almost always lead to an incorrect answer). Instead, you'll need to find the total amount of increase or decrease and then apply the formula.

In some instances, a question will ask you for the final amount as a percent of the original amount. In those cases, use this formula: $\text{Percent} = \frac{\text{final amount}}{\text{original amount}} \times 100\%$. Pay attention to the distinction between these two question types.

You need to do this:

- Calculate the actual change (increase or decrease).
- Divide by the *original* amount (not the new amount!).
- Multiply by 100%.

Explanation:

The question does not give an initial value for lemonade production, so pick 100 (often the best number to use when picking numbers for questions involving percents) and then calculate the actual change. A 25% increase from 100 is $100 + (0.25 \times 100)$ and brings the lemonade production to $100 + 25 = 125$. A 10% decrease from 125 is $125 - (0.10 \times 125)$ and brings the lemonade production to $125 - 12.5 = 112.5$. The actual increase, then, is $112.5 - 100 = 12.5$. (Again, note that simply combining the percents would get you the incorrect answer: $25\% - 10\% = 15\%$.)

Plugging this increase into the percent change formula yields the following (remember to divide by the *original* amount, 100, rather than by the new amount, 112.5):

$$\text{percent change} = \frac{12.5}{100} \times 100\% = 12.5\%$$

Enter **12.5**.

Try on Your Own

Directions

Take as much time as you need on these questions. Work carefully and methodically. There will be an opportunity for timed practice later in the book.

21

A used car dealership initially prices a car at $12,000. When the car fails to sell, the dealership reduces the price to $10,500. During a holiday sale, the dealership drops the price of the car an additional 5 percent below the reduced price. To the nearest tenth of a percent, what is the total percent discount from the car's initial price to the holiday sale price?

Ⓐ 15.5%

Ⓑ 16.9%

Ⓒ 17.5%

Ⓓ 20%

22

HINT: The first thing you'll want to do for Q22 is figure out how much additional sand and gravel was sold this year.

Last year, a company sold 280 tons of gravel and 220 tons of sand. This year, the company sold 20 percent more gravel by weight and 25 percent more sand by weight than it sold last year. By approximately what percent did the total weight of sand and gravel sold increase this year over last year?

Ⓐ 22%

Ⓑ 45%

Ⓒ 56%

Ⓓ 111%

23

HINT: Remember that when picking numbers for Q23, you don't have to pick realistic values. Pick numbers that are easy to work with in the given situation. For percent questions, the number is usually 100.

Over the past decade, the population of a certain town increased by 20 percent. If the population of the town increases 15 percent over the next decade, by what percent will the population have increased over the entire two-decade period?

Ⓐ 33%

Ⓑ 35%

Ⓒ 38%

Ⓓ 43%

24

The price of a mutual fund increased by 15 percent the first year. The following year, the price decreased by 12 percent. What is the percent change in the price of the stock for the two years?

Ⓐ −3%

Ⓑ 1.2%

Ⓒ 3%

Ⓓ 12%

25

HINT: What information do you need to determine in order to answer Q25 correctly?

There are currently 6,210 fish in a lake. If the number of fish in the lake increased by 15 percent during the last year and 20 percent during the year before that, how many more fish are in the lake currently than in the lake two years ago?

26

A movie premiered with 18 million viewers. In the second week, the number of viewers dropped to 15 million. If the number of viewers in the third week was 10 percent lower than the number in the second week, what percent of the number of viewers for the premiere is the number of viewers in the third week?

(A) 10%

(B) 25%

(C) 75%

(D) 90%

On Test Day

When a question features multiple percentages, you have to make a key strategic decision: can I do the arithmetic on the percentages themselves and get the answer right away, or do I have to calculate each percentage individually and do the arithmetic on the actual values?

For example, suppose a car traveling 50 miles per hour increases its speed by 20 percent and then decreases its speed by 20 percent. If you were to calculate $+20\% - 20\% = 0$, you might conclude the speed of the car did not change and the final speed is 50 miles per hour. However, after a 20% increase, the car's speed becomes 120% of the original: $1.2(50) = 60$. Then when the car "decreases its speed by 20 percent," that 20% is calculated based on the *new* speed, 60, not the original speed, and 20% of 60 is greater than 20% of 50. Thus, the car's final speed is lower than its starting speed: $50(1.2)(0.8) = 48$ miles per hour.

On the other hand, suppose you have to find how many more car owners than motorcycle owners live in a certain region where there are 13,450 residents, given that 60 percent of them own cars and 10 percent of them own motorcycles. It may be tempting to find 60 percent of 13,450 ($0.60 \times 13,450 = 8,070$), then find 10 percent of 13,450 ($0.10 \times 13,450 = 1,345$), and finally subtract those two numbers to get the answer ($8,070 - 1,345 = 6,725$). However, you can quickly find the difference between the two percentages ($60\% - 10\% = 50\%$) and then take 50 percent of the total to get the answer: $13,450 \times 0.50 = 6,725$.

The fundamental principles are:

- If the percentages are out of the same total, then you can do arithmetic on the percentages.
- If the totals are different, then you must convert the percentages into actual values.

Practice applying these principles on the following question.

27. There are 400 seniors and 420 juniors in a certain high school. Of the seniors, 65% are eligible for an advanced placement world history course. Among the juniors, 75% are not eligible to enroll in that course. How many more seniors than juniors could enroll in the course?

The answer and explanation can be found at the end of this chapter.

How Much Have You Learned?

Directions

For test-like practice, give yourself 15 minutes to complete this question set. Be sure to study the explanations, even for questions you answered correctly. They can be found at the end of this chapter.

1

A certain city has 2,625 total businesses. The ratio of businesses that do not require safety inspections to those that do require safety inspections is 5:2. Of the businesses that were required to have inspections, 12 percent had safety violations. How many businesses that required inspections had safety violations?

- (A) 90
- (B) 315
- (C) 660
- (D) 2,310

2

A consumer car can travel 120 miles per hour. A race car can travel 210 miles per hour. How many more miles can the race car travel in 30 seconds than the consumer car?

- (A) $\frac{3}{4}$
- (B) 1
- (C) $\frac{3}{2}$
- (D) 45

3

Company A's oil contains 4 percent zinc and company B's oil contains 9 percent zinc. Suppose a car uses 8 pints of company B's oil and a truck uses 6 quarts of company A's oil. How many times more zinc is in the car's oil than in the truck's?
(1 quart = 2 pints)

- (A) 0.34
- (B) 0.67
- (C) 1.5
- (D) 3

4

A secondhand shop acquires a piece of furniture on July 15 and prices it at 40% off of the original price. The price is marked down an additional 20 percent for every full month that it remains unsold. If the original price of the furniture was $1,050 and it is sold on September 5, what is the final selling price?

- (A) $258.05
- (B) $322.56
- (C) $504.00
- (D) $630.00

5

An amusement park is building a scale model of an airplane for a ride. The real airplane measures 220 feet from nose to tail and has a wingspan of 174 feet. If the model airplane is 36 feet long, approximately how many feet long should the wingspan be?

Ⓐ 17

Ⓑ 28

Ⓒ 35

Ⓓ 45

6

The recipe for one loaf of bread calls for 180 milliliters of milk. Drew wants to make five loaves. If 1 cup equals 236.588 milliliters, approximately how many cups of milk will Drew need?

Ⓐ $\frac{3}{4}$

Ⓑ $1\frac{1}{3}$

Ⓒ $3\frac{4}{5}$

Ⓓ $6\frac{1}{2}$

7

There are about 3 feet per meter and 1,000 meters per kilometer. Two cities are 1,800,000 feet apart. Approximately how many kilometers apart are the two cities?

8

A racing course has an adult track and a teen track, each with two straightaways. The lengths of the adult track straightaways are 100 meters and 150 meters. If the shorter teen track straightaway is proportional to that of the adult track and is 50 meters long, what is the length, in meters, of the longer teen track straightaway?

Ⓐ 25

Ⓑ 50

Ⓒ 75

Ⓓ 100

9

Last year, a farmer had 350 acres planted in corn and 160 acres planted in soybeans. This year, the farmer reduced the acreage planted in corn by 20 percent and reduced the acreage planted in soybeans by 15 percent. By approximately what percent did the farmer reduce the total acreage planted in corn and soybeans?

Ⓐ 16.4%

Ⓑ 16.9%

Ⓒ 17.5%

Ⓓ 18.4%

10

Comforters are on sale for 40 percent less than the original price. If Mandy pays a total of $89.10 at the register, including a 10% sales tax, what was the original price of the comforter?

Ⓐ $133

Ⓑ $135

Ⓒ $139

Ⓓ $141

Reflect

Directions: Take a few minutes to recall what you've learned and what you've been practicing in this chapter. Consider the following questions, jot down your best answer for each one, and then compare your reflections to the expert responses that follow. Use your level of confidence to determine what to do next.

What is a ratio?

_____

_____

_____

If you're given a ratio of one quantity to another, what can you say about the total number of quantities?

_____

_____

_____

When doing unit conversions, how can you make sure you're setting them up correctly?

_____

_____

_____

Suppose the value of something increases by 20 percent. How can you calculate the final value in the fewest number of steps? What if the value decreases by 20 percent?

_____

_____

_____

What is the percent change formula and what is the biggest pitfall to avoid when using it?

_____

_____

_____

Expert Responses

What is a ratio?

A ratio is the relative comparison of one quantity to another. For example, if the ratio of dogs to cats in an animal shelter is 3 to 5, then there are 3 dogs for every 5 cats.

If you're given a ratio of one quantity to another, what can you say about the total number of quantities?

Given a ratio, you know that the total must be a multiple of the sum of the ratio's parts. For example, if the ratio of dogs to cats is 3 to 5, then the total number of dogs and cats must be a multiple of 3 + 5, or 8. This means that when the PSAT gives you one ratio, it's actually giving you several. If you're told that dogs:cats = 3:5, then you also know that dogs:total = 3:8 and cats:total = 5:8. You can use this "hidden" knowledge to your advantage.

When doing unit conversions, how can you make sure you're setting them up correctly?

To do unit conversions correctly, set up the conversion in whichever way makes the units cancel each other out. For example, to convert 3 feet into inches, you multiply 3 feet by 12 inches per foot, because it cancels out the feet unit. If instead you multiplied 3 feet by 1 foot per 12 inches, then the resulting units would be "feet squared per inch," which makes no sense.

Suppose the value of something increases by 20 percent. How can you calculate the final value in the fewest number of steps? What if the value decreases by 20 percent?

The fastest way to increase a value by 20 percent is to multiply it by 1.2, which is 100% + 20% = 120%. Similarly, to decrease something by 20 percent, you multiply it by 0.8, which is 100% − 20% = 80%.

What is the percent change formula and what is the biggest pitfall to avoid when using it?

The percent change formula is as follows:

$$\text{Percent change} = \frac{\text{amount of increase or decrease}}{\text{original amount}} \times 100\%$$

One of the most common mistakes is to put the new amount on the bottom of the fraction rather than the original amount. Be sure to avoid that pitfall on test day.

Next Steps

If you answered most questions correctly in the "How Much Have You Learned?" section, and if your responses to the Reflect questions were similar to those of the PSAT expert, then consider Rates, Ratios, Proportions, Percents, and Units an area of strength and move on to the next chapter. Come back to this topic periodically to ensure your skills stay sharp.

If you don't yet feel confident, review those parts of this chapter that you have not yet mastered and try the questions you missed again. As always, be sure to review the explanations closely.

Answers and Explanations

Try on Your Own

1. B

Difficulty: Easy

Category: Problem-Solving and Data Analysis

Getting to the Answer: The question gives a distance and a rate, and it asks for a time. Thus, use the $D = RT$ equation:

$$\text{Distance} = \text{rate} \times \text{time}$$
$$3{,}628 \text{ miles} = 1{,}341 \text{ miles per hour} \times \text{time}$$
$$2.71 \text{ hours} \cong \text{time}$$

This matches **(B)**.

2. A

Difficulty: Medium

Category: Problem-Solving and Data Analysis

Getting to the Answer: The question gives times and heights, and it asks for a rate. Thus, use the $D = RT$ equation. In this case, D is the difference between the two heights: 3,000 m − 2,200 m = 800 m. Similarly, T is the difference between the two times: 7 pm − 3 pm = 4 hours.

$$\text{Distance} = \text{rate} \times \text{time}$$
$$800 \text{ m} = 4 \text{ h} \times \text{rate}$$
$$200 \text{ m/h} = \text{rate}$$

This matches **(A)**.

3. D

Difficulty: Hard

Category: Problem-Solving and Data Analysis

Getting to the Answer: The question gives you rates and a time, and it asks for a distance. Therefore, use the $D = RT$ equation. The time is given as 5 seconds, but the R term is more complicated because there are two balls. Think critically: every second that goes by, the first ball gets 4 feet closer to the second; at the *same time*, the second ball gets 6 feet closer to the first. Thus, the balls get 4 + 6 = 10 feet closer every second, and you can use $R = 10$ as the effective rate:

$$\text{Distance} = \text{rate} \times \text{time}$$
$$d = 10 \text{ feet per second} \times 5 \text{ seconds}$$
$$d = 50 \text{ feet}$$

Choice **(D)** is correct.

You could also get the answer by adding the individual distances of the balls. The first ball travels 4 × 5 = 20 feet, and the second ball travels 6 × 5 = 30 feet. Thus, the starting distance was 20 + 30 = 50 feet.

4. B

Difficulty: Medium

Category: Problem-Solving and Data Analysis

Getting to the Answer: Use the equation $A = RT$ to determine how many containers one crane can unload in a day, noting that there are 24 hours in a day:

$$\text{Amount} = \text{rate} \times \text{time}$$
$$\text{Amount} = 200 \text{ containers per hour} \times 24 \text{ hours per day}$$
$$\text{Amount} = 4{,}800 \text{ containers}$$

If one crane can unload 4,800 containers per day, then two cranes could unload 4,800 × 2 = 9,600 containers. This is just shy of the 10,000 containers needed, so one more crane is required. Choice **(B)** is correct.

5.   40

Difficulty: Hard

Category: Problem-Solving and Data Analysis

Getting to the Answer: Use the equation $A = RT$ to determine the rate of each pipe. In this case, $A = 1$ represents the task of filling one pool, while $A = -1$ represents the task of draining a full pool. For the water pipe:

$$\text{Amount} = (\text{water pipe rate}) \times \text{time}$$
$$1 = (\text{water pipe rate}) \times 8 \text{ hours}$$
$$\frac{1}{8} = \text{water pipe rate}$$

And for the drain pipe:

$$\text{Amount} = (\text{drain pipe rate}) \times \text{time}$$
$$-1 = (\text{drain pipe rate}) \times 10 \text{ hours}$$
$$-\frac{1}{10} = \text{drain pipe rate}$$

Add the two rates together to determine the combined rate when both pipes are active at the same time:

$$\frac{1}{8} - \frac{1}{10} = \frac{5}{40} - \frac{4}{40} = \frac{1}{40}$$

Finally, use the $A = rt$ equation one more time to determine how long it takes to fill the pool at this combined rate:

$$\text{Quantity} = \text{rate} \times \text{time}$$
$$1 = \frac{1}{40} \times \text{time}$$
$$40 = \text{time}$$

With the drain pipe working against it, the water pipe will take 40 hours to fill the pool completely. Enter **40**.

6.   B

Difficulty: Easy

Category: Problem-Solving and Data Analysis

Getting to the Answer: Let b equal the number of snowblowers produced. Set up a proportion and solve for b:

$$\frac{8 \text{ defective}}{4{,}000 \text{ produced}} = \frac{18 \text{ defective}}{b \text{ produced}}$$
$$8b = 72{,}000$$
$$b = 9{,}000$$

This matches **(B)**.

7.   A

Difficulty: Medium

Category: Problem-Solving and Data Analysis

Getting to the Answer: Draw a diagram to make sense of the situation. Find the corrected height by taking 25% of 40, which is 10, and subtracting that from 40 to get 30. Your diagram should look something like this:

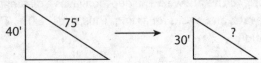

Since the question tell you that the angles must stay the same, the sides of the two triangles must be proportional. You should set up a proportion to find the longest side of the triangle. Keeping the heights on the left and the longest sides on the right, you get $\frac{40}{30} = \frac{75}{x}$. Reduce to obtain $\frac{4}{3} = \frac{75}{x}$ and cross-multiply to yield $225 = 4x$. Therefore, $x = 56.25$.

Don't stop yet! The question asks for the *difference* in escalator lengths, not the new length. Subtract 56.25 from 75 to get 18.75, which matches **(A)**.

If you noticed that the change in escalator length must be proportional to the change in floor height, you could alternatively get the answer very quickly. It's no coincidence that 25% of $75 = (0.25)(75) = 18.75$, the answer.

8.   B

Difficulty: Easy

Category: Problem-Solving and Data Analysis

Getting to the Answer: Let c equal the number of cars that can safely pass through a green light in 24 seconds. Set up a proportion and solve for c. Make sure that the units in the numerator and denominator are consistent on both sides.

$$\frac{9 \text{ cars}}{36 \text{ seconds}} = \frac{c \text{ cars}}{24 \text{ seconds}}$$
$$\frac{1 \text{ car}}{4 \text{ seconds}} = \frac{c \text{ cars}}{24 \text{ seconds}}$$
$$24 = 4c$$
$$6 = c$$

Choice **(B)** is correct.

9. C

Difficulty: Easy

Category: Problem-Solving and Data Analysis

Getting to the Answer: Set up a proportion and cross-multiply to solve:

$$\frac{31}{16} = \frac{97}{x}$$
$$1{,}552 = 31x$$
$$50.06 \approx x$$

Choice **(C)** is correct.

10. 6

Difficulty: Hard

Category: Problem-Solving and Data Analysis

Getting to the Answer: The formula for the volume of a pyramid is $V = \frac{1}{3}lwh$. The pyramid has a square base, so the length and width are equal. The proportion of length:width:height is 750:750:500, which reduces to 3:3:2. Expressed with a common multiplier, this is $3x:3x:2x$.

Plugging these proportions into the volume equation yields:

$$V = \frac{1}{3}(3x)(3x)(2x) = \frac{1}{3}(18x^3) = 6x^3$$

The question states that the student has 162 cubic inches of modeling clay, so plug in this value for V and solve for x:

$$6x^3 = 162$$
$$x^3 = 27$$
$$\sqrt[3]{x^3} = \sqrt[3]{27}$$
$$x = 3$$

Since $x = 3$ and height $= 2x$, the height of the student's model will be $2(3) = 6$ inches. Enter **6**.

11. D

Difficulty: Easy

Category: Problem-Solving and Data Analysis

Getting to the Answer: To determine the number of gallons of gasoline used during each leg of Jack's trip, set up conversion ratios to get the unwanted units to cancel out. Plugging in values for the first leg, you get:

$$180 \text{ miles} \times \frac{1 \text{ gallon}}{40 \text{ miles}} = 4.5 \text{ gallons}$$

For the second leg:

$$105 \text{ miles} \times \frac{1 \text{ gallon}}{35 \text{ miles}} = 3 \text{ gallons}$$

Together, he used $4.5 + 3 = 7.5$ gallons of gasoline, which matches **(D)**.

12. 50

Difficulty: Medium

Category: Problem-Solving and Data Analysis

Getting to the Answer: Start with the most concrete quantity: 300 liters. Then set up conversion ratios to cancel out the unwanted units and get hours.

$$300 \text{ liters} \times \frac{1000 \text{ milliliters}}{1 \text{ liter}} \times \frac{1 \text{ min}}{100 \text{ milliliters}}$$
$$\times \frac{1 \text{ hour}}{60 \text{ min}} = 50 \text{ hours}$$

Enter **50**.

13. 4.4

Difficulty: Medium

Category: Problem-Solving and Data Analysis

Getting to the Answer: Start with the given information and use conversion ratios to move from miles per hour to feet per second.

$$\frac{3 \text{ mile}}{1 \text{ hour}} \times \frac{5{,}280 \text{ ft}}{1 \text{ mile}} \times \frac{1 \text{ hour}}{60 \text{ min}} \times \frac{1 \text{ min}}{60 \text{ sec}} = \frac{4.4 \text{ ft}}{\text{sec}}$$

Enter **4.4**.

14. B

Difficulty: Medium

Category: Problem-Solving and Data Analysis

Getting to the Answer: Set up conversion ratios so that the unwanted units cancel out. The answer choices are given in hours and minutes, but it's easier to solve for minutes alone by creating one large conversion:

$$45 \text{ pages} \times \frac{500 \text{ words}}{1 \text{ page}} \times \frac{1 \text{ second}}{5 \text{ words}}$$
$$\times \frac{1 \text{ minute}}{60 \text{ seconds}} = 75 \text{ minutes}$$

Because 75 minutes is not an answer choice, convert it to hours and minutes: There are 60 minutes in an hour. 60 goes into 75 one time with a remainder of 15. 75 minutes = 1 hour and 15 minutes, **(B)**. If you selected choice C, be careful: 1.25 hours is NOT the same as 1 hour and 25 minutes.

15. A

Difficulty: Hard

Category: Problem-Solving and Data Analysis

Getting to the Answer: Solve this question step-by-step, examining units as you go. Use conversion ratios to determine the number of scans per night.

$$\frac{2 \text{ megabits}}{1 \text{ second}} \times \frac{60 \text{ seconds}}{1 \text{ minute}} \times \frac{60 \text{ minutes}}{1 \text{ hour}} \times \frac{8 \text{ hours}}{1 \text{ night}}$$
$$\times \frac{1 \text{ gigabit}}{1024 \text{ megabits}} \times \frac{1 \text{ scan}}{3.6 \text{ gigabit}}$$
$$= \frac{15.625 \text{ scan}}{\text{night}}$$

You must round this number down to 15 because the computer cannot complete the 16th scan in the time allowed. Choice **(A)** is correct.

16. C

Difficulty: Easy

Category: Problem-Solving and Data Analysis

Getting to the Answer: For discount questions, you can multiply by the complement of the discount instead of subtracting the discount. The complement is total (100%) − discount (20%) = 80%. This will give the price of the doll after the discount. Use d as the variable for the price of the discounted doll:

$$d = 0.8(\$20)$$
$$d = \$16$$

(C) is correct.

17. D

Difficulty: Medium

Category: Problem-Solving and Data Analysis

Getting to the Answer: The total budget can be represented by 100%. The percent of the budget spent on lunch is therefore 100% − 40% − 25% − 20% = 15%. You're told that the club plans to spend $225 on lunch. Let x be the total amount of the budget in dollars. Since 15% of x is 225, $0.15x = 225$. Solving this equation for x yields $x = 1{,}500$. The total budget is $1,500. Of this amount, 40% was budgeted for a guest speaker, or $0.4 \times \$1{,}500 = \$600$. Choice **(D)** is correct.

18. C

Difficulty: Medium

Category: Problem-Solving and Data Analysis

Getting to the Answer: The question asks for the percent that is NOT blue marbles, so calculate the percent of blue marbles and subtract that from 100%.

$$\frac{12}{60} = \frac{1}{5} = 20\%$$
$$100\% - 20\% = 80\%$$

Choice **(C)** is correct.

19. C

Difficulty: Hard

Category: Problem-Solving and Data Analysis

Getting to the Answer: Since Aiswarya paid $50 for a $40 haircut, she tipped the salon owner $50 − $40 = $10. Thus, $10 is p% of $40. By definition, p% is $\frac{p}{100}$, so $10 = \frac{p}{100} \times 40. Solving for p gives:

$$\frac{\$10}{\$40} = \frac{p}{100}$$
$$0.25 = \frac{p}{100}$$
$$25 = p$$

(C) is correct.

20. D

Difficulty: Hard

Category: Problem-Solving and Data Analysis

Getting to the Answer: Backsolving works well here. Start with (C). If Maxim answered 62% of the questions correctly, he answered 0.62(50) = 31 questions correctly and 50 − 31 = 19 questions incorrectly. Then his final score would be (2 × 31) − (0.5 × 19) = 52.5 points. This is less than 70, so 62% correct is too low. Eliminate (A), (B), and (C). The correct answer is **(D)**. For the record, 0.76(50) = 38 and 50 − 38 = 12, which gives (2 × 38) − (0.5 × 12) = 70 points.

Alternatively, you could set up an equation and solve algebraically. Let x represent the number of questions answered correctly:

$$2x - 0.5(50 - x) = 70$$
$$2x - 25 + 0.5x = 70$$
$$2.5x = 95$$
$$x = 38$$

The question asks for the percent of questions that Maxim answered correctly. Using the formula $\frac{part}{whole} \times 100\%$ gives $\frac{38}{50} \times 100\% = 76\%$. **(D)** is correct.

21. B

Difficulty: Medium

Category: Problem-Solving and Data Analysis

Getting to the Answer: To find the total percent discount, you'll first need to determine the total discount in actual price. The first change is given: $12,000 − $10,500 = $1,500. The second change is a 5% discount, which can be calculated using the price after the first reduction: (.05)$10,500 = $525. Therefore, the total drop in price is $1,500 + $525 = $2,025. Now, apply the percent change formula:

$$\frac{actual\ change}{original\ amount} \times 100\% = percent\ change$$
$$\frac{2,025}{12,000} \times 100\% = 16.875\%$$

Since the question asks for the percent change to the nearest tenth of a percent, round the answer to 16.9%. That's choice **(B)**.

22. A

Difficulty: Medium

Category: Problem-Solving and Data Analysis

Getting to the Answer: To find the total percent increase in weight of sand and gravel sold, first find the change in weight. The additional weight sold this year for gravel is 0.20 × 280 = 56. The additional weight sold for sand is 0.25 × 220 = 55. Therefore, the change from last year to this year is 56 + 55 = 111. Now, apply the percent change formula:

$$\frac{actual\ change}{original\ amount} \times 100\% = percent\ change$$
$$\frac{111}{500} \times 100\% = 22.2\%$$

Choice **(A)** is correct.

23. C

Difficulty: Medium

Category: Problem-Solving and Data Analysis

Getting to the Answer: You are missing one key piece of information: the initial population of the town. Since this is a percent change question, pick 100 for the initial population. (Your number doesn't have to be realistic, only easy to work with.) Over the last decade, the population increased by 20%, so that is an increase from 100 to 120. Over the next decade, if the population increases by 15%, the total population would become $120 + (0.15)120 = 120 + 18 = 138$. Therefore, the total increase in actual population over the two decades is $138 - 100 = 38$. Now, apply the percent change formula:

$$\frac{\text{actual change}}{\text{original amount}} \times 100\% = \text{percent change}$$

$$\frac{38}{100} \times 100\% = 38\%$$

Choice **(C)** is correct.

24. B

Difficulty: Medium

Category: Problem-Solving and Data Analysis

Getting to the Answer: Since the price of the mutual fund is not given and this is a percent change question, use $100 for the initial price and then calculate the changes in sequence. After the first year, the price would have been $100 \times (1 + 0.15) = \$115$. Then, the price at the end of the second year would have been $115 \times (1 - 0.12) = \$101.2$. This is a $\frac{101.2 - 100}{100} \times 100\% = 1.2\%$ increase from the original $100 price. **(B)** is correct.

25. 1710

Difficulty: Hard

Category: Problem-Solving and Data Analysis

Getting to the Answer: Work backward using the known information to find the actual number of fish in the lake for each of the past two years. You know the increase in the number of fish over the last year was 15%, so you can set up the following equation, where x represents the number of fish last year:

$$1.15x = 6,210$$

$$x = \frac{6,210}{1.15}$$

$$x = 5,400$$

Now, repeat the same process for the previous year. You know that 5,400 represents the number of fish after an increase of 20%, so you can call the original number of fish at the beginning of the first year y and use the following equation to find y:

$$1.20y = 5,400$$

$$y = \frac{5,400}{1.2}$$

$$y = 4,500$$

Now you have the starting number of fish from two years ago, so you can subtract this from the current number to find the actual change in the number of fish over the entire two years: $6,210 - 4,500 = 1,710$.

Enter **1710**.

26. C

Difficulty: Hard

Category: Problem-Solving and Data Analysis

Getting to the Answer: First, find the number of viewers for the third week. The number of viewers for the third week is 10% lower than the number for the second week (15 million), which is $15 - 0.10(15) = 13.5$ million. Divide this number by the number of viewers for the premiere (18 million) to get the percentage. The number of viewers of the third week is $\frac{13.5}{18} \times 100\% = 75\%$ of the number of viewers for the premiere. **(C)** is correct.

On Test Day

27. 155

Difficulty: Medium

Category: Problem-Solving and Data Analysis

Strategic Advice: The total numbers of seniors and juniors are different, so calculate each percentage individually and do the arithmetic on the actual values.

Getting to the Answer: Apply the given percentages to the number of students in each class to determine the number of students eligible for the course in each class and then find the difference. Be careful: the percentage for juniors is stated as those who are *not* eligible.

The number of eligible seniors is $0.65 \times 400 = 260$. The percentage of juniors who are not eligible is 75%, so the percentage who are eligible is $100\% - 75\% = 25\%$. Thus, the number of eligible juniors is $0.25 \times 420 = 105$. The difference is $260 - 105 = 155$.

Enter **155**.

How Much Have You Learned?

1. A

Difficulty: Hard

Category: Problem-Solving and Data Analysis

Getting to the Answer: Break this question into small steps. First, find the number of businesses that are required to have safety inspections. The part-to-part ratio of businesses that require inspections to those that do not is 2:5, so the ratio of those businesses that require inspections to the total number of businesses is $\frac{2}{2+5} = \frac{2}{7}$. There are 2,625 total businesses. Thus, the number of businesses that need inspections is $\frac{2}{7} \times 2,625 = 750$.

Since 12% had safety violations, $0.12 \times 750 = 90$ businesses had safety violations. Choice **(A)** is correct.

2. A

Difficulty: Medium

Category: Problem-Solving and Data Analysis

Getting to the Answer: The difference in speeds between the two vehicles is $210 - 120 = 90$ miles per hour. The speeds are given in miles per hour, but the question asks for the difference in the number of miles traveled in 30 *seconds*. Set up conversion ratios and solve:

$$30 \text{ sec} \times \frac{1 \text{ min}}{60 \text{ sec}} \times \frac{1 \text{ hour}}{60 \text{ min}} \times \frac{90 \text{ mile}}{1 \text{ hour}} = 0.75 \text{ mile}$$

Converting the decimal into a fraction, $\frac{75}{100} = \frac{3}{4}$, the race car can travel $\frac{3}{4}$ miles farther in 30 seconds, so **(A)** is correct.

3. C

Difficulty: Hard

Category: Problem-Solving and Data Analysis

Getting to the Answer: Two quantities must be in the same units if they are to be compared. Start by converting the car's pints to quarts:

$$8 \text{ pints} \times \frac{1 \text{ quart(s)}}{2 \text{ pints}} = 4 \text{ quart(s)}$$

Next, find the amount of zinc in each vehicle. Remember that $9\% = 0.09$ and $4\% = 0.04$.

Car: $0.09 \times 4 \text{ quarts} = 0.36 \text{ quarts of zinc}$

Truck: $0.04 \times 6 \text{ quarts} = 0.24 \text{ quarts of zinc}$

Finally, compare the amount in the car to the amount in the truck: $\frac{0.36}{0.24} = 1.5$. The car has 1.5 times as much zinc as the truck. This matches **(C)**.

4. C

Difficulty: Hard

Category: Problem-Solving and Data Analysis

Getting to the Answer: Draw a chart with the various price reductions for each month. Determine the percent change and new price for each date.

DATE	PERCENT OF MOST RECENT PRICE	RESULTING PRICE
Jul 15	100% − 40% = 60%	$1,050 × 0.60 = $630
Aug 15	100% − 20% = 80%	$630 × 0.80 = $504

You can stop here because the item was sold on September 5, which is not a full month after August 15. The final selling price is $504, **(C)**.

5. B

Difficulty: Medium

Category: Problem-Solving and Data Analysis

Getting to the Answer: Set up a proportion and solve:

$$\frac{\text{real wing span}}{\text{real length}} = \frac{\text{model wing span}}{\text{model length}}$$

$$\frac{174}{220} = \frac{x}{36}$$

$$6{,}264 = 220x$$

$$28.473 \approx x$$

The model airplane's wingspan is approximately 28 feet, **(B)**.

6. C

Difficulty: Easy

Category: Problem-Solving and Data Analysis

Getting to the Answer: Break this question into short steps, checking units as you go. First, find the total number of milliliters of milk Drew will need for 5 loaves:

$$5\ \text{loaves} \times \frac{180\ \text{mL}}{1\ \text{loaf}} = 900\ \text{mL}$$

Then convert the milliliters to cups:

$$900\ \text{mL} \times \frac{1\ \text{cup}}{236.588\ \text{mL}} \approx 3.804\ \text{cups}$$

Drew will need about $3.8 = 3\frac{8}{10} = 3\frac{4}{5}$ cups of milk, **(C)**.

7. 600

Difficulty: Easy

Category: Problem-Solving and Data Analysis

Getting to the Answer: Set up conversion ratios to cancel out the unwanted units and arrive at kilometers:

$$1{,}800{,}000\ \text{feet} \times \frac{1\ \text{meter(s)}}{3\ \text{feet}} \times \frac{1\ \text{kilometer(s)}}{1{,}000\ \text{meter(s)}}$$

$$= 600\ \text{kilometer(s)}$$

Enter **600**.

8. C

Difficulty: Easy

Category: Problem-Solving and Data Analysis

Getting to the Answer: Set up a proportion of the adult track's shorter to longer straightaway, and set it equal to the teen track's shorter to longer straightaway. Let x be the unknown longer straightaway on the teen track. Cross-multiply to solve for the x:

$$\frac{100}{150} = \frac{50}{x}$$

$$100x = 7{,}500$$

$$x = 75$$

Thus, **(C)** is correct.

9. D

Difficulty: Medium

Category: Problem-Solving and Data Analysis

Getting to the Answer: Begin by finding the actual change in total acreage. For corn, the acreage has been reduced by $0.20 \times 350 = 70$ acres; for soybeans, the acreage has reduced by $0.15 \times 160 = 24$ acres. Therefore, the total decrease in acreage is $70 + 24 = 94$. The total number of acres originally planted in corn and soybeans was $350 + 160 = 510$. Plug this information into the percent change formula:

$$\text{percent change} = \frac{\text{actual change}}{\text{original amount}} \times 100\%$$

$$= \frac{94}{510} \times 100\%$$

$$\approx 18.43\%$$

(D) is correct.

10. B

Difficulty: Hard

Category: Problem-Solving and Data Analysis

Getting to the Answer: Let the original price be C. If Mandy received a 40% discount, then she paid $100\% - 40\% = 60\%$. Therefore, the discounted price is $0.60C$. Because of the 10% sales tax, she must pay $100\% + 10\% = 110\%$ of this discounted price. This yields $1.10(0.60C)$. This expression should equal $89.10. Set up an equation and solve for C:

$$1.10(0.60C) = \$89.10$$
$$0.66C = \$89.10$$
$$C = \$135$$

Thus, **(B)** is correct.

Backsolving also works well for this question. When backsolving, start with either (B) or (C). Try (B) first and let the original price of the comforter be $135. If it is on sale for 40% off, then Mandy pays 60%. Thus, the comforter costs $135(0.60) = \$81$. However, she also has to pay the 10% sales tax. Therefore, she must give the cashier $81(1.10) = \$89.10$. Since this number matches the information in the question stem, **(B)** is correct. There is no need to check other answers.

[CHAPTER 8]

TABLES, STATISTICS, AND PROBABILITY

LEARNING OBJECTIVES

After completing this chapter, you will be able to:

- Draw inferences about data presented in a variety of graphical formats
- Find an unknown value given the average
- Calculate mean, median, mode, and range
- Define standard deviation
- Calculate probabilities based on data sets

How Much Do You Know?

Directions

Try the questions that follow. Show your work so that you can compare your solutions to the ones found in the "Check Your Work" section immediately after this question set. If you answered the question(s) on a specific topic correctly, and if your scratchwork looks like ours, you may be able to move quickly through the lesson covering that topic. If you answered incorrectly or used a different approach, you may want to take your time on that lesson.

1

	Number of Orders
Mango	42
Strawberry	96
Coconut	19
Pineapple	15
Banana	28

The table shows the number of orders in a day at a fruit smoothie stand. What fraction of the total number of smoothie orders is mango and banana?

Ⓐ $\dfrac{7}{20}$

Ⓑ $\dfrac{2}{5}$

Ⓒ $\dfrac{2}{3}$

Ⓓ $\dfrac{7}{10}$

2

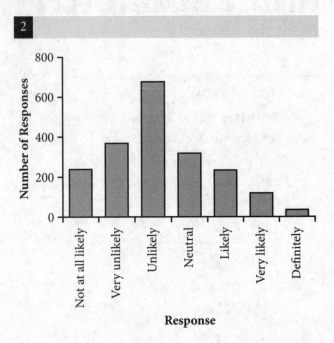

Liam surveyed a randomly selected group of 2,000 young adults on how likely they are to purchase from a company. Respondents rated their likelihood to purchase on a scale from 1 to 7, with 1 being "Not at all likely" and 7 being "Definitely." The results are summarized in the bar graph. Which of the following statements is true based on the survey results?

Ⓐ mode = 7

Ⓑ median = 3

Ⓒ mean < median

Ⓓ 4 < mean < 6

3

The average (arithmetic mean) of the data list {2, 4, 5, 8, 9, x, 3} is 5. What is the value of x?

4

	Number of Words Containing the Vowel
A	78
E	99
I	69
O	66
U	33
Y	15

The table shows the number of words out of 300 five-letter words that contain a certain vowel. What is the probability that a five-letter word randomly selected from the 300 five-letter words will contain an E?

Ⓐ 0.167

Ⓑ 0.275

Ⓒ 0.330

Ⓓ 0.990

5

	Sophomores	Juniors	Seniors
Football	414	388	450
Baseball	343	249	283
Soccer	284	347	316
Basketball	314	365	291
Total	1,355	1,349	1,340

The table summarizes the results of a survey. Students were asked to select their favorite sport. What is the approximate probability of the research group randomly selecting someone who chose baseball as their favorite sport?

Ⓐ 0.1622

Ⓑ 0.2164

Ⓒ 0.2399

Ⓓ 0.2948

Math

Check Your Work

1. A

Difficulty: Easy

Category: Problem-Solving and Data Analysis

Getting to the Answer: First, find the total number of smoothie orders for the day: $42 + 96 + 19 + 15 + 28 = 200$. Then, find the number of mango and banana smoothie orders: $42 + 28 = 70$. The fraction of the total number of smoothie orders that are mango and banana is: $\frac{70}{200} = \frac{35}{100} = \frac{7}{20}$. **(A)** is correct.

2. B

Difficulty: Medium

Category: Problem-Solving and Data Analysis

Getting to the Answer: Examine the bar chart to evaluate the choices.

(A): The bar for "Unlikely" (which is 3 on the scale given in the question) is clearly the tallest, so this is the mode. Eliminate (A), which indicates that "Definitely" (which is 7 on the scale given in the question) is the most common response.

(B): There are 2,000 responses, so the median is the average of responses 1,000 and 1,001. The total of the first two bars is about 600. Since the third bar is about 700, that means that the median response is indeed within this bar. Choice **(B)** is correct.

(C): The data is skewed to the right, meaning that the extreme values on the right will weight the mean calculation to make the mean greater than the median. Thus, (C) is not true and can be eliminated.

(D): The substantial majority of values are between 2 and 5 inclusive, so the mean has to be somewhere within that wide range. Eliminate (D), which would make the mean, or average, of this set greater than 4, but less than 6. For the record, the mean of the survey responses is *just* above 3, with an estimated value of 3.1–3.2. Calculating the mean is not required for this question, however. Stop as soon as you have enough information to answer the question, and don't do more work than necessary on test day.

3. 4

Difficulty: Medium

Category: Problem-Solving and Data Analysis

Strategic Advice: When the goal is to find a missing value in a set of data and the average is given, consider using the balance approach. We'll demonstrate both approaches starting with the average formula.

Getting to the Answer: The question requires finding the value of x in the given data set using the average of the data set. The values given in the data, besides x, are: 2, 4, 5, 8, 9, and 3. The average is given as 5. To find the missing value x, plug the known values into the average formula and solve for x:

$$\frac{2 + 4 + 5 + 8 + 9 + x + 3}{7} = 5$$

$$\frac{31 + x}{7} = 5$$

$$31 + x = 35$$

$$x = 4$$

Enter **4**.

Alternatively, to use the balance approach, write down how much each value is above or below the average of 5. For example, the first value of 2 is 3 below the average: $2 - 5 = -3$.

Now, observe that, excluding the variable, the values are $-3 + (-1) + 0 + 3 + 4 + (-2) = 1$. Without the variable, the total is 1 more than what you'd expect based on the average. So for the values to balance out to the average, the variable value must be one less than the average of 5, or $5 - 1 = 4$. Enter **4**.

4. C

Difficulty: Easy

Category: Problem-Solving and Data Analysis

Strategic Advice: Don't go on math autopilot and add up the numbers in the columns for the total. Words can contain multiple vowels, and the question gives you the total number of words: 300.

Getting to the Answer: Use the probability formula to determine the probability of selecting a word that contains an E from the 300 five-letter words:

$$\text{Probability} = \frac{\text{number of desired outcomes}}{\text{number of total possible outcomes}}$$
$$= \frac{99}{300}$$
$$= 0.33$$

Thus, the probability of selecting a five-letter word containing an E is 0.33. **(C)** is correct.

5. B

Difficulty: Medium

Category: Problem-Solving and Data Analysis

Getting to the Answer: The total possible outcomes for this selection is $1,355 + 1,349 + 1,340 = 4,044$. The total number of students who voted for baseball as their favorite sport (number of desired outcomes) is $343 + 249 + 283 = 875$. Divide this by the total to find the probability: $\frac{875}{4044} \approx 0.2164$, which makes **(B)** correct.

Tables and Graphs

LEARNING OBJECTIVES

After this lesson, you will be able to:

- Draw inferences about data presented in a variety of graphical formats
- Find an unknown value given the average

To answer a question like this:

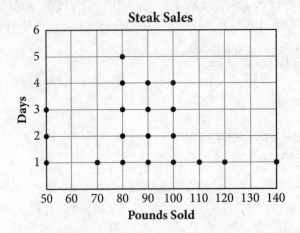

A restaurant owner sets a goal of selling an average of 90 pounds of steak per day for the first three weeks. The dot plot shows the number of pounds sold in the first 20 days. What is the minimum number of pounds the restaurant would need to sell on the last day to meet the goal?

(A) 60

(B) 80

(C) 100

(D) 140

You need to know this:

The PSAT uses some straightforward methods of representing data sets that you are likely already familiar with. For example, you may have to look up information in a table or read a bar chart. There are, however, some less common types of plots that show up from time to time that can be confusing at first glance. Graphics you may see on test day include the following:

- **Tables, bar charts, and line graphs** show up all the time in the Math sections (and in the Reading and Writing sections, too). They shouldn't be difficult to interpret, but it's helpful to keep in mind that the test maker often includes more information than you actually need. It's important to consider what the question asks for so that you find only the information that you need.

- **Frequency tables and dot plots** are ways of representing how many times a data point appears within a data set. Here is a data set (the number of appliances sold by a single salesperson over some time frame) presented as a dot plot:

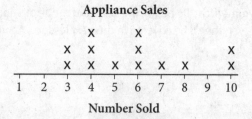

Appliance Sales

Number Sold

Each "X" represents one instance in the data set of each "number sold." So, for example, there were two different days on which this person sold 3 appliances, three different days on which this person sold 4 appliances, and so on. The data could just as easily be written as a data set {3, 3, 4, 4, 4, 5, 6, 6, 6, 7, 8, 10, 10}, or placed in a frequency table:

NUMBER SOLD	FREQUENCY
1	0
2	0
3	2
4	3
5	1
6	3
7	1
8	1
9	0
10	2

- **Histograms** look a lot like bar charts and can be read in the same way, but they are similar to frequency tables and dot plots in that they show how many times a certain value shows up in a data set for a variable. The histogram for the appliances data set would look like this:

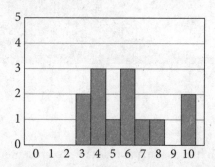

Notice that the histogram is basically the same as the dot plot for this data set. Histograms are better for representing larger data sets for which individual dots would be difficult to count.

- **Skew** is a measure of the symmetry of the data in a chart or graph.

An unskewed graph is perfectly symmetrical. Its mean, median, and mode are equal. (Don't worry if you're not familiar with these statistics terms yet; they'll be covered in the next lesson.) An unskewed graph looks like this:

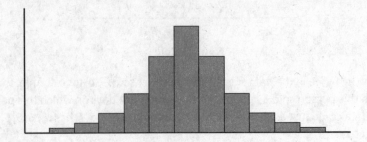

In a right-skewed graph, there are more data points on the left. The distribution is often said to have a "tail" on the right. The statistics are: Mode < Median < Mean

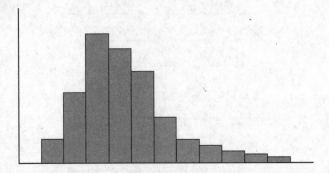

A left-skewed graph is the opposite. There are more data points on the right, and the "tail" is said to be on the left. Mean < Median < Mode

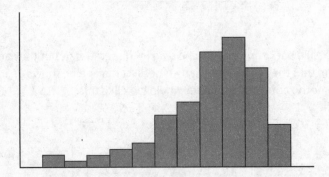

You need to do this:

- When presented with a question that uses a graph or table to present information, first inspect the format of the graph or table. What kind of graph or table is it? What information is presented on each axis? What information do you need to find in order to answer the question?

- Find the information you need from the table or graph and then use the information for any calculation the question might require, such as taking the average, finding the median, or thinking about standard deviation.

- Use the average formula, Average $= \dfrac{\text{sum}}{\text{number of items}}$, to find unknowns. For example, if you know that the average of five terms is 7, and you know that four of the terms are 3, 6, 8, and 9, you can call the last term x and plug it into the equation, then solve for x:

$$7 = \frac{3+6+8+9+x}{5}$$
$$35 = 26 + x$$
$$x = 9$$

- If the data is skewed, determine the effect on the mean, median, and mode.

Explanation:

This question gives you an average and asks for a missing value. First, set up a general equation for the average:

$$\text{Average} = \frac{\text{sum}}{\text{number of items}}$$

The event takes place over three weeks, which is 21 days, and the average is given as 90 pounds per day. Use the dot plot to calculate how many pounds were sold in the first 20 days by adding all the numbers given: $50 + 50 + 50 + 70 + 80 + 80 + 80 + 80 + 80 + 90 + 90 + 90 + 90 + 100 + 100 + 100 + 100 + 110 + 120 + 140 = 1,750$ pounds. Let p represent the missing number of pounds sold:

$$90 = \frac{1750 + p}{21}$$

Multiply both sides by 21 to get rid of the fraction and then subtract 1,750 from both sides to isolate p:

$$1,890 = 1,750 + p$$
$$p = 140$$

The correct answer is **(D)**.

PROBLEM-SOLVING AND DATA ANALYSIS

Try on Your Own

Directions

Take as much time as you need on these questions. Work carefully and methodically. There will be an opportunity for timed practice later in the book.

1

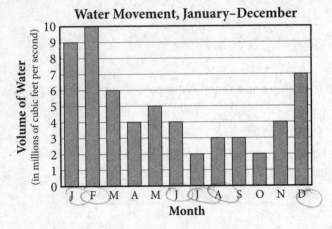

Water Movement, January–December

A researcher recorded the movement of water past a fluid motion sensor in the Atlantic Ocean along the North Carolina coast. Based on the data, which of the following would be a valid conclusion? (The summer months are June, July, and August, and the winter months are December, January, and February.)

(A) In general, a greater volume of water moves per month in the Atlantic Ocean during the winter months than during the summer months.

(B) In general, a greater volume of water moves per month in the Atlantic Ocean during the summer months than during the winter months.

(C) In general, a greater volume of water moves per month in the oceans around the world during the winter months than during the summer months.

(D) In general, a greater volume of water moves per month in the oceans around the world during the summer months than during the winter months.

2

HINT: Focus on the parts of the table that are required to answer Q2 and ignore the rest.

	Cars	Trucks	SUVs	Total
No Service	39	20	13	72
Rotate	48	36	60	144
Replace	7	8	17	32
Total	94	64	90	248

During an oil change, the technician inspects the tires and makes a recommendation: no service needed, rotate tires, or replace one or more tires. For what fraction of cars and trucks did this technician recommend a rotation?

(A) $\frac{21}{62}$

(B) $\frac{42}{79}$

(C) $\frac{18}{31}$

(D) $\frac{7}{12}$

3

Group	Proportion
A: inert, mild or no side effects	34.5%
B: inert, moderate side effects	9.2%
C: inert, severe side effects	6.2%
D: drug, mild or no side effects	9.5%
E: drug, moderate side effects	12.8%
F: drug, severe side effects	27.8%

Dr. Hunter is overseeing a treatment-resistant influenza Phase I trial with 400 healthy participants: half are given the drug and half are given an inert pill. Dr. Hunter records the severity of gastrointestinal side effects.

How many trial participants did not have severe side effects?

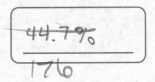

44.7%
176

3.

44.7

43.5

4

HINT: For Q4, which group in the study is of interest to the company?

Breakfast Study Results

	Breakfast ≤1 Time per Week	Breakfast 2−4 Times per Week	Breakfast 5−7 Times per Week	Total
Within Healthy Weight Range	6	15	36	57
Outside Healthy Weight Range	38	27	9	74
Total	44	42	45	131

A company provides free breakfast to its 3,000 employees. If every employee takes advantage of the free breakfast every weekday, then which of the following is closest to the number of employees who are likely to be within a healthy weight range? Assume that the study is representative and random.

(A) 825

(B) 1,030

(C) 1,900

(D) 2,400

5

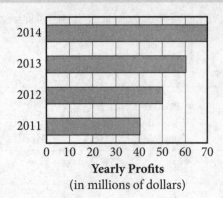

Yearly Profits
(in millions of dollars)

If the company's profits continue to grow at the same rate, in which year will it have a yearly profit that is 100% greater than its profit in 2013?

Ⓐ 2019

Ⓑ 2020

Ⓒ 2021

Ⓓ 2022

6

	TV Owners	Thursday Viewing Audience (all channels)
Under age 35	4,100	1,900
Age 35 or older	3,400	1,600
Total	7,500	3,500

On a certain evening, 20 percent of TV owners in Jonesville tuned in to Channel X. If a channel's nightly rating is defined as $\dfrac{\text{Number of channel's viewers}}{\text{Total viewing audience that night}}$, then what was Channel X's rating?

Statistics

LEARNING OBJECTIVES

After this lesson, you will be able to:

- Calculate mean, median, mode, and range
- Define standard deviation

To answer a question like this:

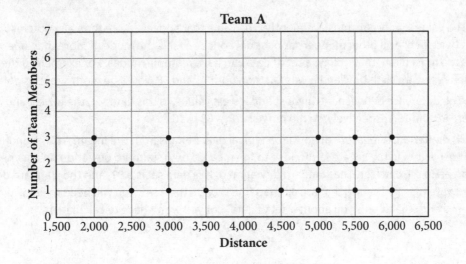

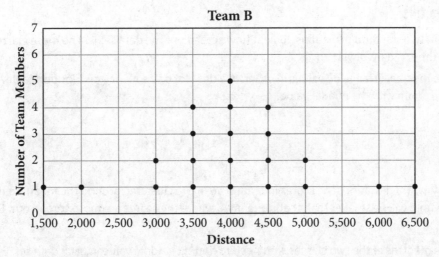

Two teams, each with 21 members on its cross-country running team, record the distances in meters run by each member. If M_A and S_A are the median and standard deviation, respectively, of team A, and M_B and S_B are the median and standard deviation, respectively, of team B, then which of the following statements is true?

Ⓐ $M_A < M_B$ and $S_A < S_B$

Ⓑ $M_A > M_B$ and $S_A < S_B$

Ⓒ $M_A > M_B$ and $S_A > S_B$

Ⓓ $M_A < M_B$ and $S_A > S_B$

You need to know this:

Below are five fundamental statistical measures you can determine for a data set. For example, suppose a nurse took a patient's pulse at different times of day and found it to be 75, 78, 71, 71, and 68.

- **Mean (also called arithmetic mean or average):** The sum of the values divided by the number of values. For this data set, the mean pulse is $\frac{75 + 78 + 71 + 71 + 68}{5} = \frac{363}{5} = 72.6$.

- **Median:** The value that is in the middle of the set *when the values are arranged in ascending order*. The pulse values in ascending order are 68, 71, 71, 75, and 78. The middle term is the third term, making the median 71. (If the list consists of an even number of values, the median is the average of the middle two values.)

- **Mode:** The value that occurs most frequently. The value that appears more than any other is 71, which appears twice (while all other numbers appear only once), so it is the mode. If more than one value appears the most often, that's okay; a set of data can have multiple modes. For example, if the nurse took the patient's pulse a sixth time and it was 68, then both 71 and 68 would be modes for this data set.

- **Range:** The difference between the highest and lowest values. In this data set, the lowest and highest values are 68 and 78, respectively, so the range is $78 - 68 = 10$.

- **Standard deviation:** A measure of how far a typical data point is from the mean. A low standard deviation means most values in the set are fairly close to the mean; a high standard deviation means there is much more spread in the data set. The standard deviation of this data set is 3.91, and the standard deviation of a data set containing five values that are all the same is 0. On the PSAT, you will need to know what standard deviation is and what it tells you about a set of data, but you won't have to calculate it.

You need to do this:

- To compare two standard deviations, look at how spread out the data set is. The more clustered the data, the lower the standard deviation.

- To find the median, arrange *all* values in order. In a dot plot or frequency distribution table, that means finding the group with the middle value.

Explanation:

Start with the standard deviation. The scores in team B are more clustered around the mean, so the standard deviation for team B will be smaller than that for team A, where the scores are more spread out. Eliminate (A) and (B).

To calculate the medians of the two classes, you need to find the middle value in each data set. Each class has 21 students, so the middle score will be the 11th term. Count from the left of each dot plot to find that the 11th score for team A is 4,500 and for team B is 4,000. So the median for team B is smaller, which makes **(C)** correct.

Try on Your Own

Directions

Take as much time as you need on these questions. Work carefully and methodically. There will be an opportunity for timed practice later in the book.

7

HINT: For Q7, think about what standard deviation means.

	Huiping	**Deanna**	**Katya**
Dive 1	8.2	9.0	7.7
Dive 2	7.3	7.1	8.4
Dive 3	8.6	6.5	7.5
Dive 4	8.0	8.6	8.1
Dive 5	9.1	6.1	8.1
Dive 6	8.4	8.9	7.2
Mean Score	8.27	7.70	7.83
Standard Deviation	0.61	1.29	0.45

Huiping, Deanna, and Katya are three varsity divers. Their diving scores for each of their six dives at a diving meet are shown in the table. According to the data, which of the following is a valid conclusion?

(A) Huiping dived the most consistently because her mean score is the highest.

(B) Katya dived the most consistently because her standard deviation is the lowest.

(C) Katya dived the least consistently because her mean score is the lowest.

(D) Deanna dived the most consistently because her standard deviation is the highest.

8

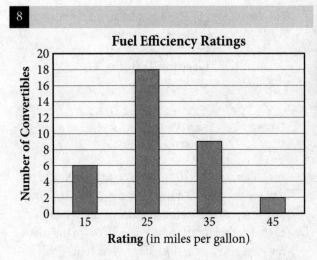

Fuel Efficiency Ratings

The bar graph shows the number of convertibles made by several manufacturers with various fuel efficiency ratings. What is the mean fuel efficiency rating for these convertibles?

(A) 25

(B) 27

(C) 30

(D) 32

9

HINT: For Q9, start by determining the sum of the number of miles for all 10 days.

Marathon Training

Distance (miles)

A runner's goal is to run an average of 5 miles per day for the first 10 days of his marathon training. The dot plot shows the number of miles he ran each day during the first 9 days. How many miles must he run on the 10th day to reach his goal?

(A) 5

(B) 5.5

(C) 6

(D) 6.5

10

Year	Number of Eligible Employees
2010	n
2011	874
2012	795
2013	732
2014	821

The table shows the number of employees at a certain company who were eligible for group health insurance each year from 2010 to 2014. If the median number of eligible employees for the five years was 821, and no two years had the same number of eligible employees, what is the least possible value for n?

(A) 733

(B) 796

(C) 822

(D) 875

11

In a local rock climbing group, the mean novice member age is 22 years and the mean experienced member age is 26 years. Which of the following can be concluded about the average age, a, of the experienced and novice members of this rock climbing group?

(A) $22 < a < 26$

(B) $a = 24$

(C) $a > 24$

(D) $a < 24$

12

HINT: Arrange the values in Q12 in ascending order to find the median and quickly identify the mode.

Data set K consists of the values 11, 4, 0, 7, 14, 1, 3, 7, and 13. Which of the following has the least value?

(A) The mode of data set K

(B) The median of data set K

(C) The mean of data set K

(D) The range of data set K

Math

Probability

To answer a question like this:

Levels Passed in Video Game

NAME	LEVELS PASSED
Imani	3
Micah	7
Corentin	5
Marco	4
Dikembe	1
Rachel	10

The table shows how many levels each player passed in the same video game. If these players represent a random sample, what is the approximate probability that a given player will pass at least four levels in this game?

(A) 33%

(B) 25%

(C) 50%

(D) 67%

You need to know this:

Probability is a fraction or decimal between 0 and 1 comparing the number of desired outcomes to the number of total possible outcomes. A probability of 0 means that an event will not occur; a probability of 1 means that it definitely will occur. The formula is as follows:

$$\text{Probability} = \frac{\text{number of desired outcomes}}{\text{number of total possible outcomes}}$$

For instance, if you roll a six-sided die, each side showing a different number from 1 to 6, there are two numbers higher than 4 (5 and 6) and six numbers total (1, 2, 3, 4, 5, and 6), so the probability of rolling a number higher than 4 is $\frac{2}{6} = \frac{1}{3}$.

To find the probability that an event will **not** happen, subtract the probability that the event will happen from 1. Continuing the previous example, the probability of **not** rolling a number higher than 4 would be:

$$1 - \frac{1}{3} = \frac{2}{3}$$

You might also be tested on the probability of two independent events both happening. Independent events are those in which the probability of one has no influence on the probability of the other. To find the probability of both events happening, multiply the probability of the first event times the probability of the second. For example, the probability of getting "heads" on a single coin toss is $\frac{1}{2}$. The probability of rolling a number greater than 4 on a six-sided die is $\frac{1}{3}$. Thus, the probability of getting "heads" on a coin toss *and* rolling a number greater than 4 on a die is $\frac{1}{2} \times \frac{1}{3} = \frac{1}{6}$.

Note that a probability can be expressed as a fraction, a decimal, or a percent; for example, a probability of $\frac{1}{2}$ can also be expressed as 0.5 or 50%.

The PSAT may test probability in the context of data tables. Using a table, you can find the probability that a randomly selected data value (whether that's a person, an object, or something else) will fit a certain profile. For example, the following table summarizing a survey on water preference might be followed by a question asking for the probability that a person randomly selected for a follow-up survey falls into a given category.

	TAP	CARBONATED	BOTTLED	TOTAL
Urban	325	267	295	887
Rural	304	210	289	803
Total	629	477	584	1,690

If the question asked for the probability of randomly selecting an urbanite who prefers tap water from all the participants of the original survey, you would calculate it using the same general formula as before:

$$\frac{\#urban, tap}{\#total} = \frac{325}{1,690} = \frac{5}{26} \approx 0.192$$

If the question asked for the probability of randomly selecting an urbanite from all participants who prefer tap water, the setup is a little different. This time, the number of total possible outcomes is the total number of participants **who prefer tap water**, which is 629, not the grand total of 1,690. The calculation is now:

$$\frac{\#urban, tap}{\#total, tap} = \frac{325}{629} \approx 0.517$$

Conversely, if you needed to find the probability of selecting someone who prefers tap water, given that the chosen participant is from an urban area, the new number of possible outcomes would be the urban participant total (887). The calculation becomes:

$$\frac{\#urban, tap}{\#total, urban} = \frac{325}{887} \approx 0.366$$

You need to do this:

- Determine the number of desired and total possible outcomes by looking at the table.
- Read the question carefully when determining the number of possible outcomes: do you need the entire set or a subset?

Explanation:

Use the probability formula: $\text{Probability} = \frac{\text{number of desired outcomes}}{\text{number of total outcomes}}$. The numerator is the number of people who passed at least four levels, which is 4. The total number of people in the data table is 6. So, $\text{Probability} = \frac{4}{6} = \frac{2}{3} \approx 0.667$. The closest answer to this is **(D)**.

Math

Try on Your Own

Directions

Take as much time as you need on these questions. Work carefully and methodically. There will be an opportunity for timed practice later in the book.

13

	Winter	Spring	Summer	Fall	Total
Apples	38	40	52	85	215
Bananas	47	53	50	30	180
Oranges	43	66	82	44	235
Pineapples	22	41	46	11	120
Total	150	200	230	170	750

The table shows the number of apples, bananas, oranges, and pineapples sold at Freddie's Fruit Stand during each of the four seasons.

Of the following, which is closest to the probability that a randomly selected fruit sold in spring will be a pineapple?

Ⓐ 5%

Ⓑ 20%

Ⓒ 24%

Ⓓ 33%

14

	Apples	Berries	Pears	Oranges	Exotics	Total
Day 1	30	32	22	18	13	115
Day 2	18	28	27	24	15	112
Day 3	37	31	18	31	22	139
Day 4	28	35	32	15	24	134
Total	113	126	99	88	74	500

Craig is selling boxes of fruit. His sales are shown in the table. Assuming that no buyer purchased more than one box of fruit, what is the probability that a randomly selected buyer purchased a box of berries or exotic fruit?

> _____

15

There is a 25% chance of rain on Saturday and a 60% chance of rain on Sunday. Assuming that the chance of rain is independent of the day, what is the probability that it will rain on Saturday but NOT rain on Sunday?

Ⓐ 10%

Ⓑ 15%

Ⓒ 65%

Ⓓ 85%

16

HINT: Take the time to make sure you're pulling the correct information from the table for Q16.

	Strongly Disagree	Disagree	Agree	Strongly Agree	Total
Freshmen	35	40	24	36	135
Sophomores	37	28	12	23	100
Juniors	24	22	36	38	120
Seniors	30	40	21	24	115
Total	126	130	93	121	470

Students at Fairview High School were asked to rate their level of agreement with a new school policy. The results are shown in the table. If under-classmen are defined as freshmen and sophomores, what is the probability that a randomly selected underclassman either agreed or strongly agreed with the new policy?

_____

17

HINT: Begin by setting up a system of equations in Q17.

Kittens at Animal Shelter X		
Color	Gray	Orange
Female		
Male		
Total	90	40

An animal shelter's current selection of kittens is shown in the table. The shelter has three times as many gray female kittens as orange female kittens and two times as many male gray kittens as male orange kittens. What is the probability that an orange kitten selected at random will be female?

Ⓐ 0.125

Ⓑ 0.25

Ⓒ 0.30

Ⓓ 0.375

On Test Day

The average formula will serve you well on questions that ask about a sum of values or the average of a set of values, but for questions that give you the average and ask for a missing value in the data set, there is an alternative that can be faster: the balance approach.

The balance approach is based on the idea that if you know what the average is, you can find the totals on both sides of the average and then add the missing value that makes both sides balance out. This approach is especially helpful if the values are large and closely spaced. Imagine that a question gives you the set $\{976, 980, 964, 987, x\}$ and tells you that the average is 970. You would reason as follows: 976 is 6 over the average, 980 is 10 over, 964 is 6 under, and 987 is 17 over. That's a total of $6 + 10 - 6 + 17 = 27$ over, so x needs to be 27 under the average, or $970 - 27 = 943$.

Try solving the question below both ways, using first the average formula and then the balance approach. If you find the latter to be fast and intuitive, add it to your test day arsenal.

	Jerseys	Shorts	T-Shirts	Tank Tops	Sweatshirts	Sweatpants
Red	6	3	4	7	8	8
Green	2	7	5	3	5	4
Blue	8	9	7	5		4

18. The table shows the types and colors of sportswear in stock at a sporting goods store. If the mean number of blue articles of clothing in stock is 7, then what is the number of blue sweatshirts the store has in stock?

The correct answer and both ways of solving can be found at the end of the chapter.

How Much Have You Learned?

Directions

For test-like practice, give yourself 13.5 minutes to complete this question set. Be sure to study the explanations, even for questions you got right. They can be found at the end of this chapter.

1

Age Group	High School Diploma Only	2-Year Degree	4-Year Degree	Total
18–25	23	12	3	38
26–35	16	19	9	44
36–45	11	13	2	26
Older than 45	2	2	0	4
Total	52	46	14	112

The table shows the distribution of job applicants by age and level of education. According to the data, which age group had the smallest percentage of people with a high school diploma only?

Ⓐ 18—25

Ⓑ 26—35

Ⓒ 36—45

Ⓓ Older than 45

2

Ray rolls two fair 6-sided dice. What is the probability that both dice show an odd prime number?

Ⓐ $\frac{1}{9}$

Ⓑ $\frac{1}{4}$

Ⓒ $\frac{1}{3}$

Ⓓ $\frac{2}{3}$

3

The Kp Index measures the energy added to Earth's magnetic field from the Sun, with 1 representing a solar calm and 5 or more indicating a magnetic storm, or solar flare. The results of measuring the Kp Index for several days in September are displayed in the table.

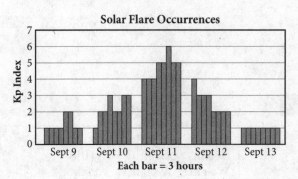

Solar Flare Occurrences

Each bar = 3 hours

During how many hours did a solar flare occur?

4

The table shows the daily costs associated with keeping a business open.

Expense	Amount
Electricity	$150/day
Trash Disposal and Cleaning	$80/day
Operational Staff	$11/hour

The business employs 10 people on operational staff who each work 8 hours a day. How much, in dollars, does it cost to keep the business open for 3 days?

5

What is the distance, on a number line, between the mode and the range of the set $\{-9, -2, 0, 0, 8, 9\}$?

Ⓐ 0

Ⓑ 1

Ⓒ 17

Ⓓ 18

6

	Below Healthy Weight Range	Within Healthy Weight Range	Above Healthy Weight Range	Total
Male	1	55	10	66
Female	8	49	5	62
Total	9	104	15	128

The table shows the number of babies born in a certain hospital in October 2018. If an infant is randomly selected from the females born at this hospital in October 2018, what is the probability that the infant is not within the healthy weight range?

Ⓐ $\dfrac{13}{128}$

Ⓑ $\dfrac{13}{62}$

Ⓒ $\dfrac{49}{128}$

Ⓓ $\dfrac{49}{62}$

7

Cinema X has 15 movie theaters, each of which averages 600 customers per day. If the cinema closes 6 of the theaters but total theater attendance stays the same, what is the average daily attendance per theater among the remaining theaters?

$$\boxed{\underline{}}$$

8

	No Mask	Regular Mask	Contoured Mask	Total
Experienced REM Sleep	14	33	78	125
Did Not Experience REM Sleep	34	29	22	85
Total	48	62	100	210

The results of a sleep study are shown in the table. Study participants were divided into three groups: the first group did not wear sleep masks, the second group wore regular sleep masks, and the third group wore contoured sleep masks. What percent of the participants who experienced REM sleep wore a contoured mask?

Ⓐ 37.1%

Ⓑ 47.6%

Ⓒ 59.5%

Ⓓ 62.4%

9

What is the average of the expressions $2x + 5$, $5x - 6$, and $-4x + 2$?

(A) $x - \dfrac{1}{3}$

(B) $x + \dfrac{1}{4}$

(C) $x + \dfrac{1}{3}$

(D) $3x + 3$

Reflect

Directions: Take a few minutes to recall what you've learned and what you've been practicing in this chapter. Consider the following questions, jot down your best answer for each one, and then compare your reflections to the expert responses that follow. Use your level of confidence to determine what to do next.

What are some common ways that the PSAT may present data?

_____

_____

_____

What is the difference between median, mode, and range?

_____

_____

_____

What does the standard deviation of a data set tell you?

_____

_____

_____

What are two ways to calculate the probability of a single event?

_____

_____

_____

Expert Responses

What are some common ways that the PSAT may present data?

The PSAT commonly presents data in tables, bar charts, line graphs, dot plots, and histograms.

What is the difference between median, mode, and range?

The median of a set with an odd number of values is the middle value, and the median of a set with an even number of numbers is the average of the two values that share the middle. Regardless of the number of numbers in the set, the mode is the most common value while the range is the biggest value minus the smallest one.

What does the standard deviation of a data set tell you?

A data set's standard deviation reflects how far apart the numbers are from each other. The standard deviation of a set whose numbers are all the same—for example, {5, 5, 5, 5}—is 0. The greater the spread among the numbers, the greater the standard deviation.

What are two ways to calculate the probability of a single event?

One way is to use the basic probability formula:

$$\text{Probability} = \frac{\text{number of desired outcomes}}{\text{number of total outcomes}}$$

Alternatively, the probability that an event happens is 1 minus the probability that it doesn't happen.

Next Steps

If you answered most questions correctly in the "How Much Have You Learned?" section, and if your responses to the Reflect questions were similar to those of the PSAT expert, then consider Tables, Statistics, and Probability an area of strength and move on to the next chapter. Come back to this topic periodically to ensure your skills stay sharp.

If you don't yet feel confident, review those parts of this chapter that you have not yet mastered, then try the questions you missed again. In particular, make sure that you understand the six terms explained in the Statistics lesson and the probability formulas explained in the Probability lesson. As always, be sure to review the explanations closely.

Answers and Explanations

Try on Your Own

1. A

Difficulty: Easy

Category: Problem-Solving and Data Analysis

Getting to the Answer: The question states that the data were collected in the Atlantic Ocean, so any conclusion drawn can be generalized only to that particular geographic region. Eliminate (C) and (D). The question defines the winter months as December, January, and February. According to the data, a greater volume of water moved during those months than during the summer months of June, July, and August, so **(A)** is correct.

2. B

Difficulty: Easy

Category: Problem-Solving and Data Analysis

Getting to the Answer: The question asks only about cars and trucks, so ignore the column for SUVs. The technician recommended a tire rotation for 48 cars and 36 trucks (a total of 84) out of the $94 + 64 = 158$ cars and trucks they serviced. This represents $\frac{84}{158} = \frac{42}{79}$ of the cars and trucks, making **(B)** correct.

3. 264

Difficulty: Easy

Category: Problem-Solving and Data Analysis

Getting to the Answer: The table indicates that 27.8% of participants who got the drug experienced severe side effects, as did 6.2% of participants who got the placebo. Add these percentages together: $27.8\% + 6.2\% = 34\%$ of participants had severe side effects. This implies that $100\% - 34\% = 66\%$ did not. The paragraph states that there were 400 participants, so 66% of $400 = 0.66 \times 400 = 264$ participants did not sustain severe side effects. Enter **264**.

4. D

Difficulty: Medium

Category: Problem-Solving and Data Analysis

Getting to the Answer: The question asks about employees who eat breakfast every weekday, so focus on the "5–7 times per week" column in the table. In the study, 36 of the 45 participants in that column were within a healthy weight range. This is equal to 80%. If the study applies to the company, then 80% of the 3,000 employees are likely to be within a healthy weight range. Multiply $0.8 \times 3,000$ to arrive at 2,400, which is **(D)**.

5. A

Difficulty: Medium

Category: Problem-Solving and Data Analysis

Getting to the Answer: According to the bar graph, the company's yearly profits have been growing by about $10 million annually. To reach yearly profits that are 100% greater than—in other words, double—its profits in 2013, the company would need yearly profits of $2 \times \$60$ million $= \$120$ million. This is $60 million more than in 2013. At $10 million more per year, reaching this target would take 6 more years. Thus, the company should double its 2013 profits in $2013 + 6 = 2019$, choice **(A)**.

6. 3/7, 0.428, 0.429, .4285, or .4286

Difficulty: Medium

Category: Problem-Solving and Data Analysis

Getting to the Answer: According to the expression provided, you need the number of viewers and the total viewing audience. The table provides the total viewing audience: 3,500 people. According to the text, the number of viewers is 20% of the number of TV owners, which is 20% of $7,500 = 0.2 \times 7,500 = 1,500$. Plug these numbers into the nightly rating equation:

$$\text{Nightly rating} = \frac{1,500}{3,500} = \frac{3}{7}$$

Entering **3/7** is easiest, but its decimal equivalent to 5 characters (rounded or truncated) is also acceptable: **0.428**, **0.429**, **.4285**, and **.4286**

7. B

Difficulty: Easy

Category: Problem-Solving and Data Analysis

Getting to the Answer: Consider the difference between mean and standard deviation: mean is a measure of center, while standard deviation is a measure of spread. The four answers all involve diving consistency, which means the explanation should involve standard deviation. Eliminate (A) and (C). Higher diving consistency means lower standard deviation (and vice versa); the only choice that reflects this—and correctly represents the data in the table—is **(B)**.

8. B

Difficulty: Easy

Category: Problem-Solving and Data Analysis

Getting to the Answer: The mean of a set of numbers is the same as the average, the sum of the values divided by the number of values. Use the graph to find the sum of the fuel efficiency ratings and then calculate the mean. To save time, multiply the frequency in each category by the rating and then divide by the total number of convertibles: $(6 \times 15) + (18 \times 25) + (9 \times 35) + (2 \times 45) = 945$. There are $6 + 18 + 9 + 2 = 35$ total convertibles, so $\frac{945}{35} = 27$. Choice **(B)** is correct.

9. C

Difficulty: Medium

Category: Problem-Solving and Data Analysis

Getting to the Answer: Understanding how averages and sums are connected is the key to answering a question like this. Recall the formula, $\text{average} = \frac{\text{sum of terms}}{\text{number of terms}}$. If the average of 10 numbers is 5, then the sum of the 10 numbers must be $5 \times 10 = 50$. Use the dot plot to find the total number of miles the runner has already run. Then, subtract this number from 50. The runner has already run $3.5 + 2(4) + 2(4.5) + 5 + 2(6) + 6.5 = 44$ miles, so he needs to run $50 - 44 = 6$ miles on the 10th day. Choice **(C)** is correct.

10. C

Difficulty: Hard

Category: Problem-Solving and Data Analysis

Getting to the Answer: The median is the middle number in a series of numbers. Arrange the number of employees from least to greatest, making sure that 821 is in the middle. Use n to balance out the number of eligible employees. Because there are two numbers below the median (732 and 795), there must be two numbers above the median, 874 and n. Be careful—n could be on either side of 874:

$$732, 795, 821, 874, n$$

or

$$732, 795, 821, n, 874$$

Since no two years had the same number, n could be anything greater than 821. Its least possible value is 822. Choice **(C)** is correct.

11. A

Difficulty: Hard

Category: Problem-Solving and Data Analysis

Getting to the Answer: To answer this question, you need to understand the assumptions each inequality makes. Start with (A). This is a reasonable conclusion to draw because the question does not specify anything about the relative quantity of experienced and novice club members, so keep (A) as a possible correct answer for the moment. Choice (B) assumes there are equal numbers of experienced and novice members. Choice (C) assumes there are more experienced than novice members, while (D) assumes there are more novice than experienced members. Because no information on the relative numbers of each group is given, (B), (C), and (D) are all incorrect, leaving **(A)** as the only option.

12. C

Difficulty: Medium

Category: Problem-Solving and Data Analysis

Getting to the Answer: First arrange the elements of data set K in increasing order: 0, 1, 3, 4, 7, 7, 11, 13, 14. The mode is 7 because that is the only value that appears twice. There are nine values, so the median is the fifth number, which is also 7. The mean is $\frac{0 + 1 + 3 + 4 + 7 + 7 + 11 + 13 + 14}{9} = \frac{60}{9} = 6\frac{2}{3}$. Finally, the range is $14 - 0 = 14$. The mean has the least value, so **(C)** is correct.

13. B

Difficulty: Easy

Category: Problem-Solving and Data Analysis

Getting to the Answer: To calculate the probability that a randomly selected spring fruit will be a pineapple, find the number of spring fruits that are pineapples and divide by the total number of spring fruits: $\frac{41}{200} = 0.205$. This is approximately 20%, so **(B)** is correct.

14. 2/5, 0.4, or .4

Difficulty: Easy

Category: Problem-Solving and Data Analysis

Getting to the Answer: According to the table, there are 126 boxes of berries and 74 boxes of exotic fruits. Add these together and divide by the total boxes sold to get $\frac{126 + 74}{500} = \frac{200}{500} = \frac{2}{5} = 0.4$. Enter **2/5, 0.4, or .4**.

15. A

Difficulty: Medium

Category: Problem-Solving and Data Analysis

Getting to the Answer: To calculate the probability of two independent events, multiply their individual probabilities together. The probability that it rains on Saturday is 25%. The probability that it does not rain on Sunday is $100\% - 60\% = 40\%$. Therefore, the probability that it rains on Saturday but not on Sunday is $(0.25)(0.40) = 0.10$, or 10%. Choice **(A)** is correct.

16. 40.42 or 40.43

Difficulty: Medium

Category: Problem-Solving and Data Analysis

Getting to the Answer: Read the question carefully to determine which rows and columns of the table you will need. First, you are told that you are looking only at underclassmen, which are defined as freshmen and sophomores. Thus, you need only consider the first two rows of the table. There are $100 + 135 = 235$ total underclassmen at the school. Next, you need to determine how many underclassmen either agreed or strongly agreed with the policy: $24 + 36 = 60$ freshmen and $12 + 23 = 35$ sophomores either agreed or strongly agreed. Thus, the probability that a randomly selected underclassman either agreed or strongly agreed with the new policy is $\frac{95}{235} \approx 0.40425$, which is approximately 40.425%. Student-produced responses will allow you to enter 5 characters for positive numbers, and you may either round or truncate at the end. Enter **40.42** or **40.43**

17. B

Difficulty: Hard

Category: Problem-Solving and Data Analysis

Getting to the Answer: Begin by setting up a system of equations to determine the number of each type of kitten. Let the number of orange female kittens be denoted by x. Since there are three times as many gray females and orange females, the number of gray females must be $3x$. Using similar logic, let the number of male orange kittens be y. There are two times as many gray males as orange males, so the gray males can be represented as $2y$.

Therefore, you obtain the following system of equations from the columns of the table.

$$\text{Gray Kittens:} \quad 3x + 2y = 90$$
$$\text{Orange Kittens:} \quad x + y = 40$$

Since you are interested in the number of female orange kittens, solve the system of equations for x. Isolate y in the second equation ($y = 40 - x$) and plug it into the first equation.

$$3x + 2y = 90$$
$$3x + 2(40 - x) = 90$$
$$3x + 80 - 2x = 90$$
$$x + 80 = 90$$
$$x = 10$$

There are a total of 40 orange kittens. Of these, 10 are female. Therefore, the probability of picking an orange kitten that is female is $\frac{10}{40} = 0.25$. Choice **(B)** is correct.

On Test Day

18. 9

Difficulty: Medium

Category: Problem-Solving and Data Analysis

Strategic Advice: When the goal is to find a missing value in a set of data and the average is given, consider using the balance approach. We'll demonstrate both approaches starting with the average formula.

Getting to the Answer: The question is about blue sportswear, so ignore the data for the other colors. The given numbers for blue sportswear are 8, 9, 7, 5, and 4. The average is given as 7. Let x represent the number of blue sweatshirts. Plugging the known values into the average formula results in the following:

$$\frac{8 + 9 + 7 + 5 + x + 4}{6} = 7$$
$$\frac{33 + x}{6} = 7$$
$$33 + x = 42$$
$$x = 9$$

Enter **9**.

Alternatively, to use the balance approach, write down how much each value is above or below the average of 7. For example, the value for jerseys is 1 above the average: $8 - 7 = 1$.

Jerseys	Shorts	T-Shirts	Tank Tops	Sweatshirts	Sweatpants
8: +1	9: +2	7: 0	5: −2		4: −3

Now, observe that, excluding sweatshirts, the values are $+1 + 2 + 0 - 2 - 3 = -2$. Without the value for sweatshirts, the total is 2 less than what you'd expect based on the average. So for the values to balance out to the average, the sweatshirts' value must be 2 more than the average of 7, or $7 + 2 = 9$. Enter **9**.

How Much Have You Learned?

1. B

Difficulty: Easy

Category: Problem-Solving and Data Analysis

Getting to the Answer: To calculate the percentage of people in each age group who had a high school diploma only, divide the number of people in that age group with only a high school diploma by the total number of applicants in that age group.

(A) $\frac{23}{38} \approx 0.605$

(B) $\frac{16}{44} \approx 0.363$

(C) $\frac{11}{26} \approx 0.423$

(D) $\frac{2}{4} = 0.5$

You are looking for the smallest value, so **(B)** is correct.

2. A

Difficulty: Hard

Category: Problem-Solving and Data Analysis

Getting to the Answer: Recall that probability $= \frac{desired}{total}$. Since the two rolls are independent of each other, you can determine the probability of getting an odd prime on each die separately and then multiply the two probabilities together. There are 6 possible rolls on the first die. The odd prime numbers between 1 and 6 are 3 and 5 (1 is not a prime number). Since there are a total of 2 desired outcomes, the probability that the first die shows an odd prime is $\frac{2}{6} = \frac{1}{3}$. The probability that the second die shows an odd prime will be exactly the same. Therefore, the probability that both show an odd prime is $\frac{1}{3}\left(\frac{1}{3}\right) = \frac{1}{9}$. Choice **(A)** is correct.

3. 15

Difficulty: Easy

Category: Problem-Solving and Data Analysis

Getting to the Answer: Read the graph carefully, including the key at the bottom that tells you that each bar represents a 3-hour period. The question tells you that a Kp Index of 5 or more indicates a solar flare. On September 11, the graph shows 4 bars at a Kp Index of 5 and 1 bar at a Kp Index of 6, for a total of five 3-hour periods during which a solar flare occurred. This represents a total of 5(3) = 15 hours. Enter **15**.

4. 3330

Difficulty: Medium

Category: Problem-Solving and Data Analysis

Getting to the Answer: Take this question one step at a time. Each person on the operational staff is paid $11 per hour. Therefore, one person working 8 hours a day makes 8($11) = $88 per day. There are 10 people on the operational staff, so together they are paid a total of 10($88) = $880 per day.

The question asks for the total expenses over three days. Electricity costs 3($150) = $450, trash disposal and cleaning costs 3($80) = $240, and operational staff costs 3($880) = $2,640. Add everything together to obtain $450 + $240 + $2,640 = $3,330. Enter **3330**.

5. D

Difficulty: Medium

Category: Problem-Solving and Data Analysis

Getting to the Answer: The mode is the number that occurs most frequently in the data set. Here, the mode is 0. The range is the difference between the biggest and smallest numbers. Here, the range is $9 - (-9) = 18$. The question asks for the distance between these two points on a number line. This can be found by subtracting the two: $18 - 0 = 18$. Choice **(D)** is correct.

6. B

Difficulty: Medium

Category: Problem-Solving and Data Analysis

Getting to the Answer: Recall that probability = $\frac{\text{desired}}{\text{total}}$. The infant is being selected from the females only, so the total is 62. Of these, $8 + 5 = 13$ are not

within the healthy weight range. Therefore, the probability that an infant randomly selected from the females is not within the healthy weight range is $\frac{13}{62}$. Choice **(B)** is correct.

7. 1000

Difficulty: Medium

Category: Problem-Solving and Data Analysis

Getting to the Answer: Originally, there were 15 theaters averaging 600 customers each per day. Therefore, the total attendance was 15(600) = 9,000 customers per day. After 6 theaters closed, the total attendance remained the same, but the number of theaters was reduced to $15 - 6 = 9$. Recalculate the average with this new denominator:

$$\text{Average} = \frac{\text{sum of terms}}{\text{\# of terms}}$$
$$= \frac{9,000}{9}$$
$$= 1,000$$

Enter **1000**.

8. D

Difficulty: Easy

Category: Problem-Solving and Data Analysis

Getting to the Answer: The question asks about participants who experienced REM sleep, so focus on this row only. Of the 125 participants who experienced REM sleep, 78 of them wore a contoured mask. This represents $\frac{78}{125} = 0.624$, or 62.4%. Choice **(D)** is correct.

9. C

Difficulty: Hard

Category: Problem-Solving and Data Analysis

Getting to the Answer: Apply the average formula to these three expressions.

$$\text{average} = \frac{\text{sum of terms}}{\text{\# of terms}}$$
$$= \frac{(2x + 5) + (5x - 6) + (-4x + 2)}{3}$$
$$= \frac{3x + 1}{3}$$
$$= x + \frac{1}{3}$$

Choice **(C)** is correct.

ADVANCED MATH

[CHAPTER 9]

ABSOLUTE VALUE AND NONLINEAR FUNCTIONS

LEARNING OBJECTIVES

After completing this chapter, you will be able to:

- Solve an equation containing an absolute value expression
- Interpret the graph of an equation containing an absolute value expression
- Interpret the domain, range, and properties of nonlinear functions and their graphs
- Evaluate the output of a given nonlinear function

How Much Do You Know?

Directions

Try the questions that follow. Show your work so that you can compare your solutions to the ones found in the "Check Your Work" section immediately after this question set. If you answered the question(s) on a specific topic correctly, and if your scratchwork looks like ours, you may be able to move quickly through the lesson covering that topic. If you answered incorrectly or used a different approach, you may want to take your time on that lesson.

1

$$\left|\frac{1}{2}x^2 - 12\right| = 6$$

In the equation shown, which of the following is a possible value of x^2?

- (A) $2\sqrt{3}$
- (B) 6
- (C) 12
- (D) 18

2

Which of the following describes all the solutions to the inequality $|x + 3| < 7$?

- (A) $x < -10$
- (B) $-10 < x < 4$
- (C) $x < -10$ or $x > 4$
- (D) $x > 4$

3

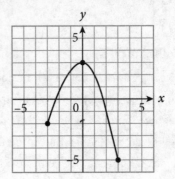

The complete graph of the function $f(x)$ in the xy-plane is shown above. What is the domain of $f(x)$?

- (A) All real numbers greater than -5
- (B) All real numbers between and including -5 and 3
- (C) All real numbers between and including -3 and 3
- (D) All real numbers

4

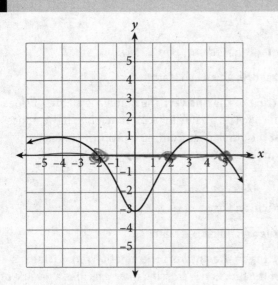

The figure shows the graph of $r(x)$. What is one value of x for which $r(x) = 0$?

$$-2, 2.5$$

5

x	$f(x)$
-4	8
-2	-6
0	-12
2	-10
4	0
6	18

Which of the following functions best describes the information in the table?

(A) $f(x) = x + 2$

(B) $f(x) = 2x - 12$

(C) $f(x) = (x - 12)(x - 4)$

(D) $f(x) = (x - 4)(x + 3)$
$\quad\quad -4 \quad 3$

Check Your Work

1. C

Difficulty: Easy

Category: Advanced Math

Getting to the Answer: Since absolute value gives a non-negative value, the expression inside the absolute value may be equal to 6 or −6. Solving for x^2 in each case gives the solutions to the equation.

$$\frac{1}{2}x^2 - 12 = 6 \qquad \frac{1}{2}x^2 - 12 = -6$$
$$\frac{1}{2}x^2 = 18 \qquad \frac{1}{2}x^2 = 6$$
$$x^2 = 36 \qquad x^2 = 12$$

Only 12 is listed as an answer choice, so **(C)** is correct.

2. B

Difficulty: Medium

Category: Advanced Math

Getting to the Answer: Since absolute value gives a non-negative value, the expression inside the absolute value may be less than 7 or greater than −7 (recall that you flip the sign of an inequality when multiplying by a negative). Solving for x in each case gives the solutions to the inequality.

$$x + 3 < 7 \qquad x + 3 > -7$$
$$x < 4 \qquad x > -10$$

Thus, the solutions are within the interval $-10 < x < 4$. **(B)** is correct.

Alternatively, you could pick numbers to test the answer choices to determine for what interval the inequality is true. For example, picking −11 gives $|-11 + 3| < 7$, which is not true because $8 > 7$. Thus, x must be greater, not less than −10. Eliminate (A) and (C). When $x = 5$, $|5 + 3| < 7$, which is also not true because $8 > 7$. Thus, x must also be less than 4. Eliminate (D); **(B)** is correct.

3. C

Difficulty: Medium

Category: Advanced Math

Getting to the Answer: The domain is all the x-values that will yield a value for $f(x)$. From left to right, notice that the graph goes from −3 to 3 and includes the endpoints. Thus, **(C)** is correct.

4. −2, 2, or 5

Difficulty: Easy

Category: Advanced Math

Getting to the Answer: The notation $r(x) = 0$ means that the function is crossing the x-axis (has a y-value of 0), so look for the x-intercepts. The function $r(x)$ intersects the x-axis at $x = -2$, 2, and 5. Enter **−2, 2,** or **5**.

5. D

Difficulty: Medium

Category: Advanced Math

Getting to the Answer: From the data, you can see the change in $f(x)$ is not constant (not linear), so eliminate (A) and (B). Next, try plugging a point from the table, for example (2, −10), into (C) and (D):

$$\begin{aligned} \text{(C): } f(2) &= (2 - 12)(2 - 4) \\ f(2) &= (-10)(-2) \\ f(2) &= 20 \\ -10 &\neq 20 \end{aligned}$$

This does not match the value of $f(x)$ in the table, so that means **(D)** is correct. On test day, there will be no need to try (D), but for the record:

$$\begin{aligned} \text{(D): } f(2) &= (2 - 4)(2 + 3) \\ f(2) &= (-2)(5) \\ f(2) &= -10 \\ -10 &= -10 \end{aligned}$$

Absolute Value

LEARNING OBJECTIVES

After this lesson, you will be able to:

- Solve an equation containing an absolute value expression
- Interpret the graph of an equation containing an absolute value expression

To answer a question like this:

If $|3x - 9| = 12$ and $x^2 - 11 = 38$, what is the value of x?

- (A) -1
- (B) -7
- (C) 7
- (D) 9

You need to know this:

The **absolute value** of a number represents its distance from zero on a number line. It is represented by a set of vertical lines around a number, variable, or expression. For example, $|x| = 4$ means that x is four units away from zero on the number line, which means that x itself could be either 4 or -4.

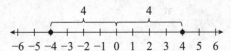

Thus, the effect of putting something inside a set of absolute value bars is to take any non-zero number and make it positive (if it wasn't already). The absolute value of 0 is simply 0.

When you see an equation involving absolute value, you'll need to consider both possible values of the expression inside the absolute value bars. Say that $|x + 8| = 11$. Then, you know that either $x + 8 = 11$ or $x + 8 = -11$, and you could solve each equation to find that $x = 3$ or $x = -19$. Both of these possible values for x satisfy the original equation; if a question asks you to narrow it down to a single value for x, you'd need more information—such as another equation.

You may see a question involving an absolute value function, where the entire function is in absolute value bars. The domain of such a function is the same as it would be if there were no absolute value bars. For instance, $f(x) = |x^2 - 3|$ has a domain of all real numbers, since any real number can be squared, while $f(x) = \left| \dfrac{1}{x + 1} \right|$ has a domain of all real numbers other than -1, since $\dfrac{1}{x + 1}$ is undefined when the denominator is 0. The range of an absolute value function will consist only of non-negative numbers because the absolute value bars turn any otherwise negative output positive.

The graph of an absolute value function will look similar to what it would look like without the absolute value bars; the only difference is that any point on the graph that would have appeared below the y-axis will instead appear an equal distance above the x-axis. For instance, consider the graphs of $f(x) = x^2 - 3x + 1$ and $f(x) = |x^2 - 3x + 1|$:

PART 2C
ADVANCED MATH

Math

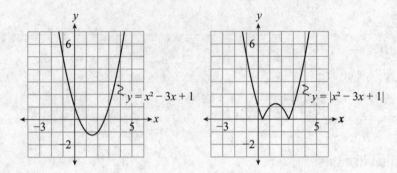

You need to do this:

- Set up equations with both the positive and negative values of the expression inside the absolute value bars.
- If needed, use any other given information to narrow down the possible values of x.

Explanation:

You need a value of x that satisfies both of these equations. Start by considering the absolute value equation. If $|3x - 9| = 12$, then either $3x - 9 = 12$ or $3x - 9 = -12$. Solve each of these equations: $3x = 21$ and $x = 7$, or $3x = -3$ and $x = -1$. Now, solve the other equation. If $x^2 - 11 = 38$, then $x^2 = 49$, and $x = \pm 7$. Thus, $x = 7$ is the only solution that satisfies both equations, and **(C)** is correct.

200 K

Try on Your Own

Directions

Take as much time as you need on these questions. Work carefully and methodically. There will be an opportunity for timed practice later in the book.

1

HINT: For Q1, domain refers to the possible *x*-values and range refers to the possible *y*-values.

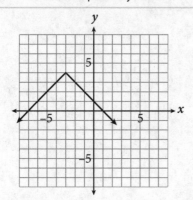

The graph of $f(x)$ is shown. Which of the following represents the domain and range of the function?

Ⓐ Domain: $f(x) \geq 4$; range: all real numbers

Ⓑ Domain: $f(x) \leq 4$; range: all real numbers

Ⓒ Domain: all real numbers; range: $f(x) \geq 4$

Ⓓ Domain: all real numbers; range: $f(x) \leq 4$

2

For what values of *x* is $|6x + 5| = 7$ true?

Ⓐ -2 and $\frac{1}{3}$

Ⓑ -2 and 3

Ⓒ 2 and $\frac{1}{3}$

Ⓓ 2 and 3

3

$|12 - 5x| = x$

What is the product of the solutions to the equation shown?

4

HINT: For Q4, the absolute value of a number is its distance from zero on a number line.

Points *c* and *d* on a number line are both 7 units from 1. Which of the following gives the coordinates *c* and *d*?

Ⓐ $|x + 1| = 7$

Ⓑ $|x - 1| = 7$

Ⓒ $|x + 7| = 1$

Ⓓ $|x - 7| = 1$

5

Which of the following expressions is true for some value of *x*?

Ⓐ $|-x + 2| + 2 = 0$

Ⓑ $|x - 2| + 2 = 0$

Ⓒ $|x + 2| - 2 = 0$

Ⓓ $|x + 2| + 2 = 0$

Nonlinear Functions

To answer a question like this:

$$f(x) = \begin{cases} -2x + 1, & x \le -3 \\ x^2 - 2, & -3 < x < 3 \\ x + 4, & x \le 3 \end{cases}$$

What is the minimum value of $f(x)$?

Ⓐ -2

Ⓑ 0

Ⓒ 7

Ⓓ $f(x)$ does not have a minimum.

You need to know this:

You learned about linear functions earlier in the book. Like a linear function, a nonlinear function takes a number as input and generates a unique output. Unlike a linear function, however, a nonlinear function's graph will be something other than a line. Here are some examples of nonlinear functions you may encounter on the PSAT:

• Parabola: A curve generated by an function in the form $f(x) = ax^2 + bx + c$. You'll learn more about parabolas in the chapter on quadratics.

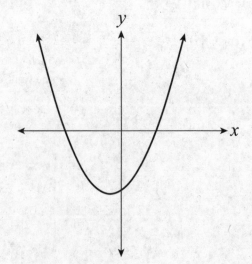

- Cubic function: A curve generated by a function with an x^3 term. The function's graph can cross the x-axis either one, two, or three times.

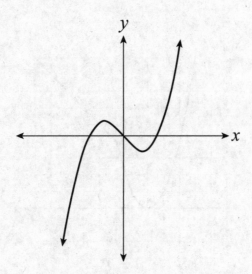

- Square root function: A curve generated by a function with a $\sqrt{x}$ term.

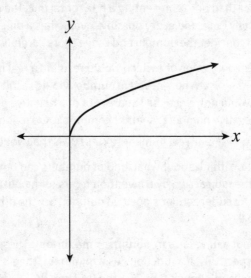

- Piecewise function: A function may have different equations for different x values. For instance, a function may be defined as $f(x) = \begin{cases} (x-2)^2, x \le 4 \\ x, x > 4 \end{cases}$

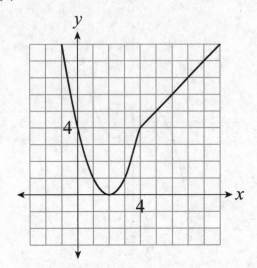

The **domain** is the set of all possible inputs to a function, and the **range** is the set of all possible outputs of a function. In a linear function, other than one representing a horizontal line, the domain and range both consist of all real numbers; a line is infinitely long, and every possible x value has a different associated y value. In a nonlinear function, you'll have to consider the domain and range more carefully.

The domain of a function includes every value of x which would result in a real number when plugged into the function. Consider the function $f(x) = \sqrt{x}$. A non-negative number would result in a real number: the positive square root. A negative number would not, since the square root of a negative number is imaginary. Thus, the domain of $f(x) = \sqrt{x}$ is all non-negative numbers. Another common issue to look out for with the domain is division by zero; the domain of $f(x) = \frac{1}{x}$ is all real numbers except 0, as that would make the function undefined.

To determine the range of a function, think about what kind of numbers can be output by the function. Consider again $f(x) = \sqrt{x}$: Since the radical sign by convention refers to the positive square root, the output of this function must be non-negative: either zero or a positive number. So, the domain of $f(x) = \sqrt{x}$ is all real numbers greater than or equal to 0.

The PSAT may sometimes ask about a function's **minimum** or **maximum**. These terms mean the least and greatest value of the function, respectively. If a function has a minimum, then its range will consist only of numbers greater than or equal to the minimum. Consider the function $f(x) = x^2$. Because squaring any real number results in a non-negative number, this function has a minimum value of 0 at the parabola's vertex, and its range is all real numbers greater than or equal to 0.

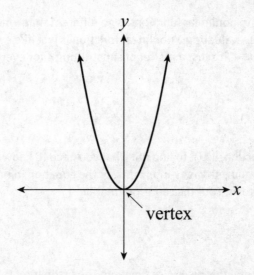

If a function has a maximum, then its range will consist only of real numbers less than or equal to the maximum. Consider the function $f(x) = -x^2$. The negative sign means that any possible output can't be positive; thus, this function has a maximum value of 0 at the parabola's vertex, and its range is all real numbers less than or equal to 0.

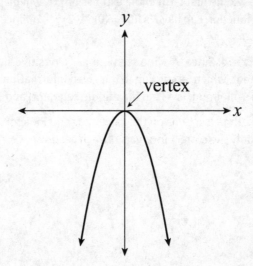

Not all functions have a maximum or minimum (for instance, $f(x) = x^3$ has a range of all real numbers). Some may have both a maximum and a minimum; $f(x) = \sin x$ has a maximum of 1 and a minimum of -1.

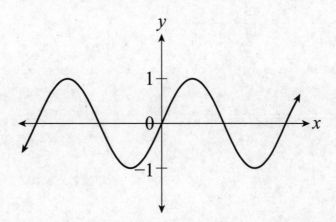

In many other ways, working with nonlinear functions is no different than what is done with linear functions earlier in the book. For example, evaluating a nonlinear function is just like evaluating a linear one. Take $f(x) = \sqrt{x} + 5$. To evaluate at $x = 4$, it's just a matter of substituting 4 for every x in the equation. $f(4) = \sqrt{4} + 5 = 2 + 5 = 7$.

You need to do this:

If you're given the graph of a function, use it to find out what you need to know about the function, such as its domain, range, minimum, maximum, its x- or y-intercepts, or the equation it may be a graph of. If you're not given a graph, use the equation to find out the same information.

Explanation:

Check for a minimum in each part of this piecewise function. The first part of the function, $-2x + 1$, is a line segment with a negative slope. Since the line decreases as the x values increase, this portion of the function will have its minimum value at its rightmost point, which, according to the function's definition, is at $x = -3$. Plug this into the line formula to get $f(-3) = -2(-3) + 1 = 7$. Now, consider the minimum of the middle piece of the function, which is defined by $x^2 - 2$. The first term in the expression, x^2, will be positive unless $x = 0$. So, the minimum value this piece of the function can have is $f(0) = (0)^2 - 2 = -2$. Since the minimum can't be greater than -2, eliminate (B) and (C).

Finally, check the third segment, $x + 4$. Since this line segment has a positive slope, its minimum value will be at the leftmost point of the segment, which, according to the given information, is at $x = 3$. Plug this in to get $f(3) = 3 + 4 = 7$. So, the function's minimum is -2, in the middle segment, and **(A)** is correct.

Alternatively, you could graph the three sections on the calculator and look for the value of the minimum point, making sure to pay attention to only the correct intervals of each section.

Try on Your Own

Directions

Take as much time as you need on these questions. Work carefully and methodically. There will be an opportunity for timed practice later in the book.

6

HINT: For Q6, remember that $f(x)$ and $g(x)$ are found on the y-axis on the graphs.

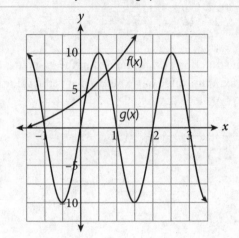

In the figure shown above, what is the value of $f(0) + g\left(\frac{1}{2}\right)$?

Ⓐ −4

Ⓑ 6

Ⓒ 10

Ⓓ 14

7

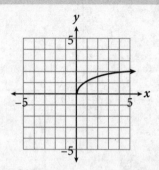

The figure shown represents the function $q(x) = \sqrt{x}$. Which statement about the function is true?

Ⓐ $q(2) = 2$

Ⓑ $q(0) = 0$

Ⓒ The range is undefined.

Ⓓ The domain is undefined.

8

x	$f(x)$
−2	16
0	4
2	0
4	4
6	16

The table shows some values for a quadratic defined by the function f. Which of the following is a factor of $f(x)$?

Ⓐ $x - 2$

Ⓑ $x - 3$

Ⓒ $x + 2$

Ⓓ $x + 3$

9

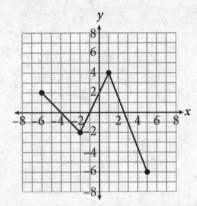

The complete graph of the function f is shown in the figure above. Which of the following is equal to -1?

Ⓐ $f(-4)$

Ⓑ $f(0)$

Ⓒ $f(1)$

Ⓓ $f(3)$

10

HINT: Begin Q10 by determining the maximum y-value.

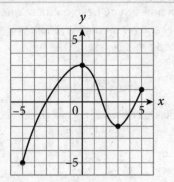

The function $f(x)$ is graphed in the xy-plane. If the maximum value of $f(x)$ is z, what is the value of $-f(z)$?

On Test Day

Remember that you can sometimes use clues from the answer choices to help you solve PSAT Math questions. Even if you are familiar with the straight math approach, solving a question by strategically using the answer choices may help you improve your efficiency on the Math section.

Try solving this absolute value question using the answer choices as clues. Then try solving the question by setting up equations and using traditional math. Which approach did you find more efficient?

11. Which of the following is the solution set of $4 = \left| \dfrac{12}{x-3} \right|$?

    (A)   {0,3}

    (B)   {0,6}

    (C)   {3,6}

    (D)   {6}

The answer and explanation can be found at the end of this chapter.

Math

How Much Have You Learned?

Directions

For test-like practice, give yourself 7.5 minutes to complete this question set. Be sure to study the explanations, even for questions you got right. They can be found at the end of this chapter.

1

$|2x + 9| = 4x - 3$

What is the set of all solutions to the equation shown?

Ⓐ $\{-6\}$

Ⓑ $\{-2, 6\}$

Ⓒ $\{-1, 6\}$

Ⓓ $\{6\}$

2

For what values of x is $|x - 6| \geq 6x - 1$ true?

Ⓐ $x \geq -1$

Ⓑ $x \leq 1$

Ⓒ $-1 \leq x \leq 1$

Ⓓ $x \leq -1$ or $x \geq 1$

3

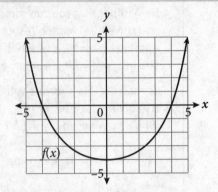

The graph of the function $f(x)$ is shown above. What is the domain of the function?

Ⓐ $y \geq -4$

Ⓑ $y > -4$

Ⓒ All real numbers

Ⓓ The domain is undefined.

4

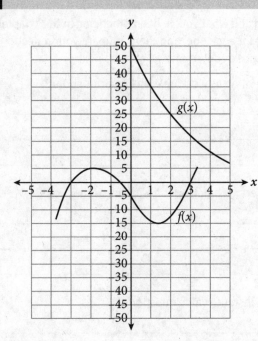

The functions $f(x)$ and $g(x)$ are graphed in the xy-plane above. What is the value of $f(-2) - g(2)$?

_____

5

Month	Number of views (in thousands)
1	3
2	9
3	27
4	81
5	244
6	729

The table shows the number of times a video has been viewed on an online platform over the past six months. Which of the following functions best describes the data shown?

Ⓐ $f(x) = x^2$

Ⓑ $f(x) = x^3$

Ⓒ $f(x) = 2^x$

Ⓓ $f(x) = 3^x$

Reflect

Directions: Take a few minutes to recall what you've learned and what you've been practicing in this chapter. Consider the following questions, jot down your best answer for each one, and then compare your reflections to the expert responses that follow. Use your level of confidence to determine what to do next.

What is one way that working with nonlinear functions is the same as working with linear functions?

_____

_____

_____

What is one way that working with nonlinear functions is different than working with linear functions?

_____

_____

_____

What two cases do you need to consider when working with absolute value questions?

_____

_____

_____

Expert Responses

What is one way that working with nonlinear functions is the same as working with linear functions?

While there are many similarities, evaluating both linear and nonlinear functions is a matter of substituting in a number for the variable given.

$$At\ x = 1, f(x) = 3x + 3 \rightarrow f(1) = 3(1) + 3 = 6$$
$$At\ x = 1, g(x) = x^2 + 7 \rightarrow g(1) = (1)^2 + 7 = 8$$

What is one way that working with nonlinear functions is different than working with linear functions?

One difference is that linear functions that are not horizontal lines have domains and ranges of all real numbers. Nonlinear functions may have limits on valid domains and ranges. For example, the range of $f(x) = x^2$ is only positive numbers and zero, since the squared term assures that there will never be a negative output to real numbers that are input into the function.

What two cases do you need to consider when working with absolute value questions?

Be sure to consider both the negative and positive case when working with absolute values. For example, $|x| = 1$, both $x = 1$ and $x = -1$ are valid solutions.

Next Steps

If you answered most questions correctly in the "How Much Have You Learned?" section, and if your responses to the Reflect questions were similar to those of the PSAT expert, then consider Absolute Value and Nonlinear Functions an area of strength and move on to the next chapter. Come back to this topic periodically to prevent yourself from getting rusty.

If you don't yet feel confident, review the lessons. Then, try the questions you missed again. As always, be sure to review the explanations closely.

Answers and Explanations

Try on Your Own

1. D

Difficulty: Easy

Category: Advanced Math

Getting to the Answer: To determine the domain, look at the x-values. Since the domain is the set of inputs, not outputs, it will not include $f(x)$. This means you can eliminate (A) and (B). Additionally, the graph is continuous (no holes or gaps in the graph) and has arrows on both sides, so the domain is all real numbers.

To determine the range, look at the y-values. For the range, the function's maximum (the vertex) is located at $(-3, 4)$, which means that the greatest possible y-value of $f(x)$ is 4. The graph is continuous and opens downward, so the range of the function is $y \leq 4$, which is the same as $f(x) \leq 4$. Choice **(D)** is correct.

2. A

Difficulty: Easy

Category: Advanced Math

Getting to the Answer: Since absolute value gives a non-negative value, the expression inside the absolute value may be equal to 7 or -7. Solving for each case gives the solutions to the equation.

$$6x + 5 = 7 \qquad 6x + 5 = -7$$
$$6x = 2 \qquad 6x = -12$$
$$x = \frac{2}{6} \qquad x = -2$$
$$x = \frac{1}{3}$$

(A) is correct.

3. 6

Difficulty: Medium

Category: Advanced Math

Getting to the Answer: Since absolute value gives a non-negative value, the expression inside the absolute value may be equal to $-x$ or x. Solving for each case gives the solutions to the equation.

$$12 - 5x = x \qquad 12 - 5x = -x$$
$$12 = 6x \qquad 12 = 4x$$
$$2 = x \qquad 3 = x$$

The question asks for the product of the solutions, which is $3(2) = 6$. Enter **6**.

4. B

Difficulty: Hard

Category: Advanced Math

Getting to the Answer: By definition, $|x|$ indicates the distance of x from 0. Thus, $|x| = 7$ indicates that x is 7 units from 0. That is, $x = 7$ or $x = -7$. Since c and d are 7 units from 1, the coordinates of c and d are $x = 1 + 7$ and $x = 1 - 7$. Subtracting 1 from both sides gives $x - 1 = 7$ and $x - 1 = -7$, which can be written more concisely as $|x - 1| = 7$. **(B)** is correct.

5. C

Difficulty: Easy

Category: Advanced Math

Getting to the Answer: The absolute value of a number is always non-negative. Note that if you isolate the absolute value term for each answer choice, you would get the absolute value term equals -2 for (A), (B), and (D)—which can never be true. Thus, **(C)** is the only answer choice that can be true (at $x = 0$ and $x = -4$) and is correct.

6. D

Difficulty: Easy

Category: Advanced Math

Getting to the Answer: Begin by finding $f(0)$ on the graph. When $x = 0$, function f has a y-value of 4. Therefore, $f(0) = 4$. Now, repeat for $g\left(\frac{1}{2}\right)$. When $x = \frac{1}{2}$ on function g, $y = 10$; thus, $g\left(\frac{1}{2}\right) = 10$. You're asked for the sum of $f(0)$ and $g\left(\frac{1}{2}\right)$, so substitute the appropriate numbers to get $4 + 10 = 14$, which is **(D)**.

7. B

Difficulty: Medium

Category: Advanced Math

Getting to the Answer: Compare each answer choice, one at a time, to the graph. The statement in (A) is not true because, at $x = 2$, y is less than 2 from the graph. For **(B)**, when $x = 0$, $q(0)$ is also zero from the graph. You can select **(B)** and move on, but for the record, the domain and range for this function are defined: they're all positive numbers and zero for both.

8. A

Difficulty: Medium

Category: Advanced Math

Getting to the Answer: A factor of a quadratic equals 0. So if $x - a$ is a factor of $f(x)$, then $x - a = 0$ and $x = a$, where a is an x-intercept of the polynomial. In other words, look for when $f(a) = 0$ in the table. According to the table, $f(2) = 0$, so $x - 2$ is a factor of $f(x)$. **(A)** is correct.

9. D

Difficulty: Easy

Category: Advanced Math

Getting to the Answer: Look where function f intersects the horizontal line $y = -1$. The function intersects at $f(-3)$, $f(-1.5)$, and $f(3)$; only $f(3)$ is listed as an option. Choice **(D)** is correct.

10. 2

Difficulty: Hard

Category: Advanced Math

Getting to the Answer: First, find the maximum value, which means the highest y-value. The maximum value occurs at the point $(0, 3)$ so 3 is the maximum value. Now plug 3 into the function. Find $f(3)$ by locating the y-value when $x = 3$. The point $(3, -2)$ means that $f(3) = -2$. Remember that the question asks for the value of $-f(z)$, which is $-f(3) = -(-2) = 2$. Enter **2**.

On Test Day

11. B

Difficulty: Medium

Category: Advanced Math

Strategic Advice: Testing and strategically eliminating answer choices can sometimes be a more efficient approach than doing traditional math. Look for patterns in the answer choices and consider whether any answer choices can be immediately eliminated.

Getting to the Answer: In the absolute value equation in the question stem, notice that one value of x is undefined; x cannot equal 3, since $3 - 3$ would yield zero in the denominator. Quickly eliminate (A) and (C), which include 3 in the solution set.

The remaining answer choices are {0,6} and {6}. The most efficient way to determine which is correct is to test $x = 0$. If 0 is a solution, the correct answer is {0,6}; if 0 is not a solution, the correct answer is {6}. Testing $x = 0$ yields:

$$4 = \left| \frac{12}{x - 3} \right|$$

$$4 = \left| \frac{12}{0 - 3} \right|$$

$$4 = |-4|$$

$$4 = 4$$

Choice **(B)** is correct.

To solve using traditional math, consider both the positive and the negative possible values of the absolute value. Set up two equations:

$$4 = \frac{12}{x - 3} \qquad\qquad -4 = \frac{12}{x - 3}$$
$$4(x - 3) = 12 \qquad\qquad -4(x - 3) = 12$$
$$4x - 12 = 12 \qquad\qquad -4x + 12 = 12$$
$$4x = 24 \qquad\qquad\qquad -4x = 0$$
$$x = 6 \qquad\qquad\qquad\quad x = 0$$

The solution is {0,6} and **(B)** is correct.

How Much Have You Learned?

1. D

Difficulty: Medium

Category: Advanced Math

Getting to the Answer: Since absolute value gives a non-negative value, the expression inside the absolute value may be equal to $-(4x - 3)$ or $4x - 3$. Solving for each case gives the solutions to the equation.

$$
\begin{array}{ll}
2x + 9 = 4x - 3 & 2x + 9 = -(4x - 3) \\
-2x = -12 & 2x + 9 = -4x + 3 \\
x = 6 & 6x = -6 \\
& x = -1
\end{array}
$$

Note that when $x = -1$, the original equation is not true.

$$
\begin{aligned}
|2(-1) + 9| &= 4(-1) - 3 \\
|-2 + 9| &= -4 - 3 \\
7 &\neq -7
\end{aligned}
$$

So, -1 can't be a solution. It's called an extraneous solution. The only solution in the set is 6. **(D)** is correct.

2. B

Difficulty: Medium

Category: Advanced Math

Getting to the Answer: Since absolute value gives a non-negative value, the expression inside the absolute value may be greater than or equal to $6x - 1$ or less than or equal to $-(6x - 1)$. Recall that you flip the sign of an inequality when multiplying by a negative. Solving for x in each case gives the solutions to the inequality.

$$
\begin{array}{ll}
x - 6 \geq 6x - 1 & x - 6 \leq -(6x - 1) \\
-5x \geq 5 & x - 6 \leq -6x + 1 \\
x \leq -1 & 7x \leq 7 \\
& x \leq 1
\end{array}
$$

Thus, the solutions are in the interval $x \leq 1$. **(B)** is correct.

Alternatively, you could pick numbers to test the answer choices to determine for what interval the inequality is true. For example, picking 2 gives $|2 - 6| \geq 6(2) - 1$, which is not true because $4 < 11$. Thus, x must be less, not greater than 1. Eliminate (D). When $x = -2$, $|-2 - 6| \geq 6(-2) - 1$, which is true because $8 > -13$. Thus, x must also be less than -1. Eliminate (A) and (C); **(B)** is correct.

3. C

Difficulty: Easy

Category: Advanced Math

Getting to the Answer: The domain of a function is all possible x-values. In this case, the arrows indicate the graph is going to continue infinitely in both directions, so every x-value is possible, meaning the domain of the function is all real numbers. **(C)** is correct.

Note that if you forgot whether it is the x- or y-value that gives you the domain, (A) would have been a tempting choice. (A) actually gives the correct *range* of the function, which is determined by all possible y-values.

4. −20

Difficulty: Medium

Category: Advanced Math

Getting to the Answer: Start by figuring out the y-values needed. On the graph, $f(-2)$ has a value of 5, while $g(2)$ has a value of 25. Therefore, $f(-2) - g(2) = 5 - 25 = -20$. Enter **−20**.

5. D

Difficulty: Medium

Category: Advanced Math

Getting to the Answer: From the data and answer choices, you can see the change in $f(x)$ is not constant (not linear). Try plugging in a point from the table, for example $(1, 3)$, into the answer choices:

(A): $f(1) = 1^2$

$\quad\quad 3 \neq 1$ Eliminate (A)

(B): $f(1) = 1^3$

$\quad\quad 3 \neq 1$ Eliminate (B)

(C): $f(1) = 2^1$

$\quad\quad 3 \neq 2$ Eliminate (C)

This means **(D)** is correct. On test day, there will be no need to try (D), but for the record:

(D): $f(1) = 3^1$

$\quad\quad 3 = 3$

[CHAPTER 10]

QUADRATICS

LEARNING OBJECTIVES

After completing this chapter, you will be able to:

- Solve a quadratic equation by factoring
- Expand quadratics using FOIL
- Recognize the classic quadratics
- Solve a quadratic equation by completing the square
- Solve a quadratic equation by applying the quadratic formula
- Use the discriminant to determine the number of real solutions to a quadratic equation
- Relate properties of a quadratic function to its graph and vice versa
- Solve a system of one quadratic and one linear equation

How Much Do You Know?

Directions

Try the questions that follow. Show your work so that you can compare your solutions to the ones found in the "Check Your Work" section immediately after this question set. If you answered the question(s) on a specific topic correctly, and if your scratchwork looks like ours, you may be able to move quickly through the lesson covering that topic. If you answered incorrectly or used a different approach, you may want to take your time on that lesson.

1

If $x^2 + 8x = 48$ and $x > 0$, what is the value of $x - 5$?

- (A) -9
- (B) -1
- (C) 4
- (D) 7

2

What is the absolute value of the difference between the roots of $4x^2 - 36 = 0$?

- (A) -6
- (B) 0
- (C) 3
- (D) 6

3

Which of the following is equivalent to $x^2 - 6x - 10 = 0$?

- (A) $(x - 3)^2 = 19$
- (B) $(x + 3)^2 = 19$
- (C) $(x - 6)^2 = 45$
- (D) $(x + 6)^2 = 45$

4

$$y = 2x^2 - 8x + c$$

The quadratic above has only one distinct, real root. What is the value of c?

- (A) -8
- (B) -4
- (C) 4
- (D) 8

5

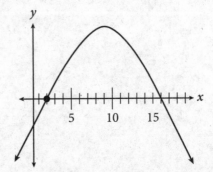

Which of the following equations could represent the above graph?

- (A) $y = -x^2 + 18x - 32$
- (B) $y = -x^2 + 14x - 32$
- (C) $y = x^2 - 14x - 32$
- (D) $y = x^2 + 18x + 32$

6

$$\begin{cases} y = x + 1 \\ y = \dfrac{1}{2}x^2 - x - \dfrac{3}{2} \end{cases}$$

If (a, b) is a solution to the system of equations shown, what is a value of a?

Check Your Work

1. B

Difficulty: Medium

Category: Advanced Math

Strategic Advice: When finding solutions to a quadratic equation, always start by rewriting the equation to make it equal to 0 (unless both sides of the equation are already perfect squares). Then, take a peek at the answer choices—if they are all integers that are easy to work with, then factoring is probably the quickest method for solving the equation. If the answers include messy fractions or square roots, then using the quadratic formula may be a better choice.

Getting to the Answer: To make the equation equal to 0, subtract 48 from both sides to get $x^2 + 8x - 48 = 0$. The answer choices are all integers, so factor the equation. Look for two numbers whose product is -48 and whose sum is 8. The two numbers are -4 and 12, so the factors are $(x - 4)$ and $(x + 12)$. Set each factor equal to 0 and solve to find that $x = 4$ and $x = -12$. The question states that $x > 0$, so x must equal 4. Before selecting an answer, don't forget to check that you answered the right question—the question asks for the value of $x - 5$, not just x, so the correct answer is $4 - 5 = -1$. **(B)** is correct.

2. D

Difficulty: Hard

Category: Advanced Math

Getting to the Answer: First, factor out a 4 to get $4(x^2 - 9)$. Notice that $x^2 - 9$ is a difference of squares, so use the formula $a^2 - b^2 = (a + b)(a - b)$ with $a^2 = x^2$ and $b^2 = 9$. This means that $a = x$ and $b = 3$. Therefore, $4(x + 3)(x - 3) = 0$. Divide both sides by 4 to get $(x + 3)(x - 3) = 0$. Set both factors equal to 0 and solve:

$$x = -3 \text{ and } x = 3$$

Remember that the question asks for the absolute difference of the roots. Think of a number line and count from -3 to 3. The distance is 6. Alternatively, just take the absolute value of the difference between the roots:

$$|3 - (-3)| = 6$$

Thus, **(D)** is correct.

3. A

Difficulty: Medium

Category: Advanced Math

Getting to the Answer: Each answer choice is in the form $(x + h)^2 = k$. Completing the square is the best approach for converting a quadratic equation in the form $ax^2 + bx + c$ to $a(x - h)^2 + k$. Since the first term has a constant of 1, completing the square is a fairly straightforward approach. Make sure to move the constant term to the right side of the equation before dividing the x-coefficient by 2 and squaring:

$$x^2 - 6x - 10 = 0$$
$$x^2 - 6x + \underline{} = 10 + \underline{}$$
$$\left(\frac{b}{2}\right)^2 = \left(-\frac{6}{2}\right)^2 = (-3)^2 = 9$$

Add 9 to both sides and factor $x^2 - 6x + 9$:

$$x^2 - 6x + 9 = 10 + 9$$
$$(x - 3)^2 = 19$$

Therefore, **(A)** is correct. Note that (C) is the result if you forgot to divide b by 2.

4. D

Difficulty: Medium

Category: Advanced Math

Getting to the Answer: In order for the quadratic to have only one root, the discriminant, $b^2 - 4ac$, must be equal to 0. In the given quadratic, $a = 2$, $b = -8$ and $c = c$. Plug the numbers given into the discriminant, set it equal to 0, and solve for c:

$$b^2 - 4ac = 0$$
$$(-8)^2 - 4(2)(c) = 0$$
$$64 - 8c = 0$$
$$64 = 8c$$
$$8 = c$$

Therefore, **(D)** is correct.

5. A

Difficulty: Hard

Category: Advanced Math

Strategic Advice: Use the visual information in the graph to eliminate answers quickly. A negative coefficient of the squared term means that the graph opens downward.

Getting to the Answer: Because the quadratic opens downward, the x^2-coefficient must be negative, so you can eliminate (C) and (D). According to the graph, the roots are $x = 2$ and $x = 16$. That means that the factored form of the quadratic is $-(x - 2)(x - 16)$.

Use FOIL to see if it matches the expanded form of the quadratic in (A) or (B):

$$-(x - 2)(x - 16) = -\left(x^2 - 16x - 2x + 32\right)$$
$$= -x^2 + 18x - 32$$

Thus, **(A)** is correct.

Another approach would be to plug the solutions for x, $x = 2$ and $x = 16$, into the equations for (A) or (B) to see which one results in $y = 0$ for both solutions:

$$(A): y = -(2)^2 + 18(2) - 32$$

$$y = -(4) + 36 - 32 = 0$$

$$\text{and}$$

$$y = -(16)^2 + 18(16) - 32$$

$$y = -256 + 288 - 32 = 0$$

(A) is correct. You do not need to check (B), but for the record at $x = 2$

$$(B): \ -(2)^2 + 14(2) - 32 = -4 + 28 - 32 = -8$$

6. 5 or −1

Difficulty: Medium

Category: Advanced Math

Getting to the Answer: Solve the system using substitution or by graphing it on your calculator. To solve via substitution, substitute the first equation for y into the second. Before you solve for x, multiply the whole equation by 2 to remove the fractions. Then, set the whole equation equal to 0 and factor:

$$x + 1 = \frac{1}{2}x^2 - x - \frac{3}{2}$$
$$2(x + 1) = 2\left(\frac{1}{2}x^2 - x - \frac{3}{2}\right)$$
$$2x + 2 = x^2 - 2x - 3$$
$$0 = x^2 - 4x - 5$$
$$0 = (x + 1)(x - 5)$$

Now, set each factor equal to 0 and solve to find that $x = -1$ and $x = 5$. You may enter either **5** or **−1**.

Note that the question asks only for a, which is the x-coordinate of the solution, so you do not need to substitute x back into an equation and solve for y.

Math

Solving Quadratics by Factoring

LEARNING OBJECTIVES

After this lesson, you will be able to:

- Solve a quadratic equation by factoring
- Expand quadratics using FOIL

To answer a question like this:

If $x^2 + x = 20$ and $x < 0$, what is the value of $x - 7$?

Ⓐ -12

Ⓑ -5

Ⓒ 5

Ⓓ 12

You need to know this:

A quadratic expression is a second-degree polynomial—that is, a polynomial containing a squared variable. You can write a quadratic expression as $ax^2 + bx + c$.

The **FOIL** acronym (which stands for First, Outer, Inner, Last) will help you remember how to multiply two binomials of the form $(a + b)(c + d)$: multiply the first terms together (ac), then the outer terms (ad), then the inner terms (bc), and finally the last terms (bd):

$$(a + b)(c + d) = ac + ad + bc + bd$$

FOIL can also be done in reverse if you need to go from a quadratic to its factors.

To solve a quadratic equation by factoring, the quadratic must be set equal to zero. For example:

$$x^2 + x - 56 = 0$$
$$(x + 8)(x - 7) = 0$$

From the binomial factors, you can find the **solutions**, also called **roots** or **zeros**, of the equation. For two factors to be multiplied together and produce zero as the result, one or both of those factors must be zero. In the example above, either $x + 8 = 0$ or $x - 7 = 0$, which means that $x = -8$ or $x = 7$.

You need to do this:

To solve a quadratic equation by factoring:

Set the quadratic equal to zero, so it looks like this: $ax^2 + bx + c = 0$.

- Factor the squared term. (For factoring, it's easiest when a, the coefficient in front of x^2, is equal to 1.)
- Make a list of the factors of c. Remember to include negatives.
- Find the factor pair that, when added, equals b, the coefficient in front of x.
- Write the quadratic as the product of two binomials.
- Set each binomial equal to zero and solve.

Explanation:

Set the equation equal to zero and factor the first term:

$$x^2 + x = 20$$
$$x^2 + x - 20 = 0$$
$$(x \pm \,?)(x \pm \,?) = 0$$

Next, consider factors of -20, keeping in mind that they must sum to 1, so the factor with the greater absolute value must be positive. The possibilities are 20×-1, 10×-2 and 5×-4. The factor pair that sums to 1 is 5 and -4. Write that factor pair into your binomials:

$$(x - 4)(x + 5) = 0$$

Set each factor equal to zero and solve:

$$(x - 4) = 0 \qquad (x + 5) = 0$$
$$x = 4 \qquad\qquad x = -5$$

The question says that $x < 0$, so $x = -5$. However, you are *not* done. The question asks for $x - 7$, which is -12. Therefore, **(A)** is correct.

Try on Your Own

Directions

Take as much time as you need on these questions. Work carefully and methodically. There will be an opportunity for timed practice later in the book.

1

Which of the following is an equivalent form of the expression $(x - 4)(x + 2)$?

Ⓐ $x^2 - 8x - 2$

Ⓑ $x^2 - 2x - 8$

Ⓒ $x^2 + 2x - 8$

Ⓓ $x^2 - 2x + 8$

2

What is the positive difference between the zeros of $g(x) = -2x^2 + 16x - 32$?

3

What positive value(s) of z satisfy the equation $4z^2 + 32z - 81 = -1$?

Ⓐ 2

Ⓑ 2 and 4

Ⓒ 2 and 10

Ⓓ None of the above

4

HINT: For Q4, is there anything you can factor out of the numerator or the denominator?

Which of the following is equivalent to $\dfrac{x^2 - 4x + 4}{2x^2 + 4x - 16}$?

Ⓐ $\dfrac{1}{2}$

Ⓑ $\dfrac{x}{x + 4}$

Ⓒ $\dfrac{x - 2}{2(x + 4)}$

Ⓓ $\dfrac{x^2 - 4x + 4}{x^2 + 2x - 8}$

5

HINT: Begin Q5 by solving for the zeros of each answer choice.

If a quadratic function $f(x)$ has solutions a and b such that $a < 0$, $b > 0$, and $|b| > |a|$, which of the following could be equal to $f(x)$?

Ⓐ $4x^2 + 4x - 24$

Ⓑ $-x^2 + x + 6$

Ⓒ $-x^2 - x + 6$

Ⓓ $3x^2 - 6x$

Classic Quadratics

LEARNING OBJECTIVE

After this lesson, you will be able to:

* Recognize the classic quadratics

To answer a question like this:

Which of the following expressions is equivalent to $36x^4y^6 - 4$?

(A) $6(x^4y^6 - 2)$

(B) $-6(x^2y^3 + 2)$

(C) $(6x^2y^2 - 2)(6x^2y^2 + 2)$

(D) $(6x^2y^3 - 2)(6x^2y^3 + 2)$

You need to know this:

Memorizing the following classic quadratics will save you time on test day:

* $x^2 - y^2 = (x + y)(x - y)$
    * This is known as a "difference of squares" because it takes the form of one perfect square minus another perfect square.
* $x^2 + 2xy + y^2 = (x + y)^2$
* $x^2 - 2xy + y^2 = (x - y)^2$

You need to do this:

When you see a pattern that matches either the left or the right side of one of the above equations, simplify by substituting its equivalent form. For example, say you need to simplify the following:

$$\frac{a^2 - 2ab + b^2}{a - b}$$

You would substitute $(a - b)(a - b)$ for the numerator and cancel to find that the expression simplifies to $a - b$:

$$\frac{a^2 - 2ab + b^2}{a - b} = \frac{(a - b)(a - b)}{a - b} = \frac{a - b}{1} = a - b$$

Explanation:

The expression $36x^4y^6 - 4$ is a difference of perfect squares. The square root of $36x^4y^6$ is $6x^2y^3$ and the square root of 4 is 2, so the correct factorization is $(6x^2y^3 - 2)(6x^2y^3 + 2)$. Hence, **(D)** is correct.

Try on Your Own

Directions

Take as much time as you need on these questions. Work carefully and methodically. There will be an opportunity for timed practice later in the book.

6

HINT: What can you do to make $(a - b)^2$ in Q6 easier to work with?

For all a and b, what is the sum of $(a - b)^2$ and $2ab$?

(A) $a^2 - b^2$

(B) $a^2 + b^2$

(C) $a^2 - 4ab + b^2$

(D) $a^2 + 4ab + b^2$

7

Which equation does NOT have a solution at $x = -4$?

(A) $y = x^2 - 8x + 16$

(B) $y = x^2 + 8x + 16$

(C) $y = x^2 - 16$

(D) $y = 4x^2 + 32x + 64$

8

Suppose $a^2 + 2ab + b^2 = c^2$ and $c - b = 4$. Assuming $c > 0$, what is the value of a?

9

In the expression $3x^2 + 12x + 12 = a(x + b)^2$, $a > 1$ and both a and b are constants. Which of the following could be the value of b?

(A) -2

(B) 2

(C) 4

(D) 12

10

HINT: For Q10, is there any variable you can factor out from each term?

$16m^2p^2 + 72mzp^2 + 81z^2p^2$

Which of the following expressions is equivalent to the expression above?

(A) $p^2(16m^2 + 9z)(8m + 9z)$

(B) $p^2(4m + 9z)^2$

(C) $2p^2m(8m + 36z + 40z^2) + z^2$

(D) $p^2(16m^2 + 72mz + 27z^2)$

Completing the Square

LEARNING OBJECTIVE

After this lesson, you will be able to:

- Solve a quadratic equation by completing the square

To answer a question like this:

Which of the following has the same roots as $30 - 8x = x^2 - y$?

(A) $y = (x - 4)^2 - 30$

(B) $y = (x - 4)^2 + 30$

(C) $y = (x + 4)^2 - 46$

(D) $y = (x + 4)^2 + 46$

You need to know this:

For quadratics that do not factor easily, you'll need one of two strategies: completing the square or the quadratic formula (taught in the next lesson). To complete the square, you'll create an equation in vertex form $(x - h)^2 = k$, where h and k are constants that represent the vertex of the parabola.

As with factoring, completing the square is most convenient when the coefficient in front of the x^2 term is 1.

You need to do this:

Here are the steps for completing the square, demonstrated with a simple example.

STEP	SCRATCHWORK
Starting point:	$x^2 + 8x - 8 = 0$
1. Move the constant to the opposite side.	$x^2 + 8x = 8$
2. Divide b, the x-coefficient, by 2, and square the quotient.	$b = 8; \left(\dfrac{b}{2}\right)^2 = \left(\dfrac{8}{2}\right)^2 = (4)^2 = 16$
3. Add the number from the previous step to both sides of the equation and factor.	$x^2 + 8x + 16 = 8 + 16$ $(x + 4)(x + 4) = 24$ $(x + 4)^2 = 24$
4. Take the square root of both sides.	$x + 4 = \pm\sqrt{24}$ $x + 4 = \pm\sqrt{4}\sqrt{6}$ $x + 4 = \pm 2\sqrt{6}$
5. Split the result into two equations and solve each one.	$x + 4 = 2\sqrt{6} \rightarrow x = 2\sqrt{6} - 4$ $x + 4 = -2\sqrt{6} \rightarrow x = -2\sqrt{6} - 4$

Explanation:

First, write the equation in standard form: $y = x^2 + 8x - 30$. Move the 30 to the other side to temporarily get it out of the way. Then, complete the square on the right-hand side, by finding $\left(\frac{b}{2}\right)^2 = \left(\frac{8}{2}\right)^2 = 4^2 = 16$ and adding the result to both sides of the equation:

$$y = x^2 + 8x - 30$$
$$y + 30 = x^2 + 8x$$
$$y + 30 + 16 = x^2 + 8x + 16$$
$$y + 46 = x^2 + 8x + 16$$

The answer choices are all written in factored form. The right side of the equation is a classic quadratic that factors as follows:

$$y + 46 = (x + 4)(x + 4)$$
$$y + 46 = (x + 4)^2$$

Finally, solve for y to get $y = (x + 4)^2 - 46$, which makes **(C)** correct.

Try on Your Own

Directions

Take as much time as you need on these questions. Work carefully and methodically. There will be an opportunity for timed practice later in the book.

11

Which of the following equations has the same solutions as $x^2 + 6x + 17 = y$?

Ⓐ $y = (x-3)^2 - 26$

Ⓑ $y = (x-3)^2 + 8$

Ⓒ $y = (x+3)^2 + 8$

Ⓓ $y = (x+3)^2 + 17$

12

Which of the following are roots for $x^2 + 10x - 8 = 0$?

Ⓐ $x = \pm\sqrt{108} - 10$

Ⓑ $x = \pm\sqrt{33} - 5$

Ⓒ $x = \pm\sqrt{33} - 25$

Ⓓ $x = \pm\sqrt{33} + 25$

13

Which of the following is equivalent to $x^2 + 4x - 4 = 0$?

Ⓐ $(x-4)^2 = 8$

Ⓑ $(x+4)^2 = 0$

Ⓒ $(x-2)^2 = 0$

Ⓓ $(x+2)^2 = 8$

14

HINT: What can you divide each term by to make the equation in Q14 easier to work with?

Which of the following values of x satisfies the equation $4x^2 + 24x + 8 = 0$?

Ⓐ $-3 - \sqrt{7}$

Ⓑ $3 - \sqrt{7}$

Ⓒ 3

Ⓓ $3 + \sqrt{7}$

The Quadratic Formula

To answer a question like this:

$4x^2 - 7x - 4 = 0$

Which of the following values of x satisfy the equation?

(A) 1 and 4

(B) $-\dfrac{7}{8} + \dfrac{\sqrt{113}}{8}$ and $-\dfrac{7}{8} - \dfrac{\sqrt{113}}{8}$

(C) $\dfrac{7}{8} + \dfrac{\sqrt{113}}{8}$ and $\dfrac{7}{8} - \dfrac{\sqrt{113}}{8}$

(D) No real solutions

You need to know this:

The quadratic formula can be used to solve any quadratic equation. It yields solutions to a quadratic equation that is written in standard form, $ax^2 + bx + c = 0$:

$$x = \frac{-b \pm \sqrt{b^2 - 4ac}}{2a}$$

The $\pm$ sign that follows $-b$ indicates that you may have two solutions, so remember to find both.

The expression under the radical ($b^2 - 4ac$) is called the **discriminant**, and its value determines the *number* of real solutions. If the discriminant is positive, the equation has two distinct real solutions. If the discriminant is equal to 0, there is only one distinct real solution. If the discriminant is negative, there are no real solutions because you cannot take the square root of a negative number.

The arithmetic can get complicated, so reserve the quadratic formula for equations that cannot be solved by factoring and those in which completing the square is difficult because $a \neq 1$.

You need to do this:

Get the quadratic equation into the form $ax^2 + bx + c = 0$. Then substitute a, b, and c into the quadratic formula and simplify.

Explanation:

In the given equation, $a = 4$, $b = -7$, and $c = -4$. Plug these values into the quadratic formula and simplify:

$$x = \frac{-b \pm \sqrt{b^2 - 4ac}}{2a}$$

$$x = \frac{-(-7) \pm \sqrt{(-7)^2 - 4(4)(-4)}}{2(4)}$$

$$x = \frac{7 \pm \sqrt{49 - (-64)}}{8}$$

$$x = \frac{7 \pm \sqrt{113}}{8}$$

$$x = \frac{7}{8} + \frac{\sqrt{113}}{8} \quad \text{or} \quad x = \frac{7}{8} - \frac{\sqrt{113}}{8}$$

The correct answer is **(C)**.

Math

Try on Your Own

Directions

Take as much time as you need on these questions. Work carefully and methodically. There will be an opportunity for timed practice later in the book.

15

HINT: For Q15, what is the value of the discriminant, $b^2 - 4ac$, when the quadratic equation has one solution?

$2x^2 - 8x + k = 0$

What value of k gives exactly one solution for x?

Ⓐ -8

Ⓑ 0

Ⓒ 8

Ⓓ 16

16

HINT: For Q16, what does the expression under the square root sign in the quadratic formula indicate?

Which of the following are the real values of x that satisfy the equation $3x^2 + 2x + 4 = 5x$?

Ⓐ 3 and -2

Ⓑ $\frac{3}{5}$ and $-\frac{2}{5}$

Ⓒ 0

Ⓓ The equation has no real solutions.

17

Which of the following are the roots of the equation $x^2 + 8x - 3 = 0$?

Ⓐ $-4 \pm \sqrt{19}$

Ⓑ $-4 \pm \sqrt{3}$

Ⓒ $4 \pm \sqrt{3}$

Ⓓ $4 \pm \sqrt{19}$

18

HINT: For Q18, remember that for a parabola to have two real solutions, the discriminant, $b^2 - 4ac$, must be greater than zero.

Which of the following quadratic equations has two real solutions?

Ⓐ $y = 2x^2 + 4x + 2$

Ⓑ $y = 5x^2 + 5x - 5$

Ⓒ $y = 5x^2 - 5x + 5$

Ⓓ $y = 2x^2 - 4x + 2$

19

$y = 8a^2 + 4a - 1$

What are the roots of the above equation?

Ⓐ $\dfrac{-1 \pm \sqrt{3}}{4}$

Ⓑ $\dfrac{-1 \pm \sqrt{3}}{2}$

Ⓒ $\dfrac{1 \pm \sqrt{3}}{4}$

Ⓓ $\dfrac{1 \pm \sqrt{3}}{2}$

Graphs of Quadratics

To answer a question like this:

Which of the following statements is true, given the equation $y = (4x - 3)^2 + 6$?

A) The vertex is (3, 6).

B) The y-intercept is (0, 15).

C) The parabola opens downward.

D) The parabola crosses the x-axis.

You need to know this:

A quadratic function is a quadratic equation set equal to y or $f(x)$ instead of 0. Remember that the solutions (also called "roots" or "zeros") of any polynomial function are the same as the x-intercepts. To solve a quadratic function, substitute 0 for y, or $f(x)$, then solve algebraically. Alternatively, you can plug the equation into your graphing calculator and read the x-intercepts from the graph. Take a look at the examples below to see this graphically.

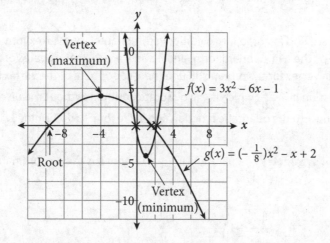

The graph of every quadratic equation (or function) is a **parabola**, which is a symmetric U-shaped graph that opens either upward or downward. To determine which way a parabola will open, examine the value of a in the quadratic equation. If a is positive, the parabola will open upward. If a is negative, it will open downward.

Like quadratic equations, quadratic functions will have zero, one, or two distinct real solutions, corresponding to the number of times the parabola crosses (or touches) the x-axis, as shown in the illustrations below. Graphing is a powerful way to determine the number of solutions a quadratic function has.

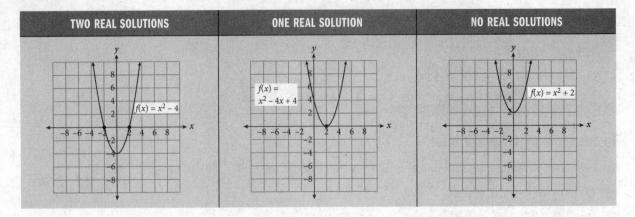

| TWO REAL SOLUTIONS | ONE REAL SOLUTION | NO REAL SOLUTIONS |

There are three algebraic forms that a quadratic equation can take: standard, factored, and vertex. Each is provided in the following table along with the graphical features that are revealed by writing the equation in that particular form.

STANDARD	FACTORED	VERTEX
$y = ax^2 + bx + c$	$y = a(x - m)(x - n)$	$y = a(x - h)^2 + k$
The y-intercept is c.	Solutions are m and n.	The vertex is (h, k).
In real-world contexts, the starting quantity is c.	The x-intercepts are m and n.	The minimum/maximum of the function is k.
Can use quadratic formula to solve.	The vertex is halfway between m and n.	The axis of symmetry is given by $x = h$.

You've already seen standard and factored forms earlier in this chapter, but vertex form might be new to you. In vertex form, a is the same as the a in standard form, and h and k are the coordinates of the **vertex** (h, k). If a quadratic function is not in vertex form, you can still find the x-coordinate of the vertex by plugging the appropriate values into the equation $h = \frac{-b}{2a}$, which is the quadratic formula without the discriminant. Once you determine h, plug this value into the quadratic function and solve for y to determine k, the y-coordinate of the vertex.

The equation of the **axis of symmetry** of a parabola is $x = h$, where h is the x-coordinate of the vertex.

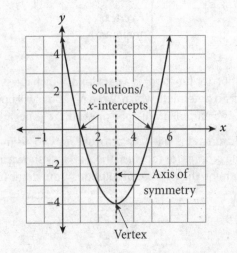

You need to do this:

To find the vertex of a parabola, get the function into vertex form, $y = a(x - h)^2 + k$, or use the formula $h = \frac{-b}{2a}$.

- To find the y-intercept of a quadratic function, plug in 0 for x.
- To determine whether a parabola opens upward or downward, look at the coefficient of a. If a is positive, the parabola opens upward. If negative, it opens downward.
- To determine the number of x-intercepts, set the quadratic function equal to 0 and solve or examine its graph.
- Graph the function on a graphing calculator and efficiently interpret the results.

Explanation:

Be careful: the equation looks like vertex form, $y = a(x - h)^2 + k$, but it's not quite there because the x has a coefficient of 4 inside the parentheses. You could rewrite the equation in vertex form, but this would involve squaring the quantity in parentheses and then completing the square, which would take quite a bit of time. You could also notice that the smallest possible value for y in this function is 6, which happens when the squared term, $(4x - 3)^2$, equals zero. To check (A), find the x-value when $y = 6$:

$$4x - 3 = 0$$
$$4x = 3$$
$$x = \frac{3}{4}$$

So the vertex is at $(\frac{3}{4}, 6)$, not (3, 6). You can also graph the quadratic with the calculator, and you will see that the vertex is at $(\frac{3}{4}, 6)$, not (3, 6). Eliminate (A). The y-intercept is indeed (0, 15); plugging 0 in for x will result in 15. Select **(B)** and move on.

For the record, the squared term is not multiplied by a negative number, so the parabola opens upward, not downward; (C) is incorrect. Because the parabola has a vertex of $(\frac{3}{4}, 6)$ and opens upward, the parabola does not cross the x-axis. (D) is incorrect.

Try on Your Own

Directions

Take as much time as you need on these questions. Work carefully and methodically. There will be an opportunity for timed practice later in the book.

20

HINT: For Q20, which form of a quadratic would you use to find its solutions?

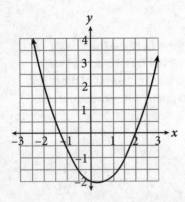

The following quadratic equations are all representations of the graph shown. Which equation enables the easiest calculation of the x-intercepts of the graph?

(A) $y = \frac{3}{4}x^2 - \frac{1}{2}x - 2$

(B) $y + \frac{25}{12} = \frac{1}{12}(3x - 1)^2$

(C) $y = \frac{1}{12}(3x - 1)^2 - \frac{25}{12}$

(D) $y = \frac{1}{4}(3x + 4)(x - 2)$

21

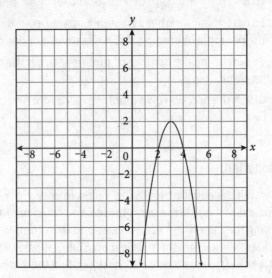

Which of the following represents the function shown in the graph?

(A) $f(x) = -(x - 3)^2 + 2$

(B) $f(x) = -2(x - 3)^2 + 2$

(C) $f(x) = -2(x + 3)^2 + 2$

(D) $f(x) = -(x + 3)^2 + 2$

22

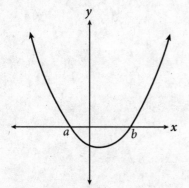

If the distance from a to b in the figure shown is 10, which of the following could be the factored form of the graph's equation?

Ⓐ $y = (x - 7)(x - 3)$

Ⓑ $y = (x - 7)(x + 3)$

Ⓒ $y = (x - 8)(x - 2)$

Ⓓ $y = (x - 1)(x + 10)$

23

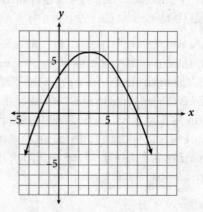

If $y = ax^2 + bx + c$ represents the equation of the graph shown in the figure, which of the following statements is false?

Ⓐ The value of a is a negative number.

Ⓑ The value of c is a negative number.

Ⓒ The y-value is increasing for $x < 3$ and decreasing for $x > 3$.

Ⓓ The zeros of the equation are $x = -2$ and $x = 8$.

24

HINT: Begin Q24 by considering what the *x*-intercepts would represent in terms of the ball's trajectory.

The path of a ball thrown by a catapult can be modeled by the quadratic equation $y = ax^2 + bx + c$, where x is the horizontal distance that the ball travels and y is the height of the ball. If one of these catapult-launched balls is launched from ground level, travels 150 feet before hitting the ground, and reaches a maximum height of 45 feet, which of the following equations represents its path?

Ⓐ $y = -0.008x^2 + 1.2x$

Ⓑ $y = -0.008x^2 - 150x$

Ⓒ $y = 45x^2 + 150x$

Ⓓ $y = 125x^2 + 25x$

Systems of Quadratic and Linear Equations

LEARNING OBJECTIVE

After this lesson, you will be able to:

- Solve a system of one quadratic and one linear equation

To answer a question like this:

In the xy-plane, two equations, $y + 2x = -4x^2 + 5$ and $y - 5 = -6x$, intersect at points $(0, 5)$ and (a, b). What is the value of $-b$?

You need to know this:

You can solve a system of one quadratic and one linear equation by substitution, exactly as you would for a system of two linear equations. Alternatively, you can plug the system into your graphing calculator.

You need to do this:

- Isolate y in both equations.
- Set the equations equal to each other.
- Put the resulting equation into the form $ax^2 + bx + c = 0$.
- Solve this quadratic by factoring, completing the square, or using the quadratic formula. (You are solving for the x-values at the points of intersection of the original two equations.)
- Plug the x-values you get as solutions into one of the original equations to generate the y-values at the points of intersection. (Usually, the linear equation is easier to work with than the quadratic.)
- Graph the equations in the graphing calculator.

Explanation:

Start by isolating y in both equations to get $y = -4x^2 - 2x + 5$ and $y = -6x + 5$. Next, set the right sides of the equations equal and solve for x:

$$-6x + 5 = -4x^2 - 2x + 5$$
$$4x^2 - 4x = 0$$
$$4x(x - 1) = 0$$
$$x = 0 \text{ or } 1$$

The question says that (0, 5) is one point of intersection for the two equations and asks for the *y*-value at the other point of intersection, so plug $x = 1$ into either of the original equations and solve for *y*. Using the linear equation will be faster:

$$y = -6(1) + 5$$
$$y = -1$$

So $(a, b) = (1, -1)$. The question asks for $-b$, which is $-(-1) = 1$. Enter **1**.

Alternatively, you could graph both equations in the graphing calculator and note the two points of intersection. Since the question gives the intersection point at (0, 5), inspect the other point of intersection on the graph to see that its *y*-value is -1. Then take the opposite: **1**.

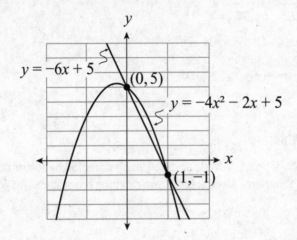

Try on Your Own

Directions

Take as much time as you need on these questions. Work carefully and methodically. There will be an opportunity for timed practice later in the book.

25

HINT: You can take a shortcut in Q25. There's no need to isolate y in the second equation.

$$\begin{cases} y = 3x \\ x^2 - y^2 = -288 \end{cases}$$

If (x, y) is a solution to the system of equations shown, what is the value of x^2?

(A) 6

(B) 36

(C) 144

(D) 1,296

26

HINT: Don't try to find solutions to all the systems in the answer choices of Q26. Backsolve instead.

One of the x-coordinates of the solutions to a system of equations is -8. Which of the following could be the system?

(A) $\begin{cases} y = -x - 1 \\ y = (x - 8)^2 - 3 \end{cases}$

(B) $\begin{cases} y = x + 8 \\ y = (x + 3)^2 - 8 \end{cases}$

(C) $\begin{cases} y = x + 8 \\ y = (x + 3)^2 - 2 \end{cases}$

(D) $\begin{cases} y = -x - 1 \\ y = (x + 5)^2 - 2 \end{cases}$

27

HINT: For Q27, what does it mean when a system of equations has only one solution?

Which system of equations has only one solution?

(A) $\begin{aligned} g(x) &= -2(x + 3)^2 - 5 \\ f(x) &= x - 5 \end{aligned}$

(B) $\begin{aligned} g(x) &= -2(x + 3)^2 - 5 \\ f(x) &= 5 \end{aligned}$

(C) $\begin{aligned} g(x) &= -2(x + 3)^2 - 5 \\ f(x) &= x + 5 \end{aligned}$

(D) $\begin{aligned} g(x) &= -2(x + 3)^2 - 5 \\ f(x) &= -5 \end{aligned}$

28

Will the graph of $f(x) = \frac{5}{2}x - 2$ intersect the graph of $f(x) = \frac{1}{2}x^2 + 2x - 3$?

(A) Yes, only at the vertex of the parabola.

(B) Yes, once on each side of the vertex.

(C) Yes, twice to the right of the vertex.

(D) No, the graphs will not intersect.

On Test Day

Remember that the PSAT doesn't ask you to show your work. If you find the algebra in a question challenging, there is often another way to get to the answer.

Try to answer this question first by setting the two functions equal to each other and solving for x and then z. Next, try plugging the values of the intersection points into one of the functions to find z. Then, try plugging it into a graphing calculator. Which approach do you find easiest? There's no right or wrong answer—just remember your preferred approach and try it first if you see a question like this on test day.

29.

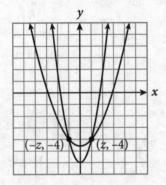

The functions $f(x) = 2x^2 - 5$ and $g(x) = 6x^2 - 7$ are graphed in the xy-plane. The points where the two functions intersect are $(z, -4)$ and $(-z, -4)$. What is the value of z?

Ⓐ $\frac{1}{2}$

Ⓑ $\frac{\sqrt{2}}{2}$

Ⓒ 0.8

Ⓓ 1.2

The correct answer can be found at the end of this chapter.

How Much Have You Learned?

Directions

For test-like practice, give yourself 15 minutes to complete this question set. Be sure to study the explanations, even for questions you answered correctly. They can be found at the end of this chapter.

1

Each of the following quadratic functions can be modeled by the equation $y = ax^2 + bx + c$. For which graph is the quantity $b^2 - 4ac$ negative?

(A)
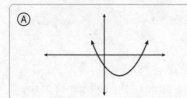

(B)
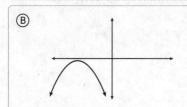

(C)
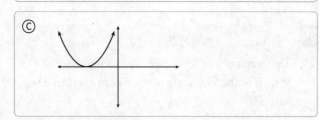

(D)
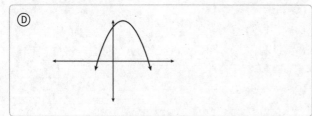

2

The x-intercepts of the equation $y = x^2 - 9x + 20$ are m and n, where $m > n$. What is the value of m?

3

Shawna throws a baseball into the air. The equation $h = -5(t^2 - 4t + 4) + 22$ represents the height of the ball in meters t seconds after it is thrown. Which of the following equations could represent the height of a second ball that was thrown by Meagan, if Meagan's ball did not go as high as Shawna's ball?

(A) $h = -10(t - 4)^2 + 27$

(B) $h = -10(t - 2)^2 + 25$

(C) $h = -8(2t - 1)^2 + 23$

(D) $h = -5(t - 2)^2 + 21$

4

Which of the following equations could represent a parabola that has a minimum value of -3 and whose axis of symmetry is the line $x = 2$?

(A) $y = (x - 3)^2 + 2$

(B) $y = (x + 3)^2 + 2$

(C) $y = (x - 2)^2 - 3$

(D) $y = (x + 2)^2 - 3$

5

Which of the following is a solution to the equation $x^2 + 24 = 14x - x^2$?

(A) -3

(B) $\frac{12}{7}$

(C) 4

(D) 7

6

Which of the following is an equivalent form of $4x^2 - 8x - 64 = 0$?

(A) $(x - 2)^2 = 12$

(B) $(x + 2)^2 = 15$

(C) $(x - 1)^2 = 17$

(D) $(x + 1)^2 = 20$

7

Which of the following is equivalent to $64x^2 - 81y^2$?

(A) $(8x + 9y)(8x - 9y)$

(B) $(9x + 8y)(9x - 8y)$

(C) $(8x + 9y)^2$

(D) $(8x - 9y)^2$

8

Which of the following quadratics has only one real solution?

(A) $4x^2 = 3x - 8$

(B) $10x = 2 - x^2$

(C) $7x^2 + 2x - 5 = 0$

(D) $3x^2 - 6x + 3 = 0$

9

$$\begin{cases} y - 3x = x^2 - 10 \\ y - 4 = -2x \end{cases}$$

What is the absolute value of the difference of the values of x for the solutions to the system of equations above?

10

The graph of $y = x^2 - 14x + c$ is a parabola. Which of the following is the y-coordinate of the vertex?

(A) c

(B) 49

(C) $c - 49$

(D) $49 - c$

Reflect

Directions: Take a few minutes to recall what you've learned and what you've been practicing in this chapter. Consider the following questions, jot down your best answer for each one, and then compare your reflections to the expert responses that follow. Use your level of confidence to determine what to do next.

What features in a quadratic equation should you look for to decide whether to factor, complete the square, or apply the quadratic formula?

Which constant in the vertex form of a quadratic function gives its maximum or minimum?

Which form of a quadratic equation gives its *y*-intercept?

Which form of a quadratic equation gives its *x*-intercepts, assuming the equation has two real roots?

How do you solve a system of one linear and one quadratic equation?

Expert Responses

What features in a quadratic equation should you look for to decide whether to factor, complete the square, or apply the quadratic formula?

Get the equation into standard form. If the coefficient in front of the squared term is 1, try factoring, but don't spend longer than about 15 seconds on the attempt. If you can't get the quadratic factored quickly, look at the coefficient on the middle term: if it is even, completing the square will be an efficient approach. Finally, the quadratic formula will work for any quadratic, no matter what the coefficients are.

Which constant in the vertex form of a quadratic function gives its maximum or minimum?

The vertex form is $y = a(x - h)^2 + k$. *The constant* k *is the* y-value at the vertex, which occurs at the maximum (if the parabola opens down) or minimum (if the parabola opens up).*

Which form of a quadratic equation gives its *y*-intercept?

The standard form, $y = ax^2 + bx + c$. *The* y-intercept is given by c.

Which form of a quadratic equation gives its *x*-intercepts, assuming the equation has two real roots?

The factored form, $y = a(x - m)(x - n)$. *The x-intercepts are at* $x = m$ *and* $x = n$.

How do you solve a system of one linear and one quadratic equation?

Put the linear equation in the form $y = mx + b$ *and the quadratic in the form* $y = ax^2 + bx + c$. *Set the right sides of the equations equal to each other and solve. Alternatively, you can graph the equations and find the intersection point(s) on the graph.*

Next Steps

If you answered most questions correctly in the "How Much Have You Learned?" section, and if your responses to the Reflect questions were similar to those of the PSAT expert, then consider Quadratics an area of strength and move on to the next chapter. Come back to this topic periodically to prevent yourself from getting rusty.

If you don't yet feel confident, review those parts of this chapter that you have not yet mastered. In particular, study the table describing the different forms of quadratics in the Graphs of Quadratics lesson. Then, try the questions you missed again. As always, be sure to review the explanations closely.

Answers and Explanations

Try on Your Own

1. B

Difficulty: Easy

Category: Advanced Math

Getting to the Answer: FOIL the binomials $(x - 4)(x + 2)$: First: $(x)(x) = x^2$. Outer: $(2)(x) = 2x$. Inner: $(-4)(x) = -4x$. Last: $(2)(-4) = -8$. Combining like terms gives: $x^2 - 4x + 2x - 8 = x^2 - 2x - 8$. The correct answer is **(B)**.

2. 0

Difficulty: Easy

Category: Advanced Math

Getting to the Answer: All the question is really asking you to do is solve for the zeros and subtract them:

$$g(x) = -2x^2 + 16x - 32$$
$$0 = -2x^2 + 16x - 32$$
$$0 = -2(x^2 - 8x + 16)$$
$$0 = x^2 - 8x + 16$$
$$0 = (x - 4)(x - 4)$$

The quadratic has only one unique solution, 4, but this is called a double zero (as a 4 can substituted into either $(x - 4)$ term to make the equation equal to zero). The positive difference between the zeros of the function is 0. Enter **0**.

3. A

Difficulty: Easy

Category: Advanced Math

Getting to the Answer: First set the equation equal to 0. From there, divide by 4, then factor as usual:

$$4z^2 + 32z - 81 = -1$$
$$4z^2 + 32z - 80 = 0$$
$$4(z^2 + 8z - 20) = 0$$
$$z^2 + 8z - 20 = 0$$
$$(z + 10)(z - 2) = 0$$

Keep in mind that while z is equal to -10 or 2, the question asks only for the positive value, which is **(A)**.

4. C

Difficulty: Medium

Category: Advanced Math

Strategic Advice: None of the choices has a remainder, suggesting that you probably will not need polynomial division for this question. Try factoring the numerator and denominator to see if something will cancel out.

Getting to the Answer: Start by factoring out a 2 in the denominator to make that quadratic a bit simpler. Once there, factor to reveal an $(x - 2)$ term that will cancel out:

$$\frac{x^2 - 4x + 4}{2(x^2 + 2x - 8)} = \frac{(x - 2)(x - 2)}{2(x + 4)(x - 2)} = \frac{(x - 2)}{2(x + 4)}$$

The correct answer is **(C)**.

5. B

Difficulty: Hard

Category: Advanced Math

Getting to the Answer: Set each answer choice equal to zero and factor to determine which one meets the criteria posed in the question: the solutions must have different signs and the positive solution must have a greater absolute value than the negative solution.

(A): $4x^2 + 4x - 24 = 4(x^2 + x - 6) = 4(x - 2)(x + 3) = 0$

The solutions are 2 and -3. They have different signs, but the negative solution has the greater absolute value. Eliminate (A).

(B): $-x^2 + x + 6 = (-1)(x^2 - x - 6)$
$= (-1)(x - 3)(x + 2) = 0$

This time, the solutions are -2 and 3, so the criteria are met. **(B)** is correct.

For the record:

(C): $-x^2 - x + 6 = (-1)(x^2 + x - 6)$
$= (-1)(x + 3)(x - 2) = 0$

This has the same solutions as (A). Eliminate (C).

(D): $3x^2 - 6x = 3x(x - 2) = 0$

The solutions are 0 and 2. Eliminate (D) and confirm that **(B)** is correct.

6. B

Difficulty: Medium

Category: Advanced Math

Getting to the Answer: Replace the first expression with $a^2 - 2ab + b^2$ and add it to $2ab$:

$$(a - b)^2 + 2ab = a^2 - 2ab + b^2 + 2ab$$
$$= a^2 + b^2$$

This matches **(B)**.

7. A

Difficulty: Medium

Category: Advanced Math

Getting to the Answer: This question can be solved two ways. One is to factor each choice and solve for the solutions, and whichever does not have a solution of $x = -4$ is correct. Another way is to plug in $x = -4$ for each choice; if the equation does not equal 0, then that choice is correct. Luckily, plugging $x = -4$ into the first choice results in 64 and not 0. Choice (A) factored would be $(x - 4)^2$, so its only unique root is $x = 4$. Hence, **(A)** is correct.

8. 4

Difficulty: Hard

Category: Advanced Math

Strategic Advice: Look for classic quadratics so you can avoid reverse-FOIL and save time: $x^2 + 2xy + y^2 = (x + y)^2$.

Getting to the Answer: Recognize that $a^2 + 2ab + b^2$ is a classic quadratic that simplifies to $(a + b)^2$. Take the square root of both sides to simplify the result:

$$(a + b)^2 = c^2$$
$$a + b = \pm c$$

The question says that c is positive. Subtracting b from both sides gives $a = c - b$. Plugging in 4 for $c - b$ gives $a = 4$. Enter **4**.

9. B

Difficulty: Medium

Category: Advanced Math

Strategic Advice: Recognizing the classic quadratic $(x + y)^2 = x^2 + 2xy + y^2$ will save you time in factoring.

Getting to the Answer: In this question, the goal is to manipulate the polynomial so that it matches the factored form given. First, recognize that 3, the coefficient of x^2, can be factored out. The resulting expression is then $3(x^2 + 4x + 4)$. Notice that $\sqrt{4} = 2$ and factor the quadratic to get $3(x + 2)(x + 2) = 3(x + 2)^2$. Now the expression is in the same form as $a(x + b)^2$. Therefore, $b = 2$, so **(B)** is correct.

10. B

Difficulty: Medium

Category: Advanced Math

Getting to the Answer: Factor out the common term p^2 to get $p^2(16m^2 + 72mz + 81z^2)$. Eliminate (D), which has a different final term. Notice that $16m^2 + 72mz + 81z^2$ is a classic quadratic:

$$16m^2 + 72mz + 81z^2 = (4m + 9z)^2$$

So the original expression is equal to $p^2(4m + 9z)^2$. Thus, **(B)** is correct. Another way to solve would have been to FOIL, or distribute, each choice and see which one results in the given expression.

11. C

Difficulty: Medium

Category: Advanced Math

Strategic Advice: Equations that are equivalent have the same solutions. Thus, you are trying to transform the given equation into another form. The answer choices are written in vertex form, so use completing the square to rewrite the equation given in the question stem.

Getting to the Answer: First, subtract 17 from both sides.

$$y - 17 = x^2 + 6x$$

To complete the square on the right hand side, compute $\left(\dfrac{b}{2}\right)^2 = \left(\dfrac{6}{2}\right)^2 = 3^2 = 9$, and add the result to both sides of the equation.

$$y - 17 + 9 = x^2 + 6x + 9$$
$$y - 8 = x^2 + 6x + 9$$

Now factor the right hand side and isolate y.

$$y - 8 = (x + 3)(x + 3)$$
$$y - 8 = (x + 3)^2$$
$$y = (x + 3)^2 + 8$$

This matches **(C)**.

12. B

Difficulty: Medium

Category: Advanced Math

Getting to the Answer: Since the first term has a constant of 1, completing the square can be used right away. Begin by moving the constant term to the right side of the equation.

$$x^2 + 10x = 8$$

Next, divide the coefficient of x by 2 and square the result. Add $\left(\frac{10}{2}\right)^2 = (5)^2 = 25$ to both sides.

$$x^2 + 10x + 25 = 8 + 25$$
$$x^2 + 10x + 25 = 33$$

Finally, factor the left hand side and solve for x.

$$(x + 5)(x + 5) = 33$$
$$(x + 5)^2 = 33$$
$$x + 5 = \pm\sqrt{33}$$
$$x = \pm\sqrt{33} - 5$$

Therefore, **(B)** is correct.

13. D

Difficulty: Medium

Category: Advanced Math

Getting to the Answer: The question presents you with an equation in standard form and asks you to rewrite it. Start by moving the constant term to the right side of the equation.

$$x^2 + 4x - 4 = 0$$
$$x^2 + 4x = 4$$

Then divide the coefficient of x by 2 and square the result. Add $\left(\frac{4}{2}\right)^2 = (2)^2 = 4$ to both sides.

$$x^2 + 4x + 4 = 4 + 4$$
$$x^2 + 4x + 4 = 8$$

Factor the resulting expression.

$$(x + 2)(x + 2) = 8$$
$$(x + 2)^2 = 8$$

Therefore, **(D)** is correct.

14. A

Difficulty: Hard

Category: Advanced Math

Getting to the Answer: Start by dividing the entire equation by 4 so that the x^2 coefficient is 1.

$$x^2 + 6x + 2 = 0$$

Factoring won't work here. When something doesn't factor cleanly, consider completing the square or using the quadratic formula. The coefficient b is even, so completing the square may be the most efficient way to go. Begin by moving the constant to the right-hand side.

$$x^2 + 6x = -2$$

Then add $\left(\frac{6}{2}\right)^2 = (3)^2 = 9$ to both sides.

$$x^2 + 6x + 9 = -2 + 9$$
$$x^2 + 6x + 9 = 7$$

Finally, factor the resulting expression and solve for x.

$$(x + 3)(x + 3) = 7$$
$$(x + 3)^2 = 7$$
$$x + 3 = \pm\sqrt{7}$$
$$x = -3 \pm \sqrt{7}$$

The question asks for just one solution, so **(A)** is the correct answer.

15. C

Difficulty: Hard

Category: Advanced Math

Getting to the Answer: Recall that a quadratic equation has one solution when its discriminant is 0. Here, $a = 2$, $b = -8$, and $c = k$. Plug these numbers into the discriminant formula, set it equal to 0, and solve for k.

$$b^2 - 4ac = 0$$
$$(-8)^2 - 4(2)(k) = 0$$
$$64 - 8k = 0$$
$$64 = 8k$$
$$8 = k$$

Choice **(C)** is correct.

16. D

Difficulty: Medium

Category: Advanced Math

Getting to the Answer: When factoring isn't easy, try a different approach. Begin by setting the equation equal to 0.

$$3x^2 + 2x + 4 = 5x$$
$$3x^2 - 3x + 4 = 0$$

Now solve for x using the quadratic formula. Here, $a = 3$, $b = -3$, and $c = 4$.

$$x = \frac{-b \pm \sqrt{b^2 - 4ac}}{2a}$$
$$= \frac{-(-3) \pm \sqrt{(-3)^2 - 4(3)(4)}}{2(3)}$$
$$= \frac{3 \pm \sqrt{9 - 48}}{6}$$
$$= \frac{3 \pm \sqrt{-39}}{6}$$

Since there is a negative number under the square root, there are no real solutions. The correct answer is **(D)**.

17. A

Difficulty: Hard

Category: Advanced Math

Strategic Advice: The roots of an equation are the same as its solutions. The equation doesn't factor, so you'll have to use a different method. The equation is already written in the form $y = ax^2 + bx + c$ and the coefficients are fairly small, so using the quadratic formula is a good option.

Getting to the Answer: In this equation, $a = 1$, $b = 8$, and $c = -3$. Plug these values into the quadratic formula and simplify.

$$x = \frac{-b \pm \sqrt{b^2 - 4ac}}{2a}$$
$$= \frac{-(8) \pm \sqrt{(8)^2 - 4(1)(-3)}}{2(1)}$$
$$= \frac{-8 \pm \sqrt{64 + 12}}{2}$$
$$= \frac{-8 \pm \sqrt{76}}{2}$$

This is not one of the answer choices, which means that you'll need to simplify the radical. Before you do, you can eliminate (C) and (D) because the non-radical part of the solutions is $\frac{-8}{2} = -4$, not 4. To simplify the radical, look for a perfect square that divides into 76.

$$x = \frac{-8 \pm \sqrt{76}}{2}$$
$$= \frac{-8 \pm \sqrt{4}\sqrt{19}}{2}$$
$$= \frac{-8 \pm 2\sqrt{19}}{2}$$
$$= \frac{2(-4 \pm \sqrt{19})}{2}$$
$$= -4 \pm \sqrt{19}$$

This matches **(A)**.

18. B

Difficulty: Medium

Category: Advanced Math

Getting to the Answer: The discriminant is the part of the quadratic formula that is underneath the square root: $b^2 - 4ac$. When the discriminant is positive, there are two real solutions.

Plug the coefficients in each answer choices into the discriminant formula and simplify. The correct answer will be positive.

(A): $a = 2$, $b = 4$, $c = 2$. The discriminant is $4^2 - 4(2)(2) = 16 - 16 = 0$, which is not positive. Eliminate (A).

(B): $a = 5$, $b = 5$, $c = -5$. The discriminant is $5^2 - (4)(5)(-5) = 25 + 100 = 125$. This is a positive number, so **(B)** has two real solutions and is correct.

On test day, you would stop here. But for the record, the discriminant of (C) is -75 and the discriminant of (D) is 0.

19. A

Difficulty: Medium

Category: Advanced Math

Getting to the Answer: Since the coefficient of the x^2 term is 8 and nothing can be factored out, using the quadratic formula is a good idea. In this equation, $a = 8$, $b = 4$, and $c = -1$.

$$x = \frac{-b \pm \sqrt{b^2 - 4ac}}{2a}$$
$$= \frac{-4 \pm \sqrt{4^2 - 4(8)(-1)}}{2(8)}$$
$$= \frac{-4 \pm \sqrt{48}}{16}$$
$$= \frac{-4 \pm \sqrt{16}\sqrt{3}}{16}$$
$$= \frac{-4 \pm 4\sqrt{3}}{16}$$
$$= \frac{4(-1 \pm \sqrt{3})}{16}$$
$$= \frac{-1 \pm \sqrt{3}}{4}$$

This matches **(A)**.

20. D

Difficulty: Medium

Category: Advanced Math

Getting to the Answer: Quadratic equations can be written in several forms, each of which reveals something important about the graph. The factored form makes it easy to calculate the solutions of the equation, which correspond to the x-intercepts on the graph. Choice **(D)** is the only equation written in factored form and is therefore correct. You can set each factor equal to 0 to find that $x = -\frac{4}{3}$ and $x = 2$, which agrees with the graph. Note that each unit on the graph is 0.5.

21. B

Difficulty: Medium

Category: Advanced Math

Getting to the Answer: All of the answer choices are in vertex form: $y = a(x - h)^2 + k$. The parabola opens downward, so the a term must be negative. Unfortunately, all of the choices have a negative a term, so you cannot eliminate any of them.

Next, examine the vertex. When a quadratic is in vertex form, $f(x) = a(x - h)^2 + k$, the vertex is (h, k). According to the graph, the vertex is (3, 2). Only (A) and (B) match this. To decide between them, plug in a point from the graph. To simplify your calculation, try (2, 0). Choice (A) is shown below.

$$f(x) = -(x - 3)^2 + 2$$
$$0 = -(2 - 3)^2 + 2$$
$$0 = -(-1)^2 + 2$$
$$0 = -1 + 2$$
$$0 = 1$$

Since this is a false statement, (A) cannot be correct. On test day, you would stop here and pick **(B)**. But for the record, here is why **(B)** is correct.

$$f(x) = -2(x - 3)^2 + 2$$
$$0 = -2(2 - 3)^2 + 2$$
$$0 = -2(-1)^2 + 2$$
$$0 = -2(1) + 2$$
$$0 = -2 + 2$$
$$0 = 0$$

22. B

Difficulty: Medium

Category: Advanced Math

Getting to the Answer: According to the graph, one x-intercept is to the left of the y-axis and the other is to the right. This tells you that one x-intercept has a positive value and the other has a negative value. You can immediately eliminate choices (A) and (C) because both factors have the same sign. To choose between (B) and (D), find the x-intercepts by setting each factor equal to 0 and solving for x. In choice (B), the x-intercepts are 7 and -3. In choice (D), the x-intercepts are 1 and -10. Choice **(B)** is correct because the x-intercepts are 10 units apart $(3 - (-7) = 10)$, while the x-intercepts in choice (D) are 11 units apart $(1 - (-10) = 11)$.

23. B

Difficulty: Medium

Category: Advanced Math

Strategic Advice: Recall that *increasing* means rising from left to right, while *decreasing* means falling from left to right. *Zero* is another way of saying x-intercept. Compare each statement to the graph to determine whether it is true, eliminating as you go. Remember that you are looking for the statement that is false.

Getting to the Answer: The parabola opens downward, so a must be negative. Eliminate (A). When a quadratic equation is written in standard form ($y = ax^2 + bx + c$), c is the y-intercept of the parabola. According to the graph, the y-intercept is above the x-axis and is therefore positive. Therefore, the statement in **(B)** is false, which means that it is the correct answer.

For the record, (C) is true because the graph rises from left to right until you get to $x = 3$, at which point it begins to fall. Choice (D) is true because the graph does indeed intersect the x-axis at -2 and 8.

24. A

Difficulty: Hard

Category: Advanced Math

Getting to the Answer: Begin by considering the shape of the parabola formed by the path of the ball. Because the ball starts and ends at ground level ($y = 0$) and travels a horizontal distance of 150 feet ($x = 150$), it must have x-intercepts of $(0, 0)$ and $(150, 0)$. The question also tells you that it reaches a maximum height of 45 feet ($y = 45$). Because the vertex is halfway between the two x-intercepts, the vertex must be at $(75, 45)$.

The vertex is above the x-intercepts, so this is a downward opening parabola. You can immediately eliminate choices (C) and (D), which have positive a values. To decide between (A) and (B), try plugging in the coordinates of the vertex or an x-intercept to see which equation holds true. The calculations for $(150, 0)$ are shown below.

(A) $y = -0.008x^2 + 1.2x$

$0 = -0.008\,(150)^2 + 1.2(150)$

$0 = -0.008(22{,}500) + 180$

$0 = -180 + 180$

$0 = 0$

(B) $y = -0.008x^2 - 150x$

$0 = -0.008\,(150)^2 - 150(150)$

$0 = -0.008(22{,}500) - 22500$

$0 = -180 - 22{,}500$

$0 = -22{,}680$

Thus, **(A)** is correct.

25. B

Difficulty: Medium

Category: Advanced Math

Getting to the Answer: Even though one of the equations in this system is not linear, you can still solve the system using substitution. You know that y is equal to $3x$, so substitute $3x$ for y in the second equation. Don't forget that when you square $3x$, you must square both the coefficient and the variable:

$$x^2 - y^2 = -288$$
$$x^2 - (3x)^2 = -288$$
$$x^2 - 9x^2 = -288$$
$$-8x^2 = -288$$
$$x^2 = 36$$

The question asks for the value of x^2, not x, so there is no need to take the square root of 36 to find the value of x. Choice **(B)** is correct.

26. D

Difficulty: Hard

Category: Advanced Math

Strategic Advice: Solving each system would be extremely time-consuming. Backsolving will be faster.

Getting to the Answer: Substitute $x = -8$, the x-value at one of the points of intersection, into each equation. The correct system will have both equations equaling the same number, which is the y-value at that point of intersection. Examine each answer choice:

(A): $y = -x - 1 = -(-8) - 1 = 8 - 1 = 7$

$y = (x - 8)^2 - 3 = (-8 - 8)^2 - 3$

$= (-16)^2 - 3 = 256 - 3 = 253$

$7 \neq 253$, so eliminate (A).

(B): $y = x + 8 = -8 + 8 = 0$

$y = (x + 3)^2 - 8 = (-8 + 3)^2 - 8$

$= (-5)^2 - 8 = 25 - 8 = 17$

$0 \neq 17$, so eliminate (B).

(C): $y = x + 8 = -8 + 8 = 0$

$y = (x + 3)^2 - 2 = (-8 + 3)^2 - 2$

$= (-5)^2 - 2 = 25 - 2 = 23$

$0 \neq 23$, so eliminate (C).

(D): $y = -x - 1 = -(-8) - 1 = 8 - 1 = 7$

$y = (x + 5)^2 - 2 = (-8 + 5)^2 - 2$

$\quad = (-3)^2 - 2 = 9 - 2 = 7$

$7 = 7$, so the two equations in (D) intersect at the point $(-8, 7)$. Thus, **(D)** is correct.

27. D

Difficulty: Hard

Category: Advanced Math

Strategic Advice: All of the choices present a system of equations that includes a parabola and a line. For a system of equations to have only one solution, the graphs must have only one point of intersection.

Getting to the Answer: Notice that all of the choices have the same parabola with a vertex of $(-3, -5)$. Choices (B) and (D) have horizontal lines, which are easy to check. Choice (B) has a horizontal line at $y = 5$, but with the parabola facing downward, the parabola will never intersect it. Choice (D) has a horizontal line at $y = -5$, which is the location of the parabola's vertex. This means that the line is tangent to the parabola and will touch it only once to create only one solution. Thus, **(D)** is correct. For the record, (A) has two points of intersection and (C) has none.

28. C

Difficulty: Easy

Category: Advanced Math

Getting to the Answer: You can graph the two functions simultaneously and observe that they intersect each other twice. You could also do a little algebraic investigating by using your calculator to tell you the values of the vertex (the minimum) and the points of intersection.

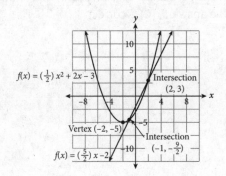

To solve algebraically, set the two equations equal to each other:

$$\frac{5}{2}x - 2 = \frac{1}{2}x^2 + 2x - 3$$

$$0 = \frac{1}{2}x^2 - \frac{1}{2}x - 1$$

$$0 = \frac{1}{2}(x^2 - x - 2)$$

$$0 = x^2 - x - 2$$

$$0 = (x + 1)(x - 2)$$

You'll see that the functions intersect each other at two locations, $x = -1$ and $x = 2$. You now need to determine the location of the parabola's vertex to compare. Using the formula given for the x-coordinate of the vertex (h), you can do this easily:

$$h = \frac{-b}{2a} = \frac{-2}{2\left(\frac{1}{2}\right)} = \frac{-2}{1} = -2$$

You need not calculate the y-coordinate (k) because you already have the answer. Both of the points of intersection, -1 and 2, occur to the right of the vertex. The answer is **(C)**.

On Test Day

29. B

Difficulty: Medium

Category: Advanced Math

Getting to the Answer: Set $f(x)$ equal to $g(x)$: $2x^2 - 5 = 6x^2 - 7$. Isolate the x^2 terms on one side to get $2 = 4x^2$, so $x^2 = \frac{1}{2}$. Take the square root of both sides to see that $x = \pm\sqrt{\frac{1}{2}} = \pm\frac{1}{\sqrt{2}}$, which means that the two intersections of the functions occur when $x = -\frac{1}{\sqrt{2}}$ and $x = \frac{1}{\sqrt{2}}$. None of the choices match, so multiply the numerator and denominator by $\sqrt{2}$ to convert these to $\pm\frac{\sqrt{2}}{2}$. From the graph, you can see that these are the values of $\pm z$, so $z = \frac{\sqrt{2}}{2}$. **(B)** is correct.

Alternatively, you could plug in the coordinates of one of the intersections into either function. Using $f(x)$, the y-coordinate is -4 and the x-coordinate is z. So, $-4 = 2z^2 - 5$. The math works out exactly the same as for the first approach: $z^2 = \frac{1}{2}$, so $z = \pm\frac{\sqrt{2}}{2}$, and, from the graph, you can determine that $z = \frac{\sqrt{2}}{2}$. Again, **(B)** is correct.

Note that you could also graph the functions on the calculator to identify the points of intersection as approximately $(-0.707, -4)$ and $(0.707, -4)$. You may or may not recognize 0.707 as $\frac{\sqrt{2}}{2}$, but by process of elimination, you know that 0.707 is not $\frac{1}{2}$, 0.8, or 1.2, which leaves $\frac{\sqrt{2}}{2}$.

How Much Have You Learned?

1. B

Difficulty: Medium

Category: Advanced Math

Getting to the Answer: The quantity $b^2 - 4ac$ is the part of the quadratic formula that is underneath the square root sign. Taking the square root of a negative quantity will produce an imaginary number. Therefore, if $b^2 - 4ac$ is negative, the quadratic will have no real solutions.

Graphically, a solution is the same as an x-intercept. There are no solutions for **(B)** because the parabola never intersects or touches the x-axis.

2. 5

Difficulty: Easy

Category: Advanced Math

Getting to the Answer: Factor the given quadratic by finding factors of 20 that add to get the middle constant -9. Notice that -4 and -5 will multiply to get 20 and add to get -9. So $x^2 - 9x + 20 = (x - 4)(x - 5)$. Set both equal to 0 and solve for x to get $x = 4$ and $x = 5$. Remember that the question asks for m, where $m > n$. In other words, it wants the larger of the two roots. Enter **5**.

3. D

Difficulty: Medium

Category: Advanced Math

Getting to the Answer: Look for an equation among the choices that has a maximum value that is less than the maximum height of Shawna's toss. To determine the peak height of Shawna's throw, convert the given equation to vertex form, $y = a(x - h)^2 + k$, where the maximum value is given by k. Notice that the polynomial within the parentheses factors to $(t - 2)^2$. Thus, you can restate the given equation as $-5(t - 2)^2 + 22$. So the

vertex of Shawna's throw is $(2, 22)$, which means that the maximum height was 22 meters.

Conveniently, the answer choices are all stated in vertex form. The only one with the k term less than 22 is **(D)**, which makes it the correct choice.

4. C

Difficulty: Medium

Category: Advanced Math

Getting to the Answer: When a quadratic equation is written in vertex form, $y = a(x - h)^2 + k$, the minimum value (or the maximum value if $a < 0$) is given by k, and the axis of symmetry is given by the equation $x = h$. The question states that the minimum of the parabola is -3, so look for an equation where $k = -3$. You can eliminate choices (A) and (B) because $k = 2$ in both equations. The question also states that the axis of symmetry is $x = 2$, so h must be 2. Be careful: this can be tricky. The equation in choice (D) is not correct because the vertex form of a parabola is written as $(x - h)$ not $(x + h)$. In other words, $(x + 2)$ should be interpreted as $(x - (-2))$, with axis of symmetry at $x = -2$. This means **(C)** is correct.

5. C

Difficulty: Medium

Category: Advanced Math

Getting to the Answer: Rearrange the equation into the standard quadratic form by moving everything to the left side of the equal sign: $2x^2 - 14x + 24 = 0$. Next, divide the equation by 2 to make factoring easier: $x^2 - 7x + 12 = 0$. Now, use reverse FOIL to determine the factors. You need factors of 12 that sum to -7. Those are -3 and -4, so your equation factors into $(x - 3)(x - 4) = 0$. That means that the solutions to the equation are $x = 3$ and $x = 4$. Since only one of these is among the answers, **(C)** is correct.

6. C

Difficulty: Hard

Category: Advanced Math

Getting to the Answer: First, divide both sides by 4, so that $4x^2 - 8x - 64 = 0$ becomes $x^2 - 2x - 16 = 0$. This cannot be solved by factoring, so use the completing the square method:

$$x^2 - 2x - 16 = 0$$
$$x^2 - 2x + \_\_ = 16 + \_\_$$
$$\left(\frac{b}{2}\right)^2 = \left(\frac{-2}{2}\right)^2 = 1$$
$$x^2 - 2x + 1 = 16 + 1$$
$$(x - 1)^2 = 17$$

Therefore, **(C)** is correct.

7. A

Difficulty: Medium

Category: Advanced Math

Getting to the Answer: Notice that this quadratic is a difference of squares, so use the pattern $a^2 - b^2 = (a + b)(a - b)$. Set a^2 equal to $64x^2$ and take the square root of both sides to find that $a = 8x$. Do the same thing with b^2 and $81y^2$ to find that $b = 9y$. Fill in $(a + b)(a - b)$ with the values you found for a and b to get $(8x + 9y)(8x - 9y)$. Therefore, **(A)** is correct.

8. D

Difficulty: Hard

Category: Advanced Math

Strategic Advice: The discriminant is the part of the quadratic formula that determines whether a quadratic equation has 1 or 2 distinct real solutions or only imaginary solutions. Note that a quadratic will have only one distinct real solution when the discriminant equals 0.

Getting to the Answer: Convert the equations into standard quadratic form, if necessary, and calculate the discriminant for each choice to see which one equals 0:

(A) converts into $4x^2 - 3x + 8 = 0$. The discriminant is $(-3)^2 - 4(4)(8) = 9 - 128 = -119$. This is not equal to 0, so eliminate (A).

(B) converts into $x^2 + 10x - 2 = 0$. The discriminant is $(10)^2 - 4(1)(-2) = 100 + 8 = 108$. Eliminate (B).

(C) is already in the proper form. The discriminant is $(2)^2 - 4(7)(-5) = 4 + 140 = 144$. Eliminate (C).

Only **(D)** is left, so it is correct. For the record, the discriminant for **(D)** does in fact equal 0. Divide through by the common factor of 3 to get $x^2 - 2x + 1 = 0$, so the discriminant is $(-2)^2 - 4(1)(1) = 0$.

9. 9

Difficulty: Hard

Category: Advanced Math

Getting to the Answer: Rearrange both equations to isolate y in terms of x:

$$y - 3x = x^2 - 10 \rightarrow y = x^2 + 3x - 10$$
$$y - 4 = -2x \rightarrow y = -2x + 4$$

Set both equations equal to each other to find where they intersect. Combine like terms on the left side of the equation:

$$x^2 + 3x - 10 = -2x + 4$$
$$x^2 + 5x - 14 = 0$$

This quadratic equation can be solved by factoring, since two factors of -14, 7 and -2, add to 5. Hence, $(x + 7)(x - 2) = 0$ and $x = -7$ and $x = 2$. The question asks for the absolute value of the difference, so subtract the roots and evaluate the absolute value:

$$|2 - (-7)| = 9$$

Enter **9**.

Alternatively, to find the points of intersection, you could graph the equations.

10. C

Difficulty: Hard

Category: Advanced Math

Strategic Advice: Vertex form is a good option when questions ask for coordinates of the vertex. One of the best methods to convert quadratic equations into vertex form is completing the square.

Getting to the Answer: The x^2 term has a coefficient of 1, so no manipulation of the equation is necessary before completing the square. Move the constant term to the right side of the equation before dividing the x term's coefficient by 2 and squaring:

$$x^2 - 14x + c = 0$$
$$x^2 - 14x + \_\_ = -c + \_\_$$
$$\left(\frac{b}{2}\right)^2 = \left(\frac{-14}{2}\right)^2 = (-7)^2 = 49$$
$$x^2 - 14x + 49 = -c + 49$$
$$(x - 7)^2 = -c + 49$$
$$(x - 7)^2 + c - 49 = 0$$

Now the equation $y = (x - 7)^2 + c - 49$ is in vertex form, $y = a(x - h)^2 + k$, where the vertex is (h, k). The y-coordinate, or k, of the vertex is $c - 49$. **(C)** is correct.

GEOMETRY AND TRIGONOMETRY

[CHAPTER 11]

GEOMETRY AND TRIGONOMETRY

LEARNING OBJECTIVES

After completing this chapter, you will be able to:

- Apply the properties of lines and angles to solve geometry questions
- Use area calculations to solve questions
- Apply scale factors to solve geometry questions
- Identify similar triangles and apply their properties
- Calculate the length of one side of a right triangle given the lengths of the other two sides
- Recognize the most common Pythagorean triples
- Calculate trigonometric ratios from side lengths of right triangles
- Calculate side lengths of right triangles using trigonometric ratios
- Describe the relationship between the sine and cosine of complementary angles

How Much Do You Know?

Directions

Try the questions that follow. Show your work so that you can compare your solutions to the ones found in the "Check Your Work" section immediately after this question set. If you answered the question(s) on a specific topic correctly, and if your scratchwork looks like ours, you may be able to move quickly through the lesson covering that topic. If you answered incorrectly or used a different approach, you may want to take your time on that lesson.

Make use of the formula sheet below as needed; you'll have these same formulas available when you take the real PSAT.

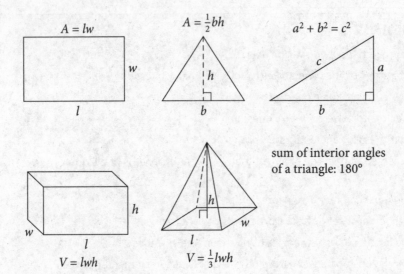

1

A rectangular patio has a width of n feet. If the length of the patio is 9 feet more than the width, what is the perimeter of the patio, in feet, in terms of n?

(A) $n + 9$

(B) $2n + 18$

(C) $4n + 9$

(D) $4n + 18$

2

The sides of a triangle are in the ratio of 15:18:21. A second triangle, similar to the first, has a longest side of length 35. What is the length of the shortest side of the second triangle?

(A) 9

(B) 20

(C) 25

(D) 30

3

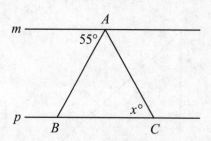

In the figure shown, m and p are parallel. Point A lies on m, and points B and C lie on p. If $AB = AC$, what is x?

(A) 45

(B) 55

(C) 70

(D) 125

4

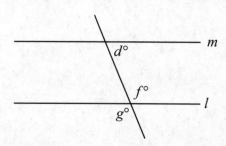

In the figure, l and m are parallel lines cut by a transversal and the measure of $\angle d$ is 68°. What is the value of $f + g$?

5

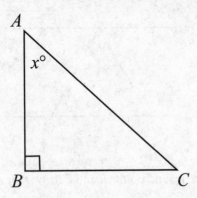

Triangle *ABC* has a hypotenuse length 15, and cos *x* = 0.6. What is the length of side *AB*?

6

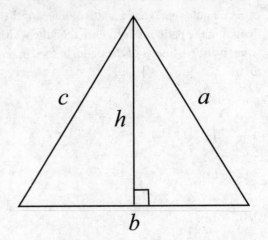

The isosceles triangle shown has an area of 55 square inches and a height, *h*, of 11 inches. If *a* = *c*, which of the following is closest to the value of *c*?

(A) 8.3

(B) 12.1

(C) 12.8

(D) 15.1

Check Your Work

1.   D

Difficulty: Easy

Category: Geometry and Trigonometry

Getting to the Answer: The perimeter of a rectangle is $2l + 2w$, where l is the length and w is the width. Since the length of the patio is 9 feet longer than the width, and the width is n feet, the length, l, is $n + 9$. Therefore, the perimeter of the patio is $2(n + 9) + 2n = 2n + 18 + 2n = 4n + 18$ feet. **(D)** is correct.

2.   C

Difficulty: Medium

Category: Geometry and Trigonometry

Getting to the Answer: When triangles are similar, the ratio of one triangle's side lengths to the other's will be the same for all three sides. The question effectively provides this ratio by providing the length of the largest side of the second triangle, which you can relate to the largest side of the first triangle: $\frac{35}{21}$. Use this information to set up a proportion, and then solve for the shortest side of the second triangle:

$$\frac{35}{21} = \frac{x}{15}$$
$$525 = 21x$$
$$25 = x$$

Choice **(C)** is correct.

3.   B

Difficulty: Medium

Category: Geometry and Trigonometry

Getting to the Answer: The question presents a pair of parallel lines cut by two transversals. The two transversals also form two sides of a triangle. Because the two transversals are equal, they form an isosceles triangle. On transversal AB, $\angle ABC$ and 55° are alternate interior angles, which makes them equal. Because base angles of an isosceles triangle have equal measures, $x°$ is also 55°. Choice **(B)** is correct.

4.   224

Difficulty: Medium

Category: Geometry and Trigonometry

Getting to the Answer: When two parallel lines are cut by a transversal, half of the angles will be acute and half will be obtuse. Each acute angle will have the same measure as every other acute angle. The same is true of every obtuse angle. Furthermore, the acute angles will be supplementary to the obtuse angles. Based on the information provided, d is an acute angle measuring 68°. Based on the figure, both f and g are obtuse angles, so d must be supplementary to both f and g. Therefore, the measure of f and g will each be $180° - 68° = 112°$. Thus, $f + g = 112 + 112 = 224$. Enter **224**.

5. 9

Difficulty: Medium

Category: Geometry and Trigonometry

Strategic Advice: When answering trigonometry questions, use the mnemonic "SOH CAH TOA" to recall the trigonometric ratios.

Getting to the Answer: You're given that the hypotenuse length of the right triangle is 15, and that $\cos x = 0.6$. Side AB is the side adjacent to x, and $\text{cosine} = \dfrac{\text{adjacent}}{\text{hypotenuse}}$. Therefore, you can use the given cosine value to solve for the adjacent side:

$$\cos x = \frac{\text{adj}}{\text{hyp}}$$
$$0.6 = \frac{AB}{15}$$
$$9 = AB$$

Enter **9**.

6. B

Difficulty: Hard

Category: Geometry and Trigonometry

Getting to the Answer: The question provides the height and area of the isosceles triangle. You can use this information and the triangle area formula to solve for the base:

$$\text{area} = \frac{1}{2}\text{base} \times \text{height}$$
$$55 = \frac{1}{2}\text{base} \times 11$$
$$110 = \text{base} \times 11$$
$$10 = \text{base}$$

Since the triangle is isosceles, and $a = c$, the two right triangles formed by the altitude have equal dimensions. That means the short leg of each is one-half of 10, or 5. Now you can use the Pythagorean theorem to find c:

$$a^2 + b^2 = c^2$$
$$5^2 + 11^2 = c^2$$
$$25 + 121 = c^2$$
$$146 = c^2$$
$$\sqrt{146} = c$$

Plug this value into the calculator; it is about 12.08, so **(B)** is correct.

Math

Lines and Angles

LEARNING OBJECTIVE

After this lesson, you will be able to:

- Apply the properties of lines and angles to solve geometry questions

To answer a question like this:

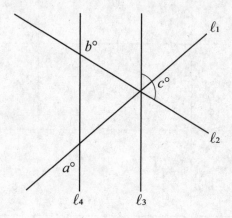

In the figure shown, lines l_3 and l_4 are parallel, and line l_1 bisects angle c. If $b = 110$, what is the value of a?

(A) 45

(B) 55

(C) 65

(D) 90

You need to know this:

A line is a one-dimensional geometrical abstraction—infinitely long with no width. Two points determine a straight line; given any two points, there is exactly one straight line that passes through them both.

A line segment is a section of a straight line of finite length with two endpoints.

An angle is formed by two lines or line segments intersecting at a point. The point of intersection is called the vertex of the angle. Angles are measured in degrees (°) or radians.

Familiarity with angle types will often unlock information that is not explicitly given in a question. This makes getting to the answer much easier for even the toughest geometry questions. First, take a look at the types of angles you should be able to recognize.

Angle Type	Angle Measurement	Example
Acute	Less than $90°$	
Right	$90°$	
Obtuse	Between $90°$ and $180°$	
Straight	$180°$	

Two angles are supplementary if together they make up a straight angle: i.e., if the sum of their measures is $180°$. In the following figure, c and d are supplementary.

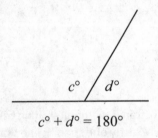

$$c° + d° = 180°$$

Two angles are complementary if together they make up a right angle: i.e., if the sum of their measures is $90°$. In the following figure, a and b are complementary.

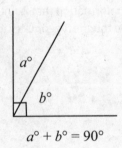

$$a° + b° = 90°$$

Note: angle pairs do not need to be adjacent to be supplementary or complementary.

Intersecting lines create angles with special relationships. When two lines intersect, adjacent angles are supplementary, and vertical angles (two angles opposite a vertex) are equal, or congruent. Take a look at the following figure for an example.

The angles marked $a°$ and $b°$ are supplementary; therefore, $a + b = 180$. The angle marked $a°$ is vertical (and thus equal) to the one marked $60°$, so $a = 60$. With this new information, you can find b: $a + b = 60 + b = 180$, so $b = 120$.

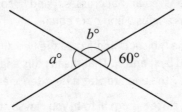

Two lines are parallel if they lie in the same plane and never intersect each other regardless of how far they are extended. If line 1 is parallel to line 2, it is written as $1 \parallel 2$.

When two parallel lines are intersected by another line (called a transversal), all acute angles are equal, and all obtuse angles are equal. Additionally, corresponding angles are angles that are in the same position but on different parallel lines/transversal intersections; they are also equal.

Alternate interior angles and alternate exterior angles are also equal. Alternate interior angles are angles that are positioned between the two parallel lines on opposite sides of the transversal, whereas alternate exterior angles are positioned on the outside of the parallel lines on opposite sides of the transversal. Consider the following figure:

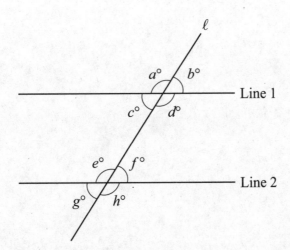

- Line 1 and Line 2 are parallel and cut by transversal ℓ.
- Angles a, d, e, and h are obtuse and equal.
- Angles b, c, f, and g are acute and equal.
- Angle pairs (b and f), (c and g), (a and e), and (d and h) are corresponding angles.
- Angle pairs (a and h) and (b and g) are alternate exterior angles.
- Angle pairs (d and e) and (c and f) are alternate interior angles.

You need to do this:

- Determine which angles in a figure are equal and which are supplementary or complementary.
- Find a missing angle by identifying its relationship to known angles in a figure.

Explanation:

Lines l_3 and l_4 are parallel. Line l_2 is a transversal that crosses l_3 and l_4, so the obtuse angles formed with the parallel lines must be equal. That means angles b and c are equal.

Additionally, the question states that line l_1 bisects angle c, so the two angles formed by the division of angle c are equal. One of those angles is formed by l_1 and l_3. That means this angle is equal to angle a; since l_1 is another transversal that crosses l_3 and l_4, the two are alternate exterior angles.

The question specifies that $b = 110$, so, since c is equal to b, you can say that $c = 110$. You've already established that a is half the value of c, so that means $a = 55$.

Choice **(B)** is correct.

Try on Your Own

Directions

Take as much time as you need on these questions. Work carefully and methodically. There will be an opportunity for timed practice later in the book.

1

HINT: In a pair of supplementary angles, 180 minus one angle will always equal the other angle. How can you use this fact in Q1?

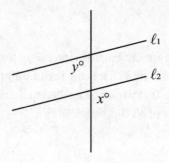

In the figure shown, l_1 and l_2 are parallel. If $y = 67$, what is the value of x?

Ⓐ 23

Ⓑ 67

Ⓒ 113

Ⓓ 123

2

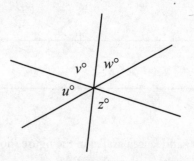

The figure shows three lines that meet at a point. Given that $z = 55$, what is the value of $u + w$?

3

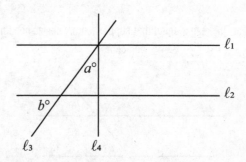

In the figure shown, line l_1 is parallel to line l_2, and line l_4 is perpendicular to line l_1. If $a = 40$, what is the value of b?

Ⓐ 30

Ⓑ 40

Ⓒ 50

Ⓓ 140

4

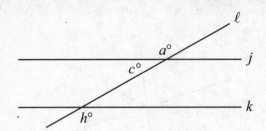

Lines j and k are parallel in the figure shown. If $h = 5c$, what is the value of $2a$?

(A) 30

(B) 60

(C) 150

(D) 300

5

HINT: For Q5, keep in mind that supplementary angles need not be adjacent.

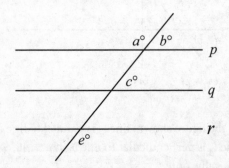

In the figure shown, lines p, q, and r are all parallel. If $c = 50$, what is the value of $a + e$?

6

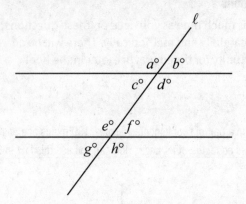

In the figure shown, line l intersects two parallel lines as shown. What is the least number of angle measures that would be needed to determine the measures of all eight angles?

(A) 1

(B) 2

(C) 4

(D) 8

Area, Perimeter, and Scale

LEARNING OBJECTIVES

After this lesson, you will be able to:

- Use area calculations to solve questions
- Apply scale factors to solve geometry questions

To answer a question like this:

A square has sides of length $x + 3$. If it had sides $\frac{1}{2}$ that length, its area would be 16. What is the value of x?

You need to know this:

The **perimeter** of a shape is the length of the shape's border. For any shape, you can find the perimeter by adding up the length of all of its sides. However, for some shapes, there are shortcuts. For an equilateral triangle, square, or another polygon with equal side lengths, you can simply multiply the side length by the number of sides. For a rectangle, the perimeter is $2(l + w)$, where l and w are the rectangle's length and width.

The **area** of a shape is the amount of space it occupies. Different shapes have different formulas for calculating their area:

- The area of a square is s^2, where s is the side length.

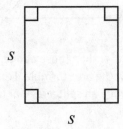

- The area of a parallelogram is $b \times h$, where b is one side of the parallelogram and h is a line perpendicular to that side and extending to its opposite side.

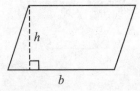

- The area of a rectangle is $l \times w$, where l and w are the rectangle's length and width, respectively.

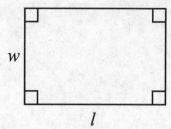

- The area of a triangle is $\frac{1}{2}bh$, where b is the base of the triangle (one of its sides) and h is its height, a line perpendicular to the base extending to the opposite vertex. Note that the height can only be a side of the triangle in a right triangle.

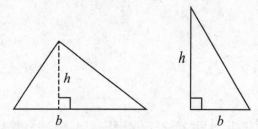

- The area of a trapezoid is $\frac{1}{2}(b_1 + b_2)h$, where b_1 and b_2 are the two parallel sides of the trapezoid and h is the height, a line connecting the two bases and perpendicular to both.

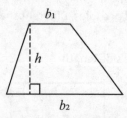

If you're asked to find the area of a polygon other than those above, it's likely that the most efficient way is to break it up into shapes for which you do know the area formula. For instance, you may not know how to calculate the area of a hexagon directly, but you can split a regular hexagon into six equilateral triangles, which you can then use the triangle area formula on.

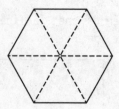

Or, consider this figure:

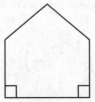

There's no area formula for this shape, but you may still see a question on the PSAT asking you to find the area of such a shape. Notice that it can be split into a rectangle and a triangle:

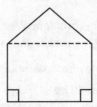

On test day, you'd be given enough information to determine the length and width of the rectangle and the base and height of the triangle, which would give you all you need to determine the area of the whole shape.

Sometimes, a PSAT question will ask you to consider what effect scaling up the size of a polygon's sides has on either the perimeter or area. Take a square that has side lengths of 1. The perimeter would be $4(1) = 4$. Then, double the side lengths to 2. The new perimeter would be $4(2) = 8$, which is also twice the original perimeter. This relationship holds for any polygon; if you multiply the side lengths by a certain number, the perimeter of the new shape is equal to the original perimeter multiplied by that same number.

Doubling the side lengths of a polygon, however, does not simply double the area. Consider again a square with side length 1; it has an area of $(1)^2 = 1$. Doubling the length of the sides yields a square with side length 2 and area $(2)^2 = 4$. This new area is 4 (or 2^2) times as big as the original. Similarly, tripling the side length results in a square with an area of $(3)^2 = 9$, which is 9 (or 3^2) times as big as the original. Thus, if you multiply the side lengths of a polygon by a number n, the area of the new polygon will be n^2 times bigger than the original.

You need to do this:

- Determine whether you can use a formula to find the area of the shape or if you have to split up the shape into smaller component shapes.
- Determine the effect of scaling up the sides of a shape on its perimeter and area.

Explanation:

You can use the formula for the area of a square, $A = s^2$ to solve for x. After the change to the side length, the new area is 16 and each side length is then $\frac{x+3}{2}$.

$$16 = \left(\frac{x+3}{2}\right)^2$$
$$4 = \frac{x+3}{2}$$
$$8 = x + 3$$
$$5 = x$$

Enter **5**.

Alternatively, you can use scale factor to solve this problem. When the side lengths of a shape are multiplied by a number, you can find the new area by multiplying the original area by the square of that number. Since the sides of this square are being multiplied by $\frac{1}{2}$, the new area would be $\left(\frac{1}{2}\right)^2 = \frac{1}{4}$ of the original area. Since the new area is 16, the original area of the square would be 64. Since the area of a square is its side length squared, you can set up the equation $(x+3)^2 = 64$. Because $x + 3$ represents the side length of a square, it must be positive; therefore, $x + 3 = 8$ and $x = 5$. Enter **5**.

Try on Your Own

Directions

Take as much time as you need on these questions. Work carefully and methodically. There will be an opportunity for timed practice later in the book.

7

A rectangular frame is f inches long. If the width of the frame is 6 inches shorter than the length, what is the perimeter of the frame, in inches, in terms of f?

- Ⓐ $2f - 6$

- Ⓑ $4f - 6$

- Ⓒ $4f - 12$

- Ⓓ $f^2 - 6f$

8

The height of a door is 4 feet greater than its width. If the area of the door is 21 square feet, what is the height of the door, in feet?

9

The area of a rectangle is x square inches. If both the length and width of the rectangle are tripled, what is the area of the new rectangle in terms of x?

- Ⓐ $3x$

- Ⓑ $9x$

- Ⓒ $3x^2$

- Ⓓ $9x^2$

10

HINT: The perimeter of an equilateral triangle is $3s$. How can you use this fact in Q10?

Triangle A and Triangle B are equilateral triangles. If the length of each side of Triangle B is twice the length of each side of Triangle A, how many times greater is the perimeter of Triangle B than the perimeter of Triangle A?

- Ⓐ 2

- Ⓑ 3

- Ⓒ 6

- Ⓓ 9

11

HINT: For Q11, a decrease by x percent can be written as $1 - \frac{x}{100}$.

The height of a triangle is increased by 20 percent, and its base is decreased by x percent. If the area of the triangle decreased by 10 percent, what is the value of x?

- Ⓐ 10

- Ⓑ 25

- Ⓒ 35

- Ⓓ 75

12

What is the combined area of a square with a length of 5 and a triangle with the same length for its base and a height of 6?

(A) 21

(B) 31

(C) 40

(D) 45

Similar Triangles

LEARNING OBJECTIVE

After this lesson, you will be able to:

- Identify similar triangles and apply their properties

To answer a question like this:

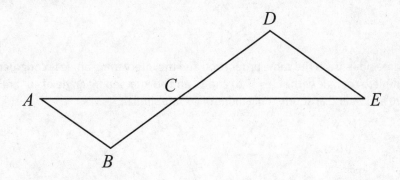

Note: Figure not drawn to scale.

In the figure shown, segments AE and BD intersect at point C, and segment DE is parallel to segment AB. If $AB = 2$, $AC = 5$, and $DE = 8$, what is the measure of EC?

You need to know this:

The corresponding angles and side lengths of **congruent triangles** are equal. **Similar triangles** have the same angle measurements and proportional sides. In the figure that follows, the two triangles have the same angle measurements, so the side lengths can be set up as the following proportion: $\frac{A}{D} = \frac{B}{E} = \frac{C}{F}$.

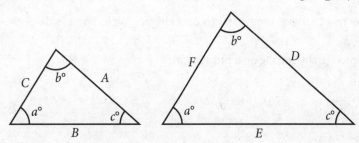

Two triangles are similar if three specific conditions are met:

- Two of their three angles are congruent (**angle-angle**). For example, two triangles that each have one 40° and one 55° angle are similar.

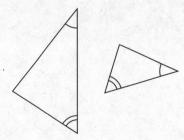

- Two of their three sides are in the same proportion and the intervening angle is congruent (**side-angle-side**). For example, a triangle with sides of 10 and 12 and an intervening angle of 40° and another triangle with sides of 20 and 24 and an intervening angle of 40° are similar.

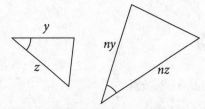

- Their three sides are in the same proportion (**side-side-side**). For example, a triangle with sides of 5, 6, and 8 and a triangle with sides of 15, 18, and 24 are similar.

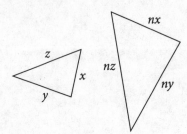

You need to do this:

- Determine whether two triangles are similar by checking for angle-angle, side-angle-side, or side-side-side relationships.
- Find a missing side length by setting up a proportion.

Explanation:

Label the figure with information from the question stem and information you can deduce from geometry principles. These two triangles are similar because they have three sets of congruent angles: one set is the set of vertical angles ($\angle ACB \cong \angle DCE$) and the others are the alternate interior angles formed by the intersection of the transversals with the two parallel segments, AB and DE. (For example, $\angle ABC \cong \angle CDE$ because they are alternate interior angles.)

Corresponding sides in similar triangles are proportional to each other, so set up a proportion to find the missing side length, EC. In this case, AB corresponds to DE and AC corresponds to EC:

$$\frac{AB}{AC} = \frac{DE}{EC}$$
$$\frac{2}{5} = \frac{8}{EC}$$
$$2(EC) = 40$$
$$EC = 20$$

Enter **20**.

Try on Your Own

Directions

Take as much time as you need on these questions. Work carefully and methodically. There will be an opportunity for timed practice later in the book.

13

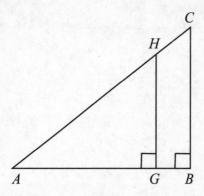

Note: Figure not drawn to scale.

In the figure shown, segment *AG* is 20 inches and segment *GB* is 4 inches. If segment *CB* is 18 inches, how long, in inches, is segment *HG*?

(A) 14

(B) 15

(C) 16

(D) 18

14

HINT: For Q14, translate carefully from English into math.

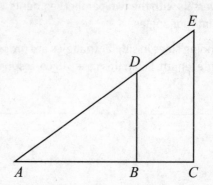

The diagram shows similar triangles *ABD* and *ACE*. Segment *AB* is 12 inches, and the area of triangle *ABD* is 48 square inches. If segment *CE* is 50% longer than segment *BD*, what is the area of triangle *ACE*, in square inches?

15

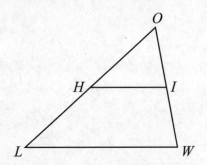

Note: Figure not drawn to scale.

Triangle *LOW* is shown. Segment *HI* is parallel to segment *LW*. If segment *OI* is 50% of segment *IW*, and segment *HI* has a length of 8, what is the length of segment *LW*?

Ⓐ 12

Ⓑ 16

Ⓒ 20

Ⓓ 24

16

HINT: Triangles with a shared angle and parallel sides are similar. How can you use this fact in Q16?

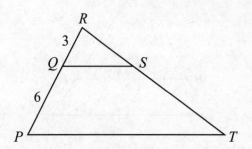

In the figure, *QS* and *PT* are parallel and the length of *QR* is 3 and the length of *PQ* is 6. If the perimeter of $\triangle QRS$ is 11 units long, how many units long is the perimeter of $\triangle PRT$?

Ⓐ 22

Ⓑ 24

Ⓒ 33

Ⓓ 66

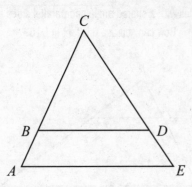

Note: Figure not drawn to scale.

In the figure above, BD is parallel to AE, and $CD = AE = 6$. If $BD = 4$, then what is the length of DE?

Ⓐ 2

Ⓑ 3

Ⓒ 4

Ⓓ 6

Pythagorean Theorem

LEARNING OBJECTIVES

After this lesson, you will be able to:

- Calculate the length of one side of a right triangle given the lengths of the other two sides
- Recognize the most common Pythagorean triples

To answer a question like this:

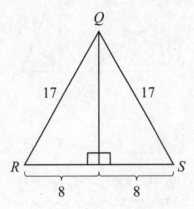

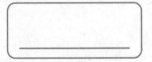

In triangle QRS, QR and QS each have a length of 17 inches. If the length of RS is 16 inches, what is the area of QRS, in square inches?

You need to know this:

The **Pythagorean theorem** states that in any right triangle (and *only* in right triangles), the square of the hypotenuse (the longest side) is equal to the sum of the squares of the legs (the shorter sides). If you know the lengths of any two sides of a right triangle, you can use the Pythagorean equation, $a^2 + b^2 = c^2$, to find the length of the third. In this equation, a and b are the legs of the triangle and c is the hypotenuse, the side across from the right angle of the triangle.

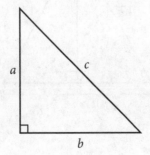

Consider an example: a right triangle has a leg of length 9 and a hypotenuse of length 14. To find the missing leg length, plug the known values into the Pythagorean equation: $9^2 + b^2 = 14^2$. This simplifies to $81 + b^2 = 196$, which becomes $b^2 = 115$. Take the square root of both sides to find that $b = \sqrt{115}$.

Some right triangles have three side lengths that are all integers. These sets of integer side lengths are called **Pythagorean triples**. The two most common Pythagorean triples on the SAT are 3:4:5 and 5:12:13. Look for multiples of these (e.g., 6:8:10 and 10:24:26) as well. Memorizing these triples now can save you valuable calculation time on test day.

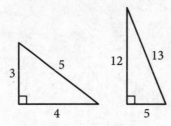

You need to do this:

- Keep in mind that the Pythagorean theorem applies only to right triangles.
- When you need to find a side length of a right triangle, look first for the common Pythagorean triples or their multiples.
- If you cannot identify any Pythagorean triples, substitute any two known side lengths into the equation $a^2 + b^2 = c^2$ to find the third.

Explanation:

The isosceles triangle *QRS* is divided into two right triangles, each with a hypotenuse of 17 inches. You're given that *RS* is 16 inches, so that means the short leg of each right triangle is half of that or 8 inches. In order to calculate the area, you'll need to find the height of *QRS*, which also happens to be the long leg of each of the two right triangles.

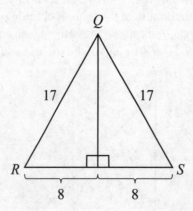

Use the Pythagorean equation to solve for the height:

$$8^2 + h^2 = 17^2$$
$$64 + h^2 = 289$$
$$h^2 = 225$$
$$h = 15$$

If you were particularly alert to Pythagorean triples, you might have noticed that each right triangle consists of an 8-15-17 triple, which would have allowed you to shortcut finding the height of *QRS*.

Now use the known base and height to calculate the area of *QRS*:

$$A = \frac{1}{2}bh = \frac{1}{2}(16)(15) = 120$$

Enter **120**.

Try on Your Own

Directions

Take as much time as you need on these questions. Work carefully and methodically. There will be an opportunity for timed practice later in the book.

18

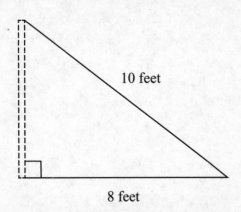

10 feet

8 feet

A playground slide is 10 feet long, and the base of the slide is 8 feet from the base of a ladder, as shown in the figure. If the ladder is perpendicular to the ground, what is the height, in feet, of the ladder?

Ⓐ   3

Ⓑ   4

Ⓒ   5

Ⓓ   6

19

HINT: In Q19, a straight line from *W* to *Z* will help to form what geometric figure?

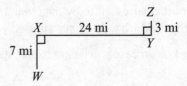

The figure shows the route of Gina's trip from her apartment to her gym. Gina travels 7 miles from *W* to *X*, 24 miles from *X* to *Y*, and 3 miles from *Y* to *Z*. If she were able to travel from *W* to *Z* directly, how much shorter, in miles, would the trip be?

Ⓐ   8

Ⓑ   10

Ⓒ   14

Ⓓ   26

20

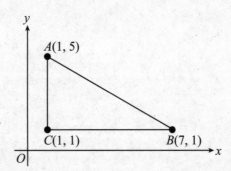

What is the length, in units, of side *AB* in the diagram?

Math

21

The longer leg of a right triangle is twice the length of the shorter leg. If the length of the shorter leg is 6 inches, what is the length, in inches, of the hypotenuse?

Ⓐ $3\sqrt{5}$

Ⓑ 12

Ⓒ $6\sqrt{5}$

Ⓓ 18

22

HINT: In Q22, remember that the side length of a triangle can never be negative.

The area of a right triangle is 48 square inches. If the longer leg is 4 inches longer than the shorter leg, what is the length, in inches, of the hypotenuse?

Ⓐ 12

Ⓑ $4\sqrt{13}$

Ⓒ 20

Ⓓ 208

K   287

Sine, Cosine, and Tangent

LEARNING OBJECTIVES

After this lesson, you will be able to:

- Calculate trigonometric ratios from side lengths of right triangles
- Calculate side lengths of right triangles using trigonometric ratios
- Describe the relationship between the sine and cosine of complementary angles

To answer a question like this:

One angle in a right triangle measures $x°$ such that $\cos x° = \frac{15}{17}$. What is the measure of $\sin(90° - x°)$?

(A) $\frac{8}{17}$

(B) $\frac{8}{15}$

(C) $\frac{15}{17}$

(D) $\frac{15}{8}$

You need to know this:

The PSAT tests three trigonometric functions: **sine**, **cosine**, and **tangent**. All three are the ratios of side lengths within a right triangle. The notation for sine, cosine, and tangent functions always includes a reference angle; for example, $\cos x$ or $\cos 9$. That's because you'll need to refer to the given angle within a right triangle to determine the appropriate side ratios.

There is a common mnemonic device for the sine, cosine, and tangent ratios: SOHCAHTOA (commonly pronounced: so-kuh-TOE-uh). Here's what it represents: **S**ine is **O**pposite over **H**ypotenuse, **C**osine is **A**djacent over **H**ypotenuse, and **T**angent is **O**pposite over **A**djacent. See the following triangle and the table for a summary of the ratios and what each equals for angle A in triangle CAB:

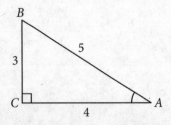

SINE (SIN)	COSINE (COS)	TANGENT (TAN)
$\dfrac{\text{opposite}}{\text{hypotenuse}}$	$\dfrac{\text{adjacent}}{\text{hypotenuse}}$	$\dfrac{\text{opposite}}{\text{adjacent}}$
$\dfrac{3}{5}$	$\dfrac{4}{5}$	$\dfrac{3}{4}$

Complementary angles (angles that sum to 90°) have a special relationship relative to sine and cosine:

- $\sin x° = \cos(90° - x°)$
- $\cos x° = \sin(90° - x°)$

In other words, if two angles add up to 90°, the sine of one equals the cosine of the other (and vice versa). For example, $\cos 30° = \sin 60°$, $\cos 60° = \sin 30°$, $\cos 45° = \sin 45°$, and so on.

You need to do this:

Apply the appropriate trigonometric ratio to a right triangle or use the relationship between the sine and cosine of complementary angles.

Explanation:

There are two ways to approach this question. You might choose to draw the triangle:

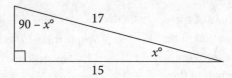

To find $\sin(90° - x°)$, put the side opposite the angle labeled $90° - x°$ over the hypotenuse. You'll get $\frac{15}{17}$, exactly the same as $\cos x°$. (Note that the third angle is $90° - x°$ because the angles of a triangle always add up to 180°, and $90° + x° + (90° - x°) = 180°$.)

Alternatively, you could use the property of complementary angles that says that $\cos x° = \sin(90° - x°)$ to find that $\sin(90° - x°) = \frac{15}{17}$.

The correct answer is **(C)**.

Try on Your Own

Directions

Take as much time as you need on these questions. Work carefully and methodically. There will be an opportunity for timed practice later in the book.

23

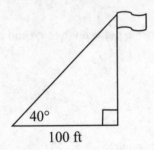

40°

100 ft

Armando wants to determine the height of a flagpole. He stands 100 feet from the base of the flagpole and measures the angle of elevation to be 40°, as shown in the figure. Which of the following is the best approximation of the height of the flagpole, in feet?

Use the following values: tan 40° = 0.839, sin 40° = 0.642, and cos 40° = 0.766.

Ⓐ   64.2

Ⓑ   76.6

Ⓒ   83.9

Ⓓ   90

24

HINT: Draw a quick sketch for Q24. Don't try to keep everything in your head!

In a right triangle with angle measure x, $\cos x = \frac{36}{39}$ and $\sin x = \frac{15}{39}$. What is the value of $\tan x$?

Ⓐ $\frac{15}{36}$

Ⓑ $\frac{39}{36}$

Ⓒ $\frac{36}{15}$

Ⓓ $\frac{39}{15}$

25

Angle theta (θ) is $3x$ degrees and angle gamma (Γ) is $6x$ degrees. If $\sin(\theta) = \cos(\Gamma)$, what is the value of x?

Ⓐ   5

Ⓑ   10

Ⓒ   30

Ⓓ   45

26

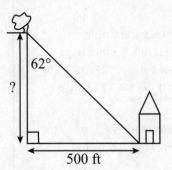

A tree is growing at the edge of a cliff, as shown in the figure. From the tree, the angle between the edge of the cliff and the base of the house is 62°. If the distance between the base of the cliff and the base of the house is 500 feet, which expression represents the height of the cliff, in feet?

Ⓐ   500 cos 62°

Ⓑ $\dfrac{500}{\tan 62°}$

Ⓒ $\dfrac{500}{\sin 62°}$

Ⓓ   500 tan 62°

27

HINT: In Q27, use the Pythagorean theorem to find the hypotenuse.

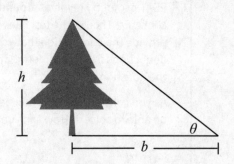

To determine the height h of a tree, Roger stands b feet from the base of the tree and measures the angle of elevation to be θ, as shown in the figure. Which of the following relates h and b?

Ⓐ $\sin \theta = \dfrac{h}{b}$

Ⓑ $\sin \theta = \dfrac{b}{h}$

Ⓒ $\sin \theta = \dfrac{b}{\sqrt{b^2 + h^2}}$

Ⓓ $\sin \theta = \dfrac{h}{\sqrt{b^2 + h^2}}$

On Test Day

PSAT geometry revolves around a small set of basic formulas and simple concepts. Though the test likes to hide the path to the solution, it will always provide the information that you need to get started. Your job is to make deductions from that information to assemble all the facts necessary to answer the question.

As you consider the question below, ask yourself what information you need to be able to solve it. How can you get that information from what you're given?

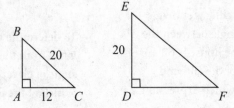

28. In the figure, triangles *ABC* and *DEF* are similar. The area of triangle *DEF* is how many times greater than the area of *ABC*?

The correct answer can be found at the end of the chapter.

How Much Have You Learned?

Directions

For test-like practice, give yourself 15 minutes to complete this question set. Be sure to study the explanations, even for questions you got right. They can be found at the end of this chapter.

1

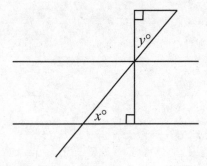

According to the figure, what is the value of $x + y$?

2

The hypotenuse of a right triangle is $2x + 4$. The length of one of its legs is x. What is the length of the other leg in terms of x?

Ⓐ $\sqrt{x^2 - 2x - 4}$

Ⓑ $4x^2 + 16x + 16$

Ⓒ $\sqrt{3x^2 + 16x + 16}$

Ⓓ $\sqrt{5x^2 + 16x + 16}$

3

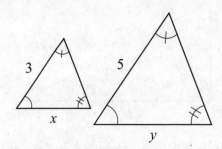

According to the figure, what is y in terms of x?

Ⓐ $\dfrac{5x}{3}$

Ⓑ $\dfrac{3x}{5}$

Ⓒ $\dfrac{5}{3x}$

Ⓓ $\dfrac{3}{5x}$

4

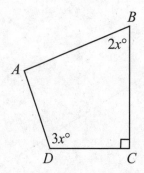

The figure shows quadrilateral $ABCD$. The measure of angle B is $2x$, and the measure of angle D is $3x$. What is the measure, in degrees, of A in terms of x?

Ⓐ $90 + 5x$

Ⓑ $180 - 5x$

Ⓒ $180 + 5x$

Ⓓ $270 - 5x$

5

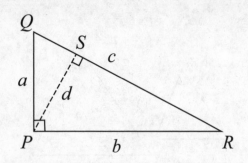

Triangle *PQR* has side lengths *a*, *b*, *c*, as shown in the figure. A dotted line segment, *d*, originates at point *P* and intersects *QR* at point *S*. What is the ratio of the length of *d* to *a*?

Ⓐ $\frac{a}{c}$

Ⓑ $\frac{b}{c}$

Ⓒ $\frac{a}{b}$

Ⓓ $\frac{b}{a}$

6

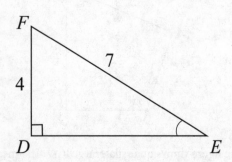

According to the figure, which of the following is equivalent to tan *E*?

Ⓐ $\frac{4}{7}$

Ⓑ $\frac{4}{\sqrt{33}}$

Ⓒ $\frac{7}{\sqrt{33}}$

Ⓓ $\frac{7}{4}$

7

The area of rectangle *R* is *x*. Rectangle *S* is formed by doubling the width of Rectangle R and adding four units to its length. Rectangle *T* is formed by subtracting eight units from the length of Rectangle *R* while maintaining Rectangle *R*'s width. Which of the following expresses the sum of the areas of Rectangles *S* and *T* in terms of *x*?

Ⓐ $2x - 8$

Ⓑ $2x - 4$

Ⓒ $2x$

Ⓓ $3x$

8

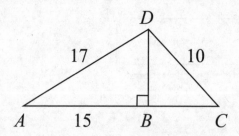

According to the figure, what is the area of triangle *BDC*?

9

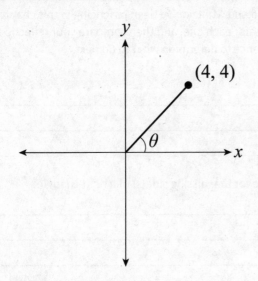

What is the value of sin θ?

Ⓐ $\dfrac{\sqrt{2}}{2}$

Ⓑ $\dfrac{\sqrt{3}}{2}$

Ⓒ 1

Ⓓ $\sqrt{2}$

10

For the area of a square to triple, what must its side length be multiplied by?

Ⓐ $\dfrac{1}{3}$

Ⓑ $\sqrt{3}$

Ⓒ 3

Ⓓ 9

Reflect

Directions: Take a few minutes to recall what you've learned and what you've been practicing in this chapter. Consider the following questions, jot down your best answer for each one, and then compare your reflections to the expert responses that follow. Use your level of confidence to determine what to do next.

What are similar triangles?

_____

_____

_____

When can you avoid using the Pythagorean theorem to solve for the missing side(s) of a right triangle?

_____

_____

_____

What are the definitions of sine, cosine, and tangent?

_____

_____

_____

What is the special relationship of sine to cosine in complementary angles?

_____

_____

_____

Expert Responses

What are similar triangles?

Two triangles are similar if their angles are congruent. Similar triangles have proportional sides.

When can you avoid using the Pythagorean theorem to solve for the missing side(s) of a right triangle?

If the two sides you're given match a Pythagorean triple, then you can use the ratio to quickly find the third side. For example, if the two legs are 10 and 24, then the triangle is a 5:12:13 triple multiplied by 2: $5 \times 2 = 10$, $12 \times 2 = 24$, so the hypotenuse must be $13 \times 2 = 26$.

What are the definitions of sine, cosine, and tangent?

Informally, sine is defined as opposite over hypotenuse, cosine as adjacent over hypotenuse, and tangent as opposite over adjacent. The acronym SOHCAHTOA can help you remember these definitions.

What is the special relationship of sine to cosine in complementary angles?

When two angles are complementary (that is, they add up to 90°), the sine of one equals the cosine of the other, and vice versa.

Next Steps

If you answered most questions correctly in the "How Much Have You Learned?" section, and if your responses to the Reflect questions were similar to those of the PSAT expert, then consider Geometry and Trigonometry an area of strength and move on to the next chapter. Come back to this topic periodically to prevent yourself from getting rusty.

If you don't yet feel confident, review those parts of this chapter that you have not yet mastered. In particular, study the properties of triangles, including trigonometry. Then, try the questions you missed again. As always, be sure to review the explanations closely.

Answers and Explanations

Try on Your Own

1. C

Difficulty: Easy

Category: Geometry and Trigonometry

Getting to the Answer: When a transversal line crosses two parallel lines, it intersects each of the parallel lines at the same angle. Therefore, the value of x is equal to the value of the angle to the right of y, making x and y supplementary.

Therefore, $x = 180 - y = 180 - 67 = 113$. Choice **(C)** is correct.

2. 125

Difficulty: Easy

Category: Geometry and Trigonometry

Getting to the Answer: When two or more angles combine to form a straight line, the sum of the angles is $180°$. Therefore, $u + v + w = 180$.

The question states that $z = 55$, and v forms a vertical angle with z, so v is also 55. Therefore, $180 - 55 = u + w$. Thus, $u + w = 125$. Enter **125**.

3. C

Difficulty: Medium

Category: Geometry and Trigonometry

Getting to the Answer: When a transversal crosses two or more parallel lines, all acute angles formed will be equal, and all obtuse angles formed will be equal.

Since l_4 is perpendicular to l_1, the angles formed by their intersection are $90°$. Therefore, angle a forms a complementary pair with the angle adjacent to it (the angle just above a).

The question specifies that $a = 40$, so the angle adjacent to it must be $90 - 40 = 50$. Because l_1 and l_2 are parallel, and l_3 is a transversal of both, the $50°$ angle that is adjacent and complementary with a corresponds with b. That means b also equals 50. Therefore, choice **(C)** is correct.

4. D

Difficulty: Hard

Category: Geometry and Trigonometry

Getting to the Answer: Since lines j and k are parallel, and line l is a transversal passing through j and k, all obtuse angles formed by the transversal will be identical, and all acute angles formed will also be identical. Therefore, obtuse angles are all equal, and acute angles are all equal.

The question specifies that $h = 5c$. Therefore, you can say that the value of each obtuse angle in the diagram is 5 times the value of each acute angle. Since an acute angle and an obtuse angle in the figure are supplementary—they sum to $180°$—you can say that $h + c = 180°$. Substituting $5c$ for h, the equations becomes $5c + c = 180°$, so $6c = 180°$. Now isolate c:

$$6c = 180°$$
$$\frac{6c}{6} = \frac{180°}{6}$$
$$c = 30°$$

The question asks for the value of $2a$. Since a is supplementary to c, $a + c = 180$. You can find a with the equation $180 - 30 = 150$. Thus, $a = 150$, and $2a = 300$.

Choice **(D)** is correct.

5. 260

Difficulty: Medium

Category: Geometry and Trigonometry

Getting to the Answer: When a transversal crosses parallel lines, all the acute angles are equal, and all the obtuse angles are equal.

In a figure where a transversal intersects parallel lines, any acute angle is supplementary to any obtuse angle, even if they are not adjacent. Since c is an acute angle, and $c = 50$, all of the obtuse angles are $180 - 50 = 130$. Angles a and e are both obtuse, with a measure of 130 each. So, $a + e = 130 + 130 = 260$.

Enter **260**.

6. A

Difficulty: Medium

Category: Geometry and Trigonometry

Getting to the Answer: At each intersection with line l, vertical angles are equal, and supplementary angles add up to 180°. Since the two lines are parallel, corresponding angles are the same. For example, $b = f$ and $a = e$. Therefore, if you know the measure of any one angle, you could determine the measures of all the angles in the figure.

Choice **(A)** is correct.

7. C

Difficulty: Easy

Category: Geometry and Trigonometry

Getting to the Answer: The perimeter of a rectangle is $2l + 2w$, where l is the length and w is the width. Since the width of the frame is 6 inches shorter than the length, or $w = f - 6$, the perimeter of the frame is $2f + 2(f - 6) = 2f + 2f - 12 = 4f - 12$ inches. **(C)** is correct.

8. 7

Difficulty: Easy

Category: Geometry and Trigonometry

Getting to the Answer: Use the formula for the area of a rectangle: $A = l \times w$. In this case, l is height and equals $w + 4$. Plugging that and the given area into the formula and solving for w gives:

$$21 = (w + 4)(w)$$
$$21 = w^2 + 4w$$
$$0 = w^2 + 4w - 21$$
$$0 = (w + 7)(w - 3)$$
$$w = -7 \text{ and } 3$$

Because the width cannot be negative, the width is 3 ft. The height is therefore $3 + 4 = 7$ ft. Enter **7**.

9. B

Difficulty: Hard

Category: Geometry and Trigonometry

Getting to the Answer: The formula for the area of a rectangle is $A = lw$, so $x = lw$. Since both the length and width of the rectangle are tripled, the length of the new rectangle is $3l$ and the width of the new rectangle is $3w$. This gives an area of $(3l)(3w)$ or $lw \times 9$. Since $x = lw$, the area of the new rectangle in terms of x is $9x$. **(B)** is correct.

10. A

Difficulty: Hard

Category: Geometry and Trigonometry

Getting to the Answer: Let x be a side of Triangle A. If the length of each side of Triangle B is twice the length of each side of Triangle A, then the length of a side of Triangle B is $2x$. The formula for the perimeter of an equilateral triangle is $3s$. Thus, the perimeter of Triangle B is $3(2x) = 6x$, and the perimeter of Triangle A is $3x$. The perimeter of Triangle B is $\frac{6x}{3x} = 2$ times greater than the perimeter of Triangle A. **(A)** is correct.

11. B

Difficulty: Hard

Category: Geometry and Trigonometry

Getting to the Answer: Let h represent the height of the original triangle and b the base. By definition, x percent is $\frac{x}{100}$. Thus, the new triangle has a height of $1.2h$ and a base of $\left(1 - \frac{x}{100}\right)b$. The new area is $A - 0.1A = 0.9A$. Plugging these into the formula for the area of a triangle, $A = \frac{1}{2}bh$, gives:

$$0.9A = \frac{1}{2}\left(1 - \frac{x}{100}\right)b(1.2h)$$
$$0.9\left(\frac{1}{2}bh\right) = \frac{1}{2}\left(1 - \frac{x}{100}\right)b(1.2h)$$
$$0.9 = \left(1 - \frac{x}{100}\right)(1.2)$$
$$0.75 = 1 - \frac{x}{100}$$
$$-0.25 = -\frac{x}{100}$$
$$25 = x$$

(B) is correct.

12. C

Difficulty: Easy

Category: Geometry and Trigonometry

Getting to the Answer: Like many combined area problems, the key is taking it one step at a time and not rushing. The square has an area equal to its side length squared: $A = s^2 = 5^2 = 25$. The triangle has an area: $A = \frac{1}{2}bh = \frac{1}{2}(5)(6) = 15$. Now, just add the two numbers: $25 + 15 = 40$. Choice **(C)** is correct.

13. B

Difficulty: Easy

Category: Geometry and Trigonometry

Getting to the Answer: In similar triangles, corresponding sides are proportional. The question states that segment *AG* is 20 inches and segment *GB* is 4 inches, so segment *AB* is 24 inches. Segment *HG* corresponds to segment *CB*, so you can set up a proportion to solve for *HG*:

$$\frac{AG}{AB} = \frac{HG}{CB}$$
$$\frac{20}{24} = \frac{HG}{18}$$
$$360 = 24(HG)$$
$$HG = 15$$

Choice **(B)** is the correct answer.

14. 108

Difficulty: Hard

Category: Geometry and Trigonometry

Strategic Advice: The figure contains a pair of similar triangles. Use the fact that their sides are in proportion to find the required length.

Getting to the Answer: The question asks for the area of triangle *ACE*. You're given that segment $AB = 12$ and the area of *ABD* is 48, so you can use the triangle area formula to find *BD*:

$$\frac{1}{2} \times \text{base} \times \text{height} = \text{area}$$
$$\frac{1}{2} \times 12 \times BD = 48$$
$$12 \times BD = 96$$
$$BD = 8$$

The question also states that segment *CE* is 50% longer than segment *BD*, so that means $CE = 8 + 0.5(8) = 12$

inches. Because the triangles are similar, the base of *ACE* must also be 50% longer than the base of *ABD*, so that is $12 + 0.5(12) = 18$ inches.

Now that you have the base and height of ACE, plug them into the area formula: $\frac{1}{2} \times 18 \times 12 = 108$ square inches. Enter **108**.

15. D

Difficulty: Hard

Category: Geometry and Trigonometry

Getting to the Answer: The question says that segment *OI* is 50% —that's half the length—of *IW*. So if you represent *OI* as *x*, you can say that *IW* is 2*x*. That means *OW* is $x + 2x = 3x$. Thus, the sides of the larger triangle are three times the sides of the smaller triangle.

The question states that side *HI* is 8, so the corresponding side *LW* is $3 \times 8 = 24$. The correct answer is **(D)**.

16. C

Difficulty: Medium

Category: Geometry and Trigonometry

Getting to the Answer: When parallel lines make a smaller triangle nested within a larger triangle as they do here, the triangles are similar (because they have the same angle measurements). Side *PR* is three times the length of *QR*, so each side of the big triangle is three times the length of the corresponding side of the smaller triangle, and therefore the ratio of the perimeters is also 3:1. Therefore, the perimeter of △*PRT* is 3 times the perimeter of △*QRS*, so that's 3×11, or 33. Choice **(C)** is correct.

17. B

Difficulty: Medium

Category: Geometry and Trigonometry

Getting to the Answer: Angle *C* is shared by both triangles. And, because *BD* is parallel to *AE*, angles *CAE* and *CBD* are congruent—they are corresponding angles. Two pairs of congruent angles mean that triangles *ACE* and *BCD* are similar by angle-angle. (You could have analyzed angles *CDB* and *CEA*, but you need only two pairs of congruent angles to conclude that two triangles are similar.)

Set up a proportion using the triangles' side lengths: $CD = 6$, $AE = 6$, and $BD = 4$. In order to find DE, you need to find CE. BD corresponds to AE and CD corresponds to CE. Use the three known side lengths to create a proportion and solve for CE:

$$\frac{BD}{AE} = \frac{CD}{CE}$$
$$\frac{4}{6} = \frac{6}{CE}$$
$$4(CE) = 36$$
$$CE = 9$$

The question asks for the length of segment DE, which is $CE - CD$, or $9 - 6 = 3$. **(B)** is correct.

18. D

Difficulty: Easy

Category: Geometry and Trigonometry

Getting to the Answer: You have a right triangle, so apply the Pythagorean theorem to solve for the missing side:

$$a^2 + b^2 = c^2$$
$$a^2 + 8^2 = 10^2$$
$$a^2 + 64 = 100$$
$$a^2 = 36$$
$$a = 6$$

Choice **(D)** is correct. If you recognized the 6:8:10 triple, you could have solved this question even more efficiently.

19. A

Difficulty: Medium

Category: Geometry and Trigonometry

Getting to the Answer: Gina's current route is $7 + 24 + 3 = 34$ miles. To find the shorter route, draw a straight line (either mentally or by reproducing the image on your provided scratch paper) from W to Z and create a right triangle. Here, the base is 24 and the height is $7 + 3 = 10$.

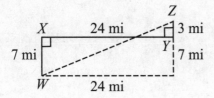

Now solve using the Pythagorean theorem.

$$a^2 + b^2 = c^2$$
$$10^2 + 24^2 = c^2$$
$$100 + 576 = c^2$$
$$676 = c^2$$
$$26 = c$$

Since the current route is 34 miles and the new route is 26 miles, Gina's new route is $34 - 26 = 8$ miles shorter. Choice **(A)** is correct. If you recognized the 10:24:26 triple, you could have solved this question even more efficiently.

20. 7.211

Difficulty: Medium

Category: Geometry and Trigonometry

Getting to the Answer: Begin by finding the lengths of CA and CB. Points A and C have the same x-coordinates, so subtract their y-coordinates to find the distance: $5 - 1 = 4$. Points C and B have the same y-coordinates, so subtract their x-coordinates to find the distance: $7 - 1 = 6$.

Now solve for AB, the hypotenuse, using the Pythagorean theorem.

$$a^2 + b^2 = c^2$$
$$4^2 + 6^2 = c^2$$
$$16 + 36 = c^2$$
$$52 = c^2$$
$$\sqrt{52} = c$$
$$7.2111 \approx c$$

For positive numbers, you are able to enter 5 characters into student-produced response boxes, so enter **7.211**.

21. C

Difficulty: Medium

Category: Geometry and Trigonometry

Getting to the Answer: Since the shorter leg is 6, the longer leg must be 2(6) = 12. Use the Pythagorean theorem and radical rules to solve for the hypotenuse.

$$a^2 + b^2 = c^2$$
$$6^2 + 12^2 = c^2$$
$$36 + 144 = c^2$$
$$180 = c^2$$
$$\sqrt{180} = c$$
$$\sqrt{36}\,\sqrt{5} = c$$
$$6\sqrt{5} = c$$

Choice **(C)** is correct.

22. B

Difficulty: Hard

Category: Geometry and Trigonometry

Getting to the Answer: Recall that the area of a triangle is $A = \dfrac{bh}{2}$. You are told that the area is 48, so this means that $bh = 2(48) = 96$.

Draw a quick sketch of the triangle described. Let the short leg be x and the long leg be $x + 4$.

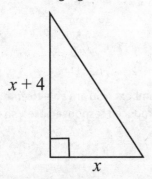

This means that $b = x$ and $h = x + 4$. Plug these values into the $bh = 96$ equation and solve for x.

$$x(x + 4) = 96$$
$$x^2 + 4x = 96$$
$$x^2 + 4x - 96 = 0$$
$$(x - 8)(x + 12) = 0$$

This yields $x = 8$ and $x = -12$. Since the side of a triangle cannot be negative, x must be 8. Plug this value of x into your diagram.

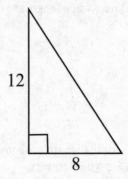

Finally, find the hypotenuse using the Pythagorean theorem.

$$a^2 + b^2 = c^2$$
$$8^2 + 12^2 = c^2$$
$$64 + 144 = c^2$$
$$208 = c^2$$
$$\sqrt{208} = c$$
$$\sqrt{16}\,\sqrt{13} = c$$
$$4\sqrt{13} = c$$

Choice **(B)** is correct.

23. C

Difficulty: Easy

Category: Geometry and Trigonometry

Getting to the Answer: You are asked to find the height of the flagpole, which is the side opposite the 40° angle. Recall that $\tan \theta = \dfrac{\text{opposite}}{\text{adjacent}}$. Let x represent the unknown side. You can conclude that $\tan 40° = \dfrac{x}{100}$. The value of $\tan 40°$ is given as 0.839, so plug this number into the equation to obtain $0.839 = \dfrac{x}{100}$. Therefore, $x = 0.839(100) = 83.9$. Select choice **(C)**.

24. A

Difficulty: Medium

Category: Geometry and Trigonometry

Getting to the Answer: Drawing a quick sketch can help you visualize the situation. Remember the acronym SOHCAHTOA to keep track of the definitions of the different trig functions. The position of angle x is arbitrary. You could have chosen a different configuration as long as you kept track of which sides were adjacent and opposite relative to x.

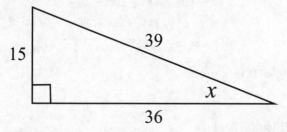

The question asks for tan x. Recall that $\tan \theta = \frac{\text{opposite}}{\text{adjacent}}$. Here, the opposite side is 15 and the adjacent side is 36. Therefore, $\tan x = \frac{15}{36}$. Choice **(A)** is correct.

25. B

Difficulty: Easy

Category: Geometry and Trigonometry

Getting to the Answer: The sine of an angle is equal to the cosine of its *complementary* angle; therefore, in degrees, $\theta + \Gamma = 90$. Set up the equation $3x + 6x = 90$. Combine terms to get $9x = 90$. Solve to find $x = 10$. Choice **(B)** is correct.

26. B

Difficulty: Medium

Category: Geometry and Trigonometry

Getting to the Answer: You are given an angle that measures 62° and the side opposite it. You are looking for the side adjacent to this angle. Since $\tan \theta = \frac{\text{opposite}}{\text{adjacent}}$, plug the given information into this formula:

$\tan 62° = \frac{500}{x}$. Solve this equation for x:

$$\tan 62° = \frac{500}{x}$$
$$x \tan 62° = 500$$
$$x = \frac{500}{\tan 62°}$$

Choice **(B)** is correct.

27. D

Difficulty: Hard

Category: Geometry and Trigonometry

Getting to the Answer: All of the answers are possible expressions for sin θ. Recall that $\sin \theta = \frac{\text{opposite}}{\text{hypotenuse}}$. The side opposite θ is h. At this point, you can eliminate (B) and (C). Since b is the adjacent side, not the hypotenuse, **(D)** must be the correct answer. If you did not see this, you could calculate the hypotenuse using the Pythagorean theorem:

$$a^2 + b^2 = c^2$$
$$b^2 + h^2 = c^2$$
$$\sqrt{b^2 + h^2} = c$$

Therefore, $\sin \theta = \frac{h}{\sqrt{b^2 + h^2}}$. Again, choice **(D)** is correct.

On Test Day

28. 1.562 or 1.563

Difficulty: Hard

Category: Geometry and Trigonometry

Getting to the Answer: Begin by examining triangle *ABC*. It is a right triangle with side lengths of 12 and 20. If you recognize that it is the common 3-4-5 right triangle multiplied by 4, you can easily conclude that the missing side is 16. If you didn't see that, you could set up the Pythagorean theorem and solve:

$$a^2 + b^2 = c^2$$
$$12^2 + b^2 = 20^2$$
$$144 + b^2 = 400$$
$$b^2 = 256$$
$$b = 16$$

The question says that the two triangles are similar. This means that they have proportional sides. Set up a proportion to find side *DF*:

$$\frac{16}{12} = \frac{20}{DF}$$
$$16DF = 240$$
$$DF = 15$$

The question asks how many times greater the area of *DEF* is than *ABC*. The area of *DEF* is $\frac{1}{2}(20)(15) = 150$. The area of *ABC* is $\frac{1}{2}(16)(12) = 96$. Therefore, triangle *DEF* is $\frac{150}{96} = 1.5625$ times greater than *ABC*. You can enter up to 5 characters for a positive answer and may either round or truncate. Enter **1.562** or **1.563**.

How Much Have You Learned?

1.   90

Difficulty: Easy

Category: Geometry and Trigonometry

Getting to the Answer: The sum of the interior angles of any triangle is 180 degrees. Call the missing angle in the bottom triangle *z*. Therefore, $x + z + 90 = 180$, or $x + z = 90$.

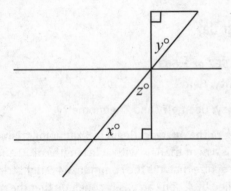

Angles *z* and *y* are vertical angles, so they are equal. Therefore, $x + y = 90$. Enter **90**.

2.   C

Difficulty: Medium

Category: Geometry and Trigonometry

Getting to the Answer: Since the length of one leg is given as *x* and the hypotenuse is given as $2x + 4$, use the Pythagorean theorem to find the missing leg, *b*:

$$a^2 + b^2 = c^2$$
$$x^2 + b^2 = (2x + 4)^2$$
$$x^2 + b^2 = (2x + 4)(2x + 4)$$
$$x^2 + b^2 = 4x^2 + 16x + 16$$
$$b^2 = 3x^2 + 16x + 16$$
$$b = \sqrt{3x^2 + 16x + 16}$$

Choice **(C)** is correct.

3.   A

Difficulty: Medium

Category: Geometry and Trigonometry

Getting to the Answer: The figure shows that both triangles have equal angles. Therefore, they are similar. Similar triangles have proportional sides, so set up a proportion and solve for *y*:

$$\frac{3}{5} = \frac{x}{y}$$
$$3y = 5x$$
$$y = \frac{5x}{3}$$

Choice **(A)** is correct.

4.   D

Difficulty: Medium

Category: Geometry and Trigonometry

Getting to the Answer: The sum of the interior angles of any quadrilateral equals 360 degrees. (Mentally connecting points A and C can show you that the quadrilateral can be thought of as made up of two triangles whose interior angles add up to 180 degrees each: 2 times 180 is 360.) Set up an equation and solve for *A* in terms of *x*:

$$90 + 3x + 2x + A = 360$$
$$5x + A = 270$$
$$A = 270 - 5x$$

Choice **(D)** is correct.

5. B

Difficulty: Hard

Category: Geometry and Trigonometry

Getting to the Answer: You are asked which ratio is equivalent to $\frac{d}{a}$. Since you are not given any numbers to work with, you must use similar triangle properties. Recall that two triangles are similar if two of their angles are the same. Consider triangles PQR and SQP. Both triangles contain a right angle and both triangles share angle Q. The two triangles are similar and therefore have proportional sides.

Examine the ratio $\frac{d}{a}$. Side d is the long leg of triangle SQP, and side a is its hypotenuse. Therefore, it must be equal to the ratio of the long leg of triangle PQR (b) to the hypotenuse of PQR (c). Thus, $\frac{d}{a} = \frac{b}{c}$. **(B)** is correct.

6. B

Difficulty: Medium

Category: Geometry and Trigonometry

Getting to the Answer: Recall that $\tan \theta = \frac{\text{opposite}}{\text{adjacent}}$. The side opposite angle E is 4, but you do not know the adjacent side. Let b be the adjacent side. Use the Pythagorean theorem to find it:

$$a^2 + b^2 = c^2$$
$$4^2 + b^2 = 7^2$$
$$16 + b^2 = 49$$
$$b^2 = 33$$
$$b = \sqrt{33}$$

Therefore, $\tan E = \frac{4}{\sqrt{33}}$. Choice **(B)** is correct.

7. D

Difficulty: Hard

Category: Geometry and Trigonometry

Getting to the Answer: Take this one step at a time. Let the width of rectangle R be w and its length be l. Therefore, its area x is lw. The width of Rectangle S is $2w$ and its length is $l + 4$, so its area is $2w(l + 4) = 2lw + 8w$. Rectangle T has a length of $l - 8$ and a width of w, so its area is $w(l - 8) = lw - 8w$. Now add these two areas: $2lw + 8w + lw - 8w = 3lw$. Since $lw = x$, this expression simplifies to $3x$. Choice **(D)** is correct.

8. 24

Difficulty: Hard

Category: Geometry and Trigonometry

Getting to the Answer: The figure shows two right triangles. Fill in the missing sides using either the Pythagorean theorem or your knowledge of common Pythagorean triples. Triangle ABD is an 8-15-17 right triangle. If you did not recognize this triple, you could have used the Pythagorean theorem:

$$a^2 + b^2 = c^2$$
$$a^2 + 15^2 = 17^2$$
$$a^2 + 225 = 289$$
$$a^2 = 64$$
$$a = 8$$

You're not done yet. Now consider triangle BDC. This is a 6-8-10 right triangle, so BC is 6. Again, if you did not recognize this triple, you could have used the Pythagorean theorem:

$$a^2 + b^2 = c^2$$
$$a^2 + 8^2 = 10^2$$
$$a^2 + 64 = 100$$
$$a^2 = 36$$
$$a = 6$$

The area formula of a triangle is $A = \frac{1}{2}bh$. Therefore, the area of triangle BDC is $\frac{1}{2}(6)(8) = \frac{1}{2}(48) = 24$. Enter **24**.

9. A

Difficulty: Hard

Category: Geometry and Trigonometry

Getting to the Answer: Sketch this out on your scratch paper. Then, draw a vertical line straight down to the x-axis. This will create a right triangle. Since the x-coordinate of the given point is 4, the base of the triangle is 4. Similarly, since the y-coordinate is 4, the height is 4. Your sketch should look something like this:

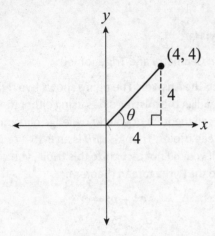

The question asks for sin ϑ. Recall that $\sin \theta = \dfrac{\text{opposite}}{\text{hypotenuse}}$.

Therefore, you must find the hypotenuse. Since this is a right triangle, use the Pythagorean theorem to find the length of the hypotenuse.

$$a^2 + b^2 = c^2$$
$$4^2 + 4^2 = c^2$$
$$16 + 16 = c^2$$
$$32 = c^2$$
$$\sqrt{32} = c$$
$$\sqrt{16} \times \sqrt{2} = c$$
$$4\sqrt{2} = c$$

The hypotenuse is $4\sqrt{2}$, so $\sin x = \dfrac{4}{4\sqrt{2}} = \dfrac{1}{\sqrt{2}}$.

Rationalize the denominator by multiplying by $\sqrt{2}$ on the top and bottom:

$$\frac{1}{\sqrt{2}} = \frac{1}{\sqrt{2}}\frac{\sqrt{2}}{\sqrt{2}} = \frac{\sqrt{2}}{\sqrt{4}} = \frac{\sqrt{2}}{2}$$

Choice **(A)** is correct.

10. B

Difficulty: Hard

Category: Geometry and Trigonometry

Getting to the Answer: Let the original side length of the square be x. The area of the square is therefore x^2. If the area of the square is tripled, its area will be $3x^2$. Let y be the side length of the larger square. Set up an equation and solve for y:

$$A = y^2$$
$$3x^2 = y^2$$
$$\sqrt{3x^2} = y$$
$$\sqrt{3}\,\sqrt{x^2} = y$$
$$\sqrt{3}\,x = y$$

The original side x must be multiplied by $\sqrt{3}$. Therefore, **(B)** is correct.

There is also an opportunity to backsolve on this question. Plugging in $\sqrt{3}\,s$ as the side length, s, into the equations for the area of a square $A = s^2$ will get an area of 3 times as large as the initial value for A.

READING AND WRITING

[CHAPTER 12]

THE METHOD FOR PSAT READING AND WRITING QUESTIONS

LEARNING OBJECTIVES

After completing this chapter, you will be able to:

- Apply the PSAT Verbal Method to PSAT Reading and Writing questions
- Identify useful keywords and use them to answer questions

How to Do PSAT Reading and Writing

LEARNING OBJECTIVES

After this lesson, you will be able to:

- Apply the PSAT Verbal Method to PSAT Reading and Writing questions
- Identify useful keywords and use them to answer questions

The PSAT Reading and Writing section contains 54 questions, divided into two 27-question modules of 32 minutes each. Every question has its own short passage (or sometimes a short pair of passages) that accompanies it. To tackle this section effectively in the 64 minutes allotted, the most successful test takers:

- **Approach the questions with a method that minimizes rereading and leads directly to correct answers.** (See "The Method for PSAT Reading and Writing Questions" section of this chapter.)
- **Read the passages strategically to focus in on the text that leads to points.** (See the "Strategic Reading" section of this chapter.)

In this chapter, we'll give you an overview of how to tackle Reading and Writing passages and questions. The following chapters in this unit will teach you the unique strategies that will help you maximize your efficiency and accuracy on each Reading and Writing question type. Chapter 16 will also provide review on the Standard English Conventions topics that are tested on the PSAT.

To get started, try the questions that follow on your own. Then, keep reading to compare your approach to ours.

Amazingly, there was a period from 1908 to 1940 when you could order an entire house by mail from Sears. In fact, Sears issued a completely separate catalog—Sears Modern Homes—specifically to market these homes by mail. Over the 33 years of the program, buyers had the choice of some 370 home designs and floor plans. What's more, the homes offered were not just simple cottages: designs ranged from modest, two-room bungalows to impressive, multi-story mansions that featured 42 intricate decorative elements, servants' quarters, and wrap-around porches.

Which choice best states the main idea of the text?

(A) The Sears Modern Homes catalog offered more mail-order houses than any other catalog of the time.

(B) It was once possible to purchase a variety of houses through a mail catalog.

(C) Two-room bungalows were the most popular home type ordered from Sears.

(D) The Sears Modern Homes catalog was a separate publication from the standard Sears Catalog.

The Sears Catalog, a mail-order catalog first introduced in 1887, offered a vastly larger selection and lower prices than a local store could do. From pocket watches to patent medicines, from women's gowns to water pumps, from hunting rifles to horse-drawn plows, _____ offered it all.

Which choice completes the text so that it conforms to the conventions of Standard English?

(A) they

(B) this

(C) it

(D) the catalog

The Method for PSAT Reading and Writing Questions

The digital PSAT presents a total of 54 questions. PSAT experts use a simple three-step method that takes advantage of this test format to help them tackle each question quickly and confidently.

THE METHOD FOR PSAT READING AND WRITING

STEP 1 What is the question asking?

- Standard English Conventions questions ONLY: Look at the answer choices for clues

STEP 2 What do I need to look for in the passage?

STEP 3 What answer strategy is best?

- Predict & Match
- Eliminate

Take another look at the first question from the set above, and then read through how and why an expert would apply the steps of the Method:

Amazingly, there was a period from 1908 to 1940 when you could order an entire house by mail from Sears. In fact, Sears issued a completely separate catalog—Sears Modern Homes—specifically to market these homes by mail. Over the 33 years of the program, buyers had the choice of some 370 home designs and floor plans. What's more, the homes offered were not just simple cottages: designs ranged from modest, two-room bungalows to impressive, multi-story mansions that featured 42 intricate decorative elements, servants' quarters, and wrap-around porches.

Which choice best states the main idea of the text?

- (A) The Sears Modern Homes catalog offered more mail-order houses than any other catalog of the time.
- (B) It was once possible to purchase a variety of houses through a mail catalog.
- (C) Two-room bungalows were the most popular home type ordered from Sears.
- (D) The Sears Modern Homes catalog was a separate publication from the standard Sears Catalog.

Step 1. What is the question asking?

The format of the PSAT provides you with an excellent time-saving strategy. Because each passage only has one question, *reading the question before you jump into the passage* will allow you to focus in on exactly what you need from the passage.

In the question above, you're asked to identify the answer choice that gives the "main idea" of the passage.

Step 2. What do I need to look for in the passage?

Next, strategically read the passage based on what the question asks. Some question types, which you'll learn about in the following chapters, can be answered by focusing on just a specific part of the passage. And whether you closely read the entire passage or only part of it, your reading approach will differ depending on the question type.

Note that, on this Main Idea question, a PSAT expert would likely read the entire passage, but would focus on the sentence(s) most likely to contain the main idea. Typically, the first or last sentence will summarize the main idea of a passage. Here, the first sentence states that houses could be mail-ordered from Sears.

Since all you need is the main idea, you should avoid getting bogged down in the details of this passage. A quick skim of the details, however, can confirm that they all support the main idea that entire houses could be ordered: the other sentences include details such as the name of the catalog that offered houses and the fact that many different types of houses were available for purchase.

Step 3. What answer strategy is best?

Finally, consider which strategy will be your best approach for answering the question efficiently and correctly. Once you have identified what the question is asking and tailored your reading approach appropriately, there are two strategies you can use to help you identify the correct answer:

- **Predict & Match**—Based on the question and your reading of the passage, make a prediction of the correct answer in your own words. Then look for an answer choice that matches your prediction.
- **Eliminate**—Analyze the answer choices one-by-one and rule out any that do not directly answer the question based upon the information in the passage.

On the Main Idea question above, use the main idea identified in the first sentence of the passage to make a **prediction** of the correct answer in your own words: *houses could be ordered from Sears by mail*. This prediction matches **(B)**, which also addresses the emphasis in the rest of the passage on the variety of available houses. Choices (A) and (C) make claims that are not supported by the passage, and choice (D) mentions just one detail from the passage rather than summarizing the big picture of the passage.

Some question types tend to lend themselves to one strategy or the other. For instance, as in the example question, Main Idea questions allow you to paraphrase the main idea from the passage in your own words, which serves as your **prediction**. When predicting, be sure to make your prediction *before looking at the answer choices*; your prediction will help you quickly identify the correct answer and avoid wasting time considering the incorrect answer choices. Check your prediction against the choices and find the *one* correct answer that **matches**. If you can't find a match, you can check the passage again and try rephrasing your prediction or try the strategy of elimination.

Eliminating entails reading the answer choices one-by-one and rejecting those that don't answer the question. Although this can be more time- consuming than predicting and matching, some questions are difficult to predict and require using this more thorough approach. Eliminate answer choices that misrepresent the passage, as well as those that fail to address the question asked. See the "Incorrect Answer Types" section that follows for information about the incorrect answer types you are most likely to encounter—and be able to quickly eliminate—on test day. Note that the digital format of the PSAT provides an option that allows you to eliminate individual answer choices by clicking an icon that appears next to each one. An icon at the far right of the question number box will enable this option, which can be very helpful for keeping track of the answer choices on test day.

While some question types may typically lend themselves to one answer strategy or the other, keep in mind that you should use whichever strategy is best for you. If you struggle to make a prediction on a Main Idea question, for instance, don't sweat it! Move on to the elimination strategy and get rid of those answer choices you recognize as incorrect.

Let's walk through the steps of the Method one more time, this time on a question that highlights the answer strategy of elimination and presents the slight adjustment you should make to the Method when answering a question about Standard English conventions.

The Sears Catalog, a mail-order catalog first introduced in 1887, offered a vastly larger selection and lower prices than a local store could do. From pocket watches to patent medicines, from women's gowns to water pumps, from hunting rifles to horse-drawn plows, _____ offered it all.

Which choice completes the text so that it conforms to the conventions of Standard English?

(A) they

(B) this

(C) it

(D) the catalog

Step 1. What is the question asking?

Note that this question stem asks you to choose the answer choice that "conforms to the conventions of Standard English." Since this question concerns English conventions, add an additional part to this step: *look at the answer choices for clues before looking at the passage*. Doing so will often enable you to identify which English convention the question is testing, which will help you focus on that issue as you read.

This question, for example, contains several pronouns in the answer choices, so you can anticipate that the question tests pronoun agreement or usage.

Step 2. What do I need to look for in the passage?

As before, strategically read the passage based on what the question asks. Since the question and answer choices indicate that the blank may contain a pronoun, read the passage with the goal of determining who is logically referred to in the blank. The blank refers to who or what "offered it all." Since the sentence contains a list of available products, it must be the Sears Catalog, referred to in the first sentence, that offered many items.

Step 3. What answer strategy is best?

Finally, consider which answer strategy—predict & match or eliminate—is your best approach. The blank must refer to the *Sears Catalog*, which offered many products. However, the answer choices contain both the noun "the catalog" and various pronouns, so evaluate the choices and **eliminate** any that do not work in the context of the passage.

First, eliminate choice (A), "they," as the "Sears Catalog" is singular and this choice is a plural pronoun. Next, consider the singular pronoun "this" in choice (B). In context, this pronoun is ambiguous, as the first sentence refers to both the "Sears Catalog" and "a local store"; the blank must refer to the "Sears Catalog," but "a local store" is closer to the blank. Thus, eliminate (B), as well as the ambiguous pronoun in (C). Choice **(D)** clarifies that the catalog offered a big selection and is correct.

Make the Method Work for You

Overall, remember that the Method for PSAT Reading and Writing is *flexible*, allowing you to efficiently answer each question using the strategy that is best for you. Always use the question to help you tailor your reading of the passage, and then determine which answer strategy—predict & match or eliminate—will enable you to confidently answer the question asked. Expert PSAT test takers consistently apply the three-step Method, but they vary their specific approach from question to question, depending on what is asked and their own strengths. As you practice PSAT questions, follow the Method, but practice both answer strategies so you can learn what works best for you.

Incorrect Answer Types

Whether you predict & match or eliminate when answering a question, being aware of the most common types of incorrect answer choices can help you focus on the correct choice and quickly rule out the incorrect choices. Incorrect answer choices on the PSAT often fall into one of five categories:

- **Out of Scope**—contains a statement that is too broad, too narrow, or beyond the purview of the passage
- **Extreme**—contains language that is too strong (*all, never, always, every, none*) to be supported by the passage
- **Distortion**—based on details or ideas from the passage but distorts or misstates what the author says or implies
- **Opposite**—directly contradicts what the correct answer must say
- **Misused Detail**—accurately states something from the passage but in a manner that incorrectly answers the question

Strategic Reading

Every question on the PSAT Reading and Writing section is accompanied by a short passage, typically about a paragraph in length. The PSAT includes passages in the following subject areas: literature, history/social studies, the humanities (topics such as the arts), and science.

The process of reading passages on the PSAT is not the same as reading materials for leisure or even for textbooks or other books you read for school. As demonstrated in the Method for PSAT Reading and Writing, your reading of each short passage should be tailored exactly to the question that is asked; you are not reading to learn everything about the passage, but only with the goal of answering a specific question. The following chapters will provide tips about how to read the passage for each particular question type. For example, as demonstrated in the Method section, you'll typically focus on the first (or possibly the last) sentence of a passage when answering a Main Idea question.

Keywords

No matter what type of question you're answering, there are special types of words you should be on the lookout for in every PSAT Reading and Writing passage. These words will help you understand the structure and viewpoints in every passage; *the test makers specifically include these words as hints to help you answer the questions asked.* PSAT keywords include:

TYPES OF KEYWORDS IN PSAT PASSAGES		
KEYWORD TYPE	**WHAT THE KEYWORDS INDICATE**	**EXAMPLES**
Opinion	the author's viewpoint	*fortunately, disappointing, I suggest, it seems likely*
Emphasis	what the author finds noteworthy	*especially, crucial, important, above all*
Continuation	a continuation of the same point	*moreover, in addition, also, further*
Contrast	a change in direction or a point of difference	*but, yet, despite, on the other hand, however*
Cause and effect	the use of evidence to support a conclusion	*thus, therefore, because, for example, to illustrate*

Keywords indicate opinions and signal structures that make the difference between correct and incorrect answers on PSAT questions. Consider this question:

> With which one of the following statements would the author most likely agree?
>
> 1. Coffee beans that grow at high altitudes typically produce dark, mellow coffee when brewed.
>
> 2. Coffee beans that grow at high altitudes typically produce light, acidic coffee when brewed.

To answer this question, look at this excerpt from its associated passage next. Pay special attention to the keywords in bold.

> Type X coffee beans grow at very high altitudes **and so** produce a dark, mellow coffee when brewed.

The continuation keywords "and so" indicate a connection between the ideas in the sentence, so choice (1) would be correct.

However, if the excerpt instead said:

> Type X coffee beans grow at very high altitudes **but** produce a **surprisingly** dark, mellow coffee when brewed.

In this case, the contrast keyword "but" and the emphasis keyword "surprisingly" indicate a contrast between Type X coffee beans and their growing at high altitudes, making choice (2) correct. The other words in the excerpts did not change at all, but the correct answer to the PSAT question would be different in each case because of the keywords the author chose to include.

Passage Blurbs

Some passages are preceded by a **short blurb** that identifies the author, the year written, and the source of the passage. They may also provide some additional context to keep in mind that will help you understand the passage. These blurbs most often accompany literature passages. Be sure to read any blurbs to help you understand the context of the passage.

Literature Passages

Many of the passages on the PSAT will be literature passages. These will be short excerpts from literary works, such as novels, short stories, and poems. Don't worry if you haven't read the source before; like every PSAT Reading and Writing question, everything you need to answer the question is found on the test. In fact, if you are familiar with the source, be careful to use only the excerpt provided on the PSAT, not your outside knowledge, to answer the question.

Literature passages are naturally less factual than other PSAT passages. When you encounter a literature passage, approach it as you would any PSAT Reading and Writing question: first analyze the question stem, then the passage, before you use an answering strategy. When reading the passage, keep in mind that literature passages often emphasize literary elements: characters, settings, themes (the main idea or message of the passage), and figurative language. Questions on literature passages often concern these types of literary elements.

Putting It All Together

By using the Method for PSAT Reading **and Writing on** every question and strategically reading every passage, expert test takers set themselves up for **success** with an approach that will be efficient and effective on every question they'll encounter. Like learning **any new skill**, mastering these strategies will take practice. So on every practice question you try, work on getting **in the** habit of following the steps: read the question, read the passage strategically, and predict & **match or eliminate** answer choices. Always read the question explanations, and reflect upon how your own approach **compares.** Keep asking yourself: *What did I do well on this question? How can I improve my strategy on a similar question in the future?* With practice, the method and strategies will become second nature by test day. Give it **a try now** by applying what you've learned to the questions that follow.

Try on Your Own

Directions

Take as much time as you need on these questions. On each question, use the three-step Method for PSAT Reading and Writing. Look for keywords as you strategically read each passage.

1

Archeologists have typically dated the beginning of human occupation of the majority of the American continents to approximately 13,000 years ago. This assumption was based upon both a lack of human archeological evidence and the premise that humans could not have traversed past broad North American glaciers prior to this timeframe. However, archeologist Ciprian Ardelean has dated what may be stone flaking tools in Chiquihuite cave in current-day Mexico to at least 18,000 years ago. If the Chiquihuite cave findings are indeed human artifacts, Ardelean implies that _____

Which choice most logically completes the text?

Ⓐ the stone flaking tools are among the most technologically advanced that have been discovered in the American continents.

Ⓑ most other human archeological evidence from the American continents has been misdated.

Ⓒ glaciers were an impassable obstacle for the humans that occupied the American continents over the past 20,000 years.

Ⓓ human occupation of certain parts of the American continents occurred earlier than archeologists previously thought.

Reading & Writing

2

The following text is from Washington Irving's 1820 short story "The Legend of Sleepy Hollow."

In the bosom of one of those spacious coves which indent the eastern shore of the Hudson, . . . there lies a small market town or rural port, which by some is called Greensburgh, . . . Not far from this village, perhaps about two miles, there is a little valley or rather lap of land among high hills, which is one of the quietest places in the whole world. <u>A small brook glides through it, with just murmur enough to lull one to repose; and the occasional whistle of a quail or tapping of a woodpecker is almost the only sound that ever breaks in upon the uniform tranquility.</u> I recollect that, when a stripling, my first exploit in squirrel-shooting was in a grove of tall walnut-trees that shades one side of the valley. I had wandered into it at noontime, when all nature is peculiarly quiet, and was startled by the roar of my own gun.

Which choice best states the function of the underlined sentence in the text as a whole?

(A) It describes a feature of the setting that also reflects a trait of the character introduced in the sentences that follow.

(B) It elaborates on the setting that is described in the previous sentence.

(C) It presents a counterpoint to the claim that is made in the previous sentence.

(D) It establishes a conflict that will likely be addressed later in the story.

3

On January 8, 1918, more than half a year before the final battles of World War I, U.S. President Woodrow Wilson shared with Congress his vision for improved postwar international relations. One of Wilson's fourteen goals for the postwar world included the creation of an international organization for collective security. The Treaty of Versailles, which officially ended the war in 1919, included the establishment of such an international organization, the League of Nations. Wilson actively advocated throughout the United States in support for the Treaty of Versailles. _____ the U.S. Congress never approved the treaty or joined the League of Nations.

Which choice completes the text with the most logical transition?

(A) Moreover,

(B) However,

(C) Indeed,

(D) Therefore,

4

Poet and monk Ukñā Suttantaprījā Ind wrote about life in Cambodia in the early twentieth century. In "Journey to Angkor Wat," written in his native Khmer _____ Ind reflects on the ancient Buddhist ruins in light of the political change occurring in Cambodia at the time.

Which choice completes the text so that it conforms to the conventions of Standard English?

(A) language,

(B) language—

(C) language

(D) language)

Reflect

Directions: Take a few minutes to recall what you've learned and what you've been practicing in this chapter. Consider the following questions, jot down your best answer for each one, and then compare your reflections to the expert responses that follow. Use your level of confidence to determine what to do next.

Identify the steps of the Method for PSAT Reading and Writing. What additional task should you perform when answering a Standard English Conventions question?

_____

_____

_____

Why do expert PSAT test takers look at the question before reading the passage?

_____

_____

_____

What are the two answer strategies you can use when answering a Reading and Writing question? When might one strategy be preferable over the other?

_____

_____

_____

What incorrect answer types can you quickly eliminate?

_____

_____

_____

What are some types of keywords that appear in PSAT passages? What is the benefit of noting keywords as you read?

_____

_____

_____

What will you do differently on future passages and their questions?

_____

_____

_____

Expert Responses

Identify the steps of the Method for PSAT Reading and Writing. What additional task should you perform when answering a Standard English Conventions question?

The steps of the Method are: 1) What is the question asking?, 2) What do I need to look for in the passage?, and 3) What answer strategy is best? When answering a Standard English Conventions question, you should look at the answer choices for clues during Step 1 before reading the passage.

Why do expert PSAT test takers look at the question before reading the passage?

Because each passage only has one question, reading the question before you jump into the passage will allow you to focus in on exactly what you need from the passage.

What are the two answer strategies you can use when answering a Reading and Writing question? When might one strategy be preferable over the other?

The two answer strategies are Predict & Match, in which you make a prediction of the correct answer in your own words before looking for a match in the answer choices and Eliminate, in which you analyze the answer choices one-by-one and rule out any that do not directly answer the question based on the information in the passage. Predicting works well when it is easy to predict the answer to the question. Eliminating works well when it is difficult to make a specific prediction.

What incorrect answer types can you quickly eliminate?

Incorrect answer choices include those that are out of scope (state something that goes beyond the passage), extreme (contain language that is too strong to be supported by the passage), distortions (misstate what the author says or implies), opposite (directly contradict what the correct answer must say), and misused details (state something from the passage but doesn't answer the question). Don't worry if you couldn't remember all these types—you'll learn to recognize them as you practice more Reading and Writing questions.

What are some types of keywords that appear in PSAT passages? Provide some examples of each type. What is the benefit of noting keywords as you read?

Keyword types include opinion (such as fortunately *and* disappointing*), emphasis (such as* especially *and* crucial*), continuation (such as* moreover *and* further*), contrast (such as* despite *and* however*), and cause-and-effect (such as* therefore *and* because*) words. These words will help you understand the structure and viewpoints in every passage; the test makers specifically include these words as hints to help you answer the questions asked.*

What will you do differently on future passages and their questions?

There is no one-size-fits-all answer to this question. Each student has individual initial strengths and opportunities in the Reading and Writing section. What's important here is that you're honestly self-reflective. Take what you need from the expert's examples and strive to apply it to your own performance. Many test takers convince themselves that they'll never get faster or more confident in PSAT Reading and Writing, but the truth is, many test takers who now routinely ace the Reading and Writing section were much slower and more hesitant before they learned to approach this section systematically and strategically.

Next Steps

If your responses to the Reflect questions were similar to those of the PSAT expert, then consider How to Do PSAT Reading and Writing an area of strength.

If you don't yet feel confident, review the information in this chapter that you have not yet mastered. Then, try the questions you missed again. As always, be sure to review the explanations closely.

In either case, make sure you apply the strategies from this chapter and the Method for PSAT Reading and Writing to *every* question you practice as you move on to the following chapters, which cover each of the Reading and Writing question types.

Answers and Explanations

Try on Your Own

1. D

Difficulty: Medium

Category: Information and Ideas

Getting to the Answer: The question stem asks which choice logically flows from the ideas in the passage. The sentence with the blank identifies that the correct answer will be something that is implied if the cave artifacts were made by humans, so look for details about these artifacts as you read the passage. The previous sentence states that Ardelean dated the tool artifacts to at least 18,000 years ago. Determine why this dating is significant. The contrast transition "However" indicates that this date contrasts with other dates; the previous sentences explain that human occupation in the Americas was previously thought to have started only 13,000 years ago. With such a clear contrast word, many students would choose the predict-and-match strategy for this question. You can predict that the archeologist would imply that the new artifacts date human occupation earlier than was previously thought. This matches **(D)**, which is correct.

Choice (A) can be eliminated because it is out of scope; the passage does not address how advanced the stone tools were. Choices (B) and (C) can be eliminated because they distort the details in the passage. For (B), the passage states that Ardelean dated the stone tools from Mexico as relatively old, but the passage never suggests that he contests the dating of other archeological artifacts. For (C), the passage states that archeologists assumed humans couldn't go past glaciers earlier than 13,000 years ago, but it never suggests that Ardelean thinks glaciers were "impassable"; if anything, his older dating of artifacts suggests that humans got around the glaciers.

2. B

Difficulty: Hard

Category: Craft and Structure

Getting to the Answer: The question stem asks for the function of an underlined sentence, so think about the structure of the passage as you read. Ask yourself, *Why did the author include this sentence?* The passage begins by discussing the setting of the story, with a valley described as "one of the quietest places in the whole world." The underlined sentence gives additional details about the valley (its murmuring brook, its occasional bird noises) that support the claim that it is quiet. The remaining sentences introduce a character (the narrator) into the quiet setting that has been described. While some students might predict an answer here, others might choose the elimination strategy. If you would choose the latter, evaluate the answer choices with the structure you just found in mind. Eliminate (A), as the character is not described as quiet; rather, he fires a loud gun. Choice **(B)** is correct; the underlined sentence uses details to elaborate on the description of the setting as quiet. Choice (C) is opposite; the underlined sentence is not a counterpoint, but rather supporting evidence, for the claim that the valley is quiet. Eliminate (D) as well, since the underlined sentence does not imply conflict, just a quiet setting.

3. B

Difficulty: Medium

Category: Expression of Ideas

Getting to the Answer: The question stem asks for the most logical transition, so as you read the passage, identify what ideas are being connected by the transition. The first idea, located in the sentence before the transition, is that Wilson advocated for the Treaty of Versailles. The second idea, located in the sentence with the transition, is that Congress never approved the treaty. These ideas contrast, so many students would predict that the correct answer will be a contrast transition word. This prediction matches **(B)**, which is correct. Choices (A) and (C) are incorrect because they are continuation transitions, while the ideas in the passage contrast. Choice (D) is incorrect because it creates an illogical cause-and-effect relationship; Congress failed to approve the treaty *despite*, not *due to*, Wilson's support for it.

4.   A

Difficulty: Easy

Category: Standard English Conventions

Getting to the Answer: Since this question asks about Standard English conventions, read the answer choices before looking at the passage. The choices signal that this question deals with punctuation, most likely testing how to set off parenthetical information, as indicated by the comma, dash, and parenthesis in the answer choices. The sentence with the blank contains the parenthetical phrase "written in his native Khmer language." Parenthetical elements should be set off from the rest of the sentence with a pair of matching punctuation marks. Since the phrase is preceded by a comma, either predict that a comma should also follow "language" or eliminate incorrect answer choices; **(A)** is correct. Choices (B) and (D) include other ways to set off parenthetical information, but a comma must be used here to result in a matching set. Choice (C) incorrectly runs the text together by omitting all punctuation.

[CHAPTER 13]

INFORMATION AND IDEAS

LEARNING OBJECTIVES

After completing this chapter, you will be able to:

- Identify the main idea of a passage
- Identify a detail explicitly stated in the text
- Identify the conclusion and evidence in an argument
- Identify additional relevant information that strengthens or weakens a claim
- Use quantitative information to logically complete or support a statement
- Determine what must be true based on given information

How Much Do You Know?

Directions

Try the questions that follow. When you're done, check your answers and reasoning against ours in the "Check Your Work" section. If they closely match, you may be able to move quickly through the chapter. If they do not, spend some extra time with the chapter to grow your PSAT Reading and Writing skills.

1

Few developments have so greatly affected American life as the automobile. The car has had a significant effect on nearly every facet of American life, including how we work, where we live, and what we believe. Interestingly, it was the process of building cars rather than the cars themselves that first brought a sea of change to the American workplace. In 1914, a Ford plant in Highland Park, Michigan used the first electric conveyor belt, greatly increasing the efficiency of automobile manufacturing. Assembly lines for the production of automobiles were quickly adopted and became highly mechanized, providing a new model for industrial business.

Which choice best states the main idea of the text?

Ⓐ The automobile has changed American life more than any other invention.

Ⓑ A new method for building automobiles changed American manufacturing processes.

Ⓒ Assembly lines have proven to be the most efficient method of producing industrial equipment.

Ⓓ Until the installation of the conveyor belt, the Ford plant in Highland Park, Michigan was unsuccessful.

2

Single-celled organisms are classified into one of three domains—Bacteria, Archaea, or Eukarya—based on specific characteristics, but the evolutionary relationships among these domains are far from clear. A comparison of the genomes showed similarities between the Bacteria and Archaea in the gene coding for enzymes, and similarities between the Archaea and Eukarya in the gene coding for protein synthesis machinery. Moreover, although the Archaea are prokaryotes, the proteins that give their chromosomes structure are similar to those within the nucleus of the Eukarya. In other words, the Archaea seem to be related, in different ways, to both the Bacteria and the Eukarya. Because the Eukarya are the most recent domain to evolve, it has been hypothesized that the first eukaryotic cell originally arose from a prokaryotic cell within the Archaea.

According to the passage, the genetic similarities between the Archaea and the Eukarya are significant because

Ⓐ they suggest an evolutionary origin for the Eukarya.

Ⓑ they imply that the origins of the Archaea are most recent.

Ⓒ they undermine the belief that the Bacteria are of more ancient origin than the Archaea.

Ⓓ they make it impossible to consider more than three domains of single-celled organisms.

3

"Old Ireland" is a late 1890s poem by Walt Whitman. In the poem, written during the time of the Irish potato famine, the speaker contrasts despair with the hope for a better future.

Which quotation from "Old Ireland" most effectively illustrates this contrast?

(A) Far hence, amid an isle of wondrous beauty,/ Crouching over a grave, an ancient sorrowful mother,/ Once a queen—now lean and tattered, seated on the ground,/

(B) At her feet fallen an unused royal harp,/ Long silent—she too long silent—mourning her shrouded hope and heir;/ Of all the earth her heart most full of sorrow, because most full of love./

(C) Yet a word, ancient mother;/ You need crouch there no longer on the cold ground, with forehead between your knees;/ O you need not sit there, veiled in your old white hair, so dishevelled;/

(D) Even while you wept there by your fallen harp, by the grave,/ What you wept for was translated, passed from the grave,/ The winds favoured, and the sea sailed it,/ And now, with rosy and new blood,/ Moves today in another country./

4

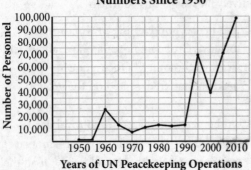

**UN Peacekeeping Personnel
Numbers Since 1950**

Years of UN Peacekeeping Operations

Decades ago, provoked by the events of World Wars I and II, world leaders began imagining a politically neutral force for international peace. The United Nations (UN) was born in 1945 as a collective political authority for global peace and security and has offered consistent relief for many of the past half-century's most difficult disasters and conflicts. It also provides a safe space for international conversation; advocates for issues such as justice, trade, hunger relief, human rights, health, and gender equality; coordinates care for those displaced by disaster and conflict; dictates environmental protection; and works toward conflict reconciliation. The UN's budget, goals, and personnel count have significantly expanded with time to meet more needs. For example, _____

Which choice most effectively uses data from the graph to complete the example?

Ⓐ the year 2010 led to an increase of approximately 100,000 in the UN peacekeeping force.

Ⓑ the year 2010 saw the UN peacekeeping force grow to approximately 100,000 strong.

Ⓒ the year 2010 saw the UN peacekeeping force decrease to just over 100,000 strong.

Ⓓ the year 2010 was the third year the UN peacekeeping force held steady at 100,000.

5

When acquiring language, newborns tend to be especially partial to their mother's voice and her native language. In this way, infants can easily learn the essential characteristics and rules of their native language. However, it is important to note that an infant's ability to learn from the nuances of her mother's speech is predicated upon her ability to separate that speech from the sounds of the dishwasher, the family dog, the bus on the street outside, and, quite possibly, other streams of speech, like a newscaster on the television down the hall or siblings playing in an adjacent room. Infants are better able to accomplish this task when the voice of interest is louder than any of the competing background noises. Therefore, a mother who wants to assist her child in language acquisition should _____

Which choice most logically completes the text?

(A) expose her child to as many spoken languages as possible.

(B) use short words composed of the basic sounds of her native language.

(C) be sure her voice is louder than other background noises.

(D) use as large a vocabulary as possible when speaking to her child.

6

Economists have hypothesized that very small loans, called microloans, for the purpose of funding small businesses, could be a useful tool to help impoverished people better their circumstances, even if only modestly. In a study conducted in 1976, an economics professor in Bangladesh extended a microloan of 27 dollars to a group of impoverished village women for the purpose of buying supplies for their business manufacturing bamboo stools.

Which finding from the study, if true, would most strongly support the hypothesis?

(A) The number of women requesting a microloan more than doubled following the first year of the study.

(B) Some borrowers used the loan to finance consumption spending and were thus unable to repay either the loan proceeds or the interest.

(C) On average, the borrowers did not increase their incomes but replaced long hours of grueling work with less onerous self-employment.

(D) Some borrowers were unable to pay the interest on the loans from their business earnings and were forced to sell off their meager possessions to avoid debt.

PART 3
READING AND WRITING

Check Your Work

1. B

Difficulty: Hard

Category: Information and Ideas

Getting to the Answer: The first two sentences introduce the automobile as an invention that had a large impact on American life, but the passage changes focus after that. Marked by the emphasis keywords "Interestingly," "first," and "sea of change," the main idea expressed in the remainder of the text is that the *process* of manufacturing cars changed American business practices. This prediction matches **(B)**, the correct answer.

Incorrect choices (A) and (C) take ideas from the passage but go too far. In the first sentence, the text states the automobile is one of a "Few" crucial inventions that changed American life, but not that it was the *most* important one. (A) also makes no mention of the change in car manufacturing processes that was the focus of the rest of the text. Similarly, the passage never states that assembly lines are the "most efficient method" for manufacturing all "industrial equipment" because the text only discusses car assembly. The success of the Ford plant is never mentioned in the passage, so (D) is also incorrect.

2. A

Difficulty: Hard

Category: Information and Ideas

Getting to the Answer: This question contains two clues. First, the question refers to the similarities between the Archaea and Eukarya. Second, the question asks why those similarities are important. Keep this paraphrase of the question in mind as you scan the text for the location of the answer. The similarities are mentioned in the last phrase of the second sentence, and the reason is introduced by the keyword "Because" at the start of the last sentence. The similarities are important because they indicate there may be an evolutionary connection between Archaea and Eukarya. Therefore, **(A)** is correct.

(B) is a distortion of information presented in the passage, which states that Eukarya has the most recent origins. (C) and (D) are not discussed in the passage at all. The similarities between Archaea and Eukarya are not connected to the origin of the Bacteria, as in (C), nor to any limitation of the number of domains, as in (D).

3. D

Difficulty: Medium

Category: Information and Ideas

Getting to the Answer: Keep the two features the question requires—an image of despair contrasted with one of hope—in mind as you read the choices. Only **(D)** contains both: despair in the weeping by the grave "you wept there by your fallen harp, by the grave" and hope "with rosy and new blood" in the life in the new country. Choice **(D)** is correct.

Incorrect choices (A), (B), and (C) all contain images of despair, but not of hope for a better future.

4. B

Difficulty: Easy

Category: Information and Ideas

Getting to the Answer: Notice that the graph gives specific information about the increases and decreases in the UN peacekeeping force over a period of time. Match the choices to the graph to find the one that best relates to the paragraph. The graph shows that the number of personnel in the year 2010 reached 100,000. Choice **(B)** is the correct answer.

(A) is incorrect because the total number of personnel, not the increase, in 2010 was 100,000. (C) and (D) are incorrect because the number of personnel increased, not decreased or held steady, in 2010.

5. C

Difficulty: Medium

Category: Information and Ideas

Getting to the Answer: The first two sentences emphasize the importance of the mother's voice and native language to infant language acquisition. The next sentence discusses how infants have difficulty separating voice streams that have equal volumes, as well as how important it is for infants to recognize their mother's speech in order to learn from it. Thus, it makes sense that a mother would aid her infant's language acquisition by speaking louder than any background sounds, which makes **(C)** correct.

Although choices (A), (B), and (D) may be true in real-life, they are never mentioned in the text and are incorrect.

6. C

Difficulty: Hard

Category: Information and Ideas

Getting to the Answer: First, identify the hypothesis and paraphrase it in your own words. The first sentence tells you that microloans may help poor people improve their lives and that the study is testing that hypothesis. Predict that the correct answer will contain some way the lives of the borrowers improved. **(C)** matches this prediction because the borrowers were able to earn the same income from better work.

Choice (A) does not address the hypothesis and is incorrect; the hypothesis is that the microloans will make the borrowers' lives better, not that the program will attract more applicants. Choices (B) and (D) make the hypothesis less likely. If borrowers could not repay the loan or the interest, their lives would be more difficult.

Main Idea Questions

To answer a question like this:

Leafcutters are probably the most important environmental engineers in the areas they occupy. For example, a single leafcutter nest can extend as far as 21 meters underground, have a central mound 30 meters in diameter with branches extending out to a radius of 80 meters, contain upwards of 1,000 individual chambers, and house up to eight million ants. Also, where they are present, leafcutters are responsible for up to 25 percent or more of the total consumption of vegetation by all herbivores.

Which choice best states the main idea of the text?

(A) Leafcutter ants constitute the largest insect population in the environments they occupy.

(B) The impact of leafcutter ants on their surroundings is significant.

(C) Few other herbivores live in the same regions as leafcutter ants.

(D) It requires the labor of millions of leafcutter ants to build a central mound.

You need to know this:

How to Identify Main Idea Questions

Main Idea questions can be identified by keywords "main idea" or "central idea" in the question stem, for instance: *Which choice best states the main idea of the text?*

How to Identify the Main Idea

The main idea is the big picture of the passage. The main idea is not just the *topic* of the passage (for instance, dogs) but the author's *main point* about that topic (perhaps, why dogs are good pets). The main idea can often be found in the first sentence, or sometimes the last sentence, of a passage. The other sentences in the passage include details that support the main idea of the passage (perhaps, details that dogs are loyal, protective, and playful—and, thus, are good pets).

When you need to identify the main idea, don't get caught up in the details of the passage. In fact, incorrect answers on Main Idea questions often address just a specific detail, rather than the overall main idea, of the passage.

Incorrect answers to a Main Idea question may be:

- **Misused Details**—Incorrect answers to Main Idea questions often address just a specific detail, rather than the overall main idea, of the passage.

- **Distortions**—Incorrect answers to Main Idea questions may be based on ideas from the passage but may distort or misstate what the author says.

- **Out of Scope**—Incorrect answers to Main Idea questions may contain ideas that are simply not covered in the passage. These incorrect answers go beyond what the passage states or logically implies.

K

The correct answer to a Main Idea question will:

- Summarize the author's main point about the topic of the passage, which is often found in the first or last sentence
- Be supported by the details within the passage

You need to do this:

THE METHOD FOR PSAT READING AND WRITING

STEP 1 What is the question asking?

STEP 2 What do I need to look for in the passage?

STEP 3 What answer strategy is best?

- Predict & Match
- Eliminate

Step 1. What is the question asking?

If the question stem asks for the "main idea" or "central ideal" of the passage, proceed through the rest of the steps of the Method with your focus on finding the main idea.

Step 2. What do I need to look for in the passage?

As discussed in the Method for PSAT Reading and Writing Questions chapter, your approach to reading the passage should vary depending on what the question asks for. Since you need to identify the main idea, focus on the first and last sentences of the passage; the main idea will often be stated there. To make sure you've identified the main idea, skim the other sentences in the passage. The other sentences should be details that provide support for the main idea you've identified.

Step 3. What answer strategy is best?

Main Idea questions lend themselves to the strategy of predicting the correct answer. Take a moment to paraphrase the main idea you identified in Step 2 in your own words. The correct answer will probably not be a word-for-word match of the wording in the passage, so having a prediction in your own words will make it easier to efficiently focus in on the answer choice that reflects the main idea. If needed, eliminate answer choices that address only specific details from the passage, as well as answer choices that are outside the scope of the passage.

Once you find the answer choice that matches your prediction and provides the main idea—not a detail—from the passage, select it and move on.

Explanation:

The question asks for the main idea, so focus on the big picture rather than the details as you read the passage. Since the first or last sentence often contains the main idea, focus on these parts of the passage. The first sentence introduces a claim, indicated by the words "most important": leafcutter ants are the most important environmental engineers. The remaining sentences are details that support this main idea, as indicated by the keywords "For example" and "Also." Predict that the main idea is that the ants are important engineers of their environment; this matches **(B)**, which is correct.

The remaining answer choices are distortions of details in the passage. Although the passage identifies that millions of ants may live in a nest, the statements in (A) and (D) are not specified in the passage; further, neither answer choice addresses the main idea that the ants are important environmental engineers. Choice (C) distorts the detail in the last sentence about consumption by herbivores.

Try on Your Own

Directions

Take as much time as you need on these questions. Work carefully and methodically. There will be an opportunity for timed practice later in the book.

1

As more and more traditional languages across the world disappear, Euskara, the traditional language of the Basque Country of Spain, is defying this trend and flourishing. In an effort to unify Spain, the language had been banned from use in public and in schools for over 40 years and had been replaced by Spanish. Prior to preservation efforts, the number of Euskara speakers was estimated to be around 25% of the population. But in 1999, the regional government instituted the General Revitalization Plan for the Basque Language and established schools where Euskara was the primary language of instruction. The results were dramatic: over 350,000 Euskara speakers have been added, 87% of 10–14-year-old children speak the language, and 56% of the population either speak or understand Euskara.

Which choice best states the main idea of the text?

- (A) Replacing Euskara with Spanish has been shown to be an historic mistake.

- (B) The General Revitalization Plan for the Basque Language has shown remarkable results in reversing the decline of Euskara.

- (C) In spite of heroic efforts by the Basque Country of Spain, Euskara, like other traditional languages, is heading for extinction.

- (D) Since the revitalization plan of the regional government was so successful, similar plans should be used to halt the decline of other traditional languages.

2

The search for life outside the planet Earth continues. Recent data received from *Curiosity*, the mechanical rover exploring the surface of Mars, has indicated the presence of sufficient organic carbon to support life. Previously, *Curiosity* reported observations that researchers interpreted as confirming the past presence of large quantities of water on the Martian surface. Organic carbon and water are two requirements for life. Despite the excitement these findings have generated, there is still no proof that life on Mars exists now or existed in the distant past.

Which choice best states the main idea of the text?

- (A) Data from the *Curiosity* rover point to large quantities of water on the Martian surface.

- (B) Life outside of Earth has yet to be found, although components necessary for life have been found on Mars.

- (C) Since the components for life have been found on Mars, researchers expect to find traces of past living organisms.

- (D) The mission of the *Curiosity* rover has reported more important information about Mars than any other mission.

3

Two Norwegian colonies in Greenland, established about 1000 C.E., disappeared after enjoying several prosperous centuries. One hypothesis proposes that cultural and sociological factors may have contributed to the demise of the Norse settlements. The Inuit tribes, recent immigrants to Greenland, had come from nearby areas to the west and had time-tested strategies to cope with the severe environment. The Norse settlers, however, seem to have viewed themselves as fundamentally European and did not adopt Inuit techniques. Inuit apparel, for example, was far more appropriate for the cold, damp environment; the remains from even the last surviving Norse settlements indicate a costume that was undeniably European in design. It seems likely that this stubborn cultural inflexibility prevented the Norse civilization in Greenland from adapting to increasingly severe environmental conditions.

Which choice best states the main idea of the text?

(A) The colonies in Greenland were Norway's most prosperous colonies.

(B) The Inuit were experts at surviving in damp, cold weather conditions.

(C) Adhering rigidly to cultural standards may have doomed the Norse colonists.

(D) If the colonists had abandoned European clothing styles, the Norse colonies would be thriving today.

4

For most of the twentieth century, it was believed that all life forms could be broadly classified into two main groups, called domains: eukaryotes, or organisms possessing a cell nucleus; and prokaryotes, or organisms lacking such a nucleus. The terms "prokaryotes" and "bacteria" were used more or less interchangeably. Only in the 1970s was it discovered that there are in fact two very distinct groups of prokaryotes, not any more related to each other than they are related to the eukaryotes: bacteria and archaea. This discovery was made by Carl Woese, who in 1990 proposed the current three-domain system based on phylogenetics, or the degree of genetic relatedness among species.

Which choice best states the main idea of the text?

(A) Eukaryotes should be included in the Archaea domain.

(B) The idea that bacteria are the most ancient life form is mistaken.

(C) The three-domain system of classification should be more widely adopted.

(D) The discovery of the Archaea domain changed the biological classification system.

5

Once the first electric conveyor belt was used in a Ford plant in 1914, assembly lines for the production of automobiles were quickly adopted and became highly mechanized, providing a new model for industrial business. In contrast to European manufacturers, which employed a higher percentage of skilled laborers to produce fewer and costlier cars, American companies focused on turning out a large quantity of affordable cars utilizing less-skilled laborers. Assembly-line production was a mixed blessing, as it enabled higher productivity and more affordable cars but resulted in less-satisfied workers with less-interesting jobs. The value of efficiency was emphasized over personal pride, craftsmanship, and investment in the work.

Which choice best states the main idea of the text?

(A) European and American cars have dramatic differences in quality.

(B) Greater efficiency and more skilled laborers can improve the American workplace.

(C) A less mechanized but less efficient factory system is preferable to assembly lines.

(D) Automobile assembly lines had both positive and negative effects on the American workplace.

6

Kigo, or seasonal words, have long been a crucial component of *haiku*, a traditional style of Japanese poetry. Past generations of poets collected *kigo* and categorized them by season because the different seasons each evoke different emotional responses from the reader. For example, *sakura*, the cherry blossoms, occur in spring, and so, evoke an image of hope and new beginnings. However, these ancient connections are being ruptured by climate change. Because cherry trees require winter freezing to flower, as temperatures in Japan rise, the trees are flowering earlier, and may not blossom at all if a winter is particularly warm. These climate shifts are rupturing the connections between *kigo* and their seasons, making traditional haiku harder to understand by modern readers.

Which choice best states the main idea of the text?

(A) A correct understanding of *kigo* is required before any poet can write *haiku*.

(B) *Kigo* anthologies will have to be extensively revised if climate change continues.

(C) Climate change has rendered *haiku*, a traditional style of Japanese poetry, meaningless.

(D) Warming temperatures may threaten the appreciation of *haiku*, a traditional style of Japanese poetry.

Reading & Writing

Detail Questions

To answer a question like this:

At least forty-seven species of leafcutter ants range from as far south as Argentina to as far north as the southern United States. These ants, as their name implies, cut sections of vegetation—leaves, flowers, and grasses—from an array of plants, taking the cut sections back into their underground nests. However, the ants don't feed on the vegetation they cut; in fact, they're unable to digest the material directly. Instead, they carry the fragments into dedicated chambers within their nests, where they cultivate a particular species of nutritious fungus on the cut vegetation. It is this fungus that the ants eat and feed to their larvae.

According to the passage, the reason that leafcutter ants bring cut vegetation into their nests is to

Ⓐ use as nesting material

Ⓑ feed the vegetation to their larvae

Ⓒ ensure they have access to a variety of vegetation

Ⓓ cultivate edible fungus on the vegetation

You need to know this:

How to Identify Detail Questions

Detail questions test your ability to interpret the details that support the main idea of a passage. Keywords that signal a Detail question include "according to the passage," "the passage indicates," and "the passage identifies"; for instance: *According to the passage, the beagle dog breed is especially proficient at which of the following skills?*

How to Locate the Relevant Detail

Although the wording of Detail questions can vary, the correct answer will always be explicitly stated in the passage. Clue words in the question stem can help you focus in on the specific detail needed to answer the question. For instance, in the example above (*According to the passage, the beagle dog breed is especially proficient at which of the following skills?*), the words "beagle," "proficient," and "skills" would indicate that you need to locate a detail about the abilities of beagle dogs. Sometimes, a single sentence in the passage may be enough to answer the question—in this case, you can ignore the other details, find the correct answer, and move on. Other times, you may need additional context from the passage in order to understand the detail needed to answer the question. Be flexible in your approach, using only as much of the passage as you need.

Although the correct answer is explicitly stated in the passage, the wording of the correct answer choice will not exactly match the wording in the passage. Rather, it will be a paraphrase of the detail in the passage. For this reason, making your own paraphrased prediction of the correct answer will help you efficiently focus in on the one correct answer choice.

Incorrect answers to a Detail question may be:

- **Misused Details**—Don't select an answer choice just because you recognize it from the passage. The most common type of incorrect answer to Detail questions mentions a detail that appears in the passage but does not answer the question that was asked.

- **Distortions**—Incorrect answers to Detail questions may reflect the relevant detail that answers the question but may misstate the detail in a way that contradicts the information in the passage.

- **Opposite**—Incorrect answers to Detail questions may even state the opposite of the details from the passage.

The correct answer to a Detail question will:

- Specifically answer the question, not just provide a detail from the passage
- Paraphrase a detail explicitly stated in the passage

You need to do this:

THE METHOD FOR PSAT READING AND WRITING

STEP 1 What is the question asking?

STEP 2 What do I need to look for in the passage?

STEP 3 What answer strategy is best?

- Predict & Match
- Eliminate

Step 1. What is the question asking?

Keywords such as "according to the passage," "the passage indicates," and "the passage identifies" signal a Detail question. Use the other clue words in the question stem to state, in your own words, exactly what the question is asking.

Step 2. What do I need to look for in the passage?

Since the first sentence of a passage typically identifies the main idea of the passage, the detail needed to answer a Detail question will likely appear in one of the sentences in the body of the paragraph. Once you've identified what the question is asking, skim the passage for clue words that reflect the detail you need. It's possible that a single sentence may be all that is required to answer the question, though be ready to read more of the passage for additional context if needed.

Step 3. What answer strategy is best?

Making a prediction can make it easier to efficiently answer Detail questions. Using the relevant detail you located in the passage, paraphrase the correct answer in your own words. Then look for a match for your prediction among the answer choices. Remember that the correct answer will not be an *exact* match for the wording in the passage. Rather, one answer choice will match the *idea* you identified in your prediction. If needed, eliminate answer choices that distort or misuse details from the passage—any detail that does not specifically answer the question.

Once you find the answer choice that matches your prediction and provides the specific answer to the question asked, select it and move on.

Explanation:

The keywords "According to the passage" indicate that this is a Detail question. The question is asking why leafcutter ants bring vegetation into their nests, so search the passage for a detail that identifies the reason. The first two sentences introduce the topic of leafcutter ants and the fact that they carry vegetation to their nests, but these sentences do not identify the reason. The next sentence, beginning "However," states that the ants *don't* eat the vegetation. The transition word "Instead" signals the reason: to cultivate fungus that they do eat. Use this reason as your prediction, which matches **(D)**.

The other answer choices can be eliminated because they either reflect details that do not specifically answer the question or they distort details from the passage. Although the ants bring vegetation into their nests, the passage never specifies that they use it as nesting material, so (A) is incorrect. Choice (B) is incorrect because the ants feed fungus, not vegetation, to their larvae. Although the passage states that the ants get cuttings from "an array of plants," the passage does not identify access to variety as the reason the ants bring the vegetation into their nests, so (C) is incorrect.

Try on Your Own

Directions

Take as much time as you need on these questions. Work carefully and methodically. There will be an opportunity for timed practice later in the book.

7

The following text is from Gustave Flaubert's 1857 novel *Madame Bovary*.

Old Rouault would not have been sorry to be rid of his daughter, who was of no use to him in the house. In his heart he excused her, thinking her too clever for farming, a calling under the ban of Heaven, since one never saw a millionaire in it. Far from having made a fortune by it, the good man was losing every year; for if he was good in bargaining, in which he enjoyed the dodges of the trade, on the other hand, agriculture properly so called, and the internal management of the farm, suited him less than most people. He did not willingly take his hands out of his pockets, and did not spare expense in all that concerned himself, liking to eat well, to have good fires, and to sleep well.

According to the passage, Old Rouault thinks that farming

(A) is an apt career for his daughter.

(B) contributes to a good night's sleep.

(C) is not a highly profitable occupation.

(D) helps meet his basic needs.

8

Though vilified in media, sharks pose a relatively low danger to humans in the water, and their unique characteristics have actually inspired life-changing innovations that are used in advancing technology and medicine. For example, a shark's skin is formed by many microscopic, overlapping teeth-like "scales" called dermal denticles that increase a shark's speed by decreasing speed discrepancy and turbulence. Paint that mimics a shark's skin has been shown to improve marine transportation outcomes by decreasing fuel costs. Furthermore, the dermal denticles of the skin create a rough texture that discourages the attachment of parasites. This same principle was applied to the medical field when surfaces in hospitals and clinics were similarly modeled: it decreased the spread of bacteria and germs by preventing them from attaching to surfaces.

According to the passage, how have the features of a shark's skin influenced innovation?

- (A) Boats that have been sprayed with paint that is modeled after shark skins have decreased fuel costs.

- (B) Whales have smooth skin that allows barnacles to attach themselves to the whale's body.

- (C) Wetsuits made with a sharkskin material increase swimmers' speed by increasing speed discrepancy.

- (D) Surfaces that have the texture like a shark's skin increase the spread of bacteria.

9

Some countries still adhere to an archaic practice of daylight savings, which was introduced and spread globally during World War I as a method to increase working hours and decrease the reliance on artificial light so that fuel could be reserved for war efforts; many countries ceased participating in the daylight savings after the war ended. In the U.S., the time shift mandate was rescinded a few months after it was enacted, but World War II brought with it a reenactment of the mandatory time shift to once again decrease fuel consumption. Just as the U.S. government did previously, the law was repealed after the cessation of the war. In 1966, a year after the U.S. President sent military troops into Vietnam, the Uniform Time Act was passed to provide a permanent, national framework for seasonal time shifts.

The passage indicates that daylight savings

- (A) was mandated in all countries since the second world war.

- (B) is a modern practice that was first implemented in the United States.

- (C) increased reliance on artificial light when implemented nationwide.

- (D) was initially implemented to conserve fuel during times of war.

10

As a major exporter of amber, along with rice and silkworm cocoons, the Southeast Asian country of Myanmar has provided the scientific community with hundreds of wonderfully preserved specimens of prehistoric creatures. In fact, the smallest fossilized dinosaur, *Oculudentavis khaungraae*, which means "eye-tooth-bird," was discovered in a piece of 99-million-year-old amber that was mined from the Hukawng Valley of northern Myanmar. Dr. Jingmai O'Connor, a lead author of the study on the *Oculudentavis khaungraae*, nicknamed it "the Cretaceous terror of insects," because, despite its diminutive size, paleontologists theorize that the *Oculudentavis khaungraae* was a fierce prehistoric predator due to its large eyes and many sharp teeth.

According to the passage, which of the following do paleontologists theorize that the *Oculudentavis khaungraae* ate?

(A) Amber

(B) Insects

(C) Fish

(D) Hukawng

11

In the wild, saltwater crocodiles have an average lifespan of 70 years, with some living up to 100 years. Typically, crocodiles in captivity may live an additional 20–30 years, when the artificial habitat and diet are structured to appropriately meet the needs of the animal based on its age and size. Unfortunately, unscrupulous people have been known to capture crocodiles, removing them from their natural habitat and displaying them for profit, and bring about the animals' premature deaths with dangerously small enclosures, insufficient water sources, and poor food quality. Furthermore, there is a shocking lack of concern for this mistreatment of crocodiles because they are at low risk for extinction and have a reputation for attacking people.

This passage indicates that a crocodile's artificial habitat size

(A) should be large enough to protect people from crocodile attacks.

(B) is best when it's as large as a crocodile's natural habitat.

(C) may have a direct impact on the number of years it will live.

(D) should be constructed to prevent unnaturally long lifespans.

12

The internationally acclaimed art piece *Under the Wave off Kanagawa* (ca. 1830–32), also known as *The Great Wave,* is a woodblock print by Katsushika Hokusai, who is considered to be one of the first masters in ukiyo-e, a Japanese style of art that rose to prominence during the 17th through 19th centuries. *The Great Wave* is one of many woodblock prints, featuring his iconic colors of indigo and Prussian blue, that the artist created to bring attention to the juxtapositions he observed in nature: the near and far, natural and manmade, and fear and respect. Today, his contrasting imagery continues to capture our attention; the closeness of a powerful wave overtakes the distant view of Japan's highest point, Mount Fuji, while the fishermen rely on the strength of their boats to survive the natural might of the ocean.

This passage indicates that a recurring theme of Katsushika Hokusai's woodblock prints was

(A) the contrast between natural subjects located close to the viewer and in the distance.

(B) the similarities between different human emotions, such as fear and respect.

(C) the use of indigo and Prussian blue to celebrate the Japanese sky and oceans.

(D) his mastery of the Japanese art style, ukiyo-e, that was popularized during the 17th century.

Command of Evidence Questions (Textual)

LEARNING OBJECTIVES

After this lesson, you will be able to:

- Identify the conclusion and evidence in an argument
- Identify additional relevant information that strengthens or weakens a claim

To answer a question like this:

Leafcutter ants in neotropical environments are most prevalent in early successional forests. Pioneer species plants—resilient species that are typically the first to inhabit difficult ecosystems—are very common in such forests. Thus, Alejandro G. Farji-Brener has hypothesized that pioneer species plants must be a preferred foraging source for the ants. To evaluate his hypothesis, Farji-Brener analyzed the foraging behavior of leafcutter ants in their natural environments.

Which finding from the analysis, if true, would most strongly support Farji-Brener's hypothesis?

Ⓐ Older leafcutter ants foraged a significantly higher number of pioneer species plants than did the younger leafcutter ants.

Ⓑ The leafcutter ants that were analyzed had to exhibit cooperative behavior in order to forage the pioneer species plants.

Ⓒ Many of the non-pioneer species plants in the forests where the ants were studied were diseased at the time of the analysis.

Ⓓ The leafcutter ants that were analyzed foraged three times as many pioneer species plants as they did other plants.

You need to know this:

How to Identify Textual Command of Evidence Questions

Textual Command of Evidence questions require you to select additional information, beyond what is provided in the passage, that would support or weaken a hypothesis or claim from the passage. These questions can be identified by keywords such as "most strongly support," "most weakens," or "most effectively illustrates." Here are some sample Textual Command of Evidence question stems:

- *Which finding from the experiment, if true, would most strongly support the hypothesis?*
- *Which quotation from the poem most effectively illustrates the claim?*

How to Identify Evidence that Supports or Weakens

Since Textual Command of Evidence questions typically ask you to support or weaken a hypothesis or claim, the first step is to identify the specific hypothesis or claim. Paraphrase the hypothesis or claim in your own words.

Next, depending on what is asked for in the question stem, think about what type of additional information could potentially strengthen, weaken, or illustrate that claim or hypothesis.

For instance, suppose someone claims that basset hounds bark louder than do German shepherds. What type of additional information would strengthen, weaken, or illustrate that claim? An experiment that records a louder average decibel level for basset hound barks than for German shepherd barks would strengthen the claim, an experiment that records the opposite would weaken the claim, and an anecdote about a basset hound—but not a German shepherd—activating a noise-activated alarm would illustrate the claim.

Incorrect answers to a Textual Command of Evidence question may be:

- **Out of Scope**—Incorrect answers to Textual Command of Evidence questions often include additional information that has no relationship to the claim or hypothesis.
- **Opposite**—Incorrect answers to Textual Command of Evidence questions may include additional information that provides the *opposite* of what is asked for in the question, for instance, information that strengthens a claim when the question asks for information that weakens the claim.

The correct answer to a Textual Command of Evidence question will:

- Provide additional information, beyond what is provided in the passage, that strengthens, weakens, or illustrates a claim or hypothesis, as identified in the question
- Have a direct, logical relationship to the claim or hypothesis

You need to do this:

THE METHOD FOR PSAT READING AND WRITING

STEP 1   What is the question asking?

STEP 2   What do I need to look for in the passage?

STEP 3   What answer strategy is best?

- Predict & Match
- Eliminate

Step 1. What is the question asking?

Textual Command of Evidence questions will ask you to strengthen, weaken, or illustrate a claim or hypothesis using additional information that is not in the passage. These questions can be identified by keywords such as "most strongly support," "most weakens," or "most effectively illustrates."

Step 2. What do I need to look for in the passage?

The question stem will mention a claim or hypothesis, so focus on identifying this claim or hypothesis as you read the passage. Paraphrase the claim or hypothesis in your own words.

Step 3. What answer strategy is best?

After identifying the claim or hypothesis, decide on your answer strategy. You might be able to quickly make a prediction about what type of additional information would help to answer the question that you have been given. If so, use your prediction to help you focus in on the one answer choice that clearly meets the criteria.

CHAPTER 13
INFORMATION AND IDEAS

If you can't make a prediction or choose not to, eliminate any answer choices one by one that fail to directly support, discredit, or illustrate the hypothesis or claim (depending on what the question asks you to do). Once you find the answer choice that is logically related to the hypothesis or claim and that addresses the task in the question stem, select it and move on.

Note that some Textual Command of Evidence questions may present a claim about a writing sample and answer choices that provide quotes from the writing sample. On these questions, follow the same steps: identify what the question is asking, paraphrase the claim, and eliminate answer choices that do not illustrate that claim.

Explanation:

The keywords "most strongly support" identify this as a Textual Command of Evidence question. You need to identify support for a hypothesis, so begin by identifying the hypothesis. The passage contains many scientific terms, but you don't need to get bogged down in the specifics to identify the relevant ideas in the passage. Fargi-Brener's hypothesis is identified in the third sentence: leafcutter ants prefer a certain plant (pioneer species) for foraging. Read the rest of the passage to put this hypothesis in context. The first part of the passage discusses why Fargi-Brener makes his hypothesis (because the plant species are common in the type of forest where the ants are common). The last sentence describes how he evaluated the hypothesis: by analyzing the ants' natural foraging behavior. Since the hypothesis is that the ants prefer pioneer species plants, predict that the needed support for the hypothesis will likely provide evidence that the ants forage the pioneer species plants more than other plants. Such support is found in **(D)**, which is correct.

The other answer choices are incorrect because they are out of scope; they would not provide direct support for the hypothesis that the ants prefer pioneer species plants. Foraging behaviors related to ant age or cooperation are irrelevant to the ants' overall preference for the plants, so (A) and (B) are incorrect. Choice (C), if anything, would weaken the hypothesis, since it provides a possible reason other than ant preference for them foraging pioneer species plants.

Try on Your Own

Directions

Take as much time as you need on these questions. Work carefully and methodically. There will be an opportunity for timed practice later in the book.

13

A beautiful and diverse ecosystem, the coral reefs support an estimated 25% of all marine life in the ocean. Wave activity causes an endless erosion of the coral reefs, but it is thought that the symbiotic relationship of coral polyps and algae renews the reef and can counteract the negative effects of erosion. Zooxanthellae, the algae that live inside the tissue of the coral, produce food through photosynthesis for their host. In turn, the coral polyps protect the algae with the polyp's calcareous exoskeletons.

Which statement, if true, would best support the passage's claim?

Ⓐ Zooxanthellae create the rich colors of the coral reef that draw in tourists, who provide essential revenue for the local cities.

Ⓑ Coral reef biologists and ecologists are continuing to study the causes of coral reef erosion.

Ⓒ When the ocean temperatures are in the right range for reef growth, a chart of the growth of coral polyps and algae correlate closely. When temperatures are in a range where reefs decay, the algae population drops sharply, and coral polyp population drops slowly.

Ⓓ Coral polyps are tiny invertebrates, related to sea anemones and jellyfish, that extract calcium carbonate from the ocean to build a resilient exoskeleton.

14

The Philippines, an archipelago, experience an average of 20 typhoons and storms each year, with a notable increase of flooding on the coast of Manila Bay. Researchers at the Stockholm Environment Institute's Asia Centre in Thailand believe the government's proposed policy changes and prevention methods, such as dike and drainage construction, are needed to address the growing number of floods that occur on their coastline.

Which statement, if true, would most strongly support the researchers' belief?

- (A) The Philippines is made up of more than 7,000 islands with a population that exceeds 100 million.

- (B) Many parts of Manila Bay appear to be slowly sinking, leaving the area more susceptible to coastal flooding.

- (C) A team of innovators has created an emergency modular raft, RE-LEAF, that can be used as a park bench until a flood is imminent, at which time it can be refolded into a raft.

- (D) The Typhoon Vamco, which hit the Philippines in 2020, is considered to have created the worst flooding experience yet.

15

While there have been many pieces of textiles discovered, the oldest piece of clothing on record is nearly 5,000 years old. The Tarkhan dress, estimated to be from Egypt's first Dynasty, is constructed of linen, which is made from fibers of the flax plant. The flax plant produces the most durable natural fibers that exist. Its cellulose structure makes linen a significantly stronger and more thermoregulating textile than cotton. Linen is also naturally resistant to moth and carpet beetles, which are known to eat animal-based textiles, such as wool and silks, and to occasionally feed on cotton and blended fabrics.

Which statement, if true, would most strongly support the claim in the text?

- (A) Based on radiocarbon dating results, the oldest verified woven flax fibers are estimated to be 34,000 years old.

- (B) A dress made out of a synthetic textile, such as polyester, would survive longer than a linen dress.

- (C) Global environmental and temperature fluctuations have eroded the quality of flax available for clothing production.

- (D) Silk, considered "The Queen of Fabric," is the most durable ancient fabric.

16

In 2007, the state of Texas rolled out its photographic traffic signal enforcement systems throughout many municipalities. Informally referred to as red-light traffic cameras, they took pictures of the front or rear of the vehicle committing an alleged traffic violation. The system would generate a ticket for the registered owner of the vehicle without verification or actual evidence that the registered owner was the driver who committed the violation. In 2019, new legislation was passed that prohibits the use of photographic traffic signal enforcement systems.

Which statement, if true, would most strongly weaken an argument for using red-light traffic cameras during the ticketing process?

- (A) Red-light traffic cameras help meet city safety outcomes because they decrease collisions at intersections.

- (B) Traffic circles, or roundabouts, are more effective in decreasing intersection collisions.

- (C) Red-light traffic cameras may violate the presumption of innocence by ticketing car owners without evidence they were the drivers.

- (D) Red-light traffic cameras are dangerous because they cause drivers to stop at yellow lights.

17

The Great Depression was a dark decade of economic crises that was fraught with widespread unemployment and mass banking panics, with an alarming number of people experiencing poverty, food scarcity, and homelessness. While economists, historians, and scholars have yet to agree on the exact cause of the Great Depression, most agree that the Great Depression was the worst financial disaster that the United States has ever experienced; no one escaped untouched by the nationwide losses.

Which statement, if true, would most strongly weaken the argument of this text?

- (A) During the Great Depression, many people saved money by renting a home instead of paying a mortgage.

- (B) During the peak of the Great Depression, nearly one-in-five people in the workforce were unemployed.

- (C) During the peak of the Great Depression, many children experienced malnutrition.

- (D) During the Great Depression, the stock market experienced a significant crash and subsequent financial losses.

18

Jean de La Fontaine, a French fabulist, published nearly 240 fables spread out through a dozen books. Many of his cleverly crafted poems reflect the traditional narrative of animals and gods employed to highlight both the flaws and foibles of human nature. In one such piece, "The Sculptor and the Statue of Jupiter," the narrator claims that being confronted with a fiction of one's own creation will inspire a more visceral emotional response than existing truths will evoke.

Which quotation from "The Sculptor and the Statue of Jupiter" most effectively supports the narrator's claim?

(A) "Indeed, the man whose skill did make / Had scarcely laid his chisel down, / Before himself began to quake, / And fear his man-ufacture's frown."

(B) "And even this excess of faith / The poet once scarce fell behind, / The hatred fear-ing, and the wrath, / Of gods the product of his mind."

(C) "Imagination rules the heart: / And here we find the fountain head / From whence the pagan errors start, / That o'er the teeming nations spread."

(D) "All men, as far as in them lies, / Create realities of dreams. / To truth our nature proves but ice; / To falsehood, fire it seems."

Command of Evidence Questions (Quantitative)

LEARNING OBJECTIVE

After this lesson, you will be able to:

- Use quantitative information to logically complete or support a statement

To answer a question like this:

Relative Nutrient Content of Leafcutter Ant Soils—Ratios of Leafcutter Ant Soils to Control Soil

NUTRIENT	NEST SOIL:CONTROL SOIL	REFUSE SOIL:CONTROL SOIL
Nitrogen	1.4:1	33:1
Phosphorus	2.0:1	48:1
Potassium	1.4:1	49:1
Carbon	4.2:1	47:1
Calcium	1.9:1	29:1
Magnesium	2.2:1	15:1

Alejandro G. Farji-Brener and Mariana Tadey have found that overall soil quality and fertility are dramatically higher where leafcutter ants are present. The ants affect the soil in two ways: first, the physical shifting of the soil that occurs as a consequence of nest construction improves soil porosity, drainage, and aeration; additionally, the ants' fungus-cultivating activities generate enormous amounts of plant waste, which the ants carry away, either into specialized chambers within the nest or to dedicated refuse piles outside. This transfer of huge volumes of organic material results in greatly enriched soil, with nutrient levels that are orders of magnitude higher than in areas where the ants are not present; for example,

———

Which choice most effectively uses data from the table to complete the example?

(A) leafcutter ants greatly increase the nutrients present in their refuse soil and increase it even more in their nest soil.

(B) the ratio of nitrogen in nest soil to control soil is the same as the ratio of potassium in nest soil to control soil.

(C) carbon in the ants' refuse soil exists in a 47 to 1 ratio in comparison to control soil.

(D) there is approximately twice as much calcium as magnesium in refuse soil.

You need to know this:

How to Identify Quantitative Command of Evidence Questions

Quantitative Command of Evidence questions are easy to identify, since they are accompanied by a graph or table. The question stem will refer to the "graph" or "table."

How to Read Tables and Graphs

To answer these Command of Evidence questions, you need to carefully analyze the graph or table to be sure you understand exactly what type of information it provides (and what information is does *not* provide). For instance, a table that displays only the *percentage* of students in a grade that have pet dogs might not provide the *actual number* of students who own dogs.

To effectively analyze the graph or table:

- Examine its titles and labels
- Identify what type of information it provides (and does *not* provide)
- Optionally, read a data point or two to make sure you understand the information presented

To answer Quantitative Command of Evidence questions, you don't necessarily need to consider *all* the information provided in the graph or table. Focus on determining exactly what data from the graph or table is relevant for logically completing the blank in the passage. The passage context near the blank will indicate what type of quantitative evidence would support the claim or detail from the passage.

Incorrect answers to a Quantitative Command of Evidence question may:

- Provide data that is true based on the graph or table but does not directly support the claim or detail from the passage
- Provide data that contradicts the information provided in the graph or table

The correct answer to a Quantitative Command of Evidence question will:

- Provide a detail that directly supports the claim or detail from the passage
- Accurately reflect the data in the graph or table

You need to do this:

> **THE METHOD FOR PSAT READING AND WRITING**
>
> **STEP 1** What is the question asking?
>
> **STEP 2** What do I need to look for in the passage?
>
> **STEP 3** What answer strategy is best?
>
> - Predict & Match
> - Eliminate

Step 1. What is the question asking?

The presence of a graph or table indicates a Quantitative Command of Evidence question. The question stem will ask you for an answer choice that provides specific support for a claim or detail from the passage, such as, *Which choice most effectively uses data from the table to complete the example?*

Step 2. What do I need to look for in the passage?

Next, read the passage. Pay careful attention to the immediate context near the blank: the passage will include a claim or detail that you will need to support with the information in the graph or table. You may need to read the entire passage to understand the full context of the provided graph or table.

Now analyze the graph or table itself. Note any titles and labels, and make sure you understand exactly what type of information the graph or table provides. You may want to read a data point or two to confirm that you understand the graph or table.

Step 3. What answer strategy is best?

You may be able to predict what kind of data from the graph or table would support the passage and be included in the correct answer, but often, you will need to evaluate the answer choices one by one. Eliminate answer choices that contradict the data in the graph or table, as well as any that do not directly support the claim or detail from the passage. If you find an answer choice that supports the claim or detail in the passage *and* is true based on the graph or table, select it and move on.

Explanation:

The presence of the table signals a Quantitative Command of Evidence question, and the question stem indicates that you need to complete an example with relevant data from the table. According to the first two sentences, the passage discusses the impact of leafcutter ants on soil. The sentence with the blank makes the claim that nutrient levels are much higher (by "orders of magnitude") where the ants are present; the correct answer will thus be an example of higher nutrient content in soil impacted by the leafcutter ants.

According to its title and labels, the table displays ratios of nutrient content in different types of soil impacted by leafcutter ants to the nutrient content in control soil (in other words, soil not impacted by the ants). For instance, calcium exists in a 29 to 1 ratio in ants' refuse soil compared to control soil. Based on the passage and table, predict that the correct answer will provide an example from the table that demonstrates the relatively higher nutrient content in the ants' nest or refuse soil.

Evaluate the answer choices, eliminating any that do not provide an example of a higher nutrient content and any that do not accurately reflect the table. Eliminate (A), as it is not true according to the table: the ants increase nutrients in their refuse soil more than in their nest soil (for example, nitrogen is in a 33:1 ratio in refuse soil but only a 1.4:1 ratio in nest soil). Also eliminate (B), as it compares the ratios of two different nutrients in nest soil rather than emphasizing a higher nutrient content in soil impacted by the ants compared to control soil. Choice **(C)** is correct because it provides an example of an increased nutrient in ants' refuse soil compared to control soil that is true based on the table. Choice (D) is also incorrect because it does not provide an example of a higher nutrient content in ants' soil compared to control soil; further, it misrepresents the table, which shows *ratios* of nutrient content compared to control soil, not the *actual amounts* of nutrient content in refuse soil, so it is not possible to compare the total amounts of calcium and magnesium.

Try on Your Own

Directions

Take as much time as you need on these questions. Work carefully and methodically. There will be an opportunity for timed practice later in the book.

 19

Exports of Tea from Qing China to the United States, in tons

	1831	1832	1833	1834
Green Teas	42,075	79,411	114,772	163,848
Black Teas	21,306	52,295	55,766	65,096
Total	63,381	131,706	170,538	228,944

South Harmon Institute of Technology economist Morgan Carney was interested in the history of Sino-American trade. After reviewing records, many of them handwritten documents in the Library of Congress, Carney noticed a curious pattern with the types of tea exported by China to the United States. It was only after consulting with historian Ajax Fowler that Carney learned that, in the 1830s, Qing dynasty China _____

Which choice most effectively uses data from the table to complete the statement?

(A) prized green teas for their medicinal qualities and thus charged an additional fee for each ton exported.

(B) exported a total of 63,381 tons of tea to the United States in 1831.

(C) favored the domestic consumption of black teas, while exporting the less favored green teas to foreigners.

(D) imported consistently greater amounts of green and black teas each year from 1831 to 1834.

Reading & Writing

20

Average Surface Fleet Enlisted Crew Positions Required, Funded, and Filled, Fiscal Years 2017 through 2020

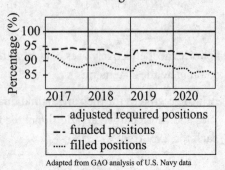

Adapted from GAO analysis of U.S. Navy data

According to Deputy Under Secretary of the Navy Victor "Pug" Henry, the United States Department of the Navy has struggled to meet its recruitment and retention goals for several years running. Even important ship postings and leadership roles have been left vacant. Henry identifies two causes: a lack of funding for various positions and a personnel shortage to fill various positions. Of those two causes, Henry points to _____.

Which choice most effectively uses data from the graph to complete the statement?

Ⓐ the lack of funding as the more important issue, since there has been an 8-15% short-fall in funding since 2017.

Ⓑ the lack of personnel as the more important issue, since there are always unfilled funded positions.

Ⓒ both as equally important, since the short-fall of funding and personnel have been equal to one another since 2017.

Ⓓ neither as especially important, since the vacant positions in the U.S. Navy are not required positions.

21

Average Percent Population Change in U.S. Cities and Towns, 2010–2018

	Population Less than 5,000	Population Between 5,000 and 9,999	Population Between 10,000 and 49,999	Population 50,000 or more
North-east	−2.0	−0.1	1.1	2.2
Mid-west	−1.4	1.2	2.1	3.0
South	1.3	6.1	7.6	10.0
West	7.8	8.3	8.1	7.8

Dr. Katarzyna Baba, a researcher at Raft College, was interested in regional population changes across the U.S. in the 2010s. Such information is important for the insight it offers into the changing fortunes of rural and urban areas, as well as the economic and political fortunes of regional areas. Dr. Baba and her team analyzed publicly available census data, sorting the information by both region and population size. The result contained a few surprises. For example, despite how its smallest towns showed minimal growth, _____

Which choice most effectively uses data from the table to complete the example?

Ⓐ the South demonstrated the greatest growth in terms of percentage of population when considering areas with a population of 50,000 or more.

Ⓑ the West demonstrated consistent growth across all population categories, with no category falling below an astonishing 7.8%.

Ⓒ the Midwest saw an increase in population in all areas with a population of 5,000 or more.

Ⓓ the Northeast saw double digit growth in terms of percentage of population when considering areas with a population of 50,000 or more.

Reading & Writing

22

Percent Change for Top 10 Languages Spoken at Home in the United States 2006–2010 to 2015–2019

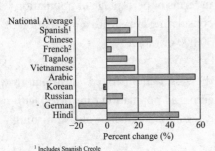

¹ Includes Spanish Creole
² Includes Cajun, Creole, and Haitian

Adapted from U.S. Census Bureau, 2006-2010 and 2015-2019 American Community Survey 5-year estimates

Dr. Natasha Barbaro, a linguist, notes that languages other than English are spoken in millions of homes, although those languages are not always what one might expect. While Spanish is the most widespread of these languages across the fifty U.S. states, it is not the only one. The frequency with which a language is spoken can be a reflection of larger, changing immigration patterns. When contrasting the languages spoken at home in the United States from 2006–2010 and 2015–2019, certain trends stand out. For example, the two languages that saw the smallest percent change in use were _____

Which choice most effectively uses data from the graph to complete the example?

Ⓐ German and Arabic, with the former declining almost 20% and the latter growing by over 50%.

Ⓑ Arabic and Hindi, with the former growing by over 50% and the latter growing by roughly 45%.

Ⓒ Tagalog and Russian, which saw growth roughly comparable to the national average of just under 10%.

Ⓓ Korean and French, with the former declining 2% and the latter growing by a mere 3%.

23

Survey of Public Opinion Concerning the Abolishment of Payroll Taxes

	Age 18–29	Age 30–44	Age 45–64	Age 65+
Support	31	41	30	19
Oppose	23	34	58	77
Undecided	47	25	12	5

Payroll taxes are automatically deducted from a worker's salary and used to fund a variety of government programs, most notably Social Security, a key welfare program for the elderly. Economist Helena Glory argues that payroll taxes are deeply unpopular with people under age thirty, with more people supporting the abolishment of payroll taxes than their continued existence. According to a public opinion research poll conducted by Humanity League Research, Glory's statement about the opinions of young people is factually correct but not the whole story. Most importantly, _____

Which choice most effectively uses data from the table to complete the statement?

(A) 77% of people age 65 or older oppose abolishing payroll taxes, as do 58% of people age 45–64, while only 31% of people age 18–29 support abolishing them.

(B) 31% of people age 18–29 support abolishing payroll taxes, but an even greater amount of people age 30–44, 41%, also support their abolishment.

(C) 30% of people age 45–64 support abolishing payroll taxes, while only 19% of people age 65 or older likewise support their abolishment.

(D) 47% of people age 18–29 are undecided on the issue of abolishing payroll taxes, while only 31% of people age 18–29 support their abolishment.

24

Seats Held by States in the U.S. House of Representatives (Out of 435 Total Seats)

	1933	1963	1993	2023
California	20	38	52	52
Illinois	27	24	20	17
New York	45	41	31	26
Texas	21	23	30	38

Bradley Kaplan Alexander, a political scientist at Purdue Global University, notes that political power in the U.S. House of Representatives is based upon population. The more people that live in a given state, the more seats will be allocated to that state during the reapportionment that takes places every ten years following the census. Alexander points to the Permanent Apportionment Act of 1929 for fixing the total number of seats in the House at 435. "Essentially," as Alexander puts it, "there are now only so many seats to go around, which creates winners and losers in terms of political power as people move between the states." He points to long-term trends, like the increasing relative population growth of _____

Which choice most effectively uses data from the table to complete the statement?

(A) California, which has continued to gain additional seats since 1933 with no signs of stopping as of 2023.

(B) Texas, which has continued to gain seats since 1933, growing from 21 seats to 38 in 2023.

(C) New York, which has continued to lose seats since 1933, declining from 45 seats to 26 in 2023.

(D) Illinois, which has continued to lose seats since 1933, declining from 27 seats to 17 in 2023.

Inference Questions

> **LEARNING OBJECTIVE**
>
> After this lesson, you will be able to:
>
> • Determine what must be true based on given information

To answer a question like this:

Leafcutter ants' foraging trails extend hundreds of meters throughout the landscape. The ants harvest a wide range of vegetation but are selective; they prefer particular plant species and typically choose younger growth. Research has also shown that the species the ants choose to harvest often have their own chemical defenses that influence the extent of the ants' cutting behavior. Thus, the leafcutter ants' harvesting practices imply that _____

Which choice most logically completes the text?

Ⓐ the amount of damage they cause to individual plants is limited.

Ⓑ most ant species harvest only a few types of plants.

Ⓒ many plants use chemical toxins as a defensive measure.

Ⓓ plant extinction due to ants' overharvesting never occurs.

You need to know this:

How to Identify Inference Questions

Inference questions can be identified by keywords such as "logically complete," "be inferred," "implies," or "based on the passage" in the question stem, for instance: *Which choice most logically completes the text?*

What an Inference Is

While the correct answer to a Detail question is something explicitly stated in the passage, the correct answer to an Inference question is *not* stated explicitly in the passage. However, you can still be confident about your answer to an Inference question because the correct answer is something *logically supported by what is stated in the passage.*

Incorrect answers to an Inference question may be:

• **Out of Scope**—Incorrect answers to Inference questions often include a statement that is related to the passage but is too broad to be logically supported by the passage. (For instance, if a passage argues that one dog breed, beagles, makes good pets, it would be out of scope to infer that the passage argues *all* dog breeds make good pets.)

• **Extreme**—Incorrect answers to Inference questions may include language that is too strong (*all*, *never*, *every*, *none*) to be supported by the passage.

• **Distortions**—Incorrect answers to Inference questions may be based on details from the passage but distort or misstate the author's ideas.

The correct answer to an Inference question will:

- Be a conclusion that can be logically supported by what is stated in the passage

You need to do this:

THE METHOD FOR PSAT READING AND WRITING

STEP 1 What is the question asking?

STEP 2 What do I need to look for in the passage?

STEP 3 What answer strategy is best?

- Predict & Match
- Eliminate

Step 1. What is the question asking?

Keywords such as "logically complete," "be inferred," "implies," or "based on the passage" in the question stem signal an Inference question. Keep in mind that the correct answer will be something that is *not* explicitly stated in the passage, but is *logically supported by the passage*.

Step 2. What do I need to look for in the passage?

If the question stem includes specific clue words, use them to help you focus in on what part of the passage the inference will be based upon. If the question stem asks you to logically complete a blank, focus on the context near the blank to determine what type of inference is required.

You will usually need to read the entire passage so that you can understand the author's logical flow of ideas. Pay special attention to transition words, such as those that indicate contrast (*but, however, although*) or logical connections (*therefore, because*). These transition words will help you paraphrase the passage in your own words.

Step 3. What answer strategy is best?

In some cases, you may be able to make at least a general prediction about the inference in the correct answer. If so, use your prediction to help you focus in on the correct answer.

Alternatively, you may need to use elimination. Immediately eliminate answer choices that are out of scope—those that make a statement that is too broad to be supported by the passage. Similarly, eliminate answer choices that use language that is too extreme (*all, never, every, none*) to be supported by the passage. Also eliminate answer choices that distort the ideas from the passage.

Remember, the correct answer to an Inference question goes a step beyond what is stated in the passage, but it always can be fully and logically supported by what is stated in the passage.

Explanation:

The words "most logically completes the text" signal that this is an Inference question, so the correct answer will be something that is not explicitly stated in the passage, but is logically supported by the passage. This question stem does not provide specific clues about the inference you will need to make, but it does direct you to the blank at the end of the passage. The last sentence states that you are looking for something implied by the ants' harvesting practices. As you read the rest of the passage, look for details about the harvesting practices so that you can make a logical prediction.

Read through the passage and paraphrase its flow of ideas. The first sentence identifies the topic of leafcutter ant foraging. The following sentences provide details about their harvesting: the ants harvest many types of plants but are selective, and plants' chemical defenses influence how much they cut. Predict that the inference in the correct answer will be related to the ants' selectivity and/or the influence of the plants on their harvesting.

Evaluate the answer choices. Choice **(A)** is correct because it is a logical inference based on the passage: if the plants' chemical defenses "influence the extent of the ants' cutting behavior," it must be the case that the ants only harvest a limited amount from these plants. Thus, the damage they cause to any single plant must be limited.

Eliminate (B) because it is beyond the scope of the passage, which discusses leafcutter ants, not all ant species. Choice (C) is also outside the scope of the passage; although the plants discussed in the passage use chemical defenses, the passage does not indicate that "many" plants do so. Eliminate (D) because it is too extreme; the passage implies that the ants limit some of their harvesting behavior, but the passage does not support the claim that plant extinction due to ants "never" occurs.

Try on Your Own

Directions

Take as much time as you need on these questions. Work carefully and methodically. There will be an opportunity for timed practice later in the book.

25

In 1721 C.E., the Norwegian missionary Hans Egede discovered that the two known Norse settlements on Greenland were completely deserted. Ever since, the reasons behind the decline and eventual disappearance of these people have been greatly debated. Greenland, established by the charismatic outlaw Erik the Red in about 986 C.E., was a colony of Norway by 1000 C.E., complete with a church hierarchy and trading community. After several relatively prosperous centuries, the colony had fallen on hard times and was no longer heard from in Europe; the ultimate fate of the settlements remained unknown until _____

Which choice most logically completes the text?

- Ⓐ the war between the colonies and Inuit groups led to the demise of the Norse colonies.

- Ⓑ Greenland was completely isolated in 1480 C.E. due to being visited by fewer and fewer trade ships.

- Ⓒ recent analyses of the central Greenland ice cores indicated that severe climate changes led to their collapse.

- Ⓓ Egede's discovery confirmed the complete downfall of the settlement.

26

The economic divide between the rich and poor grew steadily wider as the nineteenth century drew to a close. Some Americans sought to apply Charles Darwin's theory of evolution and the idea of survival of the fittest in an effort to justify people's differing economic and social standings within society. Social Darwinists argued that wealth belonged in the hands of those who were most fit to manage it. Many also believed that _____

Which choice most logically completes the text?

- Ⓐ giving assistance to the poor went against the survival of the fittest.

- Ⓑ opportunities for success were available, but Americans faced nearly insurmountable barriers in achieving them.

- Ⓒ the natural order demanded that the poor and impoverished be imprisoned for life.

- Ⓓ a federal income tax on the rich would be unconstitutional.

27

The Burgess Shale is a deposit of fossils found in British Columbia. The deposit yielded a surprisingly varied array of fossils. There were prodigious numbers of complex forms not seen since. *Hallucigenia*, so named for a structure so bizarre that scientists did not know which was the dorsal and which the ventral side, had fourteen legs. *Opabinia* had five eyes and an elongated appendage projecting from its head. By contrast, finding early chordates was rare, despite humans and all other vertebrates descending from them. The amazing diversity of the Burgess Shale led evolutionary biologist Stephen Jay Gould to believe that it was highly unlikely that _____

Which choice most logically completes the text?

Ⓐ the *Opabinia* actually had five eyes, as indicated by the fossil record.

Ⓑ the eventual success of chordates was a predictable outcome.

Ⓒ the fossils were a legitimate find and, instead, they were an elaborate fraud.

Ⓓ that chordates possessed some quality that gave them an evolutionary advantage over their competitors.

28

A hybrid is the offspring of two organisms from different species. For example, a mule is the hybrid of a male donkey and a female horse. Generally, interspecific matings represent an evolutionary dead end, producing sterile offspring, if any at all; mules are sterile, meaning they cannot produce offspring of their own. For some species of birds, however, such pairings may indeed bring evolutionary advantages to the participants. In the case of the female collared flycatchers of Gotland, three distinct factors may work to _____

Which choice most logically completes the text?

Ⓐ produce hybrids with male pied flycatchers that represent an evolutionary dead end.

Ⓑ allow them to produce reproductively capable offspring without the need for interspecific mating.

Ⓒ make interspecific pairings with male pied flycatchers reproductively beneficial.

Ⓓ create conditions that allow for male donkeys and female horses to produce non-sterile offspring.

Reading & Writing

Reading & Writing

29

French general Napoleon Bonaparte is alleged to have said that, for soldiers, "Morale is to material as three is to one." In other words, poorly armed but motivated troops are worth more than well-equipped but despairing ones. One method militaries use to improve morale is to offer creature comforts to frontline soldiers. For example, in the Pacific Theater of World War II, the U.S. Navy commissioned an ice cream barge, one able to create ten gallons of ice cream every seven minutes. The idea was that _____

Which choice most logically completes the text?

Ⓐ U.S. Navy leadership was demonstrating that they were keeping the spirits of their men in mind.

Ⓑ ice cream offered relief to the troops during the hard fighting in the Pacific Theater.

Ⓒ despair in wartime is a danger that cannot be overcome once suffered, so it must never be allowed to infect troops.

Ⓓ a soldier will not feel confident in their cause and their institutions during wartime unless bribed.

30

Rainbows have long been a part of religion and mythology in cultures around the globe, appearing as bridges between the heavens and the earth, as messages from the gods, or as weapons wielded by divine powers. Some cultures have viewed rainbows themselves as deities, or even as demonic beings from which to hide children. But in the early fourteenth century, Theodoric of Freiburg, a German friar, and Kamal al-Din al-Farisi, a Persian scientist, independently turned a scientific eye to the study of rainbows. Theodoric and al-Farisi were thousands of miles apart, but both had studied Ibn al-Haytham's *Book of Optics*. Each concluded that _____

Which choice most logically completes the text?

Ⓐ indigo and violet appear at the bottom of rainbows because those colors have shallower angles.

Ⓑ a rainbow's appearance is the result of sunlight refracting and reflecting through water droplets left after a rainfall.

Ⓒ rainbows are a relatively rare phenomenon.

Ⓓ rainbows were not, in fact, associated with any spiritual meaning.

How Much Have You Learned?

Directions

Take 7 minutes to apply the method for PSAT Reading and Writing to the following question set. Assess your work by comparing it to the expert responses at the end of the chapter.

1

Archaea are a domain of single-celled organisms that lack a cell nucleus. When they were first discovered, all archaea were believed to be extremophiles—that is, organisms that only live in extreme conditions such as very hot, cold, or chemically caustic environments. Now, scientists accept that _____

Which choice most logically completes the text?

- (A) these microorganisms exist in many habitats.
- (B) archaea are a distinct category of microorganisms.
- (C) nothing is known about these microorganisms
- (D) these organisms are no longer properly referred to as "archaebacteria."

2

Scientists assert that one of the most significant challenges in analyzing and forecasting trends in volcanic activity is a lack of access to shared, comprehensive data. In an effort to improve global communication of unrest and eruption episodes data, the World Organization of Volcano Observatories (WOVO), through funding made possible by the SGS/USAID Volcano Disaster Assistance Program and the Earth Observatory of Singapore, has created a comprehensive global database, WOVOdat, that has an online interface that uses interactive data analysis to improve the forecast of eruptions, the evaluations of potential hazards, and the mitigation of volcanic activity.

Which occurrence after the deployment of the WOVOdat, if true, would most strongly support the claim that a global database was needed?

- (A) There was a decrease in funding available from SGS/USAID Volcano Disaster Assistance Program.
- (B) There was an increase in damages caused by episodes of unrest and eruptions.
- (C) There was a decrease in international collaboration between volcano observatories.
- (D) There was an increase in the accuracy of volcanic unrest and eruption episode predictions.

3

The following text is from Jack London's 1803 novel *Call of the Wild*.

It was a hard trip, with the mail behind them, and the heavy work wore them down. They were short of weight and in poor condition when they made Dawson, and should have had a ten days' or a week's rest at least. But in two days, they dropped down the Yukon bank from the Barracks, loaded with letters for the outside. The dogs were tired, the drivers grumbling, and to make matters worse, it snowed every day. This meant a soft trail, greater friction on the runners, and heavier pulling for the dogs; yet the drivers were fair through it all, and did their best for the animals.

Which choice best states the central idea of the text?

- Ⓐ The arduous trip, which was made more laborious by the weather and the weight of the mail, was exhausting the drivers and the dogs.

- Ⓑ Neither the drivers nor the dogs were properly equipped for the inclement weather and treacherous path that plagued their journey.

- Ⓒ Historically, in the Yukon, mail delivery was a dangerous job that required well-trained sled dogs and experienced drivers.

- Ⓓ To ensure that the mail was delivered in a timely manner, the dogs and drivers rested for only two days, instead of resting for the entirety of their break period.

4

The following text is from Yei Theodora Ozaki's 1908 short story "The Tongue-Cut Sparrow" from her collection *Japanese Fairy Tales*.

But the night came on and the darkness reminded [the old man] that he had a long way to go and must think about taking his leave and return home. He thanked his kind hostess for her splendid entertainment, and begged her for his sake to forget all she had suffered at the hands of his cross old wife. He told the Lady Sparrow that it was a great comfort and happiness to him to find her in such a beautiful home and to know that she wanted for nothing. It was his anxiety to know how she fared and what had really happened to her that had led him to seek her. Now he knew that all was well he could return home with a light heart. If ever she wanted him for anything she had only to send for him and he would come at once.

According to the passage, the old man was able to return home without worry because

- Ⓐ the Lady Sparrow had forgiven his old wife for all that she had suffered at his wife's hands.

- Ⓑ he had learned how the Lady Sparrow had fared after his wife's poor treatment of her.

- Ⓒ he had enjoyed the Lady Sparrow's entertainment and her beautiful home.

- Ⓓ the Lady Sparrow would be returning with him so that she could forgive his wife for the mistreatment.

Reading & Writing

5

The fennec fox is a member of the Canidae family and may be found burrowed in the hot North African deserts. These small, nocturnal creatures have sandy-colored fur that both provides camouflage from predators and insulation on cold nights. However, their most distinct evolutionary trait, which enables them to survive during the deserts' peak temperatures, is their enormous bat-like ears. In addition to helping them hear predators and prey from 100 miles away, their ears _____

Which choice most logically completes the text?

(A) make them an easy target for flying predators to locate during the day.

(B) are their most endearing trait, which has resulted in their popularity as domesticated pets.

(C) are covered in fine, sandy-colored fur and are considered good luck by poachers.

(D) dispel body heat to help prevent their bodies from overheating.

6

Adapted from Employed persons in Japan by type, 2017 by Yuasan, License: CC-0

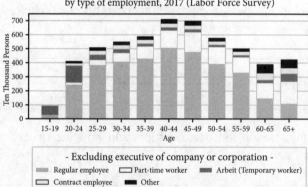

In 2017, Japan conducted a labor force census that could be used to assess the diversity of workers' ages in each type of employment within seven employment categories, exclusive of executive-level workers. When reviewing the reported data, a team of labor analysts observed that _____

Which choice most effectively uses data from the table to complete the observation?

(A) The 15-19 and the 20-24 age groups, combined, have the fewest people employed in the Arbeit (temporary workers).

(B) The 40-44 age group has the most reported workers and the highest number of other employees.

(C) The 60-64 age group has the second-fewest reported workers and the third-fewest reported regular employees.

(D) The 20-24 and the 25-29 age groups, combined, have the most people employed as part-time workers.

Reflect

Directions: Take a few minutes to recall what you've learned and what you've been practicing in this chapter. Consider the following questions, jot down your best answer for each one, and then compare your reflections to the expert responses that follow. Use your level of confidence to determine what to do next.

How should you approach reading the passage when the question stem asks you to identify its main idea?

_____

_____

_____

How can you effectively analyze graphs or tables on Quantitative Command of Evidence questions?

_____

_____

_____

How do Detail questions differ from Inference questions?

_____

_____

_____

How can predicting help you correctly answer Information and Ideas questions? What types of answer choices can you eliminate on Information and Ideas questions?

_____

_____

_____

What are the main differences you see between PSAT Information and Ideas questions and those you're used to from tests in school?

_____

_____

_____

How will you approach PSAT Reading and Writing questions more strategically as you continue to practice and improve on your performance? Are there any specific habits you will practice to make your approach to PSAT Reading and Writing more effective and efficient?

_____

_____

_____

Expert Responses

How should you approach reading the passage when the question stem asks you to identify its main idea?

On Main Idea questions, don't get caught up in the details of the passage. Instead, locate the author's main point about the topic of the passage, which can often be found in the first or last sentence. Paraphrasing the main idea in your own words can help you predict the correct answer choice.

How can you effectively analyze graphs or tables on Quantitative Command of Evidence questions?

When analyzing a graph or table, you should pay attention to its titles and labels, and you should also identify what type of information it does (and does not) provide. Reading a data point or two might help you make sure you understand the data presented. Just as importantly, make sure you carefully analyze the passage so that you can determine what data from the graph or table is relevant for logically completing the blank.

How do Detail questions differ from Inference questions?

The correct answer to a Detail question is something explicitly stated in the passage. The correct answer to an Inference question is not explicitly stated in the passage, but it is logically supported by what is stated in the passage.

How can predicting help you correctly answer Information and Ideas questions? What types of answer choices can you eliminate on Information and Ideas questions?

When you are able to do so, predicting the correct answer can increase your accuracy and speed by helping you focus in on the one correct answer and avoid spending time comparing the answer choices to one another. Main Idea and Detail questions often lend themselves to predicting. When eliminating answer choices, toss out any that misuse or distort information from the passage, any that use language that is too extreme for the passage, and any that are out of the scope of the passage.

What are the main differences you see between PSAT Information and Ideas questions and those you're used to from tests in school?

Depending on the kinds of classes and teachers you've had in high school, the skills rewarded on PSAT Information and Ideas questions may be more or less familiar. In general, Information and Ideas questions do not ask you to simply recall facts, but they instead require you to identify main ideas and details from a passage and to logically support ideas or draw inferences from a passage.

How will you approach PSAT Reading and Writing questions more strategically as you continue to practice and improve your performance? Are there any specific habits you will practice to make your approach to PSAT Reading and Writing more effective and efficient?

There is no one-size-fits-all answer here. Reflect on your own habits in answering PSAT Reading and Writing questions and give yourself an honest assessment of your strengths and weaknesses. Consider the strategies you've seen experts use in this chapter, and put them to work in your own practice to increase your accuracy, speed, and confidence.

Next Steps

If you answered most questions correctly in the "How Much Have You Learned?" section, and if your responses to the Reflect questions were similar to those of the PSAT expert, then consider Information and Ideas questions an area of strength and move on to the next chapter. Come back to this topic periodically to prevent yourself from getting rusty.

If you don't yet feel confident, review the lessons in this chapter that you have not yet mastered. Then, try the questions you missed again. As always, be sure to review the explanations closely.

Answers and Explanations

Try on Your Own

1.   B
Difficulty: Medium

Category: Information and Ideas

Getting to the Answer: Any keywords in the text that indicate emotion or the author's opinion are excellent clues to the main idea. Here, the passage opens with the author's claim that Euskara is different from traditional languages that are disappearing because Euskara is "defying this trend and flourishing." The text continues with several details supporting the claim and concludes with the author's opinion: "The results were dramatic." Predict that the correct answer will reflect this strong, positive opinion of Euskara. This prediction matches **(B)**, the correct answer.

Choice (A) is incorrect because the author does not offer an opinion on the efforts to replace Euskara with Spanish. (C) contradicts the passage; the number of Euskara speakers is growing, not decreasing. (D) is also incorrect. Although it might seem that using the same plan would assist in the preservation of other languages, the author never mentions this idea.

2.   B
Difficulty: Hard

Category: Information and Ideas

Getting to the Answer: Authors write texts to make a point. To find the point, or the main idea, ask yourself as you read, "Why did the author write this?" For this passage, the answer to that question comes at the end: the author believes that, so far, there is no proof of life on Mars. Matching this prediction to the choices yields **(B)**, the correct answer. Choice (A) is a detail from the text that the author uses to support the main idea; it is not the main idea of the passage. Incorrect choices (C) and (D) go beyond the passage. The author never discusses researchers' expectations of future discoveries (C) or compare *Curiosity's* mission with those of other devices (D).

3.   C
Difficulty: Medium

Category: Information and Ideas

Getting to the Answer: The text opens with a hypothesis: cultural factors may have contributed to the disappearance of the Norse colonies. The passage continues with an example of one possible cultural factor, contrasting Inuit and Norse clothing styles. The last sentence of the text restates the opening hypothesis and is a good prediction of the correct answer, **(C)**.

Incorrect choices (A) and (D) go beyond what is stated in the passage. You know that, before their disappearances, the colonies were prosperous, but the author does not compare them with other Norse colonies (A). Similarly, the author does not speculate as to what might have happened if the colonists had assumed Inuit clothing (D). Incorrect choice (B) restates information provided in the passage, but is not the main idea.

4.   D
Difficulty: Medium

Category: Information and Ideas

Getting to the Answer: If you are faced with a passage with a lot of unfamiliar terminology, focus on the structure, not the details, of the text. Here, an older idea is introduced in the first sentence, then that idea is updated in the third sentence. Notice that the author's tone is descriptive, so use something like, "There is a new discovery" as a prediction to start eliminating choices. The author makes no recommendations and gives no opinions, so you can immediately eliminate (A), (B), and (C). The passage discusses the discovery of a new domain of one-celled organisms, the Archaea, confirming that **(D)** is the correct answer.

5. D

Difficulty: Hard

Category: Information and Ideas

Getting to the Answer: The first sentence introduces the topic: automobile assembly lines were a new method of industrial production. The text continues with an example contrasting American and European manufacturing processes, concluding with the statement, "Assembly-line production was a mixed blessing." Using this conclusion as a prediction matches **(D)**, the correct answer.

None of the incorrect choices are mentioned in the passage. The author never makes the claim that American and European cars differ in quality (A), only that the laborers producing them are more or less skilled and that craftsmanship was or was not emphasized. The author never claimed that using more skilled laborers was necessarily good or bad, as stated in (B), instead only pointing out the variation in skill as a difference between European and American manufacturing. While the author does point out disadvantages of assembly-line production, at no point does the author indicate that a return to a less efficient factory system would be better, eliminating (C).

6. D

Difficulty: Hard

Category: Information and Ideas

Getting to the Answer: The text opens with an explanation of *kigo* and its importance to *haiku*. The contrast keyword "However" at the start of the fourth sentence introduces the author's opinion, and the main idea: climate change is affecting how people understand *kigo*. This matches the correct answer, **(D)**. "Because" at the start of the next sentence tells you that the rest of the passage will support that idea.

Incorrect choice (A) may be inferred from the passage, but is not the main idea. (B) is not mentioned in the passage, and is also incorrect. The author never speculates about how the *kigo* meanings may have to be revised. Choice (C) goes beyond the passage. The last sentence says that haiku is harder for modern readers to understand, not that it is meaningless.

7. C

Difficulty: Easy

Category: Information and Ideas

Getting to the Answer: This question is asking you to identify details about Old Rouault's opinion about farming in the passage. The passage includes many references to his opinions on both farming and being a farmer, which could result in predictions that are too broad. Elimination may be the faster strategy for this question. Eliminate choice (A) is because it is the opposite of what he says in the passage: he thinks his daughter is "too clever for farming." Choice (B) misuses a detail from the last sentence; Rouault does not make a connection between farming and sleep quality. Choice (D) is out of scope; he does not mention his basic needs, only the things for which he spares no expense. In the second and third sentences, he makes the claims that "one never saw a millionaire in [farming]" and that "far from" making a fortune, he was "losing every year." Choice **(C)** is aligned with his statements on farming and is correct.

8. A

Difficulty: Medium

Category: Information and Ideas

Getting to the Answer: Read the passage carefully for details about the application of sharkskin technology. In the third and last sentences, the author claims that mimicry of a shark's skin has "decreas[ed] fuel costs" in marine transportation and "decreas[ed] the spread of bacteria" by modeling the rough texture of sharks' skin. The correct answer will include one or both of those details. The correct choice **(A)** refers to sharkskin paint on boats that decreases fuel costs.

Choices (B) and (C) are out of scope; neither whales nor wetsuits are mentioned in the passage. Choice (D) is incorrect because it asserts the opposite of the passage; the texture does *not* increase the spread of bacteria.

9. D

Difficulty: Hard

Category: Information and Ideas

Getting to the Answer: The phrase "The passage indicates" means that this is a Detail question and that the correct answer will be explicitly stated or supported by the author. Because the passage contains a surplus of details, elimination is the strategy to use here. Eliminate choice (A) because it is a misuse of details. In the first sentence, the author states that daylight savings was introduced during the *first* world war but does not state that all countries mandated it. Choice (B) is incorrect; the author never states which country first implemented the practice. Choice (C) is a distortion of details; the author asserts that daylight saving was a method to *decrease* reliance on artificial light. Choice **(D)** is correct because the author states that daylight savings was "introduced" during World War I and was reintroduced during World War II to "once again decrease fuel consumption."

10. B

Difficulty: Medium

Category: Information and Ideas

Getting to the Answer: The phrase "According to the passage" indicates that this is Detail question and that the correct answer will be stated in the passage. The question is asking for the diet of the dinosaur discovered. In the second half of the passage, the author cites that the *Oculudentavis khaungraae* was a "fierce predator" and provides a quote that it was a "terror of insects." Predict that the correct choice refers to a diet of insects; **(B)** is correct.

Choices (A) and (D) are incorrect because neither is a food source mentioned. Choice (C) is incorrect because the passage makes no reference to the dinosaur eating anything other than insects.

11. C

Difficulty: Medium

Category: Information and Ideas

Getting to the Answer: This question is asking for passage details about the size of the crocodile's artificial habitat. In the second sentence, the author states that it may live additional years when the habitat "appropriately meet[s] the needs" of the enclosed crocodile. In the third sentence, the author claims that a small enclosure is a contributing factor to "premature death." Choice **(C)** summarizes those two details and is correct.

Choice (A) is incorrect; the author does not mention preventing attacks, only that there is a "lack of concern" about crocodile mistreatment due to the reputation that crocodiles have for attacking people. Eliminate (B) because the author does not state that the natural and artificial habitat should be comparable in size. Choice (D) distorts details in the passage; the author recommends habitats be constructed to support typical or prolonged lifespans.

12. A

Difficulty: Medium

Category: Information and Ideas

Getting to the Answer: The phrase "This passage indicates" means that this is a Detail question about a recurring theme of Katsushika Hokusai's woodblock prints. In the second sentence, the author identifies *The Great Wave* is "one of many" prints that show the juxtapositions between the "near and far, natural and manmade, and fear and respect." Predict that the correct choice will refer to one of those contrasts. Choice **(A)** matches the theme of close (near) and distant (far); this choice is correct.

Choices (B) is the opposite of the author's claim; Hokusai celebrated the *contrasts* he observed. Eliminate choice (C) because indigo and Prussian blue were part of his color palette, but were not necessarily thematic in that given way. Choice (D) is a misuse of details; being a master of an art style is not a theme of his work.

13. C

Difficulty: Medium

Category: Information and Ideas

Getting to the Answer: Start by summarizing the claim: "It is thought" that the coral reefs are an ecosystem where a symbiotic relationship between coral polyps and algae acts to renew the reef. Predict that the correct choice will support coral polyps and algae working together to counteract harmful reef erosion. Choice **(C)** shows how the population of the two correlate during growth. It is correct.

Choices (A) and (B) may be interesting facts, but they do not support the symbiotic claim. Choice (D) shows a way that coral polyps become stronger, but it does not address the algae at all.

14. B
Difficulty: Medium

Category: Information and Ideas

Getting to the Answer: The main assertion of this passage is that researchers at the Stockholm Environment Institute's Asia Centre in Thailand believe action is needed to address the "growing number" of coastal floods, with a "notable increase of flooding" in Manila Bay. Predict that the correct choice will provide evidence of the increased need to address coastal flooding. Choice **(B)** is the only choice that provides information on coastal flooding and the need for future mitigation: Manila Bay is becoming more susceptible to flooding. It is correct.

While choice (A) may be true, it does not address the need for flooding mitigation. (C) is an emergency intervention but does not address the need for it. (D) is a single moment in the past and does not reflect a future need.

15. A
Difficulty: Medium

Category: Information and Ideas

Getting to the Answer: The text claims that the flax plant produces the "most durable" natural fibers. The correct answer will provide evidence that best supports that claim. Predict that the correct answer choice will include evidence or examples of its durability. Select choice **(A)**: it states that flax fibers have been discovered that are thousands of years old and could be used as evidence of the textile's durability.

Tempting answer choices will be the ones that seem to be or might be true, but they do not act as evidence for the author. Choice (B) is about synthetics and does not support the claim. Choice (C) should be eliminated because it is irrelevant to the passage. Choice (D), if true, would not support the claim because it is about silk being the most "durable" and is, therefore, incorrect.

16. C
Difficulty: Medium

Category: Information and Ideas

Getting to the Answer: Summarize the passage: Texas implemented traffic cameras, which generated tickets for car owners without verifying the identity of the driver, and later discontinued the program. The correct choice is **(C)** because it addresses the lack of verification, or evidence, that the ticket recipient was also the driver.

None of the other traffic choices address the lack of evidence or identity verification. Choice (A) is focused on safety outcomes, which could be an argument *for* the use of the cameras. (B) is unrelated to the cameras' implementation and prohibition. (D) is about driver behavior, which is also not mentioned in the passage.

17. A
Difficulty: Medium

Category: Information and Ideas

Getting to the Answer: The argument made in this text is twofold: the Great Depression was the greatest financial disaster in the United States and that no one was unaffected by it. A statement that would weaken this text's argument would include information that undermines or disproves of one or more of the author's claims. Eliminate (B) because it supports the argument with evidence of high unemployment. Choice (C) supports the argument with evidence of food scarcity. Choice (D) is about financial losses and further supports the argument. Choice **(A)** weakens the text's claims of universal economic struggles, stating that "many people saved money," and is the correct answer.

18. D
Difficulty: Hard

Category: Information and Ideas

Getting to the Answer: The correct answer will be a stanza from the poem illustrating that the response to "a fiction of one's own creation" is more intense (visceral) than the response to truths. **(D)** is the only answer that includes both the cold reaction (ice) "our nature" has to truth and the heated reaction (fire) to falsehoods, or fiction.

Eliminate (A) and (B) because they only detail the artist's reaction ("fear," "hatred") to his creation and do not include a comparison or contrast between something made-up and something true. Choice (C) details the nationwide spread of fiction (imagination) that starts in the heart.

19. C

Difficulty: Easy

Category: Information and Ideas

Getting to the Answer: First, read the passage for clues about what information belongs in the blank. The second sentence states that the researcher "noticed a curious pattern" about the *types* of tea exports, so the correct answer will likely reflect a pattern about types of tea exports. Next, to effectively and efficiently answer a Quantitative Command of Evidence question, identify what type of information the graph or table provides (and does *not* provide). You can potentially eliminate answer choices this way. Here, the table displays exports of two types of tea (green and black) from China to the United States in four different years.

Choice (A) can be eliminated because it refers to "an additional fee," and the table makes no mention of money; only weight, year, and tea type are shown. Choice (B) is accurate according to the table, but it does not reflect a "curious pattern" about the types of tea exported, as required by the passage. Choice (D) states that China imported tea but this is contradicted by the table's title: "Exports of Tea from Qing China to the United States, in tons." By process of elimination, **(C)** is correct. It could also be discerned as the correct answer because it does not contradict any information in the table; green tea was exported in consistently greater amounts than black tea. Further, this choice reflects a "curious pattern" about the two types of tea.

20. B

Difficulty: Hard

Category: Information and Ideas

Getting to the Answer: When analyzing a graph, note any titles and labels. Make sure you understand exactly what type of information the graph provides. In this case, the graph tracks three things from 2017 through 2020: *required* crew positions, *funded* crew positions, and *filled* crew positions. Keep that information in mind

as you go through the answer choices. Also, do not ignore the passage, as it may contain vital context information for the graph. The gap between the "Required" line and the "Funded" lines must indicate the shortfall in funding. The shortfall in personnel is indicated by the gap between the "Funded" line and "Filled" line.

Choice (A) can be eliminated because it is contradicted by the graph. The line for funded crew positions never goes below 90%, meaning there could not be an 8-15% shortfall. Choice (C) can also be eliminated; the gap between the shortfall in funding and in filled positions varies a lot from year to year. Choice (D) is contradicted by the graph; required positions form the topline 100%, and the line for filled positions is always listed as below 100%. Choice **(B)** is correct because it describes the trend lines as they are featured on the graph.

21. A

Difficulty: Hard

Category: Information and Ideas

Getting to the Answer: Eliminate answer choices that contradict the data in the table, as well as any that do not directly support the claim from the passage. In the portion immediately prior to the blank, the passage notes that the "smallest towns" in an unnamed region "showed minimal growth." The passage also sets up a contrast with the word "despite," meaning there will likely be some difference between the smallest towns and the other population categories for that unnamed region.

Choices (C) and (D) can be eliminated immediately, because the table shows the Midwest and the Northeast did not see population growth, but rather decline, in their smallest category (Population Less than 5,000). Choice (B) can be eliminated because it doesn't support the passage claim: the West did *not* see a significant difference in growth between its smallest towns and its more populous locations. In fact, its growth was the same in places will less than 5,000 and with more than 50,000. Choice **(A)** is correct because only the South saw slight growth in towns with a population less than 5,000, at 1.3%, while having the greatest gains in cities with populations of 50,000 or more.

22. D

Difficulty: Medium

Category: Information and Ideas

Getting to the Answer: Quantitative Command of Evidence questions can sometimes seem intimidating with the sheer amount of information and technical terms they provide. To avoid being overwhelmed, focus on the core question being asked. Pay careful attention to the immediate context near the blank: the passage will include a claim or detail that you will need to support with the information in the graph or table. Here, the question is asking about the two languages that saw the "smallest percent change in use." According to the graph, predict that these languages are French, which grew about 3%, and Korean, which declined about 2%. This prediction matches choice **(D)**, which is correct.

Choice (A) can be eliminated because German and Arabic do not show the "smallest" change in any manner. In fact, together they represent the opposite: the largest span of change. Choice (B) can be eliminated because it is the opposite of what the question asks; Arabic and Hindi show the largest growth. Choice (C) can be eliminated because it clashes with the detail near the blank; the question is asking for the "smallest percent change," not the languages that show the closest percent change to the national average.

23. D

Difficulty: Hard

Category: Information and Ideas

Getting to the Answer: Quantitative Command of Evidence questions will ask you for an answer choice that provides specific support for a claim or detail from the passage. However, be careful to read the whole passage, as it can be necessary to understand the context of that claim or detail. In this passage, Helena Glory is arguing that young people, defined in the passage as people age 18–29, would support abolishing payroll taxes. However, Humanity League Research uses a poll to argue that while Glory is "factually correct" that more young people support than oppose abolishing payroll taxes, Glory is not telling "the whole story." So, the question is asking for evidence that would *weaken* Glory's claim that the 18–29 group wants to abolish payroll taxes.

Keeping that context in mind allows the question to be solved in a straightforward manner. Choices (A) and (B) can be eliminated because they do not address the whole claim about young people. Instead, they contrast the opinions of people age 18–29 with the opinions of people in other age brackets. Likewise, choice (C) only considers opinions of those in other age brackets. Only Choice **(D)** correctly considers only young people, noting that a majority of those age 18–29 are actually undecided on the issue of abolishing payroll taxes. Glory's claim is "not the whole story" because it is based on only discussing young people with a strong opinion for or against the issue, while ignoring the considerable percentage of those who are undecided.

24. B

Difficulty: Easy

Category: Information and Ideas

Getting to the Answer: The passage detail, which must be supported by the information in the blank, concerns a "long-term trend" related to increasing population growth, and the table shows the number of seats in the House of Representatives in four states over time. You may notice the trend that California and Texas both show general growth in seats and, thus, relative population over time. Eliminate answer choices that contradict the data provided, as well as any that do not directly support the detail from the passage.

Choice (A) is incorrect; though California gained seats over time, it held 52 seats in 1993 and 52 seats in 2023, meaning it was not continually gaining additional seats. Choices (C) and (D) can be eliminated; the question asks about a "long-term trend" of "increasing population growth," while (C) and (D) deal with states decreasing in seats and, thus, relative population. Choice **(B)** is correct because it describes the long-term trend of Texas increasing in relative population and gaining more seats.

25. D

Difficulty: Easy

Category: Information and Ideas

Getting to the Answer: Inference questions require understanding the author's logical flow of ideas, meaning you will need to read the entire passage. In this passage, the discovery of the deserted Norse colony is introduced, followed by an introduction to the long-running debate as to why it was deserted. The passage then quickly recaps the colony's history. Study the final sentence. Note how we can guess what topic the blank should address based on the structure of the passage thus far. The final sentence states that "the ultimate fate of the settlements remained unknown until…" something happened. What something? Based on the logical flow of ideas, the blank should indicate that the colony was *confirmed to be deserted*. Choice **(D)** best fits into this flow of ideas. Choices (A), (B), and (C) do not, especially as they offer specific causes for the colony being deserted, which the passage already stated was a long-running mystery.

26. A

Difficulty: Easy

Category: Information and Ideas

Getting to the Answer: The correct answer to an Inference question is not stated explicitly in the passage, but it is something logically supported by what is stated in the passage. This passage deals with the beliefs of social Darwinists, who used the theory of evolution to justify economic and social inequality. Choice **(A)** best fits that line of thinking, as social Darwinists would see charity for the poor as an act against the natural order of survival of the fittest. (B) is incorrect because it is the opposite of what social Darwinists believed. (C) is incorrect because it is too extreme; social Darwinists justified inequality, but nothing in the passage supports them wanting the poor outright removed from society. (D) is incorrect because it is out of scope.

27. B

Difficulty:Difficulty: Hard

Category: Information and Ideas

Getting to the Answer: With inference questions, it is important to determine what the question is asking. The final sentence mentions the "amazing diversity" of the Burgess Shale and how it led Gould to believe *something* was "highly unlikely." Whatever logically fills in the blank is that something.

Notice in the second to last sentence, how chordates are described as being "rare" in the Burgess Shale despite all vertebrates, including humans, being descended from them. Given the "amazing diversity" of the fossils and how few chordates there were among them, **(B)** makes the most sense. Choice (A) is a distortion; while the *Opabinia* is mentioned as having five eyes, there is no doubt cast on it having actually existed. (C) is incorrect for a similar reason. There is no indication in the passage that the Burgess Shale is anything but real. (D) is out of scope, because the passage gives no indication of *why* chordates still exist while the other animal types in the Burgess Shale are extinct.

28. C

Difficulty: Medium

Category: Information and Ideas

Getting to the Answer: When reading a passage for an inference question, pay special attention to transition words, such as those that indicate contrast. In this passage, the concept of a hybrid is introduced, as well as the idea that they are an "evolutionary dead end." Then a contrast is set up ("For some species of birds, *however*…") and furthered with the idea that interspecific pairings may bring "evolutionary advantages" in this case. You may be able to make at least a general prediction about the inference in the correct answer from this point. Pick the answer choice option that best fits that general prediction.

Choice **(C)** correctly flows from the passage, which has set up the female collared flycatchers of Gotland as a type of bird whose offspring will benefit from being a hybrid. (A) and (B) are incorrect because they do not flow from the contrast set up with the passage's opening, that the female collared flycatchers of Gotland are an exception to the standard rule that hybrids are an "evolutionary dead end." (D) is out of scope; there is nothing in the passage to indicate that birds can influence the potential fertility of mules.

29. B

Difficulty: Medium

Category: Information and Ideas

Getting to the Answer: This passage introduces the concept of morale, explains that creature comforts are one way to improve morale, then provides one example of creature comforts. Choice **(B)** is correct; the ice cream was a specific example of using creature comforts to bolster morale. (A) is out of scope; the passage gives no indication that leaders demonstrating their care for their own troops is important to morale, or that it was the primary motivation for the ice cream. (C) is too extreme; the passage states that morale is important, but it never states that a lack of morale ("despair") can *never* be overcome. (D) is a distortion and too extreme. The passage states that creature comforts are one way to improve morale, which does not mean they are the *only* way.

30. B

Difficulty: Hard

Category: Information and Ideas

Getting to the Answer: Keep the passage's logical flow of ideas in mind when deciding how to best fill in the blank. The passage begins with a discussion of the various explanations for rainbows in cultures around the world. "But" in the fourteenth century, two men "independently turned a scientific eye" to the topic of rainbows. This contrast from the passage's opening leads into the blank, where each man concluded the same thing. Select the answer choice option that best fits that flow of ideas.

Choice **(B)** is correct; this is an explanation for the rainbow that fits the "scientific eye" both men applied to the study of rainbows. (A) is a scientific explanation, it is too narrow. The passage is concerned with the existence of the rainbow itself, not with its specific colors. (C) does not match the flow of the passage, which deals with the explanation for *why* rainbows exist. (D) is a distortion; while the passage deals with finding a non-spiritual explanation for rainbows, (D) does not offer a scientific explanation.

How Much Have You Learned?

1. A

Difficulty: Easy

Category: Information and Ideas

Getting to the Answer: The words "most logically completes the text" indicate that this is an Inference question, so the correct answer will be something that is logically supported by the text but is not explicitly stated in the passage. Read through the passage and paraphrase its flow of ideas: archaea, a microorganism that lacks a nucleus, *were* thought to only live in extreme conditions. The contrast between "were" and "now" means that there is a shift in thinking. Predict that the correct inference will indicate that scientists no longer think that archaea exclusively exist in extreme habitats. Choice **(A)** matches this prediction and is correct.

Choice (B) would not be a logical completion of the thought because it is merely a rephrasing of information provided in the first sentence. Eliminate (C) because it is both inaccurate and too extreme; the text cites that scientists know the archaea's cellular structure and their habitat. (D) is out of scope; nothing related to the term "archaebacteria" is mentioned in the passage.

2. D

Difficulty: Medium

Category: Information and Ideas

Getting to the Answer: The phrase "most strongly support" signals that this is a textual Command of Evidence question that asks which statement would best support the claim that a global database was needed. The correct answer will have a direct, logical relationship to the claim that a database will "improve the forecast, . . . evaluations . . . and the mitigation of volcanic activity." Select choice **(D)**, which matches that there is an increase in the accuracy of predictions.

Choice (A) is out of scope; the amount of funding available is not mentioned in the passage. (B) is the opposite of the passage's claim that the database would improve mitigation efforts. (C) weakens the claim made in the second sentence of the passage that the database was created to "improve global communication."

3. A

Difficulty: Medium

Category: Information and Ideas

Getting to the Answer: The question stem asks for the "central idea" of the text, so take a moment to paraphrase the excerpt: carrying the letters during "a hard trip" resulted in the dogs' and drivers' "poor condition," and their short recovery time, paired with the snow, increased the difficulty they experienced on the trail. This summary matches **(A)** and is correct.

Choices (B) and (C) are out of scope. The passage mentions neither the equipment needed for the journey nor the history of the mail delivery. Choice (D) is a distortion; the passage does not state the reason they limited their rest.

4. B

Difficulty: Medium

Category: Information and Ideas

Getting to the Answer: The phrase "According to the passage" shows this to be a Detail question about why the old man was able to return home without worry. The correct answer will paraphrase a statement made explicitly in the text. In the fourth and fifth sentences, the author writes that the old man has been anxious ("his anxiety") to know what had happened to the Lady Sparrow and he could "now…return home with a light heart" because he learned "how she fared." This matches **(B)**, which is correct.

Choice (A) misuses a detail ("suffered at the hands of his cross old wife") from the second sentence; however, the passage does not mention any forgiveness. (C) is incorrect because his enjoyment and appreciation were not referred to in connection with his light-hearted return home. (D) is the opposite of what is stated in the last sentence; the old man would return to her if she had need of him.

5. D

Difficulty: Hard

Category: Information and Ideas

Getting to the Answer: The phrase "most logically completes" signals that this is an Inference question asking you which phrase best completes a sentence about the ears of fennec foxes. In the second sentence, the author claims that the fennec foxes' fur provides both camouflage and insulation. In the third sentence, the author claims that their "enormous bat-like ears" help them "survive during the desert's peak temperatures," so predict that the correct choice will refer to their ability to live in the heat of a desert habitat. Choice **(D)** describes how their ears help them during the desert's heat and is correct.

Choice (A) is a distortion; the passage states that their ears help them survive. (B) is out of scope; the foxes' domestication is not mentioned in the passage. (C) repeats a detail about their fur, but is an illogical inference, this is an informative passage about the location and physical attributes of fennec foxes.

6. C

Difficulty: Medium

Category: Command of Evidence (quantitative)

Getting to the Answer: Carefully analyze the graph to identify what type of information it provides: the number of people, organized into five-year age groups, that work in five separate types of employment. The question is very broad, so approach with the elimination strategy. Eliminate (A) because both age groups individually have the two *highest* concentrations of Arbeit employees, and therefore, when combined, do *not* have the fewest. Eliminate (B); the 40-44 age group has *fewer* Other workers than 65+, for example. **(C)** is correct; the 60-64 age group has only one age group with fewer reported workers (15-19) and the third-fewest numbers on Regular employees. On test day, select that choice and continue on to the next question. (D) is incorrect; even when combined, the 20-24 and the 25-29 age groups have a *similar* or *fewest* amount of part-time workers.

[CHAPTER 14]

CRAFT AND STRUCTURE

LEARNING OBJECTIVES

After completing this chapter, you will be able to:

- Use surrounding context to infer the meaning of a word
- Identify the word that best conveys the intended meaning
- Identify the main purpose of a paragraph
- Identify the purpose of a phrase or sentence within a paragraph
- Identify the structure of a paragraph
- Identify connections between two texts

How Much Do You Know?

Directions

Try the questions that follow. When you're done, check your answers and reasoning against ours in the "Check Your Work" section. If they closely match, you may be able to move quickly through the chapter. If they do not, spend some extra time with the chapter to grow your PSAT Reading and Writing skills.

1

The following text is from Honoré De Balzac's 1830 short story "The Elixir of Life."

At the age of sixty, Belvidéro had become enamored of an angel of peace and beauty. Don Juan was the sole fruit of this late love. For fifteen years the good man had mourned the loss of his dear Juana. His many servants and his son attributed the strange habits he had contracted to this grief.

As used in the text, what does the word "contracted" most nearly mean?

- Ⓐ Agreed
- Ⓑ Ordered
- Ⓒ Acquired
- Ⓓ Withdrawn

2

The following text is from Sherwood Anderson's 1921 short story "Unlighted Lamps."

On several occasions Mary had gone to spend a day with her father in Chicago and she was fascinated by the thought that soon she might be going there to live. Before her mind's eye floated a vision of long streets filled with thousands of people all strangers to herself. To go into such streets and to live her life among strangers would be like coming out of a waterless desert and into a cool forest carpeted with tender young grass.

As used in the text, what does the word "floated" most nearly mean?

- Ⓐ Bobbed
- Ⓑ Appeared
- Ⓒ Discussed
- Ⓓ Rested

3

As cars became more popular in the early 20th century, their effect on population distribution was _____. Unlike railroads, which helped concentrate the population in cities, the automobile contributed to urban sprawl and, eventually, to the rise of suburbs. People no longer needed to live near railroad lines or within walking distance of their jobs, and so were drawn to outlying areas with less congestion and lower property taxes. Business districts became less centralized for similar reasons.

Which choice completes the text with the most logical and precise word or phrase?

- Ⓐ absolute
- Ⓑ profound
- Ⓒ thoughtful
- Ⓓ unintelligible

4

The following text is from a short story, "The Doorman," that takes place in New York City in the 2000s.

"Dad," Simon would sigh, "just retire," meaning Simon would take care of Wallace's rent and bologna and Listerine. But of course Wallace couldn't abandon the residents of the building where he was doorman. His son didn't think he was of any use anymore, but he was wrong. The new girl in 33A, for example—who would she talk to after midnight, when she got her rumblings? And Simon clearly did not recall the time Wallace helped get that delivery man arrested, the one who swiped Mr. Harrington's wallet straight from his back pocket, and how ever since Mr. Harrington had given Wallace a crisp hundred every Veterans Day.

Which choice best states the function of the underlined sentence in the text as a whole?

- Ⓐ It introduces the detail that Wallace served in the military.
- Ⓑ It provides an example of why Wallace thinks he is still important at his job.
- Ⓒ It depicts a fundamental way in which Simon and Wallace differ.
- Ⓓ It concludes the description of the impact of Wallace's physical condition.

5

Microloans, lending people very small loans to help them lift themselves up from poverty, has demonstrated benefits, but these should not be overstated. A study in Bangladesh extended microloans to a group of impoverished women to buy supplies for their business manufacturing bamboo stools. The women made a small profit and grew their business to self-sufficiency. But in later programs, some businesses failed, and some customers used their loans for consumption spending. Some borrowers had to sell off their meager possessions to meet their obligations. Researchers examining the data found that poverty had not been reduced, but advocates point to other outcomes. Borrowers had often replaced long hours of grueling work with more fulfilling self-employment, and some used the microloans to ease the financial stresses of temporary or seasonal unemployment, crop failures, and health crises.

Which choice best states the main purpose of the text?

(A) It discusses several findings to illustrate why caution is needed when evaluating the effects of microloan programs.

(B) It encourages the use of microloans to finance consumer spending among the desperately poor.

(C) It argues that microloan organizations should replace traditional financial institutions in many parts of the world.

(D) It presents the study of the Bangladeshi women to critique the methods and results reported in later studies of the effects of microloans.

6

Text 1

Many anthropologists believe that sophisticated medical practice began in the area of modern-day Europe about 7,000 years ago. Human fossils discovered in Britain and France had small holes in the skulls that showed signs of healing. The anthropologists cite these fossils as evidence of trepanning, when ancient practitioners would open the skull to allow the disease to escape.

Text 2

India Ella Dilkes-Hall and a research team have recently excavated the oldest grave to be found in Southeast Asia. Estimated to be about 31,000 years old, the remains show evidence of surgical amputation. The carefully buried skeleton was missing the left foot, and the bone end had a very unusual growth similar to those now seen after surgical amputation. This type of surgery requires knowledge of circulation, musculature, and infection management.

Based on the texts, how would India Ella Dilkes-Hall and the research team (Text 2) most likely respond to the view of the anthropologists presented in Text 1?

- (A) It is largely correct and suggests a modification of the research team's findings.
- (B) It will likely continue to hold true until further discoveries are made.
- (C) It may have been considered correct in the past, but has been superseded by the research team's recent discovery.
- (D) It may be incorrect but is irrelevant to the research team's recent discovery.

Check Your Work

1. C

Difficulty: Medium

Category: Craft and Structure

Getting to the Answer: In the text, the servants and son believe Belvidéro's strange habits came from his grief. So Belvidéro would have "added" or "obtained" these new habits. **(C)**, "acquired," matches this prediction and is correct.

The incorrect choices are all alternative definitions of "contracted" that do not fit this context.

2. B

Difficulty: Medium

Category: Craft and Structure

Getting to the Answer: Reread the sentence containing "floated"; predict another word that could be substituted for "floated" and give the sentence the same meaning as the original one. Mary is imagining a scene in Chicago of long streets filled with lots of people she doesn't know. The image came into her mind, so "arose" or "materialized" would be good predictions. **(B)** matches and is correct.

The vision that "floated" before Mary's mind's eye is not literally floating, so (A) and (D) are incorrect. While "discussed" is an alternate meaning for "floated," it doesn't fit with the context of the vision that Mary is imagining; therefore, (C) is also incorrect.

3. B

Difficulty: Medium

Category: Craft and Structure

Getting to the Answer: In the text, the blank describes the effect cars had on population distribution. Since the next sentence state that "the automobile contributed to urban sprawl and . . . to the rise of the suburbs," look for an answer choice that means "important" or "extensive." **(B)** is correct.

Choice (A) is extreme; an "absolute" effect would imply that there were no other influences. (C) is a synonym of the word "profound" when it is used to describe an idea; however, the previous paragraph did not discuss a "thoughtful" impact of the automobile, but rather a "far-reaching" one. (D) means *impossible to understand*, and it is clear from the rest of this paragraph that the

profound effects on population distribution were both observable and understandable.

4. B

Difficulty: Medium

Category: Craft and Structure

Getting to the Answer: The underlined sentence describes an incident in which a resident showed appreciation for Wallace's help in his service as a doorman. The text is about why Wallace believes Simon is wrong to think Wallace is not "of any use anymore" at his job. Since the cited sentence supports the main idea of the paragraph by giving a reason why Wallace is of use, **(B)** is correct.

Though Wallace's military service is implied by the sentence, this is a minor detail and not the reason the sentence is included in the passage, so (A) is incorrect. Choice (C) is incorrect because, although Simon and Wallace disagree about Wallace retiring, this difference is introduced earlier in the paragraph, and the cited sentence only addresses Wallace's view. Choice (D) is incorrect because Wallace's physical condition is not mentioned in the text.

5. A

Difficulty: Medium

Category: Craft and Structure

Getting to the Answer: The text opens with a statement that microloans have been shown to be helpful, but that their benefit "should not be overstated." The passage continues with an explanation, but authors offer explanations for the purpose of defending their ideas. The first sentence is all you need to match **(A)**, the correct answer. For the record, the rest of the text says there was a successful outcome in Bangladesh, followed by some failures. Evidence supported the idea that microloans had not reduced poverty, but advocates pointed out other ways microloans had helped the poor.

Choices (B) and (C) are incorrect because, after the initial success, the author describes a number of criticisms of microloans. The text does not include any recommendations for expanding the use of microloans. (D) misstates the author's intention. Although the findings of the studies differ, the author never criticizes "the methods and results" of the studies.

6.   C

Difficulty: Medium

Category: Craft and Structure

Getting to the Answer: The anthropologists of Text 1 believe that sophisticated medicine began in Europe about 7,000 years ago. The discovery in Text 2 provides evidence of sophisticated medicine in Southeast Asia 31,000 years ago. Predict that India Ella Dilkes-Hall and the research team expect their discovery to contradict the view expressed in Text 1. **(C)** matches the prediction, and is correct.

Incorrect choices (A) and (B) are backward. The discovery discussed in Text 2 shows evidence of sophisticated medicine at a much earlier date, and would most likely replace that of Text 1. The first part of (D) is correct, but the theory to be replaced is very relevant to the new discovery, making this choice also incorrect.

Words in Context Questions

LEARNING OBJECTIVES

After this lesson, you will be able to:

- Use surrounding context to infer the meaning of a word
- Identify the word that best conveys the intended meaning

To answer a question like this:

The panspermia hypothesis, which states that life on Earth originated in outer space, can no longer be dismissed as being science fiction or the fanciful speculation of unscientific minds: it is becoming an increasingly _____ field of research within astrobiology.

Which choice completes the text with the most logical and precise word or phrase?

- Ⓐ respectable
- Ⓑ theoretical
- Ⓒ improper
- Ⓓ rejected

You need to know this:

How to Identify Words in Context Questions

Words in Context questions can be identified by the words or short phrases in their answer choices. These questions include the keyword "word," and typically appear in two types:

- *Which choice completes the text with the most logical and precise word or phrase?*
- *As used in the text, what does the word "example" most nearly mean?*

How to Predict a Word in Context

As indicated by the sample question stems above, there are two different forms of Words in Context questions: one kind will ask you to fill in a blank with a missing word or phrase, and the other kind will ask you to choose a word with the same meaning as a word from the passage.

The key to answering both types of Words in Context questions is to use the clues in the passage to make a strong prediction of the correct answer *before looking at the answer choices*. When analyzing the context of a passage:

- Determine which words in the passage indicate the meaning of the needed word.
- Consider both the immediate context around the word and, if needed, the broader context in the passage.
- Pay special attention to keywords and punctuation that indicate transitions.

Consider how to analyze the context in this short excerpt from Mary Shelley's *Frankenstein*:

On the birth of a second son, my junior by seven years, my parents gave up entirely their wandering life, and fixed themselves in their native country.

A Words in Context question might ask you: *As used in the text, what does the word "fixed" most nearly mean?*

To determine the meaning of the word "fixed," look for clues in the passage. First, consider the immediate context: someone has "fixed" themselves in their "native country." Then look at the broader context. The previous phrase states that the narrator's parents stopped their "wandering life," and the continuation transition word "and" connects these ideas: the parents stopped wandering and "fixed themselves" in their home country.

This analysis of the immediate context, the broader context, and the transition words in the passage enables you to make a prediction about the meaning of the word "fixed" as used in this passage: if being "fixed" is related to "not wandering," predict that it means *settled*. Suppose the answer choices are A) settled, B) attached, C) appointed, and D) mended. This prediction matches **(A)**. The other answer choices are alternate meanings for "fixed," but none are indicated by the context of the passage.

Incorrect answers to a Word in Context question may be words that:

- Are related to words in the passage but do not logically complete the blank
- Are synonyms of the word in the passage but do not match the context of the passage

The correct answer to a Word in Context question will:

- Provide a word that matches the context of the passage

You need to do this:

THE METHOD FOR PSAT READING AND WRITING

STEP 1   What is the question asking?

STEP 2   What do I need to look for in the passage?

STEP 3   What answer strategy is best?

  - Predict & Match
  - Eliminate

Step 1. What is the question asking?

Words in Context questions will make reference to "words" in the question stem. Some Words in Context questions will ask you to choose a missing word or phrase that logically completes a blank in the passage; others will ask you to choose a word that is closest in meaning to a word as it is used in the passage.

Step 2. What do I need to look for in the passage?

For both types of Words in Context questions, you need to use the context of the passage to determine the meaning of the word in question. Locate the blank or indicated word in the passage, and first consider the context of the phrase in which the blank or word appears. Most of the time, you will need to read the rest of the passage for additional clues to help you determine the meaning of the word. Pay careful attention to any transition words (such as *however*, *but*, *although*, *and*, *because*—words that signal connections between ideas), transition punctuation (such as a colon or dash—punctuation that signals a continuation between ideas), and other clue words.

Step 3. What answer strategy is best?

Using your analysis of context, make a prediction for the meaning of the word. Occasionally, you may find an exact match for your prediction among the answer choices. Even if there isn't an exact match, your prediction should make it easier to eliminate answer choices that give a different meaning for the word and identify the one correct meaning.

Explanation:

The question mentions a "word or phrase" and asks you to logically complete a blank, so this is a Words in Context question. The context immediately around the blank indicates that something is becoming an "increasingly _____ field of research"; since this isn't enough information to go on, examine the context of the entire passage for hints about what the research field is "increasingly" becoming. The first part of the sentence indicates that a certain hypothesis "can no longer be dismissed" as fiction or speculation. A colon indicates a logical connection between the idea that the hypothesis cannot be dismissed with it becoming an "increasingly _____ field of research," so predict that the hypothesis is becoming an *accepted* or *prevalent* field of research. This prediction matches **(A)**.

Although (B), theoretical, seems related to the passage topic of a scientific hypothesis, this choice is incorrect because the blank must logically complete the idea that the hypothesis is no longer being dismissed. Choices (C) and (D) are incorrect because they are opposite of the required meaning.

Try on Your Own

Directions

Take as much time as you need on these questions. Work carefully and methodically. There will be an opportunity for timed practice later in the book.

1

The following text is from Jane Austen's 1803 novel *Northanger Abbey*.

Everybody acquainted with Bath may remember the difficulties of crossing Cheap Street at this point; it is indeed a street of so impertinent a nature, so unfortunately connected with the great London and Oxford roads, and the principal inn of the city, that a day never passes in which parties of ladies, however important their business, whether in quest of pastry, millinery, or even (as in the present case) of young men, are not detained on one side or other by carriages, horsemen, or carts.

As used in the text, what does the word "impertinent" most nearly mean?

- (A) Unrestrained
- (B) Well structured
- (C) Irrelevant
- (D) Bold

2

There remains a tantalizing mystery: the evolution of the eukaryotic nucleus. The nucleus is a complex structure within a eukaryotic cell that is encased in a membrane and contains the cell's genetic material. There are a number of competing models for how this structure might have evolved. The most controversial of these involve viruses.

As used in the text, what does the word "models" most nearly mean?

- (A) Ideals
- (B) Hypotheses
- (C) Examples
- (D) Figurines

3

Ornithologists, scientists who specialize in the study of birds, believe that geese fly in a V-formation to conserve energy and provide visual assurance of the other geese in the flock. The lead goose flies at the lowest point of the formation, with each subsequent bird flying slightly above the one that _____ it. This staggered placement reduces wind resistance and allows the geese to view all the other flyers in the formation.

Which choice completes the text with the most logical and precise word or phrase?

Ⓐ purports

Ⓑ displaces

Ⓒ parallels

Ⓓ precedes

4

The first in-home gaming console, Magnavox Odyssey, was developed and released in 1972 by Ralph H. Baer, a German-American engineer. Despite presaging a multibillion-dollar industry, this inaugural device had _____ sales and was quickly overshadowed by the overwhelming success of the Atari 2600 system's release in 1977.

Which choice completes the text with the most logical and precise word or phrase?

Ⓐ remarkable

Ⓑ electronic

Ⓒ dismal

Ⓓ pecuniary

5

An American professional baseball player, Curtis Flood is most remembered for suing Major League Baseball (MLB) after the MLB traded him to another team without his consent. Although he lost his case against the MLB and their exemption from antitrust laws, Flood's advocacy for players' rights was _____ for future changes in the league's reserve clause.

Which choice completes the text with the most logical and precise word or phrase?

Ⓐ a catalyst

Ⓑ a regression

Ⓒ a setback

Ⓓ a detractor

6

The following text is from Charles Dickens's 1876 novel *Great Expectations*.

There were three ladies in the room and one gentleman. Before I had been standing at the window five minutes, they somehow conveyed to me that they were all toadies and humbugs, but that each of them pretended not to know that the others were toadies and humbugs: because the _____ that he or she did know it, would have made him or her out to be a toady and humbug.

Which choice completes the text with the most logical and precise word or phrase?

- (A) belief
- (B) observation
- (C) denial
- (D) admission

Reading & Writing

Purpose Questions

LEARNING OBJECTIVES

After this lesson, you will be able to:

- Identify the main purpose of a paragraph
- Identify the purpose of a phrase or sentence within a paragraph
- Identify the structure of a paragraph

To answer a question like this:

The following excerpt is from Lucy Maud Montgomery's 1908 novel *Anne of Green Gables*.

Matthew dreaded all women except Marilla and Mrs. Rachel; <u>he had an uncomfortable feeling that the mysterious creatures were secretly laughing at him</u>. He may have been quite right in thinking so, for he was an odd-looking personage, with an ungainly figure and long iron-gray hair that touched his stooping shoulders, and a full, soft brown beard which he had worn ever since he was twenty.

Which choice best states the function of the underlined portion in the text as a whole?

(A) It sets up the following sentence's alternative description of a character that was already introduced in the passage.

(B) It elaborates on a description of a character that appears earlier in the sentence.

(C) It introduces a humorous character trait of the character described in the paragraph.

(D) It contrasts the character described in the paragraph with other characters in the passage.

You need to know this:

How to Identify Purpose Questions

Purpose questions ask you to identify the purpose of a passage or a specified portion of a passage or to describe the overall structure of a passage. You can identify Purpose questions because they contain words such as "purpose," "function," or "structure." Note that in the sample questions below, the first two ask about the entire passage, and the third asks about a portion of the passage:

- *Which choice best states the main purpose of the text?*
- *Which choice best describes the overall structure of the text?*
- *Which choice best states the function of the underlined sentence in the text as a whole?*

How to Identify Purpose and Structure

On PSAT Reading and Writing, "purpose" and "function" refer to the author's *reason* for writing something, whether an entire passage or a portion of a passage. The "structure" of a passage refers to how the ideas in a passage are organized so that they can effectively achieve the author's purpose.

Identifying the Purpose of a Passage

When identifying the purpose of an entire passage, you can use many of the same strategies you used when identifying the main idea on Main Idea questions. Begin by determining the author's *main point* about the topic of the passage, which will be supported by the details in the rest of the passage. The first and last sentences are likely places to find the author's main idea.

Where Purpose questions differ from Main Idea questions is in the form of the answer choices. Whereas the correct answer to a Main Idea question summarizes the main point of the passage, the correct answer to a Purpose question will contain a verb that describes the author's specific *reason* for writing the passage. For instance, while a passage about dogs might have the main idea of *why dogs make good pets*, its purpose might be to argue that dogs make good pets. The purpose of a passage should answer the question *Why did the author write this?*

Identifying the Structure of a Passage

Passages on the PSAT are carefully crafted; each sentence and phrase intentionally contributes to the passage as a whole. If a question asks about a passage's structure, mentally map out the passage organization as you read. A few examples of basic passage structures include:

- topic and examples
- hypothesis, experiment, and results
- cause and effect
- claim and support
- counter-claim and support
- descriptive elements

Consider an example literature passage structure: perhaps a passage first introduces a character, then describes that character, then gives an example of the character behaving according to the description.

Identifying the Purpose of a Portion of the Passage

On Purpose questions that ask about the function of a specified portion of a passage, again ask yourself *Why did the author write this?* or *Why did the author include this?* To identify the purpose of a portion of a passage, first determine its overall structure, as discussed above. The placement of the specified portion will indicate its function within the passage.

For example, again consider the sample literature passage described above: a passage first introduces a character, then describes that character, then gives an example of the character behaving according to the description. If a portion appears in the example section, for instance, its function might be: *it illustrates a character's nature by providing an example*. Once again, the correct answer will include a verb that accurately reflects the function of the specified portion.

Incorrect answers to a Purpose question may:

- Include ideas from the passage but misrepresent the author's reason for writing about them
- Include verbs that misrepresent the author's reason for writing the passage or underlined portion
- Inaccurately reflect the structure of the passage

The correct answer to a Purpose question will:

- Correctly identify the author's reason for writing a passage, using an appropriate verb OR
- Correctly describe the structure of a passage in a way that accounts for every part of the passage and reflects the author's overall purpose OR
- Correctly identify the author's reason for including a portion of the passage, in light of the structure of the entire passage, using an appropriate verb

You need to do this:

THE METHOD FOR PSAT READING AND WRITING

STEP 1 What is the question asking?

STEP 2 What do I need to look for in the passage?

STEP 3 What answer strategy is best?

- Predict & Match
- Eliminate

Step 1. What is the question asking?

If the question stem contains the keyword "purpose" or "function," ask yourself: *Why did the author write/ include this?* If the question stem contains the keyword "structure," ask yourself: *How are the ideas in the passage organized?*

Step 2. What do I need to look for in the passage?

If asked about the purpose of the entire passage, identify its *main idea*, which is often reflected in the first or last sentence. Then ask yourself what the author's *reason* is for writing about that main idea. Is the author making an argument? Responding to an objection? Critiquing another idea?

If asked about the structure of the entire passage, mentally map out how the ideas in the passage are organized as you read. See if you can identify one of the commonly used passage structures, such as a topic and examples or a claim and support.

If asked about the function of a portion of the passage, analyze the structure of the passage—what role does the tested portion serve in the overall organization and structure of the passage? Ask yourself: *Why did the author decide to include this portion? What would the passage be lacking if the portion were missing?*

Step 3. What answer strategy is best?

Questions that ask about purpose lend themselves to making a prediction. Paraphrase, in your own words, the author's *reason* for writing the passage or portion. Look for an answer choice that matches your prediction. If needed, eliminate any answer choices that use an inappropriate verb (for instance, one that states the passage "critiques" an idea, when the passage never explicitly analyzes that idea). Also, eliminate any answer choices that mention ideas from the passage but misrepresent the author's purpose for mentioning them.

On questions that ask about the structure of the passage, make a prediction of the passage's overall organization if you are able. These questions often become easier to answer when you evaluate the answer choices and eliminate any that misrepresent a portion of the structure of the passage. For instance, if a passage begins by describing a character, eliminate an answer choice that begins "It describes the setting of the passage, then . . . ." Remember that the correct answer will accurately reflect the *entire* structure of the passage.

Explanation:

The keyword "function" identifies this as a Purpose question; the question asks for the reason the author included a phrase. To determine how the phrase functions within the passage, read through the passage to determine its structure. The passage begins by stating a character trait of the character Matthew. The semicolon in the first sentence signals a continuation transition between its ideas; the underlined portion continues the idea from the first part of the sentence. Indeed, the underlined portion provides a logical explanation for why Matthew "dreaded" most women: he felt they were laughing at him. You can predict that the underlined portion *gives an explanation for a character trait*. (The rest of the passage contains a physical description of Matthew.) Choice **(B)** matches the prediction and is correct.

Choice (A) is incorrect because it misrepresents the structure of the passage; the description of Matthew in the next sentence does not contrast with the previous description of him. Choice (C) is incorrect because it distorts the meaning of the underlined portion; although it mentions laughter, it does not represent a humorous character trait. Being after the semicolon, the underlined phrase also does not introduce anything. Choice (D) is incorrect because it uses an inappropriate verb; the underlined portion does not create a contrast between characters.

Try on Your Own

Directions

Take as much time as you need on these questions. Work carefully and methodically. There will be an opportunity for timed practice later in the book.

7

The following text is from Sherwood Anderson's 1921 short story "Unlighted Lamps."

In Huntersburg she had always lived under a cloud and now she was becoming a woman and the close stuffy atmosphere she had always breathed was becoming constantly more and more oppressive. It was true no direct question had ever been raised touching her own standing in the community life, but she felt that a kind of prejudice against her existed. While she was still a baby there had been a scandal involving her father and mother. The town of Huntersburg had rocked with it and when she was a child people had sometimes looked at her with mocking sympathetic eyes. "Poor child! It's too bad," they said.

Which choice best states the function of the underlined sentence in the text as a whole?

- (A) It characterizes the townspeople's subtle ostracism of Mary.

- (B) It contradicts the previous statement that the townspeople had mocking sympathy for Mary.

- (C) It reveals the concern that the townspeople had about Mary's family's financial situation.

- (D) It highlights the townspeople's lack of involvement with Mary.

8

The following text is from Wilkie Collins's 1859 novel *The Woman in White*.

Pesca's face and manner, on the evening when we confronted each other at my mother's gate, were more than sufficient to inform me that something extraordinary had happened . . . We both bounced into the parlor in a highly abrupt and undignified manner. My mother sat by the open window laughing and fanning herself. Pesca was one of her especial favorites, and his wildest eccentricities were always pardonable in her eyes. From the first moment she found out that the little Professor was deeply and gratefully attached to her son, she opened her heart to him unreservedly and took all his puzzling foreign peculiarities for granted, without so much as attempting to understand any one of them.

Which choice best states the function of the underlined sentence in the text as a whole?

- (A) It illustrates the personalities of the narrator and Pesca.

- (B) It suggests that their disruptive behavior was in fact combative.

- (C) It portrays Pesca as a bad influence on the narrator.

- (D) It provides a humorous contrast to the seriousness of the narrator's mother.

9

The following text is adapted from Henry Wadsworth Longfellow's 1879 poem "The Tides."

I saw the long line of the vacant shore,
As if the ebbing tide would flow no more.

All thought and feeling and desire, I said,
Love, laughter, and the exultant joy of song
Have ebbed from me forever! Suddenly o'er me

They swept again from their deep ocean bed,
And in a tumult of delight, and strong
As youth, and beautiful as youth, upbore me.

Which choice best describes the overall structure of the text?

(A) The speaker describes his feeling of emptiness when he doesn't see the tide, and then compares his return of positive feelings to the incoming tide.

(B) The speaker experiences regret about how he has lived his life, and then describes the ocean as having childlike characteristics.

(C) The speaker marvels at the dependability of the ocean tides, and then confronts his insignificance in light of the power of the natural world.

(D) The speaker expresses his desire to make his home by the ocean, and then reflects on the diversity of emotions that can be evoked by the ocean tides.

10

Throughout the nineteenth century, researchers attributed the disappearance of two Norse colonies in Greenland to war between the colonies and Inuit groups. This was based largely on evidence from the work *Description of Greenland*, written by Norse settler Ivar Bardarson around 1364. This book describes strained relationships between the Norse settlers and the Inuits who had recently come to Greenland. However, because there is no archaeological evidence of a war or a massacre, and the extensive body of Inuit oral history tells of no such event, modern scholars give little credence to these theories.

Which choice best states the main purpose of the text?

(A) It analyzes the motivations behind a historical event.

(B) It explains why a long-held theory is now believed to be incorrect.

(C) It disputes a modern theory with an indigenous people's oral history.

(D) It chronicles the conflict between immigrant settlers and a region's indigenous people.

11

Many linguists agree that a newborn baby's brain is preprogrammed for language acquisition, meaning that it's as natural for a baby to talk as it is for a dog to dig. According to psycholinguist Anne Cutler, an infant's language acquisition actually begins well before birth. At only one day old, newborns have demonstrated the ability to recognize the voices and rhythms heard during their last trimester in the muffled confines of the womb. During the first few months after birth, infants will subconsciously study the language used around them, taking note of the rhythmic patterns, the sequences of sounds, and the intonation of the language. By the middle of their first year, infants start displaying a preference for sounds in their native language, culminating at age one.

Which choice best states the main purpose of the text?

(A) It traces the history of a scientific inquiry.

(B) It describes an aspect of early childhood development.

(C) It explains the research that led to a new breakthrough.

(D) It presents the background of a recent medical discovery.

12

It would not be until 1861 that Louis Pasteur would propose the link between microorganisms and disease, now known as the germ theory. But during a particularly deadly outbreak of cholera in the Soho district of Westminster in London from August 31 to September 3, 1854, John Snow took to the streets. Speaking to residents of the area, he found a commonality among them: most of the victims had used a single public water pump located on Broad Street. Though he was unable to find conclusive proof that the pump was the source of the outbreak, his demonstration of a pattern in the cholera cases prompted authorities to disable the pump by removing its handle. The epidemic quickly subsided. John Snow had become one of the founders of epidemiology, the study of the occurrence and spread of disease.

Which choice best states the main purpose of the text?

(A) It summarizes the research that led to the science of epidemiology.

(B) It critiques government officials for failing to consider evidence that could have prevented further loss of life.

(C) It chronicles an episode in the history of medicine that changed the way in which research is conducted.

(D) It argues that practical actions should be taken to avoid loss of life prior to the collection of definitive data.

Connections Questions

> **LEARNING OBJECTIVE**
>
> After this lesson, you will be able to:
>
> • Identify connections between two texts

To answer a question like this:

Text 1

Confirming the panspermia hypothesis, which states that life on Earth originated in outer space, will require clear evidence that interplanetary transfer of microbes is possible. Finding such evidence is extremely challenging, the more so because alternative explanations abound for the presence of bacteria on objects in space. Living bacteria were recently found on the exterior of the International Space Station, for instance, but these bacteria had been intentionally placed by researchers.

Text 2

There is reason to believe that, billions of years ago, Mars was warmer and moister than it is now and capable of supporting life. Indeed, Mars may have been more conducive to the development of life than Earth was during the early history of the solar system. It is feasible that life developed on Mars first and was carried to Earth on space-borne debris.

Based on the texts, how would the author of Text 1 most likely respond to the evidence presented in Text 2?

(A) It is insufficient to support the panspermia hypothesis and is therefore inconclusive.

(B) It is evidence that is completely irrelevant to the panspermia hypothesis.

(C) It decisively confirms the panspermia hypothesis.

(D) It is likely correct, but additional evidence is required to confirm the panspermia hypothesis.

You need to know this:

How to Identify Connections Questions

Connections questions are easy to identify: they present two different texts (labeled "Text 1" and "Text 2") and ask a question related to both texts. A Connections question may ask about:

• How a viewpoint in one text would respond to a viewpoint from the other text

• Something the texts have in common

• How the viewpoints in the texts differ

How to Make Connections Between Texts

The key to correctly answering Connections questions is keeping straight all the viewpoints in the passages. Viewpoints could be those of the text authors, as well as those of anyone (such as a researcher) mentioned in the texts. Fortunately, you can use the question stem to identify which viewpoints you need to understand to correctly answer the question.

If the question asks about the view of an author, determine the main idea of the text, just as you would for a Main Idea question. Remember, you need to identify not just the topic of the passage but the author's main point about that topic. Paraphrase the author's view in your own words.

If the question asks about the view of someone mentioned in the passage, also paraphrase this view in your own words. These views might be explicitly stated in the passage (for example, "Some scientists have argued that . . ."), or they might be based upon information given in the passage (for instance, the results of a research study).

In either case, pay attention to any clue words in the passages that provide hints about viewpoints. Emphasis words such as "terrible" or "exciting" signal opinions. There may also be subtle words or phrases, such as "contrary to what she expected," that can provide strong hints about a viewpoint.

Make sure that you carefully distinguish between the view of the text author and the view of someone mentioned in a text—these viewpoints are not necessarily the same!

Incorrect answers to a Connections question may be:

- **Distortions**—Incorrect answers to Connections questions may distort the viewpoints in the passages by making unsupported connections between them.
- **Extreme**—Incorrect answers to Connections questions may make connections that are more extreme than those supported by the viewpoints in the passages. These incorrect answers might include extreme words, such as *always*, *never*, or *regardless*.
- **Opposites**—Incorrect answers to Connections questions may make connections that are opposite of the connection that is supported by the viewpoints in the passages.

The correct answer to a Connections question will:

- Provide a relevant and accurate connection
- Correctly reflect the viewpoints from both texts

You need to do this:

THE METHOD FOR PSAT READING AND WRITING

STEP 1 What is the question asking?

STEP 2 What do I need to look for in the passage?

STEP 3 What answer strategy is best?

- Predict & Match
- Eliminate

Step 1. What is the question asking?

When a question includes two texts, look at the question stem to determine which viewpoints are needed to answer the question. In your own words, briefly state what the question asks, for instance, *how the author of Text 2 would respond to the researchers in Text 1.*

Step 2. What do I need to look for in the passage?

Next, read the passages with the goal of identifying the viewpoints needed to answer the question. Use clue words to help you understand the nuances of each viewpoint, and make sure you keep different viewpoints (such as those of an author versus those of someone mentioned in the passage) straight. Paraphrase the two relevant viewpoints in your own words.

Step 3. What answer strategy is best?

Making a prediction about the connection between the viewpoints will make it easier to focus in on the one correct answer. Even if you are unable to make a specific prediction (such as, *the researchers in Text 2 would agree with the hypothesis presented in Text 1*), you may be able to make a general prediction about the connection (such as, *the views agree* or *the views disagree*).

Whether or not you make a prediction, eliminate answer choices that misrepresent the connection between the views. Eliminate any answer choices that distort the logical connection between the views; some answer choices may even provide the opposite of the correct connection. Also eliminate any answer choices that make connections that are too extreme; if the passages themselves lack extreme language, an extreme answer choice will likely be incorrect.

Once you identify the answer choice that presents a logical connection based on an accurate representation of both relevant viewpoints, select it and move on.

Explanation:

The question includes two texts, and the question asks how the author of Text 1 would most likely respond to evidence from Text 2, so this is a Connections question. Read the passages with these needed viewpoints in mind. The view of the author of Text 1 is introduced in the first sentence: confirming the panspermia hypothesis requires clear evidence. The clue words "extremely challenging" in the next sentence reinforce that the author thinks finding sufficient evidence will be very difficult, and the last sentence includes an example of potential evidence that the author rejects. The evidence in Text 2 concerns the possibility of life developing on Mars and traveling to Earth.

Predict the connection. The view of the author of Text 1 is that the hypothesis needs clear evidence; the evidence in Text 2 is the hypothetical transfer of life from Mars to Earth. Since the author of Text 1 demands strong evidence, predict that this author would not accept a speculation without definitive proof. This matches **(A)**, which is correct.

Choice (B) is incorrect because it distorts the connection; although the author of Text 1 would reject the evidence in Text 2, the transfer of life from Mars to Earth is certainly relevant to the hypothesis that life on Earth came from space. Choice (C) is the opposite of the logical connection since the author of Text 1 would not accept the evidence in Text 2. Choice (D) also distorts the connection; the author of Text 1 certainly would require additional evidence, but there is no indication in Text 1 that the author would consider the transfer of life from Mars "likely" to have occurred.

Try on Your Own

Directions

Take as much time as you need on these questions. Work carefully and methodically. There will be an opportunity for timed practice later in the book.

13

Text 1

Jason W. Allen won first prize in a digital art competition with an image generated with artificial intelligence (AI) software. AI art software uses a text description input by the author to create the final image, and Allen worked over 80 hours, manipulating over 900 prompts, to produce the prize-winning picture. Allen's victory shows that AI artists are true artists, since they direct the composition of a unique work of art.

Text 2

Artificial intelligence (AI) art software exploits traditional artists. When AI art software processes the words in a prompt, it accesses and copies parts of images created by human artists, then assembles these into a new composition. The human writing the prompt, the so-called AI artist, may have never held a drawing pencil, pastel, or paintbrush, much less mastered perspective, shading, and other artistic techniques.

Which choice best describes a central difference between how the authors of the texts view AI artists?

- (A) The author of Text 1 is cautious about their accomplishments, whereas the author of Text 2 embraces them.

- (B) The author of Text 1 extols the distinctive methods they employ, whereas the author of Text 2 criticizes these methods.

- (C) The author of Text 1 proposes that they be considered true artists, whereas the author of Text 2 argues that they may lack traditional skills.

- (D) The author of Text 1 proposes that AI artists be considered true artists, whereas the author of Text 2 believes they do not devote sufficient time and effort to their creations.

14

Text 1

Reducing the use of petroleum products is crucial for the future of our planet. Petroleum combustion releases toxic gases that accumulate in the atmosphere, which damage the environment, cause widespread health problems among human populations, and contribute to catastrophic weather events.

Text 2

As the need for petroleum products declines worldwide, less oil is refined. While this is expected to have many beneficial effects, there is one important drawback—the loss of the solid sulfur produced as a byproduct of the refining process. This sulfur is easily transported to factories where it is converted into sulfuric acid, a critical component of fertilizer, batteries, and solar panels. Currently, 80% of the world's sulfuric acid production is based on sulfur from petroleum refining, and this sulfur will have to be replaced as petroleum refining declines.

Which choice best states the relationship between the two texts?

Ⓐ Text 2 takes issue with the main point of Text 1.

Ⓑ Text 2 provides a supporting point to the main idea of Text 1.

Ⓒ Text 2 implies a future modification to the main point of Text 1.

Ⓓ Text 2 illustrates a practical difficulty with the main point of Text 1.

Reading & Writing

Text 1

The search for life outside of Earth has been a search for the components of life, such as water and organic carbon, and molecules, such as oxygen, that are generated by life. The problem with this approach is that it is limited to the characteristics of life on Earth. It is possible that life on other planets has a completely different biochemistry. Astrobiologists posit that alien life might use other abundant elements, such as silicon instead of carbon, and ammonia or methane instead of water.

Text 2

Titan, one of the moons of Saturn, is of particular interest to astrobiologists. Natalie Grefenstette notes that the surface of Titan is covered with lakes of liquid methane, and that, like water on Earth, methane exists there in solid, liquid, and gaseous states. The *Dragonfly* space mission in the 2030s will include mass spectrometers able to examine many of the molecules present on Titan.

Based on the texts, both authors would likely agree with which of the following claims?

(A) The *Dragonfly* mission is likely to find methane-based life on Titan.

(B) Because Titan lacks water and oxygen, the *Dragonfly* mission will likely not find life on that moon.

(C) The methods used to search for extraterrestrial life should be broadened to include biochemistries not found on Earth.

(D) Continuing to search for water, organic carbon, oxygen, and methane is the best methodology for identifying life outside of Earth.

Text 1

Mimicry, the ability of animals and insects to imitate their surroundings or other species to trick predators, is well-known. For example, the harmless milk snake has evolved similar coloration to the highly venomous coral snake. Many biologists believe that mimicry in nature is limited to visual mimicry since the differences in vocal and auditory systems between species would make tricking predators with sound much more difficult.

Text 2

Danilo Russo noticed that, as he collected bats, they made a buzzing sound similar to the sound made by local hornets. Russo and his colleague recorded both the sound made by the bats and the sound made by the hornets. They then replayed the sounds in the presence of tawny owls and barn owls, which prey upon bats. Every time either sound was played, the owls retreated as far away from the sound as possible.

Based on the texts, how would Russo and his colleague (Text 2) most likely describe the view of the biologist presented in Text 1?

Ⓐ It is plausible and has been further supported by Russo's results.

Ⓑ It has been unquestionably confirmed by Russo's results.

Ⓒ It probably is inaccurate, regardless of Russo's findings.

Ⓓ It has decreased in credibility in light of Russo's results.

17

Text 1

Human immune systems attack invaders in one of two ways: type-1 reactions are mounted against bacteria and viruses, and type-2 reactions are activated against multicellular aggressors, such as worms. Some microbiologists theorize that bacteria resistant to traditional treatments may be weakening the immune system by tricking it to mount a type-2, not a type-1, reaction.

Text 2

Ruslan Medzhitov and a team of scientists experimented with *Pseudomonas aeruginosa*, an infectious bacterium. They grew cultures of human cells and exposed the cells to a toxin produced by the bacterium. The cells produced components of a thick mucus that the body uses to trap parasitic worms, and the bacterium thrived, feeding on the mucus.

Based on the texts, how would the microbiologist (Text 1) most likely describe the findings of Medzhitov described in Text 2?

(A) They indicate that the microbiologist's theory may be correct.

(B) They demonstrate one of the limitations of the microbiologist's theory.

(C) They demonstrate that the microbiologist's theory is not compelling as a theory.

(D) They require a major refinement before they would be relevant to the microbiologist's theory.

Text 1

Although they are less productive than European breeds, African cattle are much more resistant to East Coast Fever (ECF), a fatal disease. Although vaccines and preventive treatments are available, they are expensive. Veterinary researchers theorize that it may be possible to develop cattle that are both more productive and resistant to ECF.

Text 2

Researchers conducting an East Coast Fever (ECF) vaccination study noticed that the three unvaccinated African cows that survived the disease had all been sired by the same African bull. Phil Toye and James Prendergast investigated further and identified FAFI1B, a version of a known gene that is compatible with the genes of European cattle. Of 20 African cows with two copies of FAFI1B, only one died from ECF, while 44 of 97 African cows without the gene died.

Based on the texts, how would Toye and Prendergast (Text 2) most likely describe the view of the veterinary scientists presented in Text 1?

(A) Their research refutes the theory of the veterinary scientists.

(B) Their research is irrelevant to the theory of the veterinary scientists.

(C) Their research indicates that the theory of the veterinary scientists is plausible.

(D) Their research indicates that the theory of the veterinary scientists could be true, but is seriously flawed.

How Much Have You Learned?

Directions

Take 7 minutes to apply the method for PSAT Reading and Writing to the following question set. Assess your work by comparing it to the expert responses at the end of the chapter.

1

The following text is from Honoré De Balzac's 1830 short story "The Elixir of Life."

But Don Juan's night-thoughts had left such unmistakable traces on his features, that the crew was awed into silence. The men stood motionless. The women, with wine-parched lips and cheeks marbled with kisses, knelt down and began a prayer. Don Juan could scarce help trembling when he saw splendor and mirth and laughter and song and youth and beauty and power bowed in reverence before Death.

As used in the text, what does the word "awed" most nearly mean?

- (A) Praised
- (B) Stunned
- (C) Honored
- (D) Emboldened

2

The following text is from Sherwood Anderson's 1921 short story "Unlighted Lamps."

The doctor's daughter had been to the decayed old orchard many times before. At the foot of the hill on which it stood the streets of the town began, and as she sat on the rock she could hear faint shouts and cries coming out of Wilmott Street. A hedge separated the orchard from the fields on the hillside. Mary intended to sit by the tree until darkness came creeping over the land and to try to think out some plan regarding her future . . . "Well," she told herself, "when the time comes I also shall be setting out, I shall get out of here and into the world."

As used in the text, what does the word "regarding" most nearly mean?

- (A) Honoring
- (B) Esteeming
- (C) Relating to
- (D) Brushing aside

3

In the early twentieth century, the manufacture and distribution of automobiles brought about major changes in the recreational activities of suburban and urban dwellers. For example, the 1950s saw a huge increase in drive-in movie theaters, fast-food establishments, supermarkets, and shopping centers. Most _____ of how we ate, shopped, and played changed to accommodate the car.

Which choice completes the text with the most logical and precise word or phrase?

(A) planes

(B) facets

(C) surfaces

(D) viewpoints

4

The following text is from a short story, "The Doorman," that takes place in New York City in the 2000s.

"Let me get this straight," Wallace had teased, "I screwed you up because I taught you to be happy with less?" Simon had said no, he wasn't suggesting Wallace had messed up, just that maybe the reason why Simon had a hard time accepting affluence was because he didn't grow up with it himself.

"I did the best I could," Wallace had said.

"Do you look down on us for the way we live now?" asked Simon. He had always been a serious person, even as a child, but law had made him more that way. The gulf between them held more than just seriousness, though. His wife wore the kind of jewelry that attracts scamming thieves, handsome fellows in suits catered Thanksgiving at their condo, and their children, who already had passports, ate baby food from a farm.

Which choice best states the function of the underlined sentence in the text as a whole?

(A) It elaborates on the previous sentence's description of the characters.

(B) It establishes a contrast with the previous sentence's description of the characters.

(C) It summarizes the setting introduced at the opening of the paragraph.

(D) It supports the character's criticism introduced at the start of the dialogue.

5

New developments in the sciences are discussed and disseminated in specialized magazines. The editors of these magazines use a process called peer review, where other experts examine and approve research reports before the reports are published. New research indicates that the peer review process must be viewed with caution. Nobel prize winner Vernon Smith and his student, Sabiou Inoua, cowrote an economics paper and submitted it for peer review. When Dr. Smith's name appeared as author, 23% of reviewers rejected the paper. When Mr. Inoua's name appeared, 65% of reviewers rejected the paper.

Which choice best states the main purpose of the text?

(A) It uses the work of Smith and Inoua to critique the methods and results reported in previous studies.

(B) It discusses the experience of Smith and Inoua to illustrate a potential concern with the process of peer review.

(C) It explains a significant problem in the peer review process and how Smith and Inoua tried to solve this problem.

(D) It argues that the peer review process is frequently misunderstood, as in the case of Smith's and Inoua's paper.

6

Text 1

Psychiatrists use drugs to treat patients with depression but have difficulty knowing which drug to choose. Traditionally, a trial-and-error approach is used. A doctor starts with one drug, then changes to another if the patient's symptoms don't improve. Because a wide range of dosage levels are safe, and because there is little connection between drug levels in the blood and symptom improvement, doctors do not believe that a patient's metabolism affects the choice of drug.

Text 2

Dr. David Oslin and a team of researchers used genetic testing to look for markers that would indicate whether or not a depressed patient would be able to metabolize a medication. The research team was surprised to discover that about 20% of patients in the study had better results after their doctors used a genetic test to identify specific genes that affect metabolism.

Based on the texts, how would Oslin and the research team (Text 2) most likely describe the view of the doctors presented in Text 1?

(A) It may seem plausible but is not supported by the research team's findings.

(B) It probably holds true only in conditions like those in the research team's study.

(C) It should remain the prevailing theory despite the research team's results.

(D) It is not a compelling theory regardless of any data collected by the research team.

Reflect

Directions: Take a few minutes to recall what you've learned and what you've been practicing in this chapter. Consider the following questions, jot down your best answer for each one, and then compare your reflections to the expert responses that follow. Use your level of confidence to determine what to do next.

What clues can you use to help you predict the meaning of a word on a Words in Context question?

_____

_____

_____

What questions can you ask yourself to help you answer a Purpose question?

_____

_____

_____

Why is it important to consider viewpoints when answering a Connections question?

_____

_____

_____

How can predicting help you correctly answer Craft and Structure questions? What types of answer choices can you eliminate on Craft and Structure questions?

_____

_____

_____

What are the main differences you see between PSAT Craft and Structure questions and those you're used to from tests in school?

_____

_____

_____

How will you approach PSAT Reading and Writing questions more strategically as you continue to practice and improve on your performance? Are there any specific habits you will practice to make your approach to PSAT Reading and Writing more effective and efficient?

_____

_____

_____

Expert Responses

What clues can you use to help you predict the meaning of a word on a Words in Context question?

Clues from the passage can help you predict the meaning of a word. Clues might include specific words, such as synonyms or antonyms, from the passage that indicate the meaning of the needed word, the immediate and broader context of the passage, and keywords and punctuation in the passage that indicate transitions.

What questions can you ask yourself to help you answer a Purpose question?

When answering a Purpose question about the entire passage, you can ask, "Why did the author write this?" When answering a Purpose question about a portion of the passage, you can ask, "Why did the author decide to include this portion?" and "What would the passage be lacking if the portion were missing?"

Why is it important to consider viewpoints when answering a Connections question?

Connections questions often ask about the viewpoints in two different passages, either those of the author or of someone mentioned in the text, and how they are related to one another. To correctly answer a Connections question, you should identify the two relevant viewpoints and, when possible, predict the connection between the viewpoints.

How can predicting help you correctly answer Craft and Structure questions? What types of answer choices can you eliminate on Craft and Structure questions?

When you are able to do so, predicting the correct answer can increase your accuracy and speed by helping you focus in on the one correct answer and avoid spending time comparing the answer choices to one another. Words in Context and Purpose questions often lend themselves to predicting. When eliminating answer choices, toss out any that distort the following: the intended meaning of a word used by the author (Words in Context questions), the author's purpose for writing something (Purpose questions), or viewpoints from the passage (Connections questions).

What are the main differences you see between PSAT Craft and Structure questions and those you're used to from tests in school?

Depending on the kinds of classes and teachers you've had in high school, the skills rewarded on PSAT Craft and Structure questions may be more or less familiar. In general, Craft and Structure questions do not ask you to simply recall facts, but they instead require you to analyze why or how authors wrote passages, including their choices about words and passage structure, their reasons for writing, and their viewpoints.

How will you approach PSAT Reading and Writing questions more strategically as you continue to practice and improve your performance? Are there any specific habits you will practice to make your approach to PSAT Reading and Writing more effective and efficient?

There is no one-size-fits-all answer here. Reflect on your own habits in answering PSAT Reading and Writing questions and give yourself an honest assessment of your strengths and weaknesses. Consider the strategies you've seen experts use in this chapter, and put them to work in your own practice to increase your accuracy, speed, and confidence.

Next Steps

If you answered most questions correctly in the "How Much Have You Learned?" section, and if your responses to the Reflect questions were similar to those of the PSAT expert, then consider Craft and Structure questions an area of strength and move on to the next chapter. Come back to this topic periodically to prevent yourself from getting rusty.

If you don't yet feel confident, review the lessons in this chapter that you have not yet mastered. Then, try the questions you missed again. As always, be sure to review the explanations closely.

Answers and Explanations

Try on Your Own

1.   A

Difficulty: Easy

Category: Craft and Structure

Getting to the Answer: To determine the meaning of the word "impertinent," look for clues in the passage. The immediate context refers to the "difficulties of crossing" the street and "unfortunately connected" to large roads. The author claims that ladies are frequently "detained" on either side because of "carriage, horse-men, or carts." Therefore, "impertinent" must refer to the *lack of control* over the traffic to allow pedestrians to cross. Predict that the correct choice will be *uncontrolled* or *unstructured*. Choice **(A)** most nearly matches that prediction; "Unrestrained" means *uncontrolled*.

Choice (B) is the opposite of what is intended. A well structured road would not be "unfortunately connected" or have the frequent incidents as described. Choices (C) and (D) are alternative definitions of "impertinent" that do not fit the context. The road is not *unimportant* (irrelevant), or *courageous* (bold).

2.   B

Difficulty: Medium

Category: Craft and Structure

Getting to the Answer: The immediate context reveals that "a number of competing models" exist about "how this structure might have evolved." Substitute a different word that would make sense and use that word as your prediction. *Ideas* or *theories* would be good predictions. Choice **(B)** is a match and the correct answer.

Choices (A), (C), and (D) are alternative definitions of "models" that do not fit the context. (A) may require a close read. The word "ideals" indicates a high standard to be aimed at; it does not have the same meaning as "ideas."

3.   D

Difficulty: Medium

Category: Craft and Structure

Getting to the Answer: The sentence that contains the blank pertains to the location of the geese in the formation. If the "lead" bird is at the "lowest point" and each following goose is "slightly above," then the most logical prediction for the missing word is *before* or *ahead*. Choice **(D)**, which means *in front of*, is a match and the correct answer.

Choice (A) is incorrect because "purports" means *intention* and the intent of the geese is never mentioned in the passage. (B) is incorrect because "displaces," or *takes the place of*, is the opposite of what the passage describes; each goose is following the one before it. (C) is incorrect because the geese's placement is "staggered."

4.   C

Difficulty: Medium

Category: Craft and Structure

Getting to the Answer: The sentence that contains the blank begins with the word "Despite," which signals a contrast between the device sales and the high valua-tion of the industry. Additionally, the device's sale was "overshadowed" by the release of a competing device. Predict that the correct choice is *poor* or *underwhelming*. Choice **(C)**, which means *extremely unsatisfactory*, is a match and the correct answer.

Choice (A) is incorrect because it is the opposite of the required meaning. (B) does not make sense in this context; there is no mention of the sales method being electronic. (C), "pecuniary" or *financial* is incorrect because it would not logically fit the context.

5.   A

Difficulty: Easy

Category: Craft and Structure

Getting to the Answer: The sentence that contains the blank begins with the transition word "Although," which signals a contrast between Flood's failure to obtain change with his lawsuit and his impact on "future changes." Predict that "Flood's advocacy" did the opposite of failing, it *created or caused* future changes. A catalyst is *an agent of change*, which matches the prediction. Choice **(A)** is correct.

Choices (B), (C), and (D) are incorrect because they are the opposite of the required meaning.

6.   D

Difficulty: Hard

Category: Craft and Structure

Getting to the Answer: The sentence that contains the blank includes transition punctuation (a colon) that signals a connection between "them pretend[ing] not to know that the others were toadies" and why they pretend to not know that "they were all toadies." The correct answer will contrast with the quartet's *pretending* that they are not toadies and humbugs. Eliminate (A), belief or *held as an opinion*, because the observer states that they are pretending to *not* have the opinion that they are toadies, which signals that they *do* have that opinion. Eliminate (B) because observation or *judgment*, has already occurred. Eliminate (C) because denial, which means *refusal to admit reality*, is of similar meaning as "pretend." Choice **(D)** is correct: admission of being a toady would have removed their ability to pretend that they were all not toadies.

7.   A

Difficulty: Hard

Category: Craft and Structure

Getting to the Answer: As you read, predict what the author intended in using the underlined sentence. The central idea of the text is that the townspeople of Huntersburg did not accept Mary. Predict that the dialogue shows a way that the townspeople expressed their mocking sympathy and made Mary feel oppressed. **(A)** is a good match and is correct. (B) is incorrect because the dialogue is an example of the townspeople's "mocking sympathetic eyes," not a contradiction of it.

(C) is incorrect because "poor" is not used literally as a marker of poverty. (D) is incorrect because the townspeople do not ignore Mary; instead, they have a negative attitude toward her.

8.   A

Difficulty: Medium

Category: Craft and Structure

Getting to the Answer: Throughout the paragraph, the narrator describes why his mother finds Pesca so pleasing. This introductory wording sets the stage by describing Pesca as undignified. This feature of his personality is a great match for **(A)**.

(B) is incorrect because the phrase "bounced into the parlor" implies good humor, not aggression. (C) is incorrect because the mother appreciates the bond between the narrator and Pesca. There is no suggestion of Pesca being a bad influence. (D) is incorrect because the mother is laughing, so she is not serious.

9.   A

Difficulty: Medium

Category: Craft and Structure

Getting to the Answer: Since the question asks about the structure of the passage, try to determine how the ideas in the passage are organized as you read. The speaker begins by describing what he sees: a "vacant shore" that makes it seem as if the "tide would flow no more." The speaker then says that positive qualities, such as "Love" and "laughter" have gone away from him, like the ebbed tide. The word "Suddenly" signals a change: at the end of the poem, the speaker feels positive things again sweep over him, as from the "deep ocean bed." Over the course of the poem, the speaker uses the imagery of the tide to describe feelings of despair and the return of positivity. This prediction matches **(A)**, which is correct.

You can eliminate any answer choice that misrepresents any part of the passage. Choice (B) is incorrect because although the speaker experiences the loss of feelings like love, he never indicates regret. Choice (C) is incorrect because the beginning of the poem does not suggest the "dependability" of the tides; rather, the speaker feels as though they will "flow no more." Further, the speaker never addresses his "insignificance." Choice (D) is incorrect because the speaker doesn't indicate that he wants to live by the ocean.

10. B

Difficulty: Hard

Category: Craft and Structure

Getting to the Answer: The author will identify the purpose of a text with opinion and emphasis keywords. Here, the keyword "However" signals that the author will disagree with the original claim—a claim held since the nineteenth century. This prediction is enough to identify **(B)** as the correct answer. In addition, the author clearly states at the end of the passage that "modern scholars give little credence to these theories."

Incorrect choices (A) and (D) are never discussed in the passage. There is no mention of any motivations (A) and the "strained relationships" mentioned in the text are not described as conflicts (D). (C) is backward; Inuit oral history is used to dispute nineteenth-century theory, not the modern one. This choice is also incorrect.

11. B

Difficulty: Easy

Category: Craft and Structure

Getting to the Answer: The author presented a factual description of the chronology of infant language acquisition, which matches choice **(B)**.

(C) and (D) are incorrect because the passage doesn't identify a "recent medical discovery" or "new breakthrough." (A) is incorrect because, although some of the steps in the process of language acquisition are described in the text, the history of the research into this process is not.

12. C

Difficulty: Medium

Category: Craft and Structure

Getting to the Answer: The author's purpose can be summarized as something like: "Narrate the story of how Snow's cholera research stopped an outbreak." That leads to the correct answer, **(C)**. The phrase "chronicles an episode" contains a verb that accurately describes the author's journalistic tone and focuses on the correct scope, a single event.

For the incorrect choices: (A) is too broad; the passage does not attempt to sum up the entire history of epidemiology, it only presents one seminal episode. (B) contradicts the passage; the government officials did listen to Snow. (D) summarizes a point mentioned in the passage, but the author never makes this recommendation.

13. C

Difficulty: Hard

Category: Craft and Structure

Getting to the Answer: Text 1 considers AI artists "true artists," but Text 2 says they "may have never held" traditional artists' tools or "mastered . . . artistic techniques." Predict that the two authors disagree. This prediction matches **(C)**, the correct answer.

Incorrect choice (A) is backward; the author of Text 2, not Text 1, is critical of AI artists. Incorrect choice (B) is too strong. The author of Text 1 describes the method AI artists use—writing the prompt—but doesn't praise, or extol, it. (D) is half-right, half-wrong—which makes the entire answer choice incorrect. The author of Text 2 criticizes AI artists for their lack of traditional artistic skills, not the time and effort devoted to their work.

14. D

Difficulty: Medium

Category: Craft and Structure

Getting to the Answer: The main idea of Text 1 is that the use of petroleum products should be reduced. Although Text 2 says the reduction in oil refining that comes about as a result of less petroleum use "is expected to have many beneficial effects," the contrast keyword "while" indicates the passage is going to continue with a downside. Predict that the texts share a point of agreement, but that Text 2 will point out a problem with the reduction in petroleum use. This prediction matches **(D)**, the correct answer.

Incorrect choice (A) does not recognize the central point of agreement between the texts. (B) is backward; Text 2 indicates a drawback to the reduction in petroleum use. Incorrect choice (C) distorts the argument made in Text 2. The main point of Text 1, the reduction in the use of petroleum products, is the point with which Text 2 agrees. The author of Text 2 adds an additional consideration this reduction raises, but does not argue that efforts to make the reduction should be modified.

15. C

Difficulty: Medium

Category: Craft and Structure

Getting to the Answer: Text 1 presents a problem: The search for life outside of Earth is limited to the characteristics of life on Earth. Text 2 provides a specific example of a location that has one of the possible alternative biochemistries, methane instead of water. Since it may be difficult to predict the claims that could appear in the choices, the most efficient strategy for this question is likely elimination.

Eliminate (A) and (B) because Text 1 never mentions the *Dragonfly* mission, and Text 2 never speculates on what *Dragonfly* may find. Choice **(C)** is correct; this choice restates the main idea of Text 1. In addition, the astrobiologists of Text 2 are interested in Titan because there is a lot of methane there, and methane could be supporting life as water does on Earth. These astrobiologists would want information on biochemistries different from those on Earth. Incorrect choice (D) contradicts the main idea of Text 1.

16. D

Difficulty: Easy

Category: Craft and Structure

Getting to the Answer: The biologists of Text 1 believe mimicry is limited to visual mimicry, but Russo's work indicates that the bats may be imitating the sounds of hornets to discourage the owls from attacking the bats. Predict that Russo would disagree with the biologists of Text 1. This prediction matches **(D)**, the correct answer.

Choices (A) and (B) both indicate different degrees of agreement with the biologists of Text 1, so these choices are incorrect. Incorrect choice (C) goes too far; without Russo's results, there would be no reason to believe the Test 1 biologists are incorrect.

17. A

Difficulty: Hard

Category: Craft and Structure

Getting to the Answer: The microbiologists in Text 1 believe that bacteria, which should trigger a type-1 immune reaction, are actually avoiding the immune system by getting it to mount a type-2 reaction. In Medzhitov's study, the toxin from the bacteria triggered the cells to produce mucus, which is one of the

body's defenses against worms, so this would be a type-2 reaction used against multicellular invaders. Then, the bacteria fed on the mucus and grew to a greater number. Since bacteria should trigger a type-1 reaction, not a type-2, and since the bacteria increased as a result, Medzhitov's study has provided a supporting example for the microbiologists' theory. Using this prediction yields **(A)**, the correct answer.

The incorrect choices all reflect degrees of disagreement with the theory presented in Text 1, but Medzhitov's study supported that theory.

18. C

Difficulty: Easy

Category: Craft and Structure

Getting to the Answer: The veterinary scientists in Text 1 hope to develop cattle that are both productive and resistant to ECF. Since the gene identified in Text 2 seems to protect cows from ECF, Toye and Prendergast's results support the view of the veterinary scientists. This prediction matches **(C)**, the correct answer.

Incorrect choice (A) contradicts Toye and Prendergast's results. Their results support the veterinary scientists' view, so they are relevant. Choice (B) is incorrect. (D) starts out correctly, but there is no evidence from Toye and Prendergast's results that the veterinary scientists' view is flawed, so this choice is also incorrect.

How Much Have You Learned?

1. B

Difficulty: Medium

Category: Craft and Structure

Getting to the Answer: Read enough of the text to understand the context before making a prediction. The first sentence describes an "unmistakable" change in Don Juan's features because of his thoughts. The following sentences indicate that these thoughts were solemn. The men stand "motionless," the women kneel in prayer, and Don Juan could not stop "trembling." Predict that the people were "shocked" or "surprised" into silence. Choice **(B)** is correct.

Incorrect choices (A) and (C) are based on alternative definitions for "awe" that do not fit this context. Incorrect choice (D) is opposite. "Emboldened" means to be "made more bold," but the "crew" become more subdued after seeing Don Juan's features.

2.   C

Difficulty: Easy

Category: Craft and Structure

Getting to the Answer: Mary heads into the orchard to be alone and to "think out some plan regarding her future." The next sentence describes part of this plan, so a good prediction is that she was thinking "about" her future. The prediction matches **(C)**, the correct answer.

Incorrect choices (A) and (B) are alternative meanings of "regarding," but these do not fit the context. Incorrect choice (D) is opposite. Mary is planning for her future, not brushing it aside.

3.   B

Difficulty: Medium

Category: Craft and Structure

Getting to the Answer: Reread the sentence that includes the blank and predict a word or phrase that completes the sentence. The previous sentence lists different types of new businesses made possible by cars. So the automobile changed many "aspects" or "characteristics" of how we lived. Choice **(B)** is a match for the prediction and the correct answer.

Choices (A), (C), and (D) are all alternative definitions of "facets," but they do not fit the context.

4.   A

Difficulty: Hard

Category: Craft and Structure

Getting to the Answer: The author will always provide a clue that tells you the purpose of a sentence. Here, that clue is the previous sentence, where the author says there is a "gulf" between Wallace and Simon. The text describes that gulf as "more than just seriousness," and the underlined sentence follows with examples. **(A)** is correct.

For the incorrect choices: (B) is opposite; the underlined sentence supports, not contradicts, the description in the previous sentence. (C) is not mentioned in the passage; the setting for the text is not described. The text opens with Wallace's teasing criticism, but Simon denies that criticism was intended, so (D) is also incorrect.

5.   B

Difficulty: Hard

Category: Craft and Structure

Getting to the Answer: To quickly and correctly answer a purpose question, identify the emphasis and opinion keywords. Here, the author clearly states an opinion, "the peer review process must be viewed with caution." That statement is enough to match **(B)**, the correct answer. For the record, the sentences preceding the opinion explain what the peer review process is, and the sentences that follow provide the author's evidence.

The incorrect choices are not mentioned in the text. The passage never discusses "previous studies" (A), efforts to "solve this problem" (C), or any "misunderstanding" (D).

6.   A

Difficulty: Hard

Category: Craft and Structure

Getting to the Answer: The view of the doctors in Text 1 is that a depressed patient's metabolism does not have an effect on the drug chosen for treatment. Dr. Oslin and the research team found that 20% of depressed patients in the study had better results when their doctors used the results of genetic testing that identified metabolism markers. Because the research team was "surprised" by their results, a good prediction would be "they thought the doctors would be correct, but their results make that view less likely." This prediction matches **(A)**, the correct answer.

Incorrect choices (B) and (C) are backward, the research team's study found conditions where the doctors' view was *not* true (B) and the research team's results *challenge* the prevailing theory (C). Incorrect choice (D) is too strong; the research team would use their results to challenge the view in Text 1.

[CHAPTER 15]

EXPRESSION OF IDEAS

LEARNING OBJECTIVES

After completing this chapter, you will be able to:

- Combine statements to create a logical summary that meets a given goal
- Determine the appropriate transition word or phrase to establish logical relationships within the text

How Much Do You Know?

Directions

Try the questions that follow. When you're done, check your answers and reasoning against ours in the "Check Your Work" section. If they closely match, you may be able to move quickly through the chapter. If they do not, spend some extra time with the chapter to grow your PSAT Reading and Writing skills.

1

New Zealand consists of two large islands and over seven hundred smaller islands. _____, this view of New Zealand misses something critical, a fact that was obscured for eons until humans mapped the seafloor. The islands of New Zealand are the mountains of a submerged continent, a landmass called Zealandia. Mostly submerged beneath the ocean approximately twenty-three million years ago, Zealandia is half the size of Australia. New Zealand is merely the 6% of Zealandia's landmass that is still above sea level.

Which choice completes the text with the most logical transition?

- (A) Additionally,
- (B) Subsequently,
- (C) Therefore,
- (D) However,

2

While researching a topic, a student has taken the following notes:

- Synthwave is a genre of electronic music, one that takes inspiration from 1980s movie soundtracks and features heavy use of the synthesizer and electronic drums.
- Vaporwave is a genre of electronic music, one that features slowed-down audio samples from 1980s and 1990s dance music, as well as heavy use of reverb and repetition.
- Synthwave mainly attempts to modernize certain aspects of 1980s music.
- Vaporwave mainly attempts to skewer the optimistic corporate culture of the 1980s and 1990s.

The student wants to emphasize a similarity between the two musical genres. Which choice most effectively uses relevant information from the notes to accomplish this goal?

- (A) While synthwave is primarily inspired by movie soundtracks, vaporwave is mainly influenced by dance music.
- (B) Despite vaporwave taking some influence from 1990s culture, both it and synthwave take inspiration from 1980s music.
- (C) Synthwave heavily relies on the synthesizer and electronic drums as musical instruments.
- (D) Although both vaporwave and synthwave take inspiration from the 1980s music scene, only vaporwave focuses on slowed-down audio samples.

3

Although largely forgotten in the modern day, pulp fiction magazines were once a major source of entertainment for millions of working-class people. These magazines were so named because they were printed on low-quality, ragged-edged paper made from wood pulp. This crude paper made them affordable even to people with little money, creating a large market of millions of readers, each reader having their own particular taste in fiction. _____ pulp fiction came to encompass a wide variety of genres: adventure, romance, science fiction, sports, westerns, gangster tales, spy fiction, and horror to name a few.

Which choice completes the text with the most logical transition?

(A) But,

(B) On the other hand,

(C) Despite this,

(D) Thus,

4

While researching a topic, a student has taken the following notes:

- Anna May Wong was the professional name of Wong Liu-Tsong.
- Wong starred in several silent films, most notably *The Toll of the Sea* (1921), one of the first Hollywood films in color.
- *The Toll of the Sea* (1921) was believed lost for decades, but the original camera negative was discovered in 1985.
- Wong was the first Asian-American to be the lead in a television program, a detective show called *The Gallery of Madame Liu-Tsong* (1951) on the DuMont Television Network.
- When the DuMont Television Network went out of business in the late 1950s, its video archive was dumped into New York City's Hudson River, meaning no footage of *The Gallery of Madame Liu-Tsong* (1951) survives.
- The first nationwide color broadcast on American television was in 1954, but the majority of television programming continued to be black and white until the mid-1960s.

The student wants to emphasize a difference between Wong's two projects. Which choice most effectively uses relevant information from the notes to accomplish this goal?

(A) *The Gallery of Madame Liu-Tsong* (1951) was the first television show with an Asian-American lead.

(B) Wong's acting career included a variety of roles, spanning both film and television.

(C) *The Toll of the Sea* (1921) was believed to be lost but the footage was eventually rediscovered, while no footage survives of *The Gallery of Madame Liu-Tsong* (1951).

(D) Wong completed *The Toll of the Sea* in 1921 and *The Gallery of Madame Liu-Tsong* in 1951.

5

A *gacha* game is a type of smartphone game where players pay some form of in-game currency to receive a randomized reward, such as a more powerful weapon or a new costume for a character. *Gacha* games are ostensibly free to play, but critics accuse them of encouraging a form of gambling, which can be addictive. These critics argue that the randomized rewards are akin to a payout at a slot machine. _____ it is often faster to buy the in-game currency with real-world money than it is to earn the currency via gameplay, allowing the player to purchase those randomized rewards more frequently. This fact leads some players to spend hundreds, if not thousands of dollars on their "free" *gacha* game.

Which choice completes the text with the most logical transition?

- (A) But
- (B) Despite this,
- (C) Moreover,
- (D) Yet

6

While researching a topic, a student has taken the following notes:

- In the late 1970s and early 1980s, the introduction of magnetic tape cassettes allowed consumers to watch videos at home.
- The profits from selling movies on cassette allowed movies that failed in theaters to still make money and be successful.
- In the late 1990s and early 2000s, magnetic tape cassettes gave way to a new disc-based format, one which offered vastly superior visual and audio quality for movies.
- The rise of streaming video in the late 2000s led to a steep decline in the sale of movies on disc-based media.
- Streaming video offers film studios far less profit than the physical formats, greatly increasing the importance of how much money a movie makes at the theater.

The student wants to emphasize a contrast between the two physical formats for movies. Which choice most effectively uses relevant information from the notes to accomplish this goal?

- (A) Cassette tapes and disc-based media both allowed consumers to watch movies at home, but disc-based media offered better picture and sound for those movies.
- (B) Movies that failed to make a profit in theaters could potentially still be lucrative when sold on cassette, while the disc-based format did not offer the same advantage.
- (C) Cassette tapes and disc-based media both allowed consumers to watch movies at home that had formerly been available only at theaters.
- (D) The advent of streaming video marked the decline of the disc-based format for watching movies at home.

Check Your Work

1.   D

Difficulty: Easy

Category: Expression of Ideas

Getting to the Answer: This question deals with a transition. When determining which transition is the one to use in a given situation, consider what the transition is doing. Is it a *continuation* of the ideas in the previous sentence? Does it set up a *contrast* between the ideas in the current sentence and the ones in the previous sentence? Or is it laying out events in a *cause-and-effect* situation?

In this passage, the first sentence establishes how many islands make up New Zealand. The second sentence establishes that "this view" is missing a "critical" fact. In terms of purpose, the transition connecting both sentences would be establishing a contrast between those two ideas. Choice **(D)** sets up that contrast, and it is correct. (A) is incorrect because that transition functions as a continuation of the first sentence's ideas. Choices (B) and (C) are incorrect because those transitions establish a cause-and-effect relationship between the two sentences.

2.   B

Difficulty: Easy

Category: Expression of Ideas

Getting to the Answer: This question asks for a similarity between synthwave and vaporwave, so keep that in mind as you read. The third and fourth points deal with the "missions" of their respective musical genres, and since they are not alike these points can be ignored. Based on the first and second points, a good prediction of a similarity would be, "Synthwave and vaporwave are both genres of electronic music that take influence from the 1980s," which best matches **(B)**, the correct answer. Choices (A) and (D) are incorrect because they deal with differences, not similarities. (C) is a stated point and does not address the prompt.

3.   D

Difficulty: Easy

Category: Expression of Ideas

Getting to the Answer: The sentence prior to the one with the blank establishes two ideas: pulp fiction sold to a large market of readers, and different readers had different tastes. The sentence with the blank lists several genres featured in pulp fiction magazines. Determine the type of transition that should be used to connect these two sentences, then pick the answer choice option that falls into that category.

Choice **(D)** is correct because it links the two sentences in a cause-and-effect relationship; there was a large, diverse audience for pulp fiction so it featured magazines covering many different genres. Choices (A), (B), and (C) are incorrect because these transitions are all establishing contrast.

4.   C

Difficulty: Hard

Category: Expression of Ideas

Getting to the Answer: The question asks for a difference between Wong's projects. Keep that in mind while reading the points. The first point discusses Wong's name; skim this point as it does not address the prompt. The second and third points discuss how Wong starred in *The Toll of the Sea*, a 1921 movie. The fourth and fifth points discuss a 1951 television show starring Wong. The sixth point discusses the history of color television; skim it. Summarizing the differences between the two projects makes something like "*The Toll of the Sea* was believed to be lost but a copy was eventually found, while nothing of *The Gallery of Madame Liu-Tsong* survives" a good prediction. This matches **(C)**, the correct answer.

Choice (A) is incorrect because it discusses *The Gallery of Madame Liu-Tsong* without contrasting that program with anything else, meaning (A) ignores the prompt. (B) is incorrect because it discusses Wong's career in general, not the two projects listed in the notes and prompt. (D) is incorrect because it merely lists the year each work was completed without establishing any logical relationship between the two pieces of information.

5.   C

Difficulty: Medium

Category: Expression of Ideas

Getting to the Answer: This passage deals with *gacha* smartphone games. After they are defined, criticism of *gacha* is discussed. *Gacha* are said to be akin to gambling, which can be "addictive." The sentence with the blank then establishes that it is "often faster" to buy in-game currency with "real-world" money than it is to "earn" it by playing the *gacha* game. This type of transition is a continuation, as it takes an idea introduced in the previous sentence (gambling addiction) and develops it further (spending real money to gamble faster). Choice **(C)** is the only continuation transition available, and it is correct.

Choice (A) sounds tempting if the two sentences are read as a single sentence, with "But" serving as a conjunction. However, this question is dealing with transitions, not conjunctions; "But" would be used to contrast ideas from one sentence to the next. (B) and (D) are also contrast transitions and are incorrect.

6.   A

Difficulty: Medium

Category: Expression of Ideas

Getting to the Answer: This question asks for a contrast between the two physical formats for watching movies at home. Keep that in mind as you read the points. Only the third point lists a difference between the two physical formats, stating the disc-based media had superior visual and audio quality when compared to magnetic cassette tapes. Choice **(A)** best matches this point, and it is correct.

Choice (B) is incorrect because it is contradicted by the fourth and fifth points, which state that disc-based media was profitable when it came to selling movies. (C) is incorrect because it is a similarity, not a contrast. (D) merely restates the fourth point and does not address the prompt.

Synthesis Questions

LEARNING OBJECTIVE

After this lesson, you will be able to:

• Combine statements to create a logical summary that meets a given goal

To answer a question like this:

While researching a topic, a student has taken the following notes:

• Only a few human residents but hundreds of cats currently reside on Aoshima Island in Japan.

• Fishermen originally introduced cats to Aoshima Island in the 1940s, in an attempt to control rodent populations on boats.

• About 4,000 human residents and a herd of bison, which peaked at more than 500 animals in the 1980s, currently reside on Catalina Island in California.

• Filmmakers originally introduced bison to Catalina Island in the 1920s, so that the animals could appear in several movies.

• American bison adult males can weigh more than 2,000 pounds.

The student wants to emphasize a similarity between the two locations. Which choice most effectively uses relevant information from the notes to accomplish this goal?

Ⓐ Humans introduced animal species to both Aoshima Island and Catalina Island that survived over time.

Ⓑ A large number of cats reside on Aoshima Island in Japan; Catalina Island in California, however, is home to a herd of bison.

Ⓒ The cats on Aoshima Island were intended to control rodent populations, but the bison on Catalina Island were intended to appear in several movies.

Ⓓ Cats arrived on Aoshima Island in the 1940s, and bison arrived on Catalina Island in the 1920s.

You need to know this:

How to Identify Synthesis Questions

Synthesis questions will ask you to identify which answer choice accomplishes a specific rhetorical aim. For instance, you might be asked to emphasize a similarity or a difference between ideas. The question stem will identify the rhetorical aim and then ask you which answer choice accomplishes this goal. See the question above for an example of the possible format of a Synthesis question. Also, as shown above, the passage of a Synthesis question may consist of a list of bullet point notes about a topic.

How to Synthesize Ideas

To *synthesize* means to bring different ideas together in a logical way that creates one new idea. Fortunately, synthesis question stems will always specify *how* you need to synthesize the ideas. For example, you may need to create a new idea that describes a similarity or a new idea that describes a difference.

The passage on a Synthesis question will likely contain more information than you need to meet the goal specified in the question stem. You do not need to consider all the ideas in the passage equally; as always, read the question stem first to help you identify what is being asked. Once you identify the specific rhetorical goal (such as finding a similarity), read the passage with that goal in mind. Focus on the ideas that are relevant, and, if possible, see if you can paraphrase how to achieve the goal in your own words. Mentally set aside details that are irrelevant to the goal.

Imagine, for instance, you are asked to synthesize the ideas in the notes below by emphasizing a similarity between the two dogs.

- A dog owner manages a dog daycare service and owns two dogs of her own, Astro and Bingo.
- Astro is an 8-year-old Golden Retriever who enjoys playing fetch with tennis balls.
- Bingo is a 4-year-old Labrador Retriever who enjoys playing frisbee.

Was there any information that was irrelevant to the goal? Did you focus on identifying a similarity as you read? Some information was entirely unrelated to the goal of identifying a similarity between the two dogs, such as the details about the dog owner. Some information was about *differences* between the dogs, such as their specific breeds and ages. What were the similarities? You may have noticed that they are both types of retrievers who enjoy playing. If this were a test question, you'd look for an answer choice that states one or both of these similarities.

Incorrect answers to a Synthesis question may be:

- **Opposite**—Incorrect answers to Synthesis questions may provide the *opposite* of the goal in the question stem, for instance, a difference rather than a similarity.
- **Misused Details**—Incorrect answers to Synthesis questions may include details from the passage that are irrelevant to the goal in the question stem.

The correct answer to a Synthesis question will:

- Specifically address the goal identified in the question stem using only relevant information from the passage

You need to do this:

THE METHOD FOR PSAT READING AND WRITING

STEP 1 What is the question asking?

STEP 2 What do I need to look for in the passage?

STEP 3 What answer strategy is best?

- Predict & Match
- Eliminate

Step 1. What is the question asking?

If the question stem identifies a rhetorical aim and asks you which choice "accomplish[es] this goal," it is a Synthesis question.

Step 2. What do I need to look for in the passage?

Restate the goal from the question stem in your own words—perhaps you need to find a similarity between two books or a difference between two artistic styles—and read the passage with this specific aim in mind. As you read each detail, ask yourself whether it is relevant to the goal. If not, mentally set it aside. If it is relevant, pay careful attention to that detail. When finished, try to paraphrase a statement in your own words that achieves the goal.

Step 3. What answer strategy is best?

If you paraphrased a way to achieve the goal, use it as your prediction as you look for the one correct match among the answer choices. If needed, eliminate answer choices that do the opposite of the stated goal, as well as those that use details from the passage that are irrelevant to the stated goal.

Whether you predict & match or eliminate (or both), pay careful attention to the keywords in the answer choices. They may contain contrast or continuation words that provide strong hints: if your goal is to find a similarity, for instance, an answer choice that contains contrast words such as "however" or "but" is likely incorrect. On the other hand, the correct answer will likely contain continuation words such as "both" and "and."

Explanation:

The question asks for a specific rhetorical aim and asks which answer choice "accomplish[es] this goal," so this is a Synthesis question. Before you read the passage, restate the goal in your own words: *you need a similarity between two locations.* The first two bullet points describe Aoshima Island, its current cat inhabitants, and the introduction of the cats to the island. The last two bullet points describe Catalina Island, its current bison inhabitants, and the introduction of the bison to the island. The last bullet point is about the size of the bison, so it is likely irrelevant to the goal of finding a similarity between the locations. Without getting bogged down in the details, a general similarity between the locations seems to be that both have animal populations that people introduced in the past. Use this statement as your prediction; **(A)** is correct. Note that this choice includes words that suggest similarity, such as "both" and "and."

Choices (B) and (C) are incorrect because they identify differences, as indicated by the contrast words "however" and "but." Choice (D) is incorrect because it merely states facts about the locations rather than identifying a specific similarity between them. Be careful: note that the use of "and," in this case, does not signal a similarity.

Try on Your Own

Directions

Take as much time as you need on these questions. Work carefully and methodically. There will be an opportunity for timed practice later in the book.

1

While researching a topic, a student has taken the following notes:

- The Peloponnesian war was fought between Athens and Sparta, the two most powerful city-states of ancient Greece.
- Athens encouraged education and art and was the more powerful.
- The war lasted for 26 years, but there was a 6-year truce between 2 periods of conflict.
- Sparta ultimately prevailed in the conflict.
- Lysander, a Spartan general, led the crucial battle that ended the war.

The student wants to emphasize a difference between the two city-states. Which choice most effectively uses relevant information from the notes to accomplish this goal?

Ⓐ At the start of the Peloponnesian war, Athens was the stronger city-state, but Sparta eventually won the war.

Ⓑ Although they fought an extended war, both Athens and Sparta were prosperous city-states of ancient Greece.

Ⓒ The Peloponnesian war between Athens and Sparta brought about the end of the golden age of Greece.

Ⓓ The Spartan general, Lysander, ended 26 years of conflict between Athens and Sparta.

2

While researching a topic, a student has taken the following notes:

- Interest in African art has increased worldwide as the economies of many African countries have grown.
- As interest in African art has grown, African art has become more valuable, and now commands high prices.
- Wangechi Mutu is a Kenyan artist who lives in New York and among her various themes, explores African identity in her art.
- El Anatsui was born in Ghana and has exhibited his fabrics, heavily decorated with crushed bottle caps, all over the world.
- William Kentridge, a South African artist, often deals with questions of South African politics in his art.

The student wants to emphasize a similarity shared between two, but not all three, African artists. Which choice most effectively uses relevant information from the notes to accomplish this goal?

(A) Unlike Wangechi Mutu and William Kentridge, the art of El Anatsui does not address issues unique to Africa.

(B) Fabrics, heavily decorated with crushed bottle caps, make up some of the art that has made El Anatsui famous all over the world.

(C) Wangechi Mutu, Wiliam Kentridge, and El Anatsui are all well-known African artists whose work has grown in value as the African economy has grown.

(D) Wangechi Mutu and William Kentridge both include specifically African themes in their art; Mutu considers ideas of African identity, and Kentridge explores South African politics.

3

While researching a topic, a student has taken the following notes:

- British adventure stories set during the Napoleonic Wars of the early nineteenth century remain an extremely popular literary genre.
- Born in 1792, the author Fredrick Marryat enlisted in the English navy and rose to the rank of captain.
- Marryat wrote several novels based on his naval experience, including *The King's Own*, *Peter Simple*, and *Mr. Midshipman Easy*.
- C. S. Forester, born in Cairo, Egypt in 1899, studied medicine but abandoned it for a career as a successful author and journalist.
- Forester is perhaps most famous for *The Hornblower Saga*, twelve carefully researched volumes chronicling the career of Horatio Hornblower, a fictional captain in the English Navy in the early nineteenth century.

The student wants to emphasize a difference between the two authors, Marryat and Forester. Which choice most effectively uses relevant information from the notes to accomplish this goal?

Ⓐ Set during the Napoleonic Wars, *The Hornblower Saga* made C. S. Forester's reputation as a novelist.

Ⓑ Fredrick Marryat and C. S. Forester both had very successful careers authoring historically accurate British navy adventure novels.

Ⓒ Two of the most popular authors of British navy adventure novels approached the topic from distinct perspectives: Fredrick Marryat based his books on his naval experience, while C. S. Forester relied on research and imagination.

Ⓓ *The Hornblower Saga*, *The King's Own*, *Peter Simple*, and *Mr. Midshipman Easy*, all examples of British naval adventure novels, remain among the most popular books in circulation today.

4

While researching a topic, a student has taken the following notes:

- Diamonds are the hardest naturally occurring mineral and are used extensively for industrial cutting and drilling.

- Diamonds are made of carbon in a cubic structure and are formed on Earth under conditions of high temperature and pressure over a long period of time.

- Lonsdaleite is a celestial diamond, formed by the catastrophic impact of a meteor with a dwarf planet billions of years ago and arrived on Earth in a meteor fragment.

- Lonsdaleite is made of carbon in a hexagonal structure and may be almost 60% harder than diamonds.

- Researchers hope to find a practical method of recreating lonsdaleite for use in industrial saws and drills.

The student wants to emphasize a similarity between the two minerals. Which choice most effectively uses relevant information from the notes to accomplish this goal?

(A) Although the structures differ, both diamonds and lonsdaleite are formed solely of carbon.

(B) Lonsdaleite was formed as an asteroid destroyed a dwarf planet, while diamonds are formed naturally on Earth.

(C) Industrial cutting and drilling operations frequently use diamonds because they are the hardest mineral that is found naturally on earth.

(D) The structure of lonsdaleite indicates that, if it can be replicated, lonsdaleite could augment diamonds for industrial cutting and drilling.

5

Reading & Writing

While researching a topic, a student has taken the following notes:

- *Keiro no Hi*, or Respect for the Aged Day, is a public holiday celebrated in Japan on the third Monday in September when people over the age of 55 are honored.

- Only added to the calendar in the 1960s, *Keiro no Hi* has no fixed customs or traditions, but honoring older citizens and family members with gifts or special events is common.

- *Keiro no Hi* was instituted to show respect and appreciation for the older generations and to provide a forum for them to pass on their wisdom and share their life experiences.

- Citizens over the age of 65 make up about 30% of Japan's population; many of these citizens continue to work and resent being considered "aged."

- As the population of Japan ages, a redefinition of *Keiro no Hi* may be needed to maintain the relevance of this holiday.

The student wants to emphasize a contrast between the goal and the perception of the holiday. Which choice most effectively uses relevant information from the notes to accomplish this goal?

Ⓐ Although gift-giving is common, there are no consistent traditions or customs associated with *Keiro no Hi*.

Ⓑ The growing population of Japan over the age of 65 includes some people who do not consider themselves "aged," and who want changes made in *Keiro no Hi*.

Ⓒ The holiday *Keiro no Hi* honors the aged in Japan with a day of gift-giving and memorable occasions; however, a growing number of older, active citizens, some of whom do not wish to be thought of as "aged," may require the holiday to be re-evaluated.

Ⓓ *Keiro no Hi*, a public holiday established in the 1960s, is intended to give the citizens of Japan an opportunity to honor elderly citizens and family members with gifts and special events and to learn from their experiences.

6

While researching a topic, a student has taken the following notes:

- Called SAI, the process of injecting microscopic dust particles into the atmosphere is a radical idea for cooling the poles of the Earth, which are warming faster than the rest of the planet.
- The SAI particles would drift toward the poles, reflect sunlight and drop the polar temperatures by about 2°C, slowing the melting of Arctic and Antarctic ice.
- Cloud seeding is a method of increasing snowfall or rainfall by spraying a chemical on clouds.
- The chemical serves as a nucleus around which water collects, eventually falling to the ground as rain or snow.
- Some cloud seeding projects have been successful over periods of five to ten years in increasing precipitation.

The student wants to emphasize a contrast between the particles used for SAI and the chemical used for cloud seeding. Which choice most effectively uses relevant information from the notes to accomplish this goal?

- (A) SAI dust particles remain suspended in the atmosphere, while the chemical used for cloud seeding falls to the earth.

- (B) The SAI process has not been implemented, but cloud seeding has been shown effective in some long-term studies.

- (C) SAI dust particles may be used to modify weather at the poles, and chemicals are used to modify weather through cloud seeding.

- (D) After their injection into the atmosphere, SAI dust particles accumulate over the poles and reflect sunlight away from Arctic and Antarctic ice.

Transitions Questions

LEARNING OBJECTIVE

After this lesson, you will be able to:

- Determine the appropriate transition word or phrase to establish logical relationships within the text

To answer a question like this:

Dracaena trifasciata, or the snake plant, is commonly known by the flippant nickname mother-in-law's tongue, possibly because some have related the plant's long, sharply-tipped leaves to the stereotype that mothers-in-law speak with sharp criticism. Despite any negative connotations, _____ mother-in-law's tongue is an extremely popular houseplant because its hardiness and low water requirements make it easy to maintain.

Which choice completes the text with the most logical transition?

(A) therefore,

(B) for example,

(C) however,

(D) moreover,

You need to know this:

How to Identify Transitions Questions

Transitions questions can be identified by the keywords "logical transition" and typically have the question stem, *Which choice completes the text with the most logical transition?*

How to Identify Transition Relationships

The key to answering Transitions questions is to determine what type of connection exists between the ideas in a passage. To do this, identify the two ideas that are connected by the missing transition word and paraphrase in your own words the relationship between the two ideas. The most common types of transition relationships tested on the PSAT include:

- **Continuation**—a continuation of the same point
  - *Cockapoo dogs are great pets. They are highly intelligent;* **further***, they have sociable personalities.*
  - The keyword "further" indicates a continuation of the reasons cockapoos are great pets.
- **Contrast**—a change in direction or a point of difference
  - *Cockapoo dogs are great pets;* **however***, they can develop painful knots in their fur without consistent grooming.*
  - The keyword "however" indicates a contrast between a positive feature of cockapoos (they are great pets) and a negative feature of cockapoos (they can get knots).
- **Cause and effect**—one idea causes another idea or leads to a conclusion
  - *Cockapoo dogs are great pets;* **therefore***, they were voted the most popular dog breed in New York City.*
  - The keyword "therefore" indicates a cause-and-effect relationship: because cockapoos are great pets, they were voted most popular.

In the examples above, note how the transition keywords (*further*, *however*, *therefore*) serve as clues that indicate the type of transition relationship between ideas. A different transition word can entirely change the meaning of a sentence. Consider how different transition words change the meaning of the sentence below:

- Calculus is Kiyana's strongest subject, **and** she prepared thoroughly for the exam.
- Calculus is Kiyana's strongest subject, **yet** she prepared thoroughly for the exam.
- Calculus is Kiyana's strongest subject, **so** she prepared thoroughly for the exam.

The **continuation** transition word (*and*) indicates that Kiyana's thorough preparation for the exam is a continuation of the idea that calculus is her strongest subject. The **contrast** transition word (*yet*) indicates that even though calculus is Kiyana's strongest subject, she still prepared thoroughly for the exam. Finally, the **cause-and-effect** transition word (*so*) indicates that the reason Kiyana prepared thoroughly for the exam was because calculus is her strongest subject.

The table below contains examples of common transition words used on the PSAT. Becoming familiar with these words will help you understand the connections between ideas in every Reading and Writing passage you encounter. In addition, these transition words are often answer choices on Transition questions.

TYPES OF PSAT TRANSITION KEYWORDS		
KEYWORD TYPE	**WHAT THE KEYWORDS INDICATE**	**EXAMPLES**
Continuation	a continuation of the same point	*moreover, in addition, also, further, and*
Contrast	a change in direction or a point of difference	*but, yet, despite, on the other hand, however*
Cause and effect	one idea causes another idea or leads to a conclusion	*thus, therefore, because, since, so*

Transition words are extremely helpful, but be aware that passages often include more subtle clues about the relationships between ideas. Relationships might be indicated by the content of the ideas themselves, or even by punctuation marks, so be thorough in your search for clues about the connections between ideas.

Incorrect answers to a Transitions question may be:

- **Opposite**—Incorrect answers to Transitions questions may give the opposite of the logical relationship between ideas.
- **Distortions**—Incorrect answers to Transitions questions may misrepresent the connection between ideas, such as indicating a cause-and-effect relationship where one does not logically exist.

The correct answer to a Transitions question will:

- Precisely reflect the logical relationship between the ideas in the passage

You need to do this:

> ## THE METHOD FOR PSAT READING AND WRITING
>
> **STEP 1** What is the question asking?
>
> **STEP 2** What do I need to look for in the passage?
>
> **STEP 3** What answer strategy is best?
>
> - Predict & Match
> - Eliminate

Step 1. What is the question asking?

If the question stem asks you to fill in the blank with a "logical transition," it is a Transitions question.

Step 2. What do I need to look for in the passage?

To identify the logical transition, you'll need to identify the two ideas that are connected by the blank. Then, determine the relationship between those two ideas; use transition keywords as well as additional clues, such as information in the ideas themselves and punctuation marks, to help you find the relationship.

Step 3. What answer strategy is best?

Transitions questions tend to lend themselves to the strategy of predicting the type of transition needed before looking at the answer choices. Predict a word or phrase that conveys the same type of relationship you found between the ideas: continuation, contrast, cause-and-effect, or another type of connection. Look for the answer choice that matches the meaning of your predicted transition word or phrase, and read your selection back into the passage to make sure it makes sense in context. If needed, eliminate answer choices that are opposite or distortions of the logical relationship between the ideas in the passage.

Explanation:

The keywords "logical transition" signal that this is a Transitions question, so as you read the passage, look for the two ideas that are connected by the blank. The idea before the blank is that the mother-in-law's tongue plant has negative connotations; the idea after the blank is that the plant is very popular. The sentence with the blank contains the contrast transition word "Despite," and the ideas themselves also indicate contrast (the plant's negative connotations versus its popularity). Predict that the correct answer will be a contrast transition; **(C)** is correct and logically makes sense when read into the blank.

Choice (A) is incorrect because it distorts the relationship between the ideas by indicating a cause-and-effect relationship. Choice (B) is incorrect because the plant's popularity is not an example of its negative connotations. Choice (D) is incorrect because it indicates continuation rather than the contrast relationship intended in the passage.

Try on Your Own

Directions

Take as much time as you need on these questions. Work carefully and methodically. There will be an opportunity for timed practice later in the book.

7

Public service agencies can maximize their positive outcomes by primarily implementing evidence-based programs for their agencies' participants. _____ participants experience better outcomes when agencies receive evidence-based implementation training and are diligently held accountable for program efficacy.

Which choice completes the text with the most logical transition?

(A) In addition,

(B) However,

(C) On the other hand,

(D) Finally

8

Chilean poet Pablo Neruda, a Nobel Prize laureate, was a widely read and highly influential poet of the 20th century. His body of work contains varied elements, with a profound focus on love, nature, isolation, and self-reflection. Many assert that his most famous work is his first published collection of poems, *Twenty Love Poems and a Song of Despair*; _____ his most infamous works are his letters that reflected his political activism, which resulted in his exile from Chile.

Which choice completes the text with the most logical transition?

(A) because

(B) thus,

(C) conversely,

(D) as a result,

9

The Pony Express was a system of riders that ran 2,000 miles from St. Joseph, Missouri, to Sacramento, California. The riders' routes were fraught with dangers of many kinds. In addition to being susceptible to ambush, riders often rode through rough, unfamiliar terrain and were exposed to harsh weather. _____ these challenges, only one mail delivery was lost during the Pony Express's 19 months of operation.

Which choice completes the text with the most logical transition?

- (A) In addition to
- (B) Despite
- (C) As a result of
- (D) Because of

10

Researchers in the United Kingdom have developed a new kind of biofuel that addresses several of the issues that hinder ethanol use. They extracted genes from different species of bacteria and inserted them into *E. coli* bacteria. Once this process is complete, the *E. coli* can then perform the same metabolic functions as the donor bacteria. This enables it to absorb fat molecules, convert these molecules to hydrocarbons, and then excrete the hydrocarbons as a waste product. The hydrocarbons produced by the genetically modified *E. coli* are the same as those found in commercial fossil fuels. _____ the newly created hydrocarbon molecules are interchangeable with the hydrocarbon molecules found in petroleum-based diesel fuels.

Which choice completes the text with the most logical transition?

- (A) Therefore,
- (B) Finally,
- (C) For example,
- (D) Also,

11

The following text is from Jules Verne and Michel Verne's 1889 novel *In The Year 2889*.

Every one is familiar with Fritz Napoleon Smith's system—a system made possible by the enormous development of telephony during the last hundred years. Instead of being printed, the Earth Chronicle is every morning spoken to subscribers, who, in interesting conversations with reporters, statesmen, and scientists, learn the news of the day. _____ each subscriber owns a phonograph, and to this instrument he leaves the task of gathering the news whenever he happens not to be in a mood to listen directly himself.

Which choice completes the text with the most logical transition?

(A) Secondly,

(B) However,

(C) In contrast,

(D) Furthermore,

12

It is likely that there are dangerous impacts on both the genetically modified organisms and on those who consume foods produced from genetically modified organisms. There have been insufficient human studies performed, _____ the possibility that tampering with an organism's genetic structure could cause far-reaching health consequences for the people who eat genetically modified foods must be prioritized in future scientific research.

Which choice completes the text with the most logical transition?

(A) and

(B) so

(C) or

(D) since

How Much Have You Learned?

Directions

Take 7 minutes to apply the method for PSAT Reading and Writing to the following question set. Assess your work by comparing it to the expert responses at the end of the chapter.

1

While researching a topic, a student has taken the following notes:

- Amrita Sher-Gil was a Hungarian-Indian painter of the early twentieth century.

- After her death, India designated her works as National Art Treasures and has limited the sale of her paintings abroad.

- Many of her works sought to depict the everyday life of the common people in India.

- Her work *South Indian Villagers Going to Market* (1937) features a group of villagers, including a mother speaking to her child, walking to the market.

- Her work *Haldi Grinders* (1940) features women at work grinding the spice turmeric as they sit in the forest.

The student wants to emphasize a similarity between the two works. Which choice most effectively uses relevant information from the notes to accomplish this goal?

(A) Sher-Gil completed *South Indian Villagers Going to Market* in 1937 and *Haldi Grinders* in 1940.

(B) Like many of Sher-Gil's works, both *South Indian Villagers Going to Market* and *Haldi Grinders* depict everyday life in India in the past: the former painting shows villagers going to market, and *Haldi Grinders* shows women grinding spice.

(C) Sher-Gil's paintings, which sometimes sought to depict everyday life in India in the past, have been designated as National Art Treasures of India.

(D) The subject of *South Indian Villagers Going to Market* (1937) is a group of villagers walking to market; however, the subject of *Haldi Grinders* (1940) is women grinding spice in the forest.

2

While researching a topic, a student has taken the following notes:

- Psychologists have conducted numerous studies on inattentional blindness, the phenomenon of failing to notice an unexpected stimulus.

- In a 1999 study, researchers instructed participants to count the number of times a basketball was passed among players in a pre-recorded video.

- In the 1999 study, approximately 46% of the participants did not notice that a person in a gorilla costume had walked through the center of the scene.

- In a 2013 study, researchers instructed radiologists to analyze lung scans to search for the presence of nodules that could signal the presence of lung cancer.

- In the 2013 study, 83% of the participants did not notice that a cartoon image of a gorilla had been superimposed on the scan image.

The student wants to emphasize a difference between the two studies. Which choice most effectively uses relevant information from the notes to accomplish this goal?

(A) Two studies on inattentional blindness both involved the appearance of an unexpected gorilla stimulus: a 1999 study included a gorilla appearing in a basketball game, and a 2013 study included a gorilla appearing on a lung scan.

(B) Psychological experiments on inattentional blindness typically include the introduction of an unexpected stimulus during a task that participants have been asked to perform.

(C) While both experiments tested inattentional blindness, 43% of the participants in a 1999 study failed to notice an unexpected stimulus, but 83% of the participants failed to notice an unexpected stimulus in a 2013 study.

(D) In psychology, the term inattentional blindness always refers to a failure to notice an unexpected stimulus; a wide range of different studies have attempted to analyze this phenomenon.

3

While researching a topic, a student has taken the following notes:

- Archaeologist Katherine Spielmann, along with other researchers, analyzed 17th-century Pueblo pottery from the Salinas province of New Mexico.

- The Pueblo peoples created the pottery during a period when their traditional religious practices were being threatened by Spanish colonization.

- The researchers argue that the women who created the pottery used the vessels' designs to teach and preserve traditional religious imagery.

- In areas of high Spanish influence, potters began applying thick, runny glazes to the pottery, which may indicate a purposeful obscuring of religious imagery to outsiders.

- In areas of low Spanish influence, potters increased the variety and elaborateness of the religious imagery on their pottery.

The student wants to emphasize a similarity between the pottery types created in the two different areas. Which choice most effectively uses relevant information from the notes to accomplish this goal?

- (A) Some Pueblo groups of the Salinas province of New Mexico experienced a high level of Spanish influence in the 17th century, while other Pueblo groups experienced a low level of Spanish influence during this time.

- (B) Archeological evidence of pottery indicates that the Spanish attempted to colonize the Pueblo peoples of the Salinas province of New Mexico during the 17th century.

- (C) According to researchers, the Pueblo pottery from areas of both high and low Spanish influence in the 17th century displays religious imagery, which may have been purposefully obscured or increasingly elaborated depending on where it was made.

- (D) Researchers found that 17th-century Pueblo pottery from areas of high Spanish influence shows use of a thick glaze; on the other hand, 17th-century Pueblo pottery from areas of low Spanish influence depicts an increased variety of religious imagery.

4

Much maligned as a repulsive nuisance, the opossum is actually one of North America's most interesting animals, exhibiting many notable characteristics. _____ opossums boast an incredible array of 50 razor-sharp teeth, the most of any North American land mammal. Also, because opossums are partially or totally immune, neither rabies nor snake venom presents much of a danger to them.

Which choice completes the text with the most logical transition?

- (A) However,
- (B) Moreover,
- (C) Therefore,
- (D) For example,

5

It is amazing how little the structure of the U.S. public school system has changed since its inception. Class and school sizes have varied widely and the curriculum has certainly become varied, _____ the actual system remains surprisingly similar to the way it once was. Students still change classes according to bells, even though the bell system originated during the days of factories. School is still not in session during the summer, although most students will not use that time to work on farms.

Which choice completes the text with the most logical transition?

- (A) yet
- (B) for
- (C) and
- (D) so

6

Like other ectotherms, Galapagos lava lizards are dependent on their environment for warmth. Thus, they can often be seen basking in the sun to increase their body temperature, which in turn determines their speed of locomotion. _____ the lizards can move very quickly during the day but only slowly at night.

Which choice completes the text with the most logical transition?

- (A) However,
- (B) Nevertheless,
- (C) Additionally,
- (D) Therefore,

Reflect

Directions: Take a few minutes to recall what you've learned and what you've been practicing in this chapter. Consider the following questions, jot down your best answer for each one, and then compare your reflections to the expert responses that follow. Use your level of confidence to determine what to do next.

What do Synthesis questions ask you to do, and how should you approach them strategically?

_____

_____

_____

What three types of transition words are common on the PSAT? What are some examples of each type of transition word?

_____

_____

_____

How can predicting help you correctly answer Expression of Ideas questions? What types of answer choices can you eliminate on Expression of Ideas questions?

_____

_____

_____

What are the main differences you see between PSAT Expression of Ideas questions and those you're used to from tests in school?

_____

_____

_____

How will you approach PSAT Reading and Writing questions more strategically as you continue to practice and improve your performance? Are there any specific habits you will practice to make your approach to PSAT Reading and Writing more effective and efficient?

_____

_____

_____

Expert Responses

What do Synthesis questions ask you to do, and how should you approach them strategically?

Synthesis questions ask you to bring ideas from the passage together to achieve a specific rhetorical goal (such as finding a similarity or a difference) that is identified in the question stem. You should restate this goal in your own words, and then read the passage with this specific goal in mind. Focus only on the details that are relevant to the goal, and, when finished reading, make a prediction statement that would achieve the goal. Eliminate answer choices that fail to address the specific goal.

What three types of transition words are common on the PSAT? What are some examples of each type of transition word?

The three types of transitions words on the PSAT include: continuation words (such as "moreover" and "further") that indicate a continuation of the same point, contrast words (such as "but" and "however") that indicate a change in direction or a point of difference, and cause-and-effect words (such as "therefore" and "because") that indicate that one idea causes another idea or leads to a conclusion.

How can predicting help you correctly answer Expression of Ideas questions? What types of answer choices can you eliminate on Expression of Ideas questions?

When you are able to do so, predicting the correct answer can increase your accuracy and speed by helping you focus in on the one correct answer and avoid spending time comparing the answer choices to one another. Synthesis and Transitions questions often lend themselves to predicting. When eliminating answer choices, toss out any that fail to address the specific goal (Synthesis questions) and any that distort the connection between the ideas in the passage (Transitions questions).

What are the main differences you see between PSAT Expression of Ideas questions and those you're used to from tests in school?

Depending on the kinds of classes and teachers you've had in high school, the skills rewarded on PSAT Expression of Ideas questions may be more or less familiar. In general, Expression of Ideas questions do not ask you to simply recall facts, but they instead require you to determine relationships between ideas.

How will you approach PSAT Reading and Writing questions more strategically as you continue to practice and improve your performance? Are there any specific habits you will practice to make your approach to PSAT Reading and Writing more effective and efficient?

There is no one-size-fits-all answer here. Reflect on your own habits in answering PSAT Reading and Writing questions and give yourself an honest assessment of your strengths and weaknesses. Consider the strategies you've seen experts use in this chapter, and put them to work in your own practice to increase your accuracy, speed, and confidence.

Next Steps

If you answered most questions correctly in the "How Much Have You Learned?" section, and if your responses to the Reflect questions were similar to those of the PSAT expert, then consider Expression of Ideas questions an area of strength and move on to the next chapter. Come back to this topic periodically to prevent yourself from getting rusty.

If you don't yet feel confident, review the lessons in this chapter that you have not yet mastered. Then, try the questions you missed again. As always, be sure to review the explanations closely.

Answers and Explanations

Try on Your Own

1. A

Difficulty: Easy

Category: Expression of Ideas

Getting to the Answer: This question asks for a difference between Athens and Sparta, so keep that in mind as you read the points. Only the first, second, and fourth points mention the city-states, so focus on these for your prediction. A good prediction of a difference would be, "Athens was more powerful, but Sparta prevailed in the Peloponnesian war," which matches **(A)**, the correct answer.

Incorrect choice (B) is backward, stating a similarity, not a difference between Athens and Sparta. Incorrect choices (C) and (D) are stated points but do not address the prompt. Neither choice identifies a difference between Athens and Sparta.

2. D

Difficulty: Hard

Category: Expression of Ideas

Getting to the Answer: Notice that the question stem asks about a characteristic shared by only two of the artists. Focus your attention on the last three points, since these are the only points that include the names of the African artists. Two of these, Muto and Kentridge, include African themes in their work, and this prediction matches **(D)**, the correct answer.

For the incorrect choices, (A) identifies a difference, not a similarity, among the artists; (B) only addresses one of the artists; and (C) is a similarity shared by all the artists.

3. C

Difficulty: Medium

Category: Expression of Ideas

Getting to the Answer: As usual, read the question stem first so you know what information to carefully consider. Here, you need a difference between the authors, so make a list, mentally or physically, as you read the last four points. (You can skip the first point since it doesn't mention either of the authors.) The first difference between the authors is their dates of birth: Marryat lived in the early nineteenth century, and Forester lived in the twentieth. The next difference is their careers: Marryat was a captain in the British navy, and Forester started out in medicine but was a journalist and author. The final difference is the source of their novels: Marryat used his naval experience, but Forester researched. Checking the choices for a match to one of these predictions yields **(C)**, the correct answer.

For the incorrect choices, (A) and (D) do not draw comparisons between the two authors, and (B) is a similarity between the authors, not a difference.

4. A

Difficulty: Medium

Category: Expression of Ideas

Getting to the Answer: The question asks for a similarity between diamonds and lonsdaleite, so keep that in mind as you read the points. The only similarity (mentioned in the second and fourth points) is that both minerals are made of carbon. This prediction matches **(A)**, the correct answer.

Incorrect choice (B) points out a difference, not a similarity, between the two minerals. Incorrect choice (C) does not draw a comparison between the minerals. Choice (D) states that lonsdaleite could augment diamond, and therefore, further highlights the difference between the two.

5.   C

Difficulty: Hard

Category: Expression of Ideas

Getting to the Answer: The question requires a contrast between the goals of the holiday and the perception of the holiday. Keep these two intentions in mind as you read the points. The first point just describes the holiday, so skim through this one quickly. The second point mentions "honoring older citizens and family members," so note that as a goal and move quickly to the third point. This point directly addresses the goals of the holiday; add "pass on their wisdom and share their life experiences" to the goals. A perception is mentioned in the fourth point, some older Japanese "resent being considered 'aged'." Another perception is mentioned in the final point, "a redefinition of *Keiro no Hi* may be needed." A good prediction that summarizes this information would be something like "the holiday was designed to honor older people, but may now need to be changed." Choice **(C)** matches this prediction and is correct.

Incorrect choices (B) and (D) each address only half of the question; (B) discusses perceptions, but not goals, while (D) describes goals, but not perceptions. (A) is a fact from the points that does not address either the goals or the perceptions of the holiday, so this choice is also incorrect.

6.   A

Difficulty: Hard

Category: Expression of Ideas

Getting to the Answer: The question asks for a difference between the two agents that could be used to modify the weather. Notice that the question specifies the particles and the chemical, not the processes that use them. Keep this in mind as you read the points. The first point describes the SAI process, so read this quickly. Focus on the second point that describes the action of the SAI particles. The third point describes cloud seeding, so read this point quickly. The fourth point describes the action of the seeding chemical, so read this carefully. The final point discusses the success of cloud seeding, not the chemical, so skim this point. Summarizing the differences in the second and fourth points makes something like "SAI dust particles reflect sunlight and cloud seeding chemicals serve as a nucleus for rain or snow" a good prediction. This matches **(A)**, the correct answer.

Incorrect choice (B) addresses the processes, not the agents used in the processes. Incorrect choice (C) points out a similarity between the two agents, they both modify weather. Incorrect choice (D) simply restates a fact about SAI dust particles without making a comparison with the chemical used for cloud seeding.

7.   A

Difficulty: Easy

Category: Expression of Ideas

Getting to the Answer: The phrase "logical transition" indicates that this is a Transitions question. To determine the correct transition word to use in context, first identify the relationship between the ideas it must connect. The first sentence claims that the agencies' outcomes are maximized by "implementing evidence-based programs," and the second sentence says that program participants "experience better outcomes" when there is "diligent" agency training and oversight. Both sentences identify how outcomes may be improved; therefore, a continuation transition word is needed. The correct choice is **(A)**.

Incorrect choices (B) and (C) signal contrast. (D) is incorrect because the passage is not written in sequential order.

8.   C

Difficulty: Easy

Category: Expression of Ideas

Getting to the Answer: This question is directing you to select the appropriate transition word to connect the two clauses of a sentence. The first clause identifies Neruda's "most famous" work, and the second clause *contrasts* with "most infamous" writing. Eliminate (A), (B), and (D), because they signal a cause-and-effect transition. Select **(C)**; it correctly conveys the relationship between the ideas in the sentence.

9. B

Difficulty: Easy

Category: Expression of Ideas

Getting to the Answer: Look for the relationship between the sentence that contains the blank and the previous sentence to choose the appropriate transition word. The passage opens with the long and dangerous routes that Pony Express riders traveled. The sentence that contains the blank reveals that only one delivery of mail was lost. Neither a continuation nor a cause-and-effect word would logically fit into this passage. Predict that the correct contrast transition word is *regardless of* or *despite*. Choice **(B)** is correct.

Choice (A), (C), and (D) illogically complete the sentence.

10. A

Difficulty: Medium

Category: Expression of Ideas

Getting to the Answer: Read the previous sentence in conjunction with one that contains the blank. Think about the relationship between the ideas in the two sentences. The first claims that "the hydrocarbons produced . . . are the same as . . . fossil fuels" and the second asserts that the new "molecules are interchangeable." This can be summarized as *because the new hydrocarbons are the same, the resulting molecules are interchangeable*. The correct answer choice will emphasize the cause-and-effect relationship between the ideas in the two sentences. Choice **(A)** is the only transition word that conveys a cause-and-effect relationship and is correct.

Choice (B) is incorrect because it signals continuation. Choice (C) is incorrect because the new hydrocarbons are not an example of the molecules' interchangeability. Choice (D) is incorrect because it indicates continuation rather than the cause-and-effect relationship intended in the passage.

11. D

Difficulty: Medium

Category: Expression of Ideas

Getting to the Answer: As you read the passage, look for the two ideas that are connected by the blank. The idea before the blank is that the news of the day is spoken to subscribers, instead of being printed; the idea after the blank is that subscribers have a device that can record the news. The last sentence builds upon the information presented in the preceding sentence. Predict that the correct answer will be a continuation transition; **(D)** is correct and logically makes sense when read into the blank.

Choice (A) is incorrect because it does not logically fit the sentence; there is no "first" in the previous portion of the passage. Choices (B) and (C) are incorrect because they signal a contrast rather than the continuation relationship intended by the author.

12. B

Difficulty: Hard

Category: Expression of Ideas

Getting to the Answer: This question is about choosing the appropriate transition word to connect two clauses of a sentence. The first clause is about the lack of human studies on the effect of eating genetically modified organisms, and the second clause identifies the need for such studies given the potential health risks. The ideas in the second clause are clearly a result of the information in the first, so a cause-and-effect transition is needed. Eliminate (A) and (C). Choice (D) is a cause-and-effect transition, but it would reverse the cause-and-effect relationship of the clauses, so it is incorrect. Only **(B)** correctly conveys the relationship between the ideas in the sentence.

How Much Have You Learned?

1. B

Difficulty: Medium

Category: Expression of Ideas

Getting to the Answer: The question stem asks for a similarity between two works. The last two bullet points in the passage identify the two works and describe the subjects of the paintings. The third bullet point makes a general statement about Sher-Gil's work: it often shows daily life in India. Since the descriptions of the two works entail daily life in India, you can predict that the correct synthesis statement will highlight this similarity. Choice **(B)** is correct.

Choice (A) is incorrect because it merely states when Sher-Gil completed the works; it does not indicate a specific similarity between the works. Choice (C) is incorrect because it is a statement about Sher-Gil's work in general, not the two specific paintings. Choice (D) is incorrect because it indicates a difference, rather than a similarity, between the works, as signaled by the contrast word "however."

2. C

Difficulty: Medium

Category: Expression of Ideas

Getting to the Answer: The question stem asks for a difference between two studies. The first bullet point introduces the topic of studies on inattentional blindness, and the remaining bullet points describe the studies and their results. Rather than getting bogged down in the details of the studies, you can evaluate the answer choices to determine which identifies an accurate difference based on the descriptions of the studies.

Eliminate choice (A) because it describes a similarity, not a difference, between the studies: they "both" involved an unexpected gorilla stimulus. Eliminate choice (B) because it does not discuss the two studies specifically. Choice **(C)** is correct because it identifies a difference between the studies: the significant difference in their results. Note that the contrast keywords "While" and "but" signal that this choice is about a difference. Although (D) includes the word "different," it is incorrect because it does not identify a difference between the two specific studies.

3. C

Difficulty: Hard

Category: Expression of Ideas

Getting to the Answer: The question stem asks for a similarity between two types of pottery. The first three bullet points, in turn, give the date and location of the pottery, the context in which it was made, and a use of the pottery that researchers have identified. The final bullet points describe the two specific pottery types, made in areas of high and areas of low Spanish influence. These last two bullet points identify features of the pottery that differ, but they both mention religious imagery. The idea of religious imagery also aligns with the third bullet point, which states that researchers think the potters used the pottery to convey religious imagery. You can predict that the correct synthesis statement will identify the use of religious imagery as a similarity between the pottery types; this matches **(C)**.

Choice (A) is incorrect because it does not address the pottery. Choice (B) is incorrect because, although it mentions the pottery, it does not identify a specific difference between the two types. Choice (D) is incorrect because it concerns a difference, as indicated by the phrase "on the other hand," rather than a similarity.

4. D

Difficulty: Medium

Category: Expression of Ideas

Getting to the Answer: Determine the ideas that appear before and after the blank. The first sentence describes opossums as "interesting animals" with "notable characteristics." The remaining sentences list characteristics of the opossum. Since the later sentences give examples of opossum characteristics, **(D)** is correct.

Eliminate (A) because the contrast word "However" would incorrectly indicate that the opossum's teeth are *not* an example of its notable characteristics. Choice (B) is incorrect because "Moreover" would indicate that the detail about teeth is not a supporting example but rather another claim *in addition* to the claim that opossums have notable characteristics. Choice (C) creates an illogical transition; the opossums' teeth are not the *result of* it having notable characteristics.

5. A

Difficulty: Easy

Category: Expression of Ideas

Getting to the Answer: Identify the ideas that are connected by the blank so you can determine the relationship between them. The first sentence claims that the structure of the public school system has not changed much; note that the author draws attention to this claim with the emphasis keyword "amazing." The first part of the sentence with the blank identifies changes that have happened, and the part after the blank restates that the system has not changed much. The later sentences confirm that things haven't changed much, indicated by the repeated use of the word "still." Since the sentence with the blank has two contrasting ideas, the contrast word in **(A)** is correct.

Choices (B) and (D) are incorrect because they illogically denote cause-and-effect relationships, and (C) is incorrect because "and" is a continuation transition word, while the sentence conveys contrast.

6. D

Difficulty: Hard

Category: Expression of Ideas

Getting to the Answer: Consider what two ideas are connected by the transition word in the blank. Before the blank, the passage states that the lizards' body temperature "determines their speed of locomotion," or how fast they can move. After the blank, the passage states that the lizards move quickly "during the day but only slowly at night." The information before the blank thus provides an explanation for the lizards' movement as described after the blank. A cause-and-effect transition word is thus appropriate, so **(D)** is correct.

Choices (A) and (B) are incorrect because they are contrast transitions; the ideas in the passage have a cause-and-effect, not a contrast, relationship. Choice (C) is incorrect because the detail after the blank is not merely an additional detail, but rather the result of the detail before the blank.

STANDARD ENGLISH CONVENTIONS

LEARNING OBJECTIVES

After completing this chapter, you will be able to:

- Determine the correct punctuation and/or conjunctions to form a complete sentence
- Identify and correct inappropriate uses of semicolons
- Identify and correct inappropriate uses of commas, dashes, and colons
- Use punctuation to set off simple parenthetical elements
- Identify and correct subject-verb agreement issues
- Identify and correct verb tense issues
- Identify and correct parallelism issues
- Identify and correct pronoun agreement issues
- Identify and correct modifier agreement issues
- Identify and correct inappropriate uses of apostrophes

How Much Do You Know?

Directions

Try the questions that follow. When you're done, check your answers and reasoning against ours in the "Check Your Work" section. If they closely match, you may be able to move quickly through the chapter. If they do not, spend some extra time with the chapter to grow your PSAT Reading and Writing skills.

1

Kamoya Kimeu was a Kenyan paleontologist and one of the greatest fossil hunters of all time. Born in 1940, he received little formal education, working as a goat herder until he was hired by Louis and Mary Leakey in the 1950s as a laborer on one of their research expeditions. Kimeu quickly became the Leakeys' right-hand _____ keen eye allowed him to spot fossilized bones and even identify the specific type of bone from mere fragments. After training under the Leakeys, Kimeu would go on to make some of the most important human fossil discoveries in paleontology.

Which choice completes the text so that it conforms to the conventions of Standard English?

- (A) man and his
- (B) man; and his
- (C) man, his
- (D) man. His

2

Valentina _____ the first woman in space, was born in the Soviet Union on March 6, 1937. Unlike most of the other early astronauts and cosmonauts, Tereshkova had no military background. Valentina was a mere eight years old when World War II ended. At the age of sixteen, she left school and entered the Soviet labor force, continuing her education by correspondence courses.

Which choice completes the text so that it conforms to the conventions of Standard English?

- (A) Tereshkova
- (B) Tereshkova;
- (C) Tereshkova,
- (D) Tereshkova—

CHAPTER 16
STANDARD ENGLISH CONVENTIONS

3

Green is a color rarely associated with sunrise or sunset. Yet a green flash can appear above the Sun's disk for a second or two, if atmospheric conditions are right. On westward flights toward the sunset, pilots often have a view of this rare phenomenon for long stretches of time. In the U.S. Navy, where I served for over twenty years, such green flashes typically _____ the mention of old naval folklore, how the flash was a sign of God taking the souls of mariners who died at sea up to heaven.

Which choice completes the text so that it conforms to the conventions of Standard English?

- (A) will invite
- (B) invite
- (C) invited
- (D) has invited

4

From the nation's beginning, many politicians and _____ had maintained that the ideal economy in a democracy was one in which the government played a very limited role in regulating commerce. They argued that, by permitting businesses to pursue their own interests, the government actually promoted the interests of the nation as a whole.

Which choice completes the text so that it conforms to the conventions of Standard English?

- (A) influential, business leaders
- (B) influentially business leaders
- (C) influential business leaders
- (D) influential business, leaders

5

A bouquet might just contain a hidden message in the form of the flowers selected. This is called the "language of flowers." For example, every rose is not interchangeable. Its particular color will express romantic love, mourning, happiness, or even jealousy. This allows the bouquet's creator to send an unvoiced message to _____ receives the flowers.

Which choice completes the text so that it conforms to the conventions of Standard English?

- (A) whose
- (B) whichever
- (C) whomever
- (D) whoever

K 455

6

Matter comes in four common states: solid, liquid, gas, and plasma. Under special conditions and circumstances, however, more exotic states of matter also exist. One is the Bose-Einstein condensate, _____ when a gas is cooled to near absolute zero. It is named in part after Satyendra Nath Bose, an Indian physicist whose theories were of profound importance to quantum theory.

Which choice completes the text so that it conforms to the conventions of Standard English?

- Ⓐ and forms
- Ⓑ which forms
- Ⓒ and which forms
- Ⓓ it forms

Check Your Work

1. D

Difficulty: Medium

Category: Standard English Conventions

Getting to the Answer: You must determine the correct punctuation to use between these two independent clauses. Splitting the two clauses into separate sentence is a valid solution to the problem; **(D)** is correct. A coordinating conjunction needs to have a comma before it; (A) is incorrect. A semicolon would resolve the issue without needing to use a conjunction; (B) is incorrect. As both clauses are independent, using a comma creates a run-on; (C) is incorrect.

2. C

Difficulty: Medium

Category: Standard English Conventions

Getting to the Answer: Parenthetical elements need to be separated from the rest of the sentence. There is a comma after "space," so a comma should be used after "Tereshkova." Choice **(C)** is correct. A single comma should not separate a subject from its verb; (A) is incorrect. A semicolon is used to join two independent clauses, which is not an issue presented here; (B) is incorrect. Parenthetical elements in the middle of a sentence should use either two commas or two dashes, not one of each; (D) is incorrect.

3. C

Difficulty: Medium

Category: Standard English Conventions

Getting to the Answer: As the author shifts focus from the green flashes in general to the memories of their time in the U.S. Navy, the narrative moves from the present tense to the past tense. Note the key context clue in the sentence containing the blank: "the flash was a sign. . . ." It can be helpful to double-check the other tenses, if any, within a sentence to collect every point on this type of question. **(C)** is correct because the passage shifts to past tense. Choice (A) is incorrect because future tense is inconsistent with the past tense in the rest of the sentence containing the blank. (B) is tempting but incorrect because it stays in the present tense, ignoring the contextual verb tense shift. (D) is incorrect because it is in the present perfect verb tense.

4. C

Difficulty: Medium

Category: Standard English Conventions

Getting to the Answer: This question tests how to use the words "influential" and "business" to modify "leaders" in a way that maintains the intended meaning. In this context, "business" defines the type of "leaders." You can test this by reversing the order of the modifiers: "business influential leaders" does not make logical sense. "Influential" is thus modifying "business leaders," not just "leaders," so no comma is needed between the modifiers. **(C)** is correct. (B) is incorrect because the phrase "business leaders" functions as a noun, so you need an adjective, not an adverb, to modify it.

5. C

Difficulty: Medium

Category: Standard English Conventions

Getting to the Answer: The pronouns "who" or "whom" can seem confusing. However, there is a simple way to tell when to use which pronoun. "Who" and "whoever" are *subjective* pronouns. They slot into the subject of the sentence. In other words, they are used in reference to someone performing an action. "Whom" and "Whomever" are *objective* pronouns. The action is being done upon them. Choice **(C)** is correct because "whomever" refers to someone receiving the bouquet. (A) is incorrect because "whose" is a possessive pronoun, one that expresses ownership. (B) is incorrect because "whichever" is a pronoun that refers to one member of a larger group. (D) is incorrect because the bouquet's recipient had the action of delivering the flower done upon them.

6. B

Difficulty: Hard

Category: Standard English Conventions

Getting to the Answer: The blank links two independent clauses, each containing a subject and verb ("One is . . . condensate" and "a gas is . . . cooled") and expressing a complete thought. The two clauses must be joined in a grammatically correct way. **(B)** is correct because it makes the second clause dependent. Choice (A) can be eliminated because a conjunction should keep both clauses independent, but as used here it creates a sentence where the second clause has a verb (forms) lacking a subject. Eliminate (C) because it likewise uses a conjunction to join a clause lacking a subject for its verb (forms). Eliminate (D) because it creates a run-on in which the sentence has more than one independent clause, and they are improperly joined.

The Kaplan Method with Standard English Conventions Questions

LEARNING OBJECTIVE

After this lesson, you will be able to:

* Apply the PSAT Verbal Method to PSAT Reading and Writing questions

How to Approach Standard English Conventions Questions

In the previous chapters, you've practiced applying the Method for PSAT Reading and Writing to questions that ask about Information and Ideas, Craft and Structure, and Expression of Ideas. You'll use the same method when tackling Standard English Conventions questions but with one important extra task on Step 1. Review the method, below:

THE METHOD FOR PSAT READING AND WRITING

STEP 1 What is the question asking?

* Standard English Conventions questions ONLY: Look at the answer choices for clues

STEP 2 What do I need to look for in the passage?

STEP 3 What answer strategy is best?

* Predict & Match
* Eliminate

Note that on Step 1, if you identify the question as a Standard English Conventions question (typically indicated by the stem: *Which choice completes the text so that it conforms to the conventions of Standard English?*), take a moment to glance at the answer choices before looking at the passage. Think about what Standard English conventions you notice in the answer choices. Do they contain variations on punctuation? Different verb tenses? A variety of modifying phrases or pronouns? If you identify a pattern in the answer choices, you'll have a better idea of what type of issue you'll need to correct as you read the passage.

Take a look at the question that follows and think about how you would approach it on test day. Then compare your approach to the explanation that follows.

Although hybrid electric cars have been widely available commercially in the United States since _____ less than 1% of American public school buses were electric as of the fall of 2022.

Which choice completes the text so that it conforms to the conventions of Standard English?

(A) 1999, but
(B) 1999, and although
(C) 1999,
(D) 1999;

Now consider how a PSAT expert might apply the Method for Reading and Writing to this Standard English Conventions question.

Step 1. What is the question asking?

This question asks you to choose the answer choice that "conforms to the conventions of Standard English." Since this question concerns Standard English conventions, be sure to glance at the answer choices for clues about the issue tested *before looking at the passage*. This question contains a variety of punctuation marks (commas and a semicolon) and connection words ("but," "and although"). Since these answer choices include different ways of combining the parts of a sentence, anticipate that this question will test sentence structure.

Step 2. What do I need to look for in the passage?

Since the answer choices indicate that this question tests sentence structure, be on the lookout for potential sentence fragments or run-ons as you read the passage. Consider whether the parts of the sentence before and after the punctuation are complete thoughts. The first part of the sentence ("Although hybrid electric cards have been widely available . . .") is *not* a complete thought on its own, so the part of the sentence after the punctuation must be a complete thought—otherwise, the sentence would be a fragment.

Step 3. What answer strategy is best?

After evaluating the passage for the issue you identified in Step 1, consider which answer strategy—Predict & Match or Eliminate—works best for you on the question. Here, an expert test taker might realize that a stand-alone comma should be used to connect an incomplete thought to a complete thought. Choice **(C)** appears to be correct; confirm the choice by reading the answer choice back into the sentence. Choice **(C)** correctly uses a comma to connect an incomplete thought ("Although hybrid electric cards have been widely available . . .") to a complete thought ("less than 1% . . . were electric").

Alternatively, an expert test taker might evaluate the answer choices and eliminate those that result in sentence fragments or run-ons. Choice (A) can be eliminated because a comma with a FANBOYS conjunction (here, "but") can only be used to join two complete thoughts. Choice (B) is incorrect because the addition of the word "although" results in both parts of the sentence being incomplete thoughts. Finally, choice (D) is incorrect because a semicolon can be used to connect two complete thoughts, not an incomplete thought and a complete thought.

If you were unsure about recognizing sentence fragments and run-ons on this question, don't worry. The rest of the lessons in this chapter will review the specific areas tested on Standard English Conventions questions: basic sentence structure, punctuation, verbs, pronouns, and modifiers. As you work through each lesson, practice applying the Method for Reading and Writing to every Standard English Conventions question. Use the answer choices to identify what issue is being tested, and tailor your approach to reading the passage appropriately. Then, predict or eliminate based on the best approach for you.

Sentence Structure: The Basics

LEARNING OBJECTIVES

After this lesson, you will be able to:

- Determine the correct punctuation and/or conjunctions to form a complete sentence
- Identify and correct inappropriate uses of semicolons

To answer a question like this:

San Francisco's cable cars get their name from the long, heavy cable that runs beneath the streets along which the cars _____ this cable system resembles a giant laundry clothesline with a pulley at each end. Electricity turns the wheels of the pulleys, which in turn make the cable move.

Which choice completes the text so that it conforms to the conventions of Standard English?

- (A) travel,
- (B) travel and
- (C) travel
- (D) travel;

You need to know this:

Fragments and Run-Ons

A complete sentence must have both a subject and a verb and express a complete thought. If any one of these elements is missing, the sentence is a **fragment**. You can recognize a fragment because the sentence will not make sense as written. There are some examples in the table below.

MISSING ELEMENT	EXAMPLE	CORRECTED SENTENCE
Subject	*Ran a marathon.*	*Lola ran a marathon.*
Verb	*Lola a marathon.*	
Complete thought	*While Lola ran a marathon.*	*While Lola ran a marathon, her friends cheered for her.*

The fragment *While Lola ran a marathon* is an example of a dependent clause: it has a subject (Lola) and a verb (ran), but it does not express a complete thought because it starts with a subordinating conjunction (while). Notice what the word *while* does to the meaning: While Lola ran a marathon, what happened? To fix this type of fragment, eliminate the subordinating conjunction or join the dependent clause to an independent clause using a comma. Subordinating conjunctions are words and phrases such as *since*, *because*, *therefore*, *unless*, *although*, and *due to*.

Unlike a dependent clause, an independent clause can stand on its own as a complete sentence. If a sentence has more than one independent clause, those clauses must be properly joined. If they are not, the sentence is a **run-on**: *Morgan enjoys hiking, he climbs a new mountain every summer.* There are several ways to correct a run-on, as shown in the following table.

TO CORRECT A RUN-ON	EXAMPLE
Use a period	*Morgan enjoys hiking. He climbs a new mountain every summer.*
Use a semicolon	*Morgan enjoys hiking; he climbs a new mountain every summer.*
Use a colon	*Morgan enjoys hiking: he climbs a new mountain every summer.*
Use a dash	*Morgan enjoys hiking—he climbs a new mountain every summer.*
Make one clause dependent	*Since Morgan enjoys hiking, he climbs a new mountain every summer.*
Add a FANBOYS conjunction: For, And, Nor, But, Or, Yet, So	*Morgan enjoys hiking, so he climbs a new mountain every summer.*

Semicolons

Semicolons are used in two specific ways:

- A semicolon may separate two independent clauses that are not connected by a FANBOYS conjunction (also called a coordinating conjunction), just as you would use a period.
- Semicolons may be used to separate items in a list if those items already include commas.

USE SEMICOLONS TO . . .	EXAMPLE
Join two independent clauses that are not connected by a FANBOYS conjunction	*Gaby knew that her term paper would take at least four hours to write; she got started in study hall and then finished it at home.*
Separate sub-lists within a longer list when the sub-lists contain commas	*The team needed to bring uniforms, helmets, and gloves; oranges, almonds, and water; and hockey sticks, pucks, and skates.*

You need to do this:

To recognize and correct errors involving fragments, run-ons, and semicolons, familiarize yourself with the ways in which they are tested.

- Fragments
  - If a sentence is missing a subject, a verb, or a complete thought, it is a fragment.
  - Correct the fragment by adding the missing element.
- Run-ons
  - If a sentence includes two independent clauses, they must be properly joined.
  - Employ one of the following options to properly punctuate independent clauses:
    - Use a period.
    - Insert a semicolon.
    - Use a comma and a FANBOYS (*for*, *and*, *nor*, *but*, *or*, *yet*, *so*) conjunction.
    - Use a colon.
    - Use a dash.
    - Make one clause dependent by using a subordinating conjunction (*since*, *because*, *unless*, *although*, *due to*, etc.).
- Semicolons
  - A semicolon is used to join two independent clauses that are not connected by a comma and FANBOYS conjunction.
  - Semicolons separate sub-lists within a longer list. (The items inside the sub-lists are separated by commas.)

Explanation:

If a clause could stand alone as a complete sentence, it is independent. The clauses before and after the blank are both independent clauses. Only the semicolon in **(D)** is an acceptable way to join two independent clauses, so **(D)** is correct. Choice (A) is incorrect because it results in a run-on, since two independent clauses cannot be joined by only a comma. (B) is incorrect because the FANBOYS conjunction "and" must be preceded by a comma to join independent clauses. (C) is incorrect because it eliminates all punctuation and results in a run-on.

If sentence formation or semicolons give you trouble, study the preceding information and try these Drill questions before completing the "Try on Your Own" questions. Refer to the answers that follow.

a. <u>Correct the fragment by adding a subject</u>: Drove to the store to buy ice cream.
b. <u>Correct the fragment by completing the thought</u>: Despite arriving late to the movie.
c. <u>Correct the run-on sentence with a punctuation mark</u>: I hope that Zahra can attend the study session she has a gift for clearly explaining geometry questions.
d. <u>Correct the run-on sentence with a conjunction</u>: Visiting Washington, D.C., is a great experience because you can immerse yourself in the nation's political history, another perk is the free admission at the Smithsonian museums.
e. <u>Correct the run-on sentence by making one clause dependent</u>: The early computer ENIAC could make only simple computations, it was still a landmark achievement.

Answers to Drill questions:

Note: These are not the only ways to correct the sentences; your answers may differ.

a. **Harold** drove to the store to buy ice cream.
b. Despite arriving late to the movie, **I still understood the plot.**
c. I hope that Zahra can attend the study session; she has a gift for clearly explaining geometry questions.
d. Visiting Washington, D.C., is a great experience because you can immerse yourself in the nation's political history, **and** another perk is the free admission at the Smithsonian museums.
e. **Although** the early computer ENIAC could make only simple computations, it was still a landmark achievement.

Try on Your Own

Directions

Take as much time as you need on these questions. Work carefully and methodically. There will be an opportunity for timed practice later in the book.

1

A surprising number of important discoveries have been made as the result of accidents. In 1928, bacteriologist Dr. Alexander Fleming observed that a spot of mold had contaminated one of the glass plates on which he was growing a colony of bacteria and noticed that bacteria were flourishing everywhere on the plate except in the mold's vicinity. He decided to culture the _____ that a broth filtered from it inhibited the growth of several species of bacteria. The accidental contamination eventually led to the discovery of the miracle drug, penicillin.

Which choice completes the text so that it conforms to the conventions of Standard English?

- (A) mold and found
- (B) mold; and found
- (C) mold, and found
- (D) mold. And found

2

Many of the leaders of trusts and monopolies in the 1800s unsuccessfully attempted to oppose the Sherman Antitrust Act, one of the first legislative attempts in the United States to control economic monopolies. These leaders co-opted the then cutting-edge terminology of Charles Darwin's theory of natural selection, _____ that in an unrestrained economy, power and wealth would naturally flow to the most capable according to the principles of "social Darwinism." Their monopolies were thus natural and efficient outcomes of economic development.

Which choice completes the text so that it conforms to the conventions of Standard English?

- (A) arguing
- (B) to argue
- (C) they argued
- (D) they were arguing

Reading & Writing

3

Until recently, most scientists thought that Antarctica has been covered by ice for 40 million to 52 million years and that the present ice cap is about 15 million years old. However, the discovery of remnants of a beech forest near the head of the Beardmore glacier and similar fossil finds made elsewhere suggest that western Antarctica was perhaps completely ice-free as recently as 100,000 years _____ as a result, are conducting new research to enhance their understanding of Antarctica's climate changes.

Which choice completes the text so that it conforms to the conventions of Standard English?

- (A) ago so scientists,
- (B) ago and scientists,
- (C) ago, scientists,
- (D) ago. Scientists,

4

In 1961, India passed the Maternity Benefit Act. The Act required that employers provide maternity leave, paid medical allowances, and other benefits. Breaking certain provisions in the legislation could also be punishable with prison time. Even more important than the direct effects of the Act, however, was the shift toward a new era of increasing workplace equity. The government _____ that it had to take a more active role in protecting its work-force while still building its economic power.

Which choice completes the text so that it conforms to the conventions of Standard English?

- (A) realizing finally
- (B) finally realizing
- (C) had finally realized
- (D) finally will have realized

5

Medical professionals often recommend anti-viral treatment to combat viral infections. While allergies and side effects make it impos-sible for some members of the population to take these drugs, a more significant problem is that certain viruses mutate to the point that they are becoming _____ viruses cannot be effectively combated with current antiviral measures. Despite these difficulties, antiviral treatments continue to save lives and reduce suffering.

Which choice completes the text so that it conforms to the conventions of Standard English?

- (A) antiviral-resistant these
- (B) antiviral-resistant, these
- (C) antiviral-resistant; these
- (D) antiviral-resistant; although these

6

Female artists such as Xenia Rubinos, Kali Uchis, and Mon Laferte are remaking the traditional Latin American *bolero*, a style of song that laments the pain of a broken romantic relationship. Rather than focusing on the loss of a former beloved, these are songs of _____ women reclaim their agency, shrugging off the pain of the past.

Which choice completes the text so that it conforms to the conventions of Standard English?

(A) transforming powerful

(B) transformation powerful

(C) transformation: powerful

(D) transformation, powerful

Sentence Structure: Commas, Dashes, and Colons

LEARNING OBJECTIVES

After this lesson, you will be able to:

- Identify and correct inappropriate uses of commas, dashes, and colons
- Use punctuation to set off simple parenthetical elements

To answer a question like this:

San Francisco's famous cable cars are not powered and don't generate any locomotion. Instead, each car has a powerful claw under its floor. The claw grips the cable when the car is ready to _____ releases the cable when the car needs to stop. The cars simply cling to the cable, which pulls them up and down San Francisco's steep hills.

Which choice completes the text so that it conforms to the conventions of Standard English?

Ⓐ move, and

Ⓑ move and

Ⓒ move; and

Ⓓ move—and

You need to know this:

Answer choices often move punctuation marks around, replace them with other punctuation marks, or remove them altogether. When the answer choices include commas, dashes, or colons, check to make sure the punctuation is used correctly in context.

Commas

There are two situations in which only commas are used: a series of items and introductory words or phrases.

USE COMMAS TO . . .	COMMA(S)
Set off three or more items in a series	*Jeremiah packed a sleeping bag, a raincoat, and a lantern for his upcoming camping trip.*
Separate an introductory word or phrase from the rest of the sentence	*For example, carrots are an excellent source of several vitamins and minerals.*

Commas and Dashes

In many cases, either a comma or a dash may be used to punctuate a sentence. Note that only a comma can be used to set off a leading dependent clause from an independent clause.

USE COMMAS OR DASHES TO . . .	COMMA(S)	DASH(ES)
Separate independent clauses connected by a FANBOYS conjunction (For, And, Nor, But, Or, Yet, So)	*Jess finished her homework earlier than expected, so she started an assignment that was due the following week.*	*Jess finished her homework earlier than expected—so she started an assignment that was due the following week.*
Separate a dependent clause from an independent clause when the dependent clause is first	*Because Tyson wanted to organize his locker before class, he arrived at school a few minutes early.*	*N/A*
Separate parenthetical elements from the rest of the sentence (use either two commas or two dashes, not one of each; see below for more on parentheticals)	*Professor Mann, who is the head of the English department, is known for assigning extensive projects.*	*Professor Mann—who is the head of the English department—is known for assigning extensive projects.*

Colons and Dashes

Colons and dashes introduce new ideas, often breaking the flow of the sentence. Note that the clause before the colon or dash must be able to stand on its own as a complete sentence.

USE COLONS AND DASHES TO . . .	COLON	DASH
Introduce and/or emphasize a short phrase, quotation, explanation, example, or list	*Sanjay had two important tasks to complete: a science experiment and an expository essay.*	*Sanjay had two important tasks to complete—a science experiment and an expository essay.*
Separate two independent clauses when the second clause explains, illustrates, or expands on the first sentence	*Highway 1 in Australia is one of the longest national highways in the world: it circles the entirety of the continent and connects every mainland state capital.*	*Highway 1 in Australia is one of the longest national highways in the world—it circles the entirety of the continent and connects every mainland state capital.*

Unnecessary Punctuation

Knowing when punctuation should not be used is equally important. If the answer choices include punctuation, take time to consider if it should be included at all.

DO NOT USE PUNCTUATION TO . . .	INCORRECT	CORRECT
Separate a subject from its verb	*The diligent student council, meets every week.*	*The diligent student council meets every week.*
Separate a verb from its object or a preposition from its object	*The diligent student council meets, every week.*	*The diligent student council meets every week.*
Set off elements that are essential to a sentence's meaning	*The, diligent student, council meets every week.*	*The diligent student council meets every week.*
Separate adjectives that work together to modify a noun	*The diligent, student council meets every week.*	*The diligent student council meets every week.*

Parenthetical Elements

Parenthetical elements may appear at the beginning, in the middle, or at the end of a sentence. They must be properly punctuated with parentheses, commas, or dashes for the sentence to be grammatically correct. A phrase such as *the capital of France* is considered parenthetical if the rest of the sentence is grammatically correct when it is removed. Do not mix and match; a parenthetical element must begin and end with the same type of punctuation.

PARENTHETICAL ELEMENT PLACEMENT	PARENTHESES	COMMA(S)	DASH(ES)
Beginning	*N/A*	*The capital of France, Paris is a popular tourist destination.*	*N/A*
Middle	*Paris (the capital of France) is a popular tourist destination.*	*Paris, the capital of France, is a popular tourist destination.*	*Paris—the capital of France—is a popular tourist destination.*
End	*A popular tourist destination is Paris (the capital of France).*	*A popular tourist destination is Paris, the capital of France.*	*A popular tourist destination is Paris—the capital of France.*

You need to do this:

If the answer choices include punctuation, ask yourself:

- Is the punctuation used correctly?
  The punctuation needs to be the correct type (comma, dash, or colon) and in the correct location.

- Is the punctuation necessary?
  If you cannot identify a reason why the punctuation is included, the punctuation should be removed.

Explanation:

Before you select an answer choice, make sure its punctuation marks serve a function. Punctuation here would separate the subject (claw) from part of its compound verb (grips . . . and releases). Choice **(B)** is correct. The other choices incorrectly separate the subject and verb. Choices (C) and (D) punctuate the sentence with a semicolon or dash as though joining two independent clauses.

If commas, dashes, and colons give you trouble, study the information above and try these Drill questions before completing the "Try on Your Own" questions that follow. Edit each sentence to correct the punctuation issue. Refer to the answers that follow.

a. Jamal doesn't plan to carve a jack-o'-lantern but he still had fun picking a pumpkin at the pumpkin patch.
b. Eleanor Roosevelt the longest serving First Lady of the United States considered her work on the United Nations' Declaration of Human Rights one of her greatest accomplishments.
c. I have three final exams this week Statistics, Biology, and World Literature.
d. The legendary entertainer, Johnny Carson, hosted his late-night talk show for 30 years.
e. Enabling agriculture due to its annual flooding the Nile River was truly the source of life in ancient Egypt.

Answers to drill questions:

Note: These are not the only ways to correct the sentences; your answers may differ.

a. Jamal doesn't plan to carve a jack-o'-lantern, but he still had fun picking a pumpkin at the pumpkin patch.
b. Eleanor Roosevelt, the longest serving First Lady of the United States, considered her work on the United Nations' Declaration of Human Rights one of her greatest accomplishments. OR Eleanor Roosevelt—the longest serving First Lady of the United States—considered her work on the United Nations' Declaration of Human Rights one of her greatest accomplishments.
c. I have three final exams this week: Statistics, Biology, and World Literature.
d. The legendary entertainer Johnny Carson hosted his late-night talk show for 30 years. (Commas deleted)
e. Enabling agriculture due to its annual flooding, the Nile River was truly the source of life in ancient Egypt.

Try on Your Own

Directions

Take as much time as you need on these questions. Work carefully and methodically. There will be an opportunity for timed practice later in the book.

7

After allowing the development of so many riverfront buildings, the city planners came under harsh criticism. Since the natural marshes were no longer there to serve as _____ cresting river waters freely flooded the downtown area. Despite years of increased tax revenue from the riverfront properties, the city faced its worst budget shortfall in a decade.

Which choice completes the text so that it conforms to the conventions of Standard English?

Ⓐ protection the

Ⓑ protection, the

Ⓒ protection; the

Ⓓ protection—the

8

One wonders what Auguste Rodin's reaction would be if he were to find out that his sculpture, The Thinker, is one of the most well-known pieces of art in the world today. A passionate _____ would undoubtedly swell with emotion. Whether that emotion would be pride in the lasting effects of what many consider to be the pinnacle of his work or melancholy at the cast of his sculpture placed outside of his tomb in Meudon after his tragic death is anyone's guess.

Which choice completes the text so that it conforms to the conventions of Standard English?

Ⓐ man he

Ⓑ man: he

Ⓒ man, he

Ⓓ man—he

9

To get some idea of what Siberia is like, think of a place as large as a third of the surface of the _____ and as inhospitable as Mars. This vast region spans 13.1 million square kilometers and is known for its extreme winters where the average temperature in January is −25 degrees Celsius.

Which choice completes the text so that it conforms to the conventions of Standard English?

Ⓐ Moon as remote as Pluto

Ⓑ Moon, as remote as Pluto,

Ⓒ Moon as remote as Pluto,

Ⓓ Moon, remote as Pluto,

10

Global warming poses a particular problem for coastal cities such as Jakarta, Indonesia. Scientists estimate that 70 percent of the world's fresh water is locked away in polar _____ this ice were ever to melt, sea levels would rise significantly, putting cities like Jakarta under hundreds of feet of water.

Which choice completes the text so that it conforms to the conventions of Standard English?

Ⓐ ice caps, if

Ⓑ ice caps; if

Ⓒ ice caps and if

Ⓓ ice caps; and if

11

The temperature of the Antarctic seas hovers around 29 degrees Fahrenheit, below the freezing point of blood. But even under these extreme conditions, Antarctic seas teem with _____ these waters a vital status among the Earth's ecosystems.

Which choice completes the text so that it conforms to the conventions of Standard English?

(A) life—from microscopic phytoplankton and tiny krill at the bottom of the food chain to killer whales and leopard seals at the top giving

(B) life, from microscopic phytoplankton and tiny krill at the bottom of the food chain to killer whales and leopard seals at the top; giving

(C) life; from microscopic phytoplankton and tiny krill at the bottom of the food chain to killer whales and leopard seals at the top—giving

(D) life, from microscopic phytoplankton and tiny krill at the bottom of the food chain to killer whales and leopard seals at the top, giving

12

The Vatican team that restored Michelangelo's Sistine Chapel frescoes has been criticized by other art experts for inducing a jarringly colorful transformation of the frescoes. These authorities claim the Vatican restorers did not achieve this effect solely by removing the dirt and animal glue (employed by earlier restorers to revive muted colors) from the _____ removed Michelangelo's final touches as well.

Which choice completes the text so that it conforms to the conventions of Standard English?

(A) frescoes: the team

(B) frescoes, the team

(C) frescoes and the team

(D) frescoes the team

Agreement: Verbs

LEARNING OBJECTIVES

After this lesson, you will be able to:

- Identify and correct subject-verb agreement issues
- Identify and correct verb tense issues
- Identify and correct parallelism issues

To answer a question like this:

The astronauts of *Apollo 13* _____ a routine maintenance check on the ship's equipment immediately before an explosion occurred. The impact of the blast forced them to cancel a moon landing and greatly endangered the lives of the crew.

Which choice completes the text so that it conforms to the conventions of Standard English?

- (A) have performed
- (B) will have performed
- (C) had performed
- (D) was performing

You need to know this:

Verb Tense

Verb tense indicates when an action or state of being took place: past, present, or future. The tense of the verb must fit the context of the passage. Each tense can express three different types of action.

TYPE OF ACTION	PAST	PRESENT	FUTURE
Single action occurring only once	Connor **planted** vegetables in the community garden.	Connor **plants** vegetables in the community garden.	Connor **will plant** vegetables in the community garden.
Action that is ongoing at some point in time	Connor **was planting** vegetables in the community garden this morning before noon.	Connor **is planting** vegetables in the community garden this morning before noon.	Connor **will be planting** vegetables in the community garden this morning before noon.
Action that is completed before some other action	Connor **had planted** vegetables in the community garden every year until he gave his job to Jasmine.	Connor **has planted** vegetables in the community garden since it started five years ago.	Connor **will have planted** vegetables in the community garden by the time the growing season starts.

Subject-Verb Agreement

A verb must agree with its subject in person and number:

- Person (first, second, or third)
  - First: *I **ask** a question.*
  - Second: *You **ask** a question.*
  - Third: *She **asks** a question.*
- Number (singular or plural)
  - Singular: *The apple **tastes** delicious.*
  - Plural: *Apples **taste** delicious.*

The noun closest to the verb is not always the subject: *The chair with the clawed feet is an antique.* The singular verb in this sentence, *is*, is closest to the plural noun *feet*. However, the verb's actual subject is the singular noun *chair*, so the sentence is correct as written.

When a sentence includes two nouns, only the conjunction *and* forms a compound subject requiring a plural verb form: *Saliyah and Taylor **are** in the running club.*

Collective nouns are nouns that name entities with more than one member, such as *group*, *team*, and *family*. Even though these nouns represent more than one person, they are grammatically singular and require singular verb forms:

- *The collection of paintings **is** one of the most popular art exhibits in recent years.*
- *The team **looks** promising this year.*

Parallelism

Verbs in a list, a compound, or a comparison must be parallel in form.

FEATURE	EXAMPLE	PARALLEL FORM
A list	Chloe **formulated** a question, **conducted** background research, and **constructed** a hypothesis before starting the experiment.	3 simple past verb phrases
A compound	Nineteenth-century Midwestern Native American tribes such as the Omaha taught their children **to hunt** and **to fish**, essential survival skills in the plains.	2 *to* verb forms
A comparison	Garrett enjoys **sculpting** as much as **painting**.	2 *-ing* verb forms

Note that parallelism may be tested using other parts of speech besides verbs. In general, any items in a list, compound, or comparison must be in parallel form. For example, if a list starts with a noun, the other items in the list must also be nouns; if it starts with an adjective, the other items must be adjectives, etc.

INCORRECT	CORRECT
Naomi likes *pumpkin pie and to drink coffee* on chilly weekend afternoons.	Naomi likes *pumpkin pie and coffee* on chilly weekend afternoons. or Naomi likes *to eat pumpkin pie and drink coffee* on chilly weekend afternoons.
Which of the dogs is the *most docile and better behaved?*	Which of the dogs is the *most docile and best behaved?* or Which of the dogs is the *more docile and better behaved?*
Many of the ingredients in croissants, such as salt, milk, and flour, are similar to **pancakes**.	Many of the ingredients in croissants, such as salt, milk, and flour, are similar to **those in pancakes**.

You need to do this:

If the answer choices include a verb, check that the verb:

- Reflects the correct tense: does it fit the context?
  - Agrees with the subject in person and number
  - Is parallel in form with other verbs if it appears in a list, compound, or comparison

Explanation:

When verbs are in the answer choices, make sure they agree with their subjects and match the tense of the passage. The subject of the verb tested here is "astronauts," so a plural verb is required; eliminate (D). Check the surrounding context to determine the correct tense. The actions of the sentence happened in the past (occurred, endangered), but this performance of a maintenance check happened *before* another past action in the sentence: the explosion. "Had performed" is the appropriate way to indicate the sequence of these past actions, so **(C)** is correct. The other choices are not appropriate ways to express a single past action that happened before another past action.

If verbs give you trouble, study the information above and try the following Drill questions before completing the "Try on Your Own" questions that follow. Edit each sentence to correct the verb or parallelism issue. Refer to the answers that follow.

a. The delicious flavors offered by the new ice cream shop (<u>ensure/ensures</u>) that many customers are typically lined up waiting to buy a scoop.
b. The manga club and the quiz team (<u>meet/meets</u>) in the student union on alternating Tuesdays.
c. The music textbook used in the college's World Music classes (<u>include/includes</u>) chapters about Bhaṅgrā and Afrobeat.
d. By the time the toddler finally finished his dinner, everyone else (<u>finished/had finished</u>) eating dessert.
e. Katrina's favorite activities at the amusement park include riding the wooden roller coasters, driving the bumper cars, and (<u>eating/to eat</u>) the caramel candy apples.

Answers to drill questions:

a. The delicious flavors offered by the new ice cream shop **ensure** that many customers are typically lined up waiting to buy a scoop.

b. The manga club and the quiz team **meet** in the student union on alternating Tuesdays.

c. The music textbook used in the college's World Music classes **includes** chapters about Bhaṅgrā and Afrobeat.

d. By the time the toddler finally finished his dinner, everyone else **had finished** eating dessert.

e. Katrina's favorite activities at the amusement park include riding the wooden roller coasters, driving the bumper cars, and **eating** the caramel candy apples.

Try on Your Own

Directions

Take as much time as you need on these questions. Work carefully and methodically. There will be an opportunity for timed practice later in the book.

13

Many animals existed during the Glacial Period; however, the woolly mammoth and the mastodon probably best _____ the public's current image of prehistoric Ice Age animals. Typically, these now-extinct, herbivorous precursors to the modern-day elephant were about 10 feet tall at the shoulders and weighed nearly 6,000 pounds.

Which choice completes the text so that it conforms to the conventions of Standard English?

- (A) capture
- (B) captured
- (C) will have captured
- (D) captures

14

Although they are best known today for their peculiar niche as floating commercials over sports arenas, airships, more commonly called "blimps" today, _____ widely used as passenger transportation in the early twentieth century. The most infamous was the Hindenburg. When the 804-foot Hindenburg was launched in 1936, it was the largest airship in the world.

Which choice completes the text so that it conforms to the conventions of Standard English?

- (A) was
- (B) are
- (C) were
- (D) is

15

The Sovereign Military Order of Malta, officially the Sovereign Military Hospitaller Order of Saint John of Jerusalem, of Rhodes and of Malta, or SMOM, began in 1099. The order's task was to protect and defend Christian pilgrims traveling to Jerusalem as well as _____ a hospital for their care. Though it began as a religious organization, SMOM developed into a military knighthood as a result of the volatile politics of the time.

Which choice completes the text so that it conforms to the conventions of Standard English?

- (A) providing
- (B) to provide
- (C) providing them
- (D) provided

16

Challah is a deliciously rich, beautifully braided, yeasted bread that is typically present at Jewish celebrations and holy days. Families gather together to bake the challah, setting aside a portion of it as an offering. While some traditions may change over time, challah baking continues to be a staple in many Jewish homes. Today, the global movement Challah Bake International _____ as it spreads its mission of unity and celebrates Jewish culture.

Which choice completes the text so that it conforms to the conventions of Standard English?

- (A) are thriving
- (B) thrived
- (C) began to thrive
- (D) thrives

17

At the height of their success during the 1990s, video rental companies had over 9,000 stores located throughout the world. In 1997, Reed Hastings and Marc Randolph founded a DVD-by-mail rental service that would go on to completely disrupt the movie-rental industry. By the end of 2010, the DVD-by-mail industry was worth nearly $10 billion, and its one-time competitors _____ and filed for bankruptcy.

Which choice completes the text so that it conforms to the conventions of Standard English?

- (A) closes all their stores
- (B) had closed almost all of their stores
- (C) are closing all their stores
- (D) will close almost all of its stores

18

Mycobacterium leprae is a slowly developing, rod-shaped bacillus that causes the chronic, communicable infectious disease leprosy. The disease affects the skin, eyes, nerves, and mucous membranes. It was once considered to be a diagnosis that required isolation until death, however antibiotics that successfully treated the disease were created in the late 20th century. Now, after decades of successful treatments, the scientific community believes that leprosy _____ in the near future.

Which choice completes the text so that it conforms to the conventions of Standard English?

(A) is eradicated

(B) was eradicated

(C) eradicates

(D) will be eradicated

Reading & Writing

Agreement: Pronouns

> **LEARNING OBJECTIVE**
>
> After this lesson, you will be able to:
>
> * Identify and correct pronoun agreement issues

To answer a question like this:

The public library is an invaluable treasure trove of the wisdom, research, drama, and wit of the ages, all available for easy access to eager patrons. Indeed, anyone with a card can borrow _____ free of charge.

Which choice completes the text so that it conforms to the conventions of Standard English?

(A) them

(B) it

(C) those

(D) the library's resources

You need to know this:

Pronoun Forms

A pronoun is a word that takes the place of a noun. Pronouns can take three different forms, each of which is used based on the grammatical role it plays in the sentence.

FORM	PRONOUNS	EXAMPLE
Subjective: The pronoun is used as a subject.	I, you, she, he, it, we, they, who	*Rivka is the student **who** will lead the presentation.*
Objective: The pronoun is used as the object of a verb or a preposition.	me, you, her, him, it, us, them, whom	*With **whom** will Rivka present the scientific findings?*
Possessive: The pronoun expresses ownership.	my, mine, your, yours, her, hers, his, its, our, ours, their, theirs, whose	*Rivka will likely choose a partner **whose** work is excellent.*

Note that a pronoun in subjective form can, logically, be the subject in a complete sentence. Pronouns that are in objective form cannot.

When a pronoun appears in a compound structure, dropping the other noun or pronoun will show you which form to use—for example: *Leo and me walked into town*. If you were talking about yourself only, you would say, "I walked into town," not "Me walked into town." Therefore, the correct form is subjective, and the original sentence should read: *Leo and I walked into town*.

Pronoun-Antecedent Agreement

A pronoun's antecedent is the noun it logically represents in a sentence. If the noun is singular, the pronoun must be singular; if the noun is plural, the pronoun must be plural.

ANTECEDENT	INCORRECT	CORRECT
selection	The selection of books was placed in **their** designated location.	The selection of books was placed in **its** designated location.
apples	If apples are unripe, **it** should not be purchased.	If apples are unripe, **they** should not be purchased.
woman	A woman visiting the zoo fed the giraffes all of the lettuce **they** had purchased.	A woman visiting the zoo fed the giraffes all of the lettuce **she** had purchased.
sapling	The sapling, along with dozens of flowers, was relocated to where **they** would thrive.	The sapling, along with dozens of flowers, was relocated to where **it** would thrive.

Ambiguous Pronouns

A pronoun is ambiguous if its antecedent is either missing or unclear. If a question involves a pronoun, make sure you can clearly identify the noun to which the pronoun refers. If the pronoun is ambiguous, replace it with the appropriate noun (or a rephrasing of the appropriate noun). Note that the logical antecedent may not be the noun that appears closest to the pronoun.

AMBIGUOUS PRONOUN USE	CORRECTED SENTENCE
Anthony walked with Cody to the ice cream shop, and **he** bought a banana split.	Anthony walked with Cody to the ice cream shop, and **Anthony** bought a banana split.

You need to do this:

If a question involves a pronoun, *find the logical antecedent.* Then, check that the pronoun:

- Has a clear antecedent
  - If there is no clear antecedent, the pronoun is ambiguous. Replace the pronoun with the appropriate noun (or a rephrasing of the appropriate noun).
- Uses the correct form
  - If the pronoun is the subject of a phrase or sentence, use a subjective pronoun such as *I, you, she, he, it, we, they,* or *who.*
  - If the pronoun is the object of a verb or preposition, use an objective pronoun such as *me, you, her, him, it, us, them,* or *whom.*
  - If the pronoun indicates possession, use a possessive pronoun such as *my, mine, your, yours, her, hers, his, its, our, ours, their, theirs,* or *whose.*
- Agrees with its antecedent
  - A singular antecedent requires a singular pronoun; a plural antecedent requires a plural pronoun.

Explanation:

Every pronoun on the PSAT must have a crystal-clear antecedent. In this case, it is understood from the context that the writer means that people can borrow library materials, but placing a pronoun in the blank would result in ambiguity—the noun phrase nearest the blank is "eager patrons," which is not what the writer intended to mean can be borrowed! Eliminate the pronoun answer choices, since they all result in ambiguity. **(D)** is correct because it identifies precisely what can be borrowed.

If pronouns give you trouble, study the information above and try these Drill questions before completing the "Try on Your Own" questions that follow. Select the correct choice for each sentence. Refer to the answers that follow.

a. The manager let the employee go home an hour early because (<u>the manager</u>/she) was in a good mood.
b. My parents had a great surprise for my sister and (<u>I</u>/me): a visit to the beach.
c. The manager moved the display of vintage comic books from (<u>its</u>/their) location in the back of the store to the front.
d. Fai was able to convince (him/<u>his</u>) teacher to give the class no homework over the long weekend.
e. After purchasing (<u>her</u>/she) tickets, Jen watched the singers perform in the concert.

Answers to drill questions:

a. The manager let the employee go home an hour early because **the manager** was in a good mood.

b. My parents had a great surprise for my sister and **me**: a visit to the beach.

c. The manager moved the display of vintage comic books from **its** location in the back of the store to the front.

d. Fai was able to convince **his** teacher to give the class no homework over the long weekend.

e. After purchasing **her** tickets, Jen watched the singers perform in the concert.

Try on Your Own

Directions

Take as much time as you need on these questions. Work carefully and methodically. There will be an opportunity for timed practice later in the book.

19

As we contemplate the state of literature in our modern era, it is difficult to resist longing for the epic writers of eras gone by. At times, we take great pains to merely remember that there were once authors such as Homer, Dante, and Melville: authors _____ were able to relate stories of heroic travels and struggles.

Which choice completes the text so that it conforms to the conventions of Standard English?

(A) whom

(B) which

(C) who

(D) who're

20

Nona Gaprindashvili, a pioneer in the field of chess, was inducted into the World Chess Hall of Fame in 2013, a long 35 years after she became the first woman to earn the title of Grandmaster from the World Chess Federation. She reigned as the Women's World Chess Champion from 1962–1978; it was during the year of her defeat that _____ was awarded the title of Grandmaster.

Which choice completes the text so that it conforms to the conventions of Standard English?

(A) it

(B) we

(C) she

(D) her

21

Great authors do not waste their time or ours with trivial affairs; they compel _____ to mull over great philosophical questions in stories that stand up to readers' repeated perusal. We pass these canonical writings from generation to generation, each story presenting timeless insights that bear thoughtful review and inspire meaningful discourse.

Which choice completes the text so that it conforms to the conventions of Standard English?

(A) you

(B) me

(C) one

(D) us

22

With more than 450,000 square meters of indoor and open-air space, Hanover Fairground, located in Hanover, Germany, is the largest exhibition center in the world. It is conveniently accessible via many different modes of transportation: railway, tram, bus, and car. The Fairground's sprawling layout and central location make _____ the ideal location for the largest international conventions.

Which choice completes the text so that it conforms to the conventions of Standard English?

- (A) it
- (B) their
- (C) there
- (D) them

23

After their readings of *Ulysses*, James Joyce's novel that retells Homer's *The Odyssey*, literary critics typically offer vastly different opinions of its quality. A few assert that Joyce sullied the very form of the epic genre. Whereas *The Odyssey* was a great tale of a noble hero's struggle against a seemingly insurmountable series of trials in order to restore order and honor to his household, _____ book is nearly the direct opposite. The protagonist is no hero: his actions are listless, forgettable, and undignified.

Which choice completes the text so that it conforms to the conventions of Standard English?

- (A) their
- (B) his
- (C) Joyce's
- (D) Homer's

24

Inspiration may be found in sundry sources, but only a true master of their craft is able to synthesize varied influences into a single piece of art. A titan in his industry, Akira Kurosawa was a Japanese film director _____ created movies with a unique blend of Western themes and Eastern settings. Even decades after his death, Kurosawa remains arguably the most important Japanese filmmaker in history.

Which choice completes the text so that it conforms to the conventions of Standard English?

- (A) that
- (B) he
- (C) whom
- (D) who

Reading & Writing

Agreement: Modifiers

LEARNING OBJECTIVES

After this lesson, you will be able to:

- Identify and correct modifier agreement issues
- Identify and correct inappropriate uses of apostrophes

To answer a question like this:

The populations of several bird and bat species could potentially be impacted by the further development of wind power sites. During their seasonal migrations, _____ fly through the mountainous landforms used for wind turbine locations.

Which choice completes the text so that it conforms to the conventions of Standard English?

Ⓐ many

Ⓑ they

Ⓒ many birds and bats

Ⓓ these sites

You need to know this:

A **modifier** is a word or phrase that describes, clarifies, or provides additional information about another part of the sentence. Modifier questions require you to identify the part of a sentence being modified and to use the appropriate modifier in the proper place.

In order to be grammatically correct, the modifier must be placed as close to the word it describes as possible. Use context clues in the passage to identify the correct placement of a modifier; a misplaced modifier can cause confusion and is always incorrect on test day.

Note that a common way the PSAT tests modifiers is with modifying phrases at the beginning of a sentence. Just like any other modifier, the modifying phrase grammatically modifies whatever is right next to it in the sentence. For example, consider the sentence: *While walking to the bus stop, the rain drenched Bob.* The initial phrase, *While walking to the bus stop*, grammatically modifies *the rain*, creating a nonsense sentence. After all, the rain can't walk to a bus stop! Logically, it must be that Bob walked to the bus stop, so the sentence should read: *While walking to the bus stop, Bob was drenched by the rain.*

MODIFIER/MODIFYING PHRASE	INCORRECT	CORRECT
nearly	Andre **nearly** watched the play for four hours.	Andre watched the play for **nearly** four hours.
in individual containers	The art teacher handed out paints to students **in individual containers**.	The art teacher handed out paints **in individual containers** to students.
A scholar athlete	**A scholar athlete**, maintaining high grades in addition to playing soccer were expected of Maya.	**A scholar athlete**, Maya was expected to maintain high grades in addition to playing soccer.

Adjectives and Adverbs

Use adjectives only to modify nouns and pronouns. Use adverbs to modify everything else.

- **Adjectives** are single-word modifiers that describe nouns and pronouns: *Ian conducted an **efficient** lab experiment.*
- **Adverbs** are single-word modifiers that describe verbs, adjectives, or other adverbs: *Ian **efficiently** conducted a lab experiment.*

Note that nouns can sometimes be used as adjectives. For example, in the phrase *the fashion company's autumn collection*, the word *fashion* functions as an adjective modifying *company* and the word *autumn* functions as an adjective modifying *collection*.

Comparative/Superlative

When comparing similar things, use adjectives that match the number of items being compared. When comparing two items or people, use the **comparative** form of the adjective. When comparing three or more items or people, use the **superlative** form.

COMPARATIVE (TWO ITEMS)	SUPERLATIVE (THREE OR MORE ITEMS)
better, more, newer, older, shorter, taller, worse, younger	best, most, newest, oldest, shortest, tallest, worst, youngest

Apostrophes

USE AN APOSTROPHE TO . . .	EXAMPLE
Indicate the possessive form of a single noun	*My oldest **sister's** soccer game is on Saturday.*
Indicate the possessive form of a plural noun	*My two older **sisters'** soccer games are on Saturday.*
Indicate a contraction (e.g., *don't*, *can't*)	***They've** won every soccer match this season.*

Note that plural nouns are formed without an apostrophe.

INCORRECT	CORRECT
*Sting **ray's** are cartilaginous fish related to **shark's**.*	*Sting **rays** are cartilaginous fish related to **sharks**.*
*There are many **carnival's** in this area every summer.*	*There are many **carnivals** in this area every summer.*

Possessive Nouns and Pronouns

Possessive nouns and pronouns indicate that something belongs to someone or something. In general, possessive nouns are written with an apostrophe, while possessive pronouns are not.

TO SPOT ERRORS IN POSSESSIVE NOUN OR PRONOUN CONSTRUCTION, LOOK FOR . . .	INCORRECT	CORRECT
Two nouns in a row	The **professors lectures** were both informative and entertaining.	The **professor's lectures** were both informative and entertaining.
Pronouns with apostrophes	The book is **her's**.	The book is **hers**.
Words that sound alike	The three friends decided to ride **there** bicycles to the park over **they're** where **their** going to enjoy a picnic lunch.	The three friends decided to ride **their** bicycles to the park over **there** where **they're** going to enjoy a picnic lunch.

To check whether *it's* is appropriate, replace it in the sentence with *it is* or *it has*. If the sentence no longer makes sense, *it's* is incorrect. The following sentence is correct:

The tree frog blends perfectly into its surroundings; when it holds still, it's nearly invisible.

Note that *its'* and *its's* are never correct.

You need to do this:

If a modifying phrase appears next to the blank or in the answer choices:

- Determine which word or words the phrase should be modifying.
- Make sure the modifying phrase is as *near as possible* to what it logically modifies.

If the answer choices include a modifier:

- Determine which word or words the modifier should be modifying.
- Make sure the modifier *agrees with* what it logically modifies.
  - Does the sentence require an adjective or an adverb?
  - Does the noun or pronoun show proper possession?

If the answer choices include an apostrophe, make sure it correctly indicates either possession or a contraction.

Explanation:

Make sure introductory modifiers are modifying the correct items. The introductory modifying phrase before the blank is "During their seasonal migrations," which must modify what directly follows it. The previous sentence indicates that it must be the birds and bats that fly during their seasonal migrations, so eliminate (D). "Many" in (A) and the pronoun "they" in (B) are ambiguous because they could refer to "bird and bat species" or "wind power sites." Choice **(C)** is correct because it results in the introductory phrase "During their seasonal migrations" unambiguously modifying "many birds and bats."

If modifiers give you trouble, study the information in this section and try these Drill questions before completing the "Try on Your Own" questions that follow. Edit each sentence to correct the modifier or apostrophe issue. Refer to the answers that follow.

a. The colorfully impressive plumage of the tropical birds helped make the aviary the most popular destination at the zoo.
b. Since the gym is remodeling the womens locker room, I had to change into my workout clothes at home.
c. The players on the baseball team all felt an immense sense of relief after a hard-fought victory over there long-time rivals.
d. When asked if they preferred reality programs or news documentaries, viewers reported that reality programs were most entertaining.
e. Although normally considered a children's toy, yo-yo performers are highly skilled professionals who can flawlessly execute impressive tricks.

Answers to drill questions:

Note: These are not the only ways to correct the sentences; your answers may differ.

a. The **colorful,** impressive plumage of the tropical birds helped make the aviary the most popular destination at the zoo.
b. Since the gym is remodeling the **women's** locker room, I had to change into my workout clothes at home.
c. The players on the baseball team all felt an immense sense of relief after a hard-fought victory over **their** long-time rivals.
d. When asked if they preferred reality programs or news documentaries, viewers reported that reality programs were **more** entertaining.
e. Although **the yo-yo is** normally considered a children's toy, yo-yo performers are highly skilled professionals who can flawlessly execute impressive tricks.

Try on Your Own

Directions

Take as much time as you need on these questions. Work carefully and methodically. There will be an opportunity for timed practice later in the book.

25

The upcoming elections combined with the influx of many new residents have mobilized local leaders, but efforts of the political party to register voters may undermine _____ own goal: there is no way to guarantee the new voters will support the party's candidates.

Which choice completes the text so that it conforms to the conventions of Standard English?

- (A) its
- (B) it's
- (C) they're
- (D) their

26

Madame Bovary, Flaubert's masterpiece of fiction, is seen by some critics as a cautionary tale. Their evidence is based on the behavior of the novel's main character, Emma Bovary. _____ fantasies lead to her into a dissipated life and eventual downfall.

Which choice completes the text so that it conforms to the conventions of Standard English?

- (A) Emma cares only about her immediate physical gratification and material possessions rather than the well-being of her friends and family, becoming cruel, shortsighted, and constantly dissatisfied with real life. Her

- (B) Becoming cruel, shortsighted, and constantly dissatisfied with real life, friends and family do not affect Emma's well-being as she cares only about her immediate physical gratification and material possessions. Her

- (C) Becoming cruel, shortsighted, and constantly dissatisfied with real life, Emma cares only about her immediate physical gratification and material possessions rather than the well-being of her friends and family. Her

- (D) Caring only about her immediate physical gratification and material possessions, Emma's friends and family become cruel, shortsighted, and constantly dissatisfied with real life. Her

27

In the flamboyant finale of Mozart's classic opera, *Don Giovanni*, the title villain dies in a _____ fashion that provides set designers the opportunity to imagine and recreate the fires of hell.

Which choice completes the text so that it conforms to the conventions of Standard English?

- (A) glorious dramatically

- (B) gloriously dramatic

- (C) gloriously, dramatic

- (D) glorious and dramatically

28

The vast ice fields of the continent of Antarctica reflect sunlight back into space, preventing the planet from overheating. The cold water that the icebergs generate flows north and mixes with equatorial warm water, producing currents and clouds that _____ weather patterns.

Which choice completes the text so that it conforms to the conventions of Standard English?

Ⓐ create complexly ultimate

Ⓑ create ultimate, complex

Ⓒ ultimately; complexly create

Ⓓ ultimately create complex

29

Russian filmmaker Sergei Eisenstein developed a new technique, montage, to create a cumulative emotional effect that was greater than the sum of the individual shots. Eisenstein's feature debut, a film entitled *Statchka* (*Strike* in English) released in 1925, was many _____ first experience of montage on the big screen.

Which choice completes the text so that it conforms to the conventions of Standard English?

Ⓐ moviegoer's

Ⓑ movie's goer

Ⓒ moviegoers

Ⓓ moviegoers'

30

Design museums place everyday household items under the spotlight, breaking down the barriers between commerce and creative invention. Unlike most city museums, _____ for instance, displays a collection of mass-produced objects ranging from electric type-writers to Norwegian sardine-tin labels.

Which choice completes the text so that it conforms to the conventions of Standard English?

(A) the common practice at most design museums is to display and assess objects that are readily available to the general public. London's Design Museum,

(B) the general public enjoy displays and assessments at design museums that are objects readily available to them. London's Design Museum,

(C) the objects displayed and assessed at design museums are readily available to the general public. London's Design Museum,

(D) design museums display and assess objects that are readily available to the general public. London's Design Museum,

How Much Have You Learned?

Directions

Take 7 minutes to apply the method for PSAT Reading and Writing to the following question set. Assess your work by comparing it to the expert responses at the end of the chapter.

1

Experts believe Michelangelo himself applied a veil of glaze to the Sistine Chapel frescoes to darken them after he had deemed his work too bright. The Vatican restoration team has been criticized because the solvents they used stripped away the shadows of the _____ and ultimately produced hues the painter never intended for his art.

Which choice completes the text so that it conforms to the conventions of Standard English?

- (A) frescoes, reacted chemically with Michelangelo's pigments,
- (B) frescoes reacted chemically with Michelangelo's pigments,
- (C) frescoes; reacted chemically with Michelangelo's pigments;
- (D) frescoes, reacted chemically with Michelangelo's pigments;

2

Building a functional satellite requires a tremendous degree of technical skill and a sterile manufacturing environment. Assembly teams use _____ equipment to be certain that there are no flaws in their satellite before spending millions of dollars to launch it into orbit.

Which choice completes the text so that it conforms to the conventions of Standard English?

- (A) special, cleaning solvents and computerized analysis
- (B) special, cleaning solvents and computerized, analysis
- (C) special cleaning solvents, and computerized analysis
- (D) special cleaning solvents and computerized analysis

Reading & Writing

3

A team of volunteer veterinary specialists in Rayong, Thailand are hand-raising Paradon, an endangered Irawaddy dolphin calf, after the animal was found drowning in a tidal pool by local fishermen. The rescuers chose a name for the calf that translates roughly as _____ they recognized that saving the dolphin's life would be a difficult task.

Which choice completes the text so that it conforms to the conventions of Standard English?

(A) "brotherly burden" because

(B) "brotherly burden" because,

(C) "brotherly burden"; because

(D) "brotherly burden." Because

4

Sourdough baking is experiencing a modern resurgence. Used by pioneers traveling through the American West as a way to make fresh bread, biscuits, and other baked goods without _____ sourdough has been rediscovered and prized for the light texture and slight tang it gives to the finished product.

Which choice completes the text so that it conforms to the conventions of Standard English?

(A) yeast

(B) yeast,

(C) yeast;

(D) yeast:

5

Using tree-ring dating, a Great Basin bristlecone pine dubbed "Methuselah" has been identified as one of Earth's oldest living things. _____ age was calculated to be more than 4,800 years—meaning that Methuselah predates the ancient pyramids of Giza, Egypt.

Which choice completes the text so that it conforms to the conventions of Standard English?

(A) Their

(B) His

(C) It's

(D) Its

6

The relative inaccessibility and near pristine state of Antarctica _____ it an invaluable place for scientific research. Clues to ancient climates lie buried deep in the layers of Antarctic ice—clues such as trapped bubbles of atmospheric gases, which can help scientists draw a better picture of what Antarctica was like in the past.

Which choice completes the text so that it conforms to the conventions of Standard English?

Ⓐ make

Ⓑ makes

Ⓒ made

Ⓓ is making

Reflect

Directions: Take a few minutes to recall what you've learned and what you've been practicing in this chapter. Consider the following questions, jot down your best answer for each one, and then compare your reflections to the expert responses that follow. Use your level of confidence to determine what to do next.

What additional task should you do when using the Kaplan Method for Reading and Writing on a Standard English Conventions question?

_____

_____

_____

Name at least three ways to correct a run-on sentence.

_____

_____

_____

How should parenthetical elements be punctuated?

_____

_____

_____

If the answer choices indicate that the question tests verbs, what three factors should you check about the verb?

_____

_____

_____

If the answer choices indicate that the question tests pronouns, what three factors should you check about the pronoun?

_____

_____

_____

Where should a modifying phrase be placed?

_____

_____

_____

How will you approach PSAT Reading and Writing questions more strategically as you continue to practice and improve your performance? Are there any specific habits you will practice to make your approach to PSAT Reading and Writing more effective and efficient?

_____

_____

_____

Expert Responses

What additional task should you do when using the Kaplan Method for Reading and Writing on a Standard English Conventions question?

During Step 1, once you determine that it is a Standard English Conventions question, you should look at the answer choices for clues about what specific issue (such as verb agreement) is being tested. Doing so will help you focus your reading of the passage in Step 2.

Name at least three ways to correct a run-on sentence.

There are a number of ways to fix a run-on sentence on the PSAT. The six ways that you are likely to see are: 1) use a period to create two separate sentences, 2) use a semicolon between the two independent clauses, 3) use a colon between the two independent clauses, 4) make one clause dependent, 5) add a FANBOYS conjunction after the comma, or 6) use a dash between the two independent clauses.

How should parenthetical elements be punctuated?

Parenthetical elements should be set off from the rest of the sentence by commas, parentheses, or dashes. If the parenthetical element is in the middle of the sentence, use a matching set of punctuation (for example, two dashes rather than one dash and one comma).

If the answer choices indicate that the question tests verbs, what three factors should you check about the verb?

Make sure that the verb: 1) reflects the correct verb tense based on the context of the passage, 2) agrees with its subject in person and number, and 3) is parallel in form with other verbs if it appears in a list, compound, or comparison.

If the answer choices indicate that the question tests pronouns, what three factors should you check about the pronoun?

Make sure that the pronoun: 1) has a clear and unambiguous antecedent, 2) agrees in number with its antecedent, and 3) uses the correct pronoun form (subjective, objective, or possessive).

Where should a modifying phrase be placed?

Modifying phrases should be placed as near as possible to what they logically modify.

How will you approach PSAT Reading and Writing questions more strategically as you continue to practice and improve your performance? Are there any specific habits you will practice to make your approach to PSAT Reading and Writing more effective and efficient?

There is no one-size-fits-all answer here. Reflect on your own habits in answering PSAT Reading and Writing questions and give yourself an honest assessment of your strengths and weaknesses. Consider the strategies you've seen experts use in this chapter, and put them to work in your own practice to increase your accuracy, speed, and confidence.

Next Steps

If you answered most questions correctly in the "How Much Have You Learned?" section, and if your responses to the Reflect questions were similar to those of the PSAT expert, then consider Standard English Conventions an area of strength. Come back to this topic periodically to prevent yourself from getting rusty.

If you don't yet feel confident, review the lessons in this chapter that you have not yet mastered. Then, try the questions you missed again. As always, be sure to review the explanations closely.

Answers and Explanations

Try on Your Own

1. A

Difficulty: Medium

Category: Standard English Conventions

Getting to the Answer: A quick glance at the choices indicates this question is testing the punctuation needed between the two clauses of the sentence. The first part of the sentence is an independent clause with subject-verb "He decided." The second part does not contain a subject or express a complete thought, so eliminate any answer choices that punctuates the sentence as if it contains two independent clauses: (B), a semicolon; (C), a comma and FANBOYS conjunction; and (D), a period that results in two sentences. **(A)** is correct because the word "and" joins the compound verb "decided . . . and found"; no extra punctuation is necessary.

2. A

Difficulty: Medium

Category: Standard English Conventions

Getting to the Answer: As you read, always be thinking, "Have I just read a complete idea?" The part of the sentence before the blank is an independent clause containing a subject and verb ("These leaders . . . co-opted") and expressing a complete thought. Note that this clause ends with a comma, so the correct answer will either start with a FANBOYS conjunction (For, And, Nor, But, Or, Yet, So) or make the second part of the sentence a dependent clause. None of the answer choices contains a FANBOYS conjunction, so look for the choice that makes the second clause dependent—in this case, **(A)**.

3. D

Difficulty: Easy

Category: Standard English Conventions

Getting to the Answer: A sentence is a run-on if it has two improperly joined independent clauses that could be stand-alone sentences. The first part of the sentence before the blank is an independent clause that expresses a complete thought. Expect that the correct answer will properly join this independent clause to the remainder of the sentence. "Scientists" creates another independent clause after the blank. Both a comma and a FANBOYS conjunction are required when combining two independent clauses. Eliminate (A) and (B) because they are missing the comma, and eliminate (C) because it is missing a FANBOYS conjunction. Choice **(D)** correctly divides the two independent clauses into two separate sentences.

4. C

Difficulty: Easy

Category: Standard English Conventions

Getting to the Answer: Read long sentences carefully to make sure they contain a subject and a predicate verb and express a complete thought. This sentence needs a predicate verb for the subject "the government." Filling the blank with **(C)** adds a predicate verb and forms a complete sentence. Choices (A) and (B) fail to fix the initial error; both result in a fragment. While (D) results in a complete sentence, it is incorrect because its verb tense does not match the context of the passage.

5. C

Difficulty: Medium

Category: Standard English Conventions

Getting to the Answer: A quick glance at the answer choices indicates that this question is testing the appropriate punctuation between the parts of the sentence before and after the blank. Both parts of the sentence are independent clauses; each expresses a complete thought and has a subject and predicate verb ("problem is" and "viruses cannot be"). Eliminate any answer choices that do not properly combine two independent clauses. Choice (A) is incorrect because the lack of any punctuation between independent clauses results in a run-on. (B) incorrectly uses a comma. (D) is incorrect because the word "although" turns the second clause into a dependent clause, so the clauses cannot be joined by a semicolon. **(C)** is correct because it joins two independent clauses with a semicolon.

6. C

Difficulty: Hard

Category: Standard English Conventions

Getting to the Answer: The phrases before the blank do not present a complete idea. Expect that the correct answer will complete the description of the songs and properly connect the songs to the women mentioned after the blank. Eliminate (A); this choice does not make a complete thought. The remaining choices each form two independent clauses: ". . . these are songs of transformation" and "powerful women reclaim their agency." Identify the choice that punctuates these correctly. Eliminate (B); this choice eliminates all punctuation between two independent clauses. Choice **(C)** creates two properly punctuated independent clauses and is the correct answer; the second part of the sentence describes the "transformation," so it can be introduced with a colon. Choice (D) creates a run-on, connecting two independent clauses with only a comma.

7. B

Difficulty: Medium

Category: Standard English Conventions

Getting to the Answer: This sentence begins with a subordinating clause ("Since the natural marshes . . . protection"). Because this clause is not a complete thought, it is a dependent clause that must be joined to the rest of the sentence with a comma, so **(B)** is correct. (A) runs the clauses together, while (C) and (D) punctuate the sentence as though it consisted of two independent clauses.

8. C

Difficulty: Easy

Category: Standard English Conventions

Getting to the Answer: A quick glance at the choices tells you this question is testing the punctuation needed following the introductory description of Rodin. The words "A passionate man" form an introductory phrase. An introductory phrase should be followed by a comma, so **(C)** is correct. (A) is incorrect because it is missing the required comma after the introductory phrase. In (B), the colon is used improperly: a colon can follow an independent clause only. The use of the dash in (D) is incorrect for the same reason as is the colon in (B).

9. B

Difficulty: Easy

Category: Standard English Conventions

Getting to the Answer: The sentence creates a series: attributes of locations in space that help the reader picture Siberia. Each item in the series is worded "as (*adjective*) as *Moon/Pluto/Mars*." Basic series should be punctuated with commas between each of the items, so **(B)** is correct. (A) and (C) each omit necessary commas from the series, and (D) incorrectly omits the word "as" in the second series item.

10. B

Difficulty: Medium

Category: Standard English Conventions

Getting to the Answer: Preceding and following the blank are independent clauses, each expressing a complete thought with a subject and predicate verb ("Scientists estimate" and "sea levels would rise"). Remember that semicolons combine two independent clauses, while commas can join independent clauses only when followed by a FANBOYS conjunction. Choice **(B)** is correct because it properly joins the independent clauses with a semicolon. The other answer choices are not valid ways to join independent clauses. (A) creates a run-on because it joins independent clauses with only a comma. (C) omits the necessary comma before "and." (D) adds an unnecessary "and" after the semicolon.

11. D

Difficulty: Hard

Category: Standard English Conventions

Getting to the Answer: You must determine what punctuation is correct around this long phrase that appears in the middle of a sentence. The long modifying phrase in the choices, "from microscopic . . . at the top," is parenthetical information that describes the type of life in Antarctic seas. If the phrases were removed, the sentence would still stand on its own: "Antarctic seas teem with life, . . . giving these waters a vital status among the Earth's ecosystems." Look for an answer choice that punctuates the parenthetical information appropriately, using either a pair of commas or dashes to set off the nonessential phrase. **(D)** does this with commas and is correct. (A) is incorrect because it omits the second dash needed after "top." (B) and (C) are incorrect because the use of a semicolon would indicate that two independent clauses are being joined, but each creates a dependent clause.

12. A

Difficulty: Medium

Category: Standard English Conventions

Getting to the Answer: As you approach the blank, think: "Have I read a complete idea?" The clause before the blank is an independent clause, a complete thought with subject-verb: "the restorers did not achieve." The clause after the blank will be an independent clause with the addition of the subject "team" from the choices: "the team removed." The ideas of the clauses are closely related: the first sentence states that the "effect" was not "solely" the result of "removing the dirt and animal glue," and the second sentence explains what else was done to achieve the effect ("removed Michelangelo's final touches"). Since the part of the sentence before the punctuation is an independent clause and the second part helps to explain the first, a colon effectively punctuates these two closely related clauses. Thus, **(A)** is correct. The other choices create run-on sentences by improperly joining two independent clauses.

13. A

Difficulty: Medium

Category: Standard English Conventions

Getting to the Answer: Make sure that the missing verb matches the tense of the surrounding context and agrees with its subject. The verb should be in the present tense since it refers to the "current image," so eliminate (B) and (C). The subject of the verb "capture" is the compound subject: "The woolly mammoth and the mastodon." Since a compound subject is treated as a plural, the singular verb in (D) is incorrect. Only **(A)** is left and is correct because it has the correct tense and agrees with its subject.

14. C

Difficulty: Easy

Category: Standard English Conventions

Getting to the Answer: Check whether the subject of the missing verb is singular or plural. This subject is the plural "airships," so eliminate the singular verbs in (A) and (D). It states that the use occurred almost a century ago, so you need a past tense verb; eliminate (B). Only **(C)** is left and is correct.

15. B

Difficulty: Easy

Category: Standard English Conventions

Getting to the Answer: When a subject has multiple verbs, known as compound verbs, they must all be parallel in form. The sentence begins with two verbs: "to protect and defend." The third verb must also be in the same form, "to _____," to maintain parallelism. Choice **(B)** is correct because it matches the form of the verbs used earlier in the sentence.

16. D

Difficulty: Medium

Category: Standard English Conventions

Getting to the Answer: This passage remains in the present tense from the first sentence until the last, which begins with "Today." Eliminate (B) and (C). The subject of the missing verb is the global movement; eliminate (A) because it is a plural verb. Therefore, choice **(D)** is correct because it uses the present tense, singular verb "thrives."

17. B

Difficulty: Hard

Category: Standard English Conventions

Getting to the Answer: The blank is part of a compound verb formed by the word "and." The second part of that compound verb is the past tense verb "filed." Predict that the missing verb will either be in the past tense, indicating that it happened at the same time, or the past perfect, indicating an event that happened in the past, but before the "competitors . . . filed." **(B)** matches the prediction and is correct. Closing the stores occurred in the more distant past. After the stores "had closed," the competitors "filed" for bankruptcy. The incorrect choices all use improper tenses: (A) and (C) are in the present tense, and (D) is in the future.

18. D

Difficulty: Medium

Category: Standard English Conventions

Getting to the Answer: Use context to determine the appropriate tense for the missing verb. Although the scientists' action (believes) is in the present tense, the action described in the blank occurs "in the near future." Only **(D)** is the future tense (will be), making it the correct answer.

19. C

Difficulty: Medium

Category: Standard English Conventions

Getting to the Answer: When a pronoun is blank, identify its antecedent and the correct form based on its placement in the sentence. The correct pronoun refers to people (authors), not things, so eliminate the pronoun "which," choice (B). The subjective form of the pronoun is required since the pronoun is part of the subject of the verb "were." Therefore, choice **(C)**, the subjective pronoun "who," is correct.

20. C

Difficulty: Easy

Category: Standard English Conventions

Getting to the Answer: The missing pronoun refers to the first woman, the subject, who received an award, the object. Choice **(C)** is correct because is the singular, subjective pronoun. Choice (A) is incorrect because "it" is not a pronoun applied to people. Choice (D) is incorrect because "her" is the objective form of the pronoun.

21. D

Difficulty: Medium

Category: Standard English Conventions

Getting to the Answer: A missing pronoun must match the pronouns used in the surrounding context. Determine to whom the writer is referring when they state that these authors "compelled" *someone*. In surrounding sentences, the writer uses the pronouns "we" and "ours" to refer to those impacted by these authors; the writer thus includes both the reader and herself in this designation. The correct pronoun should include the same groups, so the first-person plural "us," **(D)**, is correct. (B) is incorrect because it includes only the writer, which does not match the other surrounding pronouns. (A) is incorrect because it is in the second person, and (C) is incorrect because it is in the third person, neither of which is used elsewhere in the passage.

22. A

Difficulty: Medium

Category: Standard English Conventions

Getting to the Answer: Determine the antecedent of the missing pronoun. While "layout" and "location" are the closest, those aren't the location for conventions. The antecedent is the singular collective noun "Hanover Fairground." Eliminate (D) because "them" is plural. The blank pronoun is the object of the verb "make" and requires a singular objective pronoun. Choice **(A)** is correct. Choices (B) and (C) are incorrect because the former is possessive and the latter is not a pronoun.

23. C

Difficulty: Hard

Category: Standard English Conventions

Getting to the Answer: The missing pronoun is possessive because the "book" either belongs to or was written by someone. Therefore, the first step is identifying the most logical and least ambiguous pronoun. The context indicates that the "book" referred to in this case is the "opposite" of Homer's *The Odyssey*, so it must be the book written by Joyce. However, the writer should eliminate the grammatical ambiguity by using Joyce's name rather than a pronoun. Choice **(C)** is correct.

24. D

Difficulty: Hard

Category: Standard English Conventions

Getting to the Answer: First, determine the correct form of the missing pronoun. Kurosawa was the creator who made the movies, so the correct pronoun will be a subject pronoun that refers to people. While choice (B) meets the criteria, using the pronoun would create a poorly constructed sentence: ". . . Akira Kurosawa was a Japanese film director he created movies . . ." Choice **(D)** is correct, because "who" is the only subjective pronoun that refers to a person, without compromising the sentence clarity. Choices (A) and (C) may be eliminated because the former refers to a thing and the latter is in the objective form.

25. A

Difficulty: Medium

Category: Standard English Conventions

Getting to the Answer: The choices contain frequently confused versions of possessive pronouns and contractions, so carefully assess the context of the sentence to determine which is correct. A possessive pronoun is appropriate because the sentence is referring to the "goal" *that belongs to the* "political party," so eliminate the contractions "it's" and "they're," which mean "it is" and "they are," respectively. The "political party" is singular, so the singular possessive pronoun "its," **(A)**, is correct.

26. C

Difficulty: Hard

Category: Standard English Conventions

Getting to the Answer: A quick glance at the choices shows that the modifying phrase "becoming cruel, shortsighted, and constantly dissatisfied with real life" is moving around in the choices, so consider where that phrase should be placed. The writer intends to use that phrase to describe Emma. Only **(C)** places the modifying phrase next to "Emma," so it is correct.

27. B

Difficulty: Medium

Category: Standard English Conventions

Getting to the Answer: A glance at the choices tells you this question is testing modifiers for the noun "fashion," so the word closest to "fashion" must be an adjective. Eliminate (A) and (D) for using the adverb "dramatically" to modify "fashion." Only **(B)** uses the modifiers correctly, the adverb "gloriously" describing the adjective "dramatic" and the adjective "dramatic" describing the noun "fashion." (C) is incorrect because it separates the modifiers with an unnecessary comma.

28. D

Difficulty: Medium

Category: Standard English Conventions

Getting to the Answer: A quick glance at the choices indicates that the blank will connect the impact of Antarctic water to weather patterns. The modifier "ultimate" is not intended to modify "weather patterns," but to indicate that the creation of these weather patterns is the final part of a process; eliminate (A) and (B). (C) is incorrect because a semicolon is not used between modifiers. Only **(D)** correctly structures the modifiers so that the adverb "ultimately" modifies the verb "create" and the adjective "complex" modifies "weather patterns."

29. D

Difficulty: Medium

Category: Standard English Conventions

Getting to the Answer: The qualifier "many" that precedes the blank indicates that "moviegoers" is meant to be plural. The plural possessive is constructed by adding an apostrophe after the "s." Choice **(D)** is correct. Choice (A) is a singular possessive noun, and choice (C) is a plural noun without possession.

30. D

Difficulty: Medium

Category: Standard English Conventions

Getting to the Answer: When a blank is preceded by an introductory modifying phrase, that's a signal to identify exactly what the phrase is describing. In this question, the phrase "unlike most city museums" is setting up a contrast with *design museums*, so the phrase "design museums" should be right next to the phrase "unlike most city museums." That eliminates every choice but **(D)**, the correct answer. The incorrect choices contrast "city museums" with "the common practice" (A), "the general public" (B), and "the objects" (C).

How Much Have You Learned?

1. A

Difficulty: Medium

Category: Standard English Conventions

Getting to the Answer: Items in a series should be separated by commas. This series is lengthy, but the rule is the same. The underlined portion lists the things that the "solvents" did: "stripped," "reacted," and "produced." These should be separated by commas, so **(A)** is correct.

Semicolons, as in (C) and (D), are required only in series to separate groups of related items; when this occurs, the related items are separated by commas.

2. D

Difficulty: Medium

Category: Standard English Conventions

Getting to the Answer: The list in the choices contains two nouns ("solvents" and "equipment") and their descriptive adjectives. When more than one adjective modifies a noun, there should be commas between the adjectives only if you could change the order of the adjectives without changing the meaning. For the first noun here, "solvents," the word "cleaning" specifies the type of solvents. Thus, "special" is actually modifying "cleaning solvents." You cannot change the order of the adjectives without changing the meaning—"cleaning special solvents" does not make sense. Therefore, eliminate (A) and (B), which add a comma between "special" and "cleaning." There is no reason to separate the nouns "solvents" and "equipment" with a comma as in choice (C), so **(D)** is correct.

3. A

Difficulty: Hard

Category: Standard English Conventions

Getting to the Answer: A quick glance at the choices tells you this question is testing the punctuation connecting an independent clause ("The rescuers chose a name . . . "), with a dependent clause ("because they recognized . . . ."). No punctuation is needed and **(A)** is correct.

Choice (B) is incorrect; the comma after "because" would make the initial clause fail to express a complete idea. (C) is incorrect because a semicolon must introduce an independent, not a dependent, clause. (D) incorrectly punctuates the dependent clause as though it were a complete sentence.

4. B

Difficulty: Medium

Category: Standard English Conventions

Getting to the Answer: As you read the sentence containing the blank, mentally strip out the non-essential, modifying ideas to help you quickly identify the issue. Here, the first clause of the tested sentence reduces to "Used . . . to make fresh bread . . . " (a dependent clause) followed by "sourdough has been rediscovered . . . " (an independent clause). Eliminate (A); this choice is missing the required punctuation. Choice **(B)** correctly follows the dependent clause with a comma and is the correct answer. Select this answer choice and continue on to the next question.

Eliminate (C); a semicolon is used to connect two independent clauses. Eliminate (D); a dependent clause must be followed by a comma, not a colon.

5. D

Difficulty: Medium

Category: Standard English Conventions

Getting to the Answer: The antecedent of the blank pronoun is "a Great Basin bristlecone pine," and the "age" belongs to it, a single entity. Predict that the correct pronoun will be the singular possessive form for a thing. Choice **(D)** is correct.

Choice (A) is incorrect because "their" would refer to a group of trees, not a single one. Choice (B) is a possessive for a person, not a thing. Choice (C) is a contraction for *it is*; the possessive *its* does not contain an apostrophe.

6. A

Difficulty: Hard

Category: Standard English Conventions

Getting to the Answer: When there are verbs in the answer choices, check for tense consistency and subject-verb agreement issues. The context of the paragraph makes it clear that research in Antarctica occurs in the present, so eliminate (C), which confines the action to only the past. To determine which present tense verb is correct, find the verb's subject. Although the noun "Antarctica" is nearest, the subject is actually the compound "relative inaccessibility *and* near pristine state." Compound subjects with *and* should be treated as plural, so the plural verb "make," **(A)**, is correct.

PART 4

COUNTDOWN TO TEST DAY

CHAPTER 17

COUNTDOWN TO TEST DAY

Two to Four Months Before the Test

- Students do not typically register themselves for the PSAT, but rather they take the PSAT through their schools. Check with your school counselor or principal if needed, and see the test maker's website, **www.collegeboard.org**, for details.
- If you are homeschooled, you will need to coordinate with a local school to take the PSAT.

Two Months Before the Test

- Make sure you have an approved laptop or tablet on which to take the digital PSAT. Visit the test maker's website, **www.collegeboard.org**, to make sure you have an acceptable device. It is possible that your school may do this for you.
- If you do not have access to a device that meets the technical specifications for the exam application, you can request to borrow one from College Board. Note that a request must be made at least 30 days before your test day. Check College Board's website for the most up-to-date details.

The Week before the Test

- Focus your additional practice on the question types and/or subject areas in which you usually score highest. Now is the time to sharpen your best skills, not cram new information.
- If you have not already done so, go to **www.collegeboard.org** and download the testing application onto the laptop or tablet that you will use to take the test. If you are using a school device and are unable to download the testing application yourself, request help from your school's tech support.
- Open the testing application and complete the exam setup. Once complete, finish any additional preparation steps as prompted by the testing application.
- Most students will take the PSAT at their school, but be sure to confirm the location of your test site. Never been there before? Make a practice run to make sure you know exactly how long it will take to get from your home to your test site. Build in extra time in case you hit traffic or construction on the morning of the test.
- Get a great night's sleep the two days before the test.

The Day before the Test

- Review the methods and strategies you learned in this book.
- Put new batteries in your calculator, if using your own.
- If bringing your own laptop or tablet, charge your device overnight to make sure it is fully charged for the exam.

- Bring with you any items that the testing application or your school recommends. Consider packing your backpack or bag with the following:
  - Laptop or tablet case (or another way to help you remember to pack your device and power cord for the exam)
  - Photo ID
  - Directions to your test site location
  - Several pens or sharpened pencils with erasers (no mechanical pencils or pens that make a clicking noise)
  - Approved calculator and extra batteries, if planning to use your own rather than the built-in graphing calculator
  - Non-prohibited timepiece, if desired
  - Tissues
  - Prepackaged snacks, like granola bars
  - Bottled water, juice, or sports drink
  - Sweatshirt, sweater, or jacket

The Night before the Test

- No studying!
- Do something relaxing that will take your mind off the test, such as watching a movie or playing video games with friends.
- Set your alarm to wake up early enough so that you won't feel rushed.
- Go to bed early, but not too much earlier than you usually do. You want to fall asleep quickly, not spend hours tossing and turning.

The Morning of the Test

- Dress comfortably and in layers. You need to be prepared for any temperature.
- Eat a filling breakfast, but don't stray too far from your usual routine. If you normally aren't a breakfast eater, don't eat a huge meal, but make sure you have something substantial.
- Read something over breakfast. You need to warm up your brain so you don't go into the test cold. Read a few pages of a newspaper, magazine, or favorite novel.
- If bringing your own, make sure to pack your fully charged laptop or tablet and your power cord.
- Get to your test site early. There is likely to be some confusion about where to go and how to sign in, so allow yourself plenty of time, even if you are taking the test at your own school.
- Leave your cell phone at home or in the car. Many test sites do not allow them in the building.
- While you're waiting to sign in or be seated, read more of what you read over breakfast to stay in reading mode.

During the Test

- Be calm and confident. You're ready for this!
- Remember that while the PSAT is a more than two-hour marathon, it is also a series of shorter sections. Focus on the section you're working on at that moment; don't think about previous or upcoming sections.
- Use the methods and strategies you have learned in this book as often as you can. Allow yourself to fall into the good habits you built during your practice.
- Don't linger too long on any one question. Mark it and come back to it later.

- Can't figure out an answer? Try to eliminate some choices and take a strategic guess. Remember, there is no penalty for an incorrect answer, so even if you can't eliminate any choices, you should take a guess.

- There will be plenty of questions you *can* answer, so spend your time on those first.

- Maintain good posture throughout the test. It will help you stay alert.

- If you find yourself losing concentration, getting frustrated, or stressing about the time, stop for 30 seconds. Close your eyes, take a few deep breaths, and relax your shoulders. You'll be much more productive after taking a few moments to relax.

- Use your break effectively. During the break, go to the restroom, eat your snacks, and get your energy up for the next section.

After the Test

- Congratulate yourself! Then, reward yourself by doing something fun. You've earned it!

- If you got sick during the test or if something else happened that might have negatively affected your score, you can cancel your scores. Request information from your test proctor or visit the test maker's website for more information.

- Your scores should be available online within a week after your test.

PART 5

PRACTICE TEST

About Your Practice Test

The PSAT is an *adaptive test*. This means that, for both the Reading and Writing section and the Math section, your performance on the first module of the test section will determine the relative difficulty of the questions you see in the second module. (See chapter 1: Inside the PSAT for more information about the PSAT's structure.) Also note that on test day, the PSAT will include *pretest questions* that will not be scored, but as there is no indication of which questions they are, this paper test will grade all of the questions. While a paper test cannot simulate a digital adaptive test perfectly, the test can still give you a good estimate of your current abilities and how you might perform on the digital version of the test.

To best simulate the digital PSAT test day experience, follow these steps as you complete your Practice Test:

1. Using a timer, give yourself **32 minutes** to complete the *Routing Module of the Reading and Writing section*.

2. Use the answer key at the end of the Reading and Writing Routing Module to calculate your score. If you scored:

    - **19 or more questions correct:** Move on to *Reading and Writing Module A*.
    - **18 or fewer questions correct:** Move on to *Reading and Writing Module B*.

3. Give yourself **32 minutes** to complete *Module A or B* (see step 2) of the Reading and Writing section.

4. Take a **10 minute break**.

5. Give yourself **35 minutes** to complete the *Routing Module of the Math section*.

6. Use the answer key at the end of the Math Routing Module to calculate your score. If you scored:

    - **14 or more questions correct:** Move on to *Math Module A*.
    - **13 or fewer questions correct**: Move on to *Math Module B*.

7. Give yourself **35 minutes** to complete *Module A or B* (see step 6) of the Math section.

To score your Practice Test:

- Use the answer key to score the Reading and Writing Modules and Math Modules.
- Write down your total raw score—the total number of questions you got correct—for both of the Reading and Writing modules and both of the Math modules.
- Convert your raw scores to scaled scores as directed. The score in the right column indicates your estimated scaled score if this were an actual PSAT. Enter your scaled scores in the boxes that follow the table.
- Calculate your estimated composite, or overall, score. Simply add together your scaled scores for each section.

Reading and Writing: Routing Module

Mark your answers either on the pages that follow or on a separate sheet of paper. You will be scoring this Routing Module before going on to the final Reading and Writing Module.

DIRECTIONS

The questions in this section address a number of important reading and writing skills. Each question includes one or more passages, which may include a table or graph. Read each passage and question carefully, and then choose the best answer to the question based on the passage(s).

All questions in this section are multiple-choice with four answer choices. Each question has a single best answer.

1

Many may be familiar with the various aquatic insects and reptiles that use a body of water's surface tension to scurry across it. However, behavioral ecologist John Gould of the University of Newcastle was the first to document an insect's ability to scuttle on the underside of the water's surface. Gould reported that initially he thought the water scavenger beetle was swimming upside down, but closer observation revealed that the beetle had _____ walking method.

Which choice completes the text with the most logical and precise word or phrase?

Ⓐ   an ordinary

Ⓑ   an inverted

Ⓒ   a chaotic

Ⓓ   a speedy

CONTINUED ➡

2

The following text is from J.W. von Goethe's 1774 novel *The Sorrows Of Young Werther*.

[The physician] found me on the floor playing with Charlotte's children. Some of them were scrambling over me, and others romped with me; and, as I caught and tickled them, they made a great noise. The doctor is a formal sort of personage: he adjusts the plaits of his ruffles, and continually settles his frill whilst he is talking to you; and he thought my conduct beneath the dignity of a sensible man. I could perceive this by his countenance. But I did not suffer myself to be disturbed.

As used in the text, what does the word "conduct" most nearly mean?

- (A) Administration
- (B) Oversight
- (C) Behavior
- (D) Governance

3

The classic children's spool-and-stick toy has a design that is both _____ and versatile. The toy set comes with rods of varying lengths and wooden or plastic geometric pieces with holes. Every rod fits into every hole, so children can, without instructions, easily put together rods and the geometric spools that serve as joints in a practically limitless combination of structures.

Which choice completes the text with the most logical and precise word or phrase?

- (A) inscrutable
- (B) tedious
- (C) constricting
- (D) intuitive

4

Some financial experts put forth an intriguing theory: if impoverished people had access to very small loans, called microloans, for the purpose of funding small businesses, they could lift themselves up from poverty to self-employment and perhaps even into a position to employ others. In 1976, an economics professor in Bangladesh extended a microloan of 27 dollars to a group of impoverished village women for the purpose of buying supplies for their business manufacturing bamboo stools. The loan allowed the women to make a modest profit and grow their business to a point of self-sufficiency.

Which choice best describes the function of the second sentence in the overall structure of the text?

- (A) It illustrates the theory of microlending in practice.

- (B) It highlights the women's extreme poverty.

- (C) It critiques the lending systems of traditional financial institutions that do not offer microloans.

- (D) It proves that microloans are especially helpful to women borrowers.

5

The following text is from Sherwood Anderson's 1921 short story "Unlighted Lamps."

On several occasions Mary had gone to spend a day with her father in Chicago and she was fascinated by the thought that soon she might be going there to live. Before her mind's eye floated a vision of long streets filled with thousands of people all strangers to herself. To go into such streets and to live her life among strangers would be like coming out of a waterless desert and into a cool forest carpeted with tender young grass. In Huntersburg she had always lived under a cloud and now she was becoming a woman and the close stuffy atmosphere she had always breathed was becoming constantly more and more oppressive. It was true no direct question had ever been raised touching her own standing in the community life, but she felt that a kind of prejudice against her existed.

Which choice best describes the function of the third sentence in the overall structure of the text?

- (A) It establishes a contrast with the description in the previous sentence.

- (B) It introduces the setting that is described in the sentences that follow.

- (C) It sets up the contrast with the character's experiences presented in the sentences that follow.

- (D) It elaborates on the previous sentence's description of the character.

CONTINUED

6

Text 1

Clearly, purchasing a home is a better investment than renting a home. When you rent, you do not have an asset at the end of the rental period. When you purchase a home, you have an asset you can later resell.

Text 2

The costs of home ownership are not always obvious. Ian Mulheirn and team found that when interest payments, home repair costs, and transaction costs are included, renting a home is the financial equivalent of buying a home because home renters do not incur these costs.

Based on the texts, how would Ian Mulheirn and team (Text 2) most likely respond to the author of Text 1?

(A) They would argue that selling a purchased home may become more difficult in the future.

(B) They would agree that purchasing a home usually offers homeowners financial advantages.

(C) They would encourage the author to investigate whether all the costs of home ownership were considered.

(D) They would recommend that the author compare the purchase prices of homes in several different locations.

Practice Test

7

Text 1

Animals have evolved different camouflage strategies for different purposes. Some, like the chameleon and the octopus, change color to match the color of their surroundings, in an attempt to avoid detection. Some, like the peacock butterfly, use dramatic shapes and bright colors to attract predators to less vulnerable areas of the butterfly's body.

Text 2

João Vitor de Alcantara Viana and colleagues conducted a study to evaluate the effectiveness of animal camouflage tactics. They found that predators spent 60% more time locating camouflaged prey and that the number of predator attacks was reduced by about 25%. They were unsurprised, however, to find that the bright shapes on butterflies were not associated with reduced predator attacks.

Based on the texts, why were João Vitor de Alcantara Viana and colleagues (Text 2) not surprised with their findings on butterflies?

- (A) They anticipated that the bright eyespots would confuse the predators and make the butterflies more difficult to attack.

- (B) They thought that the predators would not be able to see the butterflies because of the motion of the bright eyespots.

- (C) They believed that the predators confused the bright eyespots with the actual eyes of a natural enemy and avoided the butterflies.

- (D) They expected that the bright eyespots led predators to attack the parts of the butterflies that would not kill the butterfly.

8

Accepted by art historians as the first truly American art movement, the Hudson River School movement began in the early nineteenth century. The first works in this style were created by landscape painters Thomas Cole, Thomas Doughty, and Asher Durand, a trio of painters who worked during the 1820s in the Hudson River Valley and surrounding locations. Heavily influenced by European romanticism, these painters set out to convey the remoteness and splendor of the American wilderness. The strongly nationalistic tone of their paintings caught the spirit of the times, and within a generation, the movement had mushroomed to include landscape painters from all over the United States.

Which choice best states the main idea of the text?

- (A) The Hudson River School movement initiated a distinctly American style of art.

- (B) Thomas Cole, Thomas Doughty, and Asher Durand were famous landscape painters.

- (C) All the landscape painters of the 1820s eventually joined the Hudson River School movement.

- (D) The Hudson River School movement was uniquely American because it rejected European romanticism.

CONTINUED ➡

9

The field of experimental archaeology entails an active, firsthand approach that might not readily be associated with the academic humanities. At the ongoing experimental archeological project Butser Ancient Farm, for instance, researchers engage in agriculture using historic farming techniques on replica farms. By using period-appropriate tools and building materials, they are able to study ancient living conditions. Elsewhere, professors Rick and Laura Brown have led their students in a variety of experimental archeological projects. For example, they recently used medieval construction practices to recreate a ceiling truss from the fire-damaged Notre Dame Cathedral.

Which choice best states the main idea of the text?

(A) Butser Ancient Farm and Notre Dame Cathedral are two historical sites that researchers have studied through experimental archaeology.

(B) The field of experimental archaeology is struggling to gain acceptance in the academic community because it employs more hands-on techniques than do many other disciplines in the humanities.

(C) Experimental archaeology involves hands-on methods, such as the use of historically accurate materials and practices to build historical structures.

(D) Professors Rick and Laura Brown are emerging leaders in the field of experimental archaeology due to their use of cutting-edge methods on the Notre Dame Cathedral.

10

The distribution of the population in a community can be affected by the available modes of transportation. Unlike railroads, which help concentrate the population in cities, the automobile can contribute to urban sprawl and, eventually, to the rise of suburbs. People no longer need to live near railroad lines or within walking distance of their jobs, and may be drawn to outlying areas with less congestion and lower property taxes. Business districts can become less centralized for similar reasons.

What is one distinction drawn in the passage between railroads and automobiles?

(A) Railroads are a more efficient mode of transportation than automobiles.

(B) Automobiles allow greater flexibility, while railroads operate on a fixed schedule.

(C) Railroads promote clustered populations, while automobiles promote dispersed populations.

(D) Automobiles replaced railroads as the preferred American mode of transportation.

Practice Test

CONTINUED

K **525**

11

Sociologists Michael Macy and Scott Golder were interested in investigating the content of the posts on a popular messaging platform. In particular, the researchers were interested in the types of emotions that users conveyed in their messages. Macy and Golder used a computer program to analyze the messages. The program detected the presence of words associated with emotions and recorded the occurrences of these words throughout the day. The researchers concluded that the level of positivity in the emotion words demonstrated an approximate U-shaped curve over the course of the day.

Which finding from Macy and Golder's research, if true, would most directly support the conclusion?

(A) The analysis indicated that the average number of messages with positive words was highest in the morning and afternoon, and the average number of messages with negative words was highest in the early evening.

(B) The analysis indicated that the average number of messages with positive words was highest in the morning and early evening, and the average number of messages with negative words was highest in the afternoon.

(C) The analysis indicated that the average number of messages that contained words associated with positive emotions was higher than the average number of messages that contained negative words.

(D) The analysis indicated that the average number of messages that contained words associated with negative emotions was higher than the average number of messages that contained positive words.

CONTINUED

Practice Test

12

Expenditures on a Child from Birth through Age 17: Average Budgetary Component Shares, 1960 versus 2012

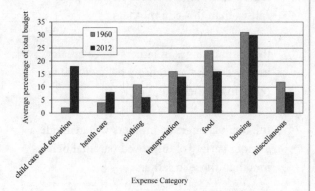

Expense Category

The average cost of raising a child to the age of 17 in the United States was around $300,000 in 2012. This total is a rough average, as differences in standard of living and costs within specific states varied widely. In addition to the gradual increase in the total cost of raising a child, the distribution of the costs among the different budgetary components shifted dramatically in some cases, as can be seen by _____

Which choice most effectively uses data from the graph to complete the statement?

Ⓐ comparing the average percentage of housing expenses in 1960 to the average percentage of housing expenses in 2012.

Ⓑ comparing the average percentage of transportation expenses in 1960 to the average percentage of transportation expenses in 2012.

Ⓒ the decrease in the average percentage of child care and education expenses during the 50-year period of 1960–2012.

Ⓓ the increase in the average percentage of child care and education expenses during the period of 1960–2012.

CONTINUED

13

Scientists have known that women's brains undergo structural changes as a result of pregnancy. They have also found a positive correlation between the decrease in brain volume during pregnancy and feelings of attachment to the new infant. These observations support the hypothesis that the brain changes are an evolutionary adaptation to improve parenting behaviors. Fathers do not undergo the physiological changes of pregnancy. However, research by Magdalena Martínez-García indicates similar, but smaller changes in the brains of new fathers that are also positively correlated with affectionate feelings towards infants. These findings suggest that _____

Which choice most logically completes the text?

(A) although similar, the brain changes in fathers may have different physiological causes than those in mothers.

(B) the brain changes in fathers cause greater improvement in parenting behaviors than those in mothers.

(C) the brain changes in mothers will generate a wider variety of improved parental behaviors than those in fathers.

(D) the brain changes in mothers occur more quickly than those in fathers.

14

During the American Civil War, inventor Richard Jordan Gatling noted that the majority of fatalities in the war were due to infected wounds. Seeking to save _____ invented the world's first successful machine gun. He hoped that by enabling one man to do the fighting of a hundred, large armies would be unnecessary and fewer soldiers would be at risk of dying from disease. This plan did not work out as Gatling expected, however.

Which choice completes the text so that it conforms to the conventions of Standard English?

(A) lives: Gatling

(B) lives; Gatling

(C) lives, Gatling

(D) lives, and Gatling

CONTINUED

15

During the Vietnam War, American military patrols would sometimes report encounters with a strange, red-furred, Bigfoot-like species. The Vietnamese called them batututs, but U.S. soldiers took to calling them Rock Apes. _____ existence has never been proven, but the rumors were so widespread that a North Vietnamese general, Hoang Minh Thao, undertook an unsuccessful expedition to find evidence of them.

Which choice completes the text so that it conforms to the conventions of Standard English?

Ⓐ It's

Ⓑ They're

Ⓒ Its

Ⓓ Their

16

Leaders of democracies often experience personal isolation. The scrutiny of the press, the pressure of their responsibilities, and the lingering paranoia that even their closest aides view the leader as a stepping stone in their own career advancement contribute to this sense of being unable to fully trust anyone. A quote by Harry Truman, U.S. president from 1945 to 1953, summarizes this view of _____ "You want a friend in Washington? Get a dog."

Which choice completes the text so that it conforms to the conventions of Standard English?

Ⓐ politics; and

Ⓑ politics, and

Ⓒ politics:

Ⓓ politics

17

Scientific theories explaining the rapid extinction of the woolly mammoth ranged from meteor showers pelting Earth to suggestions of massive volcanic eruptions. Today, however, partially due to evidence taken from the Jarkov Mammoth, the scientific community generally _____ that these creatures died out from a combination of changing climate, hunting pressures from humans, and probably even disease.

Which choice completes the text so that it conforms to the conventions of Standard English?

Ⓐ agree

Ⓑ agrees

Ⓒ agreeing

Ⓓ have agreed

Practice Test

CONTINUED 529

18

The militarization of outer space poses many dangers, but the most consequential may be the Kessler syndrome. It is a theory in which collisions between—or deliberate attacks upon—satellites in low Earth orbit (LEO) would create a cascading effect, generating a debris field of high-speed shrapnel that fills Earth orbit. Kessler syndrome could prohibit the use of satellites or even space travel for generations to come. This scenario should be carefully considered before _____ choose to risk so much for the possibility of a "secure" final frontier.

Which choice completes the text so that it conforms to the conventions of Standard English?

(A) we

(B) we as a society

(C) those of us who comprise society

(D) the citizens making up our population

19

The Battle of Waterloo, the site of the final defeat of Napoleon Bonaparte, is one of the most historically significant battles in European _____ fifty thousand soldiers died at Waterloo. Despite records of soldiers being buried in mass graves, archaeological digs at Waterloo have recovered vanishingly few skeletons. This is because, a few years after the battle, British companies dug up the bones of the dead to grind into crop fertilizer.

Which choice completes the text so that it conforms to the conventions of Standard English?

(A) history nearly

(B) history, nearly

(C) history; nearly,

(D) history. Nearly

CONTINUED

20

One of the first steps in organizing a home workspace that avoids clutter is to define a "landing zone": a dedicated site where incoming mail can be _____ sorted later into one of three categories: to act on now, to read, or to file.

Which choice completes the text so that it conforms to the conventions of Standard English?

(A) placed. The mail is

(B) placed to be

(C) placed; then

(D) placed. Then

21

British economist Normal Angell published the international best-selling book *The Great Illusion* in 1901. Arguing that international trade and economic interconnectedness meant modern war was unlikely due to it potentially costing nations so much money, _____ international peace was guaranteed through strong militaries. Unfortunately, the outbreak of World War I in 1914 proved him incorrect.

Which choice completes the text so that it conforms to the conventions of Standard English?

(A) the "great illusion" was defined as the belief

(B) and defining the "great illusion" as the belief

(C) Angell claimed the "great illusion" was that

(D) Angell's claim in *The Great Illusion* was that

CONTINUED

22

Most wild big cats, such as lions, tigers, leopards, and jaguars, have retractable claws that are only out when needed for a specific purpose. _____ these apex predators will extend their claws so that they are better equipped to hunt, fight, climb, or gain traction against the ground while they run. But one familiar big cat is not like the others: the cheetah's claws are not retractable. Zoologists believe that this trait is what enables cheetahs to run faster than the other big cats and accelerate their speed in mere seconds.

Which choice completes the text with the most logical transition?

- (A) Similarly,
- (B) On one hand,
- (C) In other words,
- (D) Despite this,

23

Some parents consider sippy cups a vital piece of a caregiving routine: they enable a child to drink independently with a decreased risk of spillage. However, recent research has begun to shed light on the potential negative effects of using sippy cups. Occupational therapists are concerned about how the rigid shape of a sippy cup's spout impedes the natural progression of an infant's swallow patterns, which may result in difficulty chewing and swallowing solid foods. _____ speech-language pathologists warn that a prolonged infantile suckle-swallow pattern may result in delays in speech and language development, as well as weaker jaw musculature.

Which choice completes the text with the most logical transition?

- (A) Consequently,
- (B) Specifically,
- (C) Additionally,
- (D) Thus,

CONTINUED

Historian J.R. McNeill claims that mosquitoes impacted geopolitical developments in the Caribbean region during the period 1620 to 1914. These insects spread the diseases of yellow fever and malaria. McNeill argues that various populations had differing levels of immunity or resistance to the diseases. _____ groups with relatively high immunity were more likely to prevail militarily against groups with relatively low immunity.

Which choice completes the text with the most logical transition?

Ⓐ Hence,

Ⓑ Similarly,

Ⓒ Next,

Ⓓ However,

While researching a topic, a student has taken the following notes:

- Mauritius, a small island off the southeast coast of Africa, was first encountered by Arab sailors around 975 and was uninhabited when it was first occupied by the Portuguese in 1511.

- The Dutch colonized the island in 1638, and, in 1715, the French took over governance.

- A successful invasion in 1810 during the Napoleonic Wars, made the British the fourth European power to rule the island.

- By the late 19th century, the population included freed slaves, Indian and Pakistani immigrants, as well as those of European descent.

- In 1947, the first legislative assembly was elected and a constitution was adopted in 1968.

- Today, Mauritius enjoys full democracy and a prosperous economy.

The student wants to emphasize the current cultural and political conditions in Mauritius. Which choice most effectively uses relevant information from the notes to accomplish this goal?

Ⓐ The population of Mauritius represents the island's colonial history.

Ⓑ Arabs, Portuguese, Dutch, French, and British influences underlie the system of government in Mauritius.

Ⓒ Mauritius owes its success in democracy to the wide diversity of the origins of its citizens.

Ⓓ Mauritius is a prosperous, democratic country with a diverse population generated by its colonial past.

Practice Test

26

While researching a topic, a student has taken the following notes:

- Research indicates that sitting for long periods impairs long-term health.
- Many people work at standing desks to improve their health.
- Because standing takes more effort than sitting does, working while standing up may divert attention to the task of standing and thus slow down mental processes.
- Working standing up may generate mild stress, proven to improve work performance.
- Yaniv Mama conducted a research study that found that standing subjects completed a difficult mental task about 20 milliseconds more quickly than seated subjects did.

The student wants to emphasize the aim and results of the research study. Which choice most effectively uses relevant information from the notes to accomplish this goal?

(A) Working standing up will either impair or improve mental processes, and Yaniv Mama researched these two outcomes.

(B) Although the physical benefits of standing are well known, Yaniv Mama found that standing benefits cognitive processes as well.

(C) The stress caused by working standing up impairs mental processes, so those who work standing up should take regular breaks.

(D) Yaniv Mama found that working standing up consumes mental attention and causes workers to take more time when solving problems.

CONTINUED

27

While researching a topic, a student has taken the following notes:

- Historian Robert Darnton employs an approach to history that focuses on researching those aspects of past cultures that seem the most strange to us today.

- He analyzes the viewpoints and meanings in individual historical documents.

- His most famous study is of a written narrative account of the 1730s "great cat massacre" in Paris.

- The cat massacre involved print shop apprentices conducting a mock trial and actual execution of cats. The cats killed included ones belonging to the wife of the master of their print shop.

- He interprets the account of the cat massacre as providing a historical critique of the apprenticeship system. He also thinks the account gives insight into what a certain historical group considered humorous.

The student wants to make a generalization about the kind of study Darnton conducted of the "great cat massacre." Which choice most effectively uses relevant information from the notes to accomplish this goal?

- (A) The 1730s cat massacre was a symbolic action that intended to criticize the Parisian apprenticeship system in print shops.

- (B) Based on his analysis of a written account of a seemingly strange event, Darnton claims that the 1730s cat massacre in Paris used humor in its critique of apprenticeships.

- (C) Historians research individual historical documents to determine aspects such as author viewpoints and meanings within the texts.

- (D) Darnton is famous for his analysis of the 1730s cat massacre in Paris, in which apprentices in a print shop were responsible for the killing of cats belonging to the shop master's wife.

IF YOU FINISH BEFORE TIME IS CALLED, YOU MAY CHECK YOUR WORK ON THIS MODULE ONLY. ON TEST DAY, YOU WON'T BE ABLE TO MOVE ON TO THE NEXT MODULE UNTIL TIME EXPIRES. **STOP**

K 535

Answer Key

Reading and Writing: Routing Module

1.	**B**	8.	**A**	15.	**D**	22.	**C**
2.	**C**	9.	**C**	16.	**C**	23.	**C**
3.	**D**	10.	**C**	17.	**B**	24.	**A**
4.	**A**	11.	**B**	18.	**B**	25.	**D**
5.	**C**	12.	**D**	19.	**D**	26.	**B**
6.	**C**	13.	**A**	20.	**A**	27.	**B**
7.	**D**	14.	**C**	21.	**C**		

Instructions

Compare your answers to the answer key and enter the number of correct answers for this stage here: _____. This is your raw score.

If you scored less than 19 correct, turn to Reading and Writing Module A and continue your test.

If you had 19 or more correct in this routing stage, turn to Reading and Writing Module B and continue your test.

Explanations will be at the end of the Practice Test.

Reading and Writing: Module A

Mark your answers either on the pages that follow or on a separate sheet of paper. You will be scoring this Module before moving on to the Math stage.

DIRECTIONS

The questions in this section address a number of important reading and writing skills. Each question includes one or more passages, which may include a table or graph. Read each passage and question carefully, and then choose the best answer to the question based on the passage(s).

All questions in this section are multiple-choice with four answer choices. Each question has a single best answer.

1

The 26.2 miles of the Boston Marathon are obviously grueling on the body, but the final stretch of the race contains _____ challenging obstacle as well. A half-mile ascent after mile marker 20 has been dubbed "Heartbreak Hill." The name was originally coined when a runner in the 1936 marathon rallied after the hill to defeat his devastated opponent. Runners today must still summon the motivation to climb the hill on legs that are already exhausted.

Which choice completes the text with the most logical and precise word or phrase?

- Ⓐ a physically
- Ⓑ a mentally
- Ⓒ a materially
- Ⓓ an aggressively

2

The following text is adapted from Sir Arthur Conan Doyle's 1887 short story "A Study in Scarlet."

As the weeks went by, my interest in him and my curiosity as to his aims in life gradually deepened and increased. His very person and appearance were such as to strike the attention of the most casual observer. In height he was rather over six feet, and so excessively lean that he seemed to be considerably taller. His eyes were sharp and piercing, save during those intervals of torpor to which I have alluded; and his thin, hawk-like nose gave his whole expression an air of alertness and decision.

As used in the text, what does the word "casual" most nearly mean?

- Ⓐ Unplanned
- Ⓑ Comfortable
- Ⓒ Relaxed
- Ⓓ Perfunctory

CONTINUED

Practice Test

3

In a 1966 article for *Scientific American*, computer scientist Anthony Oettinger anticipated how difficult it would be for computers to translate between different languages. He argued that the strict rules of computer programming might be unable to account for the _____ inherent in human language. He famously used the sentence "Time flies like an arrow" to demonstrate his claim, explaining that "Time" could function here as a noun, imperative verb, or adjective. In each instance, the meaning of the sentence changes.

Which choice completes the text with the most logical and precise word or phrase?

- (A) variations
- (B) mysteries
- (C) exceptions
- (D) grammar

4

The Green Revolution of the 1950s to 1960s has drawn some criticisms in light of its effect on the environment. However, the positive impacts of the Green Revolution's world changing advancements in agriculture far outweigh its costs. The development of high yield and disease resistant varieties of cereal grains have substantially reduced food shortages, as well as poverty and infant mortality rates, in numerous countries. Further, increases in crop production have stimulated the world economy. Countries that formerly had less stable food supplies have themselves become exporters of crops, such as rice from China and India.

Which choice best states the main purpose of the text?

- (A) It explains some major issues created by the Green Revolution and ways that scientists today are trying to minimize the damage caused by those issues.

- (B) It discusses positive and negative effects of the Green Revolution to illustrate the principle that any assessment of major world developments must entail a balanced, cautious approach.

- (C) It argues that the Green Revolution's positive effects are greater than its drawbacks by describing examples of benefits of the Green Revolution.

- (D) It rejects the criticisms of the Green Revolution by explaining why two major criticisms are unsupported by statistics about agricultural production.

CONTINUED

5

The following text is from Nicolai Gogol's 1842 short story "The Cloak." Akaky is a letter-copying clerk in a government office.

It would be difficult to find another man who lived so entirely for his duties. <u>It is not enough to say that Akaky labored with zeal; no, he labored with love.</u> In his copying, he found a varied and agreeable employment. Enjoyment was written on his face; some letters were even favorites with him; and when he encountered these, he smiled, winked, and worked with his lips, till it seemed as though each letter might be read in his face, as his pen traced it. If his pay had been in proportion to his zeal, he would, perhaps, to his great surprise, have been made even a councillor of state. But he worked, as his companions, the wits, put it, like a horse in a mill.

Which choice best states the function of the underlined sentence in the text as a whole?

- (A) It emphasizes the tedious difficulty of Akaky's work.

- (B) It sets up the contrast made later in the text between Akaky's diligence and the value of his work.

- (C) It contrasts with the description of Akaky provided in the sentences that follow.

- (D) It establishes the setting that is more fully described in the sentences that follow.

CONTINUED

Text 1

Great Zimbabwe is an ancient African settlement that was built in the 12th century and occupied through the 16th century. The European archeologists who first wrote about Great Zimbabwe in the late 19th century were astounded to find artifacts from China, Persia, Syria, and India. In their analyses, these archeologists emphasized Great Zimbabwe's connections to international trade.

Text 2

Shadreck Chirikure, an African archeologist, cites Great Zimbabwe as evidence of extensive trade among different regions of Africa. Chirikure notes that the African artifacts found on the site far outnumber the foreign artifacts. In addition, the foreign artifacts are widely distributed across the site, indicating that they were not highly valued, while the African artifacts are concentrated in areas likely occupied by community leaders.

Based on the texts, how would Chirikure (Text 2) respond to the European archeologists (Text 1)?

(A) He would agree that the foreign artifacts are the more valuable, since there are more African artifacts.

(B) He would argue that the ages of the foreign artifacts indicate they were produced earlier than the African artifacts.

(C) He would insist that African artifacts were produced earlier than the foreign artifacts.

(D) He would encourage them to consider the foreign artifacts in the context of all the artifacts.

Practice Test

7

Text 1

A 2012 study used the uranium-thorium method to date a red ochre painting in the El Castillo cave in Spain to over 40,000 years old. The date of the ancient painting affirmed archaeologists' hypothesis that cave painting by modern humans began in Europe during the Proto-Aurignacian stage.

Text 2

A team of archaeologists reported in a 2021 article that a red ochre painting of three Sulawesi warty pigs is at least 45,500 years old, based on uranium-thorium dating analysis. The well-preserved painting was found in the Leang Tedongnge cave in the Asian country of Indonesia. Archaeologist Adam Brumm, the lead author of the article, argues that the finding calls for a reanalysis of previous assumptions about the geographic origins of modern human cave painting.

Based on the texts, how would Brumm (Text 2) most likely respond to the findings of the study in Text 1?

(A) He would reject the validity of the findings about the El Castillo cave painting based upon the method that was used to date the cave painting.

(B) He would claim that the cave paintings that have been discovered in Europe are of a fundamentally different type than the cave paintings that have been discovered in Asia.

(C) He would agree that the findings support the hypothesis that modern human cave painting started in Europe during the Proto-Aurignacian stage.

(D) He would acknowledge the method used but would assert that the hypothesis that was affirmed by the findings has been called into question.

8

To create the honeycomb structure essential to his paper sculptures, Chinese visual artist Li Hingbo uses glue and whichever type of paper is best aligned with the vision he has for the finished work. Inspired by the Chinese saying "life is as fragile as paper," Hingbo considers paper to be an ideal medium: it is flexible, publicly accessible, and a powerful tool for communication. Paper may be folded into toys and lanterns and also be used to record the laws of civilization; this duality of purpose is reflected in many of Hingbo's sculptures.

Which choice best states the main idea of the text?

(A) The honeycomb structure creates flexibility in Hingbo's sculptures.

(B) The type of paper that Hingbo selects is as important as the message of his work.

(C) Paper is both Hingbo's preferred medium and an inspiration for his sculptures.

(D) Paper lanterns are both a part of Hingbo's culture and an inspiration for his artwork.

CONTINUED

9

The following text is adapted from a 1397 speech given by Bayezid the Thunderbolt, an Ottoman sultan. He is addressing a group of prisoners.

John, I am informed that you are in your own country a great lord. You are young, and in the future I hope you will be able to recover with your courage from the shame of the misfortune which has come to you in your foul knightly enterprise, and that in the desire of recovering your honor you will give me battle. If I were afraid of that and wanted to, before your release, I would make you swear that you would never bear arms against me. But no. I will not impose this oath. You will find me always ready to meet you and your people on the field of battle. Because for this purpose was I born, to carry arms and always to conquer what is ahead of me.

What is the main point of Bayezid's speech?

- (A) That he views John as an honorable knight.

- (B) That he sees John as too young to pose a threat.

- (C) That he thinks John was born to conquer others.

- (D) That he welcomes the opportunity to fight John again.

The following text is from Washington Irving's 1924 short story "The Devil and Tom Walker."

A few miles from Boston, in Massachusetts, there is a deep inlet winding several miles into the interior of the country from Charles Bay, and terminating in a thickly wooded swamp or morass. On one side of this inlet is a beautiful dark grove; on the opposite side the land rises abruptly from the water's edge into a high ridge, on which grow a few scattered oaks of great age and immense size. Under one of these gigantic trees, according to old stories, there was a great amount of treasure buried by Kidd the pirate. The inlet allowed a facility to bring the money in a boat secretly, and at night, to the very foot of the hill; the elevation of the place permitted a good lookout to be kept that no one was at hand; while the remarkable trees formed good landmarks by which the place might easily be found again.

According to the text, what is true about the inlet?

(A) It has many characteristics that make it an excellent location to hide valuables.

(B) It is difficult to navigate because of the thickly wooded swamp.

(C) It can be easily seen for several miles because of the high ridge surrounding it.

(D) It was the only hiding place Kidd the pirate used for his treasure.

Practice Test

CONTINUED

11

The following text is adapted from P. G. Wodehouse's 1923 comedic novel *The Inimitable Jeeves*. Bertie Wooster is having breakfast with a friend, Bingo, who has recently broken up with his girlfriend.

"Now look here, old friend," I said. "I know your heart is broken and all that, and at some future time I shall be delighted to hear all about it, but—"

"I didn't come to talk about that."

"No? Good egg!"

"The past," said young Bingo, "is dead."

"Right-o!"

"I have been wounded to the very depths of my soul, but don't speak about it."

"I won't."

"Ignore it. Forget it."

"Absolutely!"

I hadn't seen him so reasonable for days.

Based on the text, how does Bertie Wooster respond to his friend?

- (A) He expresses sympathy for Bingo's situation, yet he tries to change the subject when Bingo brings up his ex-girlfriend.

- (B) He is pleased to avoid discussing Bingo's breakup, despite Bingo repeatedly mentioning it.

- (C) He asks to talk to Bingo about his breakup at a later time, as the topic is too heavy for breakfast conversation.

- (D) He is preoccupied with the breakup and keeps trying to discuss it, even though Bingo insists that he is over his ex-girlfriend.

Practice Test

12

"Song of the Open Road" is a poem by Walt Whitman that was published in a collection in 1856. One theme in the poem is the speaker's conviction that genuine freedom can be found in the vastness of the outdoors: _____

Which quotation from "Song of the Open Road" most effectively illustrates the claim?

A "I think whatever I shall meet on the road I shall like, and whoever beholds me shall like me, / I think whoever I see must be happy."

B "You road I enter upon and look around, I believe you are not all that is here, / I believe that much unseen is also here."

C "Let the paper remain on the desk unwritten, and the book on the shelf unopen'd! / Let the tools remain in the workshop! let the money remain unearn'd!"

D "From this hour I ordain myself loos'd of limits and imaginary lines, . . . / I inhale great draughts of space."

CONTINUED

13

Studies are showing that there has been a continuous decline in the emotional wellness and physical health of most youth and young adults. Researchers at the University of Michigan have hypothesized that nationwide interventions that increase the youth's and young adults' exposure and time spent in nature will have a positive influence on both their emotional wellness and physical health.

Which finding, if true, would most directly support the researchers' hypothesis?

(A) After participating in a nature-based intervention, only the physical health of youths and young adults was significantly improved.

(B) Most youth and young adults declined to participate in a nature-based intervention due to increased feelings of isolation experienced when they were outside.

(C) The highest reported rates of poor emotional wellness in youth and young adults were in areas with limited access to nature.

(D) Over half of the youth and youth adults who participated in a nature-based intervention experienced a reduction in anxiety and muscle tension.

CONTINUED

14

Percentage of Population with Health Insurance and Percentage of Seniors who Graduated High School in 7 U.S. States

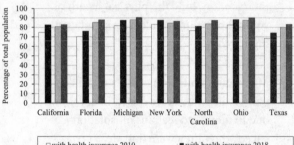

Legend: □ with health insurance 2010   ■ with health insurance 2018   ▨ graduated from high school 2010   ▪ graduated from high school 2018

In 2010, the Affordable Care Act was signed into law, which made health insurance more widely available in the United States. Although the Affordable Care Act was targeted at uninsured adults, children could be included on a parent's plan until the child reached the age of 26. Since improved health care could lead to improved attendance, and attendance in high school is correlated with graduation, it is possible that the Affordable Care Act enabled more students to graduate from high school.

Which choice best describes information from the graph that supports the author's proposal?

Ⓐ In each year, in each of the states shown, the percentage of high school students who graduated improved as the percentage of the population with health insurance increased.

Ⓑ In each year, in each of the states shown, the percentage of high school students who graduated exceeded the percentage of the population with health insurance.

Ⓒ In each year, among the seven states shown, Florida had the greatest change in both the percentage of high school students who graduated and the percentage of the population with health insurance.

Ⓓ In each year, among the seven states shown, New York had the least change in both the percentage of high school students who graduated and the percentage of the population with health insurance.

Practice Test

CONTINUED

Kenna Lehmann and colleagues utilized a computerized learning modeling to conclude that hyenas have individualized "whoops" that may allow other hyenas to identify them. Other studies about animal communication have indicated that some species repeat their calls to each other a greater number of times when their environment is noisy. When studying the hyenas, Lehmann's team found that their computer model was twice as accurate at identifying an individual hyena after hearing three whoops than one whoop. The model was most accurate at identification after hearing seven whoops. These findings suggest that

_____

Which choice most logically completes the text?

- (A) hyenas are able to identify other hyenas because each individual has a distinct number of whoops it sounds when communicating.

- (B) computer learning models are the most effective technique for studying animal vocalizations.

- (C) species that live in particularly noisy environments tend to communicate most effectively using non-auditory techniques.

- (D) increased repetition of hyena whoops increases the likelihood that they will be heard and identified by other hyenas.

16

Marine ecologist Rick Stuart Smith and professor Graham Edgar wanted to investigate the impact of increasing ocean temperatures on coral reef ecosystems in Australia. However, the researchers lacked a standard for comparison, since they did not have adequate data about other world reefs. If they compiled data from coral reefs throughout the world, _____ The researchers were determined to find out.

Which choice completes the text so that it conforms to the conventions of Standard English?

- (A) would there be sufficient evidence to evaluate the changes in Australian reefs?

- (B) would there be sufficient evidence to evaluate the changes in Australian reefs.

- (C) there would be sufficient evidence to evaluate the changes in Australian reefs?

- (D) there would be sufficient evidence to evaluate the changes in Australian reefs.

CONTINUED

17

Les Fleurs du mal is an 1857 volume of French poetry written by Charles Baudelaire that has inspired generations of writers and musicians. Exploring dark, controversial themes such as sin and death, _____ The French government officially banned six poems until 1949.

Which choice completes the text so that it conforms to the conventions of Standard English?

(A) censorship initially faced *Les Fleurs du mal.*

(B) *Les Fleurs du mal* initially faced censorship.

(C) initial censorship faced *Les Fleurs du mal.*

(D) there was poetry in *Les Fleurs du mal* that initially faced censorship.

18

Intravenous (IV) injections are only a moderately effective way to treat pneumonia. Their efficacy is limited since only a small percentage of the antibiotics in an injection actually arrives in the lungs, where the medication is needed. However, in a 2022 study, _____ showed that one small dose of antibiotics, delivered via microrobots they had developed, was effective in curing pneumonia-infected mice.

Which choice completes the text so that it conforms to the conventions of Standard English?

(A) nanoengineers Joseph Wang and Liangfang Zhang,

(B) nanoengineers Joseph Wang and Liangfang Zhang

(C) nanoengineers: Joseph Wang and Liangfang Zhang

(D) nanoengineers, Joseph Wang and Liangfang Zhang

CONTINUED

Practice Test

19

The U.S. Congress passed the Sherman Anti-trust Act, first introduced by Senator John Sherman of Ohio, in 1890. The Act made illegal "every contract, combination in the form of trust or otherwise, or conspiracy in the restraint of trade." However, many critics of the time charged that the decidedly vague wording introduced by the pro-business senators who rewrote the act before its final approval _____ in the emasculation of the law's anti-monopoly intent. Nevertheless, the Act was the first law to fight, even symbolically, against economic monopolies in the United States.

Which choice completes the text so that it conforms to the conventions of Standard English?

- (A) result
- (B) will result
- (C) resulted
- (D) has resulted

20

Astronomers now theorize that the source of Saturn's rings, a collection of icy debris that orbits the planet, _____ the moon Chrysalis. This former moon may have orbited Saturn until about 160 million years ago when its orbit destabilized. The moon is thought to have scraped the planet and fragmented into the debris that formed the rings.

Which choice completes the text so that it conforms to the conventions of Standard English?

- (A) will be
- (B) have been
- (C) was
- (D) were

CONTINUED

21

Sarah Winnemucca Hopkins wrote her 1883 autobiography, *Life Among the Piutes: Their Wrongs and Claims*, in order to draw attention to the injustices her people were experiencing under the reservation system. A compelling historical narrative that offers a rare first-hand perspective of threats to traditional _____ *Life Among the Piutes* is the first known autobiography composed by a Native American woman.

Which choice completes the text so that it conforms to the conventions of Standard English?

- (A) lifestyles.
- (B) lifestyles;
- (C) lifestyles,
- (D) lifestyles

22

Chemist Carolyn Bertozzi is the developer of the field of biorthogonal chemistry. In this subfield of chemistry, scientists use an innovative procedure to research biomolecules in living _____ to enable the study of biomolecules as they would naturally exist in cells, chemists produce certain chemical reactions that modify molecules within the cells in ways that do not interfere with their normal biological functioning.

Which choice completes the text so that it conforms to the conventions of Standard English?

- (A) cells,
- (B) cells that
- (C) cells:
- (D) cells

Practice Test

CONTINUED

23

Safia Elhillo is a spoken word artist and poet who has toured the U.S. performing works that question the truth of our histories while addressing the complexity of identity. The daughter of Sudanese immigrants, Safia celebrates her heritage and frequently speaks in a hybrid language of Arabic and English. This helps underscore how she bridges two different cultures. _____ her 2016 poem "Alien Suite" opens with an example of how the translation of an Arabic word, which can mean either "love" or "wind" in English, may completely disconnect the translated work from the author's original intent.

Which choice completes the text with the most logical transition?

Ⓐ Likewise,

Ⓑ For instance,

Ⓒ In comparison,

Ⓓ Nonetheless,

24

The 1623 Droeshout engraving of William Shakespeare appeared in the first publication of his plays. The engraving was long assumed to be based upon the so-called Flower Portrait of the playwright that was dated 1609. However, a 2005 analysis determined that the Flower Portrait actually dates to the 1800s. _____ art historians now conclude that the Droeshout engraving inspired the Flower Portrait.

Which choice completes the text with the most logical transition?

Ⓐ Nevertheless,

Ⓑ Next,

Ⓒ Similarly,

Ⓓ Consequently,

Practice Test

CONTINUED

25

A research team led by Edward H. Egelman was interested in the logistics of how bacteria use their flagella appendages to move. _____ scientists have not understood how bacteria are able to coil these single proteins into propellers that enable movement. The team utilized an improved magnification technique to view the propellers at an atomic level, which has provided a better understanding of the atomic structures that facilitate the coiling.

Which choice completes the text with the most logical transition?

Ⓐ Therefore,

Ⓑ Similarly,

Ⓒ Specifically,

Ⓓ Regardless,

26

While researching a topic, a student has taken the following notes:

- Ananse, the spider god, is a prominent figure in Akan folklore.
- He is known by the names Hapanzi, Nanzi, Anansi, Anancy, and Aunt Nancy.
- He both creates stories and steals stories from the sky god.
- He frequently uses trickery and ruses to accomplish his goals.
- He is credited with bringing stories about agriculture to his people so they could learn to care for themselves.
- In one legend, Ananse attempts to gather all knowledge into a calabash, or bottle gourd, but soon realizes that knowledge is not meant to be contained.

The student wants to make a generalization about Ananse's actions as an Akan god. Which choice most effectively uses relevant information from the notes to accomplish this goal?

Ⓐ The spider god's name, Aunt Nancy, is the result of the folklore's evolution.

Ⓑ According to Akan folklore, Ananse stole people's wisdom and kept it from them in a calabash.

Ⓒ The spider god, Ananse, used trickery to steal stories for his people so that they could learn from the stories.

Ⓓ A prominent figure in Akan folklore, the spider god is known by many names: Ananse, Hapanzi, Nanzi, Anansi, Anancy, and Aunt Nancy.

CONTINUED

27

While researching a topic, a student has taken the following notes:

- The RIPE (Realizing Increased Photosynthetic Efficiency) project seeks to increase food production on a global scale.

- Plants spend time in a non-productive state when switching between the photosynthetic processes they use when exposed to sun versus shade.

- Researchers in the RIPE project investigated whether it was possible to make photosynthesis more efficient.

- The researchers developed a bioengineering technique that reduces the time plants spend in the non-productive state when switching between photosynthetic processes.

- In field studies, the technique increased crop yields in tobacco and soybean plants.

The student wants to emphasize the aim of the research study. Which choice most effectively uses relevant information from the notes to accomplish this goal?

(A) Tobacco and soybean plants were shown to increase their crop yields after undergoing a technique that improves photosynthesis.

(B) Researchers tested a technique that changes how productive plants are when performing photosynthetic processes.

(C) The RIPE project was developed to apply bioengineering principles to plants, such as soybeans and tobacco.

(D) Researchers wanted to find a way to improve the efficiency of photosynthesis in order to positively impact food production.

IF YOU FINISH BEFORE TIME IS CALLED, YOU MAY CHECK YOUR WORK ON THIS MODULE ONLY.
ON TEST DAY, YOU WON'T BE ABLE TO MOVE ON TO THE NEXT MODULE UNTIL TIME EXPIRES.

STOP

K 555

Answer Key

Reading and Writing: Module A

1. **B**	8. **C**	15. **D**	22. **C**
2. **D**	9. **D**	16. **A**	23. **B**
3. **A**	10. **A**	17. **B**	24. **D**
4. **C**	11. **B**	18. **B**	25. **C**
5. **B**	12. **D**	19. **C**	26. **C**
6. **D**	13. **D**	20. **C**	27. **D**
7. **D**	14. **A**	21. **C**	

Instructions

Compare your answers to the answer key and enter the number of correct answers for this stage here: _____.
This is your raw score.

Take a 10-minute break and turn to the Math Routing Module to continue your test.

Explanations will be at the end of the Practice Test.

Reading and Writing: Module B

Mark your answers either on the pages that follow or on a separate sheet of paper. You will be scoring this Module before moving on to the Math stage.

DIRECTIONS

The questions in this section address a number of important reading and writing skills. Each question includes one or more passages, which may include a table or graph. Read each passage and question carefully, and then choose the best answer to the question based on the passage(s).

All questions in this section are multiple-choice with four answer choices. Each question has a single best answer.

1

The following text is from Louisa M. Alcott's 1868 novel *Little Women*.

Very few letters were written in those hard times that were not touching, especially those which fathers sent home. In this one little was said of the hardships endured, the dangers faced, or the homesickness conquered; it was a cheerful, hopeful letter, full of lively descriptions of camp life, marches, and military news; and only at the end did the writer's heart overflow with fatherly love and longing for the little girls at home.

As used in the text, what does the word "touching" most nearly mean?

- Ⓐ Communicating
- Ⓑ Neighborly
- Ⓒ Concerning
- Ⓓ Poignant

2

In "Yasmeen" (2018), the poet Safia Elhillo invested a substantial amount of time in finding the words that would best allow the biographical poem's layout to reflect the intentions of the poem. The lines of the poem are deliberately written and divided to be read as three unique poems: two of them are on opposite sides of a uniform chasm, to _____ the disconnection that is created by emigration, and the third is a combination of each line of the two poems, showing how her history changes without the separation. In doing so, the poem is a nuanced reflection of how a person's story is a combination of individual experiences (isolation) and the complex histories of their past (connection).

Which choice completes the text with the most logical and precise word or phrase?

- Ⓐ emphasize
- Ⓑ challenge
- Ⓒ cultivate
- Ⓓ disprove

CONTINUED ➡

3

Some agricultural engineers believe that plant yields cannot be improved by increasing the efficiency of photosynthesis. This view is _____ as it fails to take recent developments into account. Stephen Long has demonstrated the possibility of improving soybean yields by genetically modifying soybean plants to more quickly adjust their rates of photosynthesis.

Which choice completes the text with the most logical and precise word or phrase?

(A) tenuous

(B) disorienting

(C) nuanced

(D) unoriginal

4

The following text is adapted from J.M. Barrie's 1911 fantasy novel *Peter Pan*. In this early scene in the story, Peter Pan has just asked the tiny fairy Tinker Bell where his shadow, which had become detached from his body, is located in the children's bedroom that they have visited.

Tinker Bell said that the shadow was in the big box. She meant the chest of drawers, and Peter jumped at the drawers, scattering their contents to the floor with both hands, as kings toss halfpennies to the crowd. In a moment he had recovered his shadow, and in his delight he forgot that he had shut Tinker Bell up in the drawer.

Which choice best states the main purpose of the text?

(A) It presents Peter as a character who can display thoughtlessness.

(B) It describes the setting in which the story will take place.

(C) It provides a detailed character description of Tinker Bell and Peter.

(D) It establishes that the story takes place in a country that has a king.

5

By the mid-1950s, global public opinion was turning against above-ground nuclear testing, as many feared contamination by radioactive fallout. In response, the U.S. military began to explore the concept of subterranean nuclear testing. In the first test of this concept, codenamed Pascal-A, a nuclear weapon was lowered 500 feet below ground through a narrow shaft. The resulting explosion sent a jet of atomic fire out through the uncapped shaft and hundreds of feet into the air. During the second test, Pascal-B, a solid steel manhole cover was welded over the shaft. The force of the explosion again shot up through the shaft and punched into the manhole cover, instantly accelerating it to an estimated 150,000 mph—six times the speed needed to escape the Earth's gravity. Thus, in 1956, a simple manhole cover became the fastest-moving manmade object in history, a record it holds to this day.

Which choice best describes the function of the fourth sentence in the overall structure of the text?

(A) It establishes why the setup for Pascal-B differed from that of Pascal-A.

(B) It describes the second subterranean nuclear test.

(C) It restates why the global public was concerned about above-ground nuclear testing.

(D) It illustrates the complete lack of safety precautions being taken during the testing of nuclear bombs.

CONTINUED

6

Text 1

Great Zimbabwe is an ancient African settlement that was built in the 12th century and occupied through the 16th century. Shadreck Chirikure, an African archeologist, cites the many artifacts found there from other regions of Africa as evidence of vibrant trade within Africa.

Text 2

In 2020, 68% of Europe's exports were traded within the continent, and 59% of Asia's exports were traded within the continent, while only 17% of Africa's exports are traded within Africa.

Based on the texts, how would Shadreck Chirikuri (Text 1) most likely respond to the statistics in Text 2?

- (A) He would suggest that the extent of trade within Africa has changed since the time of Great Zimbabwe.

- (B) He would criticize African leaders for ignoring the example of Great Zimbabwe.

- (C) He would praise African governments for building strong trade relations outside the continent.

- (D) He would insist on a return to the trade practices during the time of Great Zimbabwe.

CONTINUED

Text 1

Many linguists reject the idea of linguistic determinism, instead maintaining that language itself is not a determining factor in human thoughts and actions. They claim that the limits of one's language do not rigidly constrict one's perspective or behaviors. As a simple example, if a certain language lacked a word that meant "jump," it would not follow that a speaker of that language would be unable to leap.

Text 2

Economist M. Keith Chen conducted a study in which he compared behaviors of speakers of different languages. Chen categorized the languages by whether they include a future tense (as in, "I *will* go to bed"). He found that speakers of languages *without* a strong future tense were more likely to engage in healthy proactive behaviors, such as saving for retirement.

Based on the texts, how would the linguists in Text 1 most likely respond to Chen's findings (Text 2)?

Ⓐ They would reject the validity of Chen's findings since its determination that speakers of languages with a strong future tense act differently than speakers of languages without a strong future tense supports the concept of linguistic determinism.

Ⓑ They would recommend that Chen conduct additional research to determine whether speakers of languages with and without a strong future tense are more or less likely to engage in potentially unhealthy behaviors.

Ⓒ They would argue that Chen's findings are irrelevant in the evaluation of linguistic determinism since he considered behaviors, and not just language variations, in his study.

Ⓓ They would assert that language did not itself determine the behaviors of the speakers and possibly posit an alternate explanation, such as language developing to reflect existing cultural norms, for Chen's findings.

CONTINUED

8

Although ancient Egypt may bring to mind grand-scale architecture projects and powerful government structures, ancient Egyptian elites still faced the mundane minutiae of managing their households on a day-to-day basis. The discovery and analysis of personal letters written by such elites gives a glimpse into this domestic world. A letter written by the general Nehesu, for instance, addresses an issue about sacks of grain that he had sent to his household but had gone missing, possibly due to infighting within the household. And several recovered letters of the priest Heqanakht include his responses to his household's complaints about their low food rations. As he travels, the priest also admonishes his son Merisu to carefully manage his property.

Which choice best states the main idea of the text?

(A) Generals like Nehesu and priests like Heqanakht belonged to the elite class in ancient Egypt.

(B) Ancient Egypt is best known for its architecture and system of government.

(C) Some ancient Egyptian letters reveal that elites had to manage their households.

(D) Archaeologists have discovered letters from ancient Egypt that allow them to study the historic society.

9

A Soviet textile factory worker, Valentina Tereshkova spent her free time training at a local aero club, where club members pursued flying and skydiving as hobbies. In 1959, at age 22, she made her first parachute jump. Tereshkova quickly became an expert in the field, recording over 120 jumps. When she applied for the female cosmonaut program at the dawn of the Space Age, Tereshkova's qualities drew the eye of Soviet officials. This is because the earliest Soviet space capsules were unable to decelerate fast enough when reentering Earth's atmosphere. In order to survive, cosmonauts were required to bail out of their capsules mid-descent and parachute back to the surface. Tereshkova was an ideal candidate for that task, which allowed her to become the first woman in space.

What is the main idea of the text?

(A) Tereshkova overcome discrimination to be considered for the Soviet cosmonaut program.

(B) The early Soviet space program was an incredibly dangerous experience for its cosmonauts.

(C) An experienced parachutist was desired by the Soviets since cosmonauts had to parachute during reentry.

(D) Tereshkova had mastered an important skill necessary to be an early Soviet cosmonaut.

CONTINUED

Practice Test

10

In the early 1700s, the first purely synthetic pigment was discovered when ferrous ferro-cyanide salts were exposed to oxidation and produced a rich, midnight blue color. The new pigment was colloquially called Prussian blue due to the location of its creation. Initially, its popularity was fueled by high demand from artists who used the pigment in paints, inks, lacquers, and dyes. Over a hundred years after the invention of Prussian blue, English Astronomer Sir John Herschel discovered that the compound's unique sensitivity to light allowed it to transfer drawings from one sheet to another; this process creates "blueprints." Today, Prussian blue is even prescribed in pill form to treat both radioactive cesium poisoning and thallium poisoning.

According to the passage, Prussian blue

(A) is a known cause of thallium poisoning.

(B) is a treatment for thallium poisoning.

(C) was discovered by Sir John Herschel.

(D) is created by a process called blueprinting.

11

The following text is from Washington Irving's 1924 short story "The Devil and Tom Walker."

The house and its inmates had altogether a bad name. Tom's wife was a tall termagant, fierce of temper, loud of tongue, and strong of arm. Her voice was often heard in wordy warfare with her husband; and his face sometimes showed signs that their conflicts were not confined to words. No one ventured, however, to interfere between them. The lonely wayfarer shrank within himself at the horrid clamor and clapper-clawing; eyed the den of discord askance; and hurried on his way, rejoicing, if a bachelor, in his celibacy.

According to the text, what is true about Tom?

(A) He refused to argue with his wife.

(B) His life as a bachelor was much happier.

(C) He welcomes visitors who interrupt his wife's arguments.

(D) His wife sometimes strikes him.

CONTINUED

12

Nanoengineers Joseph Wang and Liangfang Zhang hypothesized that direct application of antibiotics would be more efficient in curing infection than would a traditional IV injection. The researchers developed microrobots that could deliver antibiotics directly to the lungs of pneumonia-infected mice. They compared the success rate of a small dose of antibiotics delivered by the microrobots with the success rate of a traditional IV injection in curing pneumonia.

Which finding from Wang and Zhang's research, if true, would most directly support their hypothesis?

(A) The dosage needed to cure pneumonia via an IV injection was thousands of times larger than the dosage needed to cure pneumonia via the microrobots.

(B) The microrobot treatment had only a 50% success rate in curing pneumonia in the tested mice, while the IV injection treatment had a 100% success rate in curing pneumonia in the tested mice.

(C) The delivery of the treatment via microrobots showed an unanticipated side effect of causing additional inflammation in the lungs of the infected mice in the study.

(D) The microrobot treatment and the IV injection treatment both had a 100% success rate in curing pneumonia, but the microrobot treatment took twice as long to administer.

CONTINUED

13

R.U.R. (Rossum's Universal Robots) is a 1920 play by Karel Čapek, and it coined the word 'robot.' The play concerns artificial humans, called robots, who are treated as disposable machines despite being able to think for themselves. The head of the R.U.R. company, Harry Domin, justifies the exploitation of robots as making the world better:

Which quotation from a translation of *R.U.R.* most effectively illustrates Harry Domin's claim?

(A) "But a working machine must *not* play the piano, must not feel happy, must *not* do a whole lot of other things. A gasoline motor must not have tassels or ornaments."

(B) "The best worker is the one that is the *cheapest*. The one whose requirements are the *smallest*. Young Rossum invented a worker with the minimum amount of requirements."

(C) "But in ten years Rossum's Universal Robots will produce so much *corn*, so much *cloth*, so much everything that things will be practically without price. There will be no poverty."

(D) "Rossum's Universal Robot factory doesn't produce a uniform brand of robots. We have robots of *finer* and *coarser* grades. The best will live about *twenty* years."

CONTINUED

14

Percentage of Population with Health Insurance and Percentage of Students who Graduated High School in 7 U.S. States

State	With health insurance 2010 (%)	With health insurance 2018 (%)	Seniors graduating from high school 2010 (%)	Seniors graduating from high school 2018 (%)
California	74.7	82.7	80.7	82.9
Florida	70.2	76.1	85.3	88.0
Michigan	81.8	87.6	88.0	90.5
New York	83.1	87.6	84.4	86.5
North Carolina	76.5	81.1	83.6	87.4
Ohio	82.4	88.2	87.4	90.1
Texas	68.4	74.2	80.0	83.2

In 2010, the Affordable Care Act was signed into law, which made health insurance more widely available in the United States. Although the Affordable Care Act was targeted at uninsured adults, children could be included on a parent's plan until the child reached the age of 26. Since improved health care could lead to improved attendance, and attendance in high school is correlated with graduation, it is possible that the Affordable Care Act improved high school graduation rates, since _____

Which choice most effectively uses data from the table to complete the statement?

Ⓐ in each year, in every state shown, an improvement in the rate of health insurance correlated with an improvement in high school graduation rates.

Ⓑ in each year, in every state shown, high school graduation rates exceeded the rates of health insurance.

Ⓒ in 2018, Texas had 83.2% of high school students graduate, and 74.2% of its population covered by health insurance.

Ⓓ in 2010, Michigan had 88.0% of high school students graduate, and 81.8% of its population covered by health insurance.

15

In 1721, a Norwegian missionary discovered that the two known settlements on Greenland were completely deserted. These colonies, established by Norway about 1000 C.E., had enjoyed several centuries of relative prosperity. A new theory about the reason for the decline of these colonies is being proposed because recent analyses of the central Greenland ice core, coupled with other data, have indicated severe climate changes that some are now calling a "mini ice age." Such studies point toward a particularly warm period that occurred between the years 800 C.E. and 1300 C.E., which was then followed—unfortunately for those inhabiting even the most temperate portions of the island—by a steady decline in overall temperatures that lasted for nearly 600 years. The rise and fall of the Norse colonies in Greenland roughly mirrors this climate-based chronology indicating that _____

Which choice most logically completes the text?

(A) the colonists arrived during a time when the climate was uncharacteristically mild.

(B) climate change has not had important effects on populations earlier than our own.

(C) the settlement of Greenland by the Norse was misguided.

(D) ancient Greenland was not suitable for human habitation.

CONTINUED

16

Miami artist Romero Britto strives to create paintings and prints that reflect his "Happy Art Movement." The movement supports the production of art that promotes optimism. As such, Britto's art utilizes the bright colors of pop art and fun subject matter. For instance, his recent work *To Dream (House)* shows a home surrounded by four colorful hearts, and his 2010 painting _____ features a cartoonish reworking of Da Vinci's classic portrait.

Which choice completes the text so that it conforms to the conventions of Standard English?

Ⓐ *Mona Cat,*

Ⓑ *Mona Cat*

Ⓒ *Mona Cat—*

Ⓓ *Mona Cat:*

17

Interested in the logistics of how bacteria use their flagella appendages to move, _____ to study the atomic structures of these appendages, which the bacteria can coil into tiny propellers.

Which choice completes the text so that it conforms to the conventions of Standard English?

Ⓐ a technique called cryo-electron microscopy was used by researchers from the University of Virginia School of Medicine

Ⓑ cryo-electron microscopy, a technique at the University of Virginia School of Medicine, was used by researchers

Ⓒ there were researchers from the University of Virginia School of Medicine who utilized a technique called cryo-electron microscopy

Ⓓ researchers from the University of Virginia School of Medicine utilized a technique called cryo-electron microscopy

18

Although steam is typically associated with the nineteenth century, steam turbines remain central to electrical generation in the twenty-first century. Even nuclear reactors do not actually directly generate electricity. Instead, they produce the same thing that oil and coal power plants _____ heat. That heat warms something called a working fluid, either a liquid or gas, which is then piped through steam turbines, generating motion. The turning of the turbine generates electricity.

Which choice completes the text so that it conforms to the conventions of Standard English?

- (A) do, and
- (B) do
- (C) do—
- (D) do;

19

Akira Kurosawa's style is most famously demonstrated in his 1954 film *Seven Samurai*. Although the setting is medieval Japan, with peasants and samurai, the film's story is influenced by Western films: a village, terrorized by local bandits, turns to seven down-on-their-luck yet good-hearted samurai for the protection _____ Like movie cowboys, these samurai are romantic heroes, sure of their morals and battling clear forces of evil.

Which choice completes the text so that it conforms to the conventions of Standard English?

- (A) they need.
- (B) it needs.
- (C) he needs.
- (D) you need.

CONTINUED

Practice Test

20

The National Museum of African American History and Culture opened in Washington, D.C. in 2016. Its aptly named recent exhibition "Double Victory" explores and honors the past military service of African Americans since the time of the American Revolution. A major theme of the exhibit is that the nature of their struggles and successes, both on the home front and on the battlefields, _____ not just to gain a military victory over foreign enemies but also to secure the rights of full citizenship at home.

Which choice completes the text so that it conforms to the conventions of Standard English?

Ⓐ were

Ⓑ have been

Ⓒ being

Ⓓ was

21

A 2005 chemical analysis made headlines when it determined that the so-called Flower Portrait of William Shakespeare, long thought to have been painted during his lifetime, was actually painted not in 1609 but in the early 1800s. Paintings are not the only type of artworks that are subject to inaccurate _____ beginning in the 1950s, Brígido Lara created perhaps thousands of sculptural pieces that museums mistakenly displayed as authentic pre-Columbian artifacts.

Which choice completes the text so that it conforms to the conventions of Standard English?

Ⓐ dating, however

Ⓑ dating, however;

Ⓒ dating; however,

Ⓓ dating, however,

22

In the past, comparative coral reef research was limited, since the findings of individual dive teams were rarely compiled. In an effort to better coordinate reef research, marine biologists from the University of Tasmania created the Reef Life Survey, a collection of data from coral reefs throughout the _____ allows scientists to compare reefs and thus draw more accurate conclusions about the impact of factors like climate change on reef ecosystems.

Which choice completes the text so that it conforms to the conventions of Standard English?

Ⓐ world,

Ⓑ world, that

Ⓒ world that

Ⓓ world

CONTINUED

K 571

23

The Second Agricultural Revolution saw the widespread adoption of the four-course crop rotation. As farmers were able to leave less land lying fallow, this technique greatly increased crop yields and reduced the labor that was required for rural agriculture. _____ urban populations expanded and were able to supply workers for factories as the process of industrialization began.

Which choice completes the text with the most logical transition?

- (A) Still,
- (B) Thus,
- (C) For instance,
- (D) Specifically,

24

With its numbers dwindling due to overhunting in the nineteenth century, the bald eagle received special protections under the Bald Eagle Protection Act of 1940. _____ the act outlawed not just killing bald eagles but also interfering in any way with their nests.

Which choice completes the text with the most logical transition?

- (A) Consequently,
- (B) Similarly,
- (C) Furthermore,
- (D) Specifically,

25

Glove puppetry, a type of opera using cloth puppets with wood faces and hands, originated in seventeenth century southern China. It might not seem to have the potential to attract a mass audience in the modern world. _____ in Taiwan glove puppetry is combined with computer-generated graphics to produce popular wuxia stories, which are over-the-top martial arts tales, for popular films and television alike.

Which choice completes the text with the most logical transition?

- (A) Hence,
- (B) Further,
- (C) Nevertheless,
- (D) Consequently,

26

While researching a topic, a student has taken the following notes:

- In 2022, Kenna Lehmann and colleagues utilized a computerized learning model to analyze hyena vocalizations, or "whoops." They recorded hyenas at the Maasai Mara National Reserve in Kenya.

- The model indicated that hyenas likely have individualized "whoops" that may allow other hyenas to identify them.

- The model was twice as accurate at identifying an individual hyena after hearing three whoops than after hearing one whoop.

- The model was most accurate at identification after hearing seven whoops.

- The model's improved accuracy associated with increased whoops is evidence that hyenas repeat their vocalizations to increase the likelihood that they will be correctly identified.

The student wants to present the hyena study and its conclusions. Which choice most effectively uses relevant information from the notes to accomplish this goal?

Ⓐ As part of a 2022 study about hyenas from the Maasai Mara National Reserve, a computer learning model was used to analyze the characteristics of their whoops.

Ⓑ In 2022, researchers studied recordings of hyena whoops, which included analysis of the repetition of whoops by individual hyenas.

Ⓒ A 2022 computer learning model of Kenyan hyena whoops suggests that hyenas repeat their individual identifying whoops to improve the likelihood of identification.

Ⓓ Hyenas likely repeat their whoop vocalizations multiple times to make it easier for other hyenas to accurately identify them.

27

While researching a topic, a student has taken the following notes:

- A team from the Osaka Metropolitan University wanted to study the concept of embodied cognition.

- Embodied cognition posits that our *physical interactions* with an object are an essential component of how our brains process the meaning of the *word* for that object.

- The team showed subjects pairs of words that represent physical objects on a computer screen and asked them to compare the sizes of the objects.

- Some subjects in the study had their hands restrained from moving, while other subjects could move their hands freely.

- The restraining of hands was intended to prohibit subjects from making a physical movement, such as using their hands to demonstrate the size of an object, when reading the word pairs.

- When shown the words "fork" and "chair," subjects whose hands were restrained showed significantly less brain activity in brain scans than did subjects whose hands were not restrained.

The student wants to present the Osaka Metropolitan University's study and its conclusions. Which choice most effectively uses relevant information from the notes to accomplish this goal?

(A) A study on embodied cognition involving restrained movement while comparing the sizes of object words found less brain activity in the subjects with movement restraints.

(B) A study presented pairs of words for physical objects, such as "fork" and "chair," to subjects with and without movement restraints and required them to compare the sizes of the objects.

(C) A team of researchers discovered that subjects whose movement was limited demonstrated a significant reduction in brain activity compared to subjects whose movement was not restrained.

(D) The concept of embodied cognition can be researched by analyzing how the brain's ability to process the meaning of words for physical objects is impacted by the potential for physical movement.

IF YOU FINISH BEFORE TIME IS CALLED, YOU MAY CHECK YOUR WORK ON THIS MODULE ONLY. ON TEST DAY, YOU WON'T BE ABLE TO MOVE ON TO THE NEXT MODULE UNTIL TIME EXPIRES. STOP

574 K

Page intentionally left blank

Answer Key

Reading and Writing: Module B

1. **D**	8. **C**	15. **A**	22. **C**
2. **A**	9. **D**	16. **B**	23. **B**
3. **A**	10. **B**	17. **D**	24. **D**
4. **A**	11. **D**	18. **C**	25. **C**
5. **A**	12. **A**	19. **B**	26. **C**
6. **A**	13. **C**	20. **D**	27. **A**
7. **D**	14. **A**	21. **B**	

Instructions

Compare your answers to the answer key and enter the number of correct answers for this stage here: _____. This is your raw score.

Take a 10-minute break and turn to the Math Routing Module to continue your test.

Explanations will be at the end of the Practice Test.

Math: Routing Module

Mark your answers either on the pages that follow or on a separate sheet of paper. You will be scoring this Routing Module before going on to the final Math Module.

DIRECTIONS

- The questions in this section address a number of important math skills.

- Use of a calculator is permitted for all questions. A reference sheet, calculator, and these directions can be accessed throughout the test.

- Unless otherwise indicated:

  - All variables and expressions represent real numbers.

  - Figures provided are drawn to scale.

  - All figures lie in a plane.

  - The domain of a given function f is the set of all real numbers x for which $f(x)$ is a real number.

For **multiple-choice questions**, solve each question and choose the correct answer from the choices provided. Each multiple-choice question has a single correct answer.

For **student-produced response questions**, solve each question and enter your answer as described below:

- If you find **more than one correct answer**, enter only one answer.

- You can enter up to 5 characters for a **positive** answer and up to 6 characters (including the negative sign) for a **negative** answer.

- If your answer is a **fraction** that doesn't fit in the provided space, enter the decimal equivalent.

- If your answer is a **decimal** that doesn't fit in the provided space, enter it by truncating or rounding at the fourth digit.

- If your answer is a **mixed number** (such as $3\frac{1}{2}$), enter it as an improper fraction (**7/2**) or its decimal equivalent (**3.5**).

- Don't enter **symbols** such as a percent sign, comma, or dollar sign.

Examples

ANSWER	ACCEPTABLE WAY TO ANSWER	UNACCEPTABLE: WILL NOT RECEIVE CREDIT
3.5	3.5 3.50 7/2	31/2 3 1/2
$\frac{2}{3}$	2/3 .6666 .6667 0.666 0.667	0.66 .66 0.67 .67
$-\frac{1}{3}$	−1/3 −.3333 −0.333	−.33 −0.33

Reference:

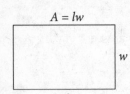

$$A = lw$$

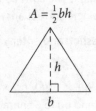

$$A = \frac{1}{2}bh$$

$$a^2 + b^2 = c^2$$

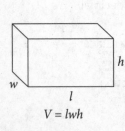

$$V = lwh$$

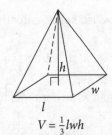

$$V = \frac{1}{3}lwh$$

sum of interior angles
of a triangle: 180°

CONTINUED ➡

1

$$\frac{4(n-2)+5}{2}=\frac{13-(9+4n)}{4}$$

In the equation above, what is the value of n?

Ⓐ $\dfrac{5}{6}$

Ⓑ $\dfrac{5}{2}$

Ⓒ   There is no value of n that satisfies the equation.

Ⓓ   There are infinitely many values of n that satisfy the equation.

2

The function $f(x)$ is defined as $f(x) = -3g(x)$, where $g(x) = x + 2$. What is the value of $f(5)$?

Ⓐ -21

Ⓑ -1

Ⓒ 4

Ⓓ 7

3

$$5(x-2) - 3x < 4x - 6$$

Solve the inequality for x.

Ⓐ $x < -2$

Ⓑ $x > -2$

Ⓒ $x < 2$

Ⓓ $x > 2$

4

$$y = x^2 - 10x + 24$$

Which of the following equivalent forms gives the x-intercepts of the parabola given by the equation shown?

Ⓐ $y = (x - 4)(x - 6)$

Ⓑ $y - 24 = x^2 - 10x$

Ⓒ $y + 1 = (x - 5)^2$

Ⓓ $y = x(x - 10) + 24$

5

If $m = \dfrac{1}{n^{-\frac{1}{4}}}$, where both $m > 0$ and $n > 0$, which of the following gives n in terms of m?

Ⓐ $n = m^4$

Ⓑ $n = \dfrac{1}{m^4}$

Ⓒ $n = \dfrac{1}{\sqrt[4]{m}}$

Ⓓ $n = m^{\frac{1}{4}}$

Practice Test

CONTINUED

6

A student is drawing the human skeleton to scale for a school assignment. The femur, or thigh bone, has an average length of 19.9 inches. If the scale factor of the drawing is one-eighth, approximately how long in inches should the student draw the femur?

Ⓐ 2

Ⓑ 2.5

Ⓒ 2.8

Ⓓ 3

7

What is the hypotenuse, in inches, of a right triangle with one leg of 20 inches and an area of 100 square inches?

Ⓐ 10

Ⓑ $10\sqrt{5}$

Ⓒ 20

Ⓓ $20\sqrt{5}$

8

$y = 3x - 1$

$y = \dfrac{5x + 8}{2}$

If (x, y) represents the solution to the system of equations shown, what is the value of y?

9

$k(10x - 5) = 2(3 + x) - 7$

If the equation shown has infinitely many solutions and k is a constant, what is the value of k?

10

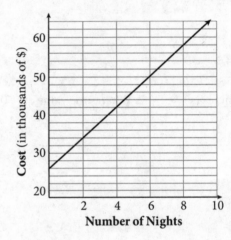

The graph shows the average cost of back surgery followed by a hospital stay. The hospital charges for the surgery itself plus all the costs associated with recovery care for each night the patient remains in the hospital. What is the average cost per night spent in the hospital?

Ⓐ $2,600

Ⓑ $4,000

Ⓒ $6,600

Ⓓ $8,000

CONTINUED ➡

Practice Test

11

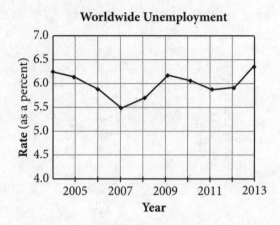

Worldwide Unemployment

The figure shows worldwide unemployment rates from 2004 to 2013. Which of the following statements is true?

(A) The graph is decreasing everywhere.

(B) The graph is increasing from 2007 to 2010.

(C) The graph is decreasing from 2004 to 2007 and from 2009 to 2011.

(D) The graph is increasing from 2007 to 2010 and decreasing from 2011 to 2013.

12

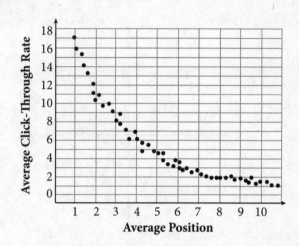

The scatterplot shows the relationship between a search result's position in a list of Internet search results and the number of people who clicked on that result's page. Which of the following regression types would be the best model for this data?

(A) A linear function

(B) A quadratic function

(C) A polynomial function

(D) An exponential function

CONTINUED ➤

13

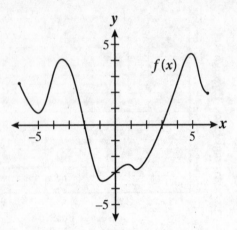

The figure shows the graph of $f(x)$. For which value(s) of x does $f(x)$ equal 0?

Ⓐ 3 only

Ⓑ −3 only

Ⓒ −2 and 3

Ⓓ −3, −2, and 3

14

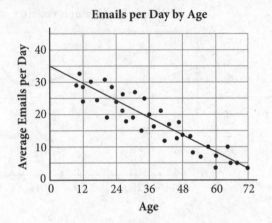

The scatterplot shows the average number of emails received daily plotted by the age of the recipient. Which of the following equations best represents the line of best fit for the data shown?

Ⓐ $y = -2.4x + 36$

Ⓑ $y = -1.2x + 40$

Ⓒ $y = -0.8x + 40$

Ⓓ $y = -0.4x + 36$

15

Main Street and 2nd Street are parallel one-way streets. Main Street runs south and 2nd Street, north. A new one-way road will run southeast and cross both streets. Cars turning off Main Street will turn 125° onto the new road. What angle would cars turning off 2nd Street make onto the new road?

Ⓐ 55°

Ⓑ 65°

Ⓒ 125°

Ⓓ 235°

CONTINUED ➡

16

Which of the following systems of inequalities has no solution?

Ⓐ $\begin{cases} y \geq x \\ y \leq 2x \end{cases}$

Ⓑ $\begin{cases} y \geq x \\ y \leq -x \end{cases}$

Ⓒ $\begin{cases} y \geq x + 1 \\ y \leq x - 1 \end{cases}$

Ⓓ $\begin{cases} y \geq -x + 1 \\ y \leq x - 1 \end{cases}$

17

A truck is carrying 410 pounds of bookcases and tables. The weight of each bookcase is 25 pounds, and the weight of each table is 37 pounds. If there are 14 total pieces of furniture in the truck, how many more bookcases than tables are on the truck?

18

$$\frac{4x}{x - 7} + \frac{5}{35 - 5x} = \frac{A}{B}$$

In the expression shown, what is A?

Ⓐ $5 + 20x$

Ⓑ $20 + 5x$

Ⓒ $4x + 5$

Ⓓ $5 - 20x$

19

If the equation of the parabola shown in the graph is written in standard quadratic form, $y = ax^2 + bx + c$, and $a = -1$, then what is the value of b?

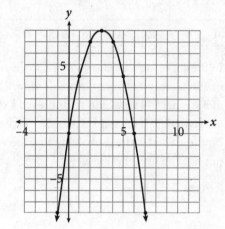

20

A stock index opened at 306, but by the end of the day, the index dropped by 2 percent. The following day, the index lost 13 percent, followed by another 12 percent loss on the third day. What was the total percent decrease over the three days?

Practice Test

21

Registered to Vote?	1	2	3	4	5	Total
Yes	112	104	228	487	163	1,094
No	28	76	48	158	54	364
Total	140	180	276	645	217	1,458

In the survey results shown in the table, responses of 1 or 2 represent an unfavorable view, a response of 3 is a neutral view, and responses of 4 or 5 are favorable. If one registered voter is chosen at random, what is the probability that the voter does not hold an unfavorable view?

(A) 40.6%

(B) 59.4%

(C) 78.1%

(D) 80.3%

22

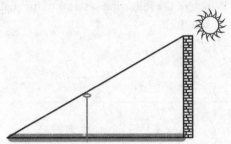

Note: Figure not drawn to scale.

A toy saber is stuck at a right angle into the ground 4 inches deep. It casts a shadow that is 4 feet long. The brick wall casts a shadow three times that long. If the wall is 7 feet 6 inches tall, how many inches long is the toy saber?

IF YOU FINISH BEFORE TIME IS CALLED, YOU MAY CHECK YOUR WORK ON THIS MODULE ONLY.
ON TEST DAY, YOU WON'T BE ABLE TO MOVE ON TO THE NEXT MODULE UNTIL TIME EXPIRES. STOP

584 K

Page intentionally left blank

Answer Key

Math: Routing Module

1.	**A**	9.	**1/5, 0.2, or .2**	17.	**4**
2.	**A**	10.	**B**	18.	**D**
3.	**B**	11.	**C**	19.	**6**
4.	**A**	12.	**D**	20.	**24.97**
5.	**A**	13.	**C**	21.	**D**
6.	**B**	14.	**D**	22.	**34**
7.	**B**	15.	**A**		
8.	**29**	16.	**C**		

Instructions

Compare your answers to the answer key and enter the number of correct answers for this stage here: _____.
This is your raw score.

If you scored less than 14 correct, turn to Math: Module A and continue your test.

If you had 14 or more correct in this routing stage, turn to Math: Module B and continue your test.

Explanations will be at the end of the Practice Test.

Math: Module A

Mark your answers either on the pages that follow or on a separate sheet of paper. You will be scoring this Module and using the results to find your final Math score.

DIRECTIONS

- The questions in this section address a number of important math skills.
- Use of a calculator is permitted for all questions. A reference sheet, calculator, and these directions can be accessed throughout the test.
- Unless otherwise indicated:
  - All variables and expressions represent real numbers.
  - Figures provided are drawn to scale.
  - All figures lie in a plane.
  - The domain of a given function f is the set of all real numbers x for which $f(x)$ is a real number.

For **multiple-choice questions**, solve each question and choose the correct answer from the choices provided. Each multiple-choice question has a single correct answer.

For **student-produced response questions**, solve each question and enter your answer as described below:

- If you find **more than one correct answer**, enter only one answer.
- You can enter up to 5 characters for a **positive** answer and up to 6 characters (including the negative sign) for a **negative** answer.
- If your answer is a **fraction** that doesn't fit in the provided space, enter the decimal equivalent.
- If your answer is a **decimal** that doesn't fit in the provided space, enter it by truncating or rounding at the fourth digit.
- If your answer is a **mixed number** (such as $3\frac{1}{2}$), enter it as an improper fraction (**7/2**) or its decimal equivalent (**3.5**).
- Don't enter **symbols** such as a percent sign, comma, or dollar sign.

Examples

ANSWER	ACCEPTABLE WAY TO ANSWER	UNACCEPTABLE: WILL NOT RECEIVE CREDIT
3.5	3.5 3.50 7/2	31/2 3 1/2
$\frac{2}{3}$	2/3 .6666 .6667 0.666 0.667	0.66 .66 0.67 .67
$-\frac{1}{3}$	−1/3 −.3333 −0.333	−.33 −0.33

Reference:

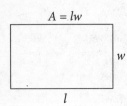

$A = lw$

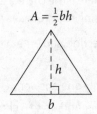

$A = \frac{1}{2}bh$

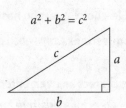

$a^2 + b^2 = c^2$

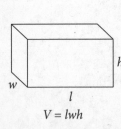

$V = lwh$

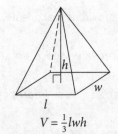

$V = \frac{1}{3}lwh$

sum of interior angles
of a triangle: 180°

CONTINUED

Practice Test

1

The "break-even point" is the point at which sales equal expenses. A company's expenses are modeled by the function $E(n) = 11{,}625 + 4.85n$, where n represents the number of units the manufacturer sells in a month. The company's sales are modeled by the function $S(n) = 9.50n$. How many units must the company sell per month to reach the break-even point?

Ⓐ 810

Ⓑ 1,225

Ⓒ 2,100

Ⓓ 2,500

2

$$4x + y = -5$$

$$-4x - 2y = -2$$

What is the y-coordinate of the solution to the system of equations shown?

Ⓐ −7

Ⓑ −3

Ⓒ 0

Ⓓ 7

3

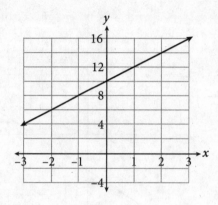

The figure shows the graph of linear function f. Where does f intersect the x-axis?

Ⓐ −5.5

Ⓑ −5

Ⓒ −4.5

Ⓓ −4

4

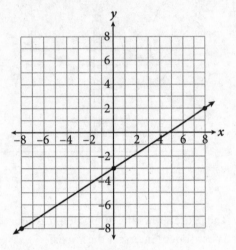

What is the average rate of change for the line graphed in the figure?

_____

5

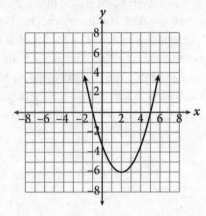

Which of the following could be the factored form of the equation graphed in the figure shown?

Ⓐ $y = \frac{1}{5}(x - 2)(x + 6)$

Ⓑ $y = \frac{1}{5}(x + 2)(x - 6)$

Ⓒ $y = \frac{2}{3}(x - 1)(x + 5)$

Ⓓ $y = \frac{2}{3}(x + 1)(x - 5)$

6

Which of the following expressions is equivalent to $25x^2 - \frac{4}{9}$?

Ⓐ $\sqrt{5x - \frac{2}{3}}$

Ⓑ $x\left(5x - \frac{2}{3}\right)$

Ⓒ $\left(5x + \frac{2}{3}\right)\left(5x - \frac{2}{3}\right)$

Ⓓ $\left(25x + \frac{2}{3}\right)\left(25x - \frac{2}{3}\right)$

CONTINUED ➡

Practice Test

7

Boeing Jets	Coach	Business	First Class
747–400	310	52	12
767–300	151	26	6
777–200	194	37	16
777–300	227	52	8

The table shows the seating configuration for several commercial airplanes. If the last seat available is on one of the two Boeing 777s, what is the probability that the seat is a Business Class seat if all seats have an equal chance of being the last one available?

Ⓐ $\frac{1}{6}$

Ⓑ $\frac{1}{4}$

Ⓒ $\frac{1}{3}$

Ⓓ $\frac{1}{2}$

8

Oil is sold by the barrel, and 1 barrel = 42 gallons. An oil company has an order for 2,500 barrels. The machine filling the barrels pumps at a rate of 37.5 gallons per minute. If the company uses 8 machines simultaneously, how long will it take to fill all the barrels in the order?

Ⓐ 5 hours and 50 minutes

Ⓑ 12 hours and 45 minutes

Ⓒ 28 hours and 30 minutes

Ⓓ 46 hours and 40 minutes

9

Alex scored approximately 12 percent lower than Chris scored on the exam. Chris scored 89. What is Alex's exam score rounded to the nearest integer?

_____

10

The value of cos 40° is the same as which of the following?

Ⓐ sin 50°

Ⓑ sin(−40°)

Ⓒ cos(−50°)

Ⓓ cos 140°

11

The ratio of the lengths of the sides of a certain right triangle is 3:4:5. If the length of the shorter leg is 9 units, what is the area of the triangle, in square units?

_____

CONTINUED

12

A tankless hot water heater costs $160 more than twice as much as a conventional hot water heater. If both water heaters cost $1,000 together, how many more dollars does the tankless water heater cost than the conventional one?

13

If $0 < \dfrac{d}{2} + 1 \le \dfrac{8}{5}$, which of the following is not a possible value of d?

Ⓐ -2

Ⓑ $-\dfrac{6}{5}$

Ⓒ 0

Ⓓ $\dfrac{6}{5}$

14

Sara is buying laundry detergent, which is on sale for 30 percent off its regular price of $8.00. She is also buying dog food, which she can buy at three cans for $4.00. Which of the following represents the total cost, before tax, if Sara buys x bottles of laundry detergent and 12 cans of dog food?

Ⓐ $C = 2.4x + 48$

Ⓑ $C = 5.6x + 16$

Ⓒ $C = 5.6x + 48$

Ⓓ $C = 8.4x + 16$

15

If $|3x - 2 + 4x| < 7$, which of the following is a possible value for x?

Ⓐ $-\dfrac{10}{7}$

Ⓑ $-\dfrac{5}{7}$

Ⓒ $\dfrac{4}{7}$

Ⓓ $\dfrac{10}{7}$

16

What are the roots of $x^2 + 10x = -5$?

Ⓐ $-5 + 2\sqrt{5}, -5 - 2\sqrt{5}$

Ⓑ $2, 5$

Ⓒ $7\sqrt{5}, -3\sqrt{5}$

Ⓓ $3\sqrt{5}, -7\sqrt{5}$

CONTINUED

Practice Test

17

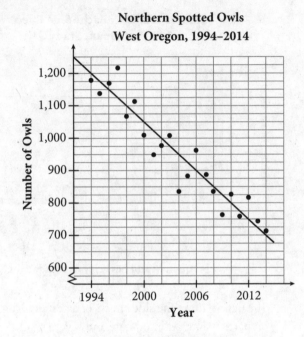

The scatterplot shows the populations of the Northern Spotted Owl in a certain region from 1994 to 2014. Based on the line of best fit shown in the figure, which of the following values most accurately reflects the average change per year in the number of Northern Spotted Owls?

Ⓐ   −25

Ⓑ   −0.04

Ⓒ   0.04

Ⓓ   25

18

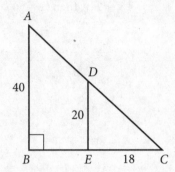

In the figure above, AB and DE are parallel. What is the length of AC?

Ⓐ $2\sqrt{181}$

Ⓑ   36

Ⓒ $4\sqrt{181}$

Ⓓ   54

19

If $x^3 - 5x^2 - 29x + k$ is evenly divisible by $x - 7$, what is the value of k?

20

If $x^2 + y^2 = 16 - 2xy$, then $(x + y)^4 =$

Ⓐ 16

Ⓑ 32

Ⓒ 128

Ⓓ 256

21

An exponential function is given in the form
$f(x) = a \bullet b^x$. If $f(0) = 3$ and $f(1) = 15$, what is the
value of $f(-2)$?

22

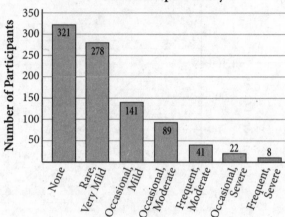

**Clinical Trial: Headache Side Effect
900-Participant Study**

Frequency and Severity of Headaches

The figure shows the side effects of a certain drug
on participants. All moderate and severe headaches are considered adverse reactions. Which of
the following best describes the data?

Ⓐ The data is symmetric with more than 50 percent of participants having adverse reactions.

Ⓑ The data is skewed to the right with more
than 50 percent of participants having adverse
reactions.

Ⓒ The data is skewed to the right with more
than 75 percent of participants failing to have
adverse reactions.

Ⓓ The data is skewed to the right with approximately 50 percent of participants having no
reaction at all.

IF YOU FINISH BEFORE TIME IS CALLED, YOU MAY CHECK YOUR WORK ON THIS MODULE ONLY. **STOP**

Page intentionally left blank

Answer Key

Math: Module A

1.	D	9.	78	17.	A
2.	D	10.	A	18.	C
3.	B	11.	54	19.	105
4.	5/8, 0.625, or .625	12.	440	20.	D
5.	D	13.	A	21.	3/25, 0.12, or .12
6.	C	14.	B	22.	C
7.	A	15.	C		
8.	A	16.	A		

Instructions

Compare your answers to the answer key and enter the number of correct answers for this module here: _____.
This is your raw score.

Go to the How to Score Your Practice Test section to determine your score.

Explanations will be at the end of the Practice Test.

Math: Module B

Mark your answers either on the pages that follow or on a separate sheet of paper. You will be scoring this Module and using the results to find your final Math score.

DIRECTIONS

- The questions in this section address a number of important math skills.

- Use of a calculator is permitted for all questions. A reference sheet, calculator, and these directions can be accessed throughout the test.

- Unless otherwise indicated:

  - All variables and expressions represent real numbers.

  - Figures provided are drawn to scale.

  - All figures lie in a plane.

  - The domain of a given function f is the set of all real numbers x for which $f(x)$ is a real number.

For **multiple-choice questions**, solve each question and choose the correct answer from the choices provided. Each multiple-choice question has a single correct answer.

For **student-produced response questions**, solve each question and enter your answer as described below:

- If you find **more than one correct answer**, enter only one answer.

- You can enter up to 5 characters for a **positive** answer and up to 6 characters (including the negative sign) for a **negative** answer.

- If your answer is a **fraction** that doesn't fit in the provided space, enter the decimal equivalent.

- If your answer is a **decimal** that doesn't fit in the provided space, enter it by truncating or rounding at the fourth digit.

- If your answer is a **mixed number** (such as $3\frac{1}{2}$), enter it as an improper fraction (**7/2**) or its decimal equivalent (**3.5**).

- Don't enter **symbols** such as a percent sign, comma, or dollar sign.

Examples

ANSWER	ACCEPTABLE WAY TO ANSWER	UNACCEPTABLE: WILL NOT RECEIVE CREDIT
3.5	3.5 3.50 7/2	31/2 3 1/2
$\frac{2}{3}$	2/3 .6666 .6667 0.666 0.667	0.66 .66 0.67 .67
$-\frac{1}{3}$	−1/3 −.3333 −0.333	−.33 −0.33

Reference:

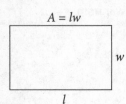

$A = lw$

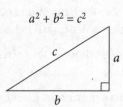

$A = \frac{1}{2}bh$

$a^2 + b^2 = c^2$

sum of interior angles
of a triangle: 180°

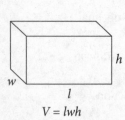

$V = lwh$

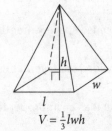

$V = \frac{1}{3}lwh$

CONTINUED ▶

1

If $f(x) = x + 1$ and $g(x) = x - 4$ then what is the value of $f(g(2))$?

(A) -2

(B) -1

(C) 2

(D) 3

2

A weed covered 3,200 acres of a farmer's cropland, so the farmer tried a new herbicide. The herbicide cleared the weed from 2,800 acres of the cropland. If there are 30,000 acres of cropland in the region, how many acres would still be covered if all the farmers in the region used the herbicide?

(A) 3,750

(B) 4,000

(C) 26,000

(D) 26,250

3

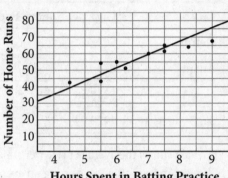

The scatterplot shows data collected from 10 major league baseball players comparing the average weekly time each one spent in batting practice and the number of home runs each hit in the season. The line of best fit for the data is also shown. What does the slope of the line represent?

(A) The estimated time spent in batting practice by a player who hits zero home runs

(B) The estimated number of single-season home runs hit by a player who spends zero hours in batting practice

(C) The estimated increase in time that a player spends in batting practice for each home run that he hits in a single season

(D) The estimated increase in the number of single-season home runs hit by a player for each hour he spends in batting practice

Practice Test

CONTINUED

4

City	Cost per Square Foot
Detroit	$62.45
Atlanta	$74.19
New York City	$288.58
San Francisco	$420.99

The table shows the average price per square foot of houses in four cities. Assuming an average home size of 1,500 to 2,000 square feet, which inequality represents how much more in dollars a house in New York City would cost than in Detroit?

Ⓐ $x \geq 226.13$

Ⓑ $62.45 \leq x \leq 288.58$

Ⓒ $93,675 \leq x \leq 432,870$

Ⓓ $339,195 \leq x \leq 452,260$

5

$$\frac{1}{3}x + \frac{1}{2}y = 5$$
$$kx - 4y = 16$$

If the system of linear equations shown has no solution, and k is a constant, what is the value of k?

6

The average wait time per ride at an amusement park increased from 5 minutes when it opened at 10 a.m. to 15 minutes at 10:30 a.m. If the wait time increased at a constant rate, which of the following functions f best models the wait time, in minutes, for h hours the amusement park is open?

Ⓐ $f(h) = \frac{1}{3}h + \frac{1}{12}$

Ⓑ $f(h) = \frac{1}{3}h + 5$

Ⓒ $f(h) = 20h + \frac{1}{12}$

Ⓓ $f(h) = 20h + 5$

7

After implementing a pollution reduction program, the Environmental Protection Agency (EPA) calculated that air pollution should decrease by approximately 8 percent each year. What kind of function could be used to model the amount of air pollution in this city over the next several years?

Ⓐ A linear function

Ⓑ A quadratic function

Ⓒ A polynomial function

Ⓓ An exponential function

CONTINUED

8

Which of the following are the roots of the equation $3x^2 - 6x - 5 = 0$?

Ⓐ $1 \pm 2\sqrt{6}$

Ⓑ $\dfrac{1 \pm 2\sqrt{2}}{3}$

Ⓒ $\dfrac{3 \pm 2\sqrt{2}}{3}$

Ⓓ $\dfrac{3 \pm 2\sqrt{6}}{3}$

9

	Jan	Feb	Mar	Apr
Company A	54	146	238	330
Company B	15	30	60	120

Company A and Company B sell two similar toys. The end-of-the-month sales figures for each are recorded in the table shown. Based on the data in the table, from which month will Company B's sales start to exceed Company's A sales?

Ⓐ   May

Ⓑ   June

Ⓒ   July

Ⓓ   August

10

Driver's Education Test Results

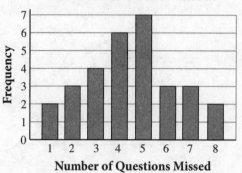

(Bar graph: x-axis "Number of Questions Missed" from 1 to 8; y-axis "Frequency" from 0 to 7. Values: 1→2, 2→3, 3→4, 4→6, 5→7, 6→3, 7→3, 8→2.)

Mr. Juno took his driver's education class to the Department of Motor Vehicles to take their driver's license test. The number of questions missed by each student in the class is recorded in the bar graph above. Which of the following statements is true?

Ⓐ   More than half of the students missed 5 or more questions.

Ⓑ   The mean number of questions missed was between 4 and 5.

Ⓒ   More students missed 3 questions than any other number of questions.

Ⓓ   Thirty-six students from Mr. Juno's class took the driver's license test that day.

CONTINUED ▶   **K**   601

11

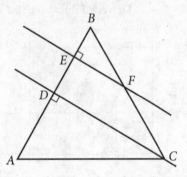

Triangle *ABC* shown is an equilateral triangle cut by two parallel lines. If the ratio of *BF* to *FC* is 3:4 and *BE* = 3, what is the length of *DE*?

12

A taxi in the city charges $3.00 for the first $\frac{1}{4}$ mile, plus $0.25 for each additional $\frac{1}{8}$ mile. Eric can spend no more than $20.00 on a taxi ride. Which inequality represents the number of miles, *m*, that Eric could travel without exceeding his limit?

- (A) $2.5 + 2m \leq 20$

- (B) $3 + 0.25m \leq 20$

- (C) $3 + 2m \leq 20$

- (D) $12 + 2m \leq 20$

13

A store models the monthly demand for an item by the function $q(p) = -200p + 3,400$, where q is the quantity sold and p is the selling price in dollars. It costs $7 to produce the item. How much more profit per month can be earned by selling the item at $12 instead of $10? (Profit = sales − costs)

14

If the graph of the equation $y = ax^2 + bx + c$ passes through the points (0, 2), (−6, −7), and (8, −14), what is the value of $a + b + c$?

- (A) 0

- (B) 0.25

- (C) 1.75

- (D) 2

15

The Midnight Zone is the layer of the Earth's oceans that is greater than 1,000 meters and less than 4,000 meters below the ocean surface. Which of the following inequalities describes all possible depths, *x*, in meters, below the ocean surface that are in the Midnight Zone?

- (A) $|x - 2,500| < 1,500$

- (B) $|x + 2,500| < 1,500$

- (C) $|x - 1,500| < 2,500$

- (D) $|x + 1,500| < 2,500$

CONTINUED

16

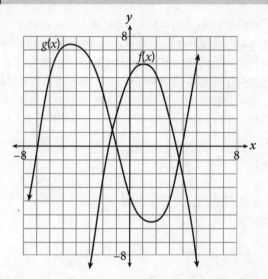

The graph shows a quadratic function $f(x)$ and a cubic function $g(x)$. Based on the graph, what is the value of $(f - g)(3)$, assuming all integer values?

_____

17

How many real values of x satisfy the quadratic equation $9x^2 - 12x + 4 = 0$?

Ⓐ 0

Ⓑ 1

Ⓒ 2

Ⓓ 4

18

At what value(s) of x do the graphs of $y = -2x + 1$ and $y = 2x^2 + 5x + 4$ intersect?

Ⓐ -8 and $\frac{1}{2}$

Ⓑ -3 and $-\frac{1}{2}$

Ⓒ -3 and 3

Ⓓ $-\frac{1}{2}$ and 3

19

Years at Company	Technicians	Sales Workers
$y < 1$	38	30
$1 \leq y \leq 3$	15	19
$y > 3$	54	48

The table shows the number of employees in each of two job positions categorized by the number of years the employees have been at the company. If four employees are chosen at random, what is the probability that all of them will have been with the company for longer than three years?

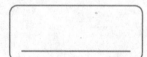

_____

CONTINUED

Practice Test

K　603

20

A bakery makes three sizes of muffins in the following ratios: mini to regular equals 5 to 2 and regular to jumbo equals 5 to 4. The bakery decided to offer only mini and jumbo muffins but wants to keep the sizes in the same ratio. What ratio of mini to jumbo should the bakery use?

Ⓐ 1:1

Ⓑ 4:2

Ⓒ 5:2

Ⓓ 25:8

21

A grain producer fills a rectangular grain bin that is x feet wide, $\frac{3}{2}x$ feet long, and $\frac{1}{2}x$ feet tall with wheat but leaves the top 5 percent of the bin empty to allow for air circulation. If the bin contains 5,700 cubic feet of wheat, what is the length, in feet, of the grain bin?

Ⓐ 10

Ⓑ 20

Ⓒ 27

Ⓓ 30

22

An elevator runs along a diagonal track approximately 170 feet long that connects the upper and lower levels of a station. The angle formed between the track and the bottom level is 30 degrees. What is the approximate vertical distance in feet between the upper and lower levels of the station?

[_____]

IF YOU FINISH BEFORE TIME IS CALLED, YOU MAY CHECK YOUR WORK ON THIS MODULE ONLY. **STOP**

Page intentionally left blank

Answer Key

Math: Module B

1. **B**
2. **A**
3. **D**
4. **D**
5. **−8/3, −2.666, or −2.667**
6. **D**
7. **D**
8. **D**

9. **C**
10. **B**
11. **4**
12. **A**
13. **800**
14. **C**
15. **A**
16. **6**

17. **B**
18. **B**
19. **.0607, .0606, 0.061, or 0.060**
20. **D**
21. **D**
22. **85**

Instructions

Compare your answers to the answer key and enter the number of correct answers for this module here: _____. This is your raw score.

Go to the How to Score Your Practice Test section to determine your score.

Explanations will be at the end of the Practice Test.

How to Score Your Practice Test

Because this is a digital and adaptive exam, scores can vary widely based on the number of correct answers. The following tables give an estimated score range based on the most common scoring logic. Please visit your online resources for the most up-to-date scoring information

If you were directed to Reading and Writing Module A:

Add the raw score from your Reading and Writing: Routing Module to your raw score from Reading and Writing: Module A.

_____ (Routing) + _____ (Module A) = _____ (Your Total Raw Reading and Writing Score)

Use this table to convert your raw score into your scaled score:

Reading and Writing		Reading and Writing		Reading and Writing	
TOTAL Raw Score	Scaled Score	TOTAL Raw Score	Scaled Score	TOTAL Raw Score	Scaled Score
0	160	21	390	42	580
1	160	22	400	43	590
2	160	23	410	44	600
3	160	24	420	45	610
4	160	25	430	46	N/A
5	160	26	440	47	N/A
6	160	27	450	48	N/A
7	170	28	450	49	N/A
8	180	29	460	50	N/A
9	190	30	470	51	N/A
10	210	31	480	52	N/A
11	240	32	490	53	N/A
12	250	33	500	54	N/A
13	260	34	510		
14	290	35	520		
15	310	36	530		
16	340	37	530		
17	350	38	540		
18	360	39	550		
19	380	40	560		
20	380	41	570		

Your scaled Reading and Writing score from the table is: _____

If you were directed to Reading and Writing Module B:

Add the raw score from your Reading and Writing: Routing Module to your raw score from Reading and Writing: Module B.

_____ (Routing) + _____ (Module B) = _____ (Your Total Raw Reading and Writing Score)

Use this table to convert your raw score into your scaled score:

Reading and Writing		Reading and Writing		Reading and Writing	
TOTAL Raw Score	Scaled Score	TOTAL Raw Score	Scaled Score	TOTAL Raw Score	Scaled Score
0	N/A	21	420	42	600
1	N/A	22	420	43	610
2	N/A	23	430	44	620
3	N/A	24	440	45	630
4	N/A	25	450	46	640
5	N/A	26	460	47	650
6	N/A	27	460	48	660
7	N/A	28	470	49	670
8	N/A	29	480	50	680
9	N/A	30	490	51	690
10	N/A	31	500	52	720
11	N/A	32	510	53	740
12	N/A	33	520	54	760
13	N/A	34	530		
14	N/A	35	540		
15	N/A	36	540		
16	N/A	37	550		
17	N/A	38	560		
18	N/A	39	570		
19	400	40	580		
20	410	41	590		

Your scaled Reading and Writing score from the table is: _____

If you were directed to Math Stage Module A:

Add the raw score from your Math: Routing Module to your raw score from Math: Module A.

_____ (Routing) + _____ (Module A) = _____ (Your Total Raw Math Score)

Use this table to convert your raw score into your scaled score:

Math		Math	
TOTAL Raw Score	Scaled Score	TOTAL Raw Score	Scaled Score
0	160	23	430
1	160	24	440
2	160	25	450
3	160	26	460
4	160	27	480
5	160	28	500
6	180	29	510
7	200	30	520
8	210	31	530
9	230	32	550
10	250	33	570
11	290	34	580
12	310	35	590
13	320	36	N/A
14	330	37	N/A
15	340	38	N/A
16	350	39	N/A
17	360	40	N/A
18	380	41	N/A
19	390	42	N/A
20	400	43	N/A
21	410	44	N/A
22	420		

Your scaled Math score from the table is: _____

If you were directed to Math Stage Module B:

Add the raw score from your Math: Routing Module to your raw score from Math: Module A.

_____ (Routing) + _____ (Module B) = _____ (Your Total Raw Math Score)

Use this table to convert your raw score into your scaled score:

Math		Math	
TOTAL Raw Score	Scaled Score	TOTAL Raw Score	Scaled Score
0	N/A	23	450
1	N/A	24	460
2	N/A	25	480
3	N/A	26	500
4	N/A	27	510
5	N/A	28	520
6	N/A	29	530
7	N/A	30	550
8	N/A	31	560
9	N/A	32	580
10	N/A	33	600
11	N/A	34	610
12	N/A	35	620
13	N/A	36	640
14	330	37	660
15	340	38	680
16	350	39	700
17	370	40	720
18	390	41	740
19	400	42	750
20	410	43	760
21	420	44	760
22	440		

Your scaled Math score from the table is: _____

To find your composite score, add your Reading and Writing score to your Math score.

_____ (Reading and Writing) + _____ (Math) = _____ (your composite score)

Reading and Writing: Routing Module Answers and Explanations

1.   B
Difficulty: Easy

Category: Craft and Structure

Getting to the Answer: The sentence that contains the blank pertains to the observations that Gould had of the beetle that appeared to be "swimming upside down," but it was revealed that the beetle was actually walking. The second sentence of the passage starts with the contrasting transition word "However," indicating that the observed beetle differs from other insects that use the water's surface tension to walk across it. Predict that the correct choice reflects this contrast, that the observed beetle has a *reversed* or *opposing* walking method. Choice **(B)**, which means *reversed in position* or *upside down*, is a match and is correct.

Choice (A) is incorrect; "ordinary," or *usual*, does not logically fit the passage, because this is the "first" documented observation. (C) is incorrect because "chaotic," or *disorderly,* is not implied in the text; the text only states that the beetle is walking underneath the surface. (D) is incorrect because the beetle's rate of motion is never mentioned.

2.   C
Difficulty: Medium

Category: Craft and Structure

Getting to the Answer: The immediate context indicates that the doctor believes the narrator's conduct to be "beneath the dignity of a sensible man." More context clues are needed to understand what the doctor observed to make that judgment. In the first two sentences, the speaker states that he was "playing," "romp[ing]," and "tickl[ing]" the children. Predict that it is the narrator's *actions* or *interactions with the children* that the doctor has determined to be undignified. Eliminate (A) and (B) because, while both are alternative meanings of "conduct," they both imply a *watchful guardianship* as opposed to the interactive engagement that the speaker has with the children. Choice **(C)** most nearly matches that prediction; "Behavior" means *the way in which one conducts oneself.* Incorrect answer choice (D), or *the act of governing*, does not logically reflect the equal engagement that both the children and narrator have in the activities.

3.   D
Difficulty: Hard

Category: Craft and Structure

Getting to the Answer: To determine the word that logically fits in the blank, examine the context of the passage to predict the word's meaning. The blank refers to an adjective, along with "versatile," that describes the toy. The rest of the passage describes features of the toy: it comes with various pieces, the pieces all fit together, it can be used without instructions, and it can be built into "practically limitless" combinations. This last feature reflects the "versatil[ity]" mentioned in the first sentence. Other features (its pieces fitting together and its not needing instructions) seem to reflect that the toy is *easy to use*. Use this, along with *versatile*, as your prediction. Choice **(D)** is correct because "intuitive" means *easily understood*.

Choice (A) is incorrect because "inscrutable" means *not easily understood*, the opposite of the required meaning. Choice (B) is incorrect because "tedious" means *boring* or *causing weariness*; nothing in the toy's description suggests that it induces boredom or tiredness. Choice (C) also provides the opposite of the required meaning, as "constricting" means *to compress* or *to inhibit*, while the toy is described as allowing for "practically limitless" combinations.

4.   A
Difficulty: Easy

Category: Craft and Structure

Getting to the Answer: In the first sentence, the author defines microloans and presents the view of "some financial experts" that microloans may help poor people improve their lives. In the second sentence, the sentence of interest, the author cites the small loan to these Bangladeshi women as an example of a microloan. This matches **(A)**, the correct answer.

For the incorrect choices: (B) distorts the author's purpose; the idea of microcredit arose to address the financial difficulties of people in poverty, but the author isn't using the example to emphasize the conditions in which these women lived. (C) is not mentioned in the text; it is not the author's purpose to criticize standard banking systems. (D) is extreme and also goes beyond the text. In the example, the loan was helpful to the women, but the passage never expands this to all "women borrowers" or says that microloans are "especially helpful to women borrowers."

5. C

Difficulty: Medium

Category: Craft and Structure

Getting to the Answer: The first sentence explains that Mary is soon to move to Chicago. The second sentence introduces her impression of the city, she will be in a place "filled with thousands of people all strangers to herself." The next sentence, the one of interest, gives Mary's opinion on what life will be like for her in Chicago. Living among strangers will be like entering "a cool forest carpeted with tender young grass." In other words, she wants to live in a place where she is not known. The remainder of the text explains why: she "lived under a cloud" in an "oppressive" atmosphere. So, the underlined sentence introduces the contrasting description of Mary's life that follows, and **(C)** is correct.

The third sentence continues, not contrasts with, the previous sentence. Eliminate (A). Although the underlined sentence contrasts Chicago with the "waterless desert" that is Huntersburg, the author's focus is the description of Mary and her feelings, not Huntersburg. Eliminate (B). Choice (D) is incorrect because the previous sentence describes Chicago, not Mary.

6. C

Difficulty: Medium

Category: Craft and Structure

Getting to the Answer: Summarize the main point of each text, then predict a relationship before you read the choices. The author of Text 1 starts off with "Clearly," an emphasis keyword that indicates "purchasing a home is a better investment than renting a home" is likely the author's main idea. Indeed, the rest of Text 1 proves to be the author's reasons for believing that main idea. As you read Text 2, identify and summarize Ian Mulheirn's view. The author introduces that view by stating "The costs of home ownership are not always obvious." Then Mulheirn and team outline some of those costs before concluding "renting a home is the financial equivalent of buying a home." So, Mulheirn and team would disagree with the author of Text 1: buying a home may not be a better investment than renting. This prediction matches **(C)**, the correct answer.

The main ideas in incorrect choices (A) and (D) are not discussed in Text 2. Mulheirn and team do not mention the difficulty of selling a home (A) or comparing purchase prices (D). Incorrect choice (B) is the view of the author of Text 1 and contradicts the view of Mulheirn and team in Text 2.

7. D

Difficulty: Hard

Category: Craft and Structure

Getting to the Answer: Every connections question must be answered using *only* information in the texts. As you read, make note, either in your mind or on your scratch paper, of the major points because the correct answer will rely on them. The first text describes two camouflage strategies and their results. The second text describes the study by João Vitor de Alcantara Viana and colleagues and its results. The question asks why João Vitor de Alcantara Viana and colleagues were *not* surprised with their findings on butterflies, so focus on the last sentence of Text 2: they were not surprised "to find that the bright eyespots on butterflies were not associated with reduced predator attacks." Refer back to Text 1 and find the discussion of butterflies: they "use dramatic shapes and colors to attract predators to less vulnerable areas of the butterfly's body." Predict that the eyespots do not prevent predator attacks, but make the predator strike a "less vulnerable area[s] of the butterfly's body." This prediction matches **(D)**, the correct answer.

The incorrect choices all bring in ideas that were not mentioned in the texts. The text never says the bright shapes on the butterflies make the butterflies harder to attack (A), keep the predators from seeing the butterflies (B), or make the predators avoid the butterflies (C).

8. A

Difficulty: Easy

Category: Information and Ideas

Getting to the Answer: This passage opens with a claim, and the rest of the paragraph provides details to support the claim. So, a good prediction for the correct answer is that the Hudson River School was "the first truly American art movement." This matches **(A)**.

Choice (B) is incorrect because Thomas Cole, Thomas Doughty, and Asher Durand are famous because they founded the Hudson River School. The text is not about them, but about the movement they started. (C) goes beyond the passage. Although many landscape painters eventually joined the Hudson River School movement, the passage does not say *all* did so. (D) contradicts the passage. The Hudson River School movement *embraced* European romanticism.

9.   C

Difficulty: Medium

Category: Information and Ideas

Getting to the Answer: The first sentence of the passage introduces its topic and main idea: experimental archaeology is "active" and uses a "firsthand" approach. The other sentences confirm that this is the main idea, as they provide two specific examples of "active, firsthand" experimental archaeology projects, in which researchers engaged in agriculture and construction. Choice **(C)** is correct because it restates this main idea and accurately sums up the projects described in the passage. Choice (A) is incorrect because it focuses on details in the passage and fails to mention the idea in the topic sentence that experimental archaeology is hands-on. Choice (B) is incorrect because it goes beyond the scope of the passage, which never claims experimental archaeology is not accepted, just that it uses an approach that might be unfamiliar. Choice (D) is incorrect because it focuses on one detail; further, the passage never claims the professors are "emerging leaders."

10.   C

Difficulty: Easy

Category: Information and Ideas

Getting to the Answer: The keyword "Unlike" at the start of the second sentence tells you the author is comparing railroads and cars. There, the author states that while railroads concentrated people in cities, the automobile "contributed to urban sprawl" and the rise of suburbs. **(C)** restates this idea in different words and is the correct answer.

Incorrect choices (A), (B), and (D) may be true statements, but these comparisons are never discussed in the passage.

11.   B

Difficulty: Medium

Category: Information and Ideas

Getting to the Answer: Begin by finding Macy and Golder's conclusion: the positivity level of the words in messages had a U-shaped curve over the day. Evaluate the choices with this conclusion in mind, looking for one that demonstrates a U-shaped pattern over time. Eliminate (A), as this description of the results would demonstrate a declining pattern—from high positivity early in the day to low positivity later in the day—rather than a U-shaped pattern. Choice **(B)** is correct, as this description of the results demonstrates a U-shaped pattern—from high to low and back to high positivity—over the course of a day. Choices (C) and (D) are incorrect because they compare the total numbers of positive and negative messages rather than tracking the positivity level throughout the day.

12.   D

Difficulty: Hard

Category: Information and Ideas

Getting to the Answer: The most important clue in the sentence with the blank is the emphasis keyword phrase "shift dramatically," which indicates the correct answer will be data that shows a big change. "Eyeballing," or quickly estimating just by looking at the graph, indicates that "child care and education" changed the most. Carefully check the years to make sure you get the comparison in the right direction. Child care and education expenses increased their share from 1960 to 2012, matching **(D)**, the correct answer.

Incorrect choices (A) and (B) mention categories that did not "shift dramatically." Housing (A) decreased in share by 1%, and transportation (B) decreased in share by 2%. Incorrect choice (C) uses the correct data but makes the wrong comparison. Child care and education increased, not decreased, its share.

13.   A

Difficulty: Hard

Category: Information and Ideas

Getting to the Answer: Inference questions must be answered using only the facts in the text. As you read, summarize the ideas in your own words. For long texts, it may be helpful to jot down notes on your scratch paper.

The first sentence says women's brains change during pregnancy. The second sentence correlates decreases in brain volume with increases in "feelings of attachment to the new infant." The third sentence presents the hypothesis that these brain changes are beneficial, to "improve parenting behaviors." The next sentence changes the focus to fathers, who "do not undergo the physiological changes of pregnancy." The contrast keyword "However" starting the next sentence, adds that fathers *do* have similar brain changes that "are also positively correlated with affectionate feelings towards infants." Now, compare the notes to the choices. **(A)** is correct. The research indicated fathers have "similar . . . changes " but "do not undergo the physiological changes of pregnancy." So if the changes in women's brains are due to pregnancy, the changes are due to some other process in the fathers. None of the incorrect choices are supported by the text. There is no mention of comparing the degree of improvement (B), the number of behaviors (C), or the speed of the changes (D).

14. C
Difficulty: Easy

Category: Standard English Conventions

Getting to the Answer: The portion of the text "Seeking to save lives" is not a complete thought, while the portion beginning "Gatling invented" is an independent clause. This question is testing how to combine these parts of the sentence using correct grammar. (B) and (D) can be eliminated automatically, as they feature punctuation used to join two independent clauses, which do not exist here. (A) can be eliminated because it uses a colon incorrectly. Colons introduce explanatory ideas, often breaking the flow of the sentence, but the clause before the colon must be able to stand on its own as a complete sentence. However, "Seeking to save lives" does not constitute an independent clause as there is no subject. This leaves **(C)**, which is correct. It could also be determined as correct because a comma can be used to set off an introductory phrase from an independent clause, as is the case here.

15. D
Difficulty: Easy

Category: Standard English Conventions

Getting to the Answer: The answer choices here are two contractions and two pronouns. To check if the contractions are appropriate here, simply plug them into the blank and see if the sentence makes sense. A

good precaution can be to unpack the contraction into the two words making it up. (A) is incorrect because "It is existence has never been proven" does not make sense. Likewise, (B) is incorrect because "They are existence has never been proven" is nonsense. This leaves the two pronoun options to choose from. (C) is a singular pronoun, and (D) is a plural pronoun. Determine whether a singular or a plural is appropriate given the context of the blank. To complicate matters, species can be both singular or plural depending on context. However, note how the sentence with the blank refers to the expedition to "find evidence of them." Since "them" is plural, in this specific context **(D)** is correct.

16. C
Difficulty: Medium

Category: Standard English Conventions

Getting to the Answer: You must determine the correct punctuation to use between these two independent clauses. Since several of the answer choices are technically correct, evaluate the content of the sentences to determine the relationship between them. The first sentence refers to a "quote," and the second sentence is the actual quote. Since the first sentence introduces the quote, a colon is appropriate, so **(C)** is correct. (A) is incorrect because a semicolon should not be followed by a conjunction, unless the semicolon is replacing commas in a list with multiple clauses. (B) is incorrect. A conjunction is unneeded here, only serving to introduce a grammar error. (D) results in a run-on.

17. B
Difficulty: Medium

Category: Standard English Conventions

Getting to the Answer: This underlined verb has the subject "community." Although this noun refers to numerous people, the collective noun itself is treated as singular. Eliminate any answer choices that use a plural verb: (A) and (D). Using the -ing form of the verb, as in (C), results in a sentence fragment. **(B)** appropriately uses a present tense singular verb; it is therefore correct.

18. B
Difficulty: Medium

Category: Standard English Conventions

Getting to the Answer: This question tests wordiness, but pure length is not the only consideration in this type of question. The correct answer choice must fully convey the writer's intended meaning. As written, (A) is the shortest answer choice, but it is difficult to determine exactly which group of people the "we" is referring to. Thus, (A) is incorrect. (C) and (D) are more specific but too wordy. **(B)** is correct because it specifies the people included in "we" using the fewest words.

19. D
Difficulty: Hard

Category: Standard English Conventions

Getting to the Answer: The portions of the text before and after the blank are each independent clauses. This question is testing how to combine (or separate) these clauses using correct punctuation. (A) is incorrect because it creates a run-on. (B) is incorrect because a comma and a FANBOYS conjunction are both needed to join two independent clauses. (C) is incorrect because, while a semicolon could join the two independent clauses, the comma after "nearly" is incorrect. **(D)** is correct because it separates the two independent clauses with a period.

20. A
Difficulty: Hard

Category: Standard English Conventions

Getting to the Answer: A quick glance at the choices indicates this question is testing the punctuation needed to correctly structure the text. The best clue indicating the correct answer is the two colons after "zone" and "categories." These have to be used in two different sentences, so eliminate (B) and (C) as each creates a single sentence. Choice **(A)** is correct; it creates two correctly punctuated sentences. Choice (D) is incorrect because "Then sorted . . . ." is not a complete idea and cannot be punctuated as a sentence.

21. C
Difficulty: Hard

Category: Standard English Conventions

Getting to the Answer: There are two clues in the text that make this challenging question a straightforward one. The comma in front of the blank and "Arguing . . ." at the start of the sentence mean that the sentence opens with a modifying clause, and the first word after the comma must be who or what is "Arguing." The second (and perhaps stronger) clue is the pronoun "him"

in the final sentence, which can only refer to "Angell," making **(C)** the correct answer.

Choice (A) is incorrect because the "great illusion" is not "Arguing." Choice (B) is incorrect because "Arguing . . . and defining . . ." is not a complete idea and cannot be punctuated as a sentence. Choice (D) is incorrect because "Angell's claim" is not a proper antecedent for "him" in the last sentence.

22. C
Difficulty: Easy

Category: Expression of Ideas

Getting to the Answer: As you read the passage, identify the two ideas that are being connected by the missing transition and determine the relationship between them. The first idea is that big cats only use their retractable claws for "a specific purpose." The following sentence repeats that information and elaborates with a specific summary of reasons they may have their claws out. Choice **(C)** provides the appropriate type of transition, indicating that second sentence reiterates the first sentence with different words.

Choice (A) is incorrect because the ideas are not similar to each other, but rather the second sentence is a rephrasing of the first. Choices (B) and (D) are incorrect because the ideas do not contrast.

23. C
Difficulty: Medium

Category: Expression of Ideas

Getting to the Answer: Begin by identifying the two ideas that are being connected by the missing transition so you can determine the relationship between them. The first idea is that occupational therapists are concerned that the swallow patterns of infants are being delayed, with harmful outcomes ("difficulty chewing and swallowing"), by the use of sippy cups with rigid spouts. The second idea is that speech-language pathologists are warning that a "prolonged . . . suckle-swallow pattern" may result in other delays ("speech and language development" and "jaw musculature"). Both ideas provide evidence of the "negative outcomes" identified by "recent research." Because the second idea is *additional* evidence; choice **(C)** is correct.

Choices (A) and (D) are incorrect because they illogically complete the passage: the occupational therapists' warnings do not cause ("Consequently" and

"Thus") the speech-language pathologists' observation. Nor is the second idea a more precise phrasing of the first idea, choice (B); rather, they are describing separate, related ideas.

24. A

Difficulty: Hard

Category: Expression of Ideas

Getting to the Answer: The question stem indicates that this question is testing transitions. As you read the passage, identify the two ideas that are being connected by the missing transition so you can determine the relationship between them. The main claim of the passage, located in the first sentence, is that disease-carrying mosquitoes impacted the history of the Caribbean region, and the rest of the passage supports the claim. The first idea connected by the transition is that different populations had different levels of immunity. The second idea is that, in a military conflict, groups with more immunity had a better chance of winning. The argument must logically be that groups with higher immunity were more likely to win conflicts *due to* the fact that populations had different levels of immunity. Choice **(A)** is a cause-and-effect transition and is correct. Choice (B) is incorrect because the ideas are not *similar*, but rather one explains the other. Choice (C) is incorrect because the ideas are not presented as sequential events. Choice (D) is incorrect because the ideas do not contrast.

25. D

Difficulty: Easy

Category: Expression of Ideas

Getting to the Answer: Use the intention of the question "to emphasize the current cultural and political conditions in Mauritius" to guide your reading. Use your scratch paper as needed to jot down the key facts. The first point mentions the discovery of Mauritius and its first occupants, the Portuguese. The second and third points provide a series of later rulers, the Dutch, French, and British. The fourth point outlines additional members of the population, "freed slaves, Indian and Pakistani immigrants." The fifth and sixth points chronicle Mauritius' transition to a "full democracy" with a "prosperous economy." Keep these notes in front of you as you evaluate the choices. Eliminate (A), which discusses the population, but not political conditions in Mauritius today. Eliminate (B); how the various

influences affected the government of Mauritius is not discussed in the text. Eliminate (C), the cause of the "success" of democracy in Mauritius is not mentioned in the passage. **(D)** must be correct; on test day, mark it confidently and move to the next question. But, for the record, **(D)** describes Mauritius as "a prosperous, democratic country," which are the "political conditions" required for the question. The "cultural" conditions demanded by the question are the "diverse population generated by its colonial past."

26. B

Difficulty: Medium

Category: Expression of Ideas

Getting to the Answer: The question asks for "the aim and results of the research study," so keep these ideas in mind as you read the points. The first two points provide some background on standing: instead of sitting at work, standing promotes health, so many people are standing while working. The third point introduces a contrast, standing "may slow down mental processes." The fourth point offers another idea, the mild stress caused by standing may "improve work performance." So far, there has been no mention of the study, so expect that the final point may resolve the conflict between the third and fourth points. Indeed, the final point mentions that Mama's research found that "standing subjects completed a difficult mental task . . . more quickly than seated subjects did." Use this final point to begin to eliminate choices. Eliminate (A); this choice sums up the question addressed by Mama's research, but neglects to report the results. Choice **(B)** is correct. On test day, mark **(B)** confidently and move to the next question; there is *always* only one correct answer. But for practice, (C) mentions one of the research questions, but the text never discusses the need to "take regular breaks." Eliminate (C). Choice (D) contradicts the last point; Mama's research showed standing subjects completed the tasks "more quickly" than did the seated subjects.

27. B

Difficulty: Hard

Category: Expression of Ideas

Getting to the Answer: Identify the goal that the correct answer will satisfy: "a generalization about the kind of study conducted." Since the generalization is about the "kind of study," the correct answer will likely provide details about the logistics or nature of the study itself, not just the study's conclusions. Look for both kinds of details as you read the bullet points. In general, according to the first two points, Darnton studies strange aspects of history and analyzes historical documents. The last three bullet points discuss the specific study of the great cat massacre. Note that the third point mentions that the study entailed analysis of a "written narrative account." The last bullet points describe the event and, finally, Darnton's interpretation: the cat massacre account provides a critique and humor. Evaluate the choices with these ideas in mind. Choice **(B)** is correct; it describes the "kind of study" in line with both Darnton's general approach to history ("analysis of a written account of a seemingly strange event") and his specific study and interpretation of the cat massacre.

Choices (A) and (D) are incorrect because they do not address the kind of study Darnton conducted; rather they reflect Darnton's interpretation of the cat massacre and a description of the massacre, respectively. Choice (C) is incorrect because it is about historians' methods in general, not Darnton's study specifically.

Reading and Writing: Module A Answers and Explanations

1.   B

Difficulty: Easy

Category: Craft and Structure

Getting to the Answer: Use the passage context to determine what kind of "challenge" is found at the end of the Boston Marathon. The contrast transition "but" signals that the challenge differs from how the marathon is described in the first part of the sentence: "grueling on the body." Predict that the challenge is *non-physical*. The rest of the passage describes more about the challenge. It is called "Heartbreak Hill" and involves a "devastated" runner and the need to "summon . . . motivation." The challenge must be *non-physical* and *emotionally or mentally difficult*. This matches **(B)**, which is correct. Choices (A) and (C) are the opposite of the required meaning. Choice (D) is not supported by the passage context; the challenge is difficult for mental reasons, not because the challenge itself is "aggressive."

2.   D

Difficulty: Medium

Category: Craft and Structure

Getting to the Answer: Predict a word that could be substituted for "casual" in context. The narrator is explaining that another man's appearance "strike[s] the attention." In other words, the man's appearance is so noteworthy (he's very tall, very lean) that even someone looking at him "casually" would notice. Predict that "casual" in context means *not paying close attention*. Choice **(D)**, *which means lacking in interest or enthusiasm*, is correct. The other answer choices are meanings of "casual" that do not match the context. An "unplanned," "comfortable," or "relaxed" observer would not be more or less likely to notice someone's appearance.

3.   A

Difficulty: Hard

Category: Craft and Structure

Getting to the Answer: Use context to predict the logical meaning of the word that fits in the blank. The word refers to something "inherent in human language," which the "strict rules" of computers might not be able to handle when translating between languages. The following sentences state that Oettinger used a sentence to "demonstrate his claim" about computers having

trouble translating. Specifically, the word "Time" could have different functions and thus result in different meanings. Predict that the quality inherent in human language that would give computers difficulty is its *irregularity* or *variability*; this matches **(A)**.

Choice (B) is incorrect because the passage does not imply that language is "mysterious," just that words can have various functions and meanings. Nor does the passage identify any "exceptions," choice (C), in language. Choice (D), "grammar," is a word related to language, but it is incorrect because the passage does not indicate that any particular "grammar" is "inherent in human language"; rather, it indicates that language contains variability.

4.   C

Difficulty: Easy

Category: Craft and Structure

Getting to the Answer: When asked to identify the purpose of a passage, think about the author's viewpoint and reason for writing as you read. The second sentence contains the author's claim: the Green Revolution's benefits "outweigh its costs." The author acknowledges criticisms but contends that the benefits are greater. The author supports the claim by providing two examples of benefits—reduced food shortages and improved world economy—in the remaining sentences. Predict that the purpose of the text is *to argue the Green Revolution was beneficial*. This matches **(C)**, which accurately summarizes the author's purpose and the structure of the passage.

Choice (A) is incorrect because the passage does not focus on negative issues. Choice (B) is incorrect because the author does not argue for a "balanced, cautious approach" to assessing the Green Revolution, but rather argues for a positive assessment. Further, the passage is about assessing the Green Revolution in particular, not about assessing world developments in general. Choice (D) is incorrect because the passage addresses benefits, not criticisms.

5. B

Difficulty: Medium

Category: Craft and Structure

Getting to the Answer: Since this question asks for "the function" of the sentence, it is a purpose question. Always answer a purpose question within the context of the entire text. The first and second sentences, including the underlined sentence of interest, describe Akaky as particularly devoted to his work. He "lived . . . entirely for his duties" and "labored with love." The next sentence adds details to this description. Then, the tone changes in the next sentence. If Akaky was paid "in proportion to his zeal," he would have a much higher position, a "councillor of state." However, as the next sentence states, Akaky works unappreciated and ignored "like a horse in a mill." Predict that the underlined sentence sets up this contrast, matching **(B)**, the correct answer.

Incorrect choice (A) misstates the text. Akaky enjoys his work; he does not find it tedious or difficult. Choice (C) also does not match the text; the sentences that follow continue, not contrast with, the description in the underlined sentence. Choice (D) is incorrect because the underlined sentence describes a character, not the setting.

6. D

Difficulty: Easy

Category: Craft and Structure

Getting to the Answer: Since there are two texts, this is clearly a connections question. Summarize the main idea of each text and predict the relationship from Chirikure's point of view (Text 2). The main idea of Text 1 is highlighted in the last sentence with the keyword "emphasized" and states the European archeologists "emphasized Great Zimbabwe's connections to international trade." The first sentence of Text 2 includes the keyword "cites" to present Chirikure's opinion: "Great Zimbabwe" is "evidence of extensive trade among different regions of Africa." Predict that the European archeologists emphasize international trade, but Chirikure highlights Great Zimbabwe's trade within Africa. Choice **(D)** matches this prediction; Chirikure uses the differences in the numbers and locations of the different types of artifacts to make his point. He would "encourage" European archeologists to do the same.

Text 2 mentions that the foreign artifacts "were not highly valued," so eliminate (A). The other incorrect choices are

not discussed in the texts. There is no mention of the ages of any artifacts. Eliminate (B) and (C).

7. D

Difficulty: Easy

Category: Craft and Structure

Getting to the Answer: As indicated in the question stem, identify the findings in Text 1 and Brumm's viewpoint in Text 2 as you read the passages. The finding in Text 1 is that a cave painting was dated to over 40,000 years ago and thus supports the hypothesis that cave painting started in Europe. In Text 2, Brumm thinks that the date of the 45,500 year old painting from Indonesia should lead to a "reanalysis" of assumptions about the "geographic origins" of cave painting. In other words, the discovery of an older painting in Asia (Indonesia) calls into question the old assumption that cave painting originated in Europe. Choice **(D)** is correct; Brumm would likely acknowledge the method used in Text 1, uranium-thorium dating, since his study used it as well, but he would think the new finding challenges the old hypothesis.

Choice (A) is incorrect because Brumm's study also used uranium-thorium dating, so he would be unlikely to reject a study for this reason. Choice (B) is incorrect because the passages don't emphasize differences in the cave paintings; in fact, they instead mention that they were both made with red ochre. Choice (C) is incorrect because it is the opposite of Brumm's view, as he argues that the hypothesis that cave painting started in Europe should be reevaluated.

8. C

Difficulty: Easy

Category: Information and Ideas

Getting to the Answer: The question stem asks for the "main idea" of the text, so take a moment to paraphrase the passage. Hingbo uses paper in sculptures because paper, like life, is both "fragile" and "flexible." The "duality" of play and function, for which the medium may be used, is reflected in his work. Eliminate (A) because it is out of scope; the passage does not explain what the honeycomb structure does. Choice (B) is a distortion; the passage only mentions that he selects the paper type that "is best aligned with" his artistic vision. Choice **(C)** states that paper is both medium and inspiration, which matches the paraphrase of the passage, and is correct. Choice (D) is a distortion of a detail in the passage: lanterns were an example of what can be created with paper.

9. D

Difficulty: Medium

Category: Information and Ideas

Getting to the Answer: Like texts, speeches are given to make a point. To find the point, or the main idea, ask yourself as you read, *Why did the speaker say this?* For this passage, the answer to that question comes at the end: Bayezid believes that he was born "to carry arms and always to conquer." Matching this prediction to the choices yields **(D)**, the correct answer. (A) is incorrect because Bayezid calls John "a great lord" but that he was in a "foul knightly enterprise" and has to "recover his honor." So, he views John as someone who has lost his honor. (B) is misusing a detail; although the speaker mentions John's youth, he does not bring it up as a negative. (C) is misuses a detail of the text; Bayezid states that he himself was born "to conquer," not John.

10. A

Difficulty: Easy

Category: Information and Ideas

Getting to the Answer: The keyword phrase "According to the text" identifies this as a detail question, and the detail needed describes "the inlet." The correct answer will be found within the passage, so as you read, make a mental or physical note of any descriptions of the inlet, and eliminate choices as you go. The first sentence describes the inlet as "deep," "several miles" long, and "terminating in a . . . swamp." Eliminate (B). The swamp ends the inlet; it does not make the swamp "difficult to navigate." The next sentence describes "a . . . dark grove" on one side of the inlet, and a "high ridge" on the other side. The emphasis keywords "great age and immense size" highlight the unusual trees on the ridge. Eliminate (C); nothing in the text implies that the inlet "can be easily seen because of" the ridge. The next sentence mentions a rumor that "Kidd the pirate" chose a "gigantic" tree under which he buried "a great amount of treasure." Eliminate (D); the text does not claim that this was the *only* place Kidd hid treasure. The only surviving choice **(A)**, must be correct. And indeed, the last sentence lists several characteristics of the inlet that make it a good hiding place: you can "bring the money

in a boat secretly, and at night," keep "a good lookout," and use "the remarkable trees" as "good landmarks."

11. B

Difficulty: Hard

Category: Information and Ideas

Getting to the Answer: The phrase "Based on the text" means that this is a Detail question and that the correct answer will be explicitly stated or supported by the author. In this case, Bertie Wooster raises the topic of Bingo's breakup, but Bingo interrupts him to insist that he did not come to breakfast to talk about that topic. Bertie agrees. Bingo then repeatedly brings up the topic of the breakup and how he does not want to talk about it, with Bertie cheering him on. The detail here is that Bingo does, in fact, want to talk about the breakup, as evidenced by him repeatedly bringing it up. Bertie mistakenly takes Bingo at his word about being over the breakup, however. **(B)** is correct because it best matches that description.

Choice (A) is incorrect because Bertie never tries to change the subject, merely congratulating Bingo on apparently getting over his breakup. (C) is incorrect because, while Bertie asks to talk about the breakup at a later time, he gives no indication in the text that the topic is too heavy for a breakfast conversation. (D) is incorrect because it is the reverse of the text; Bingo is preoccupied with the breakup, not Bertie.

12. D

Difficulty: Easy

Category: Information and Ideas

Getting to the Answer: Begin by paraphrasing the claim in your own words: *being outdoors gives freedom, and the outdoors is big* (or "vast"). Evaluate the answer choices in light of this claim. Eliminate (A), which addresses likeability and happiness, not freedom. Choice (B) mentions "unseen" elements but not freedom specifically; eliminate. Although it refers to leaving behind indoor things, (C) is incorrect because it refers to neither freedom nor the outdoors. Choice **(D)** is correct because it addresses both freedom (the speaker is "loos'd of limits") and the vastness of the outdoors ("great draughts of space").

13. D

Difficulty: Medium

Category: Information and Ideas

Getting to the Answer: The researchers have hypothesized that by spending more time in nature, youth and young adults will experience improved health, both emotionally and physically. The correct choice is **(D)** because it indicates a positive correlation between time spent in nature and improvements in both emotional (anxiety) and physical (muscle tension) health.

Incorrect choice (A) references improvement in only one outcome measure (physical health), not both emotional wellness and physical health. (B) would weaken the claim; an increased feeling of isolation when exposed to nature is the opposite of the researchers' claim. (C) is out of scope; the researchers are recommending a nationwide implementation as well as targeting both emotional and physical health.

14. A

Difficulty: Medium

Category: Information and Ideas

Getting to the Answer: The question asks for support for the author's proposal, so begin by summarizing that view in your own words. In the last line of the text, the author proposes that "the Affordable Care Act [may have] enabled more students to graduate from high school." Now, read the beginning of the text to find out the connection between the Affordable Care Act and the graph. The first two sentences explain that "the Affordable Care Act . . . made health insurance more widely available" and that "children could be included on a parent's plan." So a good way to connect the author's proposal to the graph would be something like *more health insurance could have led to more high school graduations*. Now, check the choices. **(A)** matches the prediction and the data and is correct. On test day, mark **(A)** confidently and move to the next question because there is *always* only one correct answer.

For the record, (B) overlooks New York's 2018 statistics. Furthermore, comparing the percentages of graduating high school students to the percentage of the population with health insurance does not support the author's claim; the change in each measure must be evaluated. Eliminate (B). Incorrect choices (C) and (D) each compare one state among the others, but the claim requires a comparison between the changes in the measures.

15. D

Difficulty: Easy

Category: Information and Ideas

Getting to the Answer: Since the question asks you to logically complete the text with something suggested by the study's findings, read the passage to determine what the findings are. The first sentence indicates one conclusion of the study: hyenas have individual whoops that may be used for identification. The third and fourth sentences identify another finding: the computer was better at identification when the whoops were repeated. Keep these ideas in mind as you evaluate the answer choices. Choice (A) can be eliminated because it misrepresents the findings: the hyenas were found to have "individualized 'whoops'" that may identify them, not a certain *number* of identifying whoops. Choices (B) and (C) are inferences that go beyond what can be supported by the information in the passage. Choice **(D)** is correct; the inference that hyenas are more likely to be heard and identified when they whoop more times is supported by the passage. The findings in the third and fourth sentences indicate that the computer model was more accurate when hearing more whoops, and the second sentence indicates that some species repeat their calls more often under noisy conditions, presumably to be better heard.

16. A

Difficulty: Easy

Category: Standard English Conventions

Getting to the Answer: The answer choices indicate that this question is testing how to structure the sentence, specifically, whether it should be constructed as a question. Use clues from the passage to determine whether the sentence should be a question. The sentence before the blank sets up a problem: the researchers lacked data. The sentence with the blank introduces a hypothetical: "If they compiled data . . . ." The last sentence indicates that the researchers don't know something yet, as they are "determined to find out"; this suggests the correct answer should be a question, but evaluate the choices to make sure. Choice **(A)** is correct, as it sets up the scenario as an unknown question that the researchers are determined to find out.

Choice (B) is incorrect because it is worded as a question but ends in a period. Choice (C) is incorrect because it is worded as a statement but ends in a question mark.

Choice (D) is grammatically correct, but it is the incorrect choice because it does not match the passage context of an unknown question that the researchers want to find out.

17. B
Difficulty: Easy

Category: Standard English Conventions

Getting to the Answer: The answer choices indicate that this question is likely testing the correct use of a modifying phrase. The introductory modifying phrase "Exploring dark, controversial themes such as sin and death" describes the poetry volume *Les Fleurs du mal*; the "censorship" did not "Explore dark . . . themes." Choice **(B)** is correct because it correctly places the noun *Les Fleurs du mal* immediately after the modifying phrase that describes it. Choices (A) and (C) are incorrect because they illogically have the phrase describing "censorship," and (D) is incorrect because the phrase describes the vague "there."

18. B
Difficulty: Easy

Category: Standard English Conventions

Getting to the Answer: The answer choices indicate that this question is testing comma usage around the names "Joseph Wang and Liangfang Zhang," who are identified as "nanoengineers." Choice (A) is incorrect because the comma separates the subject "Joseph Wang and Liangfang Zhang" from its verb "showed." Choice **(B)** is correct because no punctuation is needed to set off the names, which are not parenthetical because they specify which nanoengineers conducted the study. Choice (C) is incorrect because a colon would be used after an independent clause to introduce additional clarifying information. Choice (D) is incorrect because a comma should not be used to separate the modifier "nanoengineers" from "Joseph Wang and Liangfang Zhang."

19. C
Difficulty: Easy

Category: Standard English Conventions

Getting to the Answer: Unless the context in the passage indicates that the time frame has changed, verb tenses should be consistent. The context makes clear that everything described in this sentence happened in

the past. Choice **(C)**, which is in the simple past tense like the other verbs in the sentence ("charged," "introduced," and "rewrote") is correct. The other answer choices are incorrect because they are in other verb tenses: (A) is in present tense, (B) is in future tense, and (D) indicates an action that occurred in the past but has present consequences.

20. C
Difficulty: Medium

Category: Standard English Conventions

Getting to the Answer: The answer choices indicate that the question is testing verb agreement, so determine the subject and intended tense of the verb that should fit in the blank. The verb refers to the moon Chrysalis being the source of Saturn's rings. The rest of the passage describes the "former moon" hitting Saturn and turning into the debris that formed the rings. Thus, Chrysalis was and still is the source of the rings, so eliminate the future tense verb in (A). The remaining choices are all in the past tense, so next, determine the verb's subject. The singular "source" is the subject, so the singular past tense verb "was" in **(C)** is correct. Note that "rings" is not the subject; the prepositional phrase "of Saturn's rings" describes the subject "source." Choices (B) and (D) are incorrect because they are plural verbs.

21. C
Difficulty: Medium

Category: Standard English Conventions

Getting to the Answer: Since this question asks about Standard English conventions, read the answer choices before looking at the passage. The choices signal that this question deals with punctuation, most likely testing how to correctly join the parts of a sentence. The portion of the sentence before the blank is not a complete thought ("A compelling historical narrative that offers . . ."). The portion after the punctuation is a complete thought ("*Life Among the Piutes* is the first known autobiography . . ."). Predict that an incomplete thought should be joined to a complete thought by a comma. **(C)** is correct. Choices (A) and (B) are incorrect because they are ways to join two complete thoughts. Choice (D) is incorrect because it omits all punctuation.

22. C

Difficulty: Hard

Category: Standard English Conventions

Getting to the Answer: The answer choices indicate that this question is testing punctuation. Evaluate the parts of the sentence that are connected by the blank to determine what punctuation, if any, is needed. The portion before the blank is an independent clause with subject-verb "scientists use." The portion immediately after the blank is a prepositional phrase ("to enable . . . . cells"), which is connected to an independent clause with subject-verb "chemists produce." Two independent clauses must be joined by punctuation, so eliminate (B) and (D). A comma must have a FANBOYS conjunction to join independent clauses, so eliminate (A). Choice **(C)** is correct because a colon can be used after an independent clause to introduce additional clarifying information. In this sentence, the portion after the colon explains the "innovative procedure" mentioned in the portion before the blank.

23. B

Difficulty: Easy

Category: Expression of Ideas

Getting to the Answer: Identify the two ideas that are being connected by the missing transition to determine the relationship between them. The first idea is that Safia Elhillo uses both Arabic and English to include the two different cultures to which she belongs. The second idea is that one of her poems uses an example of how translating between languages can diminish the original intent of the author. Since the second idea is an *example* of how she uses the two languages in her work, choice **(B)** is correct.

Choice (A) is incorrect because the two ideas are not *alike*. Choice (C) is incorrect because the contrast transition "In comparison" would convey that the poem's content was in conflict with her being bilingual. Choice (D) is incorrect because her poem is not *in spite of* her heritage; rather, the poem "celebrates" it.

24. D

Difficulty: Medium

Category: Expression of Ideas

Getting to the Answer: The question stem indicates that this question is testing transitions. As you read the passage, identify the two ideas that are being connected by the missing transition so you can determine the relationship between them. The first idea is that an analysis now dates the Flower Portrait to the 1800s. The second idea is that art historians now think the engraving inspired the portrait; in other words, they think the engraving must have been made first. The second sentence of the passage indicates that the opposite used to be the case: historians had thought the portrait was made first, since it was dated 1609. Since the analysis led to the new conclusion, look for a cause-and-effect word in the answer choices; **(D)** is correct.

The contrast transition in (A) would be correct only if historians had rejected the analysis and stuck with their previous assumption that the portrait was older. Choice (B) is incorrect because the passage does not present the events in a sequential order. Choice (C) is incorrect because the determinations of the analysis are not *similar to* the new conclusion; rather, the analysis *led to* the new conclusion.

25. C

Difficulty: Hard

Category: Expression of Ideas

Getting to the Answer: The question stem indicates that this question is testing transitions. As you read the passage, identify the two ideas that are being connected by the missing transition so you can determine the relationship between them. The first idea is that a research team was interested in how bacteria move using their flagella. The second idea is that scientists did not understand how bacteria coiled single proteins in order to move; the passage refers to "*these* single proteins," so the proteins must be the "flagella" mentioned in the previous sentence. Thus, both ideas are related to the same structures of bacteria movement, but the second idea gives a more *specific* description of something unknown about the movement; choice **(C)** is correct.

Choice (A) is incorrect because scientists' lack of understanding of the movement was not *due to* ("Therefore") the team's interest in bacteria movement. Nor are these ideas *similar*, choice (B); rather, they are describing the *same* unknown about bacteria movement in more or less detail. Choice (D) is incorrect because the scientist's lack of understanding of the movement is not *without regard to* the team's interest in it.

26. C

Difficulty: Easy

Category: Expression of Ideas

Getting to the Answer: This question asks for a generalization about Ananse's actions, so keep that in mind as you read the points. The last four points identify who Ananse is and what he has done, so focus on those for your prediction. A good prediction would be a generalization of his actions, which include thievery and tricks, but also creation and teaching. Eliminate choice (A) because it does not address the prompt; the evolution of Ananse's name is not an *action* of his. Choice (B) misuses details and is incorrect; Ananse *attempted* to gather all knowledge but stopped after realizing it was "not meant to be contained." Choice **(C)** provides an example of a time when Ananse used thievery and tricks to help his people learn, and this is the correct answer. Incorrect choice (D) does not address the prompt; his many names are not actions.

27. D

Difficulty: Medium

Category: Expression of Ideas

Getting to the Answer: The question stem indicates that the correct answer will highlight the aim of the research study, so as you read the bullet points, look for *why* the study was conducted. The first bullet point introduces the RIPE project and identifies its goal: increasing food production. The aim of a study done by RIPE will likely be related to this goal of increasing food production. Note that the full name of the project refers to "Increased Photosynthetic Efficiency," and the third bullet point affirms that the researchers wanted to try to make photosynthesis more efficient. Predict that the study's aim was *to make photosynthesis more efficient to increase food production*. Choice **(D)** is correct.

Choice (A) is incorrect because it identifies a result rather than the aim of the study. Choice (B) accurately describes what the researchers did, but it is incorrect because it does not identify why the researchers tested the technique. Choice (C) is incorrect because it misrepresents the purpose of the RIPE project.

Reading and Writing: Module B Answers and Explanations

1. D

Difficulty: Medium

Category: Craft and Structure

Getting to the Answer: Use context to predict the meaning of "touching" as it is used in the passage. The word describes the kind of letters that were written during "hard times." The letter in the passage is sent home by a father, who must be a soldier, as he lives in a "camp" and sends "military news." The letter avoids discussing "hardships," but it is instead described as "cheerful" and "hopeful," as well as "overflow[ing] with fatherly love and longing." These details suggest that letters of the time were *emotional*, as would be sent by "homesick" fathers to their families. This prediction matches **(D)**; "poignant" means *able to affect the emotions*.

The other choices are meanings of "touching" that do not capture the emotional quality of the letters. "Communicating" in (A) is characteristic of *all* letters, so this choice does not address the emotional quality of the letter described in the passage. "Neighborly" in (B) suggests personal relationships, but not as intense as those described in the passage. Choice (C) is incorrect because the passage emphasizes the emotional quality of the letters, not their potential to "concern" the readers; in fact, the father who wrote the letter avoids topics, such as "dangers faced," that might have upset his family.

2. A

Difficulty: Hard

Category: Craft and Structure

Getting to the Answer: The clause before the blank begins by describing the layout of the first two poems that are on "opposite sides" of a great divide (chasm). The clause with the blank explains the purpose of that format, in relation to "the disconnection . . . created by emigration." Predict that the correct choice will *show* or *highlight* the parallel that she has intentionally created with her work. Choice **(A)** matches that prediction; "emphasize" conveys that *special consideration* of the relationship between the layout and the disconnection is warranted. Incorrect choice (B), "challenge," implies that she is using her work to *confront* or *dispute* the disconnection. Choice (C), "cultivate," meaning

encourage or *prepare*, does not logically complete the sentence because that is not the association asserted in the passage. (D) is incorrect because neither the poem nor the influences are provided as proof of the other.

3. A

Difficulty: Hard

Category: Craft and Structure

Getting to the Answer: Use the clues in the text to predict an appropriate word to fill the blank. The first sentence gives the opinion of "Some agricultural engineers." The important keyword comes in the next sentence, where the author states the view "fails." So a good prediction to fill the blank is a word or phrase that means the view is "wrong" or "incorrect". This prediction matches **(A)**; "tenuous" means *weak* or *lacking substance*.

None of the incorrect choices are supported by the text. (B) "disorienting" means *confusing,* (C) "nuanced" means *subtle,* and (D) "unoriginal" means *not original*. None of these, by definition, match the author's view that the agricultural engineers are "wrong."

4. A

Difficulty: Medium

Category: Craft and Structure

Getting to the Answer: Since the question stem asks for the main purpose of the text, think about *why* the author included this passage in his novel. The blurb states that this scene occurs early in the book, so the passage is likely intended to establish something for the rest of the story. The passage itself focuses on the actions of Peter: he "jump[s]" at drawers, "scatter[s]" what's in the drawers "with both hands," and, when "delight[ed]" for himself, forgets about Tinker Bell and closes her in a drawer. Further, the phrase "as kings toss halfpennies to the crowd" suggests that Peter treats the drawer contents carelessly, like a rich king tossing nearly worthless coins to a crowd. All these details paint Peter as one who acts exuberantly and without regard for others; this matches **(A)**.

Choice (B) is incorrect because the passage does not focus on the setting; it only mentions a chest of drawers. Choice (C) is incorrect because although the passage describes actions that imply qualities of Peter, it does not describe him in detail; further, the passage does not describe Tinker Bell at all. Choice (D) is incorrect because a king is mentioned to help describe Peter's actions, not to establish that there is a real king where the story takes place.

5. A

Difficulty: Hard

Category: Craft and Structure

Getting to the Answer: The first sentence explains that, in the 1950s, the public grew concerned about radioactive fallout from nuclear testing. The second sentence describes the reaction of the U.S. military to that concern; namely, they explored moving the tests underground. The third sentence describes the setup of the first subterranean test. The fourth sentence, the one of interest, explains that a jet of radioactive fire shot up the shaft that the bomb had been lowered down into. In other words, the fourth sentence shows how the first test, Pascal-A, failed in its goal of containing radioactivity. The remainder of the text explains the attempt to avoid that issue in the second test, Pascal-B, and its notable failure. So, the underlined portion illustrates a problem with Pascal-A that Pascal-B tried to solve with a different setup, meaning **(A)** is correct.

Although the fourth sentence partly describes the first subterranean nuclear test, that is not its main function in the overall structure of the text. The fourth sentence sets up why the manhole cover was welded over the shaft in Pascal-B, resulting in it becoming the fastest-moving object in human history. Thus, (B) is incorrect. (C) is incorrect because, although the fourth sentence deals with radioactivity unintentionally spreading out from a nuclear test, the Pascal-A test was an underground test, not an above-ground one like had been the focus of public attention. (D) is incorrect because the Pascal-A test trying to contain the radioactivity underground was a safety measure in and of itself.

6. A

Difficulty: Easy

Category: Craft and Structure

Getting to the Answer: Since there are two texts, this is clearly a Connections question. Summarize the main idea of each text and predict the relationship from Chirikure's point of view (Text 1). The main idea of Text 1 is highlighted in the last sentence with the keyword

"cites" and states Chirikure's opinion that Great Zimbabwe is "evidence of vibrant trade within Africa." The statistics in Text 2 indicate that, while the majority of exports from Europe and Asia stay within those continents, only 16% of African exports do so. With such a small percentage of exports trading within Africa, predict that Chirikuri would say that this situation is "different" from African trade during the time of Great Zimbabwe. This prediction matches **(A)**, the correct answer.

None of the concepts mentioned in the incorrect choices are discussed in the texts. There is no indication of any "critici[sm]" (B), "praise" (C), or "insist[ing]" (D).

7. D

Difficulty: Hard

Category: Craft and Structure

Getting to the Answer: As you read the passages, identify the view of the linguists in Text 1 and the findings made by Chen in Text 2, as indicated by the question stem. The linguists in Text 1 reject linguistic determinism, described in the rest of the passage as the idea that language can cause or limit people's thoughts and actions. In Text 2, Chen found that speakers of languages with and without a future tense behaved differently. Think about how these ideas relate: the linguists do not think language determines behavior, but Chen found evidence that speakers of languages with an essential difference behave differently. Evaluate the answer choices with this contrast in mind, but be careful to avoid answer choices that are too extreme.

Choice (A) is incorrect because it goes too far in assuming that the linguists would reject all evidence that, on the surface, seems to contradict their view. For choice (B), although the linguists might encourage Chen to conduct additional research, nothing in the passages suggests that a study specifically on *unhealthy* rather than healthy behaviors would add anything of relevance to the discussion of linguistic determinism. Choice (C) is incorrect because the linguists are concerned with language and its impact (or lack thereof) on behaviors, so Chen's study about language and behaviors would not be "irrelevant." Choice **(D)** is correct. It avoids being too extreme, indicating that the linguists would not completely reject the findings. Rather, it interprets the findings in line with a rejection of linguistic determinism: language didn't cause the behaviors in and of itself, so there must be other factors involved.

8. C

Difficulty: Medium

Category: Information and Ideas

Getting to the Answer: The question stem asks for the main idea of the text, so look for the author's main point, which is often found in the first or last sentence of the passage. The details of the passage should support the main point. The first sentence makes a passing mention of what ancient Egypt may "bring to mind," but its emphasis is on the idea that elites had to handle the "mundane" aspects of their households. The next sentence states that letters can give "a glimpse into this domestic world." The remaining sentences provide examples of letters that discuss household concerns of elites. Predict that the main idea involves *ancient Egyptian elites managing their households* and that the correct answer may mention the letters, which are discussed throughout the passage, as giving evidence of this claim. Choice **(C)** is correct.

Choice (A) is incorrect because the passage's emphasis is not on *who* the elites were, but rather on their domestic concerns. Choice (B) is incorrect because, although it refers to an idea in the first sentence, the focus of the passage is the elites' household management, not architecture and government. Choice (D) is incorrect because it omits the specific mention of managing households.

9. D

Difficulty: Hard

Category: Information and Ideas

Getting to the Answer: The question asks for the main idea, so focus on the big picture rather than the details as you read the passage. Since the first or last sentence often contains the main idea, focus on these parts of the passage. The first sentence introduces a statement: Valentina Tereshkova spent her free time at a local aero club, where members "pursued flying and skydiving." The next few sentences elaborate upon that, detailing her specific skill with a parachute. The last sentence states that Tereshkova was "an ideal candidate" and became the first woman in space. Predict that the main idea is that Tereshkova being a parachutist was important for qualifying as a cosmonaut. This matches **(D)**, which is correct.

Choice (A) is incorrect because no mention is made of discrimination against Tereshkova. In fact, the text states that she applied to the "female cosmonaut program,"

meaning Soviet officials were specifically looking for women to become cosmonauts. (B) is incorrect because, although the text mentions the dangers posed to early cosmonauts, that is a detail and not the main focus of the text. (C) is incorrect because it misuses a detail from the passage; while the need for cosmonauts to use parachutes is mentioned, it is not the main focus of the text.

10. B

Difficulty: Medium

Category: Detail

Getting to the Answer: The phrase "According to the passage" signals that this is a Detail question. The question stem is asking for a detail about Prussian blue, but because this is a broad question, opt for the elimination strategy. Eliminate (A) because it is the opposite of what is stated in the passage: "Prussian blue is. . . prescribed to treat. . . thallium poisoning." This is what choice **(B)** states and is correct. Choices (C) and (D) are both distortions of details in the passage. Herschel discovered the blueprinting process, not Prussian blue, and blueprinting is a process created by application of light to Prussian blue.

11. D

Difficulty: Hard

Category: Information and Ideas

Getting to the Answer: The keyword phrase "According to the text" identifies this as a Detail question. As you read the text and identify information about Tom, compare it to the choices. The first sentence describes the house and the second Tom's wife, so do not dwell on them. By the way, a "termagant" is a bad-tempered woman, but, if you didn't know that word, you can still get the meaning from the context. The next sentence continues the description of Tom's wife, but the first clause refers to her "wordy warfare with her husband," so eliminate (A) as Tom must be arguing with his wife. The mention of "his face" in the second clause should focus your attention. If Tom's "face . . . showed signs," there would be something to see on his face. If the "signs" showed "their conflicts were not confined to words" there must be something to see on Tom's face, like cuts or bruises, from his wife's physical conflicts. This summary matches **(D)**, the correct answer. On test day, select **(D)** with confidence and move to the next question. For practice, "the bachelor" mentioned in the text is not Tom, but "the wayfarer" who hears the terrible arguing. Eliminate (B). The text explains that "No one ventured . . . to interfere between them," but never mentions Tom's view of any interruption. Eliminate (C).

12. A

Difficulty: Easy

Category: Information and Ideas

Getting to the Answer: Begin by identifying Wang and Zhang's hypothesis: direct application of antibiotics is more "efficient" than an IV injection. In their study, the researchers used microrobots to directly apply the antibiotics. Predict that the correct answer will support their hypothesis by showing results in which *the microrobot treatment is both effective and more efficient than the IV treatment*. Choice **(A)** provides this support and is correct; the dosage needed in the IV treatment was "thousands of times larger," so the microrobot treatment was more efficient.

Choice (B) is incorrect because it shows the microrobot treatment as being much less effective than the IV treatment. (C) is also incorrect because it addresses a drawback of the microrobot treatment rather than evidence of its efficiency. (D) is incorrect because it provides the opposite of the needed support: it shows the microrobot treatment as less efficient.

13. C

Difficulty: Medium

Category: Information and Ideas

Getting to the Answer: The correct answer will be a quote from the play illustrating why "the exploitation of robots" will make "the world better" according to Domin. Only **(C)** correctly does so, as Domin claims the robots will be so productive as to eliminate poverty among humans. Choice (A) is incorrect because it provides no justification for the exploitation of the robots, only for the claim that robots should not need emotions or other "tassels or ornaments." (B) is tempting in that Domin offers a justification for exploiting the robots, that they are cheap workers with minimal needs, but it contains no evidence supporting Domin's claim that the robots will make the world a better place. (D) is incorrect because it is only Domin discussing the types of robots, not justifying their exploitation.

14. A

Difficulty: Hard

Category: Information and Ideas

Getting to the Answer: The question asks for a reason that "the Affordable Care Act [might have] improved high school graduation rates." Now, read the beginning of the text to find the connection between the Affordable Care Act and the graph. The first two sentences explain that "the Affordable Care Act . . . made health insurance more widely available" and that "children could be included on a parent's plan." So a good way to connect the author's claim to the table would be something like *more health insurance might have led to more high school graduations*. Now, check the choices. **(A)** matches the prediction and the data and is correct. On test day, mark **(A)** confidently and move to the next question because there is *always* only one correct answer.

For the record, (B) overlooks New York's 2018 statistics. Furthermore, comparing the percentages of graduating high school students to the percentage of the population with health insurance does not support the author's claim; the *change* in each measure must be evaluated. Eliminate (B). Incorrect choices (C) and (D) each compare one state among the others, but the claim requires a comparison between the changes in the measures.

15. A

Difficulty: Hard

Category: Information and Ideas

Getting to the Answer: The passage focuses on a new explanation for the disappearance of the Norse colonies, so expect that the correct answer will center on this topic. Choice **(A)** does so and is correct. Also, the beginning of the passage states that the colony was founded around the year 1000 C.E., and then, in the fourth sentence, the author writes, "a particularly warm period . . . occurred between the years 800 C.E. and 1300 C.E." The "mild," warm weather was uncharacteristic of the usually cold, harsh climate.

Incorrect choice (B) contradicts the passage. Prosperous colonies disappeared, so climate change did affect the ancient Norse settlements. Incorrect choices (C) and (D) introduce new topics that the passage did not mention. There is no mention of the wisdom behind the colonization of Greenland (C) or the suitability of ancient Greenland for human life (D).

16. B

Difficulty: Easy

Category: Standard English Conventions

Getting to the Answer: The answer choices indicate that this question is testing what punctuation, if any, should be used after the name of the painting "*Mona Cat*." No punctuation is required, since the subject "*Mona Cat*" should not be separated from its verb "features." Choice **(B)** is correct. The comma and dash in (A) and (C) would be used to set off parenthetical information, and the colon in (D) would appear after an independent clause to introduce an additional clarifying idea.

17. D

Difficulty: Easy

Category: Standard English Conventions

Getting to the Answer: The answer choices indicate that this question is testing modifying phrases. Logically, it must be the researchers who were "Interested in the logistics of . . . bacteria," so the researchers should be placed as close to this introductory descriptive phrase as possible. Choice **(D)** does so and is correct. Choices (A) and (B) are incorrect because they indicate that the technique of cryo-electron microscopy was interested in bacteria movement. Choice (C) is incorrect because it results in the phrase modifying the vague pronoun "there."

18. C

Difficulty: Medium

Category: Standard English Conventions

Getting to the Answer: Parenthetical information in a sentence must be set off by punctuation, while essential information does not require punctuation. This question tests whether the descriptive phrase "heat" is essential in this sentence. Although the phrase adds relevant information, removing the phrase still results in a sentence that makes logical sense: the reader still knows that nuclear, coal, and oil power plants all generate the same thing. Since the phrase is parenthetical, it should be set off by a comma, dash, or pair of parentheses; **(C)** is correct. Choices (A) and (D) are incorrect because they are used to separate two independent clauses, which "heat" is not. (B) is incorrect because it omits the necessary punctuation entirely.

19. B

Difficulty: Medium

Category: Standard English Conventions

Getting to the Answer: When a pronoun's antecedent is far away from the pronoun itself, it can be difficult to identify the antecedent. The description of the samurai as "down-on-their-luck yet good-hearted" can be ignored, because it merely helps to elaborate on what type of people the samurai are. So, the clause after the colon could be reduced to "a village turns to seven samurai for the protection _____." Now, the pronoun's antecedent is clearer. The village needs protection, and "village" is grammatically singular. Thus, the singular pronoun "it" is required. **(B)** is correct.

Because "village" is grammatically singular, the plural pronoun "they" is inappropriate. So, (A) is incorrect. Since "village" does not refer to a singular person, the pronouns in (C) and (D) are likewise incorrect.

20. D

Difficulty: Hard

Category: Standard English Conventions

Getting to the Answer: The answer choices indicate that this question is testing verbs, so identify the missing verb's subject and its appropriate tense as you read. The verb's subject is the singular "nature," so eliminate the plural verbs in (A) and (B). Note that "of their struggles and successes" is a prepositional phrase that describes the subject "nature," and "both on the home front and on the battlefields" is parenthetical information. Thus, no words from these phrases can be the subject of the verb "was." Choice (C) is incorrect because it results in an incomplete idea: "the nature . . . being not just to gain . . . ." Choice **(D)** uses the singular, past tense "was" to describe the "nature" of African Americans' "past military service" and is correct.

21. B

Difficulty: Hard

Category: Standard English Conventions

Getting to the Answer: The answer choices indicate that this question is testing how to join portions of a sentence. The portion before "however" is an independent clause, with subject-verb "Paintings are." The portion after "however" also contains an independent clause, with subject-verb "Brígido Lara created." Without a FANBOYS conjunction, a comma cannot join independent clauses, so eliminate (A) and (D). The remaining choices use semicolons, which can be used to join independent clauses; the choices differ in whether the contrast transition "however" is placed with the first or second clause. The intended contrast is between the first clause and the preceding sentence: the Flower Portrait painting was misdated, but other types of art can be misdated as well. Thus, "however" should be grouped with the first clause; **(B)** is correct. Choice (C) would indicate a contrast between the first clause and the second clause.

22. C

Difficulty: Hard

Category: Standard English Conventions

Getting to the Answer: The answer choices indicate that this question is likely testing sentence structure, since the choices contain commas and the possible inclusion of the word "that." Carefully determine the sentence's structure to figure out whether the comma and "that" are required. The sentence begins with an introductory prepositional phrase ("In an effort . . ."), followed by an independent clause ("marine biologists . . . created"). Finally, the next portion ("a collection of data . . .") seems to describe the "Reef Life Survey." Read the sentence with and without "that" to test which is correct. If "that" is *not* included, the end of the sentence is an independent clause ("a collection . . . allows"); two independent clauses cannot be joined by only the comma that follows "Reef Life Survey." Eliminate (A) and (D). If "that" *is* included, the entire phrase beginning "a collection of data" describes "Reef Life Survey" and is correctly preceded by a comma. A comma should not separate "that" from the noun phrase it is describing, so eliminate (B). Choice **(C)** is correct.

23. B

Difficulty: Medium

Category: Expression of Ideas

Getting to the Answer: The question stem indicates that this question is testing transitions. As you read the passage, identify the two ideas that are being connected by the missing transition so you can determine the relationship between them. The first idea is that the Second Agricultural Revolution "increased crop yields and reduced the labor that was required for rural agriculture." In other words, there were more crops and less

need for rural labor. The second idea is that cities grew and factory workers were available. The relationship between the ideas is one of cause-and-effect: *because* there was less need for rural labor, laborers could move to cities and work in factories. Choice **(B)** is a cause-and-effect transition and is correct.

Choice (A) is incorrect because the urban population did not grow *despite* ("Still") there being less demand for rural labor, but rather because of it. Choice (C) is incorrect because the urban population growth is not *an example* of increased crop yields and less rural labor. Nor is the urban growth a *more specific* instance, choice (D), of anything mentioned in the previous sentence.

24. D

Difficulty: Hard

Category: Expression of Ideas

Getting to the Answer: The question stem indicates that this question is testing transitions. As you read the passage, identify the two ideas that are being connected by the missing transition so you can determine the relationship between them. The first idea is that the bald eagle had "special protections" from the Bald Eagle Protection Act. The second idea is that the act outlawed killing bald eagles and interfering with their nests. The second idea *specifies* what kinds of "special protections" the bald eagle received from the law; **(D)** is correct.

"Consequently" in choice (A) is incorrect because the act did not outlaw actions against bald eagles *because of* the act giving special protections; rather the outlawed actions are *specific examples* of the protections. Choice (B) is incorrect because the outlawed actions are not *similar to*, but instead are *examples of*, the special protections of the act. "Furthermore" in choice (C) is incorrect because the outlawed actions are not *additional to* the special protections; they are *examples of* the special protections.

25. C

Difficulty: Hard

Category: Expression of Ideas

Getting to the Answer: The phrase "logical transition" indicates that this is a Transitions question. To determine the correct transition word to use in context, first determine the relationship between the ideas it must connect. The second sentence describes how glove puppetry "might not seem to have the potential to attract a mass audience in the modern world." The third sentence explains glove puppetry in modern Taiwan and how it uses modern technology like "computer-generated graphics." Specifically, it describes how it attracts a mass audience. Thus, a contrast transition is needed to connect the two sentences. The correct choice is **(C)**.

Choices (A) and (D) are incorrect because they are cause-and-effect transitions. (B) is incorrect because the third sentence does not continue the thought of the second sentence.

26. C

Difficulty: Medium

Category: Expression of Ideas

Getting to the Answer: The question stem indicates that you need to summarize ("present") and identify the conclusions of the study, so look for these elements as you read the bullet points. The first point describes the study's method (a computer learning model) and focus (hyena whoops). The second point provides a finding of the study: the hyenas have individual whoops that allow for identification. The last three bullet points concern another finding: repetition of the whoops increases identification accuracy. Use this summary of the study and its results as your prediction, which matches **(C)**. Choice **(C)** is correct because it "presents" the study by summarizing its method (a computer learning model of Kenyan hyena whoops) and it provides its conclusions (hyenas have individual whoops that they repeat to be identified). Choices (A) and (B) are incorrect because they omit the study's conclusions. Choice (D) is incorrect because it omits any summary of the study itself.

27. A

Difficulty: Hard

Category: Expression of Ideas

Getting to the Answer: The question stem indicates that you need to "present," or summarize, a study and describe its conclusions, so look for these elements as you read the bullet points. The first bullet point identifies that the study concerned "embodied cognition," and the second bullet point defines embodied cognition. The next three bullet points describe the procedure used in the study: subjects had to compare the sizes of object words while some had their hands restrained. The last bullet point provides a conclusion of the study: the restrained subjects showed less brain activity. Look for an answer choice that summarizes the study and its focus on embodied cognition and that identifies the study's finding about brain activity; choice **(A)** is correct.

Choice (B) is incorrect because it only summarizes the procedure of the study and does not address its conclusion. On the other hand, choice (C) is incorrect because it provides a conclusion without summarizing the specifics of the study: (C) never mentions embodied cognition or that it studied the words for physical objects. Choice (D) is incorrect because it does not discuss the study's conclusion.

Math: Routing Module Answers and Explanations

1.   A

Difficulty: Easy

Category: Algebra

Getting to the Answer: You could start by cross-multiplying to get rid of the denominators, but simplifying the numerators first will make the calculations easier. Don't forget to distribute the negative to both terms in the parentheses on the right-hand side of the equation:

$$\frac{4(n-2)+5}{2} = \frac{13-(9+4n)}{4}$$

$$\frac{4n-8+5}{2} = \frac{13-9-4n}{4}$$

$$\frac{4n-3}{2} = \frac{4-4n}{4}$$

$$4(4n-3) = 2(4-4n)$$

$$16n-12 = 8-8n$$

$$16n = 20-8n$$

$$24n = 20$$

$$n = \frac{20}{24} = \frac{5}{6}$$

Choice **(A)** is correct.

2.   A

Difficulty: Easy

Category: Algebra

Getting to the Answer: When you see an expression like $f(x)$, it means to substitute the given value for x in the function's equation. When there is more than one function involved, pay careful attention to which function should be evaluated first. You are looking for the value of $f(x)$ at $x = 5$. Because $f(x)$ is defined in terms of $g(x)$, evaluate $g(5)$ first by substituting 5 for x in the expression $x + 2$:

$$g(5) = 5 + 2 = 7$$

$$f(5) = -3g(5) = -3(7) = -21$$

Therefore, **(A)** is correct.

3.   B

Difficulty: Easy

Category: Algebra

Getting to the Answer: Solve as you would an equality, but remember, if you multiply or divide by a negative number, you must flip the symbol.

$$5(x-2) - 3x < 4x - 6$$

$$5x - 10 - 3x < 4x - 6$$

$$2x - 10 < 4x - 6$$

$$-2x < 4$$

$$x > -2$$

Choice **(B)** is correct.

4.   A

Difficulty: Easy

Category: Advanced Math

Getting to the Answer: The factored form of the equation of a parabola gives the x-intercepts directly, so factor the right side of the equation. Start by setting up the two terms. The sign of the constant term (24) is positive, so the signs in the two terms are the same. The sign of the x term (-10) is negative, so both terms have negative signs: $(x-\ )(x-\ )$. Now, think of the factors that multiply to 24 and add to 10. The factors are $(x-6)(x-4)$, making **(A)** the correct answer. Note that the remaining choices are mathematically correct, but they do not directly display the x-intercepts.

5.   A

Difficulty: Easy

Category: Advanced Math

Getting to the Answer: When you write an equation in terms of a specific variable, you are simply solving the equation for that variable. To do this, you'll need to use the property that raising a quantity to the one-fourth power is the same as taking its fourth root and that applying a negative exponent to a quantity is the same as writing its reciprocal. Rewrite the equation using these properties and then solve for n using inverse operations. Note that the inverse of taking a fourth root of a quantity is raising the quantity to the fourth power:

$$m = \frac{1}{n^{-\frac{1}{4}}}$$

$$m = \frac{\sqrt[4]{n}}{1}$$

$$(m)^4 = \left(\sqrt[4]{n}\right)^4$$

$$m^4 = n$$

Choice **(A)** is correct.

6. B

Difficulty: Easy

Category: Problem Solving and Data Analysis

Getting to the Answer: When a question involves scale factors, apply the scale factor to the given measurement to find the scaled measurement.

$$\frac{1}{8} \times 19.9 = 2.4875 \approx 2.5$$

Choice **(B)** is correct.

7. B

Difficulty: Medium

Category: Geometry and Trigonometry

Getting to the Answer: Area $= \frac{1}{2}bh$; in a right triangle, either of the legs can serve as the base or the height. So, $100 = \frac{1}{2}(20)h$ and $h = 10$. Hypotenuse$^2 = 10^2 + 20^2 = 500$, so the length of the hypotenuse is $\sqrt{500} = \sqrt{100}\sqrt{5} = 10\sqrt{5}$ inches. Choice **(B)** is correct.

8. 29

Difficulty: Medium

Category: Algebra

Getting to the Answer: When a system consists of two equations already written in terms of y, the quickest way to solve the system is to set the equations equal to each other and then use inverse operations. Don't let the fraction intimidate you—you can write the first equation as a fraction over 1 and use cross-multiplication:

$$\frac{3x - 1}{1} = \frac{5x + 8}{2}$$
$$2(3x - 1) = 5x + 8$$
$$6x - 2 = 5x + 8$$
$$6x = 5x + 10$$
$$x = 10$$

Don't stop too soon—the question is asking for the value of y, not the value of x. To find y, substitute 10 for x in either equation and simplify:

$$y = 3(10) - 1$$
$$= 30 - 1$$
$$= 29$$

Enter **29**.

9. 1/5, 0.2, or .2

Difficulty: Medium

Category: Algebra

Getting to the Answer: There are two variables but only one equation, so you can't actually solve the equation for k. Instead, recall that an equation has infinitely many solutions when the left side is identical to the right side. When this happens, everything cancels out and you get $0 = 0$, which is always true. Start by simplifying the right-hand side of the equation. Don't simplify the left side because k is already in a good position:

$$k(10x - 5) = 2(3 + x) - 7$$
$$k(10x - 5) = 6 + 2x - 7$$
$$k(10x - 5) = 2x - 1$$

Next, compare the left side of the equation to the right side. Rather than distributing the k, notice that $2x$ is a fifth of $10x$ and -1 is a fifth of -5, so if k were $\frac{1}{5}$ (or 0.2), then both sides of the equation would equal $2x - 1$, and it would therefore have infinitely many solutions. Thus, k is $\frac{1}{5}$. Enter **1/5, 0.2, or .2**.

10. B

Difficulty: Medium

Category: Algebra

Getting to the Answer: The cost per night in the hospital is the same as the unit rate, which is represented by the slope of the line. Use the grid lines and the axis labels to count the rise and the run from the y-intercept of the line (0, 26) to the next point that hits an intersection of two grid lines, (2, 34). Pay careful attention to how the grid lines are marked (by 2s on the x-axis and by 2s on the y-axis). The line rises 8 units and runs 2 units, so the slope is $\frac{8}{2}$, or 4 units. Note that units on the y-axis are thousands, which means it costs an average of $4,000 per night to stay in the hospital. Note that you could also use the slope formula and the two points to find the slope:

$$\frac{34 - 26}{2 - 0} = \frac{8}{2}$$
$$4 \times \$1,000 = \$4,000$$

Choice **(B)** is correct.

11. C

Difficulty: Medium

Category: Advanced Math

Getting to the Answer: A graph is *decreasing* when the slope is negative; it is *increasing* when the slope is positive. Eliminate (A) because there are some segments on the graph that have a positive slope. Eliminate (B) because the slope is negative, not positive, between 2009 and 2010. Choice **(C)** is correct because the slope is negative for each segment between 2004 and 2007 and also between 2009 and 2011. On test day, confidently select **(C)** and move to the next question; there is *always* only one correct answer. But for practice, (D) is incorrect because the slope is negative between 2009 and 2010, and the slope is positive between 2011 and 2012 and also between 2012 and 2013.

12. D

Difficulty: Medium

Category: Advanced Math

Getting to the Answer: You aren't given much information to go on except the shape of the graph, so you'll need to think about what the shape means. Remember, linear functions increase at a constant rate, exponential functions increase at either an increasing or decreasing rate, gradually at first and then more quickly or vice versa, and quadratics and polynomials reverse direction one or more times. The graph begins by decreasing extremely quickly, but then it almost (but not quite) levels off. Therefore, it can't be linear, and because it doesn't change direction, an exponential function, **(D)**, would be the best model for the data.

13. C

Difficulty: Medium

Category: Advanced Math

Getting to the Answer: When using function notation, $f(x)$ is simply another way of saying y, so this question is asking you to find the values of x for which $y = 0$, or in other words, where the graph crosses the x-axis. The graph crosses the x-axis at the points $(-2, 0)$ and $(3, 0)$, so the values of x for which $f(x) = 0$ are -2 and 3, which matches choice **(C)**.

14. D

Difficulty: Medium

Category: Algebra

Getting to the Answer: To determine the equation of the line of best fit, first look at the scatterplot to identify the y-intercept. For this graph, it's about 35. This means you can eliminate choices (B) and (C).

To find the slope, use two points that lie on (or very close to) the line. You can use the y-intercept, $(0, 35)$, as one of them to save time and estimate the second, such as $(72, 4)$. Use the slope formula to find the slope:

$$m = \frac{y_2 - y_1}{x_2 - x_1} = \frac{4 - 35}{72 - 0} = \frac{-31}{72} \approx -0.43$$

The equation that has the closest slope and y-intercept is **(D)**.

15. A

Difficulty: Medium

Category: Geometry and Trigonometry

Getting to the Answer: This question does not provide a graphic, so sketch a quick diagram on scratch paper of the information presented. Be sure to show the direction of traffic for each street. The question describes two parallel streets, cut by a transversal. Start with that, and then add all the details:

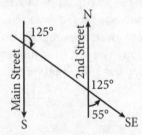

Traffic traveling south on Main Street must make a 125° turn onto the new road. This is the angle between where the traffic was initially headed and where it is headed after it makes the turn. Traffic on 2nd Street is traveling north, in the opposite direction. As shown in the diagram, the angle that the northbound traffic would make is supplementary to the corresponding angle made by the southbound traffic. When two parallel lines are cut by a transversal, corresponding angles are congruent, which means that cars turning off of 2nd Street will make a $180 - 125 = 55°$ turn onto the new road. Choice **(A)** is correct.

16. C

Difficulty: Hard

Category: Algebra

Getting to the Answer: You don't need to use algebra to answer this question, and you also don't need to graph each system. Instead, think about how the graphs would look. The only time a system of linear inequalities has no solution is when it consists of two parallel lines shaded in opposite directions. All the inequalities are written in slope-intercept form, so look for parallel lines (two lines that have the same slope but different y-intercepts). The slopes in (A) are different ($m = 1$ and $m = 2$), so eliminate this choice. The same is true for (B) ($m = 1$ and $m = -1$) and (D) ($m = -1$ and $m = 1$). This means **(C)** must be correct ($m = 1$ and $m = 1$, $b = 1$ and $b = -1$). The graph of the system is shown here:

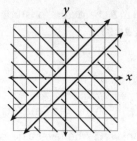

Because the shading never overlaps, the system has no solution.

17. 4

Difficulty: Hard

Category: Algebra

Getting to the Answer: Recognizing that a question like this requires a system of equations is the key to getting started. Assemble two equations using variables that make sense to help you stay organized. The two "pieces" of information given in this question are the *number* of each type of furniture and the *weight* of those items. Let b and t represent the number of bookcases and tables in the truck. The total number of items in the truck is 14, so one equation is $b + t = 14$. Bookcases weigh 25 pounds each, the tables weigh 37 pounds each, and the total weight is 410 pounds, so the second equation is $25b + 37t = 410$. Write the system vertically so you can easily combine the two equations:

$$b + t = 14$$

$$25b + 37t = 410$$

The question can be answered with either substitution or combination. To use combination, solve the system by combining the equations in such a way that one of the terms cancel out.

You can solve for either b or t first. To solve for b, there is a $37t$ in the second equation, so multiply the first equation by -37 (to create a $-37t$ term that will cancel), and then add the equations:

$$-37(b + t = 14) \rightarrow -37b - 37t = -518$$

$$25b + 37t = 410 \rightarrow \quad 25b + 37t = 410$$

$$-12b = -108$$

$$\frac{-12b}{-12} = \frac{-108}{-12}$$

$$b = 9$$

There are 9 bookcases on the truck, but don't stop too soon. You need how many *more* bookcases there are. Since there are 14 total pieces, there are $14 - 9 = 5$ tables, and there are $9 - 5 = 4$ *more* bookcases. Enter **4**.

18. D

Difficulty: Hard

Category: Advanced Math

Getting to the Answer: To add two rational expressions, the denominators must be the same, so you need to find the common denominator, rewrite both expressions using that denominator, and then add the numerators. Start with the more complex denominator: $35 - 5x$ is the same as $5(7 - x)$, which almost looks like the other denominator ($x - 7$). To make it look just right, factor out a -5 instead of a 5. The common denominator is $-5(x - 7)$. This means you need to multiply the first term by $\frac{-5}{-5}$ (which is the same as multiplying by 1). Note that you don't need to multiply the second term by anything. Adding the two rational expressions gives:

$$\frac{-5}{-5}\left(\frac{4x}{x - 7}\right) + \frac{5}{35 - 5x}$$

$$\frac{-20x}{-5x + 35} + \frac{5}{35 - 5x}$$

$$\frac{-20x}{35 - 5x} + \frac{5}{35 - 5x}$$

$$\frac{-20x + 5}{35 - 5x}$$

A is the numerator of the expression. Choice **(D)** is correct.

19. 6

Difficulty: Hard

Category: Advanced Math

Getting to the Answer: When you are given the graph of a parabola, try to use what you know about intercepts, the vertex, and the axis of symmetry to answer the question. Here, you could try to use points from the graph to find its equation, but this is not necessary because the question only asks for the value of b. As a shortcut, recall that you can find the vertex of a parabola using the formula $x = -\dfrac{b}{2a}$ (the quadratic formula without the radical part). You are given that $a = -1$. Now, look at the graph—the vertex of the parabola is $(3, 8)$, so substitute 3 for x, -1 for a, and solve for b:

$$3 = -\frac{b}{2(-1)}$$

$$3 = -\left(\frac{b}{-2}\right)$$

$$3 = \frac{b}{2}$$

$$3(2) = b$$

$$6 = b$$

As an alternate method, you could plug the value of a and the vertex (from the graph) into the vertex form of a quadratic equation and simplify:

$$y = a(x - h)^2 + k$$

$$= -1(x - 3)^2 + 8$$

$$= -1(x^2 - 6x + 9) + 8$$

$$= -x^2 + 6x - 9 + 8$$

$$= -x^2 + 6x - 1$$

The coefficient of x is b, so $b = 6$. Enter **6**.

20. 24.97

Difficulty: Hard

Category: Problem Solving and Data Analysis

Getting to the Answer: Percent change is given by the formula $\dfrac{\text{amount of change}}{\text{original amount}} \times 100\%$. To find the total percent change, you'll need to work your way through each of the days and then use the formula. Jot down the index value at the end of each day as you go. Do not round until you reach your final answer. First, calculate the value of the index at closing of the first day: it opened at 306 and decreased by 2%, which means

the value at the end of the first day was $100 - 2 = 98\%$ of the starting amount, or $306 \times 0.98 = 299.88$. This becomes the opening amount on the second day, when it decreased again by 13% to close at $100 - 13 = 87\%$ of the opening amount, or $299.88 \times 0.87 = 260.8956$. This becomes the opening amount on the third day, when it decreased by another 12% to end at $100 - 12 = 88\%$ of the opening amount, or $260.8956 \times 0.88 \approx 229.5881$. Now, use the percent change formula to calculate the percent decrease from opening on the first day (306) to closing on the third (229.588):

$$\text{Percent decrease} = \frac{306 - 229.5881}{306} \times 100\%$$

$$= \frac{76.4119}{306} \times 100\%$$

$$\approx .24971 \times 100\%$$

$$= 24.971\%$$

You can enter up to 5 characters for student-produced responses. Enter **24.97**.

21. D

Difficulty: Hard

Category: Problem Solving and Data Analysis

Getting to the Answer: Whenever a question involves a two-way table, read carefully to see which rows and/or columns you need to focus on. The question asks for the probability that the registered voter chosen will not view the issue *unfavorably*. This means the voter's view is either *neutral* or *favorable*, so look at columns 3, 4, and 5. Add the numbers together to get $228 + 487 + 163 = 878$. The probability that you're looking for is this number divided by the total number of registered voters $\times 100\%$: $878 \div 1{,}094 \times 100\% \approx 80.25\%$, or approximately 80.3%, **(D)** is correct.

Note that alternatively, since the question is asking for the probability that the voter is *not* unfavorable, you could reach the same answer by subtracting the probability of an unfavorable response from 1. So, $(1 - (112 + 104) \div 1{,}094) \times 100\% \approx 80.25\%$

22. 34

Difficulty: Hard

Category: Geometry and Trigonometry

Getting to the Answer: Copy the figure and add information from the question to the diagram. There are two right triangles—the smaller one formed by the saber, the path of the Sun's rays, and the ground; and the larger one formed by the brick wall, the path of the Sun's rays, and the ground. The two triangles share one angle (the small angle on the left side), and each has a 90-degree angle (where the saber and the brick wall each meet the ground), making the third pair of corresponding angles also congruent. Two triangles with three identical angles are similar; it follows that the sides of the triangles are proportional. You'll need to convert the height of the wall to inches because the question asks for the length of the saber in inches. (You could also convert the base lengths to inches, but it is not necessary because you can compare feet to feet in that ratio.)

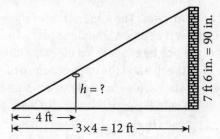

Now that you have a more detailed drawing, set up and solve a proportion:

$$\frac{\text{base of small triangle}}{\text{base of large triangle}} = \frac{\text{length of saber (in inches)}}{\text{height of wall (in inches)}}$$

$$\frac{4}{12} = \frac{h}{90}$$

$$4(90) = 12h$$

$$360 = 12h$$

$$30 = h$$

Don't forget to add the 4 inches that are stuck in the ground to find that the length of the saber is $30 + 4 = 34$ inches. Enter **34**.

Math: Module A Answers and Explanations

1. D

Difficulty: Easy

Category: Algebra

Getting to the Answer: Sales must equal expenses for the manufacturer to break even (sales = expenses). Set the functions equal to each other and solve for *n*:

$$9.5n = 11,625 + 4.85n$$
$$4.65n = 11,625$$
$$n = 2,500$$

Choice **(D)** is correct.

2. D

Difficulty: Easy

Category: Algebra

Getting to the Answer: A quick examination of the equations in the system will tell you which strategy to use to solve it. Because 4*x* and −4*x* are opposites of one another, the system is already perfectly set up to solve by elimination (combining the two equations by adding them):

$$4x + y = -5$$
$$\underline{-4x - 2y = -2}$$
$$-y = -7$$
$$y = 7$$

Choice **(D)** is correct.

3. B

Difficulty: Easy

Category: Algebra

Getting to the Answer: Finding an *x*-intercept is easy when you know the equation of the line—it's the value of *x* when *y* is 0. Notice that the answer choices are very close together. This means you shouldn't just estimate visually. Take the time to do the math. Everything you need to write the equation is shown on the graph—just pay careful attention to how the grid lines are labeled. The *y*-intercept is 10 and the line rises 2 units and runs 1 unit from one point to the next, so the slope is $\frac{2}{1} = 2$. This means the equation of the line, in slope-intercept

form, is $y = 2x + 10$. Now, set the equation equal to zero and solve for *x*:

$$0 = 2x + 10$$
$$-10 = 2x$$
$$-5 = x$$

The line will intersect the *x*-axis at −5, which is **(B)**.

4. 5/8, 0.625, or .625

Difficulty: Easy

Category: Algebra

Getting to the Answer: The average rate of change for a linear function is the same as the slope of the line. Find the slope of the line by either using the slope formula or by counting the rise and the run from one point to the next. If you start at (0, −3), the line rises 5 units and runs 8 units to get to (8, 2), so the slope, or average rate of change, is $\frac{5}{8}$ or its decimal equivalent, 0.625 or .625. Enter **5/8, 0.625, or .625**.

5. D

Difficulty: Easy

Category: Advanced Math

Getting to the Answer: A root of an equation is an *x*-value that corresponds to a *y*-value of 0. The *x*-intercepts of the graph, and therefore the roots of the equation, are $x = -1$ and $x = 5$. When $x = -1$, the value of $x + 1$ is 0, so one of the factors is $x + 1$. When $x = 5$, the value of $x - 5$ is 0, so the other factor is $x - 5$. The equation in **(D)** is the only one that contains these factors and is therefore correct.

6. C

Difficulty: Easy

Category: Advanced Math

Getting to the Answer: The expression is a difference of two squares, so write each term as a quantity squared and then use the difference of squares rule $a^2 - b^2 = (a + b)(a - b)$:

$$25x^2 - \frac{4}{9}$$
$$= (5x)^2 - \left(\frac{2}{3}\right)^2$$
$$= \left(5x + \frac{2}{3}\right)\left(5x - \frac{2}{3}\right)$$

Choice **(C)** is correct.

7. A

Difficulty: Easy

Category: Problem Solving and Data Analysis

Getting to the Answer: This question requires concentration, but no complicated calculations. First, you need to identify the rows that contain information about the seating on the 777s, which are the bottom two rows. To find the probability that the seat is a Business Class seat, find the total number of seats in that category (in only the bottom two rows), and divide by the total number of seats on the planes (in only the bottom two rows):

$$P(\text{Business Class}) = \frac{37 + 52}{194 + 37 + 16 + 227 + 52 + 8}$$
$$= \frac{89}{534} = \frac{1}{6} = 0.1\overline{6}$$

That's the equivalent of $\frac{1}{6}$, which is Choice **(A)**.

8. A

Difficulty: Easy

Category: Problem Solving and Data Analysis

Getting to the Answer: Let the units in this question guide you to the answer. You can do one conversion at a time or all of them at once. Just be sure to line up the units so they'll cancel correctly. The company uses 8 machines, each of which pumps at a rate of 37.5 gallons per minute, so the rate is actually $8 \times 37.5 = 300$ gallons per minute. Find the total number of gallons needed and then use the rate to find the time:

$$2,500\ \text{bbl} \times \frac{42\ \text{gallons}}{1\ \text{bbl}} \times \frac{1\ \text{minute}}{300\ \text{gallons}} = 350\ \text{minutes}$$

The answers are given in hours and minutes, so change 350 minutes to $350 \div 60 \approx 5.833$ hours, which is 5 hours and 50 minutes. **(A)** is correct.

9. 78

Difficulty: Easy

Category: Problem Solving and Data Analysis

Getting to the Answer: Translate carefully from English into math. If Alex's score is 12% less than Chris's score, Alex earned 100% − 12% or 88% of Chris's score. So Alex's score = $(0.88)(89) = 78.32$. Rounding to the nearest integer gives 78. Enter **78**.

10. A

Difficulty: Easy

Category: Geometry and Trigonometry

Getting to the Answer: Complementary angles (angles that sum to 90°) have a special relationship relative to trig values: the cosine of an acute angle is equal to the sine of the angle's complement and vice versa. Because only one of the answers can be correct, look for the simplest relationship (complementary angles): 50° is complementary to 40°, so cos 40° = sin 50°, which means **(A)** is correct.

11. 54

Difficulty: Easy

Category: Geometry and Trigonometry

Getting to the Answer: The formula for the area of a triangle is $A = \frac{1}{2}bh$. For a right triangle, the base and height correspond to the leg lengths. You are given the length of the shorter leg and the ratio of the side lengths. Use the ratio to find the length of the longer leg, x:

$$\frac{9}{x} = \frac{3}{4}$$
$$36 = 3x$$
$$12 = x$$

Note that the longest side of a right triangle is the hypotenuse and, in this case, would have a side length ratio of 5.

The area of the triangle is $A = \frac{1}{2}(9)(12) = 54$ square units. Enter **54**.

12. 440

Difficulty: Medium

Category: Algebra

Getting to the Answer: Translate from English into math and write a system of equations with $t =$ the cost of the tankless heater in dollars and $c =$ the cost of the conventional heater in dollars. First, a tankless heater (t) costs $160 more (+160) than twice as much as the conventional one ($2c$), or $t = 2c + 160$. Together, a tankless heater (t) and a conventional heater (c) cost $1,000, or $t + c = 1,000$. The system is:

$$\begin{cases} t = 2c + 160 \\ t + c = 1,000 \end{cases}$$

The top equation is already solved for *t*, so substitute $2c + 160$ into the second equation for *t* and solve for *c*:

$$2c + 160 + c = 1{,}000$$
$$3c + 160 = 1{,}000$$
$$3c = 840$$
$$c = 280$$

Be careful—that's not the answer! The conventional hot water heater costs $280, so the tankless heater costs $2(\$280) + \$160 = \$720$. This means that the tankless heater costs $\$720 - \$280 = \$440$ more than the conventional heater. Enter **440**.

13. A
Difficulty: Medium

Category: Algebra

Getting to the Answer: You don't need to separate this compound inequality into pieces. Just remember that whatever you do to one piece you must do to all three pieces. The fractions in this question make it look more complicated than it really is, so start by clearing them. To do this, multiply everything by the least common denominator, 10. Then solve for *d*:

$$0 < \frac{d}{2} + 1 \leq \frac{8}{5}$$
$$10(0) < 10\left(\frac{d}{2} + 1\right) \leq 10\left(\frac{8}{5}\right)$$
$$0 < 5d + 10 \leq 16$$
$$-10 < 5d \leq 6$$
$$-2 < d \leq \frac{6}{5}$$

Read the inequality symbols carefully. The value of *d* is between -2 and $\frac{6}{5}$ but does not include -2 because of the $<$ symbol. Therefore, **(A)** is the correct answer.

14. B
Difficulty: Medium

Category: Algebra

Getting to the Answer: Write an equation in words first and then translate from English into math. Keep in mind that the laundry detergent is on sale, but the dog food is not. The detergent is 30% off, which means that Sara pays only $100\% - 30\% = 70\%$ of the price, or $0.70(\$8) = \$5.60$. The dog food is three cans for $4, and she buys 12 cans. This means she buys 4 sets of 3, so she pays

$4 \times \$4 = \$16$ for the dog food. The total cost equals the detergent price ($5.60) times how many she buys (*x*) plus the total dog food price ($16). This translates as $C = 5.6x + 16$, which matches **(B)**. Note that there are variables in the answer choices, so you could also use the Picking Numbers strategy to answer this question.

15. C
Difficulty: Medium

Category: Advanced Math

Getting to the Answer: Start by simplifying inside the absolute value:

$$|3x - 2 + 4x| < 7$$
$$|7x - 2| < 7$$

Now rewrite the absolute value as two inequalities: if $|7x - 2| < 7$, either $(7x - 2) < 7$ or $-(7x - 2) < 7$. Solve each, starting with the first:

$$7x - 2 < 7$$
$$7x < 9$$
$$x < \frac{9}{7}$$

and now the other:

$$-(7x - 2) < 7$$
$$-7x + 2 < 7$$
$$7x - 2 > -7$$
$$7x > -5$$
$$x > -\frac{5}{7}$$

So the range of possible answers is $-\frac{5}{7} < x < \frac{9}{7}$, making **(C)** correct. Note that (B) is incorrect because the relationship is strictly less than, not less than or equal.

16. A
Difficulty: Medium

Category: Advanced Math

Getting to the Answer: On test day, use the method of solving a quadratic equation that is accurate and fastest for you. Because there are no factors of 5 that sum to 10, completing the square is a good strategy for this question. Take the coefficient of the *x* term and divide it by 2, square it, and add it to the two terms with *x* variables. Don't forget to add the same amount to the other side of the equation as well. This creates a perfect square of x terms, so the last step is to take the square root of both sides:

$$x^2 + 10x + 25 = -5 + 25$$
$$x^2 + 10x + 25 = 20$$
$$(x + 5)^2 = 20$$
$$x + 5 = \sqrt{20}$$
$$x + 5 = \pm 2\sqrt{5}$$
$$x = -5 + 2\sqrt{5}, -5 - 2\sqrt{5}$$

Choice **(A)** is correct.

17. A

Difficulty: Medium

Category: Problem-Solving and Data Analysis

Getting to the Answer: Examine the graph, paying careful attention to units and labels. Here, the years increase by 2 for each grid line and the number of owls by 25. The average change per year is the same as the slope of the line of best fit. Find the slope of the line of best fit using the slope formula, $m = \frac{y_2 - y_1}{x_2 - x_1}$, and any two points that lie on (or very close to) the line. Using the two endpoints of the data, (1994, 1,200) and (2014, 700), the average change per year is $\frac{700 - 1,200}{2014 - 1994} = \frac{-500}{20} = -25$, which is **(A)**. Pay careful attention to the sign of the answer—the number of owls is decreasing, so the rate of change is negative.

18. C

Difficulty: Medium

Category: Geometry and Trigonometry

Getting to the Answer: Because AB is parallel to DE, triangles ACB and DCE have the same angles and are, therefore, similar. Determine the length of DC using the Pythagorean theorem, then use the side ratio of the triangles to obtain the length of AC.

Side DC is the hypotenuse of triangle DCE, so $DC^2 = 18^2 + 20^2 = 324 + 400 = 724$, which factors to 4×181. (Use the answer choices to find the factors more quickly.) So $DC = \sqrt{4(181)} = 2\sqrt{181}$. Sides AB and DE are corresponding sides. Since $AB = 40$ and $DE = 20$, the side ratio of the triangles is 2:1. Therefore, $AC = 2DC = 4\sqrt{181}$. Choice **(C)** is correct.

19. 105

Difficulty: Medium

Category: Advanced Math

Getting to the Answer: If the polynomials are "evenly divisible," there will be no remainder. Divide the polynomials to find the value of k that will leave no remainder.

$$
\begin{array}{r}
x^2 + 2x - 15 \\
x - 7 \overline{) x^3 - 5x^2 - 29x + k} \\
\underline{-(x^3 - 7x^2)} \\
2x^2 - 29x \\
\underline{-(2x^2 - 14x)} \\
-15x + k \\
\underline{-(-15x + 105)} \\
k - 105
\end{array}
$$

In order for the difference between the two terms at the bottom to be 0, leaving no remainder, k must be 105. Enter **105**.

20. D

Difficulty: Hard

Category: Advanced Math

Getting to the Answer: The first step is to recognize that $x^2 + 2xy + y^2$, which factors to $(x + y)^2$, is hiding in the first equation:

$$x^2 + y^2 = 16 - 2xy$$
$$x^2 + 2xy + y^2 = 16$$
$$(x + y)^2 = 16$$

Rewrite $(x + y)^4$ as $((x + y)^2)^2$ and replace the $(x + y)^2$ with 16, so $16^2 = 256$. Choice **(D)** is correct.

21.   3/25, 0.12, or .12
Difficulty: Hard

Category: Advanced Math

Getting to the Answer: When a question involving a function provides one or more ordered pairs, substitute them into the function to see what information you can glean. Start with $x = 0$ because doing so often results in the elimination of a variable:

$$f(x) = a \cdot b^x$$
$$f(0) = a \cdot b^0$$
$$3 = a \cdot b^0$$
$$3 = a \cdot 1$$
$$3 = a$$

Now you know the value of a, so the equation looks like $f(x) = 3 \cdot b^x$. Substitute the second pair of values into the new equation:

$$f(x) = 3 \cdot b^x$$
$$f(1) = 3 \cdot b^1$$
$$15 = 3 \cdot b^1$$
$$15 = 3b$$
$$5 = b$$

The exponential function is $f(x) = 3 \cdot 5^x$. The final step is to find the value being asked for, $f(-2)$. Substitute -2 for x and simplify:

$$f(-2) = 3 \cdot 5^{-2} = \frac{3}{5^2} = \frac{3}{25}$$

Enter either **3/25, 0.12,** or **.12**.

22.   C
Difficulty: Hard

Category: Problem Solving and Data Analysis

Getting to the Answer: Examine the shape of the data and familiarize yourself with the title and the axis labels on the graph. Data is *symmetric* if it is fairly evenly spread out, and it is *skewed* if it has a long tail on either side. Since this data set has a long tail to the right, it is skewed to the right, so you can immediately eliminate (A). If the data were symmetric, it would have tails that were roughly equal on both sides. Choices (B), (C), and (D) all describe the data as skewed to the right, so you'll need to examine those statements more closely. For (B), "adverse reactions" include the last four bars, which represent $89 + 41 + 22 + 8 = 160$ participants total, which is not even close to 50 percent of 900, so eliminate (B). Note that you don't need to add all the bar heights to find that there were 900 participants—the title of the graph tells you that. Now look at (C)—"failed to have adverse reactions" means "None" or "Mild" (the first three bars), which represent $900 - 160 = 740$ of the 900 participants. Since 75% of $900 = 675$, and 740 is more than 675, **(C)** is correct. For (D), the "None" column contains 320 participants, which does not equal approximately 50% of 900, so it too is incorrect.

Math: Module B Answers and Explanations

1. B

Difficulty: Easy

Category: Algebra

Getting to the Answer: To solve a nested function, work from the inside out. Find the value of $g(2)$ and then use the result as input into the f function: $g(x) = x - 4$, so $g(2) = 2 - 4 = -2$. Now, solve $f(g(2))$ by plugging in -2 for $g(2)$. Since $f(x) = x + 1$, $f(-2) = -2 + 1 = -1$. Choice **(B)** is correct.

2. A

Difficulty: Easy

Category: Problem Solving and Data Analysis

Getting to the Answer: In the sample, 2,800 out of 3,200 acres were free of the weed after applying the herbicide. This is $\frac{2,800}{3,200} = 0.875 = 87.5\%$ of the area. For the whole region, $0.875(30,000) = 26,250$ acres should be free of the weed. Be careful—this is not the answer. The question asks how much of the cropland would *still be covered* by the weed, so subtract to get $30,000 - 26,250 = 3,750$ acres. **(A)** is correct.

3. D

Difficulty: Easy

Category: Problem Solving and Data Analysis

Getting to the Answer: Graphically, slope is the ratio of the change in the y-values (rise) to the change in the x-values (run). In a real-world scenario, this is the same as the unit rate. In this context, the rise describes the change in the number of home runs hit in a single season, and the run describes the change in the number of hours a player spends in batting practice. Thus, the unit rate, or slope, represents the estimated increase (since the data trends upward) in the number of single-season home runs hit by a player for each hour he spends in batting practice. **(D)** is correct.

4. D

Difficulty: Medium

Category: Algebra

Getting to the Answer: The best way to answer this question is to pretend you are a homebuyer. How much more per square foot would your house cost in New York than in Detroit? If the house was 1,500 square feet, how much more would this be? If the house was 2,000 square feet, how much more would this be?

Based on the data in the table, a house would cost $288.58 - $62.45 = $226.13 more per square foot in New York than in Detroit. If the house was 1,500 square feet, it would cost $1,500(226.13) = $339,195 more. If the house was 2,000 square feet, it would cost $2,000(226.13) = $452,260 more. So, the house would cost somewhere between $339,195 and $452,260 more, which can be expressed as the compound inequality $339,195 \leq x \leq 452,260$, **(D)**.

5. −8/3, −2.666, or −2.667

Difficulty: Medium

Category: Algebra

Getting to the Answer: Graphically, a system of linear equations that has no solution indicates two parallel lines, or in other words, two lines that have the same slope and different y-intercepts. Lines that have the same x-coefficients and the same y-coefficients will have the same slope. The most efficient approach is to notice that you can make the y-terms equivalent by multiplying the first equation by −8, then comparing the x-terms to find k. So,

$$-8\left(\frac{1}{3}x + \frac{1}{2}y = 5\right) \rightarrow -\frac{8}{3}x - 4y = -40$$

Thus, $k = -\frac{8}{3}$. Enter **−8/3, −2.666, or −2.667**.

6. D

Difficulty: Medium

Category: Algebra

Getting to the Answer: The increase in wait time is constant, so the function will be linear and can be modeled by $f(h) = mh + b$, where m is the change in wait time (in minutes per hour the park is open) and b is the wait time (in minutes) when the amusement park opened at 10 a.m. Since h is in hours, use the points $(0, 5)$ and $(0.5, 15)$ to calculate the slope, where $h = 0$ at 10 a.m. and $h = 0.5$ at 10:30 a.m.: $m = \frac{15 - 5}{0.5 - 0} = \frac{10}{0.5} = 20$. Thus, the equation of the function is $f(h) = 20h + 5$. **(D)** is correct.

7. D

Difficulty: Medium

Category: Advanced Math

Getting to the Answer: Determine whether the change in the amount of pollution is a common difference (linear function) or a common ratio (exponential function), or if it changes direction (quadratic or polynomial function). Each year, the amount of pollution should be $100\% - 8\% = 92\%$ of the year before. You can write 92% as $\frac{92}{100}$, which represents a common ratio from one year to the next. This means that the best model is an exponential function of the form $y = a \cdot (0.92)^x$. **(D)** is correct.

8. D

Difficulty: Medium

Category: Advanced Math

Getting to the Answer: The roots of an equation are the same as its solutions. Take a peek at the answer choices—they contain radicals, which tells you that the equation can't be factored. Instead, either complete the square or solve the equation using the quadratic formula, whichever you are most comfortable with. The equation is already written in the form $y = ax^2 + bx + c$, and the coefficients are fairly small, so using the quadratic formula is probably the quickest method. Jot down the values that you'll need: $a = 3$, $b = -6$, and $c = -5$. Then, substitute these values into the quadratic formula and simplify:

$$x = \frac{-b \pm \sqrt{b^2 - 4ac}}{2a}$$
$$= \frac{-(-6) \pm \sqrt{(-6)^2 - 4(3)(-5)}}{2(3)}$$
$$= \frac{6 \pm \sqrt{36 + 60}}{6}$$
$$= \frac{6 \pm \sqrt{96}}{6}$$

This is not one of the answer choices, so simplify the radical. To do this, look for a perfect square that divides into 96 and take its square root. Then, if possible, cancel any factors that are common to the numerator and the denominator:

$$x = \frac{6 \pm \sqrt{16 \times 6}}{6}$$
$$= \frac{6 \pm 4\sqrt{6}}{6}$$
$$= \frac{2(3 \pm 2\sqrt{6})}{2(3)}$$
$$= \frac{3 \pm 2\sqrt{6}}{3}$$

Choice **(D)** is correct. Be careful—you can't simplify the answer any further because you cannot divide the square root of 6 by 3.

9. C

Difficulty: Medium

Category: Advanced Math

Getting to the Answer: Look for a pattern in the sales of each company. Then, apply that pattern to see by which month Company B will sell more than Company A. Writing a function that represents each pattern will also help, but you have to be careful that you evaluate the function at the correct input value. Company A's sales can be represented by a linear function because each month the company sells 92 more of the toy than the month before, which is a constant difference. The function is $A(t) = 92t + 54$, where t is the number of months *after* January. Company B's sales can be represented by an exponential function because the sales are doubling each month, which is a constant ratio (2 for doubling). The function is $B(t) = 15(2)^t$. Find the sales for each following month until Company B's sales exceed Company A's sales.

	Apr $t = 3$	May $t = 4$	Jun $t = 5$	Jul $t = 6$
Company A	330	422	514	606
Company B	120	240	480	960

960 is greater than 606, so Company B's sales will start to exceed Company A's sales in July. Choice **(C)** is correct.

10. B

Difficulty: Medium

Category: Problem Solving and Data Analysis

Getting to the Answer: Always read the axis labels carefully when a question involves a chart or graph. *Frequency*, which is plotted along the vertical axis, tells you how many students missed a certain number of questions. Evaluate each statement as quickly as you can.

(A): Add the bar heights (frequencies) that represent students that missed 5 or more questions: $7 + 3 + 3 + 2 = 15$. Then, find the total number of students represented, which is the number that missed less than 5 questions plus the 15 you just found: $2 + 3 + 4 + 6 = 15$, plus the 15 you already found, for a total of 30 students. The statement is not true because 15 is exactly half (not more than half) of 30. Eliminate.

(B): This calculation will take a bit of time, so skip it for now.

(C): The tallest bar tells you which number of questions was missed most often, which was 5 questions, not 3 questions, so this statement is not true. Eliminate.

(D): The number of students from Mr. Juno's class who took the test that day is the sum of the heights of the bars, which you already know is 30, not 36. Eliminate.

This means **(B)** must be correct. Mark it and move on to the next question. In case you're curious, find the mean by multiplying each number of questions missed by the corresponding frequency, finding the sum, and then dividing by the total number of students, which you already know is 30:

$$\text{mean} = \frac{2 + 6 + 12 + 24 + 35 + 18 + 21 + 16}{30}$$
$$= \frac{134}{30} = 4.4\overline{6}$$

The mean is indeed between 4 and 5. **(B)** is correct.

11. 4

Difficulty: Medium

Category: Geometry and Trigonometry

Getting to the Answer: Start by marking up the figure with the information you're given. You know the length of *EB*, which is 3. You also know the triangle is cut by parallel lines, so triangle *BEF* is similar to triangle *BDC* because they have two angles in common: angle *B* and the right angle. Because the corresponding sides of

similar triangles are proportional, start with the ratio of *BF* to *FC*, which equals the ratio of *BE* and *ED*. Then, because you know the length of *BE* = 3, you can find the length of *ED*:

$$\frac{3}{4} = \frac{BF}{FC} = \frac{BE}{ED}$$
$$\frac{3}{4} = \frac{3}{ED}$$
$$ED = 4$$

Enter **4**.

12. A

Difficulty: Hard

Category: Algebra

Getting to the Answer: Pay careful attention to units, particularly when a question involves rates. The taxi charges \$3.00 for the first $\frac{1}{4}$ mile, which is a flat fee, so write 3. The additional charge is \$0.25 per $\frac{1}{8}$ mile, or $0.25 \times 8 = \$2.00$ per mile. The number of miles after the first $\frac{1}{4}$ mile is $m - \frac{1}{4}$, so the cost of the trip, not including the first $\frac{1}{4}$ mile is $2\left(m - \frac{1}{4}\right)$. This means the cost of the whole trip is $3 + 2\left(m - \frac{1}{4}\right)$. The clue "no more than \$20" means that much or less, so use the symbol $\leq$. The inequality is $3 + 2\left(m - \frac{1}{4}\right) \leq 20$, which simplifies to $2.5 + 2m \leq 20$. **(A)** is correct.

13. 800

Difficulty: Hard

Category: Algebra

Getting to the Answer: Think about this question logically and in terms of function notation. First, find the quantity that the company can expect to sell at each price using the demand function. Since profit = sales − costs, find the total profit by multiplying the quantity by the difference between the selling price and the production cost. Set up a table like the following:

Price	\$12	\$10
Quantity	$q(12) = -200(12)$ $+ 3,400$ $= -2,400 + 3,400$ $= 1,000$	$q(10) = -200(10)$ $+ 3,400$ $= -2,000 + 3,400$ $= 1,400$
Profits	$1,000(\$12 - \$7)$ $= \$5,000$	$1,400(\$10 - \$7)$ $= \$4,200$

The company will earn $5,000 − $4,200 = $800 more per month. Enter **800**.

14. C

Difficulty: Hard

Category: Algebra

Getting to the Answer: Writing quadratic equations can be tricky and time-consuming. If you know the roots, you can use factors to write the equation. If you don't know the roots, you need to create a system of equations to find the coefficients of the variable terms. You don't know the roots of this equation, so start with the point that has the nicest values (0, 2) and substitute them into the equation, $y = ax^2 + bx + c$, to get $2 = a(0)^2 + b(0) + c$, or $2 = c$. Now your equation looks like $y = ax^2 + bx + 2$. Next, use the other two points to create a system of two equations in two variables:

$(-6, -7) \rightarrow -7 = a(-6)^2 + b(-6) + 2 \rightarrow -9 = 36a - 6b$
$(8, -14) \rightarrow -14 = a(8)^2 + b(8) + 2 \rightarrow -16 = 64a + 8b$

You now have a system of equations to solve. If you multiply the top equation by 4 and the bottom equation by 3 and then add the equations, the b terms will eliminate each other:

$$4[-9 = 36a - 6b] \rightarrow -36 = 144a - 24b$$

$$3[-16 = 64a + 8b] \rightarrow \underline{-48 = 192a + 24b}$$

$$-84 = 336a$$

$$-0.25 = a$$

Now, find b by substituting $a = -0.25$ into either of the original equations. Using the top equation, you get:

$$-9 = 36(-0.25) - 6b$$

$$-9 = -9 - 6b$$

$$0 = -6b$$

$$0 = b$$

The value of $a + b + c$ is $(-0.25) + 0 + 2 = 1.75$. Choice **(C)** is correct.

15. A

Difficulty: Hard

Category: Advanced Math

Getting to the Answer: First, write an inequality that represents the scenario: "greater than 1,000 meters and less than 4,000 meters" is the same as "between 1,000 and 4,000." Thus, the possible depths below the ocean surface that are in the Midnight Zone are given by the inequality $1,000 < x < 4,000$. Now, you need to find an absolute value inequality that is equivalent to this inequality.

The inequality $1,000 < x < 4,000$ describes the interval (1,000, 4,000). To describe an interval using an absolute value inequality, think in terms of how far the endpoints of the interval are from the midpoint of the interval. The midpoint of (1,000, 4,000) is $\frac{1,000 + 4,000}{2} = 2,500$. The interval (1,000, 4,000) consists of all points that are within 1,500 of this midpoint (because $2,500 - 1,000$ is 1,500 and $4,000 - 2,500$ is 1,500). That is, (1,000, 4,000) consists of all values of x whose distances from 2,500 on a number line are less than 1,500. The distance between x and 2,500 on the number line is given by $|x - 2,500|$. Therefore, the possible values of x can be described by $|x - 2,500| < 1,500$, which is choice **(A)**.

Another strategy is to pick numbers and test the choices. Pick a depth in the given range, eliminate choices that are false, then pick a depth outside of the given range, and eliminate choices that are true. If $x = 1,500$, choices (B) and (D) are false, so eliminate these choices. If $x = 500$, (C) is true, but 500 is outside of the acceptable range, eliminate (C) and **(A)** is correct.

16. 6

Difficulty: Hard

Category: Advanced Math

Getting to the Answer: The notation $(f - g)(3)$ means to find the difference between the two functions when $x = 3$: $f(3) - g(3)$. You don't know the equations of the functions, so you'll need to read the values from the graph. Graphically, $f(3)$ means the y-value at $x = 3$ on the graph of f, which is 2. Likewise, $g(3)$ means the y-value at $x = 3$ on the graph of g, which is −4. Thus, $f(3) - g(3)$ is $2 - (-4) = 6$. Enter **6**.

17. B

Difficulty: Hard

Category: Advanced Math

Getting to the Answer: A quadratic equation can have zero, one, or two real solutions. There are several ways to determine exactly how many. You could graph the equation and see how many times it crosses the x-axis, you could calculate the discriminant (the value under the square root in the quadratic formula), or you could try to factor the equation. Use whichever method gets you to the answer the quickest. Notice that the first and last terms in the equation are perfect squares—this is a hint that it could be a perfect square trinomial, which it is. The factored form of the equation is $(3x - 2)(3x - 2)$. Both factors are the same, so there is only one real value, $x = \frac{2}{3}$, that satisfies the equation, so **(B)** is correct.

18. B

Difficulty: Hard

Category: Advanced Math

Getting to the Answer: The question asks where the graphs intersect, the point(s) at which the two graphs intersect are the points where the two equations are equal to each other. Therefore, set the equations equal and use algebra to solve for x. Because the question only asks for the x-values, you don't need to substitute the results back into the equations to solve for y.

$$-2x + 1 = 2x^2 + 5x + 4$$
$$-2x = 2x^2 + 5x + 3$$
$$0 = 2x^2 + 7x + 3$$
$$0 = (2x + 1)(x + 3)$$

Now that the equation is factored, solve for x:

$$2x + 1 = 0 \quad \text{and} \quad x + 3 = 0$$
$$2x = -1 \qquad\qquad x = -3$$
$$x = -\frac{1}{2}$$

Choice **(B)** is correct.

19. .0607, .0606, 0.061, or 0.060

Difficulty: Hard

Category: Problem Solving and Data Analysis

Getting to the Answer: First, find the probability that the first employee chosen at random will be one who has been with the company for longer than 3 years. The total number of employees who participated in the study is $38 + 30 + 15 + 19 + 54 + 48 = 204$. The total number of individuals in both job categories who have been with the company longer (greater) than 3 years is $54 + 48 = 102$. Therefore, the probability of choosing one employee who has been with the company longer than 3 years is: $\frac{102}{204} = \frac{1}{2}$. Because the same employee cannot be randomly selected more than once, the chance that another selected employee will have been with the company more than 3 years is not simply equal to $\frac{1}{2}$. Instead, assuming the first employee chosen at random has been with the company more than 3 years, the chance that a second employee chosen at random will also be is $\frac{(102 - 1)}{(204 - 1)} = \frac{101}{203}$. For a third employee, the chance is $\frac{(102 - 2)}{(204 - 2)} = \frac{100}{202} = \frac{50}{101}$, and for a fourth, the chance is $\frac{(102 - 3)}{(204 - 3)} = \frac{99}{201}$. Thus, to determine the probability that all 4 have been with the company longer than 3 years, multiply all these probabilities together: $\frac{1}{2} \times \frac{101}{203} \times \frac{50}{101} \times \frac{99}{201} \approx 0.06065$. Enter up to 5 characters for a positive number (either rounding or truncating): **.0607, .0606, 0.061, or 0.060**.

20. D

Difficulty: Hard

Category: Problem Solving and Data Analysis

Getting to the Answer: Read the question, organizing important information as you go. You need to find the ratio of mini muffins to jumbo muffins. You're given two ratios: mini to regular and regular to jumbo. Both of the given ratios contain regular muffin size units, but the regular amounts (2 and 5) are not identical. To directly compare them, find a common multiple (10). Multiply each ratio by the factor that will make the number of regular muffins equal to 10:

Mini to regular: $(5:2) \times (5:5) = 25:10$

Regular to jumbo: $(5:4) \times (2:2) = 10:8$

Now that the number of regular muffins is the same in both ratios (10), you can merge the two ratios to compare mini to jumbo directly: 25:10:8. So, the proper ratio of mini muffins to jumbo muffins is 25:8, which is **(D)**.

21. D

Difficulty: Hard

Category: Geometry and Trigonometry

Getting to the Answer: The formula for finding the volume of a rectangular prism is $V = lwh$. Leaving the top 5% of the grain bin empty is another way of saying that the bin should only be filled to 95% of its total volume, so multiply the volume by 0.95. Plug in the given dimensions of the grain bin and set it equal to 5,700. Then solve for x.

$$5,700 = x\left(\frac{3}{2}x\right)\left(\frac{1}{2}x\right)(0.95)$$
$$5,700 = 0.7125\,x^3$$
$$8,000 = x^3$$
$$\sqrt[3]{8,000} = \sqrt[3]{x^3}$$
$$20 = x$$

The question asks for the length of the grain bin, which is $\frac{3}{2}(20) = 30$ feet. Choice **(D)** is correct.

22. 85

Difficulty: Hard

Category: Geometry and Trigonometry

Getting to the Answer: Organize information as you read the question. Here, you'll definitely want to draw and label a sketch.

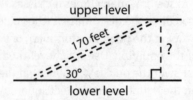

The lower level, the vertical distance between levels, and the diagonal elevator track form a right triangle. Since you're looking for the side opposite the 30° angle, use sine:

$$\sin x = \frac{\text{opp}}{\text{hyp}}$$
$$\sin 30° = \frac{\text{opp}}{170}$$
$$0.5 = \frac{\text{opp}}{170}$$
$$85 = \text{opp}$$

Enter **85**.